John Kupchik
Azuma Old Japanese

Trends in Linguistics
Documentation 40

Editors
Walter Bisang
Hans Henrich Hock

Editor responsible for this volume
Hans Henrich Hock

John Kupchik
Azuma Old Japanese

A Comparative Grammar and Reconstruction

ISBN 978-3-11-221510-4
e-ISBN (PDF) 978-3-11-107879-3
e-ISBN (EPUB) 978-3-11-107893-9
ISSN 0179-8251

Library of Congress Control Number: 2023940496

Bibliographic information published by the Deutsche Nationalbibliothek
The Deutsche Nationalbibliothek lists this publication in the Deutsche Nationalbibliografie;
detailed bibliographic data are available on the Internet at http://dnb.dnb.de

© 2025 Walter de Gruyter GmbH, Berlin/Boston
This volume is text- and page-identical with the hardback published in 2023.
Cover image: Grabara_Photography/iStock/Getty Images Plus
Typesetting: Integra Software Services Pvt. Ltd.
Printing and binding: CPI books GmbH, Leck

www.degruyter.com

Preface

I began studying the Azuma Old Japanese (AOJ) dialects in earnest in 2006, and my first publication on the topic appeared in 2007. Since then, these dialects have been my primary research focus. Initially, I was fascinated by the mystery of these dialects, and I was dissatisfied with many aspects of the previous research that had been done on them. I was particularly frustrated with the de-facto assumption that AOJ was a dialect continuum because I soon noticed this idea was not consistent with the patterns I was finding, after I separated each province's poems and analyzed the data. This had not really been investigated in a manner consistent with modern linguistic methodology. Therefore, in my 2011 doctoral dissertation, *A grammar of the Eastern Old Japanese dialects*, I tackled these issues to the best of my ability, with a focus on a comprehensive analysis of the corpus, attempting to leave no stone unturned.

Looking back on my dissertation several years later, I realized it needed many significant revisions, rewrites, and additional analyses. There were many typographical errors, topics with insufficient discussion, and my views on certain aspects of the data had evolved or changed completely over time. That led to the writing of this book, which began in 2016. My original plan was to write a book about the phonology and phonetics, but I later decided it would be better to expand it into a full grammar, which delayed the publication by roughly two years.

By the time I finished, I had rewritten most of the text of my dissertation and added a significant amount of new text, along with a few new chapters. The biggest structural difference is the removal of the more than 400 pages of phonological comparison charts: in their place are concise summaries and descriptions of the phonological developments in each topolect and dialect. I thought this would be easier to read and more useful for researchers. If anyone wants to dig into the full orthographic and phonological data, my 2011 dissertation remains available for that purpose.

I have likely introduced some confusion with the term "Azuma Old Japanese", since the title of my aforementioned dissertation employed the term "Eastern Old Japanese". Allow me to explain this difference and why I think it is important. Eastern Old Japanese is the traditional term used in Western scholarship to refer to the group of dialects spoken in eastern Japan during the eighth century. Therefore, I also used this term for my dissertation. This region was known as Azuma (< A^{n}duma) in the time of Old Japanese, and this nomenclature is still used by present-day scholars in Japan. After completing my dissertation, due to discovering linguistic innovations in specific areas of Azuma, I concluded that there were at least two major dialects present in this region that resulted from separate splits from Proto-Japanese. Labelling both "Eastern Old Japanese" would not be accurate. Therefore, I reduced the geographic region over which the Eastern Old Japanese dialect was spoken, and I introduced the term "Töpo-Suruga Old Japanese" to account for the distinct dialect spoken in the provinces of Töpotuapumi and Suruga, and which had previously been lumped in under the umbrella of Eastern Old Japanese. I also segregated the dialect spoken in Sinano province.[1] In need of a term for the entire dialect region for the present study and any future studies, I settled on "Azuma Old Japanese", which, accordingly, is an areal term, while I reserve the terms "Eastern Old Japanese" and "Töpo-Suruga Old Japanese" to reference specific, linguistically distinct dialects in that region.[2] I have been using this terminology in papers and presentations since 2012.

---

[1] However, after further examination of the data, I have since added Sinano to the Töpo-Suruga Old Japanese dialect.

[2] At the end of my dissertation, I reluctantly settled on a more confusing system of retaining the term "Eastern Old Japanese" for all of the dialects spoken across the Azuma region while I called the linguistically distinct Eastern Old Japanese dialect "true Eastern Old Japanese", abbreviated to t-EOJ. I am glad to abandon that ad hoc terminology and settle on the more coherent terminology used in this book.

Acknowledgements

Most of this book was written from 2016 – 2019, with my young son Neil playing with his toy cars on the side of my desk or putting stickers on my elbows as I typed. Occasionally he would offer me a bowl with a few lemons or oranges in it, place it on my desk, and smile. I thank him for *usually* being understanding every time I implored him that "Daddy has to write now". I also offer my heartfelt gratitude to my wife, Karen (Kèwén) Huang, for frequently going out of her way to provide me with a bit of extra time to write, even if it was just taking Neil to the store or a park for an hour. I also benefited greatly from conversations with her on various topics in this book.

I am very grateful for the support and encouragement I received from my friends, family, and colleagues while writing this book. I would especially like to thank Yukinori Takubo, Yūko Ōtsuka, Sven Osterkamp, Elisabeth Saladino, Marc Miyake, José Andrés Alonso De La Fuente, Lawrence Marceau, my parents, my siblings, and my in-laws.

I also thank the editors Birgit Sievert, Anne Rudolph, and Barbara Karlson at De Gruyter Mouton, as well as the TiLDOC series editor Hans Henrich Hock. Their support and assistance were instrumental in the publication of this book, and it was a true pleasure to work with all of them. I am also grateful to an anonymous reviewer for their helpful comments and constructive criticism. Naturally, any errors that remain are my own.

This book is dedicated to the eminent linguist David L. Stampe (June 13, 1938 – June 23, 2020), who passed away when I was in the final stages of writing this book. I consider myself very fortunate to have studied under him for several years when I was a graduate student at the University of Hawaiʻi at Mānoa, during which time he instilled in me the importance of creativity and open-mindedness in linguistic inquiry, along with the fundamentals of Natural Phonology. This has proved to be a lasting influence on my research, including the present book. As a fellow votary of poetry, I like to think he would have enjoyed reading this book.

Table of contents

Preface —— V

Acknowledgements —— VII

Glossing conventions —— XXIX

Abbreviations —— XXXI

1 Introduction —— 1
 1.1 Basic grammatical and typological characteristics of AOJ —— 3
 1.2 Verse and meter —— 3
 1.3 The linguistic situation in Japan in the eighth century CE —— 3
 1.4 Textual sources —— 4
 1.5 Major studies on AOJ —— 5
 1.6 WOJ transliteration system and phonemic reconstruction —— 5
 1.7 Orthography —— 7
 1.8 Manuscripts —— 15
 1.9 The classification of AOJ poems based on non-WOJ features —— 17
 1.10 Textual attestation format —— 20
 1.11 Translation and glossing —— 20
 1.12 Structure and aims of this book —— 21

2 Sound change, reconstruction, and subgrouping —— 23
 2.1 The phonology of Proto-Japonic, Proto-Japanese, and WOJ —— 23
 2.2 The Tōpo-Suruga Old Japanese dialect (TSOJ) —— 29
 2.3 The Eastern Old Japanese dialect (EOJ) —— 48
 2.4 The subgroups of Proto-Japanese and Proto-EOJ —— 95
 2.5 An analysis of the phonological innovations in the poems from unspecified provinces (UNP) —— 96

3 Vowel elision, *rendaku*, and assimilations —— 105
 3.1 Synchronic vowel elision (SVE) —— 105
 3.2 *Rendaku*: morpheme-based and process-based —— 112
 3.3 Synchronic vowel assimilations: progressive and regressive —— 116

4 Lexicon —— 119
 4.1 Native vocabulary —— 119
 4.2 Korean loanwords —— 120

- 4.3 Ainu loanwords —— **123**
- 4.4 Chinese loanwords —— **140**
- 4.5 Austronesian loanwords —— **141**

5 Nominals —— **143**
- 5.1 The basic syntax of nouns —— **143**
- 5.2 Morphotactics —— **143**
- 5.3 Prefixes —— **145**
- 5.4 Suffixes —— **156**
- 5.5 Reduplication —— **207**
- 5.6 Pronouns —— **209**
- 5.7 Numerals —— **237**

6 Adjectives and adjectival verbs —— **245**
- 6.1 The basic syntax of adjectives and adjectival verbs —— **245**
- 6.2 Adjectives —— **245**
- 6.3 Adjectival verbs —— **251**

7 Verbs —— **277**
- 7.1 The basic syntax of verbs —— **277**
- 7.2 Verbal grammatical categories —— **277**
- 7.3 Morphotactics —— **279**
- 7.4 Verbal classes —— **281**
- 7.5 Verbal affixes —— **292**
- 7.6 Auxiliaries —— **384**
- 7.7 Suppletive honorific and humble verbs —— **419**
- 7.8 Serial verb constructions —— **421**
- 7.9 Light verb constructions —— **423**
- 7.10 Verbal reduplication —— **425**

8 Adverbs —— **427**
- 8.1 *ito* 'simply, very, really' —— **427**
- 8.2 *kökönba* 'extremely' —— **428**
- 8.3 *sapanda* 'many, much, amply' —— **428**
- 8.4 *mata* 'again' —— **429**
- 8.5 *iya* 'plentifully, certainly' —— **430**
- 8.6 *napo* 'still' —— **430**
- 8.7 *imanda* 'yet, still' —— **430**
- 8.8 *motöna* 'incessantly, at random' —— **431**
- 8.9 *tanda* 'directly' —— **431**

8.10	*nökinde* 'extremely'	—— **431**
8.11	*sinzi* 'constantly'	—— **432**
8.12	*simaraku* 'for a while'	—— **432**
8.13	*köngötö* 'greatly'	—— **432**
8.14	*unbey* 'surely'	—— **433**
8.15	*yumey* '[not] at all'	—— **433**
8.16	*wosawosa* '[not] enough, [not] properly'	—— **433**

9 Conjunctions —— 435
- 9.1 *tömo* 'even if, even though' —— **435**
- 9.2 *monö ~ monöwo* 'although, but, considering' —— **437**
- 9.3 *monökara* 'although' —— **437**
- 9.4 *ngani* 'so that' —— **438**
- 9.5 *ngani* 'like' —— **438**
- 9.6 *sinda* 'when' —— **438**

10 Particles —— 441
- 10.1 The basic syntax of particles —— **441**
- 10.2 Focus particles —— **441**
- 10.3 Emphatic particles —— **454**
- 10.4 Question particles —— **467**
- 10.5 Restrictive particles —— **473**
- 10.6 Desiderative particle *monga[mo]* —— **476**
- 10.7 Ironic particle *ngape* —— **478**
- 10.8 Quotative particle *tö ~ te* —— **478**

Appendix A – A classification of poems in MYS Book 14 based on linguistic features —— 483

References —— 511

Index —— 519

Extended table of contents

Preface —— V

Acknowledgements —— VII

Glossing conventions —— XXIX

Abbreviations —— XXXI

1   Introduction —— 1
1.1   Basic grammatical and typological characteristics of AOJ —— 3
1.2   Verse and meter —— 3
1.3   The linguistic situation in Japan in the eighth century CE —— 3
1.4   Textual sources —— 4
1.5   Major studies on AOJ —— 5
1.6   WOJ transliteration system and phonemic reconstruction —— 5
1.7   Orthography —— 7
1.7.1   Phonograms —— 7
1.7.1.1   Disyllabic phonograms —— 11
1.7.1.2   *Kungana* phonograms —— 12
1.7.2   Logograms —— 13
1.7.3   *Kō-rui* and *otsu-rui* distinctions —— 14
1.8   Manuscripts —— 15
1.9   The classification of AOJ poems based on non-WOJ features —— 17
1.10   Textual attestation format —— 20
1.11   Translation and glossing —— 20
1.12   Structure and aims of this book —— 21

2   Sound change, reconstruction, and subgrouping —— 23
2.1   The phonology of Proto-Japonic, Proto-Japanese, and WOJ —— 23
2.1.1   The phonological changes from Proto-Japonic to Proto-Japanese —— 23
2.1.1.1   PJ and PJe consonant inventories —— 24
2.1.1.2   PJ and PJe vowel inventories —— 25
2.1.2   The phonology of WOJ —— 26
2.1.2.1   Consonants —— 26
2.1.2.2   Vowels —— 27
2.1.3   Phonotactics and prosody of OJ —— 28
2.1.4   Methodology —— 28

2.2	The Töpo-Suruga Old Japanese dialect (TSOJ) —— 29	
2.2.1	Suruga —— 30	
2.2.1.1	Vowel innovations —— 30	
2.2.1.2	A reconstruction of Suruga's vowel inventory —— 36	
2.2.1.3	A reconstruction of Suruga's consonant inventory —— 36	
2.2.2	Töpotuapumi —— 37	
2.2.2.1	Vowel innovations —— 37	
2.2.2.2	A reconstruction of Töpotuapumi's vowel inventory —— 40	
2.2.2.3	A reconstruction of Töpotuapumi's consonant inventory —— 40	
2.2.2.4	Notable phonological retentions —— 41	
2.2.3	Sinano —— 42	
2.2.3.1	Vowel innovations —— 42	
2.2.3.2	A reconstruction of Sinano's vowel inventory —— 46	
2.2.3.3	A reconstruction of Sinano's consonant inventory —— 46	
2.2.3.4	Notable phonological retentions —— 46	
2.2.4	A reconstruction of Proto-TSOJ —— 46	
2.3	The Eastern Old Japanese dialect (EOJ) —— 48	
2.3.1	Kamitukeno —— 48	
2.3.1.1	Vowel innovations —— 48	
2.3.1.2	Consonant innovations —— 51	
2.3.1.3	Notable phonological retentions —— 53	
2.3.1.4	WOJ influence in the text —— 54	
2.3.1.5	A reconstruction of Kamitukeno's vowel inventory —— 55	
2.3.1.6	A reconstruction of Kamitukeno's consonant inventory —— 55	
2.3.2	Sagamu —— 55	
2.3.2.1	Vowel innovations —— 55	
2.3.2.2	Consonant innovations —— 58	
2.3.2.3	Notable phonological retentions —— 59	
2.3.2.4	A reconstruction of Sagamu's vowel inventory —— 59	
2.3.2.5	A reconstruction of Sagamu's consonant inventory —— 60	
2.3.2.6	Subgrouping of Sagamu with Kamitukeno —— 60	
2.3.3	Muzasi —— 60	
2.3.3.1	Vowel innovations —— 60	
2.3.3.2	Consonant innovations —— 64	
2.3.3.3	Notable phonological retentions —— 65	
2.3.3.4	WOJ influence in the text —— 66	
2.3.3.5	A reconstruction of Muzasi's vowel inventory —— 67	
2.3.3.6	A reconstruction of Muzasi's consonant inventory —— 67	
2.3.4	Simotukeno —— 67	
2.3.4.1	Vowel innovations —— 67	

2.3.4.2	Consonant innovations —— 71	
2.3.4.3	Notable phonological retentions —— 72	
2.3.4.4	WOJ influence in the text —— 73	
2.3.4.5	A reconstruction of Simotukeno's vowel inventory —— 73	
2.3.4.6	A reconstruction of Simotukeno's consonant inventory —— 73	
2.3.5	Pitati —— 73	
2.3.5.1	Vowel innovations —— 74	
2.3.5.2	Consonant innovations —— 77	
2.3.5.3	Notable phonological retentions —— 77	
2.3.5.4	WOJ influence in the text —— 78	
2.3.5.5	A reconstruction of Pitati's vowel inventory —— 78	
2.3.5.6	A reconstruction of Pitati's consonant inventory —— 79	
2.3.6	Simotupusa —— 79	
2.3.6.1	Vowel innovations —— 79	
2.3.6.1.1	An unclear sound change —— 82	
2.3.6.2	Consonant innovations —— 83	
2.3.6.3	Notable phonological retentions —— 84	
2.3.6.4	WOJ influence in the text —— 85	
2.3.6.5	A reconstruction of Simotupusa's vowel inventory —— 85	
2.3.6.6	A reconstruction of Simotupusa's consonant inventory —— 85	
2.3.7	Kamitupusa —— 86	
2.3.7.1	Vowel innovations —— 86	
2.3.7.2	Consonant innovations —— 89	
2.3.7.3	WOJ influence in the text —— 89	
2.3.7.4	A reconstruction of Kamitupusa's vowel inventory —— 90	
2.3.7.5	A reconstruction of Kamitupusa's consonant inventory —— 90	
2.3.8	Mitinöku —— 90	
2.3.8.1	Vowel innovations —— 91	
2.3.8.2	Notable phonological retentions —— 92	
2.3.8.3	A reconstruction of Mitinöku's vowel inventory —— 92	
2.3.8.4	A reconstruction of Mitinöku's consonant inventory —— 93	
2.3.9	A reconstruction of Proto-EOJ —— 93	
2.3.9.1	Later EOJ subgroups —— 94	
2.4	The subgroups of Proto-Japanese and Proto-EOJ —— 95	
2.5	An analysis of the phonological innovations in the poems from unspecified provinces (UNP) —— 96	
2.5.1	Vowel innovations —— 97	
2.5.1.1	*e > /i/ —— 97	
2.5.1.2	*ui > /u/, *oi > /u/ —— 97	
2.5.1.3	*ai > /e/ —— 98	

2.5.1.4	*ə > o / C[+labial] _ —— **98**	
2.5.1.5	*a > /e/ —— **98**	
2.5.1.6	*ia > /a/ —— **99**	
2.5.1.7	*i > /u/ —— **99**	
2.5.1.8	*e > /o/ —— **100**	
2.5.1.9	*#ə > #ye —— **100**	
2.5.1.10	*o > /u/ —— **100**	
2.5.1.11	*a > /ə/ —— **101**	
2.5.1.12	Vowel metathesis —— **101**	
2.5.1.13	*na^{ŋ}g > /no^{ŋ}g/ ~ /nu^{ŋ}g/ —— **101**	
2.5.2	Consonant innovations —— **102**	
2.5.2.1	*t > s / _i —— **102**	
2.5.2.2	*r > /n/ (progressive nasal assimilation) —— **102**	
2.5.2.3	*r > /n/ (regressive nasal assimilation) —— **103**	
2.5.2.4	*r > /n/ —— **103**	
2.5.2.5	*r > /y/ —— **103**	
2.5.2.6	*#nan/^{n} > #an/^{n} —— **104**	
3	**Vowel elision, *rendaku*, and assimilations —— 105**	
3.1	Synchronic vowel elision (SVE) —— **105**	
3.1.1	SVE in EOJ —— **105**	
3.1.1.1	/i/ + /a/ → /a/ (V$_1$ elision) —— **106**	
3.1.1.2	/u/ + /a/ → /a/ (V$_1$ elision) —— **106**	
3.1.1.3	/u/ + /ə/ → /u/ (V$_2$ elision) —— **107**	
3.1.1.4	/i/ + /ə/ → /i/ (V$_2$ elision) —— **107**	
3.1.1.5	/ə/ + /i/ → /ə/ (V$_2$ elision) —— **107**	
3.1.1.6	/ə/ + /u/ → /ə/ (V$_2$ elision) —— **108**	
3.1.1.7	/e/ + /ə/ → /e/ (V$_2$ elision) —— **108**	
3.1.1.8	/e/ + /i/ → /e/ (V$_2$ elision) —— **108**	
3.1.1.9	/o/ + /a/ → /o/ (V$_2$ elision) —— **108**	
3.1.1.10	/a/ + /ə/ → /a/ (V$_2$ elision) —— **108**	
3.1.1.11	/a/ + /i/ → /a/ (V$_2$ elision) —— **108**	
3.1.1.12	/a/ + /u/ → /a/ (V$_2$ elision) —— **109**	
3.1.2	SVE in TSOJ —— **109**	
3.1.2.1	V$_1$ elision —— **109**	
3.1.2.1.1	/i/ + /a/ → /a/ (V$_1$ elision) —— **109**	
3.1.2.1.2	/ə/ + /a/ > /a/ (V$_1$ elision) —— **110**	
3.1.2.2	V$_2$ elision —— **111**	
3.1.2.2.1	/ə/ + /i/ → /ə/ (V$_2$ elision) —— **111**	
3.1.2.2.2	/e/ + /i/ → /e/ (V$_2$ elision) —— **111**	

3.2	*Rendaku*: morpheme-based and process-based —— 112	
3.2.1	Morpheme-based *rendaku* (MBR) —— 112	
3.2.2	Process-based *rendaku* (PBR) —— 115	
3.3	Synchronic vowel assimilations: progressive and regressive —— 116	
3.3.1	Regressive assimilations —— 117	
3.3.2	Progressive assimilations —— 117	
4	**Lexicon —— 119**	
4.1	Native vocabulary —— 119	
4.2	Korean loanwords —— 120	
4.3	Ainu loanwords —— 123	
4.3.1	A critical analysis of Alexander Vovin's proposed Ainu loanwords in AOJ —— 123	
4.3.1.1	Plausible (accepted) toponyms —— 123	
4.3.1.2	Problematic (rejected) toponyms —— 124	
4.3.1.2.1	EOJ *Asingara ~ Asingari* < Ainu *askar-i* 'clear place' —— 124	
4.3.1.2.2	TSOJ *Kinbey* < Ainu *kimpe* 'bear' (< *kim-pe 'mountain thing') —— 125	
4.3.1.2.3	EOJ *Kandusika* < Ainu *ka-n-toska* < *ka-ne-toska top-COP-low.cliffs 'low cliffs that are above' —— 125	
4.3.1.2.4	EOJ *Kunzi* < Ainu *kus* 'to overflow, to flood' —— 125	
4.3.1.2.5	The case of the TSOJ toponym *Sinano* —— 125	
4.3.1.3	Plausible (accepted) lexical borrowings —— 127	
4.3.1.4	Problematic (rejected) lexical borrowings —— 128	
4.3.1.4.1	EOJ *anzu* 'crumbling cliff' < ? Ainu *-as- 'to split' + *so* 'rocky shore', 'hidden rocks in the sea' —— 128	
4.3.1.4.2	EOJ *atu-* 'sea' < Ainu *atuy* 'id.' —— 129	
4.3.1.4.3	EOJ *ka* 'top' < Ainu *ka* 'id.' —— 129	
4.3.1.4.4	EOJ *ka* 'voice' < Ainu *háw* 'id.' —— 130	
4.3.1.4.5	EOJ *köndök-* 'to bless with words' < Ainu *ko-itak ~ koytak-* 'to speak to, to address words to' —— 130	
4.3.1.4.6	EOJ *ma* 'wife' < Ainu *mat* 'woman, wife' —— 131	
4.3.1.4.7	EOJ *mak-i* 'back-POSS' < Ainu *mak* 'back' + 3rd person possessive suffix *-i* —— 131	
4.3.1.4.8	EOJ *mato* 'girl' < Proto-Ainu *mat-poo woman-child 'girl, daughter' —— 132	
4.3.1.4.9	EOJ *or-ö* 'its place' < Ainu *or-o* 'place-POSS' —— 133	
4.3.1.4.10	EOJ *pa* 'year' < Ainu *pa* 'id.' —— 133	
4.3.1.4.11	EOJ *pa* 'to find' < Ainu *pa* 'id.' —— 133	
4.3.1.4.12	EOJ *paka* 'rumor, gossip' < Ainu *páhaw* 'id.' —— 133	
4.3.1.4.13	EOJ *pirö* 'oak' < Ainu *pero* or *pero-ni* 'id.' —— 134	

4.3.1.4.14	EOJ *sömö* 'not' < Ainu *somo* 'id.' —— **135**
4.3.1.4.15	EOJ *su* 'again' < Ainu *suy* 'id.' —— **135**
4.3.1.4.16	EOJ *sungu* 'to grow old' < Ainu *sukup* 'id.' —— **136**
4.3.1.4.17	EOJ *ta-ka* 'here-DIR' < Ainu *ta-ke* 'this, here-DIR' —— **136**
4.3.1.4.18	EOJ *tengo* 'maiden' < Ainu *tek* 'hand, arm' + *o* 'take in, embrace' —— **137**
4.3.1.4.19	EOJ *tora* 'together' < Ainu *tura* 'id.' —— **137**
4.3.1.5	Plausible (accepted) morphological borrowings —— **138**
4.3.1.5.1	EOJ *sinda* temporal conjunction 'when' < Ainu *hi* 'time, occasion' + *-ta* 'locative case marker' —— **138**
4.3.1.6	Problematic (rejected) morphological borrowings —— **138**
4.3.1.6.1	EOJ *i-*, nominal prefix 'thing-' < Ainu *i-* 'id.' —— **138**
4.3.1.6.2	EOJ *o-* 'locative prefix' < Ainu *o-* 'id.' —— **139**
4.3.1.6.3	EOJ *ka* 'focus particle' < Ainu *ka* 'id.' —— **140**
4.3.1.6.4	EOJ **i- ~ -y-* 'indefinite direct object prefix' < Ainu *i-* 'id.' —— **140**
4.3.2	Summary of Ainu loanwords —— **140**
4.4	Chinese loanwords —— **140**
4.5	Austronesian loanwords —— **141**

5	**Nominals** —— **143**
5.1	The basic syntax of nouns —— **143**
5.2	Morphotactics —— **143**
5.3	Prefixes —— **145**
5.3.1	Diminutive prefixes —— **145**
5.3.1.1	Diminutive *ko-* —— **145**
5.3.1.2	Diminutive *won-* —— **147**
5.3.1.2.1	Endearment function —— **147**
5.3.1.2.2	Diminutive function —— **148**
5.3.2	Locative *sa-* —— **149**
5.3.3	Honorific *mi-* —— **150**
5.3.4	Intensifying *ma-* —— **153**
5.3.5	Prefix *uti-* —— **155**
5.3.6	Prefix *i-* —— **156**
5.4	Suffixes —— **156**
5.4.1	Case suffixes —— **156**
5.4.1.1	Nominative —— **157**
5.4.1.2	Possessive *-nga* —— **158**
5.4.1.2.1	Possessive function —— **158**
5.4.1.2.1.1	Attached to an animate noun —— **158**
5.4.1.2.1.2	Attached to an inanimate noun —— **160**

5.4.1.2.2	Nominative function in embedded clauses —— 162	
5.4.1.3	Accusative/absolutive -wo —— 164	
5.4.1.3.1	Accusative function —— 164	
5.4.1.3.2	Absolutive function —— 166	
5.4.1.3.3	Use of accusative -wo as a conjunction —— 167	
5.4.1.3.4	Emphatic form -wonba —— 167	
5.4.1.4	Genitive -nö —— 168	
5.4.1.4.1	Genitive function —— 168	
5.4.1.4.2	Function of marking the subject of an embedded clause —— 172	
5.4.1.4.3	Analytic genitive construction —— 173	
5.4.1.5	Dative/Locative -ni —— 173	
5.4.1.5.1	Dative function —— 174	
5.4.1.5.2	Locative function —— 175	
5.4.1.5.3	Special temporal construction —— 178	
5.4.1.5.4	Indicating reason —— 178	
5.4.1.6	Locative -na —— 179	
5.4.1.6.1	Special construction -ana-na —— 180	
5.4.1.7	Genitive-locative -tu —— 181	
5.4.1.8	Ablative -yori ~ -yuri ~ -yo ~ -yu —— 182	
5.4.1.8.1	Examples of -yori —— 183	
5.4.1.8.2	Examples of -yuri —— 183	
5.4.1.8.3	Examples of -yo —— 184	
5.4.1.8.4	Examples of -yu —— 184	
5.4.1.9	Ablative -kara —— 185	
5.4.1.10	Allative -pe ~ -pa —— 185	
5.4.1.11	Terminative -mande —— 186	
5.4.1.12	Comitative -tö —— 189	
5.4.1.13	Comparatives -nösu ~ -nasu and -nö —— 190	
5.4.1.13.1	Examples of -nasu —— 191	
5.4.1.13.2	Examples of -nösu —— 191	
5.4.1.13.3	Examples of -nö —— 193	
5.4.1.13.4	Analytic comparative constructions —— 195	
5.4.1.14	Directive -ka ~ -ngari —— 196	
5.4.1.14.1	Example of -ka —— 196	
5.4.1.14.2	Examples of -ngari —— 196	
5.4.2	Number suffixes —— 197	
5.4.2.1	Plural -ra —— 197	
5.4.3	Diminutive suffixes —— 198	
5.4.3.1	Diminutive -ko —— 198	
5.4.3.2	Diminutive -na —— 200	

5.4.3.3	Diminutive *-ra* —— **202**
5.4.3.4	Diminutive *-rö* —— **203**
5.4.3.4.1	Diminutive function —— **204**
5.4.3.4.2	Endearment function —— **205**
5.4.3.5	Diminutive *-nö* —— **206**
5.4.3.6	A comparison of the diminutive suffixes in AOJ —— **207**
5.5	Reduplication —— **207**
5.5.1	Iteration function —— **208**
5.5.2	Plurality function —— **208**
5.6	Pronouns —— **209**
5.6.1	Personal pronouns —— **209**
5.6.1.1	First-person pronouns —— **209**
5.6.1.1.1	*wa ~ ware ~ warö* —— **210**
5.6.1.1.1.1	*wa* —— **210**
5.6.1.1.1.2	*ware ~ warö* —— **213**
5.6.1.1.1.2.1	Nominative function —— **213**
5.6.1.1.1.2.2	Possessive function —— **214**
5.6.1.1.2	*wano ~ wanu* —— **215**
5.6.1.1.3	*a ~ are* —— **216**
5.6.1.1.3.1	*a* —— **216**
5.6.1.1.3.1.1	Usage as a second-person reflexive pronoun —— **218**
5.6.1.1.3.2	*are* —— **218**
5.6.1.1.4	Summary of first-person pronouns —— **220**
5.6.1.2	Second-person pronouns —— **221**
5.6.1.2.1	*na ~ nare* —— **221**
5.6.1.2.1.1	*na* —— **221**
5.6.1.2.1.2	*nare* —— **223**
5.6.1.2.2	*imasi ~ masi* —— **223**
5.6.1.2.3	Summary of second-person pronouns —— **224**
5.6.2	Demonstrative pronouns —— **225**
5.6.2.1	Proximal pronouns —— **225**
5.6.2.1.1	*könö ~ köre* 'this' —— **225**
5.6.2.1.2	*kökö* 'here' —— **227**
5.6.2.2	Mesial pronoun *sö ~ sönö* —— **227**
5.6.2.3	Distal pronouns —— **228**
5.6.2.3.1	Distal pronoun *ka ~ kanö* —— **228**
5.6.2.3.2	Distal pronoun *wote* —— **229**
5.6.3	Interrogative pronouns —— **229**
5.6.3.1	*ta- ~ tare* 'who' —— **230**
5.6.3.2	*nani* 'why, what' —— **231**

5.6.3.3	*anze* 'why, what' —— **231**	
5.6.3.4	*andö* 'what' —— **232**	
5.6.3.5	*ika* 'how, what kind' —— **234**	
5.6.3.6	*indu* 'where' —— **234**	
5.6.3.7	*indusi* 'which' —— **235**	
5.6.3.8	*indure* 'which' —— **235**	
5.6.3.9	*itu* 'when' —— **235**	
5.6.4	Collective pronouns —— **236**	
5.6.4.1	*mïna* 'all' —— **236**	
5.6.4.2	*morö-morö* 'many' —— **237**	
5.7	Numerals —— **237**	
5.7.1	Cardinal numbers —— **237**	
5.7.1.1	Bound root *-so* 'ten' —— **238**	
5.7.2	Ordinal numbers —— **239**	
5.7.3	Numeral classifiers —— **240**	
5.7.3.1	Classifier *-tanbi* —— **240**	
5.7.3.2	Classifier *-ri* —— **240**	
5.7.3.3	Classifier *-motö* —— **241**	
5.7.3.4	Classifier *-tu* —— **242**	
5.7.3.5	Classifier *-pe* —— **242**	
5.7.3.6	Classifier *-saka* —— **242**	
6	**Adjectives and adjectival verbs —— 245**	
6.1	The basic syntax of adjectives and adjectival verbs —— **245**	
6.2	Adjectives —— **245**	
6.2.1	Bare roots used as a modifier —— **245**	
6.2.2	Usage followed by an attributive copula —— **248**	
6.2.3	Multiple adjectives before a head —— **249**	
6.2.4	*-ka* final adjectives —— **250**	
6.2.5	*-nde* final adjectives —— **250**	
6.2.6	*-nda* final adjectives —— **251**	
6.2.7	Adjectival reduplication —— **251**	
6.3	Adjectival verbs —— **251**	
6.3.1	Adjectival verb classes —— **252**	
6.3.2	Prefixes —— **252**	
6.3.2.1	Intensifying prefix *ma-* —— **252**	
6.3.3	Suffixes —— **253**	
6.3.3.1	Infinitive *-ku* —— **254**	
6.3.3.1.1	Usage as a non-final predicate —— **254**	
6.3.3.1.2	Usage as an adverbial modifier —— **255**	

6.3.3.2	Nominalizer -*ku* —— 257	
6.3.3.3	Final predication marker -*si* —— 257	
6.3.3.3.1	Final function —— 257	
6.3.3.3.2	Attributive function —— 258	
6.3.3.3.3	Final form of Class 2 adjectival verbs —— 260	
6.3.3.4	Attributive -*ki* ~ -*ke* —— 260	
6.3.3.4.1	-*ki* form —— 261	
6.3.3.4.1.1	Adnominal function —— 261	
6.3.3.4.1.2	Final predication due to an attributive-triggering particle —— 262	
6.3.3.4.1.3	Nominalization function —— 263	
6.3.3.4.2	-*ke* form —— 263	
6.3.3.4.2.1	Adnominal function —— 263	
6.3.3.4.2.2	Final predication due to an attributive-triggering particle —— 264	
6.3.3.4.2.3	Nominalization function —— 265	
6.3.3.4.3	Unclear examples —— 265	
6.3.3.5	Evidential -*ka* ~ -*ke* —— 266	
6.3.3.6	Gerund -*mi* —— 267	
6.3.3.7	Conditional gerund -*anba* —— 269	
6.3.3.8	Conjunctive gerund -*nba* —— 270	
6.3.3.9	Concessive gerund -*ndö* ~ -*ndömo* —— 271	
6.3.3.10	Nominalizer -*aku* —— 271	
6.3.3.11	Nominalizer -*sa* —— 272	
6.3.3.12	Nominalizer -*nge* —— 273	
6.3.3.13	Exclamative -*mo* —— 274	
6.3.4	Bound Auxiliaries —— 275	
6.3.4.1	Subordinative gerund -*te* —— 276	

7	**Verbs —— 277**	
7.1	The basic syntax of verbs —— 277	
7.2	Verbal grammatical categories —— 277	
7.2.1	Polarity —— 277	
7.2.2	Aspect —— 278	
7.2.3	Tense —— 278	
7.2.4	Mood —— 278	
7.2.5	Voice —— 278	
7.2.6	Retrospection —— 278	
7.2.7	Iteration and Duration —— 279	
7.2.8	Predication —— 279	
7.2.9	Honorification —— 279	
7.2.10	Humbleness —— 279	

7.3	Morphotactics —— 279	
7.4	Verbal classes —— 281	
7.4.1	Consonant-final stem verbs —— 281	
7.4.2	Vowel-final stem verbs —— 282	
7.4.3	Irregular verbs —— 283	
7.4.3.1	Strong vowel-final verbs —— 283	
7.4.3.2	kö- 'come' —— 284	
7.4.3.3	se- ~ -sö ~ 'do' —— 285	
7.4.3.4	r-final irregular verbs —— 286	
7.4.3.5	Defective verbs —— 287	
7.4.3.5.1	Copula nö —— 287	
7.4.3.5.1.1	Infinitive form n-i —— 287	
7.4.3.5.1.2	Attributive root form nö —— 289	
7.4.3.5.1.3	Contracted form n- —— 290	
7.4.3.5.2	Copula tö —— 291	
7.4.3.5.3	Copula rö —— 291	
7.5	Verbal affixes —— 292	
7.5.1	Prefixes —— 292	
7.5.1.1	Durative ari- —— 292	
7.5.1.2	Tangible kaki- —— 292	
7.5.1.3	Negative-imperative na- —— 293	
7.5.1.3.1	Special construction na-VERB-INF-sö —— 294	
7.5.1.4	Directive-locative focus i- —— 295	
7.5.1.5	Intensifying ka- —— 296	
7.5.1.6	Prefix uti- —— 297	
7.5.2	Suffixes —— 297	
7.5.2.1	Sentence non-final suffixes —— 298	
7.5.2.1.1	Infinitives —— 298	
7.5.2.1.1.1	Infinitive -i ~ -u —— 298	
7.5.2.1.1.1.1	Linking function —— 298	
7.5.2.1.1.1.2	Gerund function —— 300	
7.5.2.1.1.1.3	Adnominal function —— 302	
7.5.2.1.1.1.4	Infinitive allomorph -u —— 303	
7.5.2.1.1.2	Orthographic infinitive -e —— 305	
7.5.2.1.2	Gerunds —— 306	
7.5.2.1.2.1	Conditional gerund -anba ~ -nba —— 306	
7.5.2.1.2.1.1	Temporal construction with a following verb in the tentative mood —— 308	
7.5.2.1.2.2	Conjunctive gerund -nba —— 309	
7.5.2.1.2.2.1	Expression of reason —— 309	

7.5.2.1.2.2.2	Temporal function	309
7.5.2.1.2.3	Concessive gerund *-ndömo ~ -ndö*	311
7.5.2.1.3	Nominalizers	313
7.5.2.1.3.1	Nominalizer *-i ~ -u*	313
7.5.2.1.3.1.1	Allomorph *-u*	316
7.5.2.1.3.2	Nominalizer *-aku*	317
7.5.2.2	Sentence-final suffixes	322
7.5.2.2.1	Final predication *-u ~ -i*	322
7.5.2.2.1.1	Final predication allomorph *-i*	325
7.5.2.2.2	Attributive *-uru ~ -ur- ~ -ru- ~ -oro ~ -u ~ -o*	326
7.5.2.2.2.1	Adnominal function	328
7.5.2.2.2.2	Nominalization function	330
7.5.2.2.2.3	Usage as a final predicate due to an attributive-triggering particle	331
7.5.2.2.2.4	Usage as a final predicate without an attributive-triggering particle	332
7.5.2.2.3	Attributive *-a*	334
7.5.2.2.4	Evidential *-ure ~ -re ~ -e ~ -o*	335
7.5.2.2.5	Imperative *-e ~ -ö ~ -i ~ -rö ~ -yö*	339
7.5.2.2.5.1	Imperative *-rö ~ -yö*	342
7.5.2.2.5.2	Zero imperative	343
7.5.2.2.6	Negative-imperative *-una*	344
7.5.2.2.7	Desiderative *-ana ~ -an- ~ -n-*	345
7.5.2.2.8	Negative-tentative *-anzi*	347
7.5.2.2.9	Exclamative *-umo ~ -mo*	348
7.5.2.2.10	Subjunctive *-amasi ~ -masi*	350
7.5.2.2.11	Suppositional *-urasi ~ -rasi ~ -asi*	351
7.5.2.2.12	Verbal adjectivizer *-asi*	352
7.5.2.3	Word non-final suffixes	353
7.5.2.3.1	Negative suffix *-an- ~ -anz- ~ -n- ~ -nz-*	353
7.5.2.3.1.1	Negative-Attributive *-ana- ~ -na-*	357
7.5.2.3.2	Tentative *-am- ~ -m-*	359
7.5.2.3.3	Tentative 2 *-uram- ~ -unam-*	363
7.5.2.3.3.1	Examples of TSOJ and UNP *-uram-*	363
7.5.2.3.3.2	Examples of EOJ *-unam-*	364
7.5.2.3.4	Iterative *-ap- ~ -öp-*	365
7.5.2.3.4.1	Iterative-infinitive *-ape ~ -öpe*	368
7.5.2.3.4.1.1	Linking function	369
7.5.2.3.4.1.2	Adnominal function	369
7.5.2.3.4.1.3	Nominalization function	370

7.5.2.3.5	Passive -are- ~ -ar- ~ -aye- ~ -ye- ~ -y- —— 371	
7.5.2.3.5.1	Potential function —— 371	
7.5.2.3.5.2	Passive function —— 372	
7.5.2.3.5.3	Spontaneous action function —— 372	
7.5.2.3.6	Honorific -as- ~ -s- ~ -os- —— 374	
7.5.2.3.7	Causative -asime- ~ -asim- ~ -sime- —— 376	
7.5.2.3.8	Causative -ase- ~ -as- ~ -se- —— 377	
7.5.2.3.9	Debitive -unbe- —— 378	
7.5.2.3.10	Progressive -ar- ~ -er- ~ -ir- —— 379	
7.5.2.3.10.1	EOJ progressive -ar- —— 380	
7.5.2.3.10.2	WOJ/TSOJ progressive -er- —— 382	
7.5.2.3.10.3	Suruga TSOJ progressive -ir- —— 383	
7.6	Auxiliaries —— 384	
7.6.1	Bound auxiliaries —— 384	
7.6.1.1	Word-final bound auxiliaries —— 384	
7.6.1.1.1	Subordinative gerund -te —— 384	
7.6.1.1.2	Coordinative gerund -tutu ~ -tusi ~ -tötö —— 388	
7.6.1.1.2.1	Variant -tusi —— 390	
7.6.1.1.2.2	Variant -tötö —— 390	
7.6.1.1.3	Past tense -kV —— 390	
7.6.1.1.4	Past-attributive -si —— 392	
7.6.1.1.5	Past-evidential -sika —— 394	
7.6.1.2	Word non-final auxiliaries —— 395	
7.6.1.2.1	Perfectives -n- and -te- ~ -t- —— 396	
7.6.1.2.1.1	Perfective -n- —— 396	
7.6.1.2.1.2	Perfective -te- ~ -t- —— 400	
7.6.1.2.2	Perfective/Progressive -tar- —— 402	
7.6.1.2.3	Retrospective -ker- ~ -kar- —— 403	
7.6.1.2.3.1	EOJ form -kar- —— 404	
7.6.1.2.4	Potential -kate- ~ -kande- —— 405	
7.6.1.2.5	Negative-potential-infinitive -kane- ~ -ngane- —— 406	
7.6.1.2.6	Benefactive -kös- —— 407	
7.6.1.2.7	Conjectural -mer- —— 408	
7.6.2	Lexical auxiliaries —— 408	
7.6.2.1	Honorific auxiliaries —— 409	
7.6.2.1.1	Honorific auxiliary -tamap- —— 409	
7.6.2.1.2	Honorific auxiliary -mas- —— 409	
7.6.2.2	Humble auxiliaries —— 410	
7.6.2.2.1	Humble auxiliary -matur- —— 410	
7.6.2.3	Other auxiliaries —— 411	

7.6.2.3.1	Dummy auxiliary -ar- —— **411**	
7.6.2.3.2	Resultative auxiliary -ok- —— **412**	
7.6.2.3.3	Auxiliary -ngata 'difficult to do' and two similar forms —— **412**	
7.6.2.3.4	Directive auxiliaries —— **413**	
7.6.2.3.4.1	Directive auxiliary -kö- —— **414**	
7.6.2.3.4.2	Directive auxiliary -yuk- ~ -ik- —— **415**	
7.6.2.3.4.3	Directive auxiliary -nde- —— **416**	
7.6.2.3.4.4	Directive auxiliary -yör- —— **417**	
7.6.2.3.4.5	Directive auxiliary tuk- —— **418**	
7.7	Suppletive honorific and humble verbs —— **419**	
7.7.1	Honorific imas- —— **419**	
7.7.2	Humble tamapar- ~ tanbar- —— **420**	
7.7.3	Humble mawos- —— **420**	
7.7.4	Humble mawi- —— **421**	
7.7.5	Humble kangapur- —— **421**	
7.8	Serial verb constructions —— **421**	
7.9	Light verb constructions —— **423**	
7.10	Verbal reduplication —— **425**	

8 Adverbs —— 427

8.1	*ito* 'simply, very, really' —— **427**	
8.2	*kökönba* 'extremely' —— **428**	
8.3	*sapanda* 'many, much, amply' —— **428**	
8.4	*mata* 'again' —— **429**	
8.5	*iya* 'plentifully, certainly' —— **430**	
8.6	*napo* 'still' —— **430**	
8.7	*imanda* 'yet, still' —— **430**	
8.8	*motöna* 'incessantly, at random' —— **431**	
8.9	*tanda* 'directly' —— **431**	
8.10	*nökinde* 'extremely' —— **431**	
8.11	*sinzi* 'constantly' —— **432**	
8.12	*simaraku* 'for a while' —— **432**	
8.13	*köngötö* 'greatly' —— **432**	
8.14	*unbey* 'surely' —— **433**	
8.15	*yumey* '[not] at all' —— **433**	
8.16	*wosawosa* '[not] enough, [not] properly' —— **433**	

9 Conjunctions —— 435

9.1	*tömo* 'even if, even though' —— **435**	
9.2	*mono ~ monöwo* 'although, but, considering' —— **437**	

9.3	*monökara* 'although' —— **437**	
9.4	*ngani* 'so that' —— **438**	
9.5	*ngani* 'like' —— **438**	
9.6	*sinda* 'when' —— **438**	

10	**Particles —— 441**	
10.1	The basic syntax of particles —— **441**	
10.1.1	Attributive-triggering particles (*kakari musubi*) —— **441**	
10.1.2	Evidential-triggering particles —— **441**	
10.2	Focus particles —— **441**	
10.2.1	Topic particle *pa* —— **442**	
10.2.2	Focus particle *mo* —— **445**	
10.2.3	Focus particle *sö ~ nzö ~ nze ~ tö* —— **449**	
10.2.3.1	Variant *nzö* —— **451**	
10.2.3.2	Variant *nze* —— **451**	
10.2.3.3	Variant *tö* —— **451**	
10.2.4	Focus particle *kösö* —— **453**	
10.3	Emphatic particles —— **454**	
10.3.1	Emphatic particle *kamo* —— **454**	
10.3.1.1	Exclamation function —— **455**	
10.3.1.2	Uncertainty function —— **456**	
10.3.1.3	Special construction *-te-si kamo* —— **458**	
10.3.2	Emphatic particle *si* —— **458**	
10.3.3	Emphatic particle *mo* —— **460**	
10.3.4	Emphatic particle *ya* —— **462**	
10.3.5	Emphatic particle *yö* —— **464**	
10.3.6	Emphatic particle *ye* —— **466**	
10.3.7	Emphatic particle *na* —— **466**	
10.3.8	Emphatic particle *we* —— **467**	
10.4	Question particles —— **467**	
10.4.1	Yes/no question particle *ya* —— **468**	
10.4.1.1	Usage in ironic questions —— **469**	
10.4.2	Question particle *ka* —— **470**	
10.4.2.1	Usage in a special emphatic construction —— **472**	
10.5	Restrictive particles —— **473**	
10.5.1	Restrictive particle *nömi* —— **473**	
10.5.2	Restrictive particle *ndani* —— **474**	
10.5.3	Restrictive particle *sapey* —— **475**	
10.6	Desiderative particle *monga[mo]* —— **476**	

10.7 Ironic particle *ngape* —— **478**
10.8 Quotative particle *tö ~ te* —— **478**

Appendix A – A classification of poems in MYS Book 14 based on linguistic features —— 483

References —— 511

Index —— 519

Glossing conventions

-	morpheme boundary (inclusive of affixes, auxiliaries, and parts of a compound)
.	indicates a morpheme boundary in the glossing of portmanteau morphs, or a word boundary in the multiword English glosses of a single morpheme
*	reconstructed form
//	phonemic transcription
[ ]	phonetic transcription, or a marginal phoneme (in the phoneme charts)
C	any consonant
V	any vowel
Ø	zero morph or phone
:	corresponds to
>	changed to
<	developed from
#	word boundary (indicates the beginning or end of a word)

Translation conventions

[ ]	Words or morphemes not overtly present in the original text
(lit.)	a literal translation

Abbreviations

Grammatical Terms

1	first person
2	second person
ABL	ablative case
ABS	absolutive case
ACC	accusative case
ADJ	adjectivizer
ALL	allative case
ATTR	attributive
AVATTR	adjectival verb attributive
AVEV	adjectival verb evidential
AVFIN	adjectival verb final
AVGER	adjectival verb gerund
AVINF	adjectival verb infinitive
BEN	benefactive
CAUS	causative
CL	classifier
CNJ	conjunction
CNJC	conjectural mood
COL	collective
COM	comitative case
COMP	comparative case
CONC	concessive gerund
COND	conditional gerund
CONJ	conjunctive gerund
COOR	coordinative gerund
COP	copula
DAT	dative case
DEB	debitive mood
DES	desiderative mood
DIM	diminutive
DIR	directive case
DLF	directive-locative focus
DPT	desiderative particle
DUR	durative
EXCL	exclamative
EMP	emphatic
EPN	epenthetic consonant or vowel
EPT	emphatic particle
EV	evidential
FIN	final
FPT	focus particle
GEN	genitive case

HON	honorific
HUM	humble
IMP	imperative mood
INF	infinitive
INT	intensifier
IPT	ironic particle
ITER	iterative
LOC	locative case
NEG	negative
NML	nominalizer
NOM	nominative case
PASS	passive
PERF	perfective aspect
PLUR	plural
PN	proper name
POSS	possessive case
POT	potential
PP	perfective/progressive aspect
PREF	prefix
PROG	progressive aspect
PST	past tense
PT	particle
QUOT	quotative particle
QPT	question particle
RETR	retrospective
RPT	restrictive particle
S	singular (in regard to first or second person)
SUB	subordinative gerund
SUBJ	subjunctive mood
SUP	suppositional
TNG	tangible
TENT	tentative mood
TENT2	tentative 2 mood
TERM	terminative case
TN	toponym (or "place name")
TPT	topic particle
TRANS	transitivizing suffix

Azuma Old Japanese Provinces/Topolects

Kak	Kamitukeno Province/Topolect
Kap	Kamitupusa Province/Topolect
Mi	Mitinöku Province/Topolect
Mu	Muzasi Province/Topolect
Pi	Pitati Province/Topolect

Sa	Sagamu Province/Topolect
Sik	Simotukeno Province/Topolect
Sin	Sinano Province/Topolect
Sip	Simotupusa Province/Topolect
Su	Suruga Province/Topolect
Tö	Töpotuapumi Province/Topolect
UNP	Unknown Province

Language varieties

AOJ	Azuma Old Japanese (8th century CE dialects, Azuma region)
COJ	Central Old Japanese (8th century CE, unattested dialect)
EMC	Early Middle Chinese (approximately 600 CE)
EOJ	Eastern Old Japanese (8th century CE, eastern Azuma region)
KOJ	Kyūshū Old Japanese (8th century CE, present-day Kyūshū region)
LH	Late Han Chinese (2nd century CE)
MJ	Middle Japanese (9th century CE – 12th century CE)
NOJ	Nötö Old Japanese (8th century CE, Noto peninsula)
OJ	Old Japanese (8th century CE, cover term for all OJ dialects)
PJ	Proto-Japonic
PJe	Proto-Japanese
PR	Proto-Ryukyuan
TSOJ	Töpo-Suruga Old Japanese (8th century CE, western Azuma region)
WOJ	Western Old Japanese (8th century CE, Nara region)

Texts

BS	*Bussokuseki no Uta* (approximately 770 CE)
KK	*Kojiki Kayō* (712 CE)
MYS	*Man'yōshū* ('Collection of Ten Thousand Leaves') (759 CE)
NK	*Nihon Shoki Kayō* (720 CE)

Primary Manuscripts

GK	*Genryaku Kōhon*
NHB	*Nishi Honganji-Bon*

Other

Func   function
MK   *makura kotoba*[3]
UNC   unclear

---

[3] Literally 'pillow words', it refers to a set epithet in Japanese poetry.

1 Introduction

The Azuma Old Japanese (henceforth AOJ) dialects were spoken in Japan during the Nara period (eighth century CE) in the eastern region called Azuma that stretched from present-day Shizuoka and Nagano, east to Ibaraki, and all areas between them extending southward to the Pacific. The large northeastern area known as Mitinōku that covered present-day Fukushima, Miyagi, Iwate, and Aomori was also included in this area. AOJ is only attested in poetry.

It should be noted from the outset that I use "AOJ" as a purely areal term. My use of AOJ in reference to the different dialects in this region instead of the traditional term "Eastern Old Japanese" (EOJ) is an effort to break away from the long-held, and yet unsubstantiated, claim that the provinces in the Azuma region contained speakers of a single dialect chain (Fukuda 1965; Hōjō 1966; Mizushima 1984a; Hino 2003; Vovin 2005: xvii; Ikier 2006: 5, 64–65). The data simply do not support this hypothesis, and I hope this will become clear to the reader as they progress through the book. Based on the linguistic evidence it is undeniable there were two major dialects in Azuma, and they developed separately from Proto-Japanese, since each of these dialects shows linguistic innovations that could not have developed from the other. Moreover, this change in terminology allows me to repurpose the term "Eastern Old Japanese" for one of these distinct dialects within AOJ, whereas I term the other dialect "Tōpo-Suruga Old Japanese" (TSOJ).[4]

These AOJ dialects, as textually attested, have long been vexing for philologists and linguists, and it is in their difficulty of interpretation that several important questions naturally arise: What did these dialects sound like? How did they develop from Proto-Japanese? How did their phonology, morphology, and lexicon differ from Western Old Japanese (henceforth WOJ), the contemporaneous dialect of Nara? How did they differ from one another? This book contains my attempts to answer these questions.

AOJ is attested in twelve provinces:[5] Sinano 信濃, Tōpotuapumi 遠江, Suruga 駿河, Idu 伊豆, Kamitukeno 上毛野, Muzasi 武蔵, Sagamu 相模, Mitinōku 陸奥, Simotukeno 下毛野, Pitati 常陸, Simotupusa 下総, and Kamitupusa 上総. There is only one Idu poem (along with a variant) available to us, though most of the other provinces have a fair amount of data. There were two other provinces in Azuma from which we have no

---

[4] Previously I referred to this as "Tōpo-Suruga", abbreviated TS. I have also recently added the Sinano topolect to this subgrouping. My reason for this is discussed in Chapter 2.

[5] I write the province names phonemically in the International Phonetic Alphabet based on the eighth-century pronunciations I reconstruct for them, with four modifications: 1) /ə/ is written as ö, 2) /ɨ/ is written as ï, 3) the initial consonant is capitalized, and 4) the prenasalized voiced obstruents are written as plain voiced (e.g., /ⁿzi/ is written as zi, instead of nzi). This differs slightly from the WOJ transliteration system used throughout this book.

identifiable linguistic data: Kapï 甲斐 and Apa 安房. A map of the Azuma provinces is provided in Figure 1.1. In this book I refer to the major language varieties as "dialects" (WOJ, TSOJ, EOJ), but I use the term "topolect" when referring to the language variety of a particular province. Since "topolect" refers to the speech variety of a place or region (Mair 1991) and the AOJ data is sorted based on provinces with linguistically arbitrary boundaries, I concluded it was the most appropriate term for this study.

After the Nara period TSOJ seems to have died out completely and was replaced by a more prestigious Middle Japanese dialect, but a descendant of EOJ has managed to survive to the present-day in the Hachijō language,[6] spoken on islands to the south of Tōkyō. Pellard (2015: 13–16, 2016: 100) has raised the possibility Hachijō is instead a primary branch of Japonic, like Proto-Ryukyuan (PR) and Proto-Japanese (PJe). However, linguistic innovations shared between EOJ and Hachijō prove this is not the case (Asanuma 1999: 10; Kaneda 2001: 179; Kupchik 2016: 734, 2021a: 99). Additional evidence demonstrating the clear and unique linguistic connection between EOJ and Hachijō (Hattori 1968) is also presented in this book.

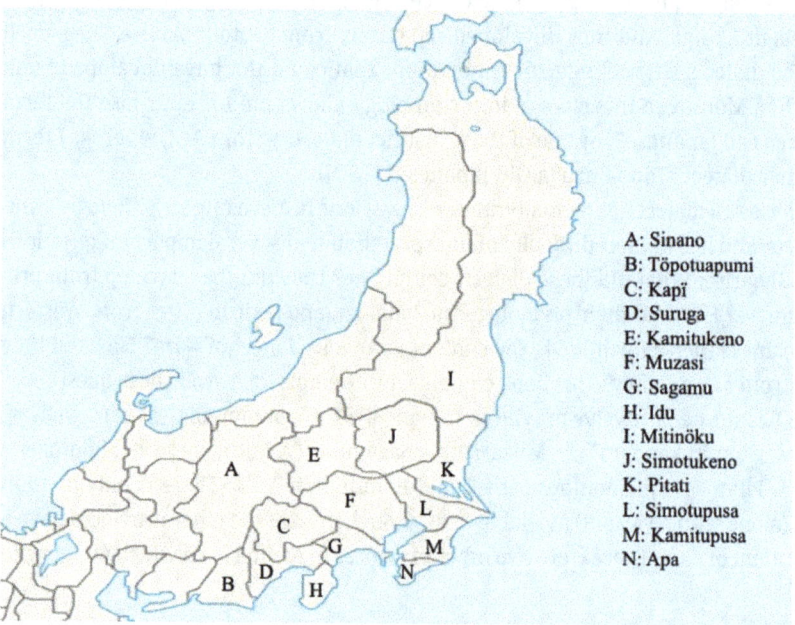

Figure 1.1: Map of the Azuma provinces in the eighth century CE.[7]

---

6 Some EOJ features have also survived in mainland Japanese dialects, including the Tōkyō dialect.
7 This map is a modified version of the one presented on http://commons.wikimedia.org/wiki/File:Provinces_of_Japan.svg

1.1 Basic grammatical and typological characteristics of AOJ

The core grammatical and typological features of these dialects differ from WOJ in mostly minor ways, and certainly less than they do in comparison to PR, which is unsurprising considering all attested OJ dialects descend from PJe, rather than Proto-Japonic (PJ). We find a basic word order of SOV, with a modifier-head phrasal structure. Suffixes are plentiful, and they include case, number, and diminutive suffixes for nouns, along with a rich morphological system in the verbs including tense, aspect, mood, and predication suffixes. However, there are also several prefixes, for both nouns and verbs. The morphology is predominantly agglutinative, but there are some portmanteau morphs as well. The phonotactic structure is a strict (C)V, with no geminate consonants or long vowels,[8] and accordingly the language was most likely syllable-timed. The details of the accent system are unknown because accent was not marked in the orthography and contemporaneous sources offer us no clues.

1.2 Verse and meter

Most of the AOJ poems consist of 31 syllables, in the structure of 5-7-5-7-7 syllables. This is known as the *tanka* ('short poem') form. One poem in the corpus (poem 4372 in book 20, from Pitati province) is a *chōka* ('long poem') composed of 91 syllables over 15 lines, in the structure 5-7-5-7-5-7-5-7-5-7-5-7-5-7-7. In addition, some poems have one or two extra syllables. In these poems, a five-syllable line is extended into a six-syllable line or a seven-syllable line is extended into an eight-syllable line. This is known as hypermetricality. An in-depth discussion of this phenomenon and other synchronic phonological processes, such as vowel elision, is presented in Chapter 3.

1.3 The linguistic situation in Japan in the eighth century CE

Outside of AOJ, there are several other attested OJ dialects that were spoken contemporaneously during the Nara period, including Western Old Japanese (WOJ), Nötö Old Japanese (NOJ), and Kyūshū Old Japanese (KOJ). WOJ, which includes the closely related topolects of Nara and Asuka, is the most well attested of any OJ

---

[8] A study of toponyms by Osterkamp (2011) suggests AOJ topolects did not automatically lengthen monosyllabic words into bimoraic long vowels, unlike Western OJ topolects.

dialect. NOJ is only attested in three poems in MYS 16 (see Vovin 2021a for analysis),[9] and the extant linguistic data we have for KOJ is similarly quite meager (Vovin 2009c, 2021a: 144–145).

In addition to these Japonic language varieties there were also widespread Ainu speakers in the eastern provinces of Japan. At least until 791 CE, when the military deputy Sakanöupey nö Tamuramarö set about to push the Ainu to the far reaches of the northeastern area of Japan, historical accounts lead us to believe the Ainu and the Japanese settlers in the eastern provinces lived side by side with few major problems, and ethnic mixing was most likely not an uncommon occurrence (Sansom 1958: 105–106). Linguistic evidence supports this notion: there are Ainu loanwords in AOJ that do not occur in WOJ (see Chapter 4). There were also people called the Kumasö and Payatö (aka Hayato) living in southern and central Kyūshū. Some scholars (Torii 1918; Nishimura 1922) have argued these people were of Southeast Asian origin, while Murayama (1975), Kakubayashi (1998), and Vovin (2021b) claim the language(s) of the Kumasö and Payatö people were Austronesian. In either case, there is no evidence these speakers had any direct contact with AOJ speakers. Loanword evidence suggests that before the eighth century there was an Amis-speaking population somewhere in southern Kyūshū (Vovin 2021b) and possibly also the northern Ryūkyū Islands (Kupchik 2021b), but it is not clear if this population was still present in Kyūshū in the eighth century, and, once again, contact with AOJ speakers seems unlikely. Finally, there were many immigrants from Korea and China, mostly in the western and central regions of Japan.

1.4 Textual sources

The primary sources of the AOJ dialects are Books 14 and 20 of the *Man'yōshū* (MYS). The poems in Book 14 are also known as the *Azuma-uta* 'Azuma poems', while the poems in Book 20 are called the *Sakimori-uta* 'Border guard poems'. In addition, we also have the nine *Pitati Fudoki* poems.

In this book I exclude the small *Pitati Fudoki* corpus and only use the MYS corpus. My decision for this is because only a few *Pitati Fudoki* poems possibly show AOJ linguistic features, and, unfortunately, their textual history shows signs of significant corruption. This is not surprising considering the earliest extant manuscript dates from the late 17th century (Aoki 1997: 27), nearly 1000 years after the poems are thought to have been composed. One example illustrating this is found

---

9 Vovin considers NOJ to be Eastern Old Japanese, but I have recently argued against that claim, due to the absence of shared innovations between NOJ and EOJ (see Kupchik 2022 for details).

in *Pitati Fudoki* song 8 in which PJ *usipo 'sea water' (cf. WOJ *usipo*) is written as *usiwo* 宇志乎 'id.'. The intervocalic lenition of *p > /w/ occurred after the Nara period, and owing to the lack of any other examples of this lenition in any other AOJ poem, it appears a later scribe altered the text in this song to fit in with the language of his time. Issues such as this make the *Pitati Fudoki* an unreliable source.

1.5 Major studies on AOJ

The major studies on AOJ can be split into three categories: commentaries, philological studies, and linguistic studies. Usually, any work on AOJ touches upon topics that fall under all three of these categories, but my description of the works is based on their main focus.

The commentaries delve into the meanings and themes of the poems as well as the meaning of the words in the poems, with translations in a modern language, such as Japanese or English, provided. They may also discuss non-linguistic topics such as the cultural, geographical, historical, or religious context of the words in the poems, as well as the authors of the poems. The major studies include Omodaka (1965, 1968), Nakanishi (1978 – 1983), Mizushima (1984c, 1986, 2003, 2009), Kinoshita (1988), Itō (1995 – 2000), and Vovin (2012a, 2013).

The philological studies have been dominated by the works of Mizushima (1972, 1984b, 1984c, 1996). His monumental works are still indispensable today.

The linguistic studies focus mainly on the phonetics, phonology, morphology, grammar, dialect features, or historical development. The major studies include Fukuda (1965), Hōjō (1966), and Mizushima (1984a, 2005). The MA thesis by Ikier (2006) on the attributive and final marking of AOJ is also notable for some important discoveries in the morphology. Kupchik (2011) was the first phonemic reconstruction and grammar of AOJ in English and serves as the foundation for the present book.

1.6 WOJ transliteration system and phonemic reconstruction

The AOJ poems were written with the WOJ orthography which consists of phonograms called *Man'yōgana*, along with some logograms. Therefore, any analysis of AOJ phonology must be viewed through the lens of this orthography. There are several different transliteration systems for WOJ, but I found all of them to be unsatisfactory for this book. Therefore, I chose the system by Kindaichi, Miller, and Ōno as a base, mainly because their *ï* and *ö* clearly indicate these are central vowels, but I made two modifications: 1) I use *ey* instead of their *ë*, and 2) the prenasalized voiced consonants are written with the digraphs *nb, nd, nz*, and *ng* instead of *b, d, z,* and *g*. I employ the digraph *ey* (adopted from Martin's Yale system) because it more clearly indicates the diphthongal nature of this vowel ([əy]), in contrast to the rest of the vowels which are monophthongs. I use the separate graph *n* for prenasalization[10] because it allows us to analyze the morphemic function of the prenasalization in a clearer manner, while being more readable than a superscript (e.g., ⁿd). It must be emphasized that these digraphs represent unitary phones, just as *ts* indicates an affricate in the Hepburn romanization system of Modern Japanese.

The WOJ transliteration system used in this book and the accompanying reconstructed WOJ phonemic values (based on Miyake 2003) are provided below.

WOJ Consonants:
p = /p/, *t* = /t/, *k* = /k/, *s* = /s/, *n* = /n/, *m* = /m/, *nb* = /ᵐb/, *nd* = /ⁿd/, *ng* = /ᵑg/, *nz* = /ⁿz/, *r* = /r/, *w* = /w/, *y* = /y/

WOJ Vowels:
After a consonant
a = /a/, *i* = /i/, *ï* = /ɨ/, *u* = /u/, *e* = /e/, *ey* = /əy/, *o* = /o/, *ö* = /ə/.

Syllable-initial
a = /a/, *i* = /i/, *u* = /u/, *o* = /ə/ ~ /o/, *wo* = /wo/, *ye* = /ye/

I follow the reconstruction of WOJ by Miyake (2003) because his detailed analysis of an enormous amount of data is unparalleled and I find his conclusions based on this analysis to be very convincing. Among the many vocalic reconstructions put forth to date[11] we find Miyake's to be closest to Arisaka's (1955). The only differences are Miyake reconstructed *ɨ for Arisaka's *ïi ([ɨi]), and *əy for Arisaka's *ǝe/*əi̯.

The orthographic practices used to transcribe the poems of the TSOJ dialect add even more support to Miyake's WOJ reconstruction. For example, WOJ phonograms with the transliteration *key* are used to write the syllables /kəy/ in WOJ, /kə/ in TSOJ, and /ke/ in EOJ. I proposed this because *kö* phonograms (WOJ /kə/, TSOJ /kə/, EOJ /kə/) are used in free variation with *key* phonograms in TSOJ (Kupchik 2007: 9). Since we only need to posit the historical deletion of *y in *kəy (< *kai) to account for this later orthographic merger in TSOJ, it can be easily explained within the framework

---

10 In Kupchik (2011) I used *N* for this, but I prefer the lowercase for its better look on the page, as well as the clearer distinction it provides between phonograms and logograms. This is because the readings of logograms are presented in capital letters, so if I were to capitalize *N* as well, *NGA* and *Nga* would be less clearly distinguished than *NGA* and *nga* are.

11 Miyake (2003: 62) lists 26 different reconstructions of WOJ vowels (and his list is not exhaustive).

of Miyake's reconstruction. On the other hand, in the popular WOJ reconstruction by Frellesvig and Whitman (2004), for example, these syllables are /ko/ (*kö*) and /ke/ (*key*). If we use this reconstruction, it is hard to find a similarly plausible phonetic reason why phonograms for these two syllables would be used in free variation in TSOJ. The same can be said about a form like TSOJ (Sinano topolect) *tönönbik-* 'to stream out': WOJ *tananbik-* 'id.'. In Miyake's reconstruction *ö* is /ə/, but in Frellesvig and Whitman's reconstruction it is /o/. The change of *a > /ə/ is a typical case of vowel reduction through centralization, but the change of *a > /o/ is rarer and more difficult to explain, especially in an environment without a neighboring labial consonant.

1.7 Orthography

In this section I present all of the phonograms and logograms used to write the AOJ poetry.

1.7.1 Phonograms

The Chinese phonograms used to transcribe the AOJ poems are listed in the tables below with their WOJ transliteration (*ongana*). The corresponding reconstructed (phonemic) readings of each phonogram in WOJ, TSOJ, and EOJ are also provided. The historical phonology underlying the TSOJ and EOJ readings is presented in Chapter 2, but some brief notes on TSOJ will be helpful here.

In TSOJ, the raising of *e > /i/ occurred in Suruga after the split from Proto-TSOJ. A few *Ce* syllables appear to have raised to *Ci* unconditionally, and that is why I list two readings for these *Ce* phonograms (e.g., *ke ~ *ki). In such cases only the reading with the unraised vowel (*Ce*) is applicable for Töpotuapumi and Sinano whereas the raised vowel reading (*Ci*) is applicable for Suruga. The raising of *o > /u/ is even more pervasive in TSOJ, but it is not restricted to Suruga, and it is for this reason that I list two readings for *Co* phonograms (e.g., *so ~ *su). When I list *ye ~ *ya, the reconstruction *ye is only applicable to the Suruga topolect. Lastly, the second reading provided for some of the coronal-initial phonograms, such as in the case of *nzə ~ *nze, only applies to the Suruga topolect.

In AOJ poetry, often there was no clear orthographic distinction between voiceless and prenasalized voiced obstruents, and that is why in Tables 1.1 – 1.5 below you will find cases in which the same phonogram is listed in two rows. For example, the phonogram 婆 *nba* could also be used to write *pa*. We can decide on the underlying reading of 婆 as *nba* due to its more common usage of writing syllables with a prenasalized voiced onset, as well as the original Chinese reading from which it derives (see Omodaka 1967: 898–899; Bentley 2016: 19, 273). This kind of orthographic free variation is more extensive in AOJ than in WOJ. For example, in WOJ, 弖 was only used to write *te* (Omodaka 1967: 897; Bentley 2016: 434–435), but in AOJ it could also be used to write word-medial *nde* (e.g., 麻左弖 *masande* 'certain' in 14:3374.3 – Muzasi).

Table 1.1: Labial-initial phonograms.

Phonograms	WOJ transliteration	WOJ reconstruction	TSOJ reconstruction	EOJ reconstruction
波泊播破伴婆	pa	*pa	*pa	*pa
比	pi	*pi	*pi	*pi
非悲飛必	pï	*pɨ	*pɨ	*pi
布不敷	pu	*pu	*pu	*pu
弊敝弁	pe	*pe	*pe	*pe
倍閇	pey	*pəy	*po ~ *pu	*pe
保寶抱富	po	*po	*po ~ *pu	*po
婆	nba	*ᵐba	*ᵐba	*ᵐba
妣婢比	nbi	*ᵐbi	*ᵐbi	*ᵐbi
夫	nbu	*ᵐbu	*ᵐbu	*ᵐbu
弊敝	nbe	*ᵐbe	*ᵐbe	*ᵐbe
倍	nbey	*ᵐbəy	*ᵐbo ~ *ᵐbu	*ᵐbe
麻萬末馬[12]	ma	*ma	*ma	*ma
美弥	mi	*mi	*mi	*mi
未	mï	*mɨ	*mɨ	*mi
牟武模無无	mu	*mu	*mu	*mu
馬賣	me	*me	*me	*me
米	mey	*məy	*mo ~ *mu	*me
毛	mo	*mo	*mo ~ *mu	*mo
母物	mö	*mə ~ *mo	*mo ~ *mu	*mo
和	wa	*wa	*wa	*wa
為	wi	*wi	*wi	*wi
恵	we	*we	*we	*we
乎袁	wo	*wo	*wo ~ *wu	*wo

---

12 Only attested in the toponym 對馬 *Tusima*, a usage that was probably inherited from Wei Zhi scribes (Bentley 2016: 173). This phonogram is otherwise only read as *me* in AOJ poetry, though logographic usage as *[U]MA* is also attested.

1.7 Orthography

Table 1.2: Coronal-initial phonograms.

Phonograms	WOJ transliteration	WOJ reconstruction	TSOJ reconstruction	EOJ reconstruction
多他	ta	*ta	*ta	*ta
知	ti	*ti	*ti	*ti
都追豆[13]	tu	*tu	*tu	*tu
弖氐天	te	*te	*te	*te
刀度	to	*to	*to ~ *tu	*to
等登得	tö	*tə	*tə ~ *te	*tə
太	nda	*ⁿda	*ⁿda	*ⁿda
治遅	ndi	*ⁿdi	*ⁿdi	*ⁿdi
豆頭	ndu	*ⁿdu	*ⁿdu	*ⁿdu
泥伱提代渥田弖	nde	*ⁿde	*ⁿde	*ⁿde
度	ndo	*ⁿdo	*ⁿdo ~ *ⁿdu	*ⁿdo
騰杼	ndö	*ⁿdə	*ⁿdə	*ⁿdə
左佐散作草	sa	*sa	*sa	*sa
斯志次吹思之師四	si	*si	*si	*si
須酒	su	*su	*su	*su
世勢西	se	*se	*se	*se
宗蘇素祖	so	*so	*so ~ *su	*so
曽	sö	*sə	*sə ~ *se	*sə
射	nza	*ⁿza	*ⁿza	*ⁿza
自	nzi	*ⁿzi	*ⁿzi	*ⁿzi
受須	nzu	*ⁿzu	*ⁿzu	*ⁿzu
是齊	nze	*ⁿze	*ⁿze	*ⁿze
叙	nzö	*ⁿzə	*ⁿzə ~ *ⁿze	*ⁿzə
奈那	na	*na	*na	*na
尓	ni	*ni	*ni	*ni
奴濃	nu	*nu	*nu	*nu
祢尼年	ne	*ne	*ne	*ne
怒努	no	*no	*no ~ *nu	*no
能乃	nö	*nə	*nə ~ *ne	*nə
良浪羅	ra	*ra	*ra	*ra
里理利	ri	*ri	*ri	*ri

---

13 In Suruga the phonogram 豆 was used to write word-initial *tu* (it represents *ndu* or *tu* when used to write a non-initial syllable), which is a practice we do not find in the WOJ poetry of the MYS (Kupchik 2011: 130). The answer lies in the orthographic systems of older WOJ texts. In the *Nihon Shoki Kayō* and the *Kojiki Kayō* this phonogram is amply attested and is in most cases used to write non-initial *ndu* syllables. However, there are a few cases in which it is used to write a word-initial *tu* syllable (NK 106 and KK 78) or a word-medial *tu* syllable (Bentley 2016: 462), which is the same phenomenon we find in the poems written in the Suruga topolect of TSOJ. This phonogram was also used to write word-medial *tu* in the Töpotuapumi topolect of TSOJ. In EOJ, however, it is only used to write *ndu*.

Table 1.2 (continued)

Phonograms	WOJ transliteration	WOJ reconstruction	TSOJ reconstruction	EOJ reconstruction
流留	ru	*ru	*ru	*ru
礼例	re	*re	*re	*re
路	ro	*ro	*ro ~ *ru	*ro
呂里[14]	rö	*rə	*rə ~ *re	*rə

Table 1.3: Palatal-initial phonograms.

Phonograms	WOJ transliteration	WOJ reconstruction	TSOJ reconstruction	EOJ reconstruction
也夜楊	ya	*ya	*ya	*ya
由遊	yu	*yu	*yu	*yu
延曳要衣	ye	*ye	*ye ~ *yə	*ye
欲用	yo	*yo	*yo ~ *yu	*yo
与與余餘	yö	*yə	*yə	*yə

Table 1.4: Velar-initial phonograms.

Phonograms	WOJ transliteration	WOJ reconstruction	TSOJ reconstruction	EOJ reconstruction
可加迦香賀河	ka	*ka	*ka	*ka
伎枳吉岐	ki	*ki	*ki	*ki
紀奇	kï	*kɨ	*kɨ	*ki
久苦九口具	ku	*ku	*ku	*ku
家價祁鷄	ke	*ke	*ke ~ *ki	*ke

---

14 In the WOJ and TSOJ poems of the MYS, as well as in nearly all EOJ topolects, the phonogram 里 is only used to write the syllable *ri*. However, exclusively in the Simotupusa topolect of EOJ, and only in MYS Book 20, it is used to write *rö*. This is an older reading of 里 that is found in Suiko period (593–628 CE) transcriptions (Bentley 2016: 340–341) and is an interesting example of some of the finer orthographic details we discover when the poems of each AOJ topolect are separated and analyzed independently of one another. Vovin (2013: 150) made this important observation and provided some thoughts on the possible implications:

> It is quite possible that the archaic phonographic usage survived on [the] periphery in Azuma. If so, this incidentally provides us the perspective on both the literacy in Azuma, and on the fact that the poems were transcribed by *sakimori* themselves, and not by *sakimori* messengers, who presented them to Opotömö-nö Yakamöti, because it is more likely that *sakimori* messengers, being themselves born and bred in Kansai would use [the] more up-to-date spelling system.

Table 1.4 (continued)

Phonograms	WOJ transliteration	WOJ reconstruction	TSOJ reconstruction	EOJ reconstruction
氣	key	*kəy	*kə	*ke
古故	ko	*ko	*ko ~ *ku	*ko
己許去	kö	*kə	*kə	*kə
賀我河何加可	nga	*ᵑga	*ᵑga	*ᵑga
藝	ngi	*ᵑgi	*ᵑgi	*ᵑgi
疑宜義	ngï	*ᵑgɨ	*ᵑgɨ	*ᵑgɨ
具	ngu	*ᵑgu	*ᵑgu	*ᵑgu
牙	nge	*ᵑge	*ᵑge ~ *ᵑgi	*ᵑge
氣	ngey	*ᵑgəy	*ᵑgə	*ᵑge
胡吾	ngo	*ᵑgo	*ᵑgo ~ *ᵑgu	*ᵑgo
其	ngö	*ᵑgə	*ᵑgə	*ᵑgə

Table 1.5: Vowel-initial phonograms.

Phonograms	WOJ transliteration	WOJ reconstruction	TSOJ reconstruction	EOJ reconstruction
阿安	a	*a	*a	*a
伊己以	i	*i	*i	*i
宇有	u	*u	*u	*u
意於	o	*ə ~ *o	*ə ~ *o	*ə ~ *o

1.7.1.1 Disyllabic phonograms

In addition to the numerous monosyllabic phonograms we also find a small number of disyllabic phonograms, but these are only used in toponyms. They appear be remnants of an older orthographic tradition, as they more closely reflect LH pronunciations than EMC pronunciations. Nearly all of them also feature an added vowel (usually an echo vowel) after the coda in lieu of a deletion of the coda, which we find in the monosyllabic phonograms. I include the reconstructed EMC and LH forms from Schuessler (2007, 2009) in Table 1.6 below.

The phonogram 蔵 is only attested in the Azuma toponym 武蔵 *Munzasi*. Unlike the other disyllabic phonograms, this one is disyllabic due to an orthographic tradition of dropping the last phonogram, *si*, when writing this toponym (Bentley 2016: 543).

Table 1.6: Disyllabic phonograms.

Phonogram	EMC	LH	WOJ trans-literation	WOJ reconstruction	TSOJ reconstruction	EOJ reconstruction
相	*sjaŋ	*siɑŋ	sanga	*saⁿga	*saⁿga	*saⁿga
駿	*tsjwenᶜ	*tsuinᶜ ¹⁵	suru	*suru	*suru	*suru
筑	*ʈjuk	*ʈuk	tuku	*tuku	*tuku	*tuku
信	*sjenᶜ	*sinᶜ	sina	*sina	*sina	*sina
對	*twậiᶜ	*tuəs	tusi	*tusi	*tusi	*tusi
中	*ʈjuŋ	*ʈuŋ	tingu	*tiⁿgu	*tiⁿgu	*tiⁿgu
藏	*dzâŋ	*dzɑŋ	nzasi	*ⁿzasi	*ⁿzasi	*ⁿzasi

1.7.1.2 *Kungana* phonograms

Kungana phonograms are Chinese characters that are used not for their meaning or phonetic Chinese-derived pronunciation, but rather for the phonetic use of the (usually monosyllabic) Japanese word that corresponds to the meaning of the Chinese character. For example, the character 江 means 'inlet' in Chinese, and the Japanese word that means 'inlet' is *ye*. When the character 江 is employed to write the Japanese syllable *ye* with no relation to the meaning 'inlet', it is being used as a *kungana* phonogram.

In the examples throughout this book, I write the transliterations of *kungana* phonograms without italics to differentiate them from regular phonograms which are transliterated in italics. There are only three of these phonograms, which are provided in Table 1.7 below.

Table 1.7: *Kungana* phonograms.

Phonogram	WOJ transliteration	WOJ reconstruction	TSOJ reconstruction	EOJ reconstruction
江	ye	*ye	*ye ~ *yə	*ye
手	te	*te	*te	*te
湍	se	*se	*se	*se

---

15 In this case we must go back in time further than LH to understand the sound correspondences. Schuessler (2009: 338) lists the Minimal Old Chinese reading as *tsjuns, but the Old Chinese reconstruction by Baxter and Sagart (2014: 252–256) supports *-r instead of *-n here, and this is a closer match to the OJ form (see Bentley 2016: 1, 418).

1.7.2 Logograms

Numerous logograms are attested in the corpus, but most are only attested once or twice. The full list is provided in Table 1.8 below. I transliterate these in uppercase italics.

Table 1.8: Logograms.

Logograms	WOJ transliteration	Meaning	WOJ reconstruction	TSOJ reconstruction	EOJ reconstruction
汝	NA	'2.S'	*na	*na	*na
吾	A ~ WA	'1.S'	*a ~ *wa	*a ~ *wa	*a ~ *wa
名	NA	'name'	*na	*na	*na
者	PA	'TPT'	*pa	*pa	*pa
葉	PA	'leaf'	*pa	*pa	*pa
邊	PE	'area'	*pe	*pe	*pe
鹿	KA	'deer'	*ka	*ka	*ka
兒	KO	'child, girl'	*ko	*ko ~ *ku	*ko
来	KÖ-	'come'	*kə	*kə	*kə
木	KÖ- ~ KÏ	'tree'	*kə- ~ *kɨ	*kə- ~ *kɨ	*kə- ~ *ke
真	MA	'true, INT-'	*ma	*ma	*ma
馬	[U]MA	'horse'	*[u]ma	*[mu]ma	*muma
身	MÏ	'body'	*mɨ	*mɨ	*mi
見	MI-	'see'	*mi-	*mi-	*mi-
水	MI	'water'	*mi	*mi	*mi
根	NE	'root'	*ne	*ne	*ne
寝眠寐	NE	'sleep'	*ne-	*ne-	*ne-
哭	NE	'sound'	*ne	*ne	*ne
莫	NA[16]	'-NEG.ATTR'	–	–	*-na
菜	NA	'vegetables'	*na	*na	*na
日	PI	'sun, day'	*pi	*pi	*pi
穂	PO	'ear of grain'	*po	*po ~ *pu	*po
目	MEY	'eye'	*məy	*mo	*me
瀬	SE	'rapids'	*se	*se	*se
栖	SU	'nest'	*su	*su	*su
渚	SU	'sandbar'	*su	*su	*su
畫	WE	'picture'	*we	*we	*we

---

[16] The negative-attributive suffix -na is only attested in EOJ. In WOJ and TSOJ the form is -n-u '-NEG-ATTR'.

Table 1.8 (continued)

Logograms	WOJ transliteration	Meaning	WOJ reconstruction	TSOJ reconstruction	EOJ reconstruction
井	WI	'well'	*wi	*wi	*wi
緒	WO	'string'	*wo	*wo	*wo
代	YÖ	'lifetime'	*yə	*yə	*yə
夜	YO	'night'	*yo	*yo ~ *yu	*yo
田	TA	'rice field'	*ta	*ta	*ta
屋	YA	'house'	*ya	*ya	*ya
楊	YA	'willow'	*ya	*ya	*ya
湯	YU	'hot spring'	*yu	*yu	*yu
江	YE	'inlet'	*ye	*ye ~ *yə	*ye
戸門	TO	'door'	*to	*to ~ *tu	*to
而	TE	'subordinative gerund'	*te	*te	*te
付	TUK-I	'attach-INF'	*tuk-i	*tuk-i	*tuk-i
道	MITI ~ NDI	'road'	*miti ~ *^{n}di	*miti ~ *^{n}di	*miti ~ *^{n}di
芝	SINBA	'grass'	*si^{m}ba	*si^{m}ba	*si^{m}ba
白	SIRA	'white'	*sira	*sira	*sira
玉	TAMA	'jewel'	*tama	*tama	*tama
長	NANGA	'long'	*na^{n}ga	*na^{n}ga	*na^{n}ga
母	PAPA	'mother'	*papa	*papa	*papa
父	TITI	'father'	*titi	*titi	*titi

1.7.3 *Kō-rui* and *otsu-rui* distinctions

Kō-rui (甲類) and *otsu-rui* (乙類) distinctions are Japanese terms used to describe the pairs of syllables that were phonemically distinct in WOJ but later merged in Middle Japanese (MJ – Heian period). For example, in WOJ the syllables *ko* /ko/ and *kö* /kə/ were phonemically distinct, but by the time of MJ they had merged to /ko/, which was written with the *hiragana* syllabogram こ. Thus, when analyzing the texts of WOJ (and AOJ), later Japanese scholars referred to WOJ *ko* syllables as こ$_1$, which is the *kō-rui* type, while they referred to WOJ *kö* syllables as こ$_2$, which is the *otsu-rui* type.[17] In addition to the pairs involving /o/ ~ /ə/ after an onset, there are also the

---

[17] *Kō-rui* and *otsu-rui* are also called 'Type-A' and 'Type-B' in some of the literature.

WOJ vowel pairs /i/ ~ /ɨ/ and /e/ ~ /əy/, which merged to /i/ and /e/, respectively, in MJ. In all of these cases the first member of the pair is the *kō-rui* type, while the second member is the *otsu-rui* type.

I do not use or reference the terms *kō-rui* and *otsu-rui* in this book for a few important reasons. First and foremost, they are not applicable to anything outside of the orthographic transition from WOJ to MJ. In other words, they are only reflective of (and referential to) phonemic mergers that occurred from WOJ to MJ. This is illustrated in Figure 1.2 below. Second, they were created due to the syllabic Japanese *hiragana* script, which did not exist at the time the AOJ poems were recorded. Lastly, in my opinion the usage of these terms in the analysis of AOJ data has hampered the progress of understanding AOJ phonology. When the AOJ data are viewed through the historical phonological developments of MJ, it is more difficult to uncover other possible phonological developments in AOJ, especially mergers of syllables that did not merge in MJ.

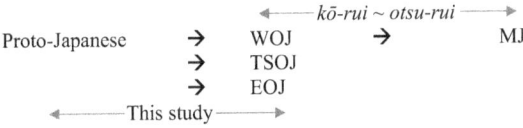

Figure 1.2: The diachronic focus of this study.

1.8 Manuscripts

The original eighth-century *Man'yōshū* manuscript has long been lost, and all extant manuscripts are copies of copies. In fact, the earliest extant manuscripts with AOJ poems[18] we have today were written over four hundred years after the first manuscript.

The earliest extant manuscript with AOJ material is the *Genryaku Kōhon* 元暦校本 (GK), which was collated in the summer of 1184 CE, during the reign of emperor Go-Toba. While this is a collated manuscript, we will probably never know which earlier manuscripts were used as source material. The text is incomplete, but very few AOJ poems are missing. Importantly, in many instances it appears linguistically truer to the ur-text than any of the subsequent manuscripts, including the *Nishi Honganji-Bon* (NHB). Compare the GK and NHB attestations against the cognate WOJ forms below:

---

[18] Some earlier MYS manuscripts do exist, and date from the mid-Heian period, but these do not contain any AOJ poems.

Book:Poem.Line	GK form	NHB form	WOJ form	Gloss
20:4403.3	久牟 kumu	久毛 kumo	kumo	'cloud'
20:4342.2	豆久利留 tukur-ir-u	豆久礼留 tukur-er-u	tukur-er-u	'make-PROG-ATTR'
20:4401.3	奈古 nak-o	奈苦 nak-u	nak-u	'cry-ATTR'
20:4330.3	比 pi	日 PI	pi	'day'

How do we know GK shows the original AOJ forms and NHB shows altered forms that were clearly influenced by WOJ or MJ phonology? First, we see the GK form *kumu* 'cloud' shows a raised vowel in the second syllable that is unattested in WOJ, therefore in GK we are most likely seeing the original innovative form in the Sinano topolect, rather than a scribal error or a change induced by WOJ influence. The NHB form, in contrast, is identical to the WOJ form. The same holds true for GK's form *tukur-ir-u* 'make-PROG-ATTR', which shows a unique progressive suffix *-ir-* in the Suruga topolect that would be undiscoverable if we followed NHB here. In the third example we find an unraised vowel in the GK form *nak-o* 'cry-ATTR', which is a retention in the Sinano topolect, rather than an innovation, but once again we can see the NHB form matches up perfectly with the WOJ form. Finally, the attestation of *pi* 'day' in the Sagamu topolect is written with a phonogram in GK, but a logogram in NHB. Thus, only GK reveals the true phonetics of the word in question. It should be noted that this is not the only example in which GK shows a phonogram where NHB shows a logogram, and when comparing the same word in two different manuscripts phonographic attestations can almost always be considered more archaic than logographic ones.

Two other Heian-period MYS manuscripts with AOJ material exist, but these include very few poems. One is the *Tenji-Bon* 天治本 which contains a small number of poems from Book 14, and the other is the *Ruijū Koshū* 類聚古集 which includes all of Book 14 and parts of Book 20.

The earliest MYS manuscript with the complete AOJ corpus is the aforementioned *Nishi Honganji-Bon* 西本願寺, which dates from the late Kamakura period (1185–1333). This is widely considered the definitive source on AOJ due to its completeness, but as described earlier, many poems show clear WOJ-isms not found in the earlier, but incomplete, GK manuscript. Consequently, the exclusive, or even primary, use of this manuscript in the reconstruction of the ur-text will inevitably lead to an obfuscation of many of the important phonological features of the AOJ dialects, and consequently render that ur-text ill-suited for any serious phonological study.

Several later MYS manuscripts exist from the Muromachi (1336–1573) to the Edo (1603–1867) periods. Among these, the *Kishū-Bon* 紀州本 (also known as the

Kanda-Bon 神田本) from the Muromachi period deserves mention because it is the second earliest complete MYS manuscript to survive to the present-day.

In contrast to most previous studies of AOJ, in this study GK is used as the primary manuscript, due to its older provenance and retention of the most AOJ linguistic features, while NHB is one of three manuscripts used in instances where GK shows a clear error as well as to supplement the poems GK lacks. NHB does not appear to be copied from GK, rather each descends from a different textual lineage. The annotated, reconstructed AOJ ur-text used for this study is available in Kupchik (2011: 871–1013).

1.9 The classification of AOJ poems based on non-WOJ features

The AOJ dialects exhibit many linguistic features not found in WOJ. In this study I classify the poems as AOJ based on *potential linguistic features*. In other words, those features that are not necessarily evident by merely examining a single attested form but instead may be discerned through the analysis of comparative data within a topolect, with other AOJ topolects, or with WOJ. A potential AOJ linguistic feature may be any one of the following: a morpheme written with one or more different phonograms in AOJ in a way that is unattested in WOJ as a "misspelling", thus potentially indicating a different phonological form; a morpheme, word, or word form not phonographically attested in WOJ; or a morphological or morphosyntactic structure not attested in WOJ. All unclear[19] sections of AOJ poems are therefore considered to contain potential AOJ linguistic features. An eastern toponym attested in an AOJ poem is not *ipso facto* a potential AOJ linguistic feature.

Table 1.9 below lists all poems from Books 14 and 20 by province, including all variants, that have at least one potential AOJ linguistic feature, as well as those that lack such features. Roughly half of the poems are from an unspecified province (henceforth abbreviated as UNP). These may include poems from provinces in Azuma that are not overtly attested (e.g., Kapï, Apa, etc.), but it is not possible to be certain. The total number of poems included for a particular province is indicated in parentheses under the province's name.[20] The poems from Book 14 that completely lack potential AOJ linguistic features are not included in this study. Such poems are written in pure WOJ and are excluded because they were either altered by a scribe when copying a manuscript, or they were originally composed in WOJ. Even in

---

[19] There are some sections of certain poems that have stubbornly resisted any coherent explanation. These appear to contain lexemes and morphology not found in OJ or any other known Japonic language variety.
[20] The complete linguistic evidence for each poem included in MYS Book 14 is presented in Appendix A.

poems with AOJ linguistic features we often find clear WOJ linguistic features that are either the product of scribal alteration or borrowing. I discuss these in Chapter 2 in an attempt to weed them out from my discussion of the historical phonology.

Some poems have variants, which replace one or more lines of the original. Whenever there is a variant and an original, regardless of the number of lines the variant replaces in the original, the original is given a lowercase "a" next to the number, while the variant is given a lowercase "b" (e.g., 3358a, 3358b). If there is a second variant, it is listed with a lowercase "c" next to the number (e.g., 3358c).

Table 1.9: All poems in the corpus included in or excluded from the present study.

PROVINCE (Total no. of included poems)	INCLUDED POEMS		EXCLUDED POEMS (MYS BOOK 14)
	MYS BOOK 14	MYS BOOK 20	
Sinano (8)	3352, 3398, 3399, 3400, 3401	4401, 4402, 4403	
Töpotuapumi (9)	3354, 3429	4321, 4322, 4323, 4324, 4325, 4326, 4327	3353
Suruga (13)	3358c, 3359a, 3359b	4337, 4338, 4339, 4340, 4341, 4342, 4343, 4344, 4345, 4346	3355, 3356, 3357, 3358a, 3358b, 3430
Kamitukeno (27)	3402, 3404, 3405a, 3405b, 3406, 3407, 3408, 3409, 3410, 3411, 3412, 3413, 3414, 3415, 3416, 3417, 3418, 3419, 3420, 3423, 3434, 3435, 3436	4404, 4405, 4406, 4407	3403, 3421, 3422
Muzasi (18)	3374, 3375, 3376a, 3376b, 3378, 3379	4413, 4414, 4415, 4416, 4417, 4418, 4419, 4420, 4421, 4422, 4423, 4424	3373, 3377, 3380, 3381
Sagamu (12)	3361, 3363, 3366, 3368, 3369, 3370, 3372, 3431, 3432	4328, 4329, 4330	3362a, 3362b, 3364a, 3364b, 3365, 3367, 3371, 3433
Mitinöku (2)	3426, 3437		3427, 3428
Simotukeno (13)	3424, 3425	4373, 4374, 4375, 4376, 4377, 4378, 4379, 4380, 4381, 4382, 4383	
Pitati (18)	3350a, 3351, 3388, 3389, 3392, 3394, 3395, 3397	4363, 4364, 4365, 4366, 4367, 4368, 4369, 4370, 4371, 4372	3350b, 3350c, 3390, 3391, 3393, 3396

1.9 The classification of AOJ poems based on non-WOJ features — 19

Table 1.9 (continued)

PROVINCE (Total no. of included poems)	INCLUDED POEMS		EXCLUDED POEMS (MYS BOOK 14)
	MYS BOOK 14	MYS BOOK 20	
Simotupusa (16)	3349, 3384, 3385, 3386, 3387	4384, 4385, 4386, 4387, 4388, 4389, 4390, 4391, 4392, 4393, 4394	
Kamitupusa (15)	3382, 3383	4347, 4348, 4349, 4350, 4351, 4352, 4353, 4354, 4355, 4356, 4357, 4358, 4359	3348
Idu (0)			3360a, 3360b
Unspecified Province (UNP) (120)	3440a, 3440b, 3442, 3444, 3445, 3446, 3447, 3448, 3450, 3451, 3452, 3453, 3456, 3458, 3460, 3461, 3463, 3464, 3465, 3466, 3468, 3469, 3471, 3472, 3473, 3474, 3476a, 3476b, 3477, 3478, 3480, 3481, 3482a, 3482b, 3483, 3484, 3485, 3486, 3487, 3488, 3489, 3492, 3493a, 3494, 3495, 3496, 3497, 3498, 3499, 3500, 3501, 3502, 3503, 3504, 3505, 3506, 3507, 3508, 3509, 3511, 3512, 3513, 3514, 3515, 3516, 3517, 3518, 3519, 3520, 3521, 3522, 3524, 3525, 3526, 3527, 3528, 3529, 3530, 3531, 3532, 3533, 3536, 3537a, 3537b, 3538a, 3538b, 3539, 3540, 3541, 3543, 3544, 3546, 3548, 3549, 3550, 3551, 3552, 3553, 3555, 3556, 3557, 3560, 3561, 3562, 3563, 3564, 3565, 3566, 3567, 3572, 3576	4425, 4426, 4427, 4428, 4429, 4430, 4431, 4432, 4436	3438a, 3438b, 3438c, 3439, 3441a, 3441b, 3443, 3449, 3454, 3455, 3457, 3459, 3462, 3467, 3470, 3475, 3479, 3490, 3491, 3493b, 3510, 3523, 3534, 3535, 3542, 3545, 3547, 3554, 3558, 3559, 3568, 3569, 3570, 3571, 3573, 3574, 3575, 3577

Thus, we find a total of 271 poems (inclusive of all variant poems) included in the present study, and 71 poems excluded from the present study. Although Book 20 contains many more poems (written in WOJ), I only included those composed by a *Sakimori* 'Border guard' or the wife of a *Sakimori*, since these people hailed from Azuma provinces. Two of the poems from Book 20 that I included (poems 4405 and 4425) do not contain any potential AOJ linguistic features, but they also do not contain any grammatical or phonological elements not found in other AOJ poems included in this study. Also, the history of transmission of Book 20 is different than that of Book 14, and it seems to have been less corrupted over time. For these reasons, I have included them.

1.10 Textual attestation format

All attestations are presented in the format *Book:Poem.Line – Topolect*. For example, "20:4343.1-2 – Suruga" indicates the poem is from *Man'yōshū* Book 20, poem number 4343, lines 1 to 2, written in the Suruga topolect. The citation of non-sequential lines is indicated by a semicolon. For example, "20:4343.1-2;5" means lines 1, 2, and 5 from poem 4343.

1.11 Translation and glossing

I provide an English translation for all examples in this book, below a morpheme-by-morpheme glossing of the transliterated text. Words that are not present in the original text but are necessary for an English translation are presented in brackets. The examples in Kupchik (2011) were thoroughly revised for this new volume and many were translated anew. I strove to make my translations highly accurate to the original text while still sounding natural in English. In this process I most often consulted the superb Japanese commentaries by Mizushima (1986, 2003) and Omodaka (1965, 1968), which provide translations into Modern Japanese along with in-depth discussions of each line and comparisons of different viewpoints from Japanese *Man'yōshū* scholars. The English commentaries and translations by Vovin (2012a, 2013) were also useful references, as they contain some helpful supplemental information and a different perspective on certain poems. My translations are influenced by these previous studies in various ways.

Throughout this book, except in sections of Chapter 3, I write all AOJ examples in the WOJ transliteration. This is the most accurate representation of the original script and ur-text. For those readers interested in reading or reciting the poems based on the reconstructed sound values of their syllables, they should refer to the tables in §1.7.

1.12 Structure and aims of this book

My goal was to write a grammar that is useful for anyone who wants to read and understand AOJ poetry in the original script, is curious about the dialects of OJ, or is interested in how lesser-known varieties of Japanese developed over time.

This is a descriptive grammar. By that, I mean that I do not employ terminology from the more specialized theoretical frameworks in linguistics such as Optimality Theory or Generative Grammar. However, the reader will often encounter terminology used in historical linguistics, morphology, and phonology. This is also a comparative grammar, in that I compare all AOJ topolects against each other, as well as against WOJ and other OJ dialects. At times, I also compare AOJ with later branches of Japanese (especially Hachijō) and Ryukyuan languages.

The book consists of two main sections. The first is a detailed phonemic reconstruction, which is presented in Chapter 2, and which includes discussions of historical sound changes. Several proto-languages and subgroupings are also reconstructed here (Proto-EOJ, Proto-TSOJ, Proto-Japanese, etc.), along with many protoforms.

The second section of the book is a reference grammar, which is presented in Chapters 3 – 10. Chapter 3 discusses notable phenomena in the synchronic phonology, and Chapter 4 discusses the lexicon, with an emphasis on loanword comparisons. Chapters 5 – 10 are devoted to the morphology, and cover the nominal, adjectival, and verbal morphology, as well as the adverbs, conjunctions, and particles. In five of these six chapters (the exception being the chapter on adverbs) I present the table below for each morpheme that is attested two or more times in the corpus.

Table 1.10: Example attestation table.

TSOJ			EOJ							UNP
Sin	Tö	Su	Kak	Mu	Sa	Mi	Sik	Pi	Sip	Kap

These tables list all attestations of a particular morpheme, to chart its linguistic (TSOJ vs. EOJ) and areal distribution. For morphemes with a high number of attestations that often include one or more debatable examples, the charts should not be taken as an exact measurement, but rather as a close approximation.

2 Sound change, reconstruction, and subgrouping

The purpose of this chapter is to describe the sound changes that occurred after the time of Proto-Japanese (PJe) in the two major dialects of Azuma: Töpo-Suruga Old Japanese (TSOJ) and Eastern Old Japanese (EOJ). I also describe changes that occurred later in specific topolects, but still before the time the poems in the MYS were recorded. In doing so, I reconstruct PJe, Proto-TSOJ, Proto-EOJ, the phoneme inventories of each AOJ topolect, and numerous protoforms. Through a synthesis of these data, near the end of the chapter I present a new subgrouping of the Old Japanese dialects based on shared linguistic innovations, as well as a detailed subgrouping of the EOJ topolects. This is followed by a discussion of phonological innovations in the UNP poems.

This chapter has many changes and revisions to the reconstruction and analysis presented in Kupchik (2011). Some are major differences, but most are better classified as minor. I will begin with an overview of Proto-Japonic (PJ), PJe, and WOJ phonology, and then move on to discuss the AOJ data in detail.

2.1 The phonology of Proto-Japonic, Proto-Japanese, and WOJ

WOJ, EOJ, and TSOJ descend directly from PJe, not PJ. Historically, there has not been a clear-cut distinction between PJe and PJ in the published research. This is because a detailed comparison of WOJ and AOJ reflexes was not attempted until Kupchik (2011: 50–482), and the data from that study, along with data from Hachijō and the other attested OJ dialects, allows us to reconstruct PJe. Miyake (2003: 66–67) refers to the previous reconstructions as "pre-OJ" and divides them into Proto-Japonic Internal and Proto-Japonic External. The former only used data from Japanese varieties, whereas the latter included Ryukyuan data. A proper reconstruction of PJ must include Proto-Ryukyuan (PR), whereas PR is not necessary to reconstruct PJe.

2.1.1 The phonological changes from Proto-Japonic to Proto-Japanese

There have been many PJ reconstructions, including Hattori (1978–1979), Whitman (1985), Martin (1987), Unger (1975, 1993) and Hino (2003). I find the reconstruction of PJ vowels proposed by Serafim (1999) to be the most plausible, with some modifications. Unfortunately, he did not publish his hypothesis, so I base my comments on the discussion of his reconstruction by Miyake (2003: 79). For the PJ consonant inventory, I follow the system described in Whitman (2012b: 27). In the next two sections I will present the PJ phoneme inventory and discuss the changes that occurred in PJe.

2.1.1.1 PJ and PJe consonant inventories

There were four approximate places of articulation for the consonants: labial, coronal (dental-alveolar), palatal, and velar. The nine consonant phonemes of PJ are shown in Table 2.1.

Table 2.1: The consonant phonemes of PJ.

	Labial	Coronal	Palatal	Velar
Plosive	*p	*t		*k
Fricative		*s		
Nasal	*m	*n		
Liquid		*r		
Glide	*w		*y	

The PJ medial sequences *np, *nt, *ns and *nk had developed into unitary prenasalized voiced obstruent phonemes by the time of PJe, shown in Table 2.2 below. There is a reasonable possibility that the phonemicization of these medial consonant sequences into prenasalized voiced obstruents occurred in Late PJ, since these unitary obstruent phonemes can be reconstructed for both PJe and PR.[21] The exact dating of PJ is unclear, but "Early PJ", at least, predates the Kofun period (300 CE – 538 CE) (Whitman 2012a: 155), and in practical terms "PJ" is used to refer to a language spoken over several centuries during the Yayoi period (300 BCE – 300 CE[22]). I assume "Late PJ" was spoken in approximately 200 – 300 CE, and possibly extending to as late as 400 CE.

There is also evidence that word-medial *ⁿr had developed in PJe from PJ *-nr- or *-mr- (see §2.3.1.3). I tentatively classify it as a marginal phoneme,[23] as indicated by its placement in brackets in the table below. Prenasalized sonorants such as [ⁿr] are rare in the world's languages (Anderson 1975),[24] but then again, so are pre-

---

[21] Thorpe (1983) reconstructed voiced obstruents for PR, but recently Vovin (2012b) has provided strong evidence we should instead reconstruct prenasalized voiced obstruents.
[22] Recently, some scholars have argued the date of the Yayoi period should be pushed back to 950 BCE (Whitman 2012a: 151).
[23] This is due to different reflexes of PJe *mura 'group' and *muⁿra 'divination' in WOJ (*mura* and *ura*, respectively). This might also help explain why only some PJe *r are reflected as /y/ in WOJ or /n/ in EOJ, if they developed as PJe *r > WOJ /y/ (sporadic) ~ /r/, PJe *ⁿr > WOJ /r/, PJe *r > EOJ /r/, and PJe *ⁿr > EOJ /n/ (sporadic) ~ /r/. At present, this remains speculative.
[24] Prenasalized alveolar trills can be found in Austronesian languages such as Fijian and the Oceanic languages of Manus Island (Blust 2007).

nasalized fricatives such as PJe and WOJ [ⁿz], which are "marked" in a language's phonology (Silverman 1995: 61).

The rest of the PJ consonant inventory continued unchanged in PJe.

Table 2.2: The consonant phonemes of PJe.

	Labial	Coronal	Palatal	Velar
Plosive	*p *ᵐb	*t *ⁿd		*k *ᵑg
Fricative		*s *ⁿz		
Nasal	*m	*n		
Liquid		*r [*ⁿr]		
Glide	*w		*y	

2.1.1.2 PJ and PJe vowel inventories

The PJ vowel phoneme inventory consisted of the six monophthongs shown in Table 2.3.

Table 2.3: The vowel phonemes of PJ.

	Front	Central	Back
High	*i		*u
Mid	*e	*ə	*o
Low			*a

There were also seven diphthongs: *oi,[25] *ui, *əi, *ai, *ia, *au, and *ua. Whether or not these were unitary phonemes or vowel sequences is not clear, but henceforth I will refer to them as diphthongs. We could also write these with a *y or *w (*oy, *aw, etc.) instead of *i or *u. I chose the latter pair for consistency with *ua and *ia.[26]

The PJe vowel phoneme inventory consisted of the same six monophthongs, which are provided in Table 2.4.

---

[25] Miyake (2003) did not include *oi, but subsequent research by Serafim (2008), Frellesvig and Whitman (2008: 39), Majtczak (2008: 26), Kupchik (2011: 117, 211), Vovin (2011b), and Pellard (2013) strongly support its reconstruction.

[26] This is a notable divergence from Kupchik (2011: 38–40), in which I wrote PJ *ai, *oi, *ui, and *əi as *ay, *oy, *uy, and *əy, respectively. At that time, I also considered *ay to be a diphthongal phoneme, but *oy, *uy, *əy, *ia, and *ua to be sequences of two phonemes, based on the later change of *ay compared to the rest, in the history of WOJ. Now I am doubtful there was any difference between *ai and the rest in regard to phonemic status.

Table 2.4: The vowel phonemes of PJe.

	Front	Central	Back
High	*i		*u
Mid	*e	*ə	*o
Low			*a

There were five diphthongs: *ui, *oi, *əi, *ai, and *ia. There were also the lexicalized compounding forms *a- (from *ai), *o- (from *oi) and *u- (from *ui). An example of *ai > *a- is PJ *kuyai-si > PJe *kuya-si 'to be regretful-ADJ'; an example of *ui > *u- is PJ *kamui-kara > PJe *kamu-kara 'deity-body'; and an example of *oi > *o- is PJ *sunkoi-s- > PJe *suᵑgo-s- 'pass-TRANS'. A notable phonological innovation from PJ to PJe is the merger of *au and *ua with *o in unbound morphs along with the change of *au > *a- in bound, compounding morphs (e.g., PJ *sirau 'white' > PJe *sira-, *siro).

In certain lexemes some vowels had already raised in PJe. One example is PJe *miⁿdo 'water', a reflex of PJ *me-nto 'water-COL' that shows a raised vowel in the initial syllable. The final syllable is probably a collective suffix since *mi* 'water' occurs independently in words like WOJ *indumi* '(water) spring' (Vovin 2009a: 162). We can reconstruct PJe *miⁿdo based on the reflexes WOJ *mindu*, TSOJ *mindu*, and EOJ *mindo*.[27] In contrast, Proto-Ryukyuan (PR) *meⁿdu 'water' shows a raised vowel in the final syllable but retains the original initial syllable vowel.[28]

2.1.2 The phonology of WOJ

I follow the reconstruction of WOJ by Miyake (2003). My reasons for this are presented in §1.6.

2.1.2.1 Consonants

There were four approximate places of articulation for the consonants: labial, coronal, palatal, and velar. The WOJ consonant inventory, shown in Table 2.5 below, was nearly identical to the PJe system; the only change was the merger of PJe *ⁿr > /r/.[29]

---

[27] The same line of the same poem in which *mindo* 'water' is attested (14:3546.4 – UNP) also has the word *se* 'fresh', cognate with WOJ *si* 'fresh'. This EOJ form shows the original PJe vowel *e, unraised. Thus, if the PJe form of 'water' were *mendo, we would expect to see *mendo* in this poem.
[28] According to Pellard (2008: 148), the modern Ryukyuan reflexes can only reflect final *u in PR.
[29] This change occurred after the change of *#muⁿr- > *#uⁿr-.

Table 2.5: The consonant phonemes of WOJ.

	Labial	Coronal	Palatal	Velar
Plosive	p ᵐb	t ⁿd		k ᵑg
Fricative		s ⁿz		
Nasal	m	n		
Liquid		r		
Glide	w		y	

2.1.2.2 Vowels

There were seven monophthong phonemes and one diphthong phoneme. Unlike the supposed diphthongs in PJ and PJe, we can be confident /əy/ in WOJ was a unitary phoneme because it counts as a single syllable in the meter of the verse. It is for this reason that I write it as /əy/ instead of /əi/.

Table 2.6: The vowel phonemes of WOJ.

	Front	Central	Back
High	i	ɨ	u
Mid	e	ə əy	o
Low		a	

Historically, the following shifts and mergers of PJe vowel sequences took place to develop the vowel system in Table 2.6. This occurred in four phases. In Phase 1 the following changes occurred in unbound morphs:
a) *ui > /ɨ/
b) *əi > /ɨ/
c) *oi > /ɨ/

Next, the following changes occurred in Phase 2:
d) *ai > /əy/
e) *ia > /e/

It is also possible change e) occurred in Phase 1 or Phase 3. I placed it here simply because *ai changed at this time.
  After that, the following mergers took place, in Phase 3:
f) *əy > e / C[-labial, -velar]_
g) *ɨ > i / C[-labial, -velar]_

It is also possible change g) occurred earlier, in Phase 2. I placed it here because it patterns with the front-shift, or decentralization, exhibited in change f).

Finally, the merger below took place, in Phase 4:

j)   *ə > o / C[+labial]_

Phase 4 is the WOJ language that is contemporaneous with the AOJ dialects in the eighth century.

2.1.3 Phonotactics and prosody of OJ

All attested OJ dialects were syllable-timed. Each syllable could be only CV word-medially and only V or CV word-initially. Outside of very few exceptions, such as onomatopoeia, the prenasalized voiced obstruents did not occur word-initially. Although Miyake (2003: 271) does not reconstruct the syllables /yi/ or /wu/ for WOJ, there is strong evidence these syllables did occur word-medially (Ramsey and Unger 1972: 286; Vovin 2009a: 420–426). However, there was no orthographic distinction between medial /yi/ and initial /i/, nor between medial /wu/ and initial /u/.

2.1.4 Methodology

I used the linguistic data sets that were separated by topolect and analyzed independently from one another in Kupchik (2011: 50–475), which were extracted from the AOJ corpus presented in Kupchik (2011: 871–1013). I corrected some errors in the original data, removed the data from the poems that were erroneously included, and added the data from the poems that were erroneously excluded (see Appendix A for the list of poems). Based on these data I reconstruct the phoneme inventories of the AOJ topolects as well as the phonological shape of many of their attested roots and affixes. I rely on the comparative method to reconstruct the protoforms in PJe, using the AOJ reflexes and the corresponding reflexes in WOJ (and other Japonic language varieties, if relevant).

The process of reconstruction begins with identifying recurrent orthographic practices and determining what phonological or phonetic phenomena they reflect. When a phonogram in the WOJ orthography is used to write a part of a word in an AOJ poem, there are three logical possibilities we must consider from a phonological and phonetic standpoint: 1) its usage is to write the same syllable as in WOJ; 2) its usage is to write a syllable that is absent in WOJ, thus the scribe tried to approximate the AOJ syllable with a phonetically similar WOJ syllable; or 3) its usage is due to a lack of phonemic contrast between two or more syllables that are phonemically distinct in WOJ. Cases of 1) are plentiful, and I trust they do not require any further explanation. However, there many cases in which a phonogram was used to write the same phonological syllable in both WOJ and AOJ, but it nevertheless indicates a sound change occurred in AOJ. A good example of this is the sporadic centralization of *a > /ə/, found in a form such as the EOJ comparative suffix -*nösu* (compare WOJ and TSOJ -*nasu*) < PJe *-nasu. Plausible cases of 2) are rare and mostly speculative, but I discuss a few in this chapter. Cases of 3) are numerous and of utmost importance – they are also less speculative than 2). The two prominent examples found in EOJ topolects are the orthographic free variation of *Ci* and *Cï* phonograms on the one hand, and *Ce* and *Cey* phonograms on the other. As I will argue in this chapter, the first pair of phonograms were used to write /Ci/ syllables in EOJ, whereas the second pair were used to write /Ce/ syllables. It is important to understand that a phonological merger between the two syllables in these pairs did not take place in EOJ topolects because *Cï* [Cɨ] and *Cey* [Cəy] syllables never developed in EOJ. However, I will show that some other cases of orthographic free variation are indeed the result of historical mergers of syllables in TSOJ and EOJ, some of which did not merge in WOJ or Middle Japanese.

Those familiar with the Middle Japanese *kana* scripts in the Heian period will find some parallels that are helpful for understanding the orthographic practices used to write the AOJ poetry. For example, in the Late Heian period /w/ was lost before the front vowels /e/ and /i/. Henceforth, the *we* syllabograms previously used to write /we/ were used in free variation with *ye* syllabograms to write /ye/ (Martin 1987: 79). The important thing to note here is they did not stop using *we* syllabograms even though the syllable /we/ no longer existed in the language. Instead, they repurposed them to expand the ways in which they could write a similar, yet distinct, syllable. Mergers were not restricted to two syllables in Heian Middle Japanese: consider the merger of medial /fe/ > /we/, which preceded the merger of /we/ > /ye/. As a result, these three series of syllabograms which were used to write three phonemically distinct medial syllables at the beginning of the Heian period were only used to write medial /ye/ by the Late Heian period. These orthographic practices are fundamentally the same as those we find in the AOJ poetry.

2.2 The Töpo-Suruga Old Japanese dialect (TSOJ)

This dialect was spoken in the provinces of Suruga, Töpotuapumi, and Sinano. As I will demonstrate, it was probably the easternmost Central Old Japanese (COJ) dialect, though it was quite divergent in regard to phonology.

2.2.1 Suruga

I begin the discussion of TSOJ with a description of the innovations that occurred in the Suruga topolect because it was the most phonologically innovative variety of TSOJ. Moreover, Suruga contains the most evidence for the unique phonological innovation *ai > *əy > /ə/ that occurred in Proto-TSOJ.

2.2.1.1 Vowel innovations

I propose the following sound changes:
a) *ai > *əy > /ə/
b) *ə > e / [-labial, -velar]_
c) *ə > o / C[+labial]_
d) Progressive vowel assimilation (in one word)
e) *ia > *e
f) Metathesis (in one word)
g) *o > /u/ (extensive)
h) *e > /i/ (extensive)

Change a) occurred before changes b) and c). These three changes are difficult to grasp without some detailed discussion and examples. Change a) was established based on the data in Tables 2.7 and 2.9.

Table 2.7: Examples of change a) in Suruga.

	Example	Phonogram(s)	Morphemic Gloss	Book:Poem.Line	WOJ	PJe
1	keymey	氣米	straw.mat	20:4338.1	kömö	*kəmə
2	key-n(ö)-	氣	tree-GEN-	20:4342.1	kö-nö, kï-nö	*kə-nə, *kəy-nə
3	keytönba	氣等婆	word	20:4346.4	kötönba	*kətᵐba

In these three examples Suruga *key* corresponds to WOJ *kö*. There are three possible explanations for this and the data in Table 2.9 below: 1) there was a change of *kə > /kəy/; 2) there was a change of *kəy > /kə/; or 3) the vowel in these syllables was not /ə/ or /əy/ but some other vowel not in WOJ, such as /ɛ/, /æ/, or /ɔ/. After considering all the data in Suruga and the other two TSOJ topolects, I concluded the most plausible explanation is hypothesis 2). In the case of the data above, this entails there was a merger of PJ *ai > *əy > /ə/ in this topolect, which is a change I also propose for the Sinano and Töpotuapumi topolects. Thus, all of the syllables shown above are phonemically /kə/, despite the fact they are each written with a *key* phonogram. I should emphasize that the usage of a *key* phonogram in the above examples is not because the syllables written with this phonogram were etymologically related to (*kai >) *kəy, but simply due to a lack of orthographic (and phonemic) contrast between *key* and *kö* phonograms in Suruga. In other words, the scribe could have chosen either type of phonogram, but in these three attestations, they chose a *key* phonogram.

Change c) was established based on the data in Table 2.8 that shows examples of *mo* and *mö* phonograms used in free variation to reflect PJe *mo or *mə syllables. It is a sound change found in WOJ (Bentley 2002), TSOJ, and EOJ (Kupchik 2007), and seems to have been a late, widespread areal change. Although by the time the AOJ poems were recorded the WOJ orthography no longer distinguished between /mo/ and /mə/ (since /mə/ no longer existed in WOJ), AOJ retains elements of older orthographic practices otherwise lost in contemporaneous WOJ writing (see §1.7.1), so it is possible they still would have distinguished between /mo/ and /mə/ orthographically if such a phonemic distinction were still present.

Table 2.8: Examples of change c) in Suruga.

	Example	Phonogram(s)	Morphemic Gloss	Book:Poem.Line	WOJ	PJe
1	kamo	加毛	EPT	20:4341.5	kamö	*kamə
2	mö	母	FPT	20:4343.5	mö	*mə
3	mo	毛	FPT	14:3358c.5	mö	*mə
4	monö	毛能	thing	20:4337.4	mönö	*mənə

In Table 2.9, I provide orthographic evidence that change c) occurred after change a).

Table 2.9: Examples showing the order of changes a) and c) in Suruga.

	Example	Phonogram(s)	Morphemic Gloss	Book:Poem.Line	WOJ	PJe
1	omey	於米	face	20:4342.5	omö	*əmə
2	mey	米	FPT	20:4345.5	mö	*mə
3	meyt-i	米知	hold-INF	20:4343.4	möt-i	*mət-i
4	-ng[a]-imey	伎米	-POSS-beloved.girl	20:4345.1	-ng[a]-imo	*-ⁿga-imo
5	keymey	氣米	straw.mat	20:4338.1	kömö	*kəmə
6	omeyp-o	於米保	think-EV	20:4343.2	omöp-ey	*əməp-ai
7	meyngur-u	米具留	encircle-ATTR	20:4339.1	meyngur-u	*maiⁿgur-o

The most remarkable feature in these data is the usage of a *mey* phonogram to transcribe reflexes of PJe *mo (example 4), *mə (examples 1, 2, 3, 5, 6), and *mai (example 7) syllables in Suruga. I reject the change of *mo to /məy/ to explain example (4) above on the grounds that it is phonetically unmotivated, and that is the primary reason why I find the hypothesis of the merger of *ai > əy > /ə/ to be the most plausible explanation for the data in Suruga and the other TSOJ topolects. I have proposed this change occurred by means of V_2 elision of Proto-TSOJ *məy (< PJe *mai), which created a merger with *mə syllables. Afterward, there was a merger of *mə with /mo/. As a consequence, the phonograms *mo*, *mö*, and *mey* were used freely to transcribe /mo/ syllables in Suruga orthography (Kupchik 2007: 8–10), which becomes even clearer when we compare the previously discussed data in Table 2.7. The data from Töpotuapumi contains evidence for the same innovation after *p-*, *y-*, and *k-*, and Sinano shows evidence for this innovation after *y-*.

Change b) was established based on the following data in Table 2.10.

Table 2.10: Examples of change b) in Suruga.

	Example	Phonogram(s)	Morphemic Gloss	Book:Poem. Line	WOJ	PJe
1	ware	和例	1.S	20:4344.3	ware	*wa-rai
2	warö	和呂	1.S	20:4343.1	ware	*wa-rai
3	töti	等知	father	20:4340.1	titi	*tete ~ *titi
4	titi	知々	father	20:4344.4	titi	*tete ~ *titi
5	te	弖	QUOT	20:4346.3	tö	*tə
6	te	弖	QUOT	20:4344.1	tö	*tə
7	nze	是	FPT	20:4346.4	nzö	*ⁿzə
8	nzö	叙	FPT	20:4337.5	nzö	*ⁿzə

Once again, there are a few possibilities to consider here. First, there is the hypothesis it is no different from the data in the labial and velar syllables, in that it reflects the same change of *əy > /ə/. In this hypothesis, the pair in (1) and (2) were both pronounced /warə/, the pair in (7) and (8) were both pronounced /ⁿzə/, and examples (5) and (6), though written *te*, were pronounced /tə/. However, it is difficult to explain why PJe *tete ~ *titi 'father' would reduce its first syllable to /tə/ in this hypothesis. As mentioned earlier in this chapter, WOJ lacked the vowel /əy/ after coronal and palatal onsets because it already merged with /e/ in this environment. However, we also know Suruga reduced *əy > /ə/ (change a)), which did not occur in WOJ.

The second hypothesis is there was a further merger of *ə > /e/ after coronal onsets, after change a) occurred. This would result in orthographic free variation of phonograms with *e* and *ö* that have coronal onsets, as of the kind we find in Table 2.10, and, importantly, it would also help explain example (3). There are many Modern Japanese dialects with *tete* (or similar) for 'father' (Satō 2003: 831–832). Hachijō also has *tete* 'father' (Asanuma 1999: 159). Therefore, it is likely that the Suruga form is the earliest attestation of the original initial *te syllable in this word.[30] In light of this evidence, I accept the second hypothesis and propose *ə merged with /e/ after coronal onsets in Suruga. The result of this sound change is *rö* and *re* phonograms were used in free variation to write Suruga /re/ syllables, *te* and *tö* phonograms were used to write /te/, and *nze* and *nzö* phonograms were used to write /ⁿze/. Based on this conclusion, I analyze (3) above phonemically as /teti/, (5) and (6) as /te/, and (7) and (8) as /ⁿze/.

Did change b) also occur after palatal initials? I am uncertain, because, as I discuss later in this chapter, evidence from Sinano and Töpotuapumi shows *ye* and *yö* phonograms were used to write /yə/, and examples (1) and (2) below also show orthographic free variation between these two phonograms. However, based on Suruga's fronting of *ə > /e/ after coronal onsets, it would be reasonable to assume the same change occurred after palatal onsets, in which case the examples in Table 2.11 below[31] would be pronounced /yesuru/ and /ye/, respectively. Unfortunately, the Suruga evidence is too limited to arrive at any clear conclusion on this matter, so I have no grounds to argue against the hypothesis they were pronounced /yəsuru/ and /yə/, respectively, as they were in the Sinano and Töpotuapumi topolects. Due to this, I only mark change b) as occurring after [+coronal] onsets.

Table 2.11: Examples possibly showing change b) after a palatal onset in Suruga.

Example	Phonogram(s)	Morphemic Gloss	Book:Poem. Line	WOJ	PJe
1 yes-uru	江須流	approach-ATTR	20:4345.3	yös-uru	*yəs-uru
2 ye	江	EPT	20:4340.1	yö	*yə

There is only one example of change d), presented in Table 2.12.

Table 2.12: Example of change d) in Suruga.

Example	Phonogram(s)	Morphemic Gloss	Book:Poem. Line	WOJ	PJe
1 kama	加麻	duck	20:4339.2	kamo	*kamo

Change f) only occurs one root, provided in Table 2.13 below. We would not expect many examples of metathesis in any topolect, due to its inherent sporadic nature.

---

30 Suruga also has *titi* 'father', shown in Table 2.10 above. Due to this and the modern Japonic reflexes I reconstruct two phonetic variants for 'father' in PJe: *tete and *titi. Suruga *töti* /teti/ shows vowel raising (change h)) in the final syllable, but not in the initial syllable.
31 They are written with the *kungana* phonogram 江.

Table 2.13: Example of change f) in Suruga.

	Example	Phonogram(s)	Morphemic Gloss	Book:Poem. Line	WOJ	PJe
1	osi	於思	rock	14:3359a.2	iso	*eso

This must have been a more recent change because the closely related Töpotuapumi topolect has *iso* for this root, and we also find two attestations of *iso* in Suruga (in 20:4338.2–3). The PJ form for 'rock, rocky shore' has been reconstructed as *eso (Vovin 2010: 127), so the Suruga form is the product of the raising of *e > /i/ and metathesis. Since Töpotuapumi also has a raised vowel (*e > /i/) in this word, this raising probably occurred prior to the metathesis in Suruga (in Proto-TSOJ).

Next, we turn to vowel raising. Examples of change g) are provided in Table 2.14 below in examples (1), (2), (4), (6), and (7).

Table 2.14: Examples of change g) in Suruga.

	Example	Phonogram(s)	Morphemic Gloss	Book:Poem. Line	WOJ	PJe
1	ar-u	阿流	exist-ATTR	20:4345.5	ar-u	*ar-o
2	pur-u	布流	fall-ATTR	14:3358c.5	pur-u	*pur-o
3	-n-o	努	-NEG-ATTR	20:4341.5	-n-u	*-n-o
4	kupusi-	苦不志	be.longing-	20:4345.5	kopïsi-, koposi-	*koposi-
5	kop-ur-aku	古布良久	long.for-ATTR-NML	14:3358c.3	kop-ur-aku	*kop-ur-a-ku
6	punzi	布自	TN ('Mt. Fuji')	14:3358c.4	–	*po-nusi 'fire-master'
7	mindu	美豆	water	20:4337.1	mindu	*miⁿdo

Rather than retention of *-o, example (3) is more likely additional evidence of a lack of contrast between *Co* and *Cu* phonograms in this topolect. In regard to example (4), although we find *kopï-* 'to long for' in the Töpotuapumi topolect of TSOJ (20:4322.2), we can reconstruct PJe *koposi 'to be longing for' based on the early WOJ form *koposi* 'to be longing for' in KK 110 (Vovin 2012a: 73). However, WOJ also has the more common doublet form *kopïsi* which is likely the result of a later analogical levelling with the WOJ verb stem *kopï-* 'to long for', perhaps due to confusion with the homophonous form *kopï-si* 'long.for.INF-PST.ATTR'. The Suruga form shows the raising of *o > /u/ in the first two syllables, but example (5) demonstrates the first syllable was also written as *ko-* in this topolect. This might be due to the orthographic practices of the different MYS books in which the words appear, or it may be more evidence that there was no contrast between *ku* and *ko* phonograms in Suruga, if all *ko had already raised to /ku/.

Example (6) deserves some discussion. Although Vovin (2018: 85–87) has argued Suruga *punzi* 'Mt. Fuji' is related to EOJ *pu* 'fire', the raising of *po- > *pu- is expected in the Suruga topolect of TSOJ (compare example 4),[32] and WOJ also shows *po-* as the compounding form of this noun. So, while his etymology of 'fire-master' is plausible in terms of morphosemantics, the *pu-* in this toponym in fact has no direct connection to the EOJ form attested in the Muzasi topolect, which is a separate, and regular, reflex from *poi in that language variety, and is morphologically free rather than bound (see §2.3.3.1 for more discussion).

As a final note on change g), it probably occurred after change c) since evidence in the other TSOJ topolects supports this.

Several examples of change h) are shown in the table below. Examples (2), (3), and (4) also provide evidence for change e), and show it occurred after change h), thus *ia first merged with *e, then the raising to /i/ occurred. I originally considered example (5) to be a case of V_1 elision (Kupchik 2011: 491), but I think a more plausible explanation is that it is the same V_2 elision that occurred in WOJ, followed by the raising of *e > /i/, since this is in accord with the rest of the examples in Table 2.15. It occurred after change b).

Table 2.15: Examples of changes e) and h) in Suruga.

	Example	Phonogram(s)	Morphemic Gloss	Book:Poem. Line	WOJ	PJe
1	kapir-i	加比利	return-INF	20:4339.4	kaper-i	*kaper-i[33]
2	ipi	已比	house	20:4343.3	ipe	*ipia
3	mi	美	wife	20:4343.5	me	*mia[34]
4	tukur-ir-u	豆久利留	make-PROG-ATTR	20:4342.2	tukur-er-u	*tukur-i-ar-o
5	panari-so	波奈利蘓	be.separated. INF-rocky.shore	20:4338.3	panare-so	*panarai-iso

---

[32] An alternative hypothesis is it is the product of regressive vowel assimilation that occurred prior to the deletion of the *-u in the penultimate syllable: *po-nusi > *punusi > *punzi*.
[33] In Kupchik (2011: 116) I analyzed this as PJe *kapi-ar-, but since PJe *ia changed to /a/ in Proto-EOJ and the EOJ cognate is *kaper-* (e.g., 20:4373.2 – Simotukeno) rather than *kapar-*, I now agree with Hino (2003: 202–203) that the PJ vowel in this morpheme was *e, and therefore the Suruga, WOJ, and EOJ forms are reflexes of PJe *kaper-.
[34] My reconstruction of this root is based on the EOJ form *ma* 'wife'. See §2.3.2.1 for a discussion.

Whether or not h) was a change in process or had already spread throughout the lexicon is unclear. The attestation of *k-e-* 'come-INF-' shown in (1) in Table 2.16 below, the only example in the entire AOJ corpus in which we find *-e* instead of expected *-i* for the infinitive suffix, supports the idea this raising was extensive. Historically, it is implausible to consider the Suruga form to be archaic (since there is no other evidence for PJ or PJe *-e ('-INF'), and there are many other attestations of the infinitive *-i* in Suruga, such as (2) below from the same poem, so I propose there was no contrast between *ki* and *ke* phonograms; both were used to write Suruga /ki/.

Table 2.16: Evidence of a lack of phonemic contrast between *ke ~ ki* (and *nge ~ ngi*) phonograms in Suruga.

	Example	Phonogram(s)	Morphemic Gloss	Book:Poem. Line	WOJ	PJe
1	k-e-	價	come-INF-	20:4337.4	k-i-	*k-i-
2	isong-i	已蘇岐	hurry-INF	20:4337.2	isong-i	*isoⁿg-i

2.2.1.2 A reconstruction of Suruga's vowel inventory

I reconstruct four to seven monophthongs and no diphthongs.

Table 2.17: The vowel phonemes of Suruga.

	Front	Central	Back
High	i	[ɨ]	u
Mid	[e]	ə	[o]
Low		a	

Marginal phonemes are indicated in brackets in Table 2.17. There are no variant spellings of a WOJ *Cï* syllable as *Ci* in this topolect, and in fact there are no *Cï* phonograms attested either, thus the phonemic status of /ɨ/ can only be presumed based on comparative evidence from the Sinano and Töpotuapumi topolects. The raising of *o > /u/ and *e > /i/ was so pervasive that this topolect may have had only four (/i, ə, u, a/) or five (/i, ɨ, ə, u, a/) vowel phonemes, the smallest inventory among all attested OJ topolects. If not, it was well on its way to such a phoneme inventory.

2.2.1.3 A reconstruction of Suruga's consonant inventory

The consonant inventory was unchanged from PJe except for the merger of PJe *ⁿr > *r, which occurred in Proto-TSOJ. In Kupchik (2011: 150) I proposed there was sufficient evidence for denasalization in the *nd-* initial syllables, but I have since grown more skeptical of that hypothesis due to the inexact way OJ scribes indicated medial voicing in the orthography.

2.2.2 Töpotuapumi

Töpotuapumi shares the distinctive TSOJ innovation of *ai > *əy > /ə/. It also shares several innovations with WOJ (verbal attributive -*u*,[35] monophthongization of PJe *oi > /ï/, etc.), but, like the two other TSOJ topolects, it shows some examples of vowel raising that are unattested in the cognate lexemes in WOJ.

2.2.2.1 Vowel innovations
I propose the following sound changes:
a) *oi > /ï/
b) *ə > o / C[+labial]_
c) *o > /u/ (potentially in process or sporadic)
d) *ai > *əi > ə / C[-coronal]_
e) *ai > *əi > e / C[+coronal]_
f) *e > /i/
g) *a > /ə/ (sporadic)
h) *ï > i / _C[+coronal]

Change a) is well supported by the examples in Table 2.18 and is shared with the Sinano topolect. There are no lexical items in the Töpotuapumi corpus that reflect PJe *ui or *əi, so we do not know how those diphthongs developed in this topolect. There are no variances in the data involving *Cï* or *Ci* syllables to indicate a lack of phonemic contrast between /ï/ and /i/ in any syllable outside of the coronal and palatal series. Change h) occurred after change a), as indicated by example (2) below.

Table 2.18: Examples of changes a) and h) in Töpotuapumi.

	Example	Phonogram(s)	Morphemic Gloss	Book:Poem. Line	WOJ	PJe
1	kopï-rasi	古非良之	long.for-SUP	20:4322.2	kop-urasi	*kopoi-urasi
2	siri	志利	back	20:4326.2	siri	*siroi

---

35 The more archaic form -*o*, which is attested in the Sinano topolect, is unattested in this topolect.

In example (1) above there is a difference in morphophonology between Töpotuapumi and WOJ (Vovin 2013: 62). In Töpotuapumi, the initial vowel of the suppositional suffix -*urasi* is deleted (V₂ elision), whereas in WOJ the final vowel of the stem *kopï-* is deleted (V₁ elision). In the case of WOJ, at least, it seems this elision occurred after the monophthongization of PJe *oi occurred.

Change b) is found in all attested OJ topolects. A few illustrative examples are provided in Table 2.19 below.

Table 2.19: Examples of change b) in Töpotuapumi.

	Example	Phonogram(s)	Morphemic Gloss	Book:Poem. Line	WOJ	PJe
1	mömö	母々	hundred	20:4326.3	momo	*momo
2	möngamo	母我毛	DPT	20:4325.2	möngamö	*məⁿgamə

The novel examples of change c) are shown in Table 2.20 below. This change may have been phonologically conditioned in some way, perhaps prosodically, because it does not occur in all possible segmental environments, even when the syllable position is taken into account. However, without any evidence to support this hypothesis, I have marked it as sporadic. In example (2) below we see the original vowel /o/ (< *o), whereas in example (1) we see the raised vowel /u/. This orthographic evidence indicates there may have been a merger between *Co* and *Cu* syllables, but the evidence is insufficient to make a confident claim.

Table 2.20: Examples of change c) in Töpotuapumi.

	Example	Phonogram(s)	Morphemic Gloss	Book:Poem. Line	WOJ	PJe
1	imu	伊牟	beloved.girl	20:4321.5	imo	*imo
2	imo	伊毛	beloved.girl	14:3354.5	imo	*imo
3	kayup-am-u	加由波牟	go.back.and.forth-TENT-FIN	20:4324.5	kayop-am-u	*kayop-am-u
4	ituma	伊豆麻	free.time	20:4327.3	itoma	*itoma
5	siru	志留	white	20:4324.2	siro	*siro

Change d) is the most unique and important one in these data, and it is an innovation shared with the Sinano and Suruga topolects. Due to this change *Cö* and *Cey* phonograms were used in free variation, as shown in Table 2.21 below. After labial onsets, there was a three-way orthographic merger between *Co*, *Cö*, and *Cey*, demonstrated by examples (1) and (2) below, because change b) occurred after change d).

Table 2.21: Examples of changes b) and d) in Töpotuapumi.

	Example	Phonogram(s)	Morphemic Gloss	Book:Poem. Line	WOJ	PJe
1	töpotuapumi	等保都安布美	TN	14:3429.1	–	*təpə t-u apomi
2	töpeytapomi	等倍多保美	TN	20:4324.1	–	*təpə t-u apomi
3	sasangö-	佐々己	raise.INF	20:4325.5	sasangey-	*sasaⁿgai
4	kangö	加其	shadow	20:4322.4	kangey	*kaⁿgai

As regards change e) (see Table 2.22), we know WOJ had already undergone a similar change of *ai > *əy > /e/ in the coronal and palatal initial syllables because a contrast between, for example, *te* [te] and *tey* [təy], was not encoded in the orthography; instead, there was a single syllable *te* [te]. But, as in Suruga, in Töpotuapumi (*ai >) *əy reduced after labial, palatal, and velar initials as well. The principal difference in the case of Töpotuapumi (and Suruga) is that monophthongization occurred by means of V₂ elision rather than through vowel fusion. Was the monophthongization of (*ai >) *əy after coronal initials also initially to /ə/ rather than to WOJ's fusional /e/? The fronting of *ə to /e/ after coronal onsets is a phonetically natural development, and we already saw ample evidence for this in the Suruga topolect (refer back to §2.2.1.1), so if Töpotuapumi did undergo an unconditioned change of (*ai >) *əy > /ə/, it is plausible that a further merger with /e/ after [+coronal] onsets occurred by the time the corpus was recorded, just as a further merger of /ə/ with /o/ occurred after [+labial] onsets.

Table 2.22: Example of change e) in Töpotuapumi.

	Example	Phonogram(s)	Morphemic Gloss	Book:Poem. Line	WOJ	PJe
1	[i]nde-	泥	go.out.INF-	20:4323.5	inde-	*iⁿdai

Change f) can be established mainly based on comparative data from Proto-Ryukyuan and EOJ, but the Töpotuapumi forms *iso* 'rock' (< PJ *eso) and *mindu* 'water' (< PJe *minⁿdo < PJ *mento), in Table 2.23 below, cannot be explained without it. It does not occur in all possible cases.

Change g) is attested in Table 2.24 below. The WOJ and EOJ forms are both *kaya*. Hachijō similarly has the reflex *kaya* (Yamada 2010: 58–59), which is also found in Ryukyuan languages (e.g., Irabu Miyako *kaya* (Tomihama 2013: 193), Yonaguni *kaya* (Ikema 2003: 87)), pointing to PJ *kaya which continued to PJe as *kaya.

Table 2.23: Examples of change f) in Töpotuapumi.

	Example	Phonogram(s)	Morphemic Gloss	Book:Poem. Line	WOJ	PJe
1	iso	伊宗	rock	20:4324.2	iso	*eso
2	mindu	美豆	water	20:4322.3	mindu	*mi^{n}do

The Töpotuapumi form is thus best explained as the result of a sporadic reduction and centralization of the word-final *a > /ə/. This sporadic change is also found in Sinano, and in some EOJ topolects, as an areal feature. Like all TSOJ topolects, there was no phonological distinction between *yö* and *ye* phonograms, and in the case of Töpotuapumi both were used to write /yə/, thus the form in Table 2.24 below was pronounced /kayə/.

Table 2.24: Example of change g) in Töpotuapumi.

	Example	Phonogram(s)	Morphemic Gloss	Book:Poem. Line	WOJ	PJe
1	kaye	加曳	reed	20:4321.4	kaya	*kaya

2.2.2.2 A reconstruction of Töpotuapumi's vowel inventory

I reconstruct seven vowel phonemes. There were no diphthongs.

Table 2.25: The vowel phonemes of Töpotuapumi.

	Front	Central	Back
High	i	ɨ	u
Mid	e	ə	[o]
Low		a	

I consider *o* to be a marginal phoneme, so I placed it in brackets. It is possible it had already raised to /u/ in some phonetic environments.

2.2.2.3 A reconstruction of Töpotuapumi's consonant inventory

The consonant inventory was unchanged from PJe except for the merger of PJe *^{n}r > *r, which occurred in Proto-TSOJ.

2.2.2.4 Notable phonological retentions

Example (1) in Table 2.26 below is also attested in the Pitati topolect of EOJ (14:3395.4) and based on this I reconstruct PJe *sapa-ⁿda 'amply-COL'. The WOJ cognate lacks the final syllable. This is either due to an irregular clipping of the final syllable in WOJ or a competition between variants, *sapa and *sapa-ⁿda, in PJe, which resulted in different reflexes in the daughter dialects. The suffix *-ⁿda seems to have had a collective meaning in PJe and is also attested in other word forms such as *iku-ⁿda 'many-COL'.

Table 2.26: Notable phonological retentions in Töpotuapumi.

	Example	Phonogram(s)	Morphemic Gloss	Book:Poem. Line	WOJ	PJe
1	sapanda	佐波太	amply	14:3354.3	sapa	*sapa-ⁿda
2	muta	牟多	together	20:4321.4	muta	*muta
3	nani	奈尔	why, what	20:4323.3	nani	*nani
4	töpeytapomi	等倍多保美	TN	20:4324.1	–	*təpə t-u apomi[36]

In regard to example (2), the EOJ form is *mita,* attested in the Simotupusa topolect (20:4394.3). Since the word is identical in TSOJ and WOJ, I prefer the hypothesis that the EOJ form is innovative, exhibiting a sporadic fronting of *u > /i/ due to the following alveolar consonant /t/ (Kupchik 2011: 395). This may also find support with the similar phonetic development of the first syllable of PJe *noⁿzi 'rainbow' in the Heian-period Kyōto Japanese reflex *niji* 'rainbow'.[37] Another possibility, proposed by Vovin (2010: 202, 2013: 154), is the WOJ and TSOJ forms were the result of a sporadic innovation of *i > /u/ due to the preceding /m/, though it is quite unlikely that both dialects would share the same sporadic innovation.

Example (3) shows this topolect also shares the form *nani* 'why, what' with WOJ, which is unattested in EOJ.

Example (4) shows the retention of PJe *-o- in -*apomi* (< PJe *apomi 'freshwater lake' < *apa-omi 'fresh-sea') (Pellard 2008: 145–146). Compare WOJ *apumi* 'freshwater lake', a reflex of this word with a raised medial vowel.

---

[36] Morphemically, this is 'distant COP-ATTR freshwater lake', meaning 'the distant freshwater lake'. This name was in reference to the large freshwater lake called Pamana (Lake Hamana in present-day Shizuoka prefecture) (Mizushima 2003: 116).

[37] Alternatively, the Heian period form might be the result of regressive vowel assimilation.

2.2.3 Sinano

Sinano shows a mix of innovations not found in WOJ, innovations shared with WOJ, and retentions not shared with WOJ. It bordered more provinces than any other province in Azuma, making it a prime candidate for being a region of dialect mixing. It is therefore probable that this topolect was influenced by multiple neighboring topolects from different branches of PJe, and there is some evidence to support this. For example, the EOJ word *tengo* 'maiden; third daughter' (< *Proto-EOJ *teŋgo) is attested in Sinano (once, in 14:3398.4), but it is unattested in Töpotuapumi, Suruga, and all OJ dialects to the west. One possibility is this word was borrowed into Sinano from the neighboring Kamitukeno topolect.[38] Another possibility is northern Sinano was part of the EOJ dialect group, but southern Sinano was part of TSOJ. There is one UNP poem that suggests this might be the case (see §2.5.1.2), though the evidence is inconclusive.

Due to such mixed linguistic evidence, in Kupchik (2011: 852) I did not classify Sinano as part of any other Azuma dialect. However, because there is evidence it shares two important innovations with the Töpotuapumi and Suruga topolects, I am now confident that we should at least add southern Sinano to the TSOJ dialect.

2.2.3.1 Vowel innovations

I propose the following sound changes:
a) *a > /ə/ (sporadic, or phonologically conditioned in some way)
b) *ə > o / C[+labial]_
c) *o > u / m_# (in nouns and particles)
d) *o > u (in the verb attributive suffix)
e) *ai (> *əy) > e / C[+coronal]_
f) *ai > *əy > ə / C[-coronal]_
g) *oi > /ɨ/
h) *əi > /ɨ/
i) *ui > /i/
j) *ia > /e/

I consider change a) to be a case of vowel centralization through phonological reduction. Some examples of this can be found in WOJ, one example is attested in

---

[38] The Sinano poem in which the word is attested mentions the toponym Panisina, which was in modern-day Kōshoku city in Hanishina district, Nagano prefecture (Mizushima 1986: 132), not far from the Nara-period border with Kamitukeno province to the east.

2.2 The Töpo-Suruga Old Japanese dialect (TSOJ)

the Töpotuapumi topolect, and other examples can be found in certain EOJ topolects, but example (1) in Table 2.27 below is attested exclusively in Sinano.

Table 2.27: Examples of change a) in Sinano.

Example	Phonogram(s)	Morphemic Gloss	Book:Poem. Line	WOJ	PJe
1 tönönbik-u	等能妣久	stream.out-ATTR	20:4403.4	tananbik-u	*tana^mbik-o
2 omö	意母	mother	20:4401.5	amö ~ omö	*amə

Change b) is the result of increased vowel labialization due the preceding consonant. A few examples are provided in Table 2.28.

Table 2.28: Examples of change b) in Sinano.

Example	Phonogram(s)	Morphemic Gloss	Book:Poem. Line	WOJ	PJe
1 mo	毛	FPT	14:3398.2	mö ~ mo	*mə
2 omo	意毛	mother	20:4402.5	amö ~ omö	*amə

Examples of change c) are provided in Table 2.29 below. Examples (1) and (3) are uniquely found in Sinano, and none of these examples are found in any other AOJ topolect. Based on these data, we can only conclude change c) occurs in nouns and particles in word-final position, and we must note change c) occurred after change b). As such, there was probably no phonological or orthographic distinction between word-final *mo*, *mö*, and *mu* phonograms in this topolect: all were used to write /mu/.

Table 2.29: Examples of change c) in Sinano.

Example	Phonogram(s)	Morphemic Gloss	Book:Poem. Line	WOJ	PJe
1 kumu	久牟	cloud	20:4403.3	kumo	*kumo
2 kamu	加牟	EPT	20:4403.5	kamö	*kamə
3 körömu	己呂武	garment	20:4401.1	körömö	*kərəmə

Example (2) occurs in WOJ in the *hapax legomenon* particle *kamu* (< *kamo* < *kamə*), which is attested in MYS 5:813.27. Vovin (2009a: 1234, 2010: 54) considers that attestation to be the result of a scribal error. I am doubtful of this, since confusion of *mo*/*mö* and *mu* phonograms is atypical in the MYS. The poem is written in the Asuka topolect of WOJ, which may have raised the vowel in this particle (*kamə > *kamo >

kamu). Whether it was a raising in Asuka WOJ or a scribal error, it does not appear to be related to the raising that occurred in Sinano.

In Sinano verbs we also find the raising of *o > /u/ in the attributive suffix (change d)), irrespective of the preceding consonant. Three examples are provided in Table 2.30 below. Examples (2) and (3) show the attributive form of the same verb written with the raised vowel (Book 14, example 2) and the original PJe vowel (Book 20, example 3), which may indicate the raising of the attributive suffix was not yet complete in this topolect, or only some areas of Sinano retained the original *-o. It might also indicate there was no contrast between [o] and [u] in the attributive suffix, in word-final position, or perhaps even the entire lexicon, due to the raising of *o > /u/. Due to a lack of strong evidence, we can only speculate on this matter.

Table 2.30: Examples of change d) in Sinano.

	Example	Phonogram(s)	Morphemic Gloss	Book:Poem. Line	WOJ	PJe
1	wor-u	乎流	exist-ATTR	14:3401.2	wor-u	*wor-o
2	nak-u	奈久	cry-ATTR	14:3352.4	nak-u	*nak-o
3	nak-o	奈古	cry-ATTR	20:4401.3	nak-u	*nak-o
4	-n[i]-ar-u	奈留	-LOC-exist-ATTR	14:3400.1	-n[i]-ar-u	*-ni-ar-o

Change e) also occurred in WOJ and EOJ. A few examples are shown in Table 2.31 below.

Table 2.31: Examples of change e) in Sinano.

	Example	Phonogram(s)	Morphemic Gloss	Book:Poem. Line	WOJ	PJe
1	sanzare	左射礼	little	14:3400.3	sanzare	*sa^{n}zarai
2	pune	布祢	boat	14:3401.2	pune	*punai

Change f) explains example (1) in Table 2.32 below. This is the defining innovation of the TSOJ dialect.

Table 2.32: Examples of change f) in Sinano.

	Example	Phonogram(s)	Morphemic Gloss	Book:Poem. Line	WOJ	PJe
1	koyö	古与	cross.over. INF	20:4403.5	koye	*koyai
2	taye	多延	cease.INF	14:3398.5	taye	*tayai
3	tamey	多米	benefit	20:4402.5	tamey	*tamai

Examples (1) and (2) indicate there was no orthographic distinction between *yö* and *ye* phonograms in Sinano: both were used to write /yə/. I think this is the best explanation as to why the scribe would use a *yö* phonogram in free variation with a *ye* phonogram (there are many examples of orthographic free variation between *Cö* and *Ce(y)* in the other TSOJ topolects as well). Although example (3) is written the same as it is in WOJ, we can predict it was pronounced /tamu/ (< *tamo < *tamə < *taməy < *tamai) in Sinano based on changes f), b), and c) and comparative data from the other TSOJ topolects.

Example (1) in Table 2.33 below demonstrates change h). There are no other clear examples of this change in TSOJ but it must have occurred before changes e) and f). Example (2) below demonstrates change g), which is also found in the other TSOJ topolects.

Table 2.33: Examples of changes i), g), and h) in Sinano.

Example	Phonogram(s)	Morphemic Gloss	Book:Poem. Line	WOJ	PJe
1 *mïna*	未奈	all	14:3398.1	*mïna*	*məina[39]
2 *sungï*	須疑	pass.INF	14:3352.5	*sungï*	*suⁿgoi-
3 *kami*	賀美	deity	20:4402.2	*kamï*	*kamui

Example (3) above is the only instance of the correspondence Sinano *i* : WOJ *ï*. It may just be a misspelling, but since it is the only clear example of a reflex of PJe *ui, I accept it as it is and offer it as change i).

There is one attestation in support of change j), shown in Table 2.34 below.

Table 2.34: Example of change j) in Sinano.

Example	Phonogram(s)	Morphemic Gloss	Book:Poem. Line	WOJ	PJe
1 -*ker-i*	家里	-RETR-INF	14:3352.5	-*ker-i*	*-k-i-ar-i[40]

---

[39] I reconstruct this with *əi based on *mərə 'many', which probably shares the same root (Martin 1987: 429; Vovin 2020: 321), and the Hachijō reflex *meNna* (Asanuma 1999: 228), which is a reflex from Proto-EOJ *məina. Frellesvig (2021: 42) reconstructs PJ *mïr > *mɨy for the first syllable, and, like Martin (1987: 479), he considers the *-na to be 'person, name', with the plausible semantic development 'many people' > 'all'. The final *-r in this form is an intriguing possibility (first proposed by Murayama 1962), though I think *ə for the preceding vowel is more plausible because I remain unconvinced of PJ *ɨ. By the time of PJe, however, this putative PJ *-r must have already lenited to *-i/-y.

[40] Morphologically, this is 'come-INF-exist-EV' (Shinmura 1927: 251).

2.2.3.2 A reconstruction of Sinano's vowel inventory

I reconstruct seven vowel phonemes. There were no diphthongs.

Table 2.35: The vowel phonemes of Sinano.

	Front	Central	Back
High	i	ɨ	u
Mid	e	ə	o
Low			a

2.2.3.3 A reconstruction of Sinano's consonant inventory

The consonant inventory was unchanged from PJe except for the merger of PJe *ⁿr > *r, which occurred in Proto-TSOJ.

2.2.3.4 Notable phonological retentions

The schwa in the second syllable of the verbal root *piröp-* 'pick up' is clearly a retention (cf. the innovative WOJ form *pirip-* 'id.', the product of progressive vowel assimilation). This is shown in (1) in Table 2.36 below. Another retention is the verbal attributive *-o* which is attested three times (cf. the innovative WOJ form *-u*, which is also attested in Sinano). One example is provided below in (2).

Table 2.36: Notable phonological retentions in Sinano.

	Example	Phonogram(s)	Morphemic Gloss	Book:Poem. Line	WOJ	PJe
1	piröp-am-u	比呂波牟	pick.up-TENT-FIN	14:3400.5	pirip-am-u	*pirəp-am-u
2	nak-o	奈古	cry-ATTR	20:4401.3	nak-u	*nak-o

2.2.4 A reconstruction of Proto-TSOJ

Based on the previously described data, I reconstruct the seven vowels of Proto-TSOJ in Table 2.37 below. The consonant inventory was identical to that of PJe except for the merger of PJe *ⁿr > *r.

There were no diphthongs or vowel sequences. PJe *oi had already changed to *ɨ, *ia had changed to *e, and *ai changed to (*əy >) *ə, except after coronals where it fronted to *e.

Table 2.37: The vowel phonemes of Proto-TSOJ.

	Front	Central	Back
High	*i	*ɨ	*u
Mid	*e	*ə	*o
Low			*a

I propose TSOJ is a Central Old Japanese (COJ) dialect, like the ancestor of the Heian-period Kyōto dialect, because it shares several of the COJ innovations that occurred after the split from PJe, including the monophthongization of *oi > *ɨ and the monophthongization of *ia to *e, neither of which can be reconstructed for Proto-EOJ. It also shares lexical and grammatical retentions with WOJ (and COJ) that do not occur in EOJ, e.g., *nani* 'what' and *-uram-* '-TENT2'. Also like WOJ, but unlike EOJ, TSOJ shows no evidence of a lack of distinction between /i/ and /ɨ/, so I reconstruct both phonemes. However, its unique innovation of *ai > *əy > /ə/ must have occurred after divergence from COJ, and the retention of the PJe attributive *-o in some forms (e.g., Sinano *nak-o* 'cry-ATTR') indicates the raising of this morpheme to *-u* began later and was not yet complete in some TSOJ topolects.

As discussed earlier, we know WOJ had already undergone the change of *ai > *əy > /e/ in the coronal and palatal initial syllables. But in TSOJ we only find this change after coronal onsets (not palatal), whereas the change *ai > *əy > /ə/ occurred after labial, palatal, and velar initials. The principal difference in the case of TSOJ in comparison to WOJ is that monophthongization of this diphthong occurred by means of V$_2$ elision rather than through fusion. It is possible this change was induced through contact with neighboring EOJ speakers, who engaged in more pervasive V$_2$ elision (Kupchik 2013b). Additionally, there is ample evidence in Suruga for a later innovation of *ə > /e/ that occurred after coronal onsets in syllables that are reflexes of PJe *Cə and PJe *Cai, whereas a further merger of these vowels with /o/ occurred after [+labial] onsets in all TSOJ topolects.

Suruga also stands apart from the other TSOJ topolects due to its sporadic progressive vowel assimilation and metathesis, and additional widespread raising of *e > /i/. Although the evidence is inconclusive, Suruga may have even undergone complete raising of *o > /u/ and *e > /i/, at least in some syllables. Sinano shows its own unique change of the raising of word-final *o > /u/ after *m. Sinano's change of *ui to /i/ may also be unique, but we have no reflexes of *ui in the other two TSOJ topolects to compare. The sporadic reduction (or centralization) of *a > /ə/ is found in Sinano and Töpotuapumi, which must have occurred after the split from Proto-TSOJ and appears to be an areal change that began in the EOJ topolects. Similarly, Töpotuapumi shows extensive raising of *o > /u/, but not in the same lexemes as in

Sinano or Suruga, indicating this change cannot be projected back to Proto-TSOJ either, but rather spread among the topolects through areal diffusion.

Fukuda (1965: 253) deserves credit as the first to notice there were important phonological similarities between the Suruga and Töpotuapumi topolects, based on their unique usage of *Cey*, *Co*, and *Cö* phonograms. Due to this, he proposed they are part of the same 'subdialect' (小方言). The data and proposals in this chapter, some of which date back to Kupchik (2007), further support his idea, though my proposal that TSOJ is not an EOJ dialect is distinct from Fukuda's view.

Hino (2003: 201) differed from Fukuda. Based on a comparison of vowel raising he grouped Sinano and Töpotuapumi together in his "Region C", whereas he grouped Suruga with topolects to the east in his "Region B". The linguistic evidence I provide in this chapter is incompatible with the inclusion of Suruga in his "Region B" dialect.

Although I group all three of these topolects together in TSOJ, I have demonstrated that Sinano forms a more tenuous linguistic link with the two other TSOJ topolects, and possibly only the southern half of the province spoke a TSOJ topolect. Töpotuapumi, in contrast, forms a strong linguistic link with Suruga, just as Fukuda noticed long ago.

2.3 The Eastern Old Japanese dialect (EOJ)

EOJ was spoken in the provinces Kamitukeno, Muzasi, Sagamu, Simotukeno, Pitati, Simotupusa, Kamitupusa, and Mitinöku. Based on its set of unique innovations, it is clearly a separate branch from PJe that did not directly descend from any other attested OJ dialect.

2.3.1 Kamitukeno

Kamitukeno shows evidence of three sound changes that occurred in Proto-EOJ, as well as several that occurred later. It is one of the more conservative topolects in respect to vowel raising.

2.3.1.1 Vowel innovations
I propose the following sound changes:
a) *ia > /a/
b) *ə > o / C[+labial]_
c) *a > /ə/ (sporadic)
d) *ui > /u/
e) *oi > /i/

f) *o > /u/ (sporadic, mainly found in the verbal attributive suffix)
g) *ai > /e/
h) *əi > /i/

The example in Table 2.38 below offers evidence for change a).

Table 2.38: Example of change a) in Kamitukeno.

Example	Phonogram(s)	Morphemic Gloss	Book:Poem. Line	WOJ	PJe
1	ipa	伊波	house	20:4406.1	ipe	*ipia

Change b) is common among all AOJ topolects. The free variation between *mo* and *mö* phonograms shown in the examples in Table 2.39 below is evidence for this change.

Table 2.39: Examples of change b) in Kamitukeno.

Example	Phonogram(s)	Morphemic Gloss	Book:Poem. Line	WOJ	PJe
1	kamo	可毛	EPT	20:4404.5	kamö	*kamə
2	kamö	加母	EPT	20:4407.5	kamö	*kamə
3	mo	毛	FPT	14:3413.2	mö	*mə
4	mö	母	FPT	14:3406.5	mö	*mə

Examples of change c) are provided in Table 2.40 below. This change is the same one we saw in the Sinano and Töpotuapumi topolects (but not Suruga), although these two topolects do not show the change in the same morpheme. Since Sinano bordered Kamitukeno, it was likely an areal change. This change can be projected back to Proto-EOJ in examples (1) and (4) below, so it seems the change spread from EOJ into TSOJ. We cannot trace example (2) below back to PJe. I consider it to be an innovative Kamitukeno variant of the Proto-EOJ diminutive *-na.[41]

The development of the PJe diphthongs *ui, *oi, and *əi is shown in Table 2.41 below.[42] Change d) only occurs in one root in these data, *kuku-* 'stem' (< PJe *kukui 'id.'), shown in example (5). It cannot be a reflex from PJe *kukoi because that would have changed to *kuki* in this topolect. Although this attestation is found in a com-

---

[41] *Pace* Vovin (2012a: 163), I consider the PJe diminutive *-ra to be unrelated to the Proto-EOJ diminutive *-na, since the PJe diminutive *-ra developed into Proto-EOJ *-rə.
[42] Changes d), e), and h) are marked without the hypothetical intermediary change to *ɨ, due to a lack of evidence for the change.

Table 2.40: Examples of change c) in Kamitukeno.

	Example	Phonogram(s)	Morphemic Gloss	Book:Poem.Line	WOJ	PJe
1	-nösu	能須	-COMP	14:3413.4	-nasu	*-nasu
2	-nö	能	-DIM	14:3402.4	–	–
3	yösör-i[43]	余曽利	be.attracted.to-INF	14:3408.3	yösör-i	*yəsar-i[44]
4	-rö	呂	-DIM	14:3409.1	-ra	*-ra

pound, I assume there was no difference in its free form, since free and "compounding" forms of nouns generally do not differ in EOJ topolects, in contrast to WOJ. We also find another attestation of *kuku* 'stem' in an UNP poem (see §2.5.1.2). This is consistent with Ryukyuan cognates that reflect PR *kukui rather than *kokoi (Vovin 2010: 142), and it is a good example of how EOJ data can contribute to the lexical reconstruction of PJ and PJe.

Table 2.41: Examples of changes d), e), and h) in Kamitukeno.

	Example	Phonogram(s)	Morphemic Gloss	Book:Poem.Line	WOJ	PJe
1	kopï-	古非	long.for-	14:3415.4	kopï-	*kopoi-
2	sungï	須宜	pass.INF	14:3423.4	sungï	*suⁿgoi-
3	nömï	能未	RPT	14:3405a.5	nömï	*nəməi
4	nangï	奈宜	pickerelweed	14:3415.3	nangï	*naⁿgVi[45]
5	kuku-	九久	stem	14:3406.2	kukï	*kukui

Change e) is supported by examples (1) and (2) above. When examining the data in Table 2.41, we should keep in mind the WOJ word *pimo* 'string' (< PJe *pimo) is written twice as *pïmo* in this topolect (in 20:4404.4 and 20:4405.3), indicating Cï phonograms were used to write /Ci/ syllables. In regard to example (2), compare EOJ *sungos-* ~ MJ *sugos-*[46] 'to pass'. This is the basis for the reconstruction of PJe *suⁿgoi- (Serafim 2008: 88–89). Example (4), which historically contains *kVi 'leek', is more difficult to reconstruct, so I leave the vowel unmarked in PJe. Since *ui changed to /u/ in this topolect, we can at least narrow it down to *koi or *kəi. Change h) is evidenced from example (3) above.

---

[43] It is possible this example is instead the result of progressive vowel assimilation or a borrowing from WOJ, since WOJ has the same reflex.
[44] I base my reconstruction on the form *yösar-* attested in 14:3478.5 – UNP.
[45] This is a reflex of PJ *na-nə kVi 'water-GEN leek' (Vovin 2011a: 164).
[46] These forms indicate the change of *-oi- > *-o- occurred in verbal morphology at the time of PJe, upon the suffixation of a morpheme that began with a consonant.

Examples of change f) are provided in Table 2.42 below, in (1), (3), (4), and (6). Examples that retain PJe *o as /o/ such as (2), and those in §2.3.1.3, show it was probably a late change still in progress. Example (5) shows this had occurred in some roots as well.

Table 2.42: Examples of change f) in Kamitukeno.

	Example	Phonogram(s)	Morphemic Gloss	Book:Poem. Line	WOJ	PJe
1	-m-u	牟	-TENT-ATTR	14:3404.5	-m-u	*-m-o
2	-m-ö	母	-TENT-ATTR	14:3418.5	-m-u	*-m-o
3	ap-u	安布	meet-ATTR	14:3413.4	ap-u	*ap-o
4	mat-am-u	麻多牟	wait-TENT-FIN	14:3406.4	mat-am-u	*mat-am-o
5	sinup-i	志濃比	yearn.for-INF	20:4405.2	sinup-i, sinop-i	*sinop-i
6	otap-ap-u	於多波布	sing-ITER-ATTR	14:3409.4	utap-ap-u	*otap-i-ap-o[47]

The free variation of *key* and *ke* phonograms shown in examples (3) and (4) in Table 2.43 below, along with the usage of a *pe* phonogram to write a syllable cognate with a WOJ /pey/ syllable in example (2), provides strong evidence for change g). Based on this, example (1) was pronounced /motəme/ in this topolect.

Table 2.43: Examples of change g) in Kamitukeno.

	Example	Phonogram(s)	Morphemic Gloss	Book:Poem. Line	WOJ	PJe
1	mötömey	物得米	search.for.INF	14:3415.5	motömey	*mətəmai
2	omop-e	於毛敝婆	think-EV	14:3435.5	omöp-ey	*əməp-ai
2	kamitukeynö	可美都氣乃	TN	14:3405b.1	–	–
3	kamitukeNO	可美都家野	TN	14:3434.1	–	–

2.3.1.2 Consonant innovations

I propose one sound change:
a) *#nan/ⁿ- > #an/ⁿ-

Change a) is supported by the two examples in Table 2.44 below. This change did not occur in TSOJ, where we find *nani* 'what' attested. Although Vovin (2005: 335,

---

[47] I reconstruct the iterative suffix as an auxiliary in PJe, which is why I add the infinitive *-i- before it. See §2.3.9.

2020: 297–298) considers the initial *n-* in WOJ *nani* 'what', *nanzö* 'why' (<*nani-se 'what-do') and *nandö* 'what' to be a segmentable morpheme in PJ, its meaning and function are unknown. I think it is more likely part of the root, and thus the WOJ form shows a retention from PJ since the initial *n-* must also be reconstructed for Proto-Ryukyuan (Thorpe 1983: 222). Specifically, Thorpe reconstructs the stem *na ~ *no 'what', but he notes Ryukyuan reflexes descend from PR **nawo(ba)* or **nowo(ba)*. He posits the *wo in these forms is the accusative suffix, in contrast to Vovin's idea of an irregular loss of medial *-n- in PR from putative *nanoi ~ *nanui 'what'. From a cross-linguistic perspective, it is not unusual to have fossilized case suffixes on interrogative words. A possibility relevant to Thorpe's PR reconstruction is that the final syllable in PJe *nani 'what' is the PJ dative/locative suffix *-ni,[48] if it were not the adverbial copula *n-i 'COP-INF', as proposed by Yamada (1954: 87). In any case, I consider the EOJ reflexes *anze* 'why' and *andö* 'what' to be innovative, the product of initial nasal deletion due to nasal dissimilation that occurred in Proto-EOJ. In addition, although not attested in EOJ, Hachijō has *ani* 'what', so we can project that form back to Proto-EOJ as well. It seems this change only occurred in the environment *#nan/ⁿ- > #an/ⁿ- because there are no words in EOJ that begin with the sequence *nan-* (< *#nan/ⁿ-). This is one of two consonant innovations that occurred in Proto-EOJ. In terms of comparative sound change within Japonic, we can find a parallel for this word-initial dissimilative deletion of a nasal in the change *#mum/ⁿ- > #um/ⁿ- that occurred in WOJ (Vovin 2005: 56–59).

Table 2.44: Examples of change a) in Kamitukeno.

	Example	Phonogram(s)	Morphemic Gloss	Book:Poem. Line	WOJ	PJe
1	andö	安杼	what	14:3404.5	nandö	*nani tə[49]
2	anze	安是	why	14:3434.5	nanzö	*nani se

The EOJ forms are a contraction of Proto-EOJ *ani tə and *ani se, but the forms were fully lexicalized by the time the poems were recorded, so there is no synchronic morpheme boundary. Although Vovin (2005: 309) analyzes *tə as either a quotative particle or a copula, I only analyze it as the quotative marker *tə because when it occurs with verbs like *ip-* 'say' and *omop-* 'think' there is no quotative marker

---

[48] This aligns with Thorpe's *na. I do not accept his reconstruction of *no for PJ, since that is more likely the result of a later regressive vowel assimilation in Ryukyuan (*nawo > *nowo). This *-ni was already fossilized in PJe, thus in the OJ dialects it was not treated as a case suffix in the synchronic grammar, as is typical of fossilized morphology.
[49] This uncontracted form is attested in NK 114 (Vovin 2005: 306), indicating the PJe form was uncontracted, or the contracted form was optional.

between the interrogative pronoun and the verb (see 14:3379.2 – Muzasi and 14:3494.5 – UNP). *se is probably the verb *se-* 'to do' (Vovin 2005: 335).

2.3.1.3 Notable phonological retentions

Examples (1) and (2) in Table 2.45 below show the PJe attributive *-o reflected as -o, while example (3) shows an unraised vowel in the adjectival verb attributive suffix -ke (< PJe *-ke). The vowels in the initial syllables of the nouns *yöki* 'snow'[50] (example 5) and *otap-* 'to sing'[51] (example 8) are similarly unraised. Example (4) shows the retention of an original initial syllable *o which was lost in WOJ through regressive vowel assimilation or sporadic fronting of *o > /i/ due to the preceding *n or following *^{n}z; Ryukyuan languages also show reflexes of *o in the initial syllable of this word, rather than *i (Hirayama, Ōshima, and Nakamoto 1966: 346).

Table 2.45: Notable phonological retentions in Kamitukeno.

Example	Phonogram(s)	Morphemic Gloss	Book:Poem.Line	WOJ	PJe
1	arapar-o	安良波路	appear-ATTR	14:3414.4	arapar-uru	*arapar-o
2	pur-o	布路	fall-ATTR	14:3423.3	pur-u	*pur-o
3	-ke	家	-AVATTR	14:3412.4	-ki	*-ke
4	nonzi	努自	rainbow	14:3414.3	*ninzi[52]	*no^{n}zi
5	yöki	与伎	snow	14:3423.3	yuki	*yoki
6	mura-	武良	divination	14:3418.3	ura-	*mu^{n}ra-
7	mundak-i	武太伎	embrace-NML	14:3404.3	undak-i	*mu^{n}dak-i
8	otap-ap-u	於多波布	sing-ITER-ATTR	14:3409.4	utap-ap-u	*otap-i-ap-o

Example (6) shows an initial *mu-* corresponding to *u-* in the WOJ form. This probably indicates there was originally an *m or *n before the *-r- in PJ. Thus, I reconstruct the PJe form as *mu^{n}ra. Vovin (2005: 57) discusses this sound correspondence with examples such as WOJ *uma* 'horse' : EOJ *muma* 'id.', and this is another corroborating example. Example (7) also shows the same correspondence, as proposed by Vovin (2013: 94).

---

[50] This is misspelled in the text as *yöki* instead of *yoki*.
[51] Analysis of this verb as *otap-* 'to sing' (< *otap-) was proposed by Vovin (2012a: 100), and it seems to be the most plausible hypothesis for the form. It is interesting the attributive *-o was raised to -u in this word form, since it retains PJe *o in the first syllable of the verb root and the attributive -o is well attested in this topolect.
[52] This is unattested in WOJ. We can reconstruct it as WOJ *ninzi based on the MJ reflex *niji*, though this is somewhat speculative since MJ does not descend directly from WOJ.

There are a few other possible retentions, though they are more speculative and may instead reflect innovations. The first is shown in example (2) in Table 2.46 below.

Table 2.46: Other possible rentations in Kamitukeno.

	Example	Phonogram(s)	Morphemic Gloss	Book:Poem.Line	WOJ	PJe
1	pitö	比等	one	14:3405a.5	pitö	*pitə (~ *pita?)
2	pita	比多	one	14:3435.5	pitö	*pitə (~ *pita?)
3	-nd-oro	度路	-go.out-ATTR	14:3419.3	-[i]nd-uru	*iⁿd-uru

As these data show, this topolect has both *pitö* and *pita* for 'one'. It is possible *pitə was a phonetic variant of *pita in PJe, with a reduced and centralized vowel in the second syllable. If so, we would have to propose both variants persisted into Proto-EOJ. However, example (2) is the only attestation of *pita* 'one' in any OJ dialect, and I was unable to find any later Japanese dialects with such a form. So, it may have just been an irregular change in this topolect.

In regard to example (3), it is the only attestation of *-oro* for the attributive suffix in any OJ dialect. It occurs in the word form *omop-i-nd-oro* 'think-INF-emerge-ATTR'. As such, it is likely an example of a synchronic progressive vowel assimilation (see §3.3.2). Moreover, the form *-uru* is also attested in this topolect (in 14:3402.3), so I am hesitant to change the PJe reconstruction from *-uru to *-oro.

2.3.1.4 WOJ influence in the text

Even in poems with EOJ linguistic features we find some clear examples of WOJ influence in the text. Example (1) in Table 2.47 below can be explained either as a borrowing of the WOJ form into Kamitukeno, or an alteration of the text by a later scribe who spoke WOJ or Middle Japanese, since the PJe form is reconstructed as *koposi. Earlier in this chapter I proposed WOJ levelled PJe *koposi to *kopïsi* 'to be longing for' based on analogy with *kopï-* 'to long for' (see §2.2.1.1), since the form *koposi* is attested once in WOJ, but it is highly unlikely Kamitukeno underwent the same change independently.

Table 2.47: Examples of WOJ influence in Kamitukeno poems.

	Example	Phonogram(s)	Morphemic Gloss	Book:Poem.Line	WOJ	PJe
1	kopisi-	古比之	be.longing.for-	20:4407.4	kopïsi-, koposi-	*koposi
2	ap-er-u	安敝流	meet-PROG-ATTR	14:3413.5	ap-er-u	*ap-i-ar-o
3	-yö	餘	-IMP	20:4405.2	-yö	*-rə
4	ipe	伊敝	house	14:3423.5	ipe	*ipia
5	-ra	良	-DIM	14:3408.4	-ra	*-ra

Example (2) should be *ap-ar-o* or *ap-ar-u* in this topolect since the change *ia > /a/ can be projected back to Proto-EOJ and the progressive *-ar-* is attested in other EOJ topolects. The presence of the WOJ progressive suffix *-er-* is strong evidence the poem was altered by some non-EOJ-speaking person or it was a borrowing from WOJ or TSOJ. The same can be said of example (3), since the Proto-EOJ form is *-rə and it is unlikely Kamitukeno underwent the same the sporadic lenition of *r > /y/ found in the WOJ reflex. Example (4) is also attested in this topolect as *ipa* 'house', so it is clear the WOJ word was either substituted here by a scribe, or it is a loanword from WOJ (Vovin 2010: 170). In regard to example (5), Kamitukeno is the only EOJ topolect with the diminutive *-ra*. Since it also has the EOJ form *-rö* (< *PJ -ra), we can conclude its *-ra* is a borrowing from WOJ (or possibly a TSOJ topolect[53]).

2.3.1.5 A reconstruction of Kamitukeno's vowel inventory
I reconstruct six vowel phonemes. There were no diphthongs.

Table 2.48: The vowel phonemes of Kamitukeno.

	Front	Central	Back
High	i		u
Mid	e	ə	o
Low			a

2.3.1.6 A reconstruction of Kamitukeno's consonant inventory
The consonant inventory was unchanged from PJe except for the merger of PJe *^{n}r > *r, which occurred in Proto-EOJ.

2.3.2 Sagamu

There are three innovations in Sagamu that can be projected back to Proto-EOJ, along with several others that occurred later.

2.3.2.1 Vowel innovations
I propose the following sound changes:
a) *a > /ə/ (occurs in two morphemes, possibly phonologically conditioned)
b) *ai > /e/

---
53 The diminutive *-ra* is not attested in TSOJ, but neither is *-rö*. I would expect to find *-ra* in TSOJ.

c) *oi > /i/ (possibly also *əi > /i/)
d) *ui > /u/
e) *ə > o / C[+labial]_
f) *ia > /a/

We find change a) in the Sinano, Töpotuapumi, and Kamitukeno topolects as well, though it occurs in a different root in Sagamu, shown in example (1) in Table 2.49 below. As mentioned in previous sections, this appears to be an areal feature that spread over both northern TSOJ and western EOJ. Since example (2) can be projected back to Proto-EOJ, it is likely this sound change began in EOJ and spread into TSOJ through contact.

Table 2.49: Examples of change a) in Sagamu.

	Example	Phonogram(s)	Morphemic Gloss	Book:Poem. Line	WOJ	PJe
1	unö-	宇能	sea-	20:4328.4	una-	*una-
2	-rö	呂	-DIM	14:3361.5	-ra	*-ra

The usage of a *key* phonogram to write a *ke* syllable, shown in example (3) in Table 2.50 below, is the evidence for change b).

Table 2.50: Examples of change b) in Sagamu.

	Example	Phonogram(s)	Morphemic Gloss	Book:Poem. Line	WOJ	PJe
1	pune	布祢	boat	14:3431.3	pune	*punai
2	sungey	須氣	sedge	14:3369.2	sungey	*suŋgai
3	keypu	氣布	today	20:4330.3	kepu	*kepu

Evidence for change c) is based on the following examples in Table 2.51. In (1) below, I am unable to determine which diphthong was in the PJe form, but *ui can be excluded based on change d).

Table 2.51: Examples of change c) in Sagamu.

	Example	Phonogram(s)	Morphemic Gloss	Book:Poem. Line	WOJ	PJe
1	sungï	須疑	cryptomeria	14:3363.5	sungï	*suŋgVi
2	siri	斯利	back, behind	14:3431.4	siri	*siroi

Example (2) above is important when we compare the Simotupusa cognate *siru* (discussed in §2.3.6.1). Since *ui became /i/ in Simotupusa, the PJe form must have been *siroi.[54]

There are two supporting examples of change d), provided in Table 2.52 below. Another likely example is the toponym Sagamu itself. This name changed to Sagami after the Nara period (Mizushima 1986: 61). If we reconstruct PJe *saⁿgamui, then it shows the expected reflex *sagamu* in the Sagamu topolect.[55] In this hypothesis the expected (though unattested) reflex in WOJ is *sagamï*, which carried on into the Heian period as Sagami.

Table 2.52: Examples of change d) in Sagamu.

	Example	Phonogram(s)	Morphemic Gloss	Book:Poem.Line	WOJ	PJe
1	tutu	都豆	earth	14:3370.4	tuti	*tutui
2	kandu	可頭	paper.mulberry	14:3432.3	kandi	*kandui

Example (1) above occurs in the phrase *pana tutu ma*, which I analyze morphemically as 'flower earth wife'.[56] Although *tutu* 'earth' is otherwise only attested as *tuti* or *tusi* in other OJ topolects, *tutui has already been proposed as the earlier form of this word (Whitman 1985: 218) and there are other examples of *ui > /u/ in the Kamitukeno topolect of EOJ, as well as in Sagamu. For context, I translate poem 14:3370 as follows.

(1) 14:3370
安思我里乃 / 波故祢能祢呂乃 / 尔古具佐能 / 波奈都豆麻奈礼也 / 比母登可受祢牟

---

54 Vovin (2011: 222, footnote 12) reconstructed *siroy, presumably based on the final vowel in WOJ *usiro* 'back'. If WOJ *usiro* is a reflex of PJe *u-siroi, it is the only example of the reduction of PJe *oi > /o/ in a free (non-compounding) form in WOJ.

55 In most other EOJ topolects we would expect to find the reflex *sagami*, based on their shared sound change *ui > /i/.

56 This is a new proposal. It may mean either 'flowers and earth' (cf. Simotukeno EOJ *amey tuti* 'heaven and earth' in 20:4374.1) or 'flower of the earth' (cf. WOJ *pana tatibana* 'flower of the mandarin orange (tree)' in 14:3574.2); I chose the latter. Most other scholars (see Mizushima 1986: 81–82) analyze it morphemically as *pana t-u tuma* 'flower COP-ATTR spouse', with wide-ranging speculation on the contextual meaning (since this phrase is otherwise unattested in any other OJ text), but there are no other attestations of the attributive copular form *t-u* in EOJ, and 'wife' works better in the context compared to 'spouse'.

*asingari-nö / pakone-nö ne-rö-nö / niko n-gusa-nö / pana **tutu** ma nar-e ya*[57] */ pimö tök-anz-u ne-m-u*
TN-GEN / TN-GEN peak-DIM-GEN / soft COP.ATTR-grass-COMP / flower **earth** wife be-EV IPT / cord untie-NEG-INF sleep-TENT-ATTR
'Are [you] a wife [who is] a flower of the **earth**, like the soft grass on the small peak of Pakone in Asigari? (Certainly not!) Why would [I] sleep with [you] without untying [my] cords?'

A metaphorical comparison of a woman to a plant is also found in poems 14:3415 – Kamitukeno and 14:3498.1-3 – UNP.

There is one example of change e), shown in Table 2.53 below in the comparison of the word-final syllable. This change occurred in all attested OJ dialects.

Table 2.53: Example of change e) in Sagamu.

	Example	Phonogram(s)	Morphemic Gloss	Book:Poem. Line	WOJ	PJe
1	möngamo	母我毛	DPT	20:4329.5	möngamö	*maⁿgamə

Change f) is supported by the example in Table 2.54 below.

Table 2.54: Example of change f) in Sagamu.

	Example	Phonogram(s)	Morphemic Gloss	Book:Poem. Line	WOJ	PJe
1	ma	麻	wife	14:3370.4	me	*mia

EOJ *ma* 'wife' is also attested in 14:3502.1 – UNP.

2.3.2.2 Consonant innovations

I propose the following two sound changes:
a) *r > /n/ (morphologically conditioned)
b) *#nan/ⁿ- > #an/ⁿ-

---

[57] This line is one of the few incontrovertible examples of hypermetricality in EOJ poetry, with eight syllables instead of the expected seven, and no adjacent vowels to elide. This hypermetricality serves as additional evidence that *tutu* 'earth' is more likely in this line than *t-u tuma* 'COP-ATTR spouse' because the poet would only have exceeded the meter if absolutely necessary. They could have chosen *pana tuma* 'flower spouse', *pana n-duma* 'flower COP.ATTR-spouse' or *pana t-u ma* 'flower COP-ATTR wife' instead and retained the seven-syllable meter, if that were really the intended meaning.

The tentative 2 suffix -*unam*- in example (1) in Table 2.55 below supports change a). I consider this change to be the result of regressive nasal assimilation due to the influence of the [m]. This is found sporadically in various languages around the world (cf. Tongan *nima* 'five' and Hawaiian *lima* 'id.', both reflexes from Proto-Polynesian *lima). In fact, we even find it in WOJ, in the doublet *oyanzi* 'same' and *onanzi* 'id.', the latter of which survived past the Nara period.

Table 2.55: Examples of changes a) and b) in Sagamu.

	Example	Phonogram(s)	Morphemic Gloss	Book:Poem. Line	WOJ	PJe
1	mit-unam-u	美都奈武	fill-TENT2-ATTR	14:3366.5	mit-uram-u	*mit-uram-o
2	anze	安是	why	14:3369.4	nanzö	*nani se

Change b) is supported by example (2) above. Both changes a) and b) can be projected back to Proto-EOJ. Although the coexistence of these two changes may seem counterintuitive, they are in fact quite distinct, because in (1) the second nasal, and the one that triggers the assimilation, is [m] only when preceded by an [r], whereas in (2) the nasal that triggers dissimilation is [n], and only when preceded by a word-initial [n] and the vowel [a]. This illustrates an interesting structural pressure in Proto-EOJ between nasals and liquids in certain adjacent syllables.

2.3.2.3 Notable phonological retentions

The attributive -*u* is most common in this topolect, though there is one attestation of the form -*o* (provided in Table 2.56), which shows an unraised vowel from PJe.

Table 2.56: A notable phonological retention in Sagamu.

	Example	Phonogram(s)	Morphemic Gloss	Book:Poem. Line	WOJ	PJe
1	pik-o	比古	pull-ATTR	14:3431.3	pik-u	*pik-o

2.3.2.4 A reconstruction of Sagamu's vowel inventory

I reconstruct six vowel phonemes. There were no diphthongs.

Table 2.57: The vowel phonemes of Sagamu.

	Front	Central	Back
High	i		u
Mid	e	ə	o
Low			a

There is little evidence to reconstruct /ɨ/, so I omit it. There is only one *Cï* phonogram in the Sagamu corpus, which is used to write the word *sungï* 'cryptomeria' in 14:3363.5. None of the *Ci* phonograms in the corpus are used to write a word with a WOJ cognate that contains a /Cɨ/ syllable.

2.3.2.5 A reconstruction of Sagamu's consonant inventory
The consonant inventory was unchanged from PJe except for the merger of PJe *ⁿr > *r, which occurred in Proto-EOJ.

2.3.2.6 Subgrouping of Sagamu with Kamitukeno
Unlike the other EOJ topolects, Sagamu and Kamitukeno do not show the changes *oi > /u/[58] or *ui > /i/. Instead, they show *oi > /i/ and *ui > /u/. Therefore, they constitute an early split from Proto-EOJ, before these changes occurred. These topolects do share the changes *ia > /a/, *ai > /e/, the reduction of *a to /ə/ in the diminutive and comparative suffixes, and two important sporadic consonant sound changes, all of which firmly link them with the other EOJ topolects.

2.3.3 Muzasi

The Muzasi topolect shows evidence for the sound changes unique to Proto-EOJ as well as sound changes that occurred later. There are some important differences in this topolect that indicate it was part of a separate subdialect, distinct from the Sagamu and Kamitukeno topolects.

2.3.3.1 Vowel innovations
I propose the following sound changes:
a) *oi > /u/

---

[58] Mitinöku also lacks evidence for this change. The difference is there are no reflexes of PJ *oi in the Mitinöku corpus, so we simply do not know what its reflex was.

b) *ui > /i/
c) *əi > /i/
d) *o > /u/
e) *ai > /e/
f) *ia > /a/
g) *ə > o / C[+labial]_
h) *a > /ə/ (only attested in two suffixes)
i) *e > /i/ (only attested word-finally in two suffixes)
j) *i > /a/ (progressive vowel assimilation in one toponym)

Evidence in support of changes a) and b) is shown in Table 2.58 below.

Table 2.58: Examples of changes a) and b) in Muzasi.

Example	Phonogram(s)	Morphemic Gloss	Book:Poem. Line	WOJ	PJe
1 -pu	布	fire	20:4419.2	pï, po-	*poi
2 paru	波流	needle	20:4420.5	pari	*paroi
3 tuku	都久	moon	20:4413.5	tukï, tuku-	*tukoi
4 tuti	都知	earth	20:4418.5	tuti	*tutui

Muzasi shows strong evidence for *oi > /u/ in examples (1) – (3), whereas example (4) illustrates the change *ui > /i/. This allows use to confidently reconstruct *paroi, instead of *parui, in example (2). The reconstruction of PJe *poi in (1) is consistent with PJ *poi (Vovin 2011b: 222; Pellard 2013: 90). Similarly, the reconstruction of PJe *tukoi in example (3) is consistent with PR *tuko(i) (Thorpe 1983: 229–230, 355) and PJ *tukoj (Whitman 2012b: 26).

Change c) is supported by one example, provided in Table 2.59.

Table 2.59: Example of change c) in Muzasi.

Example	Phonogram(s)	Morphemic Gloss	Book:Poem. Line	WOJ	PJe
1 oti-	於知	fall-	20:4418.5	oti-	*ətəi

Examples of change d) are provided in Table 2.60 below. Since the attributive -o is also amply attested in this topolect, the change to -u can be considered a late, areal change that was not yet complete.

Table 2.60: Examples of change d) in Muzasi.

	Example	Phonogram(s)	Morphemic Gloss	Book:Poem. Line	WOJ	PJe
1	ip-am-u	伊波武	say-TENT-ATTR	14:3379.2	ip-am-u	*ip-am-o
2	yar-am-u	也良牟	send-TENT-ATTR	20:4417.5	yar-am-u	*yar-am-o
3	pur-am-u	布良武	-TENT-ATTR	14:3376a.2	pur-am-u	*pur-am-o
4	-m-u	无	-TENT-ATTR	20:4413.4	-m-u	*-m-o
5	kopusi-	古布志	be.longing.for-	20:4419.5	kopïsi-, koposi-	*koposi
6	maru	麻流	round	20:4416.3 20:4420.2	maro	*maro

Muzasi is otherwise very conservative with vowel height, showing no other examples of *o > /u/ except in the word *ukera* 'Atractylodes japonica' < PJe *wokera (14:3376a.4, 14:3379.4), which is only attested as *ukera* in EOJ, and thus the vowel raising in this root may have occurred in Proto-EOJ.[59] Examples of words in Muzasi that retain PJe *o include *tor-* 'to hold' (20:4417.3), *kado* 'gate' (20:4418.1), *sonde* 'sleeve' (20:4423.3), *sinop-* 'to long for' (20:4421.5), *no* 'field' (20:4417.2), *imo* 'beloved girl' (20:4423.4), and *-yori* '-ABL' (14:3375.4). This demonstrates PJe *oi developed differently from *o, and the change of *oi > /u/ was more likely a fusional process with the [+back] and [+round] features of [o] gaining the [+high] feature of [i]. A merger of *oi with *ui (as [ui]) before the change to /u/ can be ruled out because the Muzasi topolect does not show /ü/ as a reflex of PJe *ui.

Examples (4) – (7) in Table 2.61 below show evidence of change e). The free variation between *key* and *ke* phonograms shown in examples (1) – (3) indicates the syllable /kəy/ did not exist in this topolect.

Table 2.61: Examples of change e) in Muzasi.

	Example	Phonogram(s)	Morphemic Gloss	Book:Poem. Line	WOJ	PJe
1	-key	氣	-AVATTR	20:4414.3	-ki	*-ke
2	-key	氣	-AVATTR	20:4419.3	-ki	*-ke
3	-key	氣	-AVATTR	20:4419.5	-ki	*-ke
4	tukey-	都氣	be.attached-	20:4420.4	tukey-	*tukai-
5	ware	和礼	1.S	20:4416.4	ware	*wa-rai
6	wakare	和可礼	separate. INF	14:3375.3	wakare	*wakarai
7	pure-	布礼	touch-	20:4418.4	pure-	*purai-

---

59 This word is not phonographically attested in WOJ. We can only reconstruct PJe *wokera based on the MJ cognate *wokera*.

Examples of change f) are provided in Table 2.62 below. This change occurred in Proto-EOJ.

Table 2.62: Examples of change f) in Muzasi.

Example	Phonogram(s)	Morphemic Gloss	Book:Poem. Line	WOJ	PJe
1 ipa	伊波	house	20:4416.4	ipe	*ipia
2 ipa	伊波	house	20:4419.1	ipe	*ipia
3 ipa	伊波	house	20:4423.4	ipe	*ipia

The free variation between *mo* and *mö* phonograms in the examples in Table 2.63 below offer evidence for change g).

Table 2.63: Examples of change g) in Muzasi.

Example	Phonogram(s)	Morphemic Gloss	Book:Poem. Line	WOJ	PJe
1 imö	伊母	beloved.girl	20:4415.4	imo	*imo
2 imo	伊毛	beloved.girl	20:4423.4	imo	*imo
3 kamö	可母	EPT	14:3379.2	kamö	*kamə
4 kamo	可毛	EPT	20:4418.5	kamö	*kamə

Examples of change h) are shown in Table 2.64 below. All of the Muzasi forms can be reconstructed for Proto-EOJ, indicating it was an old change.

Table 2.64: Examples of change h) in Muzasi.

Example	Phonogram(s)	Morphemic Gloss	Book:Poem. Line	WOJ	PJe
1 -rö	呂	-DIM	14:3375.5	-ra	*-ra
2 -rö	呂	-DIM	20:4413.4	-ra	*-ra
3 -nösu	乃須	-COMP	20:4415.3	-nasu	*-nasu

There are three examples of change i), which are provided in Table 2.65 below. It only occurs in two suffixes, in final position. The form *-ki* for the adjectival attributive suffix may be due to WOJ influence, since there are more attestations of the form *-key* /ke/ in this topolect.

Table 2.65: Examples of change i) in Muzasi.

Example	Phonogram(s)	Morphemic Gloss	Book:Poem. Line	WOJ	PJe
1	-kani	加尔	-NEG.POT.INF	20:4417.3	-kane	*-kane
2	-ki	伎	-AVATTR	14:3379.5	-ki	*-ke
3	-ki	伎	-AVATTR	20:4413.3	-ki	*-ke

Change j) is attested twice, in one toponym. This is shown in Table 2.66.

Table 2.66: Examples of change j) in Muzasi.

Example	Phonogram(s)	Morphemic Gloss	Book:Poem. Line	WOJ	PJe
1	asingara	安之我良	TN	20:4421.3	asingari	*asi^{n}gari
2	asingara	安之我良	TN	20:4423.1	asingari	*asi^{n}gari

Since *asingara* is the only form of this toponym attested in Muzasi, I consider it a completed sound change in this topolect, unlike in the case of the Sagamu topolect, where both *asingari* and *asingara* are attested (see §3.3.2).

2.3.3.2 Consonant innovations

I propose the following three consonant innovations:
a) *t > s /_i
b) *#^{n}an/^{n}- > #an/^{n}-
c) *#mu^{n}r > #ur-

Change a) is supported by the free variation between *ti* and *si* phonograms demonstrated in the data in Table 2.67 below. It was a later change that occurred after the split from Proto-EOJ. Examples (1) – (3) are the only ones in the Muzasi corpus with a *ti* phonogram. Examples (4) – (7) show *si* phonograms were used to write syllables that correspond to WOJ *ti* syllables, and which can be projected back to PJe as *ti. Examples (3) and (5) show the same word form written with a *ti* phonogram and a *si* phonogram. Therefore, it is clear there was no contrast between [ti] and [si] in Muzasi (there was only /si/), due to the proposed change *t > s/_i. For a cross-linguistic perspective, this change has also occurred in many other languages, including Finnish and Tongan. Within Japonic, it also occurred independently in the Southern Ryukyuan language Hateruma many centuries after it occurred in EOJ, after the change *te > *ti (Thorpe 1983: 293).

Table 2.67: Examples of change a) in Muzasi.

Example		Phonogram(s)	Morphemic Gloss	Book:Poem. Line	WOJ	PJe
1	oti-	於知	fall-	20:4418.5	oti-	*ətəi-
2	tuti	都知	earth	20:4418.5	tuti	*tutui
3	tat-i	多知	stand-INF	14:3375.3	tat-i	*tat-i
4	kasi	加志	go.on.foot	20:4417.5	kati	*kati
5	tas-i	多志	stand-INF	20:4423.2	tat-i	*tat-i
6	tasi	多之	sword	20:4413.1	tati	*tati
7	lös-i	母志	hold-INF	20:4420.5	möt-i	*mət-i

There is one example of change b), which I provide in Table 2.68. See §2.3.1.2 for a detailed discussion. This change occurred in Proto-EOJ.

Table 2.68: Example of change b) in Muzasi.

Example		Phonogram(s)	Morphemic Gloss	Book:Poem. Line	WOJ	PJe
1	andö	安杼	what	14:3379.2	nandö	*nani tə

Change c) is supported by the two attestations in Table 2.69.

Table 2.69: Examples of change c) in Muzasi.

Example		Phonogram(s)	Morphemic Gloss	Book:Poem. Line	WOJ	PJe
1	ura	宇良	divination	14:3374.2	ura	*muⁿra
2	ura	宇良	divination	14:3374.5	ura	*muⁿra

It is possible these are examples of WOJ influence in the text and should instead be listed in §2.3.3.4. However, the form *mura* 'divination' is only attested in the Kamitukeno topolect, which is part of a different subdialect of EOJ compared to Muzasi. Since a similar change occurred in WOJ but is otherwise unattested in AOJ, it may have been induced by WOJ contact or borrowed from WOJ. As mentioned in §2.3.1.3, the PJe form was *muⁿra.

2.3.3.3 Notable phonological retentions

Examples (1) – (3) in Table 2.70 below show the PJe verbal attributive suffix *-o reflected as -o.

Table 2.70: Notable phonological retentions in Muzasi.

	Example	Phonogram(s)	Morphemic Gloss	Book:Poem. Line	WOJ	PJe
1	-m-o	毛	-TENT-ATTR	20:4415.5	-m-u	*-m-o
2	[o]mop-am-ö	毛波母	think-TENT-ATTR	20:4419.5	omöp-am-u	*əməp-am-o
3	pap-o	波保	crawl-ATTR	20:4421.4	pap-u	*pap-o
4	-rö	呂	-IMP	20:4420.4	-yö	*-rə
5	-key	氣	-AVATTR	20:4414.3	-ki	*-ke

Example (4) shows a retention of *r-, which sporadically lenited to y- in WOJ. Example (5) is one of three attestations of -key /ke/ 'AVATTR' in this topolect.

2.3.3.4 WOJ influence in the text

In example (1) in Table 2.71 below, it is clear kopïsi was inserted into the Muzasi text by a WOJ speaker, since the Muzasi form of the word is kopusi- (shown in Table 2.60).

Table 2.71: WOJ influence in the Muzasi poems.

	Example	Phonogram(s)	Morphemic Gloss	Book:Poem. Line	WOJ	PJe
1	kopïsi-	古非思	be.longing. for-	14:3376a.1	kopïsi-, koposi-	*koposi
2	ipe	伊弊	house	20:4415.4	ipe	*ipia
3	-ke-	家	-AVEV	14:3376a.1	-ke-	*-ke-a[r-e]-[60]
4	-ker-i	家里	-RETR-FIN	14:3374.5	-ker-i	*-k-i-ar-i[61]

Similarly, in example (2), we find WOJ ipe 'house' instead of the expected EOJ form ipa, even though ipa is attested in this topolect. Examples (3) and (4) are not attested as -ka- and -kar-i, respectively, in this topolect, but we do find them in the closely related Kamitupusa and Simotupusa topolects (as well as in UNP poems). Examples (2) – (4) should all have the vowel /a/ instead of /e/, due to the changes *-i-a > /a/ and *-e-a > /a/ that occurred in Proto-EOJ.

---

[60] Morphologically, this is '-AVATTR-exist-EV' (Vovin 2009a: 476–477).
[61] Morphologically, this is 'come-INF-exist-EV' (Shinmura 1927: 251).

2.3.3.5 A reconstruction of Muzasi's vowel inventory
I reconstruct six vowel phonemes. There were no diphthongs.

Table 2.72: The vowel phonemes of Muzasi.

	Front	Central	Back
High	i		u
Mid	e	ə	o
Low			a

This topolect shows free variation between *Ci* and *Cï* phonograms, indicating there was no /ɨ/ phoneme (e.g., Muzasi *kukï* 'mountain cave' (14:3375.2), WOJ *kuki* 'id.').

2.3.3.6 A reconstruction of Muzasi's consonant inventory
The consonant inventory was unchanged from PJe except for the merger of PJe *^{n}r > *r, which occurred in Proto-EOJ.

2.3.4 Simotukeno

Much like the closely related Muzasi topolect, Simotukeno shows evidence of the innovations that occurred in Proto-EOJ, as well as some that occurred after the split from Proto-EOJ.

2.3.4.1 Vowel innovations
I propose the following sound changes:
a) *ai > /e/
b) *oi > /u/
c) *ui > /i/
d) *əi > /e/
e) *ia > /a/
f) *ə > o / C[+labial]_
g) *o > /u/ (in the attributive suffix)
h) *a > /ə/
i) *ai > a (in compounds)
j) *yam- > /yum/

Changes a) and d) are evidenced from the following data in Table 2.73.

Table 2.73: Examples of changes a) and d) in Simotukeno.

	Example	Phonogram(s)	Morphemic Gloss	Book:Poem.Line	WOJ	PJe
1	-key	氣	-AVATTR	20:4376.5	-ki	*-ke
2	ke	家	container	14:3424.5	key	*-kai
3	key-nö	氣乃	tree-GEN	20:4375.1	kö-nö, kï-nö	*kə-nə, *kəi-nə
4	ape-	阿敝	join.INF	20:4377.5	apey-	*apai-
5	sunbey	須倍	way	20:4379.4	sunbe	*suᵐbe

Examples (1) and (2) show the lack of an orthographic distinction between *key* and *ke* phonograms (both were used to write /ke/ in this topolect), while examples (4) and (5) show the same lack of contrast between *pe* and *pey* phonograms. There are many other examples of this in Simotukeno. Examples (1) and (5) also show a retention of PJe *e.

In example (3), we see the reflex /ke/ from PJe *kə- ~ *kəi 'tree'. Since /kə/ is an attested form of 'tree' before the genitive in WOJ and TSOJ, we could posit a sporadic fronting of *kə > /ke/ in Simotukeno. However, there are no other examples of that change in this topolect (or anywhere else in AOJ), and WOJ also has the form *kï-nö* 'tree-GEN' (e.g., MYS 10:1875.2), indicating the free form of the root could also precede the genitive in PJe. In light of this, I think it is more likely the diphthong *əi changed to /e/ in Simotukeno, and the form in (3) is a development from PJe *kəi-nə, rather than *kə-nə. Although the orthographic form *key-nö* 'tree-GEN' is also attested in Suruga (discussed in §2.2.1.1), in that topolect I already demonstrated there was no contrast between *key* and *kö* phonograms, due to the merger of *kai > *kəy > /kə/, and thus the form is phonemically /kə-nə/. In contrast, in Simotukeno there is no evidence for this merger. Instead, there is ample evidence for the merger of *kai with /ke/, like in the other EOJ topolects. Thus, the Suruga and Simotukeno forms, though orthographically identical, were different phonologically. Only a careful analysis of each topolect's corpus can reveal such important distinctions.

Change b) is supported by examples (1) and (2) in Table 2.74 below, while change c) is supported by examples (3) and (4). In regard to example (1), the compounding form *kamu-* 'deity' is attested in WOJ (e.g., MYS 15:3621.5). It is also attested once in EOJ, in an UNP poem (14:3516.3), before the genitive -*nö*. Therefore, this bound form must date to PJe or earlier. However, the EOJ data indicates the free form *kamui persisted at least into Proto-EOJ, alongside the compounding allomorph *kamu-.

Table 2.74: Examples of changes b) and c) in Simotukeno.

	Example	Phonogram(s)	Morphemic Gloss	Book:Poem. Line	WOJ	PJe
1	kami	可美	deity	20:4374.2	kamï, kamu-	*kamui
2	tuti	都知	earth	20:4374.1	tuti	*tutui
3	tuku	都久	moon	20:4378.1	tukï, tuku-	*tukoi
4	sungu	須具	pass.NML[62]	20:4378.2	sungï	*suⁿgoi

As regards example (4), in other EOJ topolects we find *sungï* for the infinitive form of 'pass', even in those topolects in which the change *oi > /u/ occurred, but this is the only example in all of AOJ of the nominalized form of the verb. Importantly, it shows that while the infinitive form was analogically levelled in EOJ topolects so that it did not end in -*u*, the nominalized form did not face the same pressure, thus creating a unique phonological contrast between the two forms. There are two other examples of a nominalized verb with final /u/ as a reflex of PJe *oi: one is attested in the Kamitupusa topolect (see §2.3.7.1), and one is attested in UNP (see §2.5.1.2 and §4.3.1.6.2).

The data in Tables 2.73 and 2.74 demonstrate Simotukeno is the only attested OJ language variety to have three distinct reflexes from the PJe diphthongs *ui, *oi, and *əi, as well as the only variety to merge PJe *ai and *əi > /e/.

Change i) is supported by example (1) in Table 2.75 below, while change e) is supported by examples (2) and (3).

Table 2.75: Examples of changes i) and e) in Simotukeno.

	Example	Phonogram(s)	Morphemic Gloss	Book:Poem. Line	WOJ	PJe
1	puna-	布奈	boat-	20:4381.3	puna-	*punai
2	ipa	伊波	house	20:4375.3	ipe	*ipia
3	tat-ar-i	多々里	stand-PROG-INF	20:4375.5	tat-er-i	*tat-i-ar-i

Change f) is supported by the following pairs of examples in Table 2.76 below: (1) & (2) and (3) & (4). Many other supporting examples are also attested in this topolect.

---

[62] This analysis agrees with Kinoshita (1988: 154) and Mizushima (2003: 498).

Table 2.76: Examples of change f) in Simotukeno.

	Example	Phonogram(s)	Morphemic Gloss	Book:Poem.Line	WOJ	PJe
1	mo	毛	FPT	20:4383.4	mö	*mə
2	mö	母	FPT	20:4377.1	mö	*mə
3	amo	阿毛	mother	20:4378.3	amö, omö	*amə
4	amö	阿母	mother	20:4383.5	amö, omö	*amə

Change g) is supported by examples (1) – (3) in Table 2.77 below. Example (4) demonstrates the change was not complete or did not occur yet after /n/.

Table 2.77: Examples of change g) in Simotukeno.

	Example	Phonogram(s)	Morphemic Gloss	Book:Poem.Line	WOJ	PJe
1	tananbik-u	多奈妣久	stream.out-ATTR	20:4380.5	tananbik-u	*tanaᵐbik-o
2	tat-u	多都	stand-ATTR	20:4373.5	tat-u	*tat-o
3	yösör-u	与曽流	approach-ATTR	20:4379.2	yösör-u	*yəsar-o
4	-n-o	努	-PERF-ATTR	14:3425.4	-n-uru[63]	*-n-o

This topolect, like Muzasi, is otherwise conservative in regard to vowel height. Examples of unraised reflexes of PJe *o include *ito* 'door' (20:4380.1), *tonzi* 'housewife' (20:4377.1), *ito* 'simply, very, really' (20:4379.4), *sonde* 'sleeve' (20:4379.5), and *sora* 'sky' (14:3425.4).

The two examples[64] in Table 2.78 below support change h). This change is shared with other EOJ topolects as well as areally with the Sinano and Topötuapumi topolects of TSOJ.

Table 2.78: Examples of change h) in Simotukeno.

	Example	Phonogram(s)	Morphemic Gloss	Book:Poem.Line	WOJ	PJe
1	-nösu	能須	-COMP	14:3424.3	-nasu	*-nasu
2	yösör-u	与曽流	approach-ATTR	20:4379.2	yösör-u	*yəsar-o

---

[63] This appears to be a late form that replaced earlier *-n-o (Vovin 2021a: 178).

[64] It is possible example (2) is instead the result of progressive vowel assimilation or a borrowing from WOJ, since WOJ has the same reflex.

Change j) is one of the more unusual ones we find in AOJ, but there are two similar examples in UNP poems (discussed in §2.5.1.13). The one supporting example in this topolect is provided in Table 2.79 below.

Table 2.79: Example of change j) in Simotukeno.

	Example	Phonogram(s)	Morphemic Gloss	Book:Poem. Line	WOJ	PJe
1	yum-ap-i	由麻比	be.sick-ITER-NML	20:4382.3	yam-ap-i	*yam-ap-i

This occurs in the phrase *ata yum-ap-i*, meaning 'sudden illness'. Clearly the Simotukeno form is innovative, since the Hachijō cognate is *atayami* 'sudden illness' (Asanuma 1999: 22), and we also find /a/ in the initial syllable of Ryukyuan cognates such as Iejima Okinawan *yaɲuŋ* 'to be hurt, to feel pain' (Oshio 2009: 517). As proposed in Kupchik (2011: 329–330), this seems to be a rounding of *a > /u/ due to the following /m/. However, it only occurs in the environment with a preceding /y/ or /n/, therefore it is likely the alveo-palatal nature of these consonants also affected the vowel. I suspect they triggered the raising of the vowel, while the /m/ triggered the rounding of it. I also previously proposed the vowels in these syllables may have been long, to account for cases where this rounding did not occur, but that idea is more speculative.

2.3.4.2 Consonant innovations

I propose the following sound change:
a) *t > s / _i

Examples of this change are in (1) and (3) in Table 2.80 below. Example (2) demonstrates a lack of contrast between *ti* and *si* phonograms in this topolect. It is in fact the only *ti* phonogram in Simotukeno's corpus.

Table 2.80: Examples of change a) in Simotukeno.

	Example	Phonogram(s)	Morphemic Gloss	Book:Poem. Line	WOJ	PJe
1	tas-i	多志	stand-INF	20:4383.4	tat-i	*tat-i
2	tuti	都知	earth	20:4374.1	tuti	*tutui
3	sisi	志志	father	20:4376.3	titi	*tete ~ *titi

2.3.4.3 Notable phonological retentions

In EOJ we find three phonetically distinct focus particles that all appear to have the same function: *tö*, *sö*, and *nzö*. I support the hypothesis that the EOJ focus particle *tö* is a retention from the PJ focus particle *tə, which developed into Proto-Ryukyuan as *do (Yamada 1954, Thorpe 1983: 209) but was lost in WOJ (Serafim and Shinzato 2013: 136–137). We should also mention in this context the proposal by Omodaka (1965: 97) that the EOJ focus particle *tö* is cognate with WOJ *nzö*. I am not persuaded by Thorpe's idea that EOJ *tö* and PR *do* are cognate with the WOJ concessive gerund -*dö* (1983: 250); rather I follow the proposal by Serafim and Shinzato (2013: 138) that in PJ there were two focus particles: *sə and *tə.[65] I do not accept Serafim and Shinazo's hypothesis of palatalization to account for this (which necessitates *tə was the original particle, and *sə was secondary), because other clear examples of such consonant palatalization are lacking for PJ phonology. Instead, I follow Mizushima (1984a: 358–360) who proposed a fortition of *z or *s to /t/ to account for this. We can sharpen Mizushima's hypothesis by claiming it could only be *sə that underwent sporadic fortition to *tə (since we cannot reconstruct the focus particle *ⁿzə for PJ), and that this must have occurred not in PJe or OJ, but in PJ or pre-PJ. For PJe, we must reconstruct *tə, *sə, and *ⁿzə.

As examples (1), (2), and (3) in Table 2.81 below illustrate, all three of these focus particles are attested in this topolect.

Table 2.81: Notable phonological retentions in Simotukeno.

	Example	Phonogram(s)	Morphemic Gloss	Book:Poem. Line	WOJ	PJe
1	nzö	叙	FPT	20:4376.5	nzö	*ⁿzə
2	sö	曽	FPT	20:4380.5	sö	*sə
3	tö	登	FPT	14:3425.4	–	*tə
4	sunbe	須敝	way	20:4381.5	sunbe	*suᵐbe
5	kaper-i	可敝理	return-INF	20:4373.2	kaper-i	*kaper-i
6	-key	氣	-AVATTR	20:4376.5	-ki	*-ke

Example (4) is only valid if this word is not the product of WOJ influence (in which case the PJe form should be reconstructed as *suᵐbia). A clearer example of this is (5), which is *kapir-* in the Suruga topolect of TSOJ and can be confidently reconstructed as PJe *kaper-. In contrast, example (6) shows a retention of PJe *e in Simotukeno that has raised to /i/ in WOJ.

---

65 To be accurate they reconstruct *t(j)ə, but since I do not accept the post-consonantal glide *j for PJ, I have modified this to *tə. In addition, they were incorrect in claiming EOJ does not have any attestations of *nzö*, which led to their reconstruction of only *sə and *tə for PJe.

2.3.4.4 WOJ influence in the text

The example in Table 2.82 below is best explained as the result of WOJ influence, since the expected EOJ reflex is *pa*.

Table 2.82: WOJ influence in the Simotukeno poems.

	Example	Phonogram(s)	Morphemic Gloss	Book:Poem. Line	WOJ	PJe
1	*pey*	倍	area, side, direction	20:4379.2	*pe*	*pia

2.3.4.5 A reconstruction of Simotukeno's vowel inventory

I reconstruct six vowel phonemes. There were no diphthongs.

Table 2.83: The vowel phonemes of Simotukeno.

	Front	Central	Back
High	i		u
Mid	e	ə	o
Low			a

I do not reconstruct *ɨ because there is no evidence for it. There are two attestations of *kami* 'deity' (20:4374.2, 20:4380.3), which are cognate with WOJ *kamï* (< PJe *kamui). This probably indicates the change in this topolect was from *ui > /i/, without an intermediary change to *ɨ. Moreover, there are no *pï, nbï, mï, kï,* or *ngï* phonograms attested in this topolect, as well as no variances involving *ki, pi,* or *nbi* phonograms.

2.3.4.6 A reconstruction of Simotukeno's consonant inventory

The consonant inventory was unchanged from PJe except for the merger of PJe *ⁿr > *r, which occurred in Proto-EOJ.

2.3.5 Pitati

The Pitati topolect shows the same core innovations found in the other EOJ topolects, as well as some later changes shared with certain other topolects.

2.3.5.1 Vowel innovations

I propose the following sound changes:

a) *ai > /e/
b) *ə > o / C[+labial]_
c) *o > /u/ (sporadic)
d) *oi > /u/
e) *ui > /i/
f) *ai > /a/ (in compounds)
g) *i > /a/ (progressive vowel assimilation in one toponym)
h) *əi > /ə/ (in verbal compounds)
i) *e > /i/ (sporadic)
j) *ə > i / t_ (sporadic)

Examples supporting change a) are provided in Table 2.84 below. These data show a lack of orthographic contrast between *e* and *ey* phonograms, indicating both were used to write syllables with /e/.

Table 2.84: Examples of change a) in Pitati.

	Example	Phonogram(s)	Morphemic Gloss	Book:Poem. Line	WOJ	PJe
1	nar-unbe	奈流弊	make.a.living-DEB	20:4364.4	nar-unbey	*nar-uᵐbai
2	sumeyra	須米良	emperor	20:4370.4	sumera	*sumera
2	kapeyr-i	可閇理	return-INF	20:4372.15	kaper-i	*kaper-i
3	kaper-i	可敝里	return-NML	20:4368.5	kaper-i	*kaper-i
4	pune	布祢	boat	20:4363.2	pune	*punai

Change b) is supported by the free variation between *mo* and *mö* phonograms shown in the examples in Table 2.85 below. There are many other examples in this topolect.

Table 2.85: Examples of change b) in Pitati.

	Example	Phonogram(s)	Morphemic Gloss	Book:Poem. Line	WOJ	PJe
1	imo	伊毛	beloved.girl	14:3389.1	imo	*imo
2	imö	伊母	beloved_girl	20:4363.5	imo	*imo
3	kamo	可毛	EPT	14:3351.2	kamö	*kamə
4	kamö	可母	EPT	20:4364.5	kamö	*kamə

Examples in support of change c) are plentiful, and a selection are provided in Table 2.86 below. Example (3) indicates this was a late change, since it must have occurred after change b).

Table 2.86: Examples of change c) in Pitati.

	Example	Phonogram(s)	Morphemic Gloss	Book:Poem.Line	WOJ	PJe
1	mindu	美豆	water	14:3392.3	mindu	*mi^{n}do
2	imu	伊牟	beloved.girl	20:4364.3	imo	*imo
3	sakimuri	佐岐牟理	border.guard	20:4364.1	sakimöri	*saki-məri
4	ipap-am-u	伊波々牟	pray-TENT-ATTR	20:4372.12	ipap-am-u	*ipap-am-o
5	tat-am-u	多々牟	stand-TENT-ATTR	20:4364.2	tat-am-u	*tat-am-o
6	-m-u	武	-TENT-ATTR	14:3397.5	-m-u	*-m-o
7	kuye	久江	cross.over.INF	20:4372.4	koye	*koyai

Change d) is supported by examples (1) and (2) in Table 2.87 below, whereas change e) is supported by example (4). Example (3) is the product of analogical levelling (we would expect the reflex *kopu*), since infinitive forms of verbs could not end in -*u*. We find this in other EOJ topolects as well.

Table 2.87: Examples of changes d) and e) in Pitati.

	Example	Phonogram(s)	Morphemic Gloss	Book:Poem.Line	WOJ	PJe
1	tuku	都久	moon	14:3395.2	tukï	*tukoi
2	yuru	由流	lily	20:4369.2	yuri	*yuroi
3	kopi	古比	long.for.INF	20:4371.5	kopï	*kopoi
4	kami	可美	deity	20:4370.2	kamï	*kamui

Change f) only occurred in compounding forms, as shown in Table 2.88 below. Example (2) can be projected back to PJe and is a change shared with WOJ. Example (1) is probably also quite old, since it occurs only once in the verbal word form *wasura-kö*- forget-come-, which means 'starting to forget'. This was probably a set phrase that only survived in poetry, since *wasure*- 'to forget' is also attested in this topolect (in 20:4367.2).

Table 2.88: Examples of change f) in Pitati.

	Example	Phonogram(s)	Morphemic Gloss	Book:Poem.Line	WOJ	PJe
1	wasura-	和須良	forget-	14:3394.4	wasure-	*wasurai
2	puna-	布奈	boat-	20:4365.3	puna-	*punai

Change h) occurred before change a) and seems to be restricted to compounding verb forms. There is only one possible supporting example, which is provided in Table 2.89 below.

Table 2.89: Example of change h) in Pitati.

Example	Phonogram(s)	Morphemic Gloss	Book:Poem. Line	WOJ	INV
1 orö-	於呂	lower-	20:4363.2	ori-	*ərəi-

This example occurs in the line *mi-pune orö-suwe* HON-boat lower-place.INF 'lower the boat into place'. Alternatively, the verb in this line might be analyzed as *orös-u* 'make.lower-FIN', with the following *we* being the same emphatic particle attested in the Kamitukeno topolect (see §10.3.8). If we accept the latter analysis, then there is no basis to claim change h) occurred.

An example of change i) is provided in Table 2.90 below. Importantly, this shows it was a late change, since it occurred after change a).

Table 2.90: Example of change i) in Pitati.

Example	Phonogram(s)	Morphemic Gloss	Book:Poem. Line	WOJ	PJe
1 tungi	都岐	tell.INF	20:4365.5	tungey	*tuⁿgai

The form *tungey* 'tell.INF' is also attested in this topolect (20:4363.5), indicating a lack of phonemic contrast between *ngi* and *ngey* phonograms when writing this verb, and perhaps being an important example of how scribes exploited any merger of syllables, even down to cases that only occur in one lexeme in one topolect. There is no evidence that all *ⁿge syllables had raised to /ⁿgi/. In fact, the Pitati topolect is otherwise rather conservative in regard to the raising of *e > /i/.

There is one example in support of change j), which is shown in Table 2.91 below.

Table 2.91: Example of change j) in Pitati.

Example	Phonogram(s)	Morphemic Gloss	Book:Poem. Line	WOJ	PJe
1 timar-i	知麻利	stay-INF	20:4372.11	tömar-i	*təmar-i

This is phonetically similar to the change of *ə > /e/ after coronal onsets proposed for Suruga in §2.2.1.1 as well as the change of *ə > /e/ after /s/ in Mitinöku proposed in §2.3.8.1. Considering Heian-period Kyōto Japanese also underwent a similar change in *tigaf-* 'to differ' < PJe *ta^ngap- 'id.' (cf. WOJ *tangap-* 'id.' (KK 22), TSOJ *tangap-* 'id.' (14:3359a.5)), this is an excellent example of a parallel innovation[66] in Japanese dialects.

2.3.5.2 Consonant innovations
I propose the following two sound changes:
a) *t > s / _i
b) *#nan/ⁿ- > #an/ⁿ-

Examples of change a) are provided in (1) and (2) in Table 2.92 below, while an example of change b) is in (3).

Table 2.92: Examples of changes a) and b) in Pitati.

Example	Phonogram(s)	Morphemic Gloss	Book:Poem. Line	WOJ	PJe
1 tatinbana	多知波奈	mandarin.orange	20:4371.1	tatinbana	*tatiᵐbana
2 tas-i	多思	rise-INF	14:3395.2	tat-i	*tat-i
3 andö	阿杼	what	14:3397.5	nandö	*nani tə

Change b) occurred in Proto-EOJ (see §2.3.1.2), whereas change a) occurred later and is shared with three other EOJ topolects (Muzasi, Simotukeno, and Simotupusa).

2.3.5.3 Notable phonological retentions
There are many unchanged reflexes from PJe *e and *o in this topolect. Examples of the former are (3) and (4) in Table 2.93 below, while examples of the latter are (1) and (2). Example (5) shows a retention of word initial *m- in the sequence *mum-, which was regularly deleted in WOJ through a process of nasal dissimilation.

Example (6) is not phonographically attested in WOJ, but the Middle Japanese reflex is *nuno*, which is probably more innovative, showing a regressive spread of labialization from the *o. Alternatively, the Pitati form *nino* may be more innovative, showing a sporadic fronting of *u > /i/ in the environment *nun-, due to the alveolar articulation of /n/. It is difficult to decide between these two hypotheses, but I tentatively reconstruct PJe *nino.

---

[66] See §2.3.7.2 for a different example.

Table 2.93: Notable phonological retentions in Pitati.

	Example	Phonogram(s)	Morphemic Gloss	Book:Poem. Line	WOJ	PJe
1	mayo	麻欲	cocoon	14:3350a.2	–[67]	*mayo
2	-m-ö	母	-TENT-ATTR	20:4367.3	-m-u	*-m-o
3	-ke	家	-AVATTR	20:4369.4	-ki	*-ke
4	sake-	佐祁	be.safe-	20:4372.14	saki-	*sake-
5	muma	牟麻	horse	20:4372.9	uma	*muma
6	nino	尓努	cloth	14:3351.5	–	*nino

2.3.5.4 WOJ influence in the text

There are a few clear cases in which WOJ words or morphemes were inserted into the text of poems with EOJ linguistic features, which are shown in Table 2.94 below.

Table 2.94: WOJ influence in the Pitati poems.

	Example	Phonogram(s)	Morphemic Gloss	Book:Poem. Line	WOJ	PJe
1	ipe	伊敞	house	20:4364.3	ipe	*ipia
2	-ki	伎	-AVATTR	20:4364.4	-ki	*-ke

In example (1), the Proto-EOJ word for 'house' is *ipa < PJe *ipia, whereas the WOJ reflex is *ipe* (this is also the Proto-TSOJ form of the word). As regards example (2), the form *-ke* is also well attested in this topolect (e.g., 20:4369.4), so the raised vowel form *-ki* is probably due to WOJ influence.

2.3.5.5 A reconstruction of Pitati's vowel inventory

I reconstruct six vowel phonemes. There were no diphthongs.

Table 2.95: The vowel phonemes of Pitati.

	Front	Central	Back
High	i		u
Mid	e	ə	o
Low		a	

---

67 The Middle Japanese form is *mayu*, showing the raising of PJe *o > /u/. There are no phonographic attestations of this word in WOJ.

I do not reconstruct *ɨ because there is no evidence for it. There is one attestation in which a *Cï* phonogram is used to write the reflex of a PJe *Ci syllable (*pïk-ey* 'pull-EV' in 14:3397.4, instead of *pik-ey*), indicating there was no orthographic or phonemic contrast between *Cï* and *Ci* phonograms.

2.3.5.6 A reconstruction of Pitati's consonant inventory
The consonant inventory was unchanged from PJe except for the merger of PJe *ⁿr > *r, which occurred in Proto-EOJ.

2.3.6 Simotupusa

This topolect shows evidence of the sound changes that occurred in Proto-EOJ, as well as some changes that occurred after the split from Proto-EOJ.

2.3.6.1 Vowel innovations
I propose the following sound changes:
a) *a > ə ~ o /#_mo (sporadic)
b) *e > ə ~ o /#_Cu (sporadic)
c) *ə > o / C[+labial, -velar]_
d) *oi > /u/
e) *ui > /i/
f) *əi > /i/
g) *ai > /e/
h) *ia > /a/
i) *u > i / m_t
j) *o > u (sporadic)
k) *e > i (sporadic)

The example supporting change a) is provided in (2) in Table 2.96 below, while the example supporting change b) is provided in (1). Example (1) shows a retention of the PJe vowel height in the first syllable, though it has either centered to [ə] due to the backness of the following [u] or backed and rounded to [o] due to the backness and labiality of the following [u]. In other words, regressive vowel assimilation. There is no orthographic or phonemic contrast between [o] and [ə] in word-initial position, but it is probable that both sounds were allophones of /o/, depending on the subsequent vowels in the word. Thus, [osu] is a more likely pronunciation than [əsu]. Example (2) is also probably the result of regressive vowel assimilation, through the sound changes *amə > *əmə > *əmo > [omo].

Table 2.96: Examples of changes a) and b) in Simotupusa.

Example	Phonogram(s)	Morphemic Gloss	Book:Poem.Line	WOJ	PJe
1 osu	於須	rock	14:3385.4	iso	*eso
2 omo	於毛	mother	20:4386.4	amö ~ omö	*amə

The free variation between *mo* and *mö* phonograms shown in Table 2.97 below serves as evidence for change c).

Table 2.97: Examples of change c) in Simotupusa.

Example	Phonogram(s)	Morphemic Gloss	Book:Poem.Line	WOJ	PJe
1 imo	以毛	beloved.girl	20:4390.4	imo	*imo
2 imö	伊母	beloved.girl	20:4391.5	imo	*imo
4 mo	毛	FPT	14:3385.5	mö	*mə
5 mö	母	FPT	20:4386.5	mö	*mə

Change d) is supported by example (4) in Table 2.98 below. I consider example (5) to be the result of analogical levelling because nominalized verb roots may only terminate in -*i* or -*e* in this topolect. This is why we see *kopi* instead of expected *kopu*. In a few other EOJ topolects, however, only the infinitive forms were levelled out, and the nominalized forms retained the reflex -*u* (<*-oi). See §2.3.7.1 for a discussion of the forms *kopï* 'long.for.INF' and *kopu* 'long.for.NML' in the Kamitupusa topolect.

Change e) is supported by examples (2) and (3) below.
Change f) is supported by example (1) below.

Table 2.98: Examples of changes d), e), and f) in Simotupusa.

Example	Phonogram(s)	Morphemic Gloss	Book:Poem.Line	WOJ	PJe
1 nömi	能美	RPT	20:4355.1	nömï	*nəməi
2 kami	加美	deity	20:4391.2	kamï	*kamui
3 tusi	都之	earth	40:4392.1	tuti	*tutui
4 siru	志流	behind	20:4385.3	siri	*siroi
5 kopi	古比	long.for.NML	20:4386.4	kopï	*kopoi

The examples in Table 2.99 below offer evidence for change g).

Table 2.99: Examples of change g) in Simotupusa.

Example	Phonogram(s)	Morphemic Gloss	Book:Poem. Line	WOJ	INV
1	pe	弊	pot	20:4393.4	pey	*pai
2	pe	弊	prow	20:4389.2	pey	*pai
3	[i]p-e	弊	say-EV	20:4388.1	ip-ey	*ip-ai
4	pune	布祢	boat	20:4384.4	pune	*punai

Change h) is supported by the two examples in Table 2.100 below.

Table 2.100: Examples of change h) in Simotupusa.

Example	Phonogram(s)	Morphemic Gloss	Book:Poem. Line	WOJ	PJe
1	popom-ar-e	保々麻例	be.unopened-PROG-EV	20:4387.3	pupum-er-e	*popom-i-ar-ai
2	omop-ape-	於毛波弊	think.INF-endure-	20:4389.5	omöp-i-apey-	*əməp-i-apai-

Example (2) occurs in the line in *omop-ape-n-aku n-i* think.INF-endure-NEG.ATTR-NML COP-INF '[I] was unable to think about it' (Vovin 2013: 148–149). In WOJ there is a logographic attestation of the same line as 念不堪國 OMÖP-I-APEY-N-AKU N-I in MYS 6:962.5. The line is hypermetrical with eight syllables instead of the expected seven, but it is unclear which vowel ([i] or [a]), if any, in *omöp-i-apey-* was elided in WOJ recitation (or perhaps -*i-a-* fused to [e]?). In MYS 18:4083.5 we also find 尓奈比安倍 *ninap-i-apey-* carry-INF-endure- 'able to carry', where once again both the infinitive -*i* and the initial vowel of *apey-* 'endure' are written, unlike in Simotupusa.

There is only one supporting example of i), which I provide in Table 2.101 below. I discussed the WOJ and TSOJ cognates in §2.2.2.4. It is possible Simotupusa is the conservative topolect here and the PJe form was *mita, but I find this less likely due to the sporadic change *#mi > *mu that is unlikely to have occurred independently in both WOJ and TSOJ.

Table 2.101: Example of change i) in Simotupusa.

Example	Phonogram(s)	Morphemic Gloss	Book:Poem. Line	WOJ	PJe
1	mita	美他	together	20:4394.3	muta	*muta

The six examples in Table 2.102 below offer evidence for change j). Examples (2) – (4) all involve the attributive suffix -*u* (<*-o), whereas examples (1) and (5) show the raising of *o > /u/ in the second syllable of each word.

Table 2.102: Examples of changes j) and k) in Simotupusa.

	Example	Phonogram(s)	Morphemic Gloss	Book:Poem. Line	WOJ	PJe
1	osu	於須	rock	14:3385.4	iso	*eso
2	watar-am-u	和多良牟	cross-TENT-ATTR	20:4394.4	watar-am-u	*watar-am-o
3	s-unam-u	須奈牟	do-TENT2-ATTR	20:4391.4	s-uram-u	*s-uram-o
4	top-am-u	刀波牟	ask-TENT-ATTR	20:4392.5	top-am-u	*top-am-o
5	opuse	於不世	assign.INF	20:4389.4	opose	*oposai
6	popom-ar-e	保々麻例	be.unopened-PROG-EV	20:4387.3	pupum-er-e	*popom-i-ar-ai
7	pi	比	side	14:3385.4	pe	*pia

Example (7) shows evidence for change k). It seems to be the result of a borrowing of the WOJ (or TSOJ) form, followed by vowel raising, since the expected reflex in EOJ topolects is *pa*.

2.3.6.1.1 An unclear sound change

There is one vowel correspondence in Simotupusa that can be explained by two different sound changes. There is not enough evidence to decide which one is more plausible, so I mark it as unclear.

Table 2.103: An unclear vowel correspondence in Simotupusa.

	Example	Phonogram(s)	Morphemic Gloss	Book:Poem. Line	WOJ	PJe
1	-tö-	等	-PERF-	20:4390.3	-te-	*-tai-

The example in Table 2.103 above could be explained as a sporadic change of Proto-EOJ *-te- > /-tə-/ in this perfective morpheme. Alternatively, it may reflect a change of *-ta- > /-tə-/ only fossilized in this poem, if the PJe perfective *-tai- lost its final vowel in certain concatenations in Proto-EOJ through V_2 elision, prior to the sound change *ai > /e/. This would be similar to the Pitati form *wasura-* 'forget-', described in §2.3.5.1. However, the Simotupusa form would show an additional change of vowel centralization (*a > /ə/) that is not found in the Pitati form but is well attested in other morphemes in other AOJ topolects, as well as in certain Proto-EOJ morphemes. There are no other attestations of this perfective morpheme in Simotupusa.

2.3.6.2 Consonant innovations
I propose the following three sound changes:
a) *t > s / _i
b) *-tutu > /tusi/
c) *r > n / _am (sporadic regressive nasal assimilation in one morpheme)

Change a) is supported by the example in Table 2.104 below, and several other examples are found in neighboring EOJ topolects.

Table 2.104: Example of change a) in Simotupusa.

Example	Phonogram(s)	Morphemic Gloss	Book:Poem. Line	WOJ	PJe
1 tusi	都之	earth	20:4392.1	tuti	*tutui

Change b) is only attested in the coordinative gerund, which is shown in the example in Table 2.105 below. It is possible the scribe was trying to write a syllable [tsu] or [tsɨ], if *t had affricated before *u in this topolect. However, this is the only example in which EOJ ~ WOJ *tu* corresponds to Simotupusa *si* (or *si* in any other AOJ topolect), and there are thirteen *tu* phonograms attested in this topolect's corpus. So, perhaps it is just an irregular change of *-tutu > /tusi/ in this morpheme. It is also possible the Simotupusa form is different morphologically, though I am unable to present any coherent analysis of -*tusi* consisting of two or more morphemes, except the highly speculative hypothesis it is a truncated, or more archaic, form of the coordinative gerund (retaining the pre-reduplicative form *-tu > -*tutu*?), followed by *s-i* 'do-INF'.

Table 2.105: Example of change b) in Simotupusa.

Example	Phonogram(s)	Morphemic Gloss	Book:Poem. Line	WOJ	PJe
1 -tusi	都之	-COOR	20:4386.5	-tutu	*-tutu

Change c) is supported by the attestations of the second tentative suffix in examples (1) and (2) in Table 2.106 below. This sporadic change can be projected back to Proto-EOJ.

Table 2.106: Examples of change c) in Simotupusa.

	Example	Phonogram(s)	Morphemic Gloss	Book:Poem. Line	WOJ	PJe
1	s-unam-u	須奈牟	do-TENT2-ATTR	20:4391.4	s-uram-u	*s-uram-o
2	ayok-unam-ey	阿用久奈米	waver-TENT2-EV	20:4390.5	?-uram-ey[68]	*ayok-uram-ai

2.3.6.3 Notable phonological retentions

In regard to example (1) in Table 2.107 below, I think there are two hypotheses worth considering. First, it could be that PJe *wə had the reflex /we/ in this topolect. Second, it is possible a we phonogram was used to write a Simotupusa /wə/ syllable, which did not exist in WOJ, but can be reconstructed for PJe. Since the accusative case marker is attested eleven times in this topolect and is written invariably as -wo (< PJe *-wo), either hypothesis is plausible. Accepting the second hypothesis would entail Simotupusa is the only known OJ topolect with a phonemic or phonetic distinction between [wo] and [wə]. There is no other relevant data to push us toward one hypothesis over the other.

Table 2.107: Notable phonological retentions in Simotupusa.

	Example	Phonogram(s)	Morphemic Gloss	Book:Poem. Line	WOJ	PJe
1	töwerap-i	等恵良比	shake-NML	20:4385.2	töworap-i	*təwərap-i[69]
2	popom-ar-e	保々麻例	be.unopened-PROG-EV	20:4387.3	pupum-er-e	*popom-i-ar-ai
3	-tamap-o	他麻保	-HON-ATTR	20:4389.4	-tamap-u	*-tamap-o
4	yuk-o	由古	go-ATTR	20:4385.1	yuk-u	*yuk-o
5	-key	氣	-AVATTR	20:4394.5	-ki	*-ke

In example (2) we see the retention of two PJe *o vowels, both of which raised to /u/ in the WOJ cognate.

Examples (3) and (4) show a retention of the PJe attributive *-o. A raised vowel allomorph (-u) is also attested in this topolect.

Example (5) shows a retention of PJe *e in this topolect.

---

[68] The verb ayok- 'waver' is not phonographically attested in WOJ, but it is attested as ayuk- ~ ayug- in the Heian and Kamakura periods (NKD).
[69] Historically -ap- is the iterative suffix, but it appears to have been fossilized on this verb since PJe because the form töwor- does not occur in OJ.

2.3.6.4 WOJ influence in the text

In contrast to most other EOJ topolects, there is very little WOJ influence evident in the text. Example (1) shows the raised vowel form of this suffix, typical of WOJ, whereas the form -*key* is also attested in this topolect. For example (2), the Proto-EOJ word for 'house' was *ipa (< PJe *ipia), so it is clear that the WOJ form is being used here, though we cannot rule out borrowing from WOJ[70] or TSOJ into Simotupusa (instead of scribal alteration), since *ipa* 'house' is not attested in this topolect.

Table 2.108: WOJ influence in the Simotupusa poems.

Example	Phonogram(s)	Morphemic Gloss	Book:Poem.Line	WOJ	PJe
1 -*ki*	伎	-AVATTR	14:3386.2	-*ki*	*-ke
2 *ipe*	以弊	house	20:4388.3	*ipe*	*ipia

2.3.6.5 A reconstruction of Simotupusa's vowel inventory

I reconstruct six vowel phonemes. There were no diphthongs.

Table 2.109: The vowel phonemes of Simotupusa.

	Front	Central	Back
High	i		u
Mid	e	ə	o
Low			a

I do not reconstruct *ɨ because there is no evidence for it. Free variation between C*i* and C*ï* phonograms is apparent in the data, e.g., Simotupusa *tanbï* 'journey' (20:4388.1), WOJ *tanbi* 'id.'; Simotupusa *kopi* 'long.for.INF' (20:4386.4), WOJ *kopï* 'id.'.

2.3.6.6 A reconstruction of Simotupusa's consonant inventory

The consonant inventory was unchanged from PJe except for the merger of PJe *ⁿr > *r, which occurred in Proto-EOJ. Although in Kupchik (2011: 425–426) I proposed there was some evidence for denasalization in the *ng*- and *nd*- initial syllables, in the intervening years I have grown more skeptical of that hypothesis due to the inexact manner in which OJ scribes indicated medial voicing with Chinese phonograms.

---

70 First proposed by Vovin (2010: 170).

2.3.7 Kamitupusa

Like the other EOJ topolects, Kamitupusa shares the innovations that occurred in Proto-EOJ but also shows some innovations that occurred later.

2.3.7.1 Vowel innovations
I propose the following sound changes:
a) *ə > o / C[+labial]_
b) *ai > /e/
c) *ia > /a/
d) *a > /ə/ (sporadic, phonologically conditioned?)
e) *əi > /i/
f) *ui > /i/
g) *oi > /u/

The free variation between *mo* and *mö* phonograms shown in Table 2.110 offers evidence for change a).

Table 2.110: Examples of change a) in Kamitupusa.

	Example	Phonogram(s)	Morphemic Gloss	Book:Poem. Line	WOJ	PJe
1	mo	毛	EPT	20:4358.5	mö	*mə
2	mö	母	FPT	20:4347.4	mö	*mə
3	kamo	可毛	EPT	20:4356.5	kamö	*kamə
4	kamö	加母	EPT	20:4347.5	kamö	*kamə

Change b) is supported by the examples in Table 2.111. Examples (2) and (3) show free variation between *pe* and *pey* phonograms to write the same noun, indicating a lack of phonemic contrast between these syllables.

Table 2.111: Examples of change b) in Kamitupusa.

	Example	Phonogram(s)	Morphemic Gloss	Book:Poem. Line	WOJ	PJe
1	kapeyr-i	加倍理	return-INF	20:4350.5	kaper-i	*kaper-i
2	pey	閇	prow	20:4359.5	pe	*pe
3	pe	敝	prow	20:4359.2	pe	*pe

Example (1) in Table 2.112 below offers evidence for change c). Example (2) indicates there was a lack of orthographic and phonemic contrast between *Ce* and *Cey* phonograms in this topolect.

Table 2.112: Examples of changes c) and d) in Kamitupusa.

Example	Phonogram(s)	Morphemic Gloss	Book:Poem. Line	WOJ	PJe.
1	karam-ar-u	可良麻流	wrap.around-PROG-ATTR	20:4352.4	karam-er-u	*karam-i-ar-o
2	ipey	伊閇	house	20:4347.1	ipe	*ipia
3	kömo	許毛	duck	20:4354.1	kamo	*kamo

Example (3) above offers support for change d), which is a well-attested sound change in EOJ topolects. Vovin (2013: 104) proposed this example is the result of regressive vowel assimilation, but that is unlikely. The Kamitupusa form is phonemically /kəmo/, and we would expect to find /komo/ if it were a case of regressive vowel assimilation.

Change e) is supported by example (1) in Table 2.113 below, while change f) is supported by example (5).

Table 2.113: Examples of changes e), f), and g) in Kamitupusa.

Example	Phonogram(s)	Morphemic Gloss	Book:Poem. Line	WOJ	PJe
1	nömi	能美	RPT	20:4355.1	nömi	*nəməi
2	kopï	古非	long.for.INF	20:4347.2	kopï	*kopoi
3	kopu	故布	long.for.NML	14:3382.5	kopï	*kopoi
4	sungï	須義	pass.INF	20:4349.4	sungï	*suⁿgoi
5	kami	可美	deity	20:4350.2	kamï	*kamui

In regard to change g), we see two different reflexes of PJe *kopoi in examples (2) and (3) above. In example (2), it is the infinitive form of the verb. This form cannot be *kopu* because the verb paradigm lacked an infinitive -*u* in this position, so it was levelled out under the influence of -*i*. I have already discussed examples of this in other EOJ topolects. This also explains the infinitive form in (4). Example (3) shows the root of the nominalized form the verb did not face the same pressures and remains as *kopu*, the expected reflex of PJe *kopoi in this topolect.[71] It precedes the topic particle *pa* in the line, just like the similar example *sungu* 'to pass.NML' (20:4378.2 – Simotukeno) discussed in §2.3.4.1. I provide an analysis and translation of this line in (2) below.

(2) 14:3382.5
汝者故布婆曽母
NA PA kopu pa sö-m-ö
2.S TPT long.for.NML TPT do-TENT-ATTR
'You shall love [me].'

Sentences with two topic particles are well attested in OJ poetry, and, unlike Modern Japanese where such constructions are contrastive, both particles can be topical (Vovin 2020: 1075–1076). Compare the poem in (3) below, written in WOJ, showing the same pattern of a noun followed by the topic particle and the tentative form of the verb *se-* 'do'.

(3) 20:4446.3
麻比波勢牟
mapi pa se-m-u
present TPT do-TENT-FIN
'[I] will give [you] a present.' (Vovin 2013: 216–217)

The phonological form *sö-* 'do' in (2) above is unusual (normally it is *se-*), but it is also attested in the negative-imperative construction *na*-VERB-*sö*. The form *se-m-u* 'do-TENT-ATTR' is attested once in this topolect in 14:3383.5, but (2) is the only Kamitupusa attestation of this word form with an unraised vowel in the attributive,[72] which may have favored the (more archaic?) allomorph *sö-* 'do' in this topolect. Among the various reconstructions offered for this verb in PJ,[73] I find Frellesvig and Whitman's *sə 'do' (2004: 294) to be the most persuasive, since its irregular

---

[71] Perhaps forms like this ending in /u/ were permitted in EOJ topolects due to their phonological and syntactic similarity to attributive forms like *yuk-u* 'go-ATTR', which can also function as nominals, as well as the fact that nouns faced no restriction in ending in *-u*. An example of *yuk-u* preceding the topic particle *pa* is attested in 20:4425.2 – UNP.

[72] Actually, there are only two other attestations of *se-m-o* in all of EOJ: 14:3418.5 – Kamitukeno and 14:3426.4 – Mitinöku. There is also a form *si-m-u* do-TENT-ATTR attested once in 14:3556.5 – UNP, showing another unique form of the verb 'to do' before the tentative suffix.

[73] Vovin mentions the reconstructions *sai and *sia as possibilities (2010: 187) and he claims we cannot decide between them, but if it were *sia, the Proto-EOJ reflex would be *sa, so that reconstruction can be rejected with confidence. His PJ *sai is a reasonable possibility, though it is harder

conjugation is identical to that of *kə 'come'. I view the later change of *sə to *se-* as the result of an irregular fronting of *ə > /e/ after the coronal-initial *s- in the initial position of a phonological word, which is why it did not affect the negative-imperative construction *na-VERB-sə. The occurrence of this vowel fronting only after a coronal onset is why we only find *kö-* 'come', never *ke-*, in OJ. The Kamitupusa form in (2) above indicates the forms /sə/ and /se/ persisted as doublets in some pockets of Japan, at least into the Nara period. This fronting of *ə > /e/ after coronal onsets was already described in the Suruga topolect of TSOJ (§2.2.1.1), where it was shown to be an extensive sound change, similar in kind, but a separate, later development.

2.3.7.2 Consonant innovations
I propose one consonant innovation in Kamitupusa:
a) *#w- > [p] ~ [b]

Table 2.114: Example of change a) in Kamitupusa.

	Example	Phonogram(s)	Morphemic Gloss	Book:Poem.Line	WOJ	PJe
1	pakare	波可礼	be.separated.NML	20:4352.5	wakare	*wakarai

This is a sporadic fortition of PJe *#w-, which may have been to [p] or [b]. It is difficult to decide which of these two sounds is more plausible, since both fortitions are attested cross-linguistically. If the fortition were to [b], this resulted in an allophone of /ᵐb/ in word-initial position that did not have prenasalization. Interestingly, the fortition of *#w- > [b] occurred independently in the Southern Ryukyuan languages several centuries later, serving as another example of drift, or parallel innovation, in Japonic languages (see the discussion under Table 2.91). It should be noted there are two attestations of *wakare* 'be.separated.INF' in this topolect (20:4348.2, 20:4349.5), which means the change of *#w- > [p] ~ [b] in this word probably only occurred in a certain speech community in Kamitupusa.

2.3.7.3 WOJ influence in the text
In example (1) in Table 2.115 below, the EOJ form is *-pa*, whereas the WOJ form is *-pe*. Since the WOJ form is attested in this example, I consider it due to some sort of WOJ influence.

---

to explain the OJ allomorph *-sö* with this, as well as its irregular conjugation. Earlier, Vovin (2005: 335) offered the reconstruction *søi [səi].

Table 2.115: WOJ influence in the text.

	Example	Phonogram(s)	Morphemic Gloss	Book:Poem. Line	WOJ	PJe
1	-pe	敝	-ALL	20:4359.4	-pe	*-pia
2	ipey	伊閇	house	20:4347.1	ipe	*ipia

Likewise, for example (2), we would expect *ipa* in an EOJ topolect. There are two other attestations of this lexeme in Kamitupusa and they are also written *ipey*. Since the change *ia > /a/ is attested in this topolect and it can be projected back to Proto-EOJ, the Kamitupusa form *ipey* [ipe] must be either due to the influence of a WOJ scribe or because it is a loanword from WOJ or TSOJ.

2.3.7.4 A reconstruction of Kamitupusa's vowel inventory

I reconstruct six vowel phonemes. There were no diphthongs.

Table 2.116: The vowel phonemes of Kamitupusa.

	Front	Central	Back
High	i		u
Mid	e	ə	o
Low			a

I do not reconstruct *ɨ because there is no evidence for it. Free variation between *Ci* and *Cï* phonograms is apparent in the data, e.g., Kamitupusa *ipap-ï* 'pray-INF' (20:4347.5), WOJ *ipap-i* 'id.'; Kamitupusa *k-ï* 'come-INF' (20:4349.2), *k-i* 'id.' (14:3382.4), WOJ *k-i* 'id.'.

2.3.7.5 A reconstruction of Kamitupusa's consonant inventory

The consonant inventory was unchanged from PJe except for the merger of PJe *ⁿr > *r, which occurred in Proto-EOJ.

2.3.8 Mitinöku

There are only two poems from Mitinöku in the corpus with AOJ features, and both are from Book 14 (poems 3426 and 3437). Due to this small corpus, there is comparatively little we can infer from the data.

2.3.8.1 Vowel innovations

I propose the following sound changes:
a) *ai > /e/
b) *ə > o / C[+labial]_
c) *əi > /e/

Change a) is supported by the two examples in Table 2.117 below, which show a lack of orthographic and phonemic contrast between *me* and *mey* phonograms. This change can be projected back to Proto-EOJ.

Table 2.117: Examples of change a) in Mitinöku.

	Example	Phonogram(s)	Morphemic Gloss	Book:Poem. Line	WOJ	PJe
1	ser-asime	西良思馬	bend-CAUS.INF	14:3437.4	?-asimey[74]	*səi-wor-asimai
2	pak-am-e	波可馬	string-TENT-EV	14:3437.5	pak-am-ey	*pak-am-ai

Change b) is evidenced from the example in Table 2.118 below.

Table 2.118: Example of change b) in Mitinöku.

	Example	Phonogram(s)	Morphemic Gloss	Book:Poem. Line	WOJ	PJe
1	kamo	可毛	EPT	14:3437.5	kamö	*kamə

Change c) is supported by only one example, which is provided in Table 2.119 below.

Table 2.119: Example of change c) in Mitinöku.

	Example	Phonogram(s)	Morphemic Gloss	Book:Poem. Line	WOJ	PJe
1	ser-asime	西良思馬	bend-CAUS.INF	14:3437.4	–	*səi-wor-asimai

The root *ser-* 'bend' in (1) is attested in MJ as *sor-* 'id.'. We can reconstruct this as consisting of PJe *səi 'back' and *wor- 'bend' (Martin 1987: 756). Thus, the MJ form can be explained by the following sequence of changes: *səi-wor- > *si-

---

[74] The root *ser-* 'bend' is unattested in WOJ, but the causative suffix *-asimey* is attested.

wor- > *sɨ-or > sor-.[75] The final change occurred through V_1 elision. In Mitinöku, the changes progressed in this way: *səi-wor- > *se-wor > *se-or > ser-, with the final change being the result of V_2 elision. The change of *əi > /e/ also occurred in the neighboring Simotukeno topolect, indicating these two topolects were closely related.

As a final note, the variance between the Mitinöku form and the MJ cognate is unlikely to be due to a misspelling, since mistakenly writing *se* for *sö*, as far as I can tell, is not attested in any WOJ text.

2.3.8.2 Notable phonological retentions

The only notable retention in this province is the attributive suffix *-o*, which is unchanged from PJe *o, and is provided in example (1) in Table 2.120 below. Other attributive forms are not attested in this topolect.

Table 2.120: A notable phonological retention in Mitinöku.

Example	Phonogram(s)	Morphemic Gloss	Book:Poem. Line	WOJ	PJe
1	-m-o	毛	-TENT-ATTR	14:3426.4	-m-u	*-m-o

2.3.8.3 A reconstruction of Mitinöku's vowel inventory

I reconstruct the following six vowel phonemes.

Table 2.121: The vowel phonemes of Mitinöku.

	Front	Central	Back
High	i		u
Mid	e	ə	o
Low		a	

I do not reconstruct *ɨ because there is no evidence for it.

---

[75] It is also possible PJe *səi 'back' did not fusionally reduce to *sɨ prior to V_1 elision, but rather developed into the compounding allomorph *sə- through V_2 elision. Either way, the later V_1 elision produced the same result. Due to the Mitinöku reflex, however, we must reconstruct PJe *səi-wor-, not *sə-wor-.

2.3.8.4 A reconstruction of Mitinöku's consonant inventory

The consonant inventory was identical to that of PJe except for the merger of PJe *^{n}r > *r, which occurred in Proto-EOJ.

2.3.9 A reconstruction of Proto-EOJ

Based on the previously described data, I reconstruct the six vowel phonemes of Proto-EOJ in Table 2.122. There were also the diphthongs *ui, *oi, and *əi. The consonant inventory was identical to that of PJe except for the merger of PJe *^{n}r > *r.

Table 2.122: The vowel phonemes of Proto-EOJ.

	Front	Central	Back
High	*i		*u
Mid	*e	*ə	*o
Low			*a

The phonological innovations that define Proto-EOJ as a distinct subgroup from Proto-Japanese are as follows:
  PJe *ia > Proto-EOJ *a[76]
  PJe *-e-a > Proto-EOJ *a[77]
  PJe *ai > Proto-EOJ *e
  PJe *#nan/^{n}- > Proto-EOJ *#an/^{n}- (e.g., *nani se > *na^{n}ze > *a^{n}ze 'why'; *nani tə > *na^{n}də > *a^{n}də 'what'; *nani > *ani 'what')[78]

There are also four sporadic phonological innovations in specific morphemes that occurred in Proto-EOJ. These further strengthen Proto-EOJ as a valid subgroup:
  PJe *-uram- > Proto-EOJ *-unam-[79] 'non-past tentative suffix'
  PJe *-ra > Proto-EOJ *-rə 'diminutive suffix'
  PJe *-nasu > Proto-EOJ *-nəsu 'comparative suffix'
  PJe *-kate- > Proto-EOJ *-ka^{n}de- 'potential auxiliary'

---

[76] Hachijō reflects this change in its progressive suffix -*ar*- (Kaneda 2001: 206), which is a retention of the EOJ progressive suffix -*ar*-.
[77] This change only occurred at word boundaries. It is necessary to explain the Proto-EOJ adjectival evidential form *-ka- < *-kare- < *-ke-ar-e '-AVATTR-exist-EV'.
[78] Hachijō reflects this change in its interrogative pronouns, e.g., *ani* 'what', *aNdō* 'what' (Asanuma 1999: 25).
[79] This is retained in Hachijō as -*unou*- (Kaneda 2001: 179).

The fixed morpheme order of the negative and iterative suffixes as -NEG-ITER- is a morphological innovation that occurred in Proto-EOJ (it does not occur in TSOJ). In pre-WOJ, the order was fixed as -ITER-NEG-. It is unclear which order, if any, was original, though as I have argued previously (Kupchik 2011: 728), it is likely the iterative suffix was grammaticalized separately in WOJ and EOJ, from a PJe auxiliary (it is not found in the Ryukyuan languages, and thus cannot be projected back to PJ). Perhaps one of the two languages initially grammaticalized it, and the second followed suit through contact with the first. In EOJ, the iterative is a true suffix and, like the tentative, it fits in a suffix slot after the negative (and progressive), whereas in WOJ it retains more of its original auxiliary nature, in that the negative in the verbal word form appears to be negating the iterative -*apey* instead of the verbal root. In an unknown OJ dialect we even find the iterative suffixed to the attributive -*uru* in MYS 16:3791.94 (Vovin 2021a: 44), further strengthening the hypothesis of a late, independent grammaticalization in different OJ dialects. Other Proto-EOJ morphological innovations include the diminutive suffix *-na, the usage of two diminutive suffixes in sequence, and possibly also the ironic particle *ngape*.

Lexical innovations in Proto-EOJ include *teⁿgo 'third daughter, maiden', *mama 'cliff', and *mek- 'walk'. All of these have cognates in Hachijō.

2.3.9.1 Later EOJ subgroups

There are two clear subgroups from Proto-EOJ that each share at least two innovations. The first was spoken in Kamitukeno and Sagamu provinces. Based on geography the unattested Kapï topolect was probably also part of this dialect since it bridged the gap between Kamitukeno and Sagamu. I will refer to this as Western EOJ because these provinces were the westernmost in Azuma with EOJ speakers. The other subgroup was spoken in Muzasi, Pitati, Simotukeno, Mitinöku, Simotupusa, and Kamitupusa provinces.[80] I will refer to this as Coastal EOJ since all of these provinces bordered the sea except Simotukeno. Each subgroup developed Proto-EOJ *ui and *oi in a distinct manner, as illustrated in Figure 2.1.

Due to a paucity of data, the Mitinöku topolect of EOJ does not show any reflexes of Proto-EOJ *oi or *ui, but I group it in Coastal EOJ because it has the same unique reflex of Proto-EOJ *əi found in the Simotukeno topolect (> /e/).

It is unclear when the change *ə > o / C[+labial]_ occurred, though it is found in all EOJ topolects. It is possible it occurred in Proto-EOJ, but we know it was a late change in TSOJ and WOJ. Since it is found in all OJ dialects of the eighth century, it appears to have spread by areal diffusion rather quickly.

---

[80] It is likely the OJ topolect spoken in the province Apa, situated directly south of Kamitupusa, was also part of this dialect group, but that presumption is only based on geography.

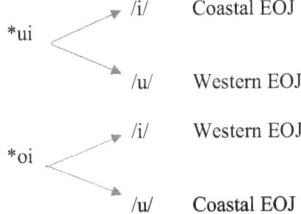

Figure 2.1: Different reflexes of Proto-EOJ *ui and *oi in EOJ dialects.

The change of *t > s/_i was another one that occurred in Coastal EOJ. Its absence in Kamitupusa and Mitinöku indicates it was a late change that occurred after these two topolects diverged from the Coastal EOJ core. It probably began in the Muzasi-Pitati-Simotupusa subgroup and spread by areal diffusion to neighboring Simotukeno, since Simotukeno subgroups with Mitinöku.

2.4 The subgroups of Proto-Japanese and Proto-EOJ

Figure 2.2 below illustrates the historical development of Proto-EOJ and the other Old Japanese dialects from Proto-Japanese. I do not include the Ryukyuan languages in this tree diagram because Proto-Ryukyuan is a separate branch from Proto-Japonic.

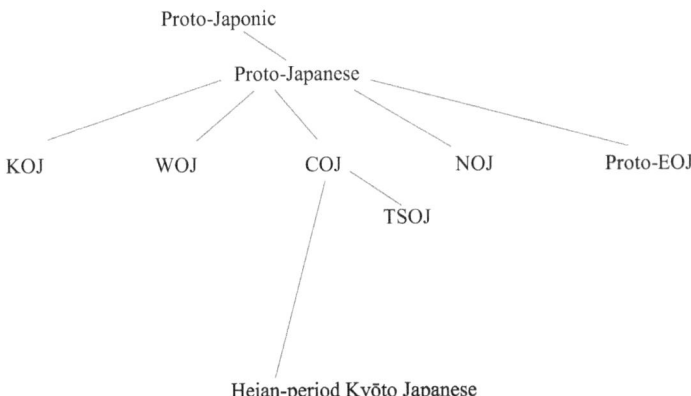

Figure 2.2: The subgroups of Proto-Japanese.

In Figure 2.3 below I present my proposed subgroupings of the EOJ dialects based on shared innovations.

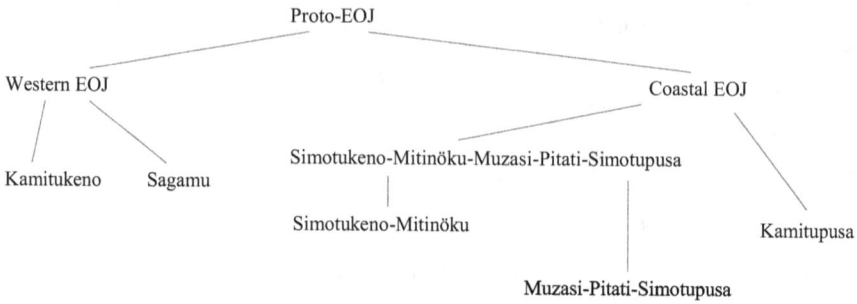

Figure 2.3: The subgroups of Proto-EOJ.

Hino (2003: 201) proposed the following EOJ dialect regions based on vowel raising, irrespective of whether the raisings occurred in the same morphemes in two or more AOJ topolects:
 REGION C: Sinano & Töpotuapumi
 REGION B: Suruga, Kamitukeno, Muzasi, Sagamu, Idu, Pitati, Simotupusa
 REGION A: Simotukeno & Kamitupusa

As I have demonstrated in this chapter, a comparison of shared linguistic innovations does not support his Region B or Region A as valid EOJ dialect regions, and in his Region C a different OJ dialect was spoken (TSOJ).

Ikier (2006: 63–65) accepted Hino's dialect divisions but he also proposed a dialect spoken in the provinces Kamitukeno, Muzasi, Pitati, and Simotupusa. His conclusion was based on a quantitative study of shared "interrelations" (vowel, consonant, and allomorphic alternations), without any discrimination between shared innovations and shared retentions. If we remove Kamitukeno, his dialect aligns with one of the subgroups I propose above, based on the shared innovation of *t > s/_i.

2.5 An analysis of the phonological innovations in the poems from unspecified provinces (UNP)

There are 120 AOJ poems that are not attributed to any specific province. I refer to these as "unspecified province" poems, abbreviated as UNP. In this section I will discuss the vowel and consonant innovations apparent in the data.

2.5.1 Vowel innovations

What follows below are the forms in the data that differ from cognate WOJ forms, which are evidence for phonological innovations.

2.5.1.1 *e > /i/

The examples provided in Table 2.123 below show the raising of *-e > -i. These cases are unique to UNP, but we also find this raising in the commonly attested UNP adjectival verb attributive suffix -ki, a reflex from PJe *-ke, which is a reflex that is also found in WOJ and several AOJ topolects.

Table 2.123: Examples of *e > /i/ in UNP.

	Example	Phonogram(s)	Morphemic Gloss	Book:Poem.Line	WOJ	PJe
1	-n-i	尔	-PERF-IMP	14:3440a.5	-n-e	*-n-e
2	namï	奈未	taste.NML	14:3460.3	namey	*namai
3	si-	思	do-	14:3556.5	se-	*se-

Example (2) developed as *namai > *name > /nami/.

2.5.1.2 *ui > /u/, *oi > /u/

These sound changes are found in a few different roots, which are shown in Table 2.124 below.

Table 2.124: Examples of *ui > /u/ and *oi > /u/ in UNP.

	Example	Phonogram(s)	Morphemic Gloss	Book:Poem.Line	WOJ	PJe
1	kuku[81]	久君	stem	14:3444.2	kukï	*kukui
2	kamu	可牟	deity	14:3516.3	kamï, kamu-	*kamui
3	tuku	都久	moon	14:3476.3	tukï, tuku-	*tukoi
4	tuku	都久	moon	14:3565.5	tukï, tuku-	*tukoi
5	oyu	於由	grow.older.NML	14:3473.5	oyi	*oyoi

---

[81] There is another possible attestation of kuku in the word mikuku (14:3525.1 – UNP), if we analyze it as mi-kuku 'water-stalk' (Vovin 2012a: 213). However, there is a second plausible etymology that does not involve kuku 'stalk, stem', so I do not list it in Table 2.124.

These changes occurred in EOJ (but not TSOJ). Therefore, it is clear these words are attested in poems written in EOJ. Moreover, since *ui > /u/ only occurred in the Sagamu and Kamitukeno topolects, examples (1) and (2) must be either from one of those areas or from an overtly unattested province such as Kapï.[82] Similarly, *oi > /u/ occurred in six attested EOJ topolects, so examples (3) – (5) are most likely written in one of those topolects.

In regard to example (4), based on evidence from toponyms (Mizushima 1986: 396), Vovin (2012a: 250) proposed poem 14:3565 might be attributed to Sinano province, but the word for 'moon' is unfortunately unattested in TSOJ, and in Sinano *oi became /i/, so we would expect *tukï* 'moon'. Still, as mentioned earlier in this chapter, it is possible northern Sinano was part of the EOJ dialect group and southern Sinano was part of the TSOJ dialect group, in which case *tuku* would be a possible reflex for the northern area.

2.5.1.3 *ai > /e/

There are numerous attestations of a *Ce* phonogram used to write a word that is written with a *Cey* phonogram in WOJ, as well as the inverse. We saw evidence for this sound change in the EOJ topolects, but not in TSOJ, so it is probable that the UNP poems that evidence this change were written in EOJ. Fifteen examples were presented in Kupchik (2007: 28–31), which I will not repeat here.

2.5.1.4 *ə > o / C[+labial] _

This sound change is unsurprisingly well attested throughout the UNP poems, just as it is throughout the AOJ poems that are overtly linked to a province. 61 supporting examples were presented in Kupchik (2007: 24–28), which I will not repeat here. Since it is a change shared by both EOJ and TSOJ, it cannot be used to link these poems to any specific topolect.

2.5.1.5 *a > /e/

We find this sound change once in the form shown in Table 2.125 below.

---

[82] Vovin (2012a: 136) claimed poem 14:3444 is from Pitati province, due to the form *-an-ap-* '-NEG-ITER' that appears in another Pitati poem (14:3394.5), along with some earlier speculation (e.g., Mizushima 1986: 212) that a toponym in the poem might be located in Pitati. However, the same form *-n-ap-* '-NEG-ITER' is attested in the Kamitukeno topolect (in 14:3419.5), and more importantly this morpheme order can be reconstructed for Proto-EOJ. Furthermore, in the Pitati topolect *ui became /i/, so we can rule it out based on this linguistic evidence.

Table 2.125: Example of *a > /e/ in UNP.

Example	Phonogram(s)	Morphemic Gloss	Book:Poem. Line	WOJ	PJe
1 pe	敞	leaf	14:3456.2	pa	*pa

The PJe form for 'leaf' was clearly *pa and not *pe, so I conclude the UNP attestation of *pe* 'leaf' is due to a sporadic raising and fronting of *a > /e/ in this one root.

2.5.1.6 *ia > /a/

I reconstruct the PJe word for 'house' as *ipia, thus the UNP attestation *ipa* 'house' in Table 2.126 below shows V₁ elision of the PJe sequence *ia, while the WOJ form shows a fusional reduction of this sequence to /e/.

Table 2.126: Example of *ia > /a/ in UNP.

Example	Phonogram(s)	Morphemic Gloss	Book:Poem. Line	WOJ	PJe
1 ipa	伊波	house	20:4427.1	ipe	*ipia

The form *ipa* 'house' is also attested in the Muzasi, Simotukeno, and Kamitukeno topolects, but this sound change can be projected back to Proto-EOJ.

2.5.1.7 *i > /u/

The phonetic motivation for this sound change in the example in Table 2.127 below is unclear, but it is perhaps a sporadic rounding and backing of the vowel due to the preceding /p/. Ryukyuan reflexes confirm the PJ form ended in *-i, rather than *-u (Thorpe 1983: 311–312).

Table 2.127: Example of *i > /u/ in UNP.

Example	Phonogram(s)	Morphemic Gloss	Book:Poem. Line	WOJ	PJe
1 nipu	尔布	new	14:3460.3	nipi	*nipi

2.5.1.8 *e > /o/

This sound change is unusual for AOJ, but the UNP form *tor-* 'shine' is more likely the innovative one, since we can reconstruct *ter- 'shine' in PJ (cf. Old Ryukyuan *ter-* 'shine') and PJe.

Table 2.128: Example of *e > /o/ in UNP.

	Example	Phonogram(s)	Morphemic Gloss	Book:Poem. Line	WOJ	PJe
1	tor-e	刀礼	shine-EV	14:3561.3	ter-e	*ter-ai

2.5.1.9 *#ə > #ye

There is one example supporting this sound change.

Table 2.129: Example of *#ə- > /ye/ in UNP.

	Example	Phonogram(s)	Morphemic Gloss	Book:Poem. Line	WOJ	PJe
1	yenbi	叡比	sash	20:4428.4	onbi	*əᵐbi

The UNP form appears to be the result of a sporadic fronting and raising of the vowel due to the vowel /i/ in the following syllable.

2.5.1.10 *o > /u/

This sound change is evident in the many attestations of the verbal attributive suffix *-o > -u. Two lexical examples are provided below in Table 2.130.

Table 2.130: Examples of *o > /u/ in UNP.

	Example	Phonogram(s)	Morphemic Gloss	Book:Poem. Line	WOJ	PJe
1	ukera	宇家良	ukera	14:3503.4	–	*wokera
2	yun-öpe-nba	由乃敞波	sleep-ITER-COND	14:3476b.5	–	*yor-

Example (1) is unattested in WOJ but it is attested in MJ as *wokera*. Similarly, example (2) is not attested outside of EOJ until MJ, where we find *-yor-* 'sleep-'. The existence of this UNP verb is more speculative that the other examples I provide, but I consider it plausible enough to include.

2.5.1.11 *a > /ə/

This sound change is mainly found in EOJ. A few UNP examples are provided below in Table 2.131. There are 32 other attestations of example (2) in UNP.

Table 2.131: Examples of *a > /ə/ in UNP.

	Example	Phonogram(s)	Morphemic Gloss	Book:Poem.Line	WOJ	PJe
1	-nö	能	-DIM	14:3528.3	–	–
2	-rö	呂	-DIM	14:3495.1	-ra	*-ra
3	yösör-i	余曾里	approach-INF	14:3512.5	yösör-i	*yəsar-i

In regard to example (1), we only find this diminutive suffix (< Proto-EOJ *-na) attested in the Kamitukeno topolect of EOJ, so this poem was probably written in that topolect. Example (3) may instead be an example of progressive vowel assimilation, or a borrowing from WOJ which has the same reflex.

2.5.1.12 Vowel metathesis

Metathesis is attested just once, in the example below.

Table 2.132: Example of vowel metathesis in UNP.

	Example	Phonogram(s)	Morphemic Gloss	Book:Poem.Line	WOJ	PJe
1	yande	夜提	branch	14:3493a.5	yenda	*yeⁿda

2.5.1.13 *naᵑg > /noᵑg/ ~ /nuᵑg/

This change is evident in the initial syllable vowels in the two examples shown in Table 2.133 below. In Kupchik (2011: 330) I reconstructed PJ *naamkar- 'to flow' to explain the raising and rounding of the initial syllable's vowel.[83] However, this reconstruction is not plausible for PJe, for which we must reconstruct *naᵑgar-, and therefore it is not relevant to the data in question. We should also keep in mind the similar change of *yam > /yum/ in the Simotukeno topolect of EOJ, discussed in §2.3.4.1.

---

[83] At present I would revise it to PJ *namkar-, but this necessitates it was possible to have syllable-final *-m in PJ that was not homorganic with the following onset, and I am unaware of other evidence for reconstructing this phonotactic structure.

Table 2.133: Examples of *naᵑg > /noᵑg/ ~ /nuᵑg/ in UNP.

	Example	Phonogram(s)	Morphemic Gloss	Book:Poem. Line	WOJ	PJe
1	nungan-ape	奴我奈敝	flow-ITER.INF	14:3476b.4	nangar-	*naᵑgar-
2	nongan-ape	努賀奈敝	flow-ITER.INF	14:3476a.4	nangar-	*naᵑgar-

2.5.2 Consonant innovations

There are relatively few consonant innovations to be found in these data.

2.5.2.1 *t > s / _i
This change occurs in the two examples provided in Table 2.134 below.

Table 2.134: Example of *t > s/ _i in UNP.

	Example	Phonogram(s)	Morphemic Gloss	Book:Poem. Line	WOJ	PJe
1	pendas-i	敝太思	be.separated-INF	14:3445.5	pendat-i	*peⁿdat-i
2	tusi	都之	earth	20:4426.1	tuti	*tutui

This change is only found in the Muzasi, Simotukeno, Pitati, and Simotupusa topolects, therefore the UNP poems in which this change appears were almost certainly composed in one of those EOJ topolects.

2.5.2.2 *r > /n/ (progressive nasal assimilation)
This change occurred in the verb root-final consonant in the two examples in Table 2.135 below. The most plausible explanation for these forms is progressive nasal assimilation due to the preceding prenasalized voiced ng.

Table 2.135: Examples of *r > /n/ (progressive assimilation) in UNP.

	Example	Phonogram(s)	Morphemic Gloss	Book:Poem. Line	WOJ	PJe
1	nungan-ape	奴我奈敝	flow-ITER.INF	14:3476b.4	nangar-	*naᵑgar-
2	nongan-ape	努賀奈敝	flow-ITER.INF	14:3476a.4	nangar-	*naᵑgar-

2.5.2.3 *r > /n/ (regressive nasal assimilation)

This change only occurs in the tentative 2 suffix -*unam*-, which is attested six times in the UNP poems. Here we see regressive, rather than progressive, nasal assimilation due to the following *m*. The PJe form of this suffix was *-*uram*-.

Table 2.136: Examples of *r > /n/ (regressive assimilation) in UNP.

	Example	Phonogram(s)	Morphemic Gloss	Book:Poem. Line	WOJ	PJe
1	kop-unam-o	故布奈毛	long.for-TENT2-ATTR	14:3476a.2	kop-uram-u	*kop-uram-o
2	kopusi-k[u]-ar-unam-ö	故布思可流奈母	be.longing.for-AVINF-exist-TENT2-ATTR	14:3476a.5	kopïsi-k[u]-ar-uram-u	*koposi-ku-ar-uram-o
3	omop-unam-u	於毛布奈牟	think-TENT2-ATTR	14:3496.3	omöp-uram-u	*əmə p-uram-o
4	yuk-unam-ö	由久奈母	go-TENT2-ATTR	14:3526.4	yuk-uram-u	*yuk-uram-o
5	omop-os-unam-ö	於毛抱須奈母	think-HON-TENT2-ATTR	14:3552.4	omöp-os-uram-u	*əmə p-əs-uram-o
6	mat-unam-o	麻都那毛	wait-TENT2-ATTR	14:3563.4	mat-uram-u	*mat-uram-o

2.5.2.4 *r > /n/

The example in Table 2.137 below is the only attestation of this sound change in AOJ that was not induced by a preceding or following nasal.

Table 2.137: Example of *r > /n/ in UNP.

	Example	Phonogram(s)	Morphemic Gloss	Book:Poem. Line	WOJ	PJe
1	yun-öpe-nba	由乃敝波	sleep-ITER-COND	14:3476b.5	–	*yor-

Vovin proposed this verb developed from a conversion of the noun *yoru* 'night' and the UNP form underwent (sporadic) nasalization of *r > /n/ (2012a: 165).

2.5.2.5 *r > /y/

The example in Table 2.138 below shows a sporadic lenition of *r > /y/ in one verb root.

Table 2.138: Examples of *r > /y/ in UNP.

	Example	Phonogram(s)	Morphemic Gloss	Book:Poem. Line	WOJ	PJe
1	mindaye-	美太要	confuse-	14:3563.3	mindare-	*mi^{n}darai-

2.5.2.6 *#nan/^{n} > #an/^{n}

There are many examples of this sound change in the UNP poems, and I provide two in Table 2.139 below.

Table 2.139: Examples of *nan/^{n} > #an/^{n} in UNP.

	Example	Phonogram(s)	Morphemic Gloss	Book:Poem. Line	WOJ	PJe
1	andö	安騰	what	14:3564.3	nandö	*nani tə
2	anze	安是	why	14:3576.5	nanzö	*nani se

As discussed earlier in §2.3.1.2, this change occurred in Proto-EOJ, but did not occur in TSOJ. Therefore, the UNP poems that show this change must reflect the language of EOJ.

3 Vowel elision, *rendaku*, and assimilations

In this chapter I discuss these three types of morphophonological alternation in a comprehensive manner. These occurred mainly synchronically, meaning they were not lexicalized and were in most cases optional. I will also discuss comparative data from WOJ when it has explanatory value, and briefly touch upon some diachronic data when it is relevant or useful.

3.1 Synchronic vowel elision (SVE)

SVE refers to the elision of one of two adjacent vowels (V_1 or V_2) in different word forms. I have previously published a comprehensive study of this topic in EOJ (see Kupchik 2013b). In this section I will summarize the main results of that study and add the results from the TSOJ topolects of Sinano, Töpotuapumi, and Suruga.

In a departure from the rest of the book, I write the AOJ examples in §3.1.1 ~ §3.1.2.2.2 in the International Phonetic Alphabet (IPA), based on the reconstruction summarized in Chapter 2, without the original *Man'yōgana* script. I decided to do this because the IPA transcription makes the analysis of SVE easier to understand in the examples. I also implemented one common modification: the usage of /y/ instead of /j/ to represent a palatal glide. In each example the surface forms are placed after the arrow, while the pre-SVE forms precede the arrow.

3.1.1 SVE in EOJ

V_2 elision is dominant in EOJ, as first noted by Wenck (1959). I have demonstrated that SVE is entirely predictable in EOJ based on the sequence of vowels (Kupchik 2013b), as we can see in Table 3.1 below.[84] The rule is simply that all vowel sequences undergo V_2 elision (the default type) except the sequences /i/ + /a/ and /u/ + /a/, which undergo V_1 elision. The latter two sequences exhibit a maximal increase in sonority from V_1 to V_2, which triggers V_1 elision instead of the default V_2 elision. As demonstrated in Chapter 2, the eight EOJ topolects do not show a phonemic distinction between *Ce* and *Cey* syllables, thus I write both as /e/ below. Similarly, all EOJ topolects lack a phonemic distinction between *Ci* and *Cï*, therefore both are written as /i/ below. The vowel *ö* has been phonemically reconstructed as /ə/ in all AOJ topolects.

---

[84] I also included data from UNP poems that contain EOJ linguistic features.

Table 3.1: Vowel sequences and elision types in EOJ.

Vowel Sequence	V₁ Elision	V₂ Elision
/i/ + /a/	+	
/u/ + /a/	+	
/u/ + /ə/		+
/i/ + /ə/		+
/ə/ + /i/		+
/ə/ + /u/		+
/e/ + /ə/		+
/e/ + /i/[85]		+
/o/ + /a/		+
/a/ + /ə/		+
/a/ + /i/[86]		+
/a/ + /u/		+

Below, I provide an example of SVE involving each sequence of vowels.

3.1.1.1 /i/ + /a/ → /a/ (V₁ elision)

1. /mikətə n-i s**i** **a**r-e-ᵐba/ → /mikətənis**a**reᵐba/
   command COP-INF EPT exist-EV-CONJ
   'As it is a command...' (20:4393.2 – Simotupusa)

3.1.1.2 /u/ + /a/ → /a/ (V₁ elision)

2. /kopusi-k**u** **a**r-unam-o/ → /kopusik**a**runamo/
   be.longing.for-AVINF exist-TENT2-ATTR
   '[She] will long for [me]!' (14:3476a.5 – UNP)

---

[85] This combination is not discussed in Kupchik (2013b), as it was not discovered until the writing of this book.
[86] This combination is not discussed in Kupchik (2013b), as it was not discovered until the writing of this book.

3.1.1.3 /u/ + /ə/ → /u/ (V₂ elision)

3. /tək-ur-ak**u** **ə**mop-e-ᵐba/ → /təkurak**u**mopeᵐba/
    untie-ATTR-NML think-EV-CONJ
    'Because [I] think that the [cord she tied] has come undone...' (20:4427.5 – UNP)

3.1.1.4 /i/ + /ə/ → /i/ (V₂ elision)

4. /ko-rə-wo s**i** **ə**mop-e-ᵐba/ → /korəwos**i**mopeᵐba/
    girl-DIM-ACC EPT think-EV-CONJ
    'Because [I am] thinking of a sweet girl...' (14:3504.5 – UNP)

3.1.1.5 /ə/ + /i/ → /ə/ (V₂ elision)

5. /kət**ə** **i**ta-ku ar-i-t-umo/ → /kət**ə**takaritumo/
    word be.painful-AVINF exist-INF-PERF-EXCL
    'The rumors have been painful!' (14:3482b.5 – UNP)

The first part of the above example, /kətə ita-ku/, occurs in WOJ poetry as /kətita-ku/ (MYS 2:114.5[87]), with V₁ elision instead of V₂ elision. This is a good example that demonstrates the synchronic rules for elision in EOJ and WOJ were not the same. It is important to be aware of these differences because they function as another piece of evidence in determining if a poem is written in EOJ or WOJ. For example, based on the rules in Table 3.1, we would expect the phrase *kötö ide-* 'words go out' to show V₂ elision in a poem written in EOJ. However, in WOJ, this phrase shows V₁ elision (in MYS 4:776.1[88]). There is an example, provided below, of this V₁ elision in a poem attributed to Sagamu province (an EOJ topolect) that lacks any potential EOJ linguistic features. This V₁ elision serves as a strong piece of evidence that the poem was written in WOJ.

6. /kət**ə** **i**ⁿde-t-uru kamo/ → /kət**i**ⁿdeturukamo/
    word go.out.INF-PERF-ATTR EPT
    '[I] wonder, will [I] tell [her my feelings]?' (14:3371.5 – Sagamu)

---

[87] The form in question is attested here and elsewhere only logographically in WOJ. The reading is based on later Heian-period *kana* transliterations of the MYS.
[88] This is a logographic attestation. The reading is based on later Heian-period *kana* transliterations of the MYS.

3.1.1.6 /ə/ + /u/ → /ə/ (V₂ elision)

7. /ipa-nə upe-ni/ → /ipanəpeni/
   rock-GEN above-LOC
   'Above the rocks...' (14:3518.1 – UNP)

3.1.1.7 /e/ + /ə/ → /e/ (V₂ elision)

8. /kopusi-ⁿge əmop-am-o/ → /kopusiⁿgemopamo/
   be.longing.for-AVNML think-TENT-ATTR
   '[I] am sure [I] will long for [it]!' (20:4419.5 – Muzasi)

3.1.1.8 /e/ + /i/ → /e/ (V₂ elision)

9. /iⁿza ne-sime ito-ra/ → / iⁿzanesimetora/
   well sleep-CAUS.INF dear.one-DIM
   'Well, let's sleep [together], deary.' (14:3409.5 – Kamitukeno)

For further discussion on the above example, see §4.3.1.4.19.

3.1.1.9 /o/ + /a/ → /o/ (V₂ elision)

10. /na-wo andə kamo si-m-u/ → /nawoⁿdəkamosimu/
    2.S-ACC what EPT do-TENT-ATTR
    'What should [I] do about you?' (14:3556.5 – UNP)

3.1.1.10 /a/ + /ə/ → /a/ (V₂ elision)

11. /na pa aⁿdə ka əmop-u/ → /napaaⁿdəkamopu/
    2.S TPT what QPT think-ATTR
    'What do you think?' (14:3494.5 – UNP)

3.1.1.11 /a/ + /i/ → /a/ (V₂ elision)

12. /ma ⁿ-gupasi ma-ito-ni/ → / maⁿgupasimatoni /
    true COP.INF-beautiful INT-dear.one-LOC
    'Upon a truly beautiful, dear girl...' (14:3407.2 – Kamitukeno)

3.1.1.12 /a/ + /u/ → /a/ (V₂ elision)

13. /n-uru-ᵑga upe-ni/ → /nuruᵑgapeni/
    sleep-ATTR-POSS above-LOC
    'Besides sleeping [with her]...' (14:3465.3 – UNP)

3.1.2 SVE in TSOJ

SVE also occurs in topolects of TSOJ. In the subsections that follow I present all examples of SVE in these three topolects and discuss the implications of these data. As in the previous sections in this chapter I write all examples in the IPA, based on the reconstruction summarized in Chapter 2. The only exception is a potential WOJ example, which is written in the reconstruction presented by Miyake (2003). The data is much more limited in the case of TSOJ, but from what we have available, this dialect seems to follow rules for elision similar to those found in EOJ.

Table 3.2: Vowel sequences and elision types in TSOJ.

Vowel Sequence	V₁ Elision	V₂ Elision
/i/ + /a/	+	
/ə/ + /i/		+
/e/ + /i/		+
/ə/ + /a/*	+	

*Unclear example

3.1.2.1 V₁ elision
There are three attested examples of this type of elision, as well as another possible example presented in §3.1.2.1.2.

3.1.2.1.1 /i/ + /a/ → /a/ (V₁ elision)

14. /tukusi-ni ar-u/ → /tukusi-n-aru/
    TN-LOC exist-ATTR
    'In Tukusi...' (20:4340.3 – Suruga)

15. /sinanu-n**i a**r-u/ → /sinanun**a**ru/
    TN-LOC exist-ATTR
    'In Sinano...' (14:3352.1 – Sinano)

16. /sinanu-n**i a**r-u/ → /sinanun**a**ru/
    TN-LOC exist-ATTR
    'In Sinano...' (14:3400.1 – Sinano)

This sequence of vowels elides identically in EOJ.

3.1.2.1.2 /ə/ + /a/ > /a/ (V₁ elision)

In a Suruga poem (example 17) that was excluded from the corpus because it lacks any potential AOJ linguistic features, we find this sequence produces V₁ elision. This sequence of vowels is not attested in EOJ with SVE, but we can predict that it would show V₂ elision.

17. /yəsi kəs**ə a**r-uram-əy/ → /yəsikəs**a**ruraməy/
    reason FPT exist-TENT2-EV
    'There must be a reason!' (14:3430.5 – Suruga)

In all other WOJ examples, however, the sequence *kösö ar-* does not exhibit elision, even in a hypermetrical line. This is demonstrated in the example below from MYS Book 15, in which line 2 has eight syllables instead of the standard seven.

18. /ipe sima pa na n-i **kəsə ar**-i-ker-e/
    house island TPT name COP-INF **FPT exist**-INF-RETR-EV
    "'Home island' was just a name.' (MYS 15:3718.1-2 – WOJ)

Is this V₁ elision a feature of TSOJ? That is a reasonable possibility, in which case an argument could be made to add poem 3430 to the Suruga corpus. However, it is also plausible the vowel sequence in WOJ, if it were forced to elide, would exhibit V₁ elision, but we simply do not have any attested examples clearly showing this in a non-AOJ text. Considering this, it may be preferable to err on the side of caution and presume the Suruga poem is still written in WOJ. This situation raises a few interesting questions: if the poems of MYS Book 14 that appear to be written in pure WOJ, like poem 3430, were originally written in AOJ but were later altered by scribes, did the scribes alter the vowel elision as well, or just the segmental phonology? Or were the poems recorded in WOJ from the beginning? There is a third possibility that I think is also worthy of consideration: the poem was originally written in WOJ by a native speaker of a TSOJ topolect, and although they produced the segmental phonology accurately, their own rules of vowel elision snuck in.

3.1.2.2 V₂ elision
There are two attested vowel sequences that result in V₂ elision.

3.1.2.2.1 /ə/ + /i/ → /ə/ (V₂ elision)

19. /mon**ə i**p-aⁿz-u k-i-n-i-te/ → /mon**ə**paⁿzukinite/
    thing say-NEG-INF come-INF-PERF-INF-SUB
    '[I] came [out] here without saying a word [to my mother or father]. . .'
    (20:4337.4 – Suruga)

20. /papa t**ə i**p-u pana-nə/ → /papat**ə**pupananə/
    mother QUOT say-ATTR blossom-GEN
    'The flower called 'mother'. . .' (20:4323.4 – Töpotuapumi)

This vowel sequence elides identically in EOJ.

3.1.2.2.2 /e/ + /i/ → /e/ (V₂ elision)

21. /saⁿzar**e i**si mo/ → /saⁿzar**e**simo/
    small stone FPT
    'Small stones.' (14.3400.3 – Sinano)

The phrase *sanzare isi* is attested with an unelided vowel in 14:3542.1 – UNP, in a hypermetrical line containing six syllables instead of the expected five. However, that poem does not contain any AOJ linguistic features, therefore it appears to have been written in pure WOJ. In addition, WOJ may have phonetically diphthongized the sequence /e/ + /i/ into [ej], in which case the syllable count would remain a metrical five syllables. This may be another case of an AOJ topolect exhibiting elision in a manner different from WOJ. However, similar to the example from Suruga discussed in §3.1.2.1.2, with only one example here, and no unambiguous attestations in WOJ showing us how this sequence elides in that dialect, it is not possible to reach a strong conclusion on this point. In EOJ, we find V₂ elision in the sequence /e/ + /i/.

3.2 *Rendaku*: morpheme-based and process-based

Rendaku, or 'sequential voicing', is a common term in Japanese linguistics. It refers to a non-initial morpheme in a compound that undergoes voicing of its onset obstruent. In the case of the Old Japanese dialects, this voicing was also prenasalized, and it could occur in phrases as well as in compounds. There are two types of *rendaku* in AOJ: morpheme-based and process-based.

3.2.1 Morpheme-based *rendaku* (MBR)

In Kupchik (2012: 12) I first introduced the term "morpheme-based *rendaku*", abbreviated as MBR. MBR refers to the word-boundary elision of the vowel of a nasal-initial syllable of a grammatical morpheme or word form (in the case of the infinitive copula *n-i*), which in turn fuses with the following voiceless onset, prenasalizing and voicing it in the output. This idea originated in the work of Hashimoto (1932), Hamada (1952), and Unger (1975, 1993). Prenasalized voiced onsets are restricted from participating because they are already prenasalized and voiced. MBR is well attested in all dialects of Old Japanese and it is the historical source of many of the *rendaku* forms found in Modern Japanese. Many of the AOJ forms that show MBR are synchronic and optional in application, so the extended forms without MBR can be posited to exist based on morphosyntactic and lexical evidence. It should also be noted that in most cases it is clear MBR occurs when an underlying line is hypermetrical, and it never occurs at the boundary between two lines. Due to this, we can conclude its function in poetry was to stabilize the meter, or rhythm, of a single line of verse.

The grammatical morphemes and word forms that participate in MBR are the dative/locative *-ni*, the genitive *-nö*, the copula-infinitive *n-i*, and the attributive copula *nö*.[89] These are some of the most frequently attested morphemes in the corpus, which probably contributes to their participation in MBR. An example of each is given below in examples (22) – (25).

22. 20:4368.1-2 – Pitati
    久自我波々 / 佐氣久阿利麻弖
    *kunzi-**n**-gapa pa / sakey-ku ari-mat-e*
    TN-**GEN**-river TPT / be.safe-AVINF DUR-wait-IMP
    'Keep waiting for me safely, [at] Kunzi river!'

---

[89] In Kupchik (2012) I also included the demonstrative pronoun *könö* 'this' and an MBR form *kön-*, but I have since abandoned that interpretation.

The underlying form of line 1 in example (22) is *kunzi-nö kapa pa.*

23. 14:3537b.1-2 – UNP
    宇麻勢胡之 / 牟伎波武古麻能
    *uma-se-**n**-gos-i / mungi pam-u koma-nö*
    horse-fence-**LOC**-cross-INF / grain munch-ATTR horse-COMP
    'Like a horse that crosses the fence to munch on grain...'

The underlying form of line 1 in example (23) is *uma-se-ni kos-i.*

24. 14:3412.4-5 – Kamitukeno
    可奈師家兒良尓 / 伊夜射可里久母
    *kanasi-ke KO-ra-ni / iya **n**-zakar-i-[i]k-umö*
    be.dear-AVATTR girl-DIM-DAT / more.and.more **COP.INF**-be.far.from-INF-go-EXCL
    '[I] am going further and further away from [my] dear, darling girl!'

The underlying form of line 5 in example (24) is *iya n-i sakar-i-k-umö.*

25. 14:3489.5 – UNP
    左祢度波良布母
    *sa-ne **n**-do parap-umö*
    LOC-sleep.NML COP.ATTR-place clear.away-EXCL
    '[As I] clear away a place for us to sleep!'

The underlying form of the line in example (25) is *sa-ne nö to parap-umö.*

Normally we only find one occurrence of MBR in a line, but there is one extreme case shown below in which the underlying line is nine syllables and two implementations of MBR are used to contract it into seven syllables.

26. 14:3497.1-2 – UNP
    可波加美能 / 祢自路多可我夜
    *kapa kami-nö / ne-**n**-ziro taka **n**-gaya*
    river upper.part-GEN / root-**GEN**-white high **COP.ATTR**-grass
    'The tall grass [with] white roots in the upper area [of] the river...'

The underlying form of line 2 in example (26) is *ne-nö siro taka nö kaya.*

In AOJ, most likely due to the size of the corpus, we do not find attestations of the exact same sequence of morphemes without MBR, but we do find this in WOJ. I demonstrate this in the WOJ examples that follow.⁹⁰

27. 15:3632.3 – WOJ
波麻藝欲伎
pama-n-giyo-ki
beach-GEN-be.clean.AVATTR
'The beach is clean.'

In example (27) we find six underlying syllables, which are contracted to five syllables in the output through the implementation of MBR. In the next example, we find an attestation of the same sequence of morphemes, but without MBR. This is because there are seven underlying syllables, and the line requires seven syllables to be metrical. Thus, MBR is unnecessary and the genitive *-nö* surfaces.

28. 7:1239.5 – WOJ
濱之浄奚久
PAMA-NÖ KIYO-keku
beach-GEN be.clean-AVATTR.NML
'The cleanliness of the beach.'

The example above is a logographic attestation, but the character 之 is always used logographically to write the genitive *-nö* rather than the contracted form *-n-*. Moreover, if we analyzed it as *-n-*, we would need to posit the line was hypometrical with six syllables instead of the expected seven.

In the following two examples we see the same phenomenon occurring. In example (29) below MBR occurs because the line requires five syllables in the output, but the underlying syllable count is six. MBR of the genitive morpheme makes the line metrical.

29. 5:855.1-2 – WOJ
麻都良河波 / 可波能世比可利
matura-n-gapa / *kapa-nö se pikar-i*
TN-GEN-river / river-GEN rapids shine-FIN
'The river rapids of Matura river are shining.'

---

90 I first pointed these out in a conference presentation in Japan in early 2013 (See Kupchik 2013a).

In the next example we find the same sequence of morphemes, but MBR does not occur because the line is already underlyingly metrical at seven syllables.

30. 5:857.2-3 – WOJ
末都良能加波尓 ／ 和可由都流
matura-nö kapa-ni* / *waka-yu tur-u
TN-GEN river-LOC / young-sweetfish fish-ADN
'Fish for young sweetfish at Matura river.'

This evidence demonstrates how MBR was employed to make a hypermetrical line of poetry metrical. MBR and SVE both act to maintain metricality in verse. This holds true for WOJ, TSOJ, and EOJ, which means MBR and SVE were active at least as early as PJe. Both MBR and SVE also interact with each other. In EOJ and TSOJ, the evidence suggests MBR is preferred to SVE when both are available options to maintain metricality. This is because we can find metrical lines with unrealized SVE, but there are no attested metrical lines with unrealized MBR. There are also attestations that remain hypermetrical with unrealized SVE, such as 14:3480.3 – UNP. In contrast, there are no examples that are hypermetrical with unrealized MBR.

3.2.2 Process-based *rendaku* (PBR)

There is another type of *rendaku* in AOJ, which I call process-based *rendaku* (PBR). PBR involves reduplicating the root and prenasalizing and voicing the onset of the reduplicant. Its function is pluralization, and there is no synchronically derivable morpheme from the resulting prenasalized onset of the reduplicant. It is only attested a few times in AOJ (once in TSOJ and twice in EOJ), all of which are provided below.

31. 20:4323.1-2 – Töpotuapumi
等伎騰吉乃 ／ 波奈波左家登母
töki-ndöki*-nö / *pana pa sak-e-ndömö
time-REDUP-GEN / flower TPT bloom-EV-CONC
'The **seasonal** [lit. 'of seasons' or 'of times'] flowers [all] bloom, but...'

32. 20:4391.1-3 – Simotupusa
久尓具尓乃 ／ 夜之里乃加美尓 ／ 奴作麻都理
kuni-nguni*-nö / *yasirö-nö kami-ni* / *nusa matur-i
province-REDUP-GEN / shrine-GEN deity-DAT / paper.offering offer-INF
'[I] make paper offerings to the deities in the shrines of [many] **provinces**.'

33. 20:4381.1-3 – Simotukeno
久尔具尔乃 / 佐岐毛利都度比 / 布奈能里弓
kuni-nguni-*nö* / *sakimori tundop-i* / *puna-nör-i-te*
province-REDUP-GEN / border.guard gather-INF / boat-ride-INF-SUB
'Border guards from [many] **provinces** gather [here], and sail [off] on a boat...'

The reduplication itself is not adequate to indicate plurality – without the PBR prenasalization and voicing, reduplication usually has an iterative function in AOJ. Unlike MBR, PBR is not productive in application and is therefore not used to adjust the metricality, or rhythm, of a line of poetry.

3.3 Synchronic vowel assimilations: progressive and regressive

In the EOJ and UNP poems we can find a few examples of synchronic vowel assimilations, and both regressive and progressive assimilations are attested. This phenomenon should not be confused with vowel harmony in languages like Finnish in which we find only suffixes changing their vowels to assimilate to root vowels, which is a systematic type of progressive assimilation with few or no exceptions. In contrast, the AOJ attestations demonstrate isolated (either textually or geographically) cases of vowel assimilations, possibly indicative of a phonological system in a state of flux. We might speculate this to be the result of contact with speakers of other languages, such as Old Ainu or Old Koreanic dialects, but it is also possible it was an internal development.

This is not unique to EOJ, among Old Japanese dialects. In fact, WOJ exhibits more examples of vowel assimilations than EOJ (both progressive and regressive), as well as consonant assimilations that are unattested in AOJ.[91] Examples of WOJ vowel assimilations include MJ *niji*[92] : EOJ *nonzi* 'rainbow'; WOJ *pirip-* : TSOJ *piröp-* 'pick up'; and WOJ *yösör-* : EOJ *yösar-* 'be attracted to'. It is possible some of these assimilations in WOJ were not lexicalized and instead only applied based on some condition such as speech rate or phrasal prosody.

---

[91] A good example is the WOJ word *pukum-* 'to hold, contain, wrap in' which is also attested in WOJ as *kukum-* (regressive assimilation) (Vovin 2009b: 25).
[92] Unattested in WOJ, but it is possible the MJ form reflects the WOJ form.

3.3.1 Regressive assimilations

In the Sagamu topolect of EOJ there are two examples that show the synchronic regressive vowel assimilation of *ko* /ko/ 'girl' > *kö* /kə/ when the diminutive suffix *-rö* /rə/ is attached. The attestations are 14:3361.5 and 14:3369.5. *Ko* /ko/ 'girl' is otherwise a very stable and frequently attested word in AOJ with no misspellings or other spellings indicative of a vowel assimilation. The non-assimilated form *ko-rö* 'girl-DIM' is also attested in Sagamu in 14:3368.5, indicating the forms with regressive assimilation were optional in this topolect.

Another example can be found in 14:3458.5 – UNP, in which we find the form *ikunduk-* 'to catch one's breath, to sigh'. The cognate WOJ form is *ikinduk-* 'id.'. This example demonstrates the regressive assimilation of *i > /u/ does not spread beyond one syllable (and occurred after *rendaku* application), since the initial /i/ remains intact in the UNP form. The non-assimilated form *ikinduk-* 'id.' is also attested in the Pitati topolect of EOJ in 14:3388.4, and in UNP in 14:3527.4.

3.3.2 Progressive assimilations

There are two examples of synchronic progressive vowel assimilation, both in EOJ. The first involves the Azuma toponym *Asingari*, which is also attested as *Asingara*[93] in the Sagamu and Muzasi topolects. Attestations of *Asingari* include 14:3368.1 and 14:3431.1, whereas attestations of *Asingara* are found in 14:3363.3 and 20:4421.3. This appears to be an optional assimilation because we find both *Asingari* and *Asingara* attested in the Sagamu topolect.

The other example is found in the Kamitukeno word form *omop-i-nd-oro* 'think-INF-emerge-ATTR', attested in 14:3419.3. The attributive form *-uru* is also attested in this topolect, so this example is likely the result of synchronic progressive vowel assimilation induced by the vowels in the root *omop-*.

---

[93] Vovin (2009c: 3–5) proposed this was due to a "sound assimilation" but did not claim it was synchronic.

4 Lexicon

The lexicons of the AOJ dialects are comprised primarily of Japonic stock, but there are also strata consisting of Korean loanwords, Ainu loanwords, Chinese loanwords, and possibly one Austronesian loanword. In this chapter I discuss the previous proposals for the loanwords from these languages. But first, I begin with a brief overview of the native vocabulary.

4.1 Native vocabulary

There are very few lexical differences between TSOJ and EOJ in the native vocabulary,[94] so I discuss them together here under the umbrella of AOJ. Among the Japonic stock, the basic nouns in AOJ with plentiful attestations include *ko* 'girl', *yama* 'mountain', *pana* 'flower', *kötö* 'word', *pitö* 'person', *kapa* 'river', *tanbi* 'journey', *kami* 'deity', *ne* 'peak', and *pimo* 'cord, string'.

Kinship terms include *titi* 'father', *papa* 'mother', *ko* 'child', and *tuma* 'spouse'. The frequently attested *imo*, literally 'younger sister', is always used in the AOJ poems to mean 'beloved girl', referring to one's wife or female lover. Likewise, the frequently attested *se*, literally 'older brother', is always used in the AOJ poems to mean 'beloved man', referring to one's husband or male lover.

The word *wo* 'yes' is attested just once, and *ina* 'no' is attested twice.

The body part terms attested are *te* ~ *ta-* 'hand', *a* ~ *asi* 'foot', *omö(te)* ~ *kapo* 'face', *mayo* 'eyebrow', *mey* ~ *ma-* 'eye', *kösi* 'waist', *kata* 'shoulder (blade)', *panda* 'skin', and *kasira* 'head, head hair'.

The AOJ poems contain the earliest, full phonographic attestations of some nouns that are phonographically unattested in WOJ but appear in later periods of Japanese, such as *nonzi* 'rainbow' (this is cognate with MJ *niji* 'id.'), *kaperute* 'maple tree', and *mungi* 'barley', as well as some nouns that are phonographically attested in WOJ which contain more conservative phonetic features in AOJ, such as *muma* 'horse' (compare WOJ *uma* 'id.' and MJ *muma* 'id.'), *yöki* 'snow' (compare WOJ *yuki* 'id.' and later Japanese *yuki* 'id.'), *tawore* 'saddle' (compare WOJ *tawori* 'id.'), and *mayo* 'cocoon' (compare WOJ and later Japanese *mayu* 'id.').

---

94 Examples of lexical innovations in EOJ include *tengo* 'third daughter, maiden', *mama* 'cliff', and *mek-* 'walk'. These are discussed later in this chapter. Phonological differences between TSOJ and EOJ in the native vocabulary are discussed in Chapter 2. Differences between EOJ and TSOJ in morphology and grammatical words, including pronouns, are discussed in Chapters 5–10.

In regard to the Japonic verbs, as expected we find basic verbs such as *kö-* 'come', *yuk-* ~ *ik-* 'go', *ar-* 'exist', *nö* 'copula', *se-* 'do', *ne-* 'sleep', and *ip-* 'say' attested very frequently in AOJ. Verbs related to eating and drinking, however, are not very common, with *pam-* 'eat (soft food)' attested three times, *nöm-* 'drink' attested just once, and WOJ *kup-* 'eat (hard food)' not attested at all. As many of the poems are love poems, we find verbs such as *kopï-* 'love, long for', *nak-* 'cry', and *omop-* 'think' attested many times. AOJ also shows us the earliest attested forms of some verbs that retain an original unraised *o, such as *ayok-* 'waver' (compare later JP *ayuk-* ~ *ayug-* 'id.') and *sungos-* 'pass' (compare WOJ *sungus-* 'id.' and later JP *sugos-* 'id.').

4.2 Korean loanwords

EOJ *amo* ~ *omo* 'mother' and TSOJ *omo* 'id.' (cf. WOJ *amo* ~ *omo* 'id.'), which is a doublet with the native Japonic word *papa* 'id.', may be a borrowing of pre-Middle Korean *émà 'mother' into PJe (Vovin 2010: 234[95]). The initial vowel correspondence is problematic, and the comparison remains speculative due to this.[96] There are two other imperfect comparisons that are worth mentioning: EOJ *asa* 'morning' (also attested in WOJ), possibly borrowed into PJe from an earlier form of Middle Korean *àchóm* 'morning' – the problem here is the correspondence of Middle Korean *-ch-* to OJ *-s-* is irregular (Vovin 2010: 224); and EOJ *mötö* 'root' (also attested in WOJ), possibly borrowed into PJe from an earlier form of Middle Korean *míth* 'base, bottom, root' – once again the vowel correspondence is irregular (Whitman 1985: 240; Vovin 2010: 202).

Vovin (2009b: 45, 2010: 178) proposes AOJ *sonde* 'sleeve' (also attested in WOJ) is a borrowing of Old Korean *swon-toy[97] 'hand-place' into PJe, and I think this is

---

[95] This comparison and the other comparisons I discuss in this section originated in Martin (1966) or Whitman (1985). Their comparisons were in the context of a genetic relationship between Japanese and Korean, whereas Vovin argued that these are loanwords from Korean into Japonic.

[96] Due to the sound correspondences in the initial syllable, Vovin (2010: 234–235) proposes EOJ *amo* 'mother' is unrelated to OJ *omo* 'mother', though I disagree with that viewpoint (I reconstruct PJe *amə 'mother'), since *amo* 'mother' is also phonographically attested in WOJ (in NK 82), and it is easy to explain the variant OJ form *omo* as the result of regressive vowel assimilation or initial vowel reduction of *a > /ə/. If the Korean comparison is too problematic, I believe it should be tossed out, rather than splitting up the Japonic forms into one 'native' and one 'borrowed', as Vovin does. Unfortunately, this word is not attested in Old Korean, but it is worth noting that the Middle Korean forms *àpí* 'father' and *èpí* 'id.' differ in their initial vowels, and it seems *àpí* is more archaic (Vovin 2010: 235).

[97] Probably phonetically [sontʌy], which would have been borrowed into PJe as *soⁿdai. Whitman's etymology is Korean (*swómó or *swómá > *-m- loss >) *sô 'sleeve' + OJ *të (< *tai) 'hand,

a plausible etymology. Other plausible Korean loanwords include: EOJ *kasi* 'go on foot' (attested in WOJ as *kati*), borrowed into PJe from Proto-Korean *ketu- 'walks' (> Middle Korean :*ket*-) (Vovin 2010: 150); EOJ *asa* 'hemp' (also attested in WOJ), borrowed into PJe from Proto-Korean *asam 'hemp' (Vovin 2010: 173); EOJ *rö* 'copula' (also attested in WOJ), borrowed into WOJ[98] from a later form of the Old Korean copula *itwo, after consonant lenition to *ilwo occurred (Vovin 2009a: 549); EOJ *sa* 'arrow' (also attested in WOJ), borrowed into PJe from an earlier form of Middle Korean *sál* 'arrow' (Vovin 2010: 173); EOJ *tuti ~ tusi ~ tutu* 'earth' (attested in WOJ as *tuti*), borrowed into PJe[99] from Old Korean *twùtú- 'earth' (Vovin 2010: 124); EOJ *kuku* 'stem, stalk' (attested in WOJ as *kuki*), borrowed into PJ[100] from an earlier form of Middle Korean *kwokwoli* 'stem, stalk' (Vovin 2010: 142); EOJ *tura* 'bowstring' (attested in WOJ as *turu*), borrowed into PJ from an earlier form of Middle Korean *cwúl* 'rope' (Vovin 2010: 166–167); EOJ *taku* 'paper mulberry (bark)' (also attested in WOJ), borrowed into PJe from an earlier form of Middle Korean *tàk* 'mulberry tree' (Vovin 2012a: 123); EOJ *sasa* 'bamboo grass' (also attested in WOJ), borrowed into PJe from an earlier form of Middle Korean *sàsól* 'bamboo branch' (Vovin 2010: 174–175); EOJ *sömey-* 'dye' (also attested in WOJ), borrowed into PJe (or PJ) from an earlier form of Middle Korean *sùmúy-* 'soaks, permeates' (Vovin 2010: 181–182); and EOJ *sima* 'island' (also attested in WOJ), borrowed into PJ from Proto-Korean *sima 'island' (> Middle Korean :*syem*) (Vovin 2010: 183–184).

I propose EOJ *kuma* 'offering to the deities' is attested once in 14:3419.4 (Kam-itukeno topolect). This is a borrowing of an earlier form of Middle Korean :*kwoma* 'paying respect' that is also attested in WOJ. The connection between the WOJ word and the Korean word originated with Whitman (1985: 223), and Vovin put forth the hypothesis it is a loanword from Korean into WOJ (2010: 142). There is also some helpful discussion of this comparison in Francis-Ratte (2016: 192–193). I provide the attestation below with my translation.

---

arm' (1985: 233). I think this etymology is also worth consideration, but it works better without *-m- loss. Thus, *swomo-te > *sonde* through deletion of *-o- and fusion of *-m-t- > -*nd*-.
98 There is only one attestation in EOJ, so it is likely a borrowing from WOJ.
99 Vovin argues it was borrowed into WOJ due to his false claim that it is "attested only once" in EOJ. It is actually attested five times in EOJ: twice as *tuti* (20:4374.1 – Simotukeno and 20:4418.5 – Muzasi), once as *tutu* (14:3370.4 – Sagamu), and twice as *tusi* (20:4392.1 – Simotupusa and 20:4426.1 – UNP). Due to these widespread attestations as well as the Sagamu form *tutu* that could not have been borrowed from WOJ, I think this word was borrowed into PJe.
100 Vovin argues it was a borrowing into (Proto-)Japanese, but cognates in Southern Ryukyuan that he was apparently unaware of, such as Tarama Miyako *fukŋ* 'stalk' (Tokuyama & Celik 2020: 420), support a PJ-era loan.

1. 14:3419.3-5 – Kamitukeno
於毛比度路 / **久麻許曽之都**等 / 和須礼西奈布母
omop-i-ndoro / **kuma kösö s-i-t-u**[101] *tö* / *wasure se-n-ap-umö*
think-INF-emerge-ATTR / **offering.to.the.deities** FPT do-INF-PERF-FIN QUOT / forget.NML do-NEG-ITER-EXCL
'[I] recall **making the offering to the deities** – [I] will not forget [you]!'

The focus particle *kösö* normally co-occurs with the evidential form of the predicate verb, unlike in example (1), and in WOJ this is a strict rule with no exceptions (Vovin 2009a: 1202). However, in an EOJ (UNP) poem shown in example (2) below, this focus particle occurs after the attributive form a verb and precedes the final form of an adjectival verb, similar to example (1).

2. 14:3509.3-5 – UNP
宿奈敝杼母 / 古呂賀於曽伎能 / **安路許曽要志**母
NE-n-ap-e-ndömö / *ko-rö-nga osöki-nö* / ***ar-o kösö ye-si-mö***
sleep-NEG-ITER-EV-CONC / girl-DIM-POSS upper.garment-GEN / **exist-ATTR FPT be.good-AVFIN-EXCL**
'Although [we] are not sleeping together, **it is so nice to have** [my] dear girl's upper garment!'

Mizushima (1984a: 593–612) provides an extraordinarily detailed discussion of the many hypotheses offered to explain line 4 in example (1), and sides with the view *kuma* means 'hidden place'. He analyzes the line as *kuma kös-ö s-i-tutö* hidden. place cross-ATTR do-INF-COOR 'while doing the crossing of the hidden place', but as pointed out in Kupchik (2011: 847–848), there are several inexplicable phonetic and grammatical problems with this. None of the previous analyses of this line involved *kuma* 'offering to the deities'. Kupchik (2011: 847–848) left line 4 unanalyzed, as did Vovin (2012a: 110). Vovin also earlier claimed WOJ *kuma* 'offering to the deities' is not attested in EOJ or Ryukyuan (2010: 142), but I propose there is a Ryukyuan cognate in Yoron *kuma* 'divination' (Kiku and Takahashi 2005: 191) and possibly also Tarama Miyako *kuma* 'millet, grain' (Tokuyama and Celik 2020: 172).[102]

Another Korean loanword, *paka* 'place', is discussed in §4.3.1.4.12.

---

[101] Compare *nipey s-u* food.offering do-FIN 'make a food offering [to the deities]' in 14:3386.3 – Simotupusa.
[102] I raise this possibility because OJ texts attest *kuma* in the context of a rice offering (Omodaka 1967: 269), and in the Heian period it is consistently, if not exclusively, used in reference to a rice offering (Ōno, Satake, and Maeda 1990: 425; NKD).

4.3 Ainu loanwords

4.3.1 A critical analysis of Alexander Vovin's proposed Ainu loanwords in AOJ

There is no question that Alexander Vovin has made the most effort to discover Ainu loanwords in AOJ (see Vovin 2009c, 2012, 2013). However, until now no critical analysis of his proposals has been put forth (except Kupchik 2016, which only discusses one word). In the below sections I offer my own critical assessment of Vovin's proposals, dividing them into plausible (accepted) and problematic (rejected) toponyms, lexical borrowings, and morphological borrowings. This exercise was necessary to explain to the reader why in some cases throughout this book I adopt a translation consistent with an Ainu loanword proposed by Vovin, but in other cases I do not. When Vovin's AOJ-Ainu comparisons were first published, as well as several years after, I considered them to be convincing. However, after I started writing this book, I began to look at them more critically and with an open mind. Soon, problematic aspects of many of his comparisons started jumping out at me, and other, more plausible explanations came into focus.

In doing this I was inspired by Vovin (2010) and his assessment of the comparison of Korean and Japonic words put forth by Whitman (1985). I present my criticism in the same amicable spirit Vovin presented his criticism to Whitman:

> I may be wrong in my conclusion...However, I hope at least that this...will trigger a lively and friendly discussion and will help to reinvigorate the field. Without such discussion, the truth cannot emerge. (Vovin 2010: 240)

4.3.1.1 Plausible (accepted) toponyms
The great contribution of Vovin's research is the identification of many toponyms in Azuma that are of Ainu origin. I consider the comparisons below to be plausible.
- *Akina* < Ainu *ay-kina* 'arrow grass'. Attested in 14:3431.2 – Sagamu.
- *Andikama* < Ainu *anci* 'obsidian' + *kama* 'flat rock, rock'. Attested in 14:3551.1 – UNP and 14:3553.1 – UNP.
- *Asikanga* < Ainu *askan(-ne)* '(be) beautiful' + *kat* 'view, appearance'. Attested in the postscript to 20:4379 – Simotukeno.
- *Inasa* < Ainu *inaw-san* 'the place where *inaw* [are offered]'. Attested in 14:3429.2 – Töpotuapumi.
- *Kake* < Ainu *ka-kes* 'upper end'. Attested in 14:3553.2 – UNP.
- *Munza* < Ainu *mun* 'unedible grass' + *sa* 'shore, plain'. Attested in the postscript to 20:4355 – Kamitupusa.

- *Munzasi* < Ainu *mun* 'unedible grass' + *sa* 'shore, plain' + *-hi* third person singular possessive,[103] i.e., 'grass plain' or 'grass shore'. Attested in 14:3374.1 – Muzasi, 14:3375.1 – Muzasi, 14:3376a.3 – Muzasi, 14:3376b.3 – Muzasi, and 14:3379.3 – Muzasi.
- *Nipey* < Ainu *nipet* 'wood river' (*ni* 'tree, wood' + *pet* 'river'). Attested in 20:4324.3 – Töpotuapumi.
- *Nipu* < Ainu toponym *Nipu* 'storage in the forest on the riverbank for frozen salmon' (< *ni* 'tree' + *pu* 'storage'). Attested in 14:3560.2 – UNP.
- *Pita* < Ainu *pitar* 'stone field' < *pit-tar 'pebbles-continue one after another'. Attested in 14:3563.1 – UNP.
- *Punzi* < Ainu *pun* 'raise' + *sir* 'ground, place, mountain'.[104] Attested in 14:3358c.4 – Suruga.
- *Sirupa* < Ainu *sirpa* 'cape' (*sir* 'land' + *pa* 'head'). Attested in 20:4324.2 – Töpotuapumi.
- *Tayupi* < Ainu *tay-yúpe* 'dead shark' (*ray* ~ *tay* (< *day) 'die' + *yúpe* 'shark'). Attested in 14:3549.1 – UNP.
- *Töya* < Ainu *to-ya* 'lake shore' (*to* 'lake' + *ya* 'shore, dry land'). Attested in 14:3529.1 – UNP.
- *Tukupa* < Ainu *tuk* 'small mountain' + *pa* 'head, top'. Attested in 14:3350a.2 – Pitati, 14:3351.1 – Pitati, 14:3388.1 – Pitati, 14:3389.3 – Pitati, 14:3392.1 – Pitati, 14:3394.2 – Pitati, 14:3395.1 – Pitati, 20:4367.3 – Pitati, 20:4369.1 – Pitati, and 20:4371.4 – Pitati.

4.3.1.2 Problematic (rejected) toponyms

There are only five toponym comparisons that I consider to be too problematic or speculative to accept.

4.3.1.2.1 EOJ *Asingara* ~ *Asingari* < Ainu *askar-i* 'clear place'

The form *asingari* is only attested in the Sagamu topolect of EOJ (14:3368.1, 14:3369.1, 14:3370.1, 14:3431.1, 14:3432.1), whereas the form *asingara* is attested in both the Sagamu (14:3361.1, 14:3363.4) and Muzasi (20:4421.3) topolects. Here, the Ainu cluster *-sk-* is borrowed as *-sing-*, but in the comparison below (§4.3.1.2.3) it is borrowed as *-sik-*. The prenasalized voicing of Ainu /k/ to /ng/ is unexpected

---

[103] Also note Bentley's earlier proposal that this is from Ainu 'grass fortress' (2006: 369, footnote 43).
[104] Vovin has since abandoned this etymology in favor of an internal (Japonic) etymology, *po-nu-si 'fire-master' (2018: 85–87), which is preferable due to the closer semantic link to a volcano. I only list the Ainu etymology here because it remains plausible.

because in the Ainu word the -k- is not intervocalic. I think this EOJ toponym more likely contains *asi* 'reed'.

4.3.1.2.2 TSOJ *Kinbey* < Ainu *kimpe* 'bear' (< *kim-pe 'mountain thing')

This is attested in 14:3354.1 – Töpotuapumi. There are two problems here. First, as Vovin notes (2012a: 35), it is unclear if the TSOJ toponym should be read as *kipey* or *kinbey*; if it is *kipey* then the comparison is invalid. Second, I could not find an Ainu dialect that has *kimpe* 'bear'. We do find *kimpe* 'bear' listed as an entry in Kayano (2002: 209), but the example provided in that entry is written *kimunpe*, so the entry may be erroneous. Similarly, we find *kimúnpe* 'bear' in the Yakumo (Hattori 1964: 185), Chitose (Nakagawa 1995: 159), and Saru (Tamura 1996: 305) dialects. For these reasons, I find the comparison too speculative to accept. Vovin (2012a: 35) also mentions an alternative hypothesis that it is comprised of Ainu *kim* 'mountain' and *pet* 'river'. This seems to work better in terms of morphosemantics, though the phonetic speculation remains.

4.3.1.2.3 EOJ *Kandusika* < Ainu *ka-n-toska* < *ka-ne-toska top-COP-low.cliffs 'low cliffs that are above'

This is attested in 14:3384.1 – Simotupusa, 14:3385.1 – Simotupusa, and 14:3386.2 – Simotupusa. The correspondence of EOJ *n* : Ainu *-ne-* conflicts with Vovin's proposal of the WOJ toponym *Kanipa* < Ainu *ka-ne-pa* 'upper-COP-bank' in poem 20:4456.4. I also wonder why these two toponyms have a copula after *ka* 'upper', but EOJ *Kake* < Ainu *ka-kes* 'upper end' does not.

4.3.1.2.4 EOJ *Kunzi* < Ainu *kus* 'to overflow, to flood'

This is attested in 20:4368.1 – Pitati, as the name of a river. The correspondence of EOJ *-nzi* : Ainu *-s* conflicts with the correspondence of EOJ *-Ø* : Ainu *-s* in Vovin's proposal of the EOJ toponym *Kake* < Ainu *ka-kes* 'upper end'.

4.3.1.2.5 The case of the TSOJ toponym *Sinano*

This toponym is attested in 14:3352.1 – Sinano, 14:3399.1 – Sinano, and 14:3400.1 – Sinano. Its pronunciation in the eighth century, as well as its etymology, are matters of debate that lack a consensus view. Universally written as 信濃 in the MYS, Vovin (2012a: 32–33) points out the phonogram 濃 is otherwise only used to write *nu* in the MYS. However, when we examine the attestations of this phonogram in the MYS, we find there are only 10 in total, and six are used to write the toponym Sinano ~ Sinanu, leaving us just four other examples to compare. Three of these are WOJ attestations that should undoubtedly be read *nu*. However, one is found in an EOJ poem (20:4405.2 – Kamitukeno topolect). In this attestation the phonogram 濃 is used to write the second character of the word *sinop-* 'to yearn for', leading scholars to believe it should be read as *sinup-* in this instance. Both *sinop-* and *sinup-* 'to yearn for' are well attested phonographically in the MYS (in both AOJ and WOJ), though *sinop-* is the more dominant form. Consequently, in this case the reading is not so clear. Regardless, Kojima, Kinoshita, and Satake (1973: 446), Tsuchiya (1977: 203), Kinoshita (2001), and Vovin (2012: 32–33) follow the viewpoint that the toponym was pronounced Sinanu, which later changed to Sinano in the Heian period. The majority of scholars (Takagi, Gomi, and Ōno 1959: 409; Kubota 1967: 139; Omodaka 1965: 15; Nakanishi 1981: 242; Mizushima 1986: 29; Itō 1997: 278; and Satake et al. 2002: 309), on the other hand, prefer the hypothesis that it was pronounced Sinano in the Nara period.

I take a different stance from previous scholars. I think it was pronounced both Sinano and Sinanu when the MYS was recorded. The pronunciation Sinanu was a short-lived development in the eighth century from the earlier pronunciation Sinano, through the raising of *o > /u/, which is common in TSOJ. To be clear, I propose it was pronounced Sinanu by speakers in Sinano and the other two TSOJ provinces, but speakers of WOJ and EOJ referred to it as Sinano. My reasons for this are as follows. First, as Mizushima (1986: 29) points out, in the *Wamyō Ruijushō* (938 CE) it is written phonographically as 之奈乃 *sinano*. This was nearly two hundred years after the MYS was compiled and thus is not conclusive evidence on its own, but recently analyzed evidence from seventh-century *mokkan*[105] show this province was also written as 科野 *sinano* (Tateno 2012: 19), a *kungana* representation of the pronunciation. This is excellent evidence for an original final *no* syllable because the character 野 'field' could only be phonographically employed as WOJ *no* 'field'. As a final piece of evidence, vowel lowering (*u > /o/) is not a well-supported sound change in Heian-period Japanese.[106]

As for the etymology of this toponym, setting aside those etymologies that are clearly implausible, Vovin (2012a: 33) proposes Sinanu is of Ainu origin, namely *sinnam* (<*sir-nam 'vicinity-be.cold') *nup* 'cold field'.[107] He mentions that *sinnam*

---

[105] Wooden tablets used for writing from the late Asuka period through the Edo period. See Piggott (1990) for an excellent introduction to *mokkan* in English.
[106] This is probably an understatement, since I have been unable to find a single clear case of this vowel lowering in MJ.
[107] Vovin (2011a: 50) also proposed the MK *siranupi* in MYS 5.794.3 means 'white (western) land', consisting of WOJ *sira* 'white' and Ainu *nup-i* 'field-POSS'. I do not find his hypothesis to be convincing, as it requires us to accept two speculative claims: 'white' is used symbolically to mean 'Western' (I am not aware of any other examples of this in OJ, and Vovin does not provide any either), and there was a semantic change in OJ of 'field' > 'land'. He also does not explain why WOJ

means 'to be cold' only in Sakhalin Ainu, whereas it means 'to be cold (to the touch)' in other Ainu dialects. Indeed, I was able to find *sinnam* attested in the Raichishka (Sakhalin) dialect, in the form *sinnam'an* 'to be cold' (Hattori 1964: 225), but it is not listed in the other Ainu dialects (in Hattori 1964) nor in the other dialect dictionaries I searched (Tamura 1996, Kayano 2002, Nakagawa 1995). I could only find *nam* 'to be cold, tepid (to the touch)' in the Saru dialect (Tamura 1996: 404), with the possibly related form *yam* 'to be cold' attested in the Chishima (Kurile) dialect. The more common word for 'to be cold' in Ainu dialects is *me'an*. The weak point of Vovin's proposed etymology is it requires us to posit Ainu *u was borrowed as Proto-TSOJ *o (due to the *mokkan* evidence), even though Proto-TSOJ had *u. This is a minor variance that I would accept if there were no stronger internal (or other external) etymology available. However, as I will demonstrate, that is not the case here.

I would like to propose two internal (Japonic) etymologies for Sinano. First, Sinano may be a phonologically innovative form of OJ *sira no* 'white field(s)'. In this hypothesis, the change of medial *-r-> -n- in *sira* is due to regressive nasal assimilation (induced by the nasal onset of *no* 'field'), a sporadic phenomenon that is well attested in Azuma. Sinano province was well known for its snowy weather and therefore 'white fields' were certainly a common and distinctive sight in the province during the cold months. There are two minor issues with this idea: 1) there are no other examples of *-r- > -n- in the poems attributed to Sinano province, and 2) there are no other examples of *sira* 'white' changing to *sina* in AOJ. I do not think either problem makes this hypothesis worth discarding, but they do weaken it somewhat. My other proposal is that it consists of OJ *sina* 'sun' (Murayama 1970)[108] and *no* 'field'. This hypothesis is phonetically perfect.

4.3.1.3 Plausible (accepted) lexical borrowings

There are five lexical comparisons that I consider to be strong enough to accept. Interestingly, most of these words relate to aspects of nature. The first four were proposed by Vovin (2012a), whereas I proposed the fifth (*tengo*) in Kupchik (2016).

---

borrowed the Ainu possessive form *nup-i* (> *nupi*) whereas TSOJ borrowed the Ainu bare form *nup* (> *nu*).

108 Kupchik (2021b) proposed this was an Austronesian loanword in PJ, in which case *sinano* would only be half Japonic. Whether or not one accepts that is not relevant for this proposed etymology, since, regardless of its origin, Murayama (1970) demonstrated that OJ *sina* clearly meant 'sun'.

- TSOJ *karinba* 'sakura' < Ainu *karinpa* 'sakura [bark]'.[109] Attested in 14:3399.3 – Sinano.
- TSOJ *na* 'river' < Ainu *nay* 'id.'. Attested in 14:3401.1 – Sinano.
- EOJ *pinzi* 'sandbank' < Ainu *pis* 'shore', *pis-i* 'its shore'. Attested in 14:3448.4 – UNP.
- EOJ *ya* 'shore' < Ainu *ya* 'shore, dry land'. Attested in 14:3562.1 – UNP.
- EOJ *tengo* 'third daughter, maiden' < Ainu **dE* 'three' + EOJ *nö ko* 'COP.ATTR girl'.[110] See §4.3.1.4.18 for a list of attestations and further discussion, including a comparison with Vovin's etymology.

TSOJ *na* 'river' may have only been part of a toponym (*Tinguma na* 'Tiguma river'), rather than a true loanword. EOJ *pinzi* 'sandbank' is also attested in KOJ, which either means it is a more ancient loanword, or the word was borrowed twice (as suggested in Kupchik 2021a).

4.3.1.4 Problematic (rejected) lexical borrowings

I find the following comparisons to be too problematic or speculative to accept. Most of these comparisons are *hapax legomena*.

4.3.1.4.1 EOJ *anzu* 'crumbling cliff' < ? Ainu **-as-* 'to split' + *so* 'rocky shore', 'hidden rocks in the sea'

This is attested in 14:3539.1 – UNP and 14:3541.1 – UNP. I reject this comparison for three main reasons. First, we do not find Vovin's reconstructed **-as-* 'to split' used in Ainu as a free verb. Second, the borrowing of Ainu **o* as /u/ conflicts with most other cases in which the proposed sound correspondence is Ainu **o* > EOJ /ə/. And third, if the Ainu wanted to name an area of 'crumbling cliffs' as 'splitting rock', wouldn't they use their word for 'rock', which is *sirar*? Or perhaps even *suma* 'stone'? There is one other possible issue with this comparison. Vovin mentions two sources that claim Ainu *so* can mean 'hidden rocks in the sea' or 'rocky shore', but 'hidden rocks in the sea' might be a semantic extension from Ainu *so* 'waterfall' in

---

[109] This is attested in WOJ as *kaninba* (showing regressive nasal assimilation) (Omodaka 1967: 204–205), which suggests a borrowing into PJe, unless it was borrowed twice.

[110] The intervening attributive copula *nö* was reduced to the prenasalization of the following onset, as is commonly found in AOJ. In regard to the proposed underlying construction *te nö* 'third', we can find several words in Japanese that contain a borrowed Chinese numeral, followed by the attributive copula *nö*, in order to indicate the numeral is ordinal. For example, *san no ito* 'third string (on a *shamisen*)', *san no tani* 'third valley', and *ni no tsugi* 'secondary'. EOJ **te nö ko* (> *tengo*) 'third daughter' follows the same pattern.

some variety of Ainu (since it is not listed in Hattori 1964), and Ainu *so* 'rocky shore' looks like a borrowing of EOJ *iso* 'rocky shore' (it is also not listed in Hattori 1964).

4.3.1.4.2 EOJ *atu-* 'sea' < Ainu *atuy* 'id.'
This is a *hapax legomenon* attested in 14:3503.1 – UNP. It occurs in the line *anzeka-ngata*, which Vovin analyzes as *atu-ka-n-gata* sea-top-COP.ATTR-tideland 'sea tideland' (lit. 'tideland that is on top of the sea'). It is strange the poet would refer to a tideland as being 'on top of' the sea, since the sea washes over the tideland at high tide. Vovin's entire hypothesis is based on his selection of the character 齋 (*itu*) 'to be holy', which is only attested in the GR manuscript. He chose this in favor of 齊 (*nze*) 'to put in order' which is found in nearly every other manuscript. He states (2012a: 192): "Although most manuscripts present 齊 and not 齋, the direction of a scribal mistake is most likely to be 齋 > 齊, and not 齊 > 齋, because the former includes omission, and the latter addition. Addition is unlikely as a source of a scribal mistake." However, GR does contain mistakes. Also, in his translation of MYS Book 16, for example, he accepts Keichū's earlier proposal that in the *Amagasaki-Bon* 果 'fruit' is a mistake for 昊 'face' in 16:3791.74 (Vovin 2021a: 43), and that is a case of addition in a scribal error.

Since the character 齋 is not attested as an *ongana* phonogram in OJ, he selects the *kungana* reading *itu* instead,[111] and proposes the first vowel was elided after combination with the preceding *a*. Normally I also follow GR but based on all the evidence I think it is more likely that GR contains a mistake here. Therefore, I consider *anzeka* to be a toponym near the sea (note: there was a lake called Anze in Pitati province that is mentioned in the *Pitati Fudoki* (Nakanishi 1985: 417; Mizushima 1986: 303[112])), and the tideland the poet mentions was located there. Even if Vovin is correct about the character, I still must reject his Ainu origin hypothesis on semantic grounds.

4.3.1.4.3 EOJ *ka* 'top' < Ainu *ka* 'id.'
This is attested in 14:3409.3 – Kamitukeno, 14:3503.1 – UNP, and 14:3518.3 – UNP. I think the two clear attestations of this comparison are better analyzed as involving OJ *kami* 'upper, top'. This is because the syllable *mi* is known to contract to *n* in EOJ in word-final position, as we find, for example, in *yunduka* (<*yumi-tuka) 'bow handle' (14:3486.2 – UNP). When *mi* occurs before a nasal onset, the *mi* is deleted

---

[111] There are no other attestations of this character used as *kungana* phonogram in OJ.
[112] I make this point to show the name *Anze* was used in reference to a body of water, not to imply the Pitati lake is what *Anzeka* refers to in poem 14:3503. Indeed, since a tideland is mentioned, it is unlikely to be this lake, because, scientifically speaking, only seas and oceans are tidal.

entirely because an *mn/*mm cluster is prohibited, thus the first nasal deletes. As such, in 14:3409.3 and 14:3518.3, the form is *ka-numa* (<*kamnuma < *kami-numa) 'upper marsh'. As already explained in the discussion of Vovin's proposal of EOJ *atu* 'sea' above, I consider the attestation in 14:3503.1 to be a toponym that is likely unrelated to *kami* 'upper, top' (or if it is, the development is internally transparent as *kangata* < *kami-kata 'upper tideland', thus there is no reason to involve Ainu here).

4.3.1.4.4 EOJ *ka* 'voice' < Ainu *háw* 'id.'

This is attested in 14:3361.4 – Sagamu and 20:4430.4 – UNP. In both attestations it occurs in the line *ka-nar-u ma sindum-i*, which I analyze as INT-sound-ATTR period be.quiet-INF 'the period of intense sound subsides (lit. 'quiets down')'. Vovin proposes the *ka* is Ainu *haw* 'voice', but the verbal intensifying prefix *ka-* is well attested in OJ, and is unproblematic here, so I do not see a compelling reason to reject the internal explanation. The borrowing of Ainu initial *h as EOJ /k/ is also lacking other clear examples.

4.3.1.4.5 EOJ *köndök-* 'to bless with words' < Ainu *ko-itak ~ koytak-* 'to speak to, to address words to'

This is a *hapax legomenon* attested in 14:3506.2 – UNP. Vovin proposes the Ainu word was borrowed into EOJ as *köndak-, and then underwent progressive vowel assimilation to *köndök-*. Other progressive assimilations do occur in EOJ (though rarely), but I remain skeptical in this case because it is required to explain a hypothetical loanword that is attested just once, and that is too easy a wand to wave. The semantic change from 'to speak to' to 'to bless with words' is also speculative, and though I might accept it if the phonetics were stronger, I think this comparison should be rejected. The interpretation of this word as *kö-n-töki* silkworm-GEN-time 'time of silkworms',[113] in the lines *nipi muro-nö kö-n-döki* 'time of a new house for silkworms' (Mizushima 1986: 307), is preferable, since the custom of building a new house for silkworms is attested, but the custom of Japonic speakers using an Ainu phrase to bless a new room is not. Lastly, line 5 of the same poem contains *könö körö* 'this time', which is a phonetic and semantic play on *köndöki* 'time of silkworms', but the semantic aspect of this word play is lost if we change *köndöki* to 'blessing with words'.

---

[113] The word 'silkworm' was *ko* in OJ, but the regressive vowel assimilation of *ko* > *kö* (due to a following morpheme that contains *ö* in its initial syllable) is also attested twice with the word *ko* 'child' in the Sagamu topolect. See §3.3.1.

4.3.1.4.6 EOJ *ma* 'wife' < Ainu *mat* 'woman, wife'

This is attested in 14:3502.1 – UNP. I also propose it is attested once in a poem written in the Sagamu topolect (14:3370.4), though Vovin does not make this connection. An Ainu origin should be rejected because the EOJ word is a regular reflex from PJe **mia* 'wife'. The other OJ reflexes of this word are *me* in WOJ and *mi* in TSOJ (Suruga topolect), both of which are regular in those dialects. This is the same sound correspondence of the PJe diphthong **ia* we see, for example, in PJe **ipia* 'house' > EOJ *ipa*, WOJ *ipe*, Suruga TSOJ *ipi*.

4.3.1.4.7 EOJ *mak-i* 'back-POSS' < Ainu *mak* 'back' + 3rd person possessive suffix *-i*

This is a *hapax legomenon* attested in 20:4413.4 – Muzasi. Vovin proposes the line this word occurs in should be analyzed as *se-rö-nga mak-i kö-m-u* beloved-DIM-POSS back-POSS come-TENT-ATTR 'my dearly beloved will come back'. He notes there are the OJ verbs *makar-* 'to go' and *makey-* 'to send', but there are no attestations of *mak-* 'to go' (a point discussed earlier and in more detail in Mizushima 2003: 699). I agree that EOJ *mak-* 'to go' is too speculative to accept.

Ainu *mak* is a noun that does not simply mean 'back' as glossed by Vovin, but also 'inside, behind' (Tamura 1996: 373–374). Vovin does not explain why it is suffixed with a possessive marker.

There are three reasons why I reject this comparison. First, Japonic languages do not use nouns meaning 'back, behind, inside' (such as Japanese *se* 'back', *usiro* 'back', or *siri* 'back, behind') before the verb *kö-* 'come' to convey the meaning 'to come back'. For example, we do not find constructions such as hypothetical OJ *siri kö-m-u* back come-TENT-ATTR 'I will come back'. I was also unable to find examples in Ainu where *mak* 'back, behind, inside' is used in a verb phrase to mean 'to come back', and Vovin does not provide any either.

Second, there is an important orthographic issue at play. The usage of 馬 in the MYS as a phonogram is otherwise always read as *me* (outside of archaic toponyms), while its *kungana* reading at the start of a word is always *uma* (not *ma*) (Mizushima 2003: 699). Therefore, I select the *ongana* reading *me*,[114] and analyze the verb as *mek-*, which rules out the Ainu comparison completely.

Lastly, and most importantly, in Hachijō there is a verb *mik-* 'to walk, to go by walking' (Asanuma 1999: 218; Yamada 2010: 82–83; Naitō 1979: 187). Based on this, I propose the EOJ form *mek-* is the earlier form of this word, since the raising of **e > /i/* did occur in the initial syllable in some other Hachijō words (e.g., Hachijō *mido* 'eye of a needle' (Naitō 1979: 188), Japanese *medo* 'id.'; Hachijō *ikubo* 'dimple'

---

114 This *ongana* is also attested in 14:3450.5 – UNP.

(Asanuma 1999: 32), Japanese *ekubo* 'id.', etc.). This appears to be another word unique to the Eastern branch of PJe (like *mama* 'cliff'[115]) since it does not occur in other OJ dialects. I could not find it in the Ryukyuan languages or Modern Japanese dialects either, which supports the hypothesis it is yet another lexical innovation that occurred in Proto-EOJ. I translate poem 20:4413 as follows:

3. 20:4413 – Muzasi
麻久良多之 / 己志尒等里波伎 / 麻可奈之伎 / 西呂**我馬**伎己無 / 都久乃之良奈久

makura tasi / *kösi-ni tör-i-pak-i* / *ma-kanasi-ki* / *se-rö-nga* **mek-i**-*kö-m-u* / *tuku-nö sir-an-aku*

head.rest long.sword / waist-LOC hold-INF-wear-INF / INT-be.dear-ATTR / beloved-DIM-POSS **walk-INF**-come-TENT-ATTR / month-GEN know-NEG.ATTR-NML

'Not knowing the month [my] dearly beloved, who wears a long sword at [his] waist [during the day] and [places it] at [his] headrest [during the night], will come **walking** [back]...'

4.3.1.4.8 EOJ *mato* 'girl' < Proto-Ainu *mat-poo woman-child 'girl, daughter'

This is a *hapax legomenon* attested in 14:3407.2 – Kamitukeno. If EOJ borrowed Ainu *matpoo* 'girl' we would expect the first consonant in the medial cluster to delete, not the second, and the word to be imported as *mapo*. This is because, when borrowing words, onsets are given priority to codas, and this is especially true in languages without coda consonants (Uffmann 2015: 648), such as OJ. To give a few cross-linguistic examples, loanwords from English into Japanese such as *hebon* (< Hepburn) and *waishatsu* (< white shirt) demonstrate this (Smith 2006), as do loanwords from French into the Eastern Gbe language Fon, such as [vītô] (< Victor) (Kenstowicz 2003: 102). Vovin states the deletion of C_2 in a medial -CC- cluster is "expected" (2012a: 98), though he does not provide any reference or evidence for this claim.

I do think Vovin was correct that the meaning of this is close to 'girl', but I propose it consists of the intensifying prefix *ma*- and EOJ *ito* 'dear (one)', also attested twice in other poems (see §4.3.1.4.19). The combination of these morphemes resulted in the form *ma-to* due to V_2 elision (< *ma-ito), and the meaning was 'a real (or true) dear'.[116]

---

[115] See Vovin (2012a: 27) and Lawrence (2013).
[116] Compare *ma-ko* INT-girl 'true girl' in 20:4414.3 – Muzasi.

4.3.1.4.9 EOJ *or-ö* 'its place' < Ainu *or-o* 'place-POSS'

This is a *hapax legomenon* attested in 20:4363.2 – Pitati. Similar to Mizushima (2003: 370–371) and most other MYS scholars I analyze this as EOJ *orö-* 'lower' or possibly *orös-u we* 'let.down-FIN EPT'. Either way, there is no Ainu word involved. See §2.3.5.1 for a discussion.

4.3.1.4.10 EOJ *pa* 'year' < Ainu *pa* 'id.'

This is a *hapax legomenon* attested in 20:4378.2 – Simotukeno. Like nearly every other MYS scholar (see Mizushima 2003: 498), I analyze this as the topic particle *pa* (shown in example 4 below), so I reject this comparison.

4. 20:4378.1-2 – Simotukeno
   都久比**夜**波 / 須具**波**由氣等毛
   *tuku pi ya **pa** / sungu **pa** yuk-ey-ndömo*
   month day EPT **TPT** / pass.NML **TPT** go-EV-CONC
   'Although the months and days pass [by]…'

See §2.3.4.1 for further discussion.

4.3.1.4.11 EOJ *pa* 'to find' < Ainu *pa* 'id.'

This is a *hapax legomenon* attested in 14:3499.4 – UNP. Like Omodaka (1965: 198) and Mizushima (1986: 297), I analyze this as the topic particle *pa*. It is also not likely for Japonic speakers to borrow a verb but not integrate it into one of their verbal paradigms: no verbs in OJ have roots that end in -*a*, and bare verb roots (non-infinitival) are not used in isolation in OJ either. For these reasons, I must reject this comparison.

4.3.1.4.12 EOJ *paka* 'rumor, gossip' < Ainu *páhaw* 'id.'

This is a *hapax legomenon* attested in 14:3385.3 – Simotupusa. It appears in the line *ar-i-si paka*, which Vovin translates as 'a rumor that [the maiden] was [there]'. There are two reasons why I reject this comparison. First, I could not find any uncontroversial Ainu loanwords in OJ that demonstrate the borrowing of Ainu *h as /k/, and deletion of the medial [h] during importation to EOJ is equally likely. Second, Vovin (2021a: 184) has recently proposed WOJ *n-baka* -GEN-place 'place' is a borrowing of Old Korean *pàká* 'place' (> Middle Korean *pà* 'place'). This is an important discovery, and although Vovin claims this word is unattested in EOJ, I propose the *paka* in this EOJ poem is the same word, and the borrowing from Old Korean occurred in PJe, rather than in WOJ. Thus, I translate the poem as follows:

5. 14:3385 – Simotupusa
可豆思賀能 / 麻萬能手兒奈我 / 安里之**波可** / 麻末乃於須比尓 / 奈美毛登杼呂尓
kandusika-nö / *mama-nö* te*NGO-na-nga* / *ar-i-si* **paka** / *mama-nö osu-pi-ni* / *nami mo töndörö n-i*
TN-GEN / cliff-GEN maiden-DIM-POSS / exist-INF-PAST.ATTR **place** / cliff-GEN rocky.shore-side-LOC / wave FPT roaring COP-INF
'Waves were also roaring on the side of the rocky shore [near] the cliffs, the **place** where the maiden from the cliffs of Kandusika was...'

The three WOJ attestations (MYS 4:512.2, 10:2133.2, and 16:3887.4) are all *nbaka* rather than *paka* because they occur in a context in which a genitive *-nö* is necessary (or, at least, grammatical). In fact, they all occur in the same phrase, *kar-i-n-baka* cut-NML-GEN-place 'place of cutting'. However, in this EOJ attestation that occurs after the past-attributive *-si*, a genitive would be ungrammatical, so we see the bare noun *paka* 'place' instead. As a final point, even if the Ainu word were equally plausible phonetically, I would argue the Old Korean word still fits better in the context.

4.3.1.4.13 EOJ *pirö* 'oak' < Ainu *pero* or *pero-ni* 'id.'

This is a *hapax legomenon* that occurs in the phrase *pirö-nbasi* (14:3538a.1 – UNP), which Vovin proposes means 'oak bridge'. I reject this comparison because I think it is more likely this phrase contains OJ *pirö* 'wide'. Although Vovin thinks it is unlikely that the phrase *pirö-nbasi* would mean 'wide bridge' in this poem, I do not share his skepticism since 広橋 Hirobashi (< *pirə-ᵐbasi) is both a toponym in Nara and a Japanese surname.[117] Thus, the UNP attestation may have been the name of a specific wide bridge in Azuma. I also prefer the interpretation of this poem by Kubota (1967: 256), also accepted by Mizushima (1986: 359), which entails the rider does not make his horse cross the 'wide bridge' because the sound of the hooves would alert others to his visit, and he wishes to visit in secret. *Pirö* 'wide' emphasizes that the bridge was easy to cross (and thus there was no physical obstacle), but something else held the rider back. If we change this to 'oak bridge', the contrast is lost, and the poem becomes somewhat prosaic.

---

[117] In contrast, I could not find any toponyms or surnames in Japan that translate to 'oak bridge'.

4.3.1.4.14 EOJ *sömö* 'not' < Ainu *somo* 'id.'

This is a *hapax legomenon* attested in 14:3382.5 – Kamitupusa. I reject this comparison because I analyze the EOJ form as *sö-m-ö* 'do-TENT-ATTR'. See §2.3.7.1 for a discussion.

4.3.1.4.15 EOJ *su* 'again' < Ainu *suy* 'id.'

This is attested in 14:3363.3 – Sagamu, 14:3487.3 – UNP, and 14:3564.3 – UNP. I reject the attestations in 14.3487.3 and 14.3564.3 because I find the analysis of a reduplication of *s-u* 'do-FIN' (Mizushima 1986: 395) to be more plausible in both cases. Other cases of verbal reduplication are attested in EOJ to indicate an iterative action (see §7.10 for several examples).

The only attestation in which *su* 'again' might be plausible is in 14:3363.3. This is a poem from Sagamu province, one of only two topolects in which Proto-EOJ *ui is reflected as /u/ (not /i/). So, phonetically, it is unproblematic. The same cannot be said about the proposed attestation in 14:3487.3, since that poem is written in the Simotupusa topolect which changed *ui > /i/.

Even so, I still find a Japonic explanation for *su* in 14:3363.3 to be preferable to an Ainu one. Let's examine the poem in detail, analyzing *su* in line 3 as *s-u* 'do-FIN', rather than *su* 'again'.

6. 14:3363 – Sagamu
   和我世古乎 / 夜麻登敝夜利弖 / 麻都之太須 / 安思我良夜麻乃 / 須疑乃木能末可
   *wa-nga se-ko-wo / yamatö-pe yar-i-te / mat-u sinda **s-u** / asingara yama-nö / sungï-nö KÖ-nö ma ka*
   1S-POSS beloved-DIM-ACC / TN-ALL send-INF-SUB / wait-ATTR CNJ **do-FIN** / TN mountain-GEN / cryptomeria-GEN tree-GEN space QPT
   '[I] sent my beloved to Yamato, and when [I] wait for [him], **[I] do [it]**...perhaps [he will come back] through the cryptomeria trees on Mt. Asingara?'

When the poet says, 'do [it]' (*s-u*), the action they are referring to is not 'when [I] wait' (*mat-u sinda*)[118] but rather the watching for her beloved through the cryptomeria trees and wondering how he will make his way back, implied by lines 4 and 5 in the poem. Compare the syntactically similar line below, with a verb in the attributive form followed by the temporal conjunction *sinda* and a verb.

---

[118] As Vovin (2009c: 27) notes, unlike OJ *töki* 'time', EOJ *sinda* 'when' does not function as a noun meaning 'time'.

7. 14:3461.5 – UNP
安家努思太久流
ake-n-o sinda k-uru
brighten.INF-PERF-ATTR CNJ come-ATTR
'[You only] came when it dawned.'

4.3.1.4.16 EOJ *sungu* 'to grow old' < Ainu *sukup* 'id.'

This is a *hapax legomenon* attested in 20:4378.2 – Simotukeno. Like most other scholars (see Mizushima 2003: 498) I analyze this attestation as *sungu* 'pass.NML', and therefore reject Vovin's Ainu etymology. See §2.3.4.1 for a discussion.

4.3.1.4.17 EOJ *ta-ka* 'here-DIR' < Ainu *ta-ke* 'this, here-DIR'

This is a *hapax legomenon* attested in 20:4387.5 – Simotupusa. Phonetically, the vowel in the last syllable of the EOJ form is a problem because we must posit a progressive vowel assimilation to account for it. Other progressive assimilations do occur in EOJ, but as explained in the discussion of EOJ *köndök-* above, I am skeptical whenever it is required to explain a hypothetical loanword that is attested just once.

The other previous proposals claim it is *taka* 'high' or *ta-ga* 'who-NOM' (Mizushima 2003: 570–573), but neither works very well. I propose the *-ka* is a directive suffix cognate with the PR allative suffix *-ka (Thorpe 1983: 214) and it is suffixed to OJ *ta* 'rice field'. As such, I translate poem 20:4387 as follows:

8. 知波乃奴乃／ 古乃弖加之波能 ／ 保々麻例等 ／ 阿夜尓加奈之美 ／ 於枳弖 他加枳奴
tinba-nö nu-nö / ko-nö te kasipa-nö / popom-ar-e-ndö / aya n-i kanasi-mi / ok-i-te ta-ka k-i-n-u
TN-GEN field-GEN / child-GEN hand oak-GEN / be.unopened-PROG-EV-CONC / mysterious COP-INF be.dear-GER / leave.behind-INF-SUB **rice.field-DIR** come-INF-PERF-FIN
'Although the buds of the oak trees in Tiba field, with leaves like a child's hand, have not yet blossomed, [I] left [her] behind and came **to the rice field**, because [she] is mysteriously dear [to me].'[119]

---

[119] We must read between the lines to grasp that the girl was so 'mysteriously dear [to him]' it was painful for the author, and he left due to that. The first three lines of the poem are a metaphor for this girl having not yet reached maturity. Her beauty is described as 'mysterious' because it was not normal to be attracted to girl of her age (Mizushima 2003: 568). OJ *kanasi-* can also mean 'sad',

There are no other attestations of the directive *-ka* in OJ,[120] but the EOJ directive *-ngari* (unattested in WOJ or TSOJ) is clearly related, in much the same way the OJ ablative suffixes *-yo* and *-yori* are related to one another.

4.3.1.4.18 EOJ *tengo* 'maiden' < Ainu *tek* 'hand, arm' + *o* 'take in, embrace'
This is attested in 14:3384.2,5 – Simotupusa, 14:3385.2 – Simotupusa, 14:3398.4 – Sinano, 14:3442.2 – UNP, 14:3477.2 – UNP, 14:3485.5 – UNP, and 14:3540.2 – UNP. In Kupchik (2016) I rejected this in favor of a different Ainu etymology. An interested reader should see that article, but to summarize, I proposed it is a loan blend consisting of Ainu **dE* 'three' and EOJ (*nö ko* >) *n-go* 'COP.ATTR-girl', meaning 'third daughter' with semantic extension to 'maiden'. In Hachijō, *tego* survives with the meaning 'third daughter'. I consider Vovin's hypothesis to be more unlikely, due to the conversion from verb to noun required, the lack of a noun *teko* in Ainu meaning 'maiden', as well as the weaker semantic link to the meaning 'third daughter'.

4.3.1.4.19 EOJ *tora* 'together' < Ainu *tura* 'id.'
This is attested in 14:3409.5 – Kamitukeno and 14:3518.5 – UNP. There are a few issues with this comparison. First and foremost, there is a syntactic problem. OJ *muta ~ mita* 'together' always occurs after a genitive suffix, whereas EOJ *tora* only occurs after the causative-imperative form of the verb *ne-* 'sleep'. As Vovin mentions (2012a: 100), the initial-syllable vowel *o* in EOJ is also a problem, since we would expect *u*; there is no evidence the Ainu form is a reflex of **tora*.

I agree with Mizushima (1986: 156) that *tora* was used to refer to a 'dear girl'. However, he considers it to be a development from *ko-ra* 'girl-DIM'. This is implausible due to the irregular change of **k > /t/* that is otherwise unattested. Instead, I think this word form is *ito-ra*[121] dear.one-DIM 'deary': the initial [i] was elided due to V_2 elision, which is dominant in EOJ (see Chapter 3, as well as Kupchik 2013b). Although in WOJ *ito* 'dear' is not attested in isolation (Vovin 2021a: 177), in Modern Japanese we can find *ito* 'girl' in the dialects of Kyōto, Nara, Wakayama, Okuyama, and Takachi, as well as *itosama* 'girl' in Nagasaki prefecture (Satō 2003: 1239).

---

and *aya n-i* can also mean 'extremely', so we could also translate the line as 'because it is extremely sad', in reference to the situation.
120 In this context we should also keep in mind a cognate of the EOJ locative *-na* can be reconstructed for PR, even though it was lost in WOJ and TSOJ. The EOJ adjective nominalizer suffix *-ngey* (see §6.3.3.12) is similarly only attested once, though it survived into Modern Japanese.
121 Further supporting this analysis is the fact that poem 14:3409 is from Kamitukeno, which is the only EOJ topolect with the diminutive suffix *-ra*.

4.3.1.5 Plausible (accepted) morphological borrowings

I accept the following comparison.

4.3.1.5.1 EOJ *sinda* temporal conjunction 'when' < Ainu *hi* 'time, occasion' + *-ta* 'locative case marker'

This is attested in 14:3363.3 – Sagamu, 14:3461 – UNP, 14:3478.3-4 – UNP, 14:3515.2 – UNP, 14:3520.2 – UNP, 14:3533.2 – UNP, 20:4367.2 – Pitati, and 20:4407.3 – Kamitukeno. It is not attested in WOJ or TSOJ, but it is attested once in KOJ (Vovin 2009c: 31). Vovin (2009c: 24–31) convincingly argues that it is a borrowing of Ainu *hi-ta* [hida] 'time-LOC', based not only on sound correspondences, but also on syntactic parallels, as can be seen in the following Ainu example from Nakagawa and Nakamoto (1997: 38):

9. *sirpopke* **hi-ta** *ku-sinot-rusuy*
   be.warm **time-LOC** 1.S-play-DES
   '**When** it is warm, I want to play.'

This conjunction is possibly related to Taketomi *sina* (Maeara 2011: 493), Yoron *sjaa* (Kiku and Takahashi 2005: 254) and Amami *sira* (Osada, Suyama, and Fujii 1980: 479),[122] all of which are temporal conjunctions that follow the infinitive form of the verb,[123] as is also attested twice in EOJ (see §9.6 for examples). If these Ryukyuan forms are valid cognates, then the date of borrowing must have been much earlier than proposed by Vovin (2009c), unless it was borrowed separately from Ainu speakers in the northern Ryūkyū Islands or southern Kyūshū.

4.3.1.6 Problematic (rejected) morphological borrowings

The following four comparisons are too problematic for me to accept.

4.3.1.6.1 EOJ *i-*, nominal prefix 'thing-' < Ainu *i-* 'id.'

This is a *hapax legomenon* attested in 20:4428.4 – UNP. Vovin proposes **i-epi* 'thing-sash' to account for the attestation of *yenbi*, which is cognate with WOJ *onbi* 'sash' (< PJe **əᵐbi). Semantically, this is quite odd, and the lack of any other attestations of this Ainu prefix in OJ further increases the implausibility. It is more likely the original **ə fronted to **ye sporadically in this unknown AOJ topolect, perhaps due

---

122 The development of medial PR *-ⁿd- > Amami-Okinawan *-r-* is also apparent in the reflexes of PR *-maⁿde 'terminative case marker' > Inō (Tokunoshima) *-mari* and Sesoko Okinawan *-marii* (Thorpe 1983: 217).

123 I am grateful to Wayne Lawrence for informing me of the Ryukyuan forms as possible cognates.

to the /i/ in the following syllable.[124] Vovin proposes the topolect might be Suruga (TSOJ), but the allative suffix -pa (< *pia) and the other morphology in the poem show this cannot be the case because these are hallmark features of EOJ, not TSOJ.

4.3.1.6.2 EOJ o- 'locative prefix' < Ainu o- 'id.'

This is a *hapax legomenon* attested in 14:3473.5 – UNP. Acceptance of this prefix requires us to posit an EOJ verb *yun-* 'to sleep' that Vovin proposes is also found in poem 14:3476b.5 – UNP. The evidence for this in poem 14:3473 is weak. Moreover, Vovin glosses *yun-i* 'sleep-NML' as 'dream', but nominalization of *ne* 'sleep', for example, is not used to mean 'dream' in Japanese.

Taking into consideration the known EOJ reflexes of PJe *oi and *ui and the form *oyu* in 14:3473.5, there is another interpretation of this poem that I would like to put forth.

10. 14:3473 – UNP
左努夜麻尓 / 宇都也乎能登乃 / 等抱可騰母 / 祢毛等可兒呂賀 / **於由**尓 美要都留

sano yama-ni / ut-u ya wonö [o]tö-nö / töpo-ka-ndömö / ne-m-o ka tö KO-rö-nga / **oyu** *n-i mi-ye-t-uru*

TN mountain-LOC / hit-ATTR EPT axe sound-COMP / be.far-AVEV-CONC / sleep-TENT-ATTR FPT QUOT girl-DIM-POSS / **grow.older.NML** COP-INF see-PASS.INF-PERF-ATTR

'[She] is far away, like the sound of an axe that strikes on Mt. Sano, but I suddenly see my dear girl **has grown older**, asking [me], 'Shall [we] sleep [together]?'.'[125]

The OJ verb *oyi-* 'to grow older' is a reflex of PJe *oyoi or *oyui. As demonstrated in Chapter 2, most EOJ topolects reflect PJe *oi as /u/, and *ui as /i/. So, I consider PJe *oyoi to be more likely. The nominalized form *oyu* 'grow.older.NML' is paralleled by EOJ *sungu* 'pass.NML' (< *sungoi) in the Simotukeno topolect and *kopu* 'long.for. NML' (< *kopoi) in the Kamitupusa topolect.

---

124 This is quite similar to the attested forms *ye-* [ye] and *yö-* [yə] 'to be good' in OJ.
125 This interpretation of the poem entails the author had a vision of her in which she matured more than when he last saw her, but there is no implication that the girl became elderly. This interpretation is thematically similar to KK 93.

4.3.1.6.3 EOJ *ka* 'focus particle' < Ainu *ka* 'id.'

I could not find a discussion of this supposed focus particle *ka* in Vovin (2012a) or (2013). He claims it is in attested in 14:3361 – Sagamu and 20:4386 – Simotupusa (Vovin 2013: 13), but there is no mention of it in his description of either poem (Vovin 2012a: 48–49, 2013: 145). So, I must reject it as a ghost word.

4.3.1.6.4 EOJ **i- ~ -y-* 'indefinite direct object prefix' < Ainu *i-* 'id.'

This is attested in 14:3526.5 – UNP and 20:4427.4 – UNP. In regard to the attestation in 14:3526.5, Vovin proposes it occurs as the second morpheme in the word form *na-y-ömöp-ar-i-sö-n-e* NEG.IMP-UNC-think-PROG-do-DES-IMP '[I] wish [you] are not thinking [that]'. However, there are no other phonographic attestations of the negative-imperative prefix *na-* attaching to a vowel-initial verb root in any OJ dialect. Thus, the *-y-* may simply be epenthetic (as Vovin suggested to me earlier), though there are no other cases of such epenthesis in OJ. I think a singular case of epenthesis is more likely than a morphological borrowing from Ainu that has no other clear attestations.

The second attestation, in 20:4427.4, involves EOJ *yusup-* 'to tie', possibly related to WOJ *musunb-* 'id.'. Vovin proposes the Ainu morpheme is word-initial in the EOJ word, and the sound changes progressed as **i-musup-* > **iusup* > *yusup-*. As he mentions, the condition for the deletion of the medial **-m-* is unclear and is unsupported by other examples. Due to this I think it is too speculative to accept.

4.3.2 Summary of Ainu loanwords

Although most of Vovin's Ainu loanwords in AOJ poetry do not stand up to scrutiny, a small number remain plausible, as do most of his toponym etymologies. Based on this, I agree that there were linguistic changes in EOJ and TSOJ that were induced by contacts with Ainu speakers as they colonized the Azuma region, but, considering the weight of the available evidence, I am of the opinion they were not to the degree envisioned by Vovin.

4.4 Chinese loanwords

There are only two clear, early Chinese loanwords in AOJ. One is buried inside the word *yanangi* 'willow tree' (20:4386.2 – Simotupusa). This probably consists of a borrowing of *ya* 'willow' from EMC **yaŋ* 'willow', while the rest of the word is Japonic in origin (Vovin 2009b: 45). Another is *WE* 'picture' (attested in 20:4327.2 – Töpotuapumi), from LH **γue^C* (Vovin 2005: 56).

4.5 Austronesian loanwords

I do not consider any of the proposals of Austronesian loanwords in AOJ to be plausible except *sina* 'sun', which dates to PJ (Kupchik 2021b[126]), and which is possibly found in the Azuma toponym *Sinano* (see §4.3.1.2.5). I have selected a few of the proposed Austronesian loanwords to illustrate some of the common problems with these comparisons.

Kumar and Rose (2000: 229) propose a precursor to Old Javanese *sawak-* 'to call out' was borrowed into pre-OJ as *sawak-* 'to make noise'. This word is not attested in TSOJ, but it is attested in EOJ in 14:3349.4 – Simotupusa, 20:4364.2 – Pitati, and 20:4354.2 – Kamitupusa. In terms of semantics this comparison is not a very close match. The authors dismiss the comment by Omodaka (1967: 344) that the OJ word contains an onomatopoetic morpheme *sawa*, and they further imply this *sawa* does not occur elsewhere in OJ. This is misleading because in EOJ we find *sawawe* 'noisy' attested in 14:3552.2 – UNP and *sawe-sawe* 'rustling' in 14:3481.2 – UNP, while in WOJ we find *sawi-sawi* 'rustling' (MYS 4:503.2) and *sawa-sawa n-i* 'noisily' (KK 63). Due to the shared semantics and close phonetics of these OJ words (including *sawak-*), they most likely all descend from an onomatopoeia for 'noise' in PJe, which I will reconstruct as *sawai. This makes for an unconvincing comparison with Old Javanese *sawak-* 'to call out'.

An Austronesian loanword origin for the OJ locative prefix *sa-* has been proposed by Vovin (2005: 90–91). For AOJ examples, see §5.3.2. This comparison is functionally and phonetically unproblematic, however no other Japonic prefix shows a clear Austronesian link, and the prefix consists of just two phonemes, so the possibility it is a look-alike is strong. Furthermore, we would expect to see a significant number of clear Austronesian lexical borrowings in Japonic if Japonic speakers went so far as to borrow Austronesian prefixes, but so far convincing evidence for this has not been put forth.

Recently, Vovin (2021b) proposed OJ *a* 'foot' is a loanword from Batanic *ai* ~ *ay* 'foot'. This word is attested in both EOJ (14:3387.1 – Simotupusa and 14:3533.4 – UNP) and WOJ,[127] so we must project it back to PJe. As has been well established (see Chapter 2), *ai was a diphthong or vowel sequence in PJe. It changed independently in the different OJ dialects and was a late change in WOJ (to /əy/), after

---

[126] Murayama (1970) was the first to propose an Austronesian origin (Proto-Malayo-Polynesian *t'inaʀ 'sun, light') for Old Ryukyuan *sina* 'sun' ~ *sino* '(sun) light' and WOJ *sina* 'sun'. However, he considered Japanese to be a "mixed" language, with a Malayo-Polynesian component and an Altaic component. He stated clearly, "the Malayo-Polynesian elements in Japanese do not exist there simply as loanwords" (Murayama 1976: 419).
[127] In TSOJ, we only find *asi* 'foot' attested, but it contains the same *a.

*əi had monophthongized to /ɨ/. Therefore, we would expect Batanic *ai ~ ay* to be borrowed as *ai in PJe, and the reflexes in OJ dialects to be *a-* in compounds and *ey ~ e* in isolation. Since at least one of the attestations in EOJ does not occur in a compound (14:3533.4 – UNP) and there is no OJ (or later Japanese) attestation of *ey ~ e* for 'foot', I must reject this comparison. Moreover, there is ample evidence to reconstruct *a 'foot' for Proto-Ryukyuan as well, which means it is a PJ word. The evidence is *a-* fossilized in compounds such as PR *agom- 'to climb a tree with one's legs' (<*a-nə-kom- 'foot-GEN-cross.legs-'[128]) and *abumi 'stirrups' (< *a-nə-pum-i 'foot-GEN-step.on-NML'). The PR word *ado 'heel' seems to also have this *a-* fossilized (< *a-nə-to 'foot-GEN-place'?). This is congruous with Vovin's hypothesis (even though he argues against it being a PJ word), since he proposes the word was borrowed between 300 BCE and 400 CE, and most of this time period predates the split of PJ into PR and PJe. However, the insurmountable phonetic problems with the comparison make this a moot point.

Vovin (2021b) also proposed an Austronesian origin of the OJ directive-locative focus prefix *i-* (see §7.5.1.4 for AOJ examples). His hypothesis entails it is a borrowing of an Amis nominal prefix *i-*.[129] It is highly unlikely Japonic speakers would borrow a noun prefix from another language and only use it on verbs. Since this prefix consists of just one vowel phoneme, the chance of it being a look-alike is once again very high.

---

[128] In mainland Japanese, and in OJ, this means 'to sit cross-legged'. I reconstruct *agom- rather than *agum- due to the Muromachi-period Mikawa dialect cognate *agom-* 'to straddle something' (Doi 1985: 60).

[129] It must be mentioned that van Hinloopen Labberton (1924: 270) was the first to propose the OJ directive-locative focus prefix *i-* is Austronesian in origin. In his hypothesis it is cognate with an obsolete Malayo-Polynesian *i-* prefix, in the context of a proposed genetic relationship between Japanese and Malayo-Polynesian.

5 Nominals

The nominals include nouns, pronouns, and numbers. The nominal morphology of the AOJ dialects consists of prefixes and suffixes that encode case, classification, diminutivity, honorification, intensification, and number. Reduplication is also attested with the functions of iteration and plurality. In this chapter all of the nominal morphology is presented and differences between TSOJ and EOJ are noted.

5.1 The basic syntax of nouns

Both TSOJ and EOJ have a modifier-head constituent order, thus nouns may be preceded by modifiers such as adjectives and attributivized verbs, but they are not followed by such modifiers. Particles always follow nouns.

5.2 Morphotactics

The maximal noun word form consists of two prefixes and five suffixes, in the following fixed order:

    INT-[DIM/LOC/HON]-root-DIM[1]-DIM[2]-PLUR-CASE[1]-CASE[2]

An example of a word form with two prefixes is provided in (1):

1. 14:3464.3-4 – UNP
   麻乎其母能 ／ 於夜自麻久良波
   ma-won-gömö-nö / oyanzi makura pa
   INT-DIM-reed-GEN / same pillow TPT
   'The same pillow, [made] of **really small reeds**. . .'

Although there are no attested examples of the maximal noun word form in TSOJ or EOJ, there is an UNP example in the corpus that may[130] show three different suffixes in one word form, and they combine in the order root-DIM-PLUR-CASE:

---

[130] An alternative analysis for this form would be *imö-nö-ra-ni* 'beloved girl-DIM-DIM-LOC.'

2. 14:3528.3-4 – UNP
   伊母能良尔 / 毛乃伊波受伎尔弖
   imö-nö-ra-ni / *monö ip-anz-u k-i-n-i-te*
   beloved.girl-DIM-PLUR-DAT / thing say-NEG-INF come-INF-PERF-INF-SUB
   '[I] came without saying anything **to [my] darling girls**.'

In addition, in more than one poem we find two diminutive suffixes attested in the same word form. This usage seems to be for emphasis, and is only attested in EOJ and UNP:

3. 14:3544.4-5 – UNP
   勢奈那登布多理 / 左宿而久也思母
   *se-**na-na**-tö puta-ri* / *sa-NE-TE kuyasi-mö*
   beloved.man-**DIM-DIM**-COM two-CL / LOC-sleep.INF-SUB be.regretful.AVFIN-EXCL
   '[I] slept there with [my] **dear, darling beloved,** [and now I] regret [it]!'

As for case marker combinations, the accusative case suffix *-wo* can be followed by the comitative case suffix *-tö* in EOJ:

4. 20:4385.3-5 – Simotupusa
   志流敝尔波 / 古乎等都麻乎等 / 於枳弖等母枳奴
   siru pe-ni pa / *ko-**wo-tö** tuma-**wo-tö*** / *ok-i-te tö mö k-i-n-u*
   behind area-LOC TPT / child-**ACC-COM** spouse-**ACC-COM** / leave.behind-INF-SUB FPT EPT come-INF-PERF-FIN
   '[I] left [my] **wife and child** behind to come [out here].'

Finally, the terminative case marker *-mande* can be followed by the locative case marker *-ni* in both EOJ and TSOJ:

5. 20:4339.4-5 – Suruga
   加比利久麻弖尔 / 已波比弓麻多祢
   *kapir-i-k-u-**mande-ni*** / *ipap-i-te mat-an-e*
   return-INF-come-ATTR-**TERM-LOC** / pray-INF-SUB wait-DES-IMP
   'Please pray and wait for [me] **until** [I] return.'

5.3 Prefixes

There are several nominal prefixes, which is quite peculiar for an SOV language. Most likely this is residue from an earlier SVO word order, as suggested by Vovin (2009a: 589).

The prefixes can be divided into four categories: diminutives, locatives, honorifics, and intensifiers. There is also one unclear prefix that may be another intensifier, as well as an unclear prefix that may mark an object.

5.3.1 Diminutive prefixes

The diminutive prefixes are *ko-* and *won-*.

5.3.1.1 Diminutive *ko-*

The diminutive prefix *ko-* most likely shares the same origin as the diminutive suffix *-ko*, and was also likely the earlier form, before prefixes shifted to suffixes in the language. It is attested prefixed to the following roots: *sungey* 'sedge', *yande* 'branch', *nangï* 'pickerelweed', and possibly also *nara* 'oak'. I provide all attestations below. It is only attested with a diminutive meaning. Vovin (2005: 79, 2020: 98) notes that this prefix is not phonographically attested in the WOJ poems of the MYS,[131] but it is attested in the WOJ poems of the KK and NK.

6. 14:3424.1-3 – Simotukeno
之母都家野 / 美可母乃夜麻能 / **許奈良**能須
simötukeNO / *mikamö-nö yama-nö* / ***kö-nara**-nösu*
TN / TN-GEN mountain-GEN / **DIM-oak**-COMP
'Like the **little oaks** on the mountain of Mikamo in Simotukeno...'

In example (6) the diminutive is misspelled as *kö-*. This example is not clear because it is possibly *kö-* 'tree' instead of the diminutive *ko-* (Omodaka 1967: 303).

---

131 One exception is 14:3454.2. Vovin (2012a: 144) classifies this poem as being written in WOJ (and I agree with him), rather than AOJ. Accordingly, we must consider this to be a phonographic attestation of this prefix in a WOJ poem in the MYS. Unlike all other attestations in the MYS, this attestation has an endearment meaning.

7. 14:3445.1-3 – UNP
   美奈刀能也 / 安之我奈可那流 / 多麻古須氣
   *minato-nö ya / asi-nga naka-n[i] ar-u / tama **ko-sungey***
   harbor-GEN EPT / reed-POSS inside-LOC exist-ATTR / jewel **DIM-sedge**
   'The jewel[-like] **small sedges** that are among the reeds in the harbor...'

8. 14:3493a.3-4 – UNP
   牟可都乎能 / 四比乃故夜提能
   *muka-tu wo-nö / sipi-nö **ko-yande**-nö*
   opposite.side-GEN.LOC mountain.ridge-GEN / chinquapin-GEN **DIM-branch-**COMP
   'Like the **little branches** of the chinquapin trees on the mountain ridge across the way...'

9. 14:3498.1-2 – UNP
   宇奈波良乃 / 根夜波良古須氣
   *una-para-nö / NE yapara **ko-sungey***
   sea-plain-GEN / root be.soft **DIM-sedge**
   '**Small sedges** [with] soft roots [growing near] the sea...'

10. 14:3576.1-4 – UNP
    奈波之呂乃 / 古奈宜我波奈乎 / 伎奴尔須里 / 奈流留麻尔末仁
    *napa-sirö-nö / **ko-nangï**-nga pana-wo / kinu-ni sur-i / nar-uru manima n-i*
    seedling-enclosure-GEN / **DIM-pickerelweed**-POSS flower-ACC / robe-LOC rub-NML / get.used.to-ATTR as COP-INF
    'As [I] get used to rubbing the flowers of the **little pickerelweed** from the seedling nursery on [my] robes [to dye them]...'

Table 5.1: Attestations of the diminutive *ko-* across the provinces.

	TSOJ					EOJ					UNP
Sin	Tö	Su	Kak	Mu	Sa	Mi	Sik	Pi	Sip	Kap	
0	0	0	0	0	0	0	1	0	0	0	4

5.3.1.2 Diminutive *won-*

The diminutive prefix *won-* is attested in TSOJ, EOJ, and UNP. Most attestations show a prenasalization at the end of the prefix, but three do not,[132] and in one case it is unclear because the following onset consonant is a nasal. For WOJ, Vovin (2005: 78) considers *wo-* to be the synchronic form but *won- (or *bon-) to be the earlier form, and he presents a possible etymology: a borrowing from Ainu *pon* 'little'. The borrowing of Ainu *p as *w or *b in PJe is irregular and lacks a satisfactory explanation.[133] This prefix has functions of both endearment and diminutivity, with the latter being more commonly attested.

5.3.1.2.1 Endearment function

11. 14:3354.5 – Töpotuapumi
    伊毛我乎杼許尓
    *imo-nga **won-dökö**-ni*
    beloved.girl-POSS **DIM-bed**-LOC
    'In the **warm bed** of [my] beloved girl. . .'

12. 14.3436.2-3 – Kamitukeno
    乎尓比多夜麻乃 / 毛流夜麻乃
    ***wo-nipita** yama nö / mor-u yama-nö*
    DIM-TN mountain COP.ATTR / guard-ATTR mountain-GEN
    '[The trees] on **Mt. Nipita**, the guarded mountain. . .'

13. 14:3484.5 – UNP
    伊射西乎騰許尓
    *inza se **won-dökö**-ni*
    well do.IMP **DIM-bed**-LOC
    'Well, do [it], in [my] **warm bed**.'

---

[132] OJ orthography does not make a consistent distinction between voiceless and prenasalized voiced obstruents, so perhaps these three examples without clear prenasalization are a product of that orthographic ambiguity.

[133] Based on the original comparison by Martin (1966: 240), Vovin (2010: 111) also proposed Proto-Korean *pantah ~ *patol as the source of WOJ *wata* 'sea', showing another possible case of this irregular correspondence.

5.3.1.2.2 Diminutive function

14. 14:3524.1-3 – UNP
    麻**乎其母**能 / **布能末**知可久弖 / 安波奈敝波
    *ma-**won-gömö-nö** / **pu-nö ma** tika-ku-te / ap-an-ap-e-nba*
    INT-**DIM-wild.rice-GEN** / **joint-GEN space** be.near-INF-SUB / meet-NEG-ITER-EV-CONJ
    'Since, [like] the really **small gaps in the [woven] wild rice** [mat], [we] are near [one another], yet [we] do not meet. . .'

Examples (15) – (17) below do not show clear prenasalization at the end of this prefix, even though *won-* precedes an onset that can be prenasalized in each example.

15. 14:3527.1-3 – UNP
    於吉尓須毛 / **乎加母**能毛己呂 / 也左可杼利
    *oki-ni sum-o / **wo-kamö**-nö mokörö / yasaka-n-döri*
    offing-LOC live-ATTR / **DIM-duck**-GEN similarity / TN-GEN-bird
    'The birds of Yasaka [are] similar to **little ducks** that live in the offing.'

16. 14:3538b.1-2 – UNP
    乎波夜之尓 / 古麻乎波左佐氣
    ***wo-payasi**-ni* / *koma-wo pasasangey*
    DIM-forest-LOC / horse-ACC let.run.free.INF
    '[I] let [my] horse run free in the **grove**.'

17. 20:4430.1-3 – UNP
    阿良之乎乃 / 伊**乎佐**太波佐美 / 牟可非多知
    *ara-si wo-nö / i-**wo-sa**-n-da-pasam-i / mukap-ï-tat-i*
    rough-FIN man-GEN / PREF-**DIM-arrow**-LOC-hand-pinch-INF / face-INF-stand-NML
    '[Like a] rough man who stands facing [a target] with [his] hand gripping **a small arrow**. . .'

Table 5.2: Attestations of the diminutive *won-* across the provinces.

TSOJ			EOJ								UNP
Sin	Tö	Su	Kak	Mu	Sa	Mi	Sik	Pi	Sip	Kap	
0	1	0	1	1	0	0	0	2	0	0	6

5.3.2 Locative *sa-*

The locative prefix *sa-* indicates a general location, something akin to 'there', as in the common example *sa-ne* LOC-sleep.NML 'sleep [there]'. As Vovin (2005: 83) notes, it marks the entire noun phrase, rather than a single noun. The locative prefix *sa-* most often attaches to nominalized forms of verbs, including gerunds, but it also attaches to nouns.

18. 14:3366.1-2 – Sagamu
    麻可奈思美 / <u>佐祢</u>尓和波由久
    ma kanasi-mi / ***sa-ne**-ni wa pa yuk-u*
    so be.dear-AVGER / **LOC-sleep.NML**-LOC 1.S TPT go-ATTR
    'Since [she] is truly dear [to me], [I] will go **and sleep** [with her].'

19. 14:3414.5 – Kamitukeno
    <u>佐祢</u>乎<u>佐祢</u>弖婆
    ***sa-ne**-wo **sa-ne**-te-nba*
    LOC-sleep.NML-ACC **LOC**-sleep.INF-PERF-COND
    'If [only I] had **slept there** [with you]...'

In example (19), both the object and the verb take the prefix *sa-*. This may be an example of agreement.

20. 20:4369.1-2 – Pitati
    都久波祢乃 / <u>佐由</u>流能波奈能
    tukupa ne-nö / ***sa-yuru**-nö pana-nö*
    TN peak-GEN / **LOC-lily**-GEN flower-COMP
    'Like **the blossoms of a lily** on the peaks of Mt. Tukupa...'

Example (20) shows the locative *sa-* prefixed to a noun root but marking the entire noun phrase.

21. 20:4394.3-5 – Simotupusa
    由美乃美他 / <u>佐尼</u>加和多良牟 / 奈賀氣己乃用乎
    yumi-nö mita / ***sa-ne** ka watar-am-u* / *nanga-key könö yo-wo*
    bow-GEN together / **LOC-sleep.NML** QPT cross.over-TENT-ATTR / be.long-AVATTR this night-ACC
    'Shall [I] get through this long night, **sleeping together** with [my] bow?'

22. 14:3497.3-4 – UNP
安也尔阿夜尔 / **左宿佐寐**弖許曽
aya n-i aya n-i / ***sa-NE sa-NE**-te kösö*
extreme COP-INF extreme COP-INF / **LOC-sleep.NML LOC-sleep.INF**-SUB FPT
'[We] **slept [together] there** so very often…'

23. 14:3530.1-2 – UNP
左乎思鹿能 / 布須也久草無良
***sa-wo-siKA**-nö* / *pus-u ya kusa mura*
LOC-male-deer-GEN / lie.down-ATTR EPT grass group
'A patch of grass where a **stag** lies down…'

24. 14:3536.1-4 – UNP
安加胡麻乎 / 宇知弖**左乎**妣吉 / 己許呂妣吉
aka n-goma-wo / *ut-i-te **sa-wo**-n-bik-i* / *kökörö-n-bik-i*
red COP.ATTR-horse-ACC / strike-INF-SUB **LOC-string**-GEN-pull-INF / heart-GEN-pull-INF
'Just as [he] whips [his] red horse and tugs on [its] **reins**, so [he] tugs on [my] heart.'

Table 5.3: Attestations of the locative *sa-* across the provinces.

TSOJ			EOJ							UNP
Sin	Tö	Su	Kak	Mu	Sa	Mi	Sik	Pi	Sip	Kap	
0	0	0	1	0	1	0	0	1	1	0	6

5.3.3 Honorific *mi-*

The honorific prefix *mi-* has the functions of honorification and beautification. It is widely attested across AOJ (in TSOJ, EOJ, and UNP) and can be found prefixed to the following noun roots: *saka* 'hill', *kötö* 'word', *tate* 'shield', *kesi* 'garment', *pune* 'boat', *ikusa* 'war', *naka* 'center', *ura* 'bay', and *yama* 'mountain'. Due to their semantics, a few forms may have already been lexicalized. For example, *mi-kötö* 'HON-word' means '[imperial/sovereign] command' and *mi-tate* 'HON-shield' means 'soldier'.

25. 20:4403.1-2 – Sinano
意保枳美能 / **美己等**可之古美
opo kimi-nö / **mi-kötö** kasiko-mi
great lord-GEN / **HON-word** be.august-AVGER
'Because [my] sovereign's **command** is august...'

26. 20:4321.1-2 – Töpotuapumi
可之古伎夜 / **美許等**加我布理
kasiko-ki ya / **mi-kötö** kangapur-i
be.august-AVATTR EPT / **HON-word** receive.HUM-INF
'Having received the august [imperial] **command**...'

27. 20:4423.1-3 – Muzasi
安之我良乃 / **美佐可**尓多志弖 / 蘇埿布良婆
asingara-nö / **mi-saka**-ni tas-i-te / sonde pur-anba
TN-GEN / **HON-slope**-LOC stand-INF-GER / sleeve wave-COND
'If [I] wave [my] sleeves, standing on the great **slope** of Asigara...'

28. 20:4328.1-2 – Sagamu
於保吉美能 / **美許等**可之古美
opo kimi-nö / **mi-kötö** kasiko-mi
great lord-GEN / **HON-word** be.august-AVGER
'Because [my] sovereign's **command** is august...'

29. 20:4373.3-5 – Simotukeno
意富伎美乃 / 之許乃**美多弖**等 / 伊埿多都和例波
opo kimi-nö / sikö nö **mi-tate** tö / inde-tat-u ware pa
great lord-GEN / lowly COP.ATTR **HON-shield** COP / go.out.INF-rise-ATTR 1.S TPT
'I, who will leave [today] to be a lowly **soldier** for my sovereign...'

30. 14:3350a.4-5 – Pitati
伎美我**美家思**志 / 安夜尓伎保思母
kimi-nga **mi-kesi** si / aya n-i ki posi-mö
lord-POSS **HON-garment** EPT / extreme COP-INF wear.NML be.desired-EXCL
'[I] so desperately want to put on [my] lord's **garment**!'

In example (30), the noun *kesi* 'garment' takes the honorific prefix *mi*- due to the preceding possessive form *kimi-nga* lord-POSS 'lord's'.

31. 20:4363.1-2 – Pitati
    奈尓波都尓 / **美布祢**於呂須恵
    nanipa tu-ni / ***mi-pune*** *orö-suwe*
    TN harbor-LOC / **HON-boat** lower-place.INF
    'Lowering the **boat** in Nanipa harbor and fixing it in place. . .'

32. 20:4394.1-2 – Simotupusa
    於保伎美乃 / **美己等**加之古美
    opo kimi-nö / ***mi-kötö*** *kasiko-mi*
    great lord-GEN / **HON-word** be.august-AVGER
    'Because [my] sovereign's **command is** august. . .'

33. 14:3463.3-5 – UNP
    己許呂奈久 / 佐刀乃**美奈可**尓 / 安敝流世奈可毛
    kökörö na-ku / *sato-nö **mi-naka**-ni* / *ap-er-u se-na kamo*
    heart not.exist-INF / village-GEN **HON-inside**-LOC / meet-PROG-ATTR beloved.man-DIM EPT
    'Oh [my] darling beloved, [with] whom [I] am meeting inconsiderately in the **great center** of the village. . .'

34. 14:3508.1-3 – UNP
    芝付乃 / **御宇良**佐伎奈流 / 根都古具佐
    SINBATUKI-nö / ***MIura***[134] *saki-n[i] ar-u* / *NEtuko-n-gusa*
    TN-GEN / **TN** cape-LOC exist-ATTR / UNC-GEN-grass
    'The *netuko* grass found at **Miura** cape in Sibatuki. . .'

In example (34) we see a logographic attestation of the honorific prefix *mi-*. Though a toponym, its etymology is transparent as *MI-ura* 'HON-bay'.

35. 14:3513.1-3 – UNP
    由布佐礼婆 / **美夜麻**乎左良奴 / 尓努具母能
    yupu sar-e-nba / ***mi-yama**-wo sar-an-u* / *nino n-gumö-nö*
    evening come-EV-CONJ / **HON-mountain**-ACC leave-NEG-ATTR / cloth COP.ATTR-cloud-COMP
    '[She is] like the cloth[-like] clouds that do not leave the **great mountain** even when night has set in.'

---

[134] Since the medial sequence *-iu-* does not reduce to one vowel here, this word form was probably phonetically [miwura] or [miyura].

36. 20:4432.2 – UNP
美許登尔阿礼婆
mi-kötö n-i ar-e-nba
HON-word COP-INF exist-EV-CONJ
'Since [these] are **commands** [from the emperor]...'

Table 5.4: Attestations of the honorific *mi-* across the provinces.

TSOJ			EOJ							UNP
Sin	Tö	Su	Kak	Mu	Sa	Mi	Sik	Pi	Sip	Kap	
2	1	0	0	2	1	0	1	4	0	0	5

5.3.4 Intensifying *ma-*

The prefix *ma-* has a function of intensifying the meaning of the noun to which it attaches. It can also mark an object that undergoes an intense action. This prefix is a grammaticalization of the adjective *ma* 'true', which is attested once in WOJ (Vovin 2005: 71), and once in EOJ (in 14:3424.4-5 – Simotukeno). For examples of this prefix attached to adjectives, see §6.3.2.1.

37. 20:4342.1-3 – Suruga
麻氣婆之良 / 寶米弓豆久利留 / 等乃能其等
ma-key n-basira / pomey-te tukur-ir-u / tönö-nö ngötö
INT-tree COP.ATTR-pillar / bless.INF-SUB make-PROG-ATTR / mansion-GEN like
'Like the mansion with pillars of **hearty timber** that were blessed during construction...'

38. 14:3404.1-3 – Kamitukeno
可美都氣努 / 安蘇能麻素武良 / 可伎武太伎
kamitukeyno / aso-nö ma-so mura / kaki-mundak-i
TN / TN-GEN **INT**-hemp group / TNG-embrace-NML
'[Like] holding a bundle of **fine hemp** from the fields of Aso [in] Kamitukeno close to [my] bosom...'

39. 14:3437.1-3 – Mitinöku
美知能久能 / 安太多良末由美 / 波自伎於伎弓
mitinöku-nö / andatara **ma-yumi** / panzik-i-ok-i-te
TN-GEN / TN **INT-bow** / take.off-INF-put-INF-SUB
'[I] take off [the string on my] **fine bow** [from] Adatara in Mitinöku...'

40. 20:4368.3-4 – Pitati
志富夫祢尔 / 麻可知之自奴伎
sipo-n-bune-ni / **ma-kandi** sinzi nuk-i
tide-GEN-boat-LOC / **INT-oar** constantly pierce-INF
'Constantly thrusting the **oar** on the tide boat...'

The ma- in example (40) indicates the rudders undergo an intensive action (in this case, 'thrusting').

41. 20:4388.1-2 – Simotupusa
多飛等弊等 / 麻多妣尔奈理奴
tapï tö [i]p-e-ndö / **ma-tanbi** n-i nar-i-n-u
journey QUOT say-EV-CONC / **INT-journey** COP-INF become-INF-PERF-FIN
'Although [it] was said to be [just] 'a journey', [this] has become **such a [trying] journey**.'

42. 14:3463.1-2 – UNP
麻等保久能 / 野尔毛安波奈牟
ma-töpo-ku nö / NO-ni mo ap-ana-m-u
INT-be.distant-NML COP.ATTR / field-LOC FPT meet-DES-TENT-FIN
'[I] would like to meet with you in the fields that are **quite a distance** [away].'

43. 20:4427.3-5 – UNP
麻由須比尔 / 由須比之比毛乃 / 登久良久毛倍婆
ma-yusup-i-ni / yusup-i-si pimo-nö / tök-ur-aku [o]mop-ey-nba
INT-tie-NML-LOC / tie-INF-PST.ATTR cords-GEN / come.undone-ATTR-NML think-EV-CONJ
'When [I] think that the cord [she] tied, in **a tight knot**, has come undone...'

44. 14:3461.3-4 – UNP
真日久礼弓 / 与比奈波許奈尔
MA-PI kure-te / yöpi-na pa kö-na-ni
INT-sun set.INF-SUB / evening-LOC TPT come-NEG.ATTR-LOC
'[It is] because [you] did not come during the evening after **the bright sun** set.'

Table 5.5: Attestations of the intensifying prefix *ma-* across the provinces.

TSOJ			EOJ								UNP
Sin	Tö	Su	Kak	Mu	Sa	Mi	Sik	Pi	Sip	Kap	
0	0	1	1	4	1	1	0	1	2	1	15

5.3.5 Prefix *uti-*

This prefix is attested three times in UNP. It also attaches to verbs (see §7.5.1.6 for examples). The meaning of this prefix is difficult to discern, so I gloss it as 'PREF'. It is possibly an intensifying prefix.

45. 14:3482a.1-2 – UNP
可良許呂毛 / 湏蘇乃**宇知可倍**
*kara körömo / suso-nö **uti-kapey***
TN robe / hem-GEN **PREF-cross.over.NML**
'[Like] **the seams** on the hem of Kara robes...'

46. 14:3482b.1-2 – UNP
可良許呂毛 / 須素能**宇知可比**
*kara körömo / suso-nö **uti-kap-i***
TN robe / hem-GEN **PREF-cross.over-NML**
'[Like] **the seams** on the hem of Kara robes...'

47. 14:3505.1-3 – UNP
宇知比佐都 / 美夜能瀬河泊能 / 可保婆奈能
***uti-pi** sat-u / miyanöSE kapa-nö / kapo-n-bana-nö*
PREF-sun shine.upon-ATTR / TN river-GEN / face-GEN-flower-COMP
'Like the morning glories along Miyanöse river that the **sun** shines upon...'

Table 5.6: Attestations of the prefix *uti-* across the provinces.

TSOJ			EOJ								UNP
Sin	Tö	Su	Kak	Mu	Sa	Mi	Sik	Pi	Sip	Kap	
0	0	0	0	0	0	0	0	0	0	0	3

5.3.6 Prefix *i-*

This prefix may mark the indirect object in a sentence. If so, it could be a borrowing of the Ainu indirect object prefix *e-* (with subsequent raising). Alternatively, it could be the directive-locative focus prefix *i-* (see §7.5.1.4). In WOJ, one or more nouns cannot come between that prefix and the verb (Vovin 2013: 197), but perhaps in some AOJ topolect this was possible. Unfortunately, it is only attested once, so we can do little but speculate here.

48. 20:4430.1-3 – UNP
    阿良之乎乃 / **伊乎佐**太波佐美 / 牟可非多知
    ara-si wo-nö / ***i-wo-sa**-n-da-pasam-i* / *mukap-ï-tat-i*
    rough-FIN man-GEN / **PREF-DIM-arrow**-LOC-hand-pinch-INF / face-INF-stand-NML
    '[Like a] rough man who stands facing [a target] with [his] hand gripping **a small arrow**...'

5.4 Suffixes

The suffixes encode case, number, and diminutivity.

5.4.1 Case suffixes

There are nine case suffixes attested in TSOJ and fifteen in EOJ. I analyze these as suffixes because nothing can come between them and the word form except another case marker, a number suffix, or a diminutive suffix. Vovin (2005: 110), on the other hand, views them as 'agglutinative case markers'. The case suffixes are the possessive *-nga*, genitive *-nö*, accusative/absolutive *-wo*, terminative *-mande*, dative/locative *-ni*, locative *-na*, genitive-locative *-tu*, comparative *-nö*, comparative *-nösu* ~ *-nasu*, comitative *-tö*, allative *-pe* ~ *-pa*, directive *-ka*, directive *-ngari*, ablative *-yo* ~ *-yu*, ablative *-yori* ~ *-yuri*, and ablative *-kara*. The nominative is unmarked (except in embedded clauses, where it can be marked by the possessive *-nga* or the genitive *-nö*).

Table 5.7 below shows the maximal nominal declension for the root *imo* 'beloved girl' in TSOJ and EOJ, based on attested morphology.[135] Phonetic variants are listed together, while morphological variants are listed separately.

---

[135] All of these suffixes are attested, but not all of them are attested attached to *imo* 'beloved girl'.

Table 5.7: Maximal nominal declension of *imo* 'beloved girl' in AOJ.

Case	TSOJ		EOJ	
	Word form	Contracted form	Word form	Contracted form
NOM	*imo*		*imo*	
POSS	*imo-nga*	*imo-ng-*	*imo-nga*	*imo-ng-*
ACC/ABS	*imo-wo*		*imo-wo*	
GEN	*imo-nö*	*imo-n-*	*imo-nö*	*imo-n-*
DAT/LOC	*imo-ni*	*imo-n-*	*imo-ni*	*imo-n-*
LOC	–		*imo-na*	*imo-n-*
ABL	–		*imo-yo ~ imo-yu*	
ABL	*imo-yuri*		*imo-yori ~ imo-yuri*	
ABL	–		*imo-kara*	
ALL	–[136]		*imo-pa ~ imo-pe*[137]	
DIR	–		*imo-ka*	
DIR	–		*imo-ngari*	
TERM	*imo-mande*		*imo-mande*	
COM	*imo-tö*		*imo-tö*	
COMP	*imo-nö*	*imo-n-*	*imo-nö*	*imo-n-*
COMP	*imo-nasu*		*imo-nösu*	

Perhaps the most striking feature in the chart above is that the genitive, dative/locative, locative, and comparative cases all syncretize in their contracted, fusional forms where they are reduced to the prenasalization of the following consonant onset. The genitive and comparative *-nö* are also syncretic in their underlying, uncontracted forms.

5.4.1.1 Nominative
The nominative case functions as a marker of the subject of a verb. It is morphologically unmarked in main clauses. Due to this, I do not gloss it as a morpheme in the examples.

---

[136] We would expect *-pe*, since this was the form in COJ/WOJ, and PJe *ia developed into /e/ in TSOJ.
[137] Allative *-pe* in EOJ is a borrowing from TSOJ or WOJ, since native *-pa* is attested (as the expected reflex from PJe *pia in EOJ).

49. 20:4343.5 – Suruga
和加美可奈志母
wa-nga mi kanasi-mö
1.S-POSS wife be.sad.AVFIN-EXCL
'**My wife** [must] be so sad!'

50. 14:3361.5 – Sagamu
許呂安礼比毛等久
kö-rö are pimo tök-u
girl-DIM 1.S cord undo-FIN
'[My] **dear girl and I** untie [our] cords.'

51. 20:4389.1-3 – Simotupusa
志保不尼乃 / 弊古祖志良奈美 / 尓波志久母
sipo pune-nö / pe kos-o sira nami / nipasi-ku mö
tide boat-GEN / prow surpass-ATTR white wave / be.sudden-INF FPT
'[It is as] sudden [as] **the white waves that surpass the prow of a tide boat**.'

5.4.1.2 Possessive -*nga*

The possessive case marker -*nga* is used with nominals to express a relation between a possessor and a possessed. It is similar to the genitive in this regard, though the genitive is used mainly with inanimate nouns and describes general connections rather than possessions. Due to the presence of a genitive case suffix in the AOJ dialects we might expect the possessive case suffix to be used exclusively with animate nouns, but in fact it is used with both animate and inanimate nouns as well as attributivized verbs, so any underlying animacy feature associated with it appears to have eroded by the time these poems were recorded.

In AOJ the possessive can lose its final vowel, creating the allomorph -*ng-*. However, this only occurs in the set phrase *wa-ng[a]-imo* 1.S-POSS-beloved.girl 'my beloved girl'. This phrase is also attested in EOJ without the elision of [a], so it seems to have been a synchronic variant, at least in EOJ.

5.4.1.2.1 Possessive function
The possessive function may occur with animate or inanimate nouns.

5.4.1.2.1.1 Attached to an animate noun
The animate nouns to which this suffix attaches are all human.

52. 14:3398.4-5 – Sinano
    伊思井乃**手兒我** / 許登奈多延曽祢
    isiWI-nö **te*NGO*-*nga*** / *kötö na-taye-sö-n-e*
    TN-GEN **maiden-POSS** / word NEG.IMP-cease.INF-do-DES-IMP
    '[There is] a **maiden** from Isiwi [whose] words [I] wish would never cease!'

53. 20:4402.5 – Sinano
    意毛知々可多米
    omo titi-nga tamey
    mother father-POSS benefit
    'For the sake **of [my] mother and father**…'

54. 14:3354.5 – Töpotuapumi
    伊**毛我**乎杼許尓
    imo*-*nga *won-dökö-ni*
    beloved.girl-POSS DIM-bed-LOC
    'In the warm bed **of [my] beloved girl**…'

55. 20:4383.5 – Simotukeno
    阿**母我**米母我母
    amö-nga *mey möngamö*
    mother-POSS eye DPT
    '[I] long for [my] **mother's** eyes.'

56. 14:3350a.4-5 – Pitati
    伎**美我**美家思志 / 安夜尓伎保思母
    kimi-nga *mi-kesi si* / *aya n-i ki posi-mö*
    lord-POSS HON-garment EPT / extreme COP-INF wear.NML be.desired-EXCL
    '[I] so desperately want to put on [my] **lord's** garment!'

57. 20:4386.1-2 – Simotupusa
    和**加**可都乃 / 以都毛等夜奈枳
    wa-nga *kandu-nö* / *itu-motö yanaki*
    1.S-POSS gate-GEN / five-CL willow
    'The five willows near **my** gate…'

58. 14:3383.5 – Kamitupusa
奈我目保里勢牟
***na-nga** MEY por-i se-m-u*
2.S-POSS eye desire-NML do-TENT-FIN
'[I] dream of **your** eyes.'

59. 14:3509.3-5– UNP
宿奈敝杼母 / 古呂賀於曾伎能 / 安路許曾要志母
*NE-n-ap-e-ndömö / **ko-rö-nga** osöki-nö / ar-o kösö ye-si-mö*
sleep-NEG-ITER-EV-CONC / **girl-DIM-POSS** upper.garment-GEN / exist-ATTR FPT be.good-AVFIN-EXCL
'Although [we] are not sleeping together, it is so nice to have [my] **dear girl's** upper garment!'

5.4.1.2.1.2 Attached to an inanimate noun

The inanimate nouns include toponyms and attributivized verbs. I also include plants here (such as *kaye* 'reed, grass' and *asi* 'reed'), though some may consider those to be animate.

60. 20:4321.4-5 – Töpotuapumi
加曳我牟多祢牟 / 伊牟奈之尓志弖
***kaye-nga** muta ne-m-u / imu na-si n-i s-i-te*
reed-POSS together sleep-TENT-ATTR / beloved.girl NEG-FIN COP-INF do-INF-SUB
'Will [I] sleep **among the reeds**, without [my] beloved girl?'

61. 20:4404.3-5 – Kamitukeno
和藝毛古賀 / 都氣之非毛我乎 / 多延尓氣流可毛
*wa-ng-imo-ko-nga / tukey-si **pïmo-nga** wo / taye-n-i-keyr-u kamo*
1.S-POSS-beloved.girl-DIM-POSS / be.attached.INF-PST.ATTR **string-POSS** cord / break.INF-PERF-INF-RETR-ATTR EPT
'Oh, the **cord** that my darling girl tied [over my robes] has come undone!'

62. 14:3375.1-3 – Muzasi
武蔵野乃 / 乎具奇我吉藝志 / 多知和可礼
*munzasi NO-nö / **won-gukï-nga** kingisi / tat-i-wakare*
TN field-GEN / **DIM-mountain.cave-POSS** pheasant / rise-INF-separate.NML
'[Like] the ascent of a **small mountain** pheasant in Muzasi Plain. . .'

63. 14:3445.2-4 – UNP
    安之我奈可那流 / 多麻古須氣 / 可利己和我西古
    ***asi-nga** naka-n[i] ar-u / tama-ko-sungey / kar-i kö wa-nga se-ko*
    reed-POSS inside-LOC exist-ATTR / jewel-DIM-sedge / chop.down-INF come.
    IMP 1.S-POSS beloved.man-DIM
    'Chop down the jewel[-like] small sedges that are **among the reeds** and come [back here], my darling man.'

Example (64) below shows the possessive attached to a toponym:

64. 14:3405a.2-3 – Kamitukeno
    乎度能**多杼里我** / 可波治尔毛
    *wondo-nö **tandöri-nga** / kapa-ndi-ni mo*
    TN-GEN **TN-POSS** / river-road-LOC FPT
    'On **Tadöri's** river road in Wodo...'

Examples (65) and (66) show the possessive attached to the attributive form of a verb:

65. 20:4338.4-5 – Suruga
    波々乎波奈例天 / **由久我**加奈之佐
    *papa-wo panare-te / **yuk-u-nga** kanasi-sa*
    mother-ACC part.from.INF-SUB / **go-ATTR-POSS** be.sad-AVNML
    'The sadness of parting from [my] mother and **going** [away]...'

66. 20:4425.3-4 – UNP
    刀布比登乎 / **美流我**登毛之佐
    *top-u pitö-wo / **mi-ru-nga** tömosi-sa*
    ask-ATTR person-ACC / **see-ATTR-POSS** be.favored-AVNML
    '[Oh,] the enviousness **of looking** at those who ask...'

Examples (67) and (68) show the possessive attached to an interrogative pronoun:

67. 20:4425.1-2 – UNP
    佐伎毛利尔 / 由久波**多我**世登
    *sakimori n-i / yuk-u pa **ta-nga** se tö*
    border.guard COP-INF / go-ATTR TPT **who-POSS** beloved.man QUOT
    '**Whose husband** is that, going to be a border guard?'

68. 14:3424.5 – Simotukeno
多賀家可母多牟
ta-*nga* ke ka möt-am-u
who-POSS container QPT hold-TENT-ATTR
'**Whose** [food] container shall [she] hold?'

5.4.1.2.2 Nominative function in embedded clauses

As mentioned above, the possessive -*nga* may be used as a nominative marker in embedded clauses. In such examples the verb is always in an attributive form.

69. 20:4413.3-4 – Muzasi
麻可奈之伎 / 西呂我馬伎己无
ma-kanasi-ki / **se-rö-nga** mek-i-kö-m-u
INT-be.dear-AVATTR / **beloved.man-DIM-POSS** walk-INF-come-TENT-ATTR
'[My] **dearly beloved** shall come walking [back].'

70. 20:4329.3-5 – Sagamu
布奈可射里 / 安我世牟比呂乎 / 美毛比等母我毛
puna-kanzar-i / **a-nga** se-m-u pi-rö-wo / mi-m-o pitö möngamo
boat-decorate-NML / **1.S-POSS** do-TENT-ATTR day-DIM-ACC / see-TENT-ATTR person DPT
'[I] wish someone would witness the special day when **I** do the boat-decorating.'

71. 20:4364.3-5 – Pitati
伊敝能伊牟何 / 奈流敝伎己等乎 / 伊波須伎奴可母
ipe-nö **imu-nga** / nar-unbe-ki kötö-wo / ip-anz-u k-i-n-u kamö
house-GEN **beloved.girl-POSS** / make.a.living-DEB-AVATTR word-ACC / say-NEG-INF come-INF-PERF-ATTR EPT
'[I] wonder, did [I] come [here] without saying [what my] **darling** at home must do to make a living?'

72. 14:3385.1-3 – Simotupusa
可都思加能 / 麻萬能手兒奈我 / 安里之波可
kandusika-nö / mama-nö **teNGO-na-nga** / ar-i-si paka
TN-GEN / cliff-GEN **maiden-DIM-POSS** / exist-INF-PST.ATTR place
'The place where the **dear maiden** from the cliffs of Kandusika was...'

73. 20:4347.3-5 – Kamitupusa
奈我波氣流 / 多知尓奈里弖母 / 伊波非弖之加母
na-nga *pak-eyr-u* / *tati n-i nar-i-te mö* / *ipap-ï-te-si kamö*
2.S-POSS wear-PROG-ATTR / sword COP-INF become-INF-SUB FPT / pray-INF-PERF-PST.ATTR EPT
'[I] want to become the sword **you** are wearing and pray for [you].'

74. 14:3453 – UNP
可是能等乃 / 登抱吉**和伎母賀** / 吉西斯伎奴 / 多母登乃久太利 / 麻欲比伎尓家利
kanze-nö [o]tö-nö / *töpo-ki **wa-ng[a]-imö-nga*** / *ki-se-si kinu* / *tamötö-nö kundar-i* / *mayop-i-k-i-n-i-ker-i*
wind-GEN sound-COMP / be.far-AVATTR **1.S-POSS-beloved.girl-POSS** / wear-CAUS-PST.ATTR robe / sleeve.edge-GEN descend-NML / become.frayed-INF-come-INF-PERF-INF-RETR-FIN
'The edge of the sleeve of the robe that **my beloved girl**, who is far away like the sound of the wind, had [me] wear has become frayed.'

The second possessive in example (74) is used to mark a nominative, while the first is used in a possessive function.

75. 14:3539.4-5 – UNP
比等豆麻古呂乎 / 伊吉尓**和我**須流
pitö-n-duma ko-rö-wo / *iki-ni **wa-nga** s-uru*
person-GEN-spouse girl-DIM-ACC / breath-LOC **1.S-POSS** do-ATTR
'I sigh for a dear girl [who is] another man's wife.'

Table 5.8: Attestations of the possessive *-nga* across the provinces.

Func	TSOJ			EOJ								UNP
	Sin	Tö	Su	Kak	Mu	Sa	Mi	Sik	Pi	Sip	Kap	
POSS	3	5	6	10	13	3	0	4	5	4	8	35
NOM	0	1	1	4	2	2	0	1	2	4	1	21

The data in Table 5.8 show that the possessive function is more common in every topolect except Simotupusa (where the nominative function is equally common). This, along with the fact that the nominative function does not yet occur with final predicates, supports the idea that the nominative function is secondary.

5.4.1.3 Accusative/absolutive -wo

The suffix -wo is predominantly used as an accusative marker. There are a few examples of its usage as an absolutive marker, but it only attaches to the intransitive subject of an adjectival verb gerund. It also has a secondary function of attaching to an attributive form of a verb to indicate the meaning 'even though', which is described in §5.4.1.3.3.

5.4.1.3.1 Accusative function

The accusative function is well attested across the topolects.

76. 20:4403.3-5 – Sinano
阿乎久牟乃 /等能妣久夜麻乎 / 古与弓伎怒加牟
*awo kumu-nö / tönönbik-u **yama-wo** / koyö-te k-i-n-o kamu*
blue cloud-GEN / stream.out-ATTR **mountain-ACC** / cross.INF-SUB come-INF-PERF-ATTR EPT
'Oh, [I] came [here], having crossed **the mountain** where the blue clouds stream out...'

77. 14:3429.1-4 – Töpotuapumi
等保都安布美 / 伊奈佐保曽江乃 / 水乎都久思 / 安礼乎多能米弖
*töpotuapumi / inasa posö-YE-nö / MIwo-tu kusi / **are-wo** tanömey-te*
TN / TN narrow-estuary-GEN / water.channel-GEN.LOC stalk / **1.S-ACC** make.trust.INF-SUB
'[You] made **me** trust [you], as [I trust] the buoys in the channel of the narrow estuary of Inasa in Töpotuapumi...'

78. 14:3359a.4-5 – Suruga
伊麻思乎多能美 / 波播尓多我比奴
***imasi-wo** tanöm-i / papa-ni tangap-i-n-u*
2.S-ACC trust-INF / mother-DAT defy-INF-PERF-FIN
'[I] defied [my] mother and put [my] trust in **you**.'

79. 20:4341.1-3 – Suruga
多知波奈能 / 美袁利乃佐刀尓 / 父乎於伎弓
*tatinbana-nö / miwori-nö sato-ni / **TITI-wo** ok-i-te*
TN-GEN / TN-GEN village-LOC / **father-ACC** leave.behind-INF-SUB
'Leaving [my] **father** behind in the village of Miwori in Tatibana...'

5.4 Suffixes — 165

80. 14:3402.1-3 – Kamitukeno
比能具礼尓 / 宇須比乃夜麻乎 / 古由流日波
pi-nö kure-ni / ***usupi-nö yama-wo*** / *koy-uru PI pa*
sun-GEN darken.NML-LOC / **TN-GEN mountain-ACC** / cross-ATTR day TPT
'[On] the day [my beloved] crossed over **Mt. Usupi** during the sunset. . .'

81. 14:3379.1-2 – Muzasi
和我世故乎 / 安杼可母伊波武
*wa-nga **se-ko-wo*** / *andö kamö ip-am-u*
1.S-POSS **beloved.man-DIM-ACC** / what EPT say-TENT-ATTR
'[I] wonder, what could [I] say [about] my **beloved man**?'

82. 20:4328.5 – Sagamu
知々波々乎於伎弖
titi papa-wo *ok-i-te*
father mother-ACC leave.behind-INF-SUB
'Leaving [my] **father and mother** behind. . .'

83. 20:4374.1-2 – Simotukeno
阿米都知乃 / 可美乎伊乃里弖
amey tuti-nö / ***kami-wo*** *inör-i-te*
heaven earth-GEN / **deity-ACC** pray-INF-SUB
'Praying to **the deities** of heaven and earth. . .'

84. 14:3394.3-5 – Pitati
夜麻乃佐吉 / 和須良延許婆古曽 / 那乎可家奈波賣
yama-nö saki / *wasura-kö-nba kosö* / ***na-wo*** *kake-n-ap-am-e*
mountain-GEN brow / forget-come-COND FPT / **2.S-ACC** call.out-NEG-ITER-TENT-EV
'When [I] start to forget [our meeting at] the brow of the mountain, [I] shall stop calling out **for you**!'

85. 14:3384 – Simotupusa
可都思加能 / 麻末能手兒奈乎 / 麻許登賀聞 / 和礼尓余須等布 / 麻末乃弖胡奈乎
kandusika-nö / *mama-nö* ***tengo-na-wo*** / *ma-kötö kamo* / *ware-ni yös-u tö [i]p-u* / *mama-nö* ***tengo-na-wo***
TN-GEN / cliff-GEN **maiden-DIM-ACC** / INT-word EPT / 1.S-DAT make.approach-ATTR QUOT say-FIN / cliff-GEN **maiden-DIM-ACC**
'[I] wonder, is it true that [some] say I am intimate with **a darling maiden** from the cliff in Kadusika? **A darling maiden** from the cliff. . .'

86. 20:4348.2 – Kamitupusa
波々乎和加例弖
***papa-wo** wakare-te*
mother-ACC be.separated.INF-SUB
'[I] am separated from [my] **mother**...'

87. 14:3440a.3-4 – UNP
奈礼毛阿礼毛 / 余知乎曽母弓流
*nare mo are mo / **yöti-wo** sö möt-er-u*
2.S FPT 1.S FPT / **same.age-ACC** FPT hold-PROG-ATTR
'You and I both have [children] **of the same age**.'

88. 14:3456.5 – UNP
安乎許登奈須那
***a-wo** kötö nas-una*
1.S-ACC word produce-NEG.IMP
'Do not spread rumors [about] **me**.'

89. 14:3539.1-2 – UNP
安受乃宇敝尔 / 古馬乎都奈伎弖
*anzu-nö upe-ni / **koMA-wo** tunang-i-te*
crumbling.cliffs-GEN above-LOC / **horse-ACC** tie.up-INF-SUB
'Having tied [my] **horse** above the crumbling cliffs...'

5.4.1.3.2 Absolutive function

This usage is attested only three times in the corpus: twice in EOJ and once in UNP. It is only attested as marking the intransitive subject of an adjectival verb gerund in a dependent clause.

90. 14:3434.3 – Kamitukeno
野乎比呂美
***NO-wo** pirö-mi*
field-ABS be.wide-AVGER
'Because **the field** is wide...'

91. 14:3426.1-2 – Mitinöku
安比豆祢能 / 久尓乎佐杼抱美
*apindu ne-nö / **kuni-wo** sa n-döpo-mi*
TN peak-GEN **land-ABS** thus COP.INF-be.far-AVGER
'Because the **land of the Apidu peaks** is so far [away]...'

92. 14:3540.4-5 – UNP
    安可故麻我 / **安我伎乎**波夜美 / 許等登波受伎奴
    aka koma-nga / ***a-n-gak-i-wo*** *paya-mi* / *kötö tö [i]p-anz-u k-i-n-u*
    red horse-POSS / **foot-GEN-scrape-NML-ABS** be.fast-AVGER / word QUOT say-NEG-INF come-INF-PERF-FIN
    'Because [my] **red horse's gallop** is swift, [I] came [back] without saying a word.'

5.4.1.3.3 Use of accusative *-wo* as a conjunction

The accusative *-wo* has a special function where it attaches to the attributive form of verbs to indicate the meaning 'even though', 'but', or 'because', much like a conjunction.

93. 14:3376a.1-2;5 – Muzasi
    古非思家波 / 素弖毛**布良武乎** / 伊呂尓豆奈由米
    kopïsi-ke-nba / *sonde mo **pur-am-u-wo*** / *irö-ni [i]nd-una yumey*
    be.longing.for-AVEV-CONJ / sleeve FPT **wave-TENT-ATTR-ACC** / color/feelings-LOC go.out-NEG.IMP at.all
    'When [you] are longing [for me], [I] **shall wave** [my] sleeve [for you], **but** do not let [your] face reveal even a hint of [your] true feelings [for me]!'

94. 14:3395.3-5 – Pitati
    安比太欲波 / 佐波太**奈利怒乎** / 萬多祢天武可聞
    apinda yo pa / *sapanda **nar-i-n-o-wo*** / *mata ne-te-m-u kamo*
    interval night TPT / many **be-INF-PERF-ATTR-ACC** / again sleep.INF-PERF-TENT-ATTR EPT
    '**Since** there **have been** many nights in between [our meetings], [I] wonder if [I] shall sleep [with her] again.'

95. 14:3544.1-3 – UNP
    阿須可河泊 / 之多**尓其礼留乎** / 之良受思天
    asuka-n-gapa / *sita **ningör-er-u-wo*** / *sir-anz-u s-i-te*
    TN-GEN-river / below **be.muddy-PROG-ATTR-ACC** / know-NEG-NML do-INF-SUB
    'The bottom of Asuka river **is muddy**, **but** [I] did not know [that]...'

5.4.1.3.4 Emphatic form *-wonba*

The emphatic accusative *-wonba* is attested just once.

96. 14:3452.1-2 – UNP
    於毛思路伎 / **野乎婆**奈夜吉曽
    omosiro-ki / ***NO-wonba*** *na-yak-i-sö*
    be.lovely-AVATTR / **field-ACC.EMP** NEG.IMP-burn-INF-do
    'Do not burn the lovely **field**!'

Table 5.9: Attestations of the accusative/absolutive -*wo* across the provinces.

Func	TSOJ			EOJ								UNP
	Sin	Tö	Su	Kak	Mu	Sa	Mi	Sik	Pi	Sip	Kap	
ACC	2	2	3	8	10	5	0	5	9	11	4	60
ABS	0	0	0	1	0	0	1	0	0	0	1	1

5.4.1.4 Genitive -*nö*

The genitive suffix -*nö* is the most common case suffix, and it is amply attested in all AOJ topolects as well as in UNP. It has two functions: 1) genitive marker and 2) marker of the subject of an embedded clause. It has two orthographic forms: -*nö*, and a contracted, fusional form -*n*-, which prenasalizes the following obstruent.

5.4.1.4.1 Genitive function

The genitive function is the most commonly attested.

97. 14:3399.1-2 – Sinano
    信濃道者 / **伊麻能**波里美知
    sinanu-NDI PA / ***ima-nö*** *par-i miti*
    TN-road TPT / **now-GEN** clear-INF road
    'The road to Sinano [is] cleared **now**. . .'

98. 20:4402.1-2 – Sinano
    知波夜布留 / **賀美乃**美佐賀尓
    tipayanburu / ***kami-nö*** *mi-saka-ni*
    MK / **deity-GEN** HON-slope-LOC
    'On the sacred slope **of the Tipayaburu deity**. . .'

99. 14:3354.1-3 – Töpotuapumi
伎倍**比等乃** / 萬太良夫須麻尓 / 和多佐波太
kipey **pitö-nö** / mandara n-busuma-ni / wata sapanda
TN **person-GEN** / speckled COP.ATTR-bed.covers-LOC / cotton amply
'[Like] the cotton [that is] amply [placed] inside the speckled bed covers **of the people** from Kipey. . .'

100. 20:4323.1-2 – Töpotuapumi
等伎騰吉乃 / 波奈波左家登母
töki-ndöki-nö / pana pa sak-e-ndömö
time-REDUP-GEN / flower TPT bloom-EV-CONC
'The **seasonal** flowers [all] bloom, but. . .'

101. 14:3359a.1-3 – Suruga
駿河能宇美 / 於思敝尓於布流 / 波麻都豆良
surunga-nö umi / osi-pe-ni op-uru / pama tundura
TN-GEN sea / rock-shore-LOC grow-ATTR / shore vine
'Like the vines that grow on the rocky shore along the sea **of Suruga**. . .'

102. 20:4341.1-3 – Suruga
多知波奈能 / **美袁利乃**佐刀尓 / 父乎於伎弖
tatinbana-nö / **miwori-nö** sato-ni / TITI-wo ok-i-te
TN-GEN / **TN-GEN** village-LOC / father-ACC leave.behind-INF-SUB
'Leaving my father behind in the village **of Miwori in Tatibana**. . .'

103. 14:3404.1-3 – Kamitukeno
可美都氣努 / **安蘇能**麻素武良 / 可伎武太伎
kamitukeyno / **aso-nö** ma-so mura / kaki-mundak-i
TN / **TN-GEN** INT-hemp group / TNG-embrace-INF
'[Like] holding a bundle of fine hemp **from Aso** [in] Kamitukeno close to [my] bosom. . .'

104. 14:3378.1-3 – Muzasi
伊利麻治能 / 於保屋我**波良能** / 伊波為都良
irima-ndi-nö / opoYA-nga **para-nö** / ipawi tura
TN-road-GEN / **TN-POSS field-GEN** / UNC vine
'The *ipawi* vines **in the field** of Opoya, **on the road to Irima**. . .'

105. 14:3361.1-3 – Sagamu
安思我良能 / 乎弓毛許乃母尓 / 佐須和奈乃
***asingara*-nö** / *wote mo könö mö-ni* / *sas-u wana-nö*
TN-GEN / that side this side-LOC / thrust-ATTR trap-COMP
'Like the [noise from the] traps set here and there **in Asigara**...'

106. 20:4330.1-4 – Sagamu
奈尓波都尓 / 余曽比余曽比弖 / **氣布能**比夜 / 伊田弖麻可良武
nanipa tu-ni / *yösöp-i yösöp-i-te* / ***keypu*-nö** *pi ya* / *inde-te makar-am-u*
TN harbor-LOC / prepare-INF prepare-INF-SUB / **today-GEN** day QPT go.out.INF-SUB depart-TENT-ATTR
'Preparing [the boats] in Nanipa harbor, [I wonder], will [we] depart and [sail] out **today**?'

107. 14:3437.1-3 – Mitinöku
美知能久能 / 安太多良末由美 / 波自伎於伎弖
***mitinöku*-nö** / *andatara ma-yumi* / *panzik-i-ok-i-te*
TN-GEN / TN INT-bow / take.off-INF-put-INF-SUB
'[I] take off [the string on my] fine bow [from] Adatara **in Mitinöku**...'

108. 14:3425.1-4 – Simotukeno
志母都家努 / **安素乃**河泊良欲 / 伊之布麻努受 / 蘓良由登伎努与
simötukeno / ***aso*-nö** *kapara-yo* / *isi pum-anz-u* / *sora-yu tö k-i-n-o yö*
TN / **TN-GEN** river.bank-ABL / stone step-NEG-INF / sky-ABL FPT come-INF-PERF-ATTR EPT
'[I] came from the sky without stepping [on] the stones from the riverbank **of Aso** in Simotukeno!'

109. 14:3388.1-2 – Pitati
筑波祢乃 / 祢呂尓可須美為
***tukupa ne*-nö** / *ne-rö-ni kasumi wi*
TN peak-GEN / peak-DIM-LOC mist sit.INF
'The mist sitting on the smaller peak **of Mt. Tukupa**....'

110. 14:3385.1-3 – Simotupusa
可都思加能 / 麻萬能手兒奈我 / 安里之波可
***kandusika*-nö** / ***mama*-nö** te*NGO*-na-nga / *ar-i-si paka*
TN-GEN / **cliff-GEN** maiden-DIM-POSS / exist-INF-PST.ATTR place
'The place where the dear maiden **from the cliffs of Kadusika** was...'

111. 20:4388.3-5 – Simotupusa
以弊乃母加 / 枳世之己呂母尔 / 阿可都枳尔迦理
ipe-nö [i]mö-nga / ki-se-si körömö-ni / aka tuk-i-n-i-kar-i
house-GEN beloved.girl-POSS / wear-CAUS-PST.ATTR garment-LOC / dirt attach-INF-PERF-INF-RETR-FIN
'Dirt is stuck to the garment that [my] beloved **at home** had [me] wear.'

112. 20:4353.3-5 – Kamitupusa
和伎母古賀 / 伊倍其登母遅弓 / 久流比等母奈之
wa-ng[a]-imö-ko-nga / **ipey-n-götö** möt-i-te / k-uru pitö mö na-si
1.S-POSS-beloved.girl-DIM-POSS / **house-GEN-word** hold-INF-SUB / come-ATTR person FPT not.exist-FIN
'There is no one who comes with **news** of my beloved girl.'

Example (112) contains the contracted allomorph -n-.

113. 14:3444.1-4 – UNP
伎波都久能 / 乎加能久君美良 / 和礼都賣杼 / 故尔毛乃多奈布
kipatuku-nö / **woka-nö** kuku-mira / ware tum-e-ndö / ko-ni mo nöt-an-ap-u
TN-GEN / **hill-GEN** stem-leek / 1.S pluck-EV-CONC / basket-LOC FPT fill.up-NEG-ITER-FIN
'I pluck the **stem-leeks on Kipatuku hill**, but the basket is not filling up.'

114. 14:3458.2-4 – UNP
等里能乎加恥志 / 奈可太乎礼 / 安乎祢思奈久与
töri-nö woka-ndi si / naka n-dawore / a-wo ne si nak-u yö
TN-GEN hill-road EPT / inside COP.ATTR-saddle / 1.S-ACC voice EPT make.cry-FIN EPT
'Oh, [riding on that] saddle in the middle of the road to **Töri** hill makes me cry out loud!'

115. 14:3497.1-2 – UNP
可波加美能 / 祢自路多可我夜
kapa kami-nö / ne-n-ziro taka n-gaya
river upper.part-GEN / root-GEN-white high COP.ATTR-grass
'The tall grass [with] white roots **in the upper area [of] the river**...'

116. 14:3576.1-3 – UNP
奈波之呂乃 / 古奈宜我波奈乎 / 伎奴尓須里
napa-sirö-nö / *ko-nangï-nga pana-wo* / *kinu-ni sur-i*
seedling-enclosure-GEN / DIM-pickerelweed-POSS flower-ACC / robe-LOC rub-NML
'Rubbing the flowers of the little pickerelweed **in the seedling nursery** on [my] robes [to dye them]. . .'

117. 20:4427.1-2 – UNP
伊波乃伊毛呂 / 和乎之乃布良之
ipa-nö imo-rö / *wa-wo sinöp-urasi*
house-GEN beloved.girl-DIM / 1.S-ACC yearn.for-SUP
'It seems that [my] darling girl **at home** yearns for me.'

5.4.1.4.2 Function of marking the subject of an embedded clause
This function is only attested four times, which most likely indicates it is a secondary function.

118. 20:4413.5 – Muzasi
都久乃之良奈久
tuku-nö sir-an-aku
moon-GEN know-NEG.ATTR-NML
'Not knowing **the month** [when]. . ..'

119. 20:4375 – Simotukeno
麻都能氣乃 / 奈美多流美礼波 / 伊波比等乃 / 和例乎美於久流等 / 多々里之毛己呂
matu-nö key-nö / *nam-i-tar-u mi-re-nba* / *ipa-pitö-nö* / *ware-wo mi-okur-u tö* / *tat-ar-i-si mokörö*
pine-GEN tree-GEN / be.lined.up-INF-PP-ATTR see-EV-CONJ / **house-person-GEN** / 1.S-ACC see.INF-send.off-FIN QUOT / stand-PROG-INF-PST.ATTR similarity
'When [I] see the **pine trees** lined up, [it is] similar to how [my] **family members** were standing, intending to see me off.'

120. 20:4367.1-2 – Pitati
阿我母弓能 / 和須例母之太波
a-nga [o]möte-nö / *wasure-m-ö sinda pa*
1.S-POSS **face-GEN** / forget-TENT-ATTR CNJ TPT
'When [she] forgets my **countenance**. . .'

121. 14:3382.1-4 – Kamitupusa
宇麻具多能 / 祢呂乃佐左葉能 / 都由思母能 / 奴礼弖和伎奈婆
umanguta-nö / ***ne-rö-nö sasa-PA-nö*** / ***tuyu simö-nö*** / *nure-te wa k-i-n-anba*
TN-GEN / **peak-DIM-GEN bamboo.grass-leaf-GEN** / **dew frost-GEN** / get.wet.INF-SUB 1.S come-INF-PERF-COND
'If I come [to you], wet [with] **dew and frost from the bamboo grass leaves on the peaks of Umaguta**. . .'

Example (121) contains four genitive suffixes, and the genitive in the third line marks the subject of a subordinative clause.

Table 5.10: Attestations of the genitive *-nö* across the provinces.

TSOJ			EOJ							UNP
Sin	Tö	Su	Kak	Mu	Sa	Mi	Sik	Pi	Sip	Kap	
13	11	10	38	16	24	2	20	28	25	20	166

5.4.1.4.3 Analytic genitive construction

Rarely, the genitive *-nö* may be dropped, with the genitive relation expressed solely by noun juxtaposition. This is shown in the following two examples:

122. 20:4380.4-5 – Simotukeno
伊古麻多可祢尓 / 久毛曽多奈妣久
ikoma *taka ne-ni* / *kumo sö tanambik-u*
TN high peak-LOC / cloud FPT stream.out-ATTR
'[I see] clouds streaming out over the high peak **[of] Mt. Ikoma**.'

123. 14:3473.1-2 – UNP
左努夜麻尓 / 宇都也乎能登乃
sano yama-ni / *ut-u ya **wonö** [o]tö-nö*
TN mountain-LOC / strike-ATTR EPT **axe** sound-COMP
'Like the sound **[of] an axe** striking on Sano mountain. . .'

5.4.1.5 Dative/Locative *-ni*

The suffix *-ni* is another very common case marker, in fact it is attested in every topolect except Mitinöku. It has two primary functions and a secondary function. The primary functions are a marker of the dative case and a marker of the locative case ('in', 'at', or 'to'[138]). The secondary function involves attaching to the attributive form of verbs to create a concessive clause which can either indicate reason ('because. . .'), or temporality ('when'). It has the allomorphs -ni and -n-. The allomorph -n- appears due to vowel elision, and it is found before the verb ar- 'exist'. It is also a fusional form that prenasalizes the onset of the following consonant and is quite common when the locative is situated between two nouns.

5.4.1.5.1 Dative function
The dative function is attested a small number of times.

124. 14:3359a.4-5 – Suruga
伊麻思乎多能美 / 波播尔多我比奴
imasi-wo tanöm-i / ***papa-ni*** *tangap-i-n-u*
2.S-ACC trust-NML / **mother-DAT** defy-INF-PERF-FIN
'[I] defied [my] **mother** and put [my] trust in you.'

125. 14:3375.4-5 – Muzasi
伊尔之与比欲利 / 世呂尔安波奈布与
in-i-si yöpi-yori / ***se-rö-ni*** *ap-an-ap-u yö*
depart-INF-PST.ATTR evening-ABL / **beloved.man-DIM-DAT** meet-NEG-ITER-FIN EPT
'Since the evening [he] departed, [I] have not met **my beloved**!'

126. 20:4376.1-4 – Simotukeno
多妣由伎尔 / 由久等之良受弖 / 阿母志志尔 / 己等麻乎佐受弖
tanbi yuk-i-ni / *yuk-u tö sir-anz-u-te* / ***amö sisi-ni*** / *kötö mawos-anz-u-te*
journey go-NML-LOC / go-FIN QUOT know-NEG-INF-SUB / **mother father-DAT** / word say.HUM-NEG-INF-SUB
'[I] did not know that [I] would be going on a journey, and [I] did not inform [my] **mother and father**. . .'

127. 20:4366.5 – Pitati
伊母尔志良世牟
imö-ni *sir-ase-m-u*
beloved.girl-DAT know-CAUS-TENT-FIN
'[It] would let [my] **beloved girl** know [how I feel].'

---

[138] 'to' is more accurately a lative function, but I will subsume it under the category of a locative because it only occurs a few times.

5.4.1.5.2 Locative function

The locative function is widely attested.

128. 14:3352.1-3 – Sinano
 信濃奈流 / 須我能安良能尓 / 保登等藝須
 sinano-n[i] ar-u / ***sunga-nö ara nö-ni*** / *potötöngisu*
 TN-LOC exist-ATTR / TN-GEN wild field-LOC / cuckoo
 'The cuckoo **in the wild fields of Suga in Sinano**...'

In example (128) we see the allomorph *-n* of the locative in the first line.

129. 20:4401.1-4 – Sinano
 可良己呂武 / 須宗尓等里都伎 / 奈古古良乎 / 意伎弖曽伎怒也
 kara körömu / ***suso-ni** tör-i-tuk-i* / *nak-o ko-ra-wo* / *ok-i-te sö k-i-n-o ya*
 TN garment / **hem-LOC** take-INF-attach-INF / cry-ATTR child-PLUR-ACC leave.behind-INF-SUB FPT come-INF-PERF-ATTR EPT
 'Oh, [I] have come [here], leaving behind my sobbing children who clung **to the hem** of [my] Kara robes!'

130. 14:3354.1-3 – Töpotuapumi
 伎倍比等乃 / 萬太良夫須麻尓 / 和多佐波太
 kipey pitö-nö / ***mandara n-busuma-ni*** / *wata sapanda*
 TN person-GEN / **speckled COP.ATTR-bed.covers-LOC** / cotton amply
 '[Like] the cotton [that is] amply [placed] **inside the speckled bed covers** of the people from Kipey...'

131. 20:4322.3-5 – Töpotuapumi
 乃牟美豆尓 / 加其佐倍美曳弖 / 余尓和須良礼受
 *nöm-u **mindu-ni*** / *kangö sapey mi-ye-te* / *yö-ni wasur-are-nz-u*
 drink-ATTR **water-LOC** / shadow RPT see-PASS.INF-SUB / lifetime-LOC forget-PASS-NEG-FIN
 'So much as seeing [her] shadow **in the water** that [I] drink, [makes me realize I] cannot forget her in this lifetime.'

132. 14:3405a.1-4 – Kamitukeno
 可美都氣努 / 乎度能多杼里我 / 可波治尓毛 / 兒良波安波奈毛
 kamitukeyno / *wondo-nö tandöri-nga* / ***kapa-ndi-ni*** *mo* / *KO-ra pa ap-ana-m-o*
 TN / TN-GEN TN-POSS / **river-road-LOC** FPT / girl-DIM TPT meet-DES-TENT-ATTR
 '[I] want [my] darling girl to meet [me] **on** Tadöri's **river road** in Wodo [in] Kamitukeno.'

133. 20:4406.1-2 – Kamitukeno
和我伊**波呂尔** / 由加毛比等母我
*wa-nga **ipa-rö-ni*** / *yuk-am-o pitö mönga*
1.S-POSS **house-DIM-LOC** / go-TENT-ATTR person DPT
'[I] wish someone would go **to my dear home**...'

134. 20:4414.5 – Muzasi
之末**豆**多比由久
***sima-n**-dutap-i-yuk-u*
island-LOC-go.along-INF-go-INF
'[I] will go and pass by **island after island**...'

135. 20:4329.1-2 – Sagamu
夜蘇久尔波 / **奈尔波尔**都度比
ya-so kuni pa / ***nanipa-ni*** *tundop-i*
eight-ten province TPT / **TN-LOC** gather-INF
'[Those from] many provinces gather **in Nanipa**...'

136. 14:3351.1-2 – Pitati
筑波**祢尔** / 由伎可母布良留
*tukupa **ne-ni*** / *yuki kamö pur-ar-u*
TN **peak-LOC** / snow EPT fall-PROG-ATTR
'[I] wonder [if] snow is falling **on Mt.** Tukupa?'

137. 14:3385.4-5 – Simotupusa
麻末乃**於須比尔** / 奈美毛登杼呂尔
*mama-nö **osu-pi-ni*** / *nami mo töndörö n-i*
cliff-GEN **rocky.shore-side-LOC** / wave FPT roaring COP-INF
'Waves were also roaring **on the side of the rocky shore** [near] the cliffs.'

138. 20:4385 – Simotupusa
由古**作枳尔** / 奈美奈等惠良比 / 志流**敝尔**波 / 古乎等都麻乎等 / 於枳弖等母枳奴
*yuk-o **saki-ni*** / *nami na-töwerap-i* / *siru **pe-ni** pa* / *ko-wo-tö tuma-wo-tö* / *ok-i-te tö mö k-i-n-u*
go-ATTR **ahead-LOC** / wave NEG.IMP-shake-INF / behind **area-LOC** TPT / child-ACC-COM spouse-ACC-COM / leave.behind-INF-SUB FPT EPT come-INF-PERF-FIN
'Waves, do not shake [me] **as [I] go ahead**! I left [my] wife and child **behind** to come [out here].'

139. 14:3383.1-2 – Kamitupusa
宇麻具多能 / 祢呂尓可久里為
umanguta-nö / ***ne-rö-ni*** *kakur-i-wi*
TN-GEN / **peak-DIM-LOC** hide-INF-sit.NML
'[I] remain hiding [away] in **the small peak of Umaguta**...'

140. 20:4355 – Kamitupusa
余曽尓能美 / 々弓夜和多良毛 / 奈尓波我多 / 久毛為尓美由流 / 志麻奈良奈久尓
yösö-ni *nömi* / *mi-te ya watar-am-o* / *nanipa-n-gata* / ***kumo wi-ni*** *mi-y-uru* / *sima nar-an-aku n-i*
elsewhere-LOC RPT / see.INF-SUB QPT cross-TENT-ATTR / TN-GEN-tideland / cloud sit.NML-**LOC** see-POT-ATTR / island be-NEG.ATTR-NML COP-INF
'Shall [I] cross over [to the island, even though I] only gazed **into the distance**? Being that it is not an island that [one] can see **through the clouds sitting [over] the Nanipa tidelands**...'

141. 14:3366.1-2 – Sagamu
麻可奈思美 / 佐祢尓和波由久
ma-kanasi-mi / ***sa-ne-ni*** *wa pa yuk-u*
INT-be.dear-AVGER / **LOC-sleep.NML-LOC** 1.S TPT go-ATTR
'Since [she] is truly dear [to me], [I] will go **and sleep** [with her].'

142. 14:3461.1-2 – UNP
安是登伊敝可 / 佐宿尓安波奈久尓
anze tö ip-e ka / ***sa-NE-ni*** *ap-an-aku n-i*
why QUOT say-EV QPT / **LOC-sleep.NML-LOC** meet-NEG.ATTR-NML COP-INF
'Why did [we] not meet **to sleep together**?'

143. 14:3463.1-2 – UNP
麻等保久能 / 野尓毛安波奈牟
ma-töpo-ku nö / ***NO-ni*** *mo ap-ana-m-u*
INT-distant-NML COP.ATTR / **field-LOC** FPT meet-DES-TENT-FIN
'[I] would like to meet [you] **in** the **fields** that are quite a distance [away].'

144. 20:4431 – UNP
佐左賀波乃 / 佐也久志毛<u>用尓</u> / 奈々弁加流 / <u>去呂毛尓</u>麻世流 / 古侶賀波太波毛
sasa-nga pa-nö / *sayak-u simo **yo-ni*** / *nana-pe k-ar-u* / ***körömo-ni** mas-er-u* / *ko-rö-nga panda pa mo*
bamboo.grass-POSS leaf-GEN / rustle-ATTR frost **night-LOC** / seven-CL wear-PROG-ATTR / **robe-LOC** be.superior-PROG-ATTR / girl-DIM-POSS skin TPT EPT
'Oh, [my] darling girl's skin [would] be better than **the robes** [I] am wearing in seven layers **on** [this] frosty **night** when the bamboo grass leaves are rustling!'

5.4.1.5.3 Special temporal construction
The following example shows the locative *-ni* used in a temporal construction, attached to the terminative case *-mande* with the meaning 'until'.

145. 20:4339.3-5 – Suruga
由伎米久利 / <u>加比利久麻弖尓</u> / 已波比弖麻多祢
yuk-i-meyngur-i / ***kapir-i-k-u-mande-ni*** / *ipap-i-te mat-an-e*
go-INF-encircle-INF / **return-INF-come-ATTR-TERM-LOC** / pray-INF-SUB wait-DES-IMP
'Please pray and wait for [me] **until [I] return** from [my travels] around [the provinces].'

5.4.1.5.4 Indicating reason
There is a special usage of the locative *-ni* that is only possible when this suffix attaches to the attributive form of a verb or adjectival verb. It indicates a reason for the action, something akin to 'since' or 'because'.

146. 14:3411.5 – Kamitukeno
曽能可抱<u>与吉尓</u>
*sönö kapo **yö-ki-ni***
that face **be.good-AVATTR-LOC**
'**Since** that [hidden] face [of his] **is handsome**...'

147. 20:4330.3-5 – Sagamu
氣布能比夜 / 伊田弖麻可良武 / 美流波々**奈之尓**
keypu-nö pi ya / *inde-te makar-am-u* / *mi-ru papa **na-si-ni***
today-GEN day QPT / go.out.INF-SUB depart-TENT-ATTR / see-ATTR mother **not.exist-AVFIN-LOC**
'[I wonder], will [we] depart and [sail] out today? [I ask] **because [my] mother is not here** to watch. . .'

148. 14:3442.4-5 – UNP
夜麻尓可祢牟毛 / 夜杼里波**奈之尓**
yama-ni ka ne-m-u mo / *yandör-i pa **na-si-ni***
mountain-LOC QPT sleep-TENT-ATTR FPT / lodge-NML **not.exist-AVFIN-LOC**
'Shall [I] sleep in the mountains, **since there is no** lodging [here]?'

In examples (147) and (148) the second -*ni* is suffixed to the final adjectival verb suffix -*si*, rather than the adjectival verb attributive suffix -*ki* ~ -*ke*. This is a special feature unique to the adjectival verb *na*- 'not exist'.

149. 14.3461.3-5 – UNP
真日久礼弖 / 与比奈波**許奈尓** / 安家奴思太久流
MA-PI kure-te / *yöpi-na pa **kö-na-ni*** / *ake-n-o sinda k-uru*
INT-sun grow.dark.INF-SUB / evening-LOC TPT **come-NEG.ATTR-LOC** / dawn.INF-PERF-ATTR CNJ come-ATTR
'[It is] **because [you] did not come** during the evening after the bright sun set. [You only] came when it dawned.'

Table 5.11: Attestations of the dative/locative -*ni* across the provinces.

TSOJ			EOJ								UNP
Sin	Tö	Su	Kak	Mu	Sa	Mi	Sik	Pi	Sip	Kap	
5	5	10	22	13	10	0	10	16	11	15	97

5.4.1.6 Locative -*na*

The locative -*na* is attested in the Kamitukeno topolect of EOJ and in UNP. It is not attested in WOJ (Vovin 2005: 151) or TSOJ,[139] but the PR *-*na* distributive locative is

---

[139] There is a possibility example (152) was written in the Suruga topolect of TSOJ, based on the placename Ano (Mizushima 1986: 217).

a cognate (Thorpe 1983: 212–213). In EOJ this suffix means 'to' or 'over (something)' on a spatial noun, whereas when attached to a temporal noun it means 'during' or 'throughout' (similar to its function in the Ryukyuan languages).

150. 20:4407.1-3 – Kamitukeno
比奈久毛理 / 宇須比乃佐可乎 / 古延志太尓
***pi-na** kumor-i / usupi-nö saka-wo / koye sinda-ni*
sun-LOC become.cloudy-INF / TN-GEN slope-ACC / cross.INF CNJ-LOC
'When [I] crossed Usupi hill with clouds **over the sun**...'

151. 14:3461.4 – UNP
与比奈波許奈尓
***yöpi-na** pa kö-na-ni*
evening-LOC TPT come-NEG.ATTR-LOC
'[It is] because [you] did not come **during the evening**...'

152. 14:3447.2 – UNP
安努奈由可武等
***ano-na** yuk-am-u tö*
TN-LOC go-TENT-FIN QUOT
'[I] thought that [I] would go **to Ano**.'

5.4.1.6.1 Special construction *-ana-na*

This construction means 'without' or 'not (doing)'. It consists of the EOJ negative-attributive suffix *-ana* (§7.5.2.3.1.1) and the locative *-na*. The identification of the locative *-na* in this construction was first made by Thorpe (1983: 242), who compared it to the similar PR construction *-aⁿda-na. This construction is semantically distinct from the EOJ construction *-ana-ni* '-NEG.ATTR-LOC', which means 'because not (doing)'. Both constructions were analogically levelled out in WOJ, replaced by *-anz-u n-i* -NEG-INF COP-INF 'without (doing)' and *-an-u-ni* -NEG-ATTR-LOC 'because not (doing)'.

153. 14.3408.2 – Kamitukeno
祢尓波都可奈那
*ne-ni pa tuk-**ana-na***
peak-LOC TPT reach-**NEG.ATTR-LOC**
'**Without** reaching the peak...'

154. 14.3436.4-5 – Kamitukeno
宇良尓賀礼勢奈那 / 登許波尓毛我母
ura-n-gare se-na-na / *tökö pa n-i mongamö*
top.branch-GEN-wither.NML do-NEG.ATTR-LOC / eternal leaf COP-INF DPT
'I wish [the trees] had eternal leaves, **without withered top branches**.'

155. 14.3487.4-5 – UNP
宿莫奈那里尓思 / 於久乎可奴加奴
NE-NA-na nar-i-n-i-si / *oku-wo kan-u kan-u*
sleep-NEG.ATTR-LOC become-INF-PERF-INF-PST.ATTR / future-ACC worry.about-FIN worry.about-FIN
'[I] worry about [our] future again and again, [because] it turned out that [we] **did not sleep** [together].'

156. 14:3557.4-5 – UNP
和須礼波勢奈那 / 伊夜母比麻須尓
wasure pa se-na-na / *iya [o]möp-i mas-u-ni*
forget.NML TPT do-NEG.ATTR-LOC / more.and.more think-NML increase-ATTR-LOC
'[I] think of [her] more and more, **without forgetting** [anything about her].'

Table 5.12: Attestations of the locative *-na* across the provinces.

TSOJ			EOJ								UNP
Sin	Tö	Su	Kak	Mu	Sa	Mi	Sik	Pi	Sip	Kap	
0	0	0	3	0	0	0	0	0	0	0	4

5.4.1.7 Genitive-locative *-tu*

The genitive-locative *-tu* is attested in TSOJ and in UNP. Due to the scarcity of this suffix in the texts, Vovin considers AOJ *-tu* to be a loan from WOJ (Vovin 2005: 157). An alternate explanation is that it was simply no longer productive, and since it was clearly not widely generalized in PJe, it was fossilized in just a few phrases by the time the AOJ poems were recorded.

157. 14:3448.1-2 – UNP
波奈治良布 / 己能牟可都乎乃
pana-n-dir-ap-u / *könö* **muka-tu** *wo nö*
flower-GEN-scatter-ITER-ATTR / this **opposite.side-GEN.LOC** mountain.ridge COP.ATTR
'It is the mountain ridge **across the way**, where the flowers are scattering.'

158. 14:3493a.3-5 – UNP
牟可都乎能 / 四比乃故夜提能 / 安比波多我波自
muka-tu *wo-nö* / *sipi-nö ko-yande-nö* / *ap-i pa tangap-anzi*
opposite.side-GEN.LOC mountain.ridge-GEN / chinquapin-GEN DIM-branch-COMP / meet-NML TPT differ-NEG.TENT
'[Our] meeting shall be indistinguishable from how the small branches of the chinquapin trees on the mountain ridge **across the way** [touch each other].'

159. 14:3524.4-5 – UNP
於吉都麻可母能 / 奈氣伎曽安我須流
oki-tu *ma-kamö-nö* / *nangeyk-i sö a-nga s-uru*
offing-GEN.LOC INT-duck-COMP / lament-NML FPT 1.S-POSS do-ATTR
'Like the ducks **in the offing**, [I] lament…'

Table 5.13: Attestations of the genitive-locative *-tu* across the provinces.

TSOJ			EOJ								UNP
Sin	Tö	Su	Kak	Mu	Sa	Mi	Sik	Pi	Sip	Kap	
0	1	0	3	0	0	0	0	0	0	0	3

5.4.1.8 Ablative *-yori ~ -yuri ~ -yo ~ -yu*

The ablative case indicates the origin of an action. There are four orthographic forms of this case marker: *-yori*, *-yuri*, *-yo*, and *-yu*. The form *-yo* is also attested once in a comparative function and the form *-yu* is attested once in an instrumental function, but in most cases there is no functional difference between the four forms. Thus, I view the forms *-yo* and *-yu* as contracted variants of *-yori* and *-yuri*, respectively, though Vovin (2005: 179) convincingly argues that *-yo* and *-yu* are the original forms, so my use of the term "contracted variant" is in a purely synchronic sense. It is possible the contracted forms *-yo* and *-yu* were used to avoid hypermetrical lines because none of the four attested forms occur in a hypermetrical line. Further supporting this is the fact that while *-yuri* is restricted to just two attestations in topolects that lack attestations of other ablative forms, the other three forms appear to coexist in free variation in some topolects.

I do not view these as allomorphs of a single morpheme, since allomorphy is confined within the domain of a single language variety. The fact that some forms are attested only in certain topolects, paired with the free variation exhibited among the forms, prevents us from labelling these variants as allomorphs in TSOJ or EOJ. The original form was likely *yo, which acquired a formant *ri (Itabashi 1991) and raised to /yuri/ in some dialects, or optionally raised to /yu/, without the additional *ri, in some dialects. Thorpe (1983: 214–215) earlier proposed a distributive morpheme *-ri in Proto-Ryukyuan, and I think this is plausible for the etymology of AOJ *-yuri* ~ *-yori*.

5.4.1.8.1 Examples of *-yori*
The form *-yori* is attested twice.

160. 14:3375.4-5 – Muzasi
 伊尓之**与比欲利** / 世呂尓安波奈布与
 in-i-si **yöpi-yori** / *se-rö-ni ap-an-ap-u yö*
 depart-INF-PST.ATTR **evening-ABL** / beloved.man-DIM-DAT meet-NEG-ITER-FIN EPT
 '**Since** the **evening** he departed, [I] have not met [my] beloved!'

161. 20:4373.1-2 – Simotukeno
 祁布**与利**波 / 可敝理見奈久弖
 kepu-yöri *pa* / *kaper-i-MI na-ku-te*
 today-ABL TPT / return-INF-see.NML not.exist-INF-SUB
 '**From today**, without looking back. . .'

Example (161) shows a misspelling as *-yöri*.

5.4.1.8.2 Examples of *-yuri*

162. 20:4321.3-4 – Töpotuapumi
 阿須**由利**也 / 加曳我牟多祢牟
 asu-yuri *ya* / *kaye-nga muta ne-m-u*
 tomorrow-ABL QPT / reed-POSS together sleep-TENT-ATTR
 'Will [I] sleep among the reeds **from tomorrow**?'

163. 20:4365.2-3 – Pitati
    奈尔波能**都由利** / 布奈与曽比
    *nanipa-nö **tu-yuri** / puna yösöp-i*
    TN-GEN **harbor-ABL** / boat prepare-INF
    '[I] prepared the boat [to depart] **from** Nanipa **harbor**.'

5.4.1.8.3 Examples of -*yo*

164. 14:3417.4-5 – Kamitukeno
    与曽尓**見之欲**波 / 伊麻許曽麻左礼
    *yösö-ni **MI-si-yo** pa / ima kösö mas-ar-e*
    elsewhere-LOC **see.INF-PST.ATTR-ABL** TPT / now FPT be.superior-PROG-EV
    'Now [things] are better **than [when I] was looking** elsewhere.'

Example (164) demonstrates the ablative -*yo* used in a comparative function.

165. 14:3425.1-4 – Simotukeno
    志母都家努 / 安素乃**河泊良欲** / 伊之布麻努受 / 蘓良由登伎努与
    *simötukeno / aso-nö **kapara-yo** / isi pum-anz-u / sora-yu tö k-i-n-o yö*
    TN / TN-GEN **river.bank-ABL** / stone step-NEG-INF / sky-ABL FPT come-INF-PERF-ATTR EPT
    '[I] came from the sky without stepping [on] the stones **from the riverbank of Aso in Simotukeno**!'

5.4.1.8.4 Examples of -*yu*

166. 14:3425.3-4 – Simotukeno
    伊之布麻受 / **蘓良由**登伎努与
    *isi pum-anz-u / **sora-yu** tö k-i-n-o yö*
    stone step-NEG-INF / **sky-ABL** FPT come-INF-PERF-ATTR EPT
    '[I] came **from the sky** without stepping [on] the stones!'

The ablative -*yu* may also be used in an instrumental function, as example (167) shows:

167. 20:4417.4-5 – Muzasi
多麻能余許夜麻 / **加志由**加也良牟
tama-nö yökö yama / ***kasi-yu*** *ka yar-am-u*
TN-GEN horizontal mountain / **go.on.foot-ABL** QPT send-TENT-ATTR
'Shall [I] send [my beloved to traverse] Tama's flat mountain **on foot**?'

Table 5.14: Attestations of the ablative *-yori* ~ *-yuri* ~ *-yo* ~ *-yu* across the provinces.

Form	TSOJ			EOJ								UNP
	Sin	Tö	Su	Kak	Mu	Sa	Mi	Sik	Pi	Sip	Kap	
-yori	0	0	0	0	1	0	0	1	1	0	0	0
-yuri	0	1	0	0	0	0	0	0	1	0	0	0
-yo	0	0	0	1	0	0	0	1	0	0	0	1
-yu	0	0	0	0	1	0	0	1	0	0	0	3

The Simotukeno topolect of EOJ is notable for showing three forms (*-yori*, *-yo*, and *-yu*), and even including more than one form in a single poem (14:3425). It is somewhat surprising that the uncontracted forms *-yori* and *-yuri* are unattested in the large UNP corpus.

5.4.1.9 Ablative *-kara*

The ablative *-kara* is attested just once (Yamada 1954: 470).

168. 14:3541.1-3 – UNP
安受**倍可良** / 古麻能由胡能須 / 安也波刀文
*anzu **pey-kara***[140] / *koma-nö yuk-o-nösu* / *ayapa tomo*
crumbling.cliffs **side-ABL** / horse-GEN go-ATTR-COMP / dangerous CNJ
'Even though [it] is as dangerous as riding my horse **from the side** of the crumbling cliffs. . .'

5.4.1.10 Allative *-pe* ~ *-pa*

The allative is attested twice as *-pe* and once as *-pa*. As reflexes of PJe *pia, *-pa* is the expected form in EOJ, and *-pe* ~ *-pi* is the expected form in TSOJ (though it is unattested in those topolects). The attestations of *-pe* in EOJ are thus best explained

---

[140] An alternative interpretation is *anzu [u]pey-kara* crumbling.cliffs above-ABL 'from above the crumbling cliffs.'

as the result of borrowing from TSOJ or WOJ, or due to other WOJ influence in the text. The form *-pa* is unattested in WOJ.

169. 20:4422.1-2 – Muzasi
和我世奈乎 / 都久之倍夜里弓
wa-nga se-na-wo / **tukusi-pey** *yar-i-te*
1.S-POSS beloved.man-DIM-ACC / **TN-ALL** send-INF-SUB
'[I] sent my dearly beloved **to Tukusi**. . .'

170. 14:3363.1-2 – Sagamu
和我世古乎 / 夜麻登敞夜利弓
wa-nga se-ko-wo / **yamatö-pe** *yar-i-te*
1.S-POSS beloved.man-DIM-ACC / **TN-ALL** send-INF-SUB
'[I] sent [my] dearly beloved **to Yamato**. . .'

171. 20:4428.1-2 – UNP
和我世奈乎 / 都久志波夜利弓
wa-nga se-na-wo / **tukusi-pa** *yar-i-te*
1.S-POSS beloved.man-DIM-ACC / **TN-ALL** send-INF-SUB
'[I] sent my dearly beloved **to Tukusi**. . .'

Table 5.15: Attestations of the allative *-pe* ~ *-pa* across the provinces.

Form	TSOJ			EOJ								UNP
	Sin	Tö	Su	Kak	Mu	Sa	Mi	Sik	Pi	Sip	Kap	
-pe	0	0	0	0	1	1	0	0	0	0	0	0
-pa	0	0	0	0	0	0	0	0	0	0	0	1

5.4.1.11 Terminative *-mande*

The terminative case marker *-mande* indicates the end point of an action. It is difficult to conclude whether it was really part of the nominal declension because in all attestations it only attaches to the attributive form of a verb, as noted by Vovin (2005: 196). This is somewhat peculiar, as every other case suffix in the corpus is attested attached to a noun root at least once, and it is attested in WOJ attached to noun roots. Perhaps this indicates the grammaticalization of *-mande* was not complete in the AOJ dialects, and *-mande* still functioned as a bound, postposed noun. Or perhaps it is simply the byproduct of the size of the corpus.

Another peculiarity of this suffix in AOJ is that, unlike in WOJ, it is never attested after the attributive allomorph -*uru*, even in cases in which we would expect to find that allomorph.

This is the only case suffix that may be followed by the locative -*ni*, which is more evidence for its original postpositional (or nominal) status.

172. 20:4326.4-5 – Töpotuapumi
母々与伊弖麻勢 / 和我**伎多流麻弖**
mömö yö inde-mas-e / *wa-nga **k-i-tar-u-mande***
hundred year go.out.INF-HON-IMP / 1.S-POSS **come-INF-PP-ATTR-TERM**
'[I] hope [my parents] will live for a hundred years, **until I return** [to them]!'

173. 20:4339.4-5 – Suruga
加比利久麻弖尓 / 已波比弖麻多祢
***kapir-i-k-u-mande**-ni* / *ipap-i-te mat-an-e*
return-INF-come-ATTR-TERM-LOC / pray-INF-SUB wait-DES-IMP
'Please pray and wait for [me] **until [I] return**.'

In example (173) above and examples (174) – (176) below, we see the form *k-u-mande* 'come-ATTR-TERM', instead of the expected *k-uru-mande*. See §7.4.3.2 for a discussion.

174. 14:3414 – Kamitukeno
伊香保呂能 / 夜左可能為提尓 / 多都努自能 / **安良波路萬代**母 / 佐祢乎佐祢弖婆
ikapo-rö-nö / *ya-saka-nö winde-ni* / *tat-u nonzi-nö* / ***arapar-o-mande** mö* / *sa-ne-wo sa-ne-te-nba*
TN-DIM-GEN / eight-CL-GEN dam-LOC / rise-ATTR rainbow-GEN / **appear-ATTR-TERM** FPT / LOC-sleep.NML-ACC LOC-sleep.INF-PERF-COND
'If [only I] had slept there [with you], **until** a rainbow **appeared** over the tall dam in Ikapo...'

175. 20:4404.1-2 – Kamitukeno
奈尓波治乎 / 由伎弖**久麻弖**等
nanipa-ndi-wo / *yuk-i-te **k-u-mande** tö*
TN-road-ACC / go-INF-SUB **come-ATTR-TERM** QUOT
'**Until** [I] returned [from my] journey on Nanipa road...'

176. 20:4372.15 – Pitati
可閇利久麻弖尓
kapeyr-i-k-u-mande-ni
return-INF-come-ATTR-TERM-LOC
'Until [I] return…'

177. 20:4350.5 – Kamitupusa
加倍理久麻泥尓
kapeyr-i-k-u-mande-ni
return-INF-come-ATTR-TERM-LOC
'Until [I] return…'

178. 14:3448.3-5 – UNP
乎那能乎能 / 比自尓**都久麻提** / 伎美我与母賀母
*wona-nö wo-nö / pinzi-ni **tuk-u-mande** / kimi-nga yö möngamö*
TN-GEN mountain.ridge-GEN / sandbar-LOC **reach-ATTR-TERM** / lord-POSS life DPT
'[I] want [my] lord's life [to last] **until** the Wona mountain ridge **reaches** a sandbar.'

179. 14:3458.4-5 – UNP
安乎祢思奈久与 / **伊久豆君麻弖**尓
*a-wo ne si nak-u yö / **ikunduk-u-mande**-ni*
1.S-ACC voice EPT make.cry-FIN EPT / **sigh-ATTR-TERM**-LOC
'[It] makes me cry out loud, **until [I] heave a sigh**!'

180. 14:3494.1-3 – UNP
兒毛知夜麻 / 和可加敞流弖能 / **毛美都麻弖**
*KOmoti yama / waka kaperute-nö / **momit-u-mande***
TN mountain / young maple-GEN / **leaves.turn.color-ATTR-TERM**
'**Until** the young maples [on] Komoti mountain **turn red**…'

Table 5.16: Attestations of the terminative -*mande* across the provinces.

TSOJ			EOJ								UNP
Sin	Tö	Su	Kak	Mu	Sa	Mi	Sik	Pi	Sip	Kap	
0	1	2	2	0	0	0	0	1	0	1	3

5.4.1.12 Comitative -*tö*

The comitative case suffix -*tö* marker has a meaning that translates roughly to 'with' or 'together with'. It may also function as an instrumental marker in certain contexts, as shown in example (183) below.

181. 20:4324 – Töpotuapumi
 等倍多保美 / 志留波乃**伊宗等** / 尓問乃**宇良等** / 安比弓之阿良婆 / 己等母加由波牟
 töpeytapomi / *sirupa-nö* ***iso-tö*** / *nipey-nö* ***ura-tö*** / *ap-i-te si ar-anba* / *kötö mö kayup-am-u*
 TN / TN-GEN **rocky.shore-COM** / TN-GEN **bay-COM** / meet-INF-SUB EPT exist-COND / word FPT go.back.and.forth-TENT-FIN
 'If only Töpeytapomi's **rocky shore** of Sirupa and Nipey **bay** were close **to one another**! [Then we] could exchange words...'

182. 20:4345.1-4 – Suruga
 和伎米故等 / 不多利和我見之 / 宇知江須流 / 々々河乃祢良波
 wa-ng-imey-ko-tö / *puta-ri wa-nga MI-si* / *uti-yes-uru* / *surunga-nö ne-ra pa*
 1.S-POSS-beloved.girl-DIM-COM / *two-CL* 1.S-POSS see.INF-PST.ATTR PREF-approach-ATTR / TN-GEN peak-PLUR TPT
 'The peaks of Suruga, where [the waves] crash, which I gazed upon **with my darling girl**...'

183. 20:4420.4-5 – Muzasi
 安我**弓等**都氣呂 / 許礼乃波流母志
 a-nga ***te-tö*** *tukey-rö* / *köre nö paru mös-i*
 REFL-POSS **hand-COM** attach-IMP / this COP.ATTR needle hold-INF
 'Hold this needle and attach [the cords] **with** your own **hands**.'

184. 20:4385.3-5 – Simotupusa
 志流敝尓波 / **古乎等都麻乎等** /於枳弓等母枳奴
 siru pe-ni pa / ***ko-wo-tö tuma-wo-tö*** / *ok-i-te tö mö k-i-n-u*
 behind area-LOC TPT / **child-ACC-COM spouse-ACC-COM** / leave.behind-INF-SUB FPT EPT come-INF-PERF-FIN
 '[I] left [my] **wife and child** behind to come [out here].'

Example (184) shows double case marking in the order -ACC-COM.

185. 14:3444.5 – UNP
西奈等都麻佐祢
se-na-tö tum-as-an-e
beloved.man-DIM-COM pluck-CAUS-DES-IMP
'Please let [me] pluck [them] **with [my] dearly beloved**!'

186. 14:3544.4-5 – UNP
勢奈那登布多理 / 左宿而久也思母
se-na-na-tö puta-ri / sa-NE-TE kuyasi-mö
beloved.man-DIM-DIM-COM two-CL / LOC-sleep.INF-SUB be.regretful.AVFIN-EXCL
'[I] slept there **with [my] dear, darling beloved**, [and now I] regret it!'

187. 14:3450.1-4 – UNP
乎久左乎等 / 乎具佐受家乎等 / 斯抱布祢乃 / 那良敝弖美礼婆
wokusa wo-tö / **wongusa-n-suke-wo-tö** / sipo pune-nö / naranbe-te mi-re-nba
TN man-COM / **TN-GEN-help-man-COM** / tide boat-COMP / line.up.INF-SUB see-EV-CONJ
'When [I] see **the man [from] Wokusa and the assistant [from] Wogusa** lined up like tide boats. . .'

188. 14:3492.4-5 – UNP
奈里毛奈良受毛 / **奈等**布多里波毛
nar-i mo nar-anz-u mo / **na-tö** puta-ri pa mo
be-INF FPT be-NEG-INF FPT / **2.S-COM** two-CL TPT FPT
'Whatever may be, at least [I shall be] **with you**!'

Table 5.17: Attestations of the comitative -tö across the provinces.

	TSOJ				EOJ						UNP
Sin	Tö	Su	Kak	Mu	Sa	Mi	Sik	Pi	Sip	Kap	
0	2	1	0	1	0	0	0	0	3	0	7

5.4.1.13 Comparatives -nösu ~ -nasu and -nö

There are three comparative suffixes in the corpus: -nösu, -nasu, and -nö. While there are distributional differences between them, there does not appear to be any difference in meaning.

5.4.1.13.1 Examples of -nasu

The form -nasu is only attested three times: once in TSOJ and twice in UNP. This is the widely attested WOJ form of the suffix, so it is probable that one or more of the UNP examples are due to WOJ influence, unless they are written in a TSOJ topolect.

189. 14:3358c.4-5 – Suruga
布自乃多可祢尓 / 布流<u>由伎奈須</u>毛
punzi-nö taka ne-ni / pur-u **yuki-nasu** mo
TN-GEN high peak-LOC / fall-ATTR snow-COMP FPT
'**Like the snow** that falls on the high peak of Mt. Puzi...'

190. 14:3531.3-5 – UNP
麻欲婢吉能 / 与許夜麻敝呂能 / <u>**思之奈須於母敝流**</u>
mayo-n-bik-i-nö / yökö yama pe-rö-nö / **sisi-nasu omöp-er-u**
eyebrow-GEN-pull-NML-COMP / horizontal mountain area-DIM-GEN / **wild. animal-COMP think-PROG-ATTR**
'[She] **likens [me] to a wild beast** of the low mountainous area that stretches out like eyebrows...'

191. 14:3548.1-2 – UNP
奈流世呂尓 / 木都能<u>余須奈須</u>
nar-u se-rö-ni / KÖtu-nö **yös-u-nasu**
make.sound-ATTR rapids-DIM-LOC / tree.debris-GEN **approach-ATTR-COMP**
'**Like** the tree debris **approaching** the roaring rapids...'

5.4.1.13.2 Examples of -nösu

The comparative suffix -nösu is exclusive to EOJ[141] and can be projected back to Proto-EOJ. However, only three EOJ topolects have this form attested, with most of the attestations being from UNP. In all examples except (194) it occurs after the attributive form of a verb, so its usage as a comparative of attributivized verbs appears to be the primary function, as noted by Hendricks (1994: 246).

---

[141] Hendricks (1994: 244) and Vovin (2005: 203–204) mention a WOJ attestation in KK, but I do not find this to be a convincing example.

192. 14:3413.4-5 – Kamitukeno
奈美尓**安布能須** / 安敝流伎美可母
*nami-ni **ap-u-nösu*** / *ap-er-u kimi kamö*
wave-DAT **meet-ATTR-COMP** / meet-PROG-ATTR lord EPT
'Oh, meeting [you, my] lord, [is] **like encountering** a wave!'

193. 20:4415.1-3 – Muzasi
志良多麻乎 / 弖尓刀里母之弖 / **美流乃須**母
sira tama-wo / *te-ni tor-i-mös-i-te* / ***mi-ru-nösu*** *mö*
white pearl-ACC / hand-LOC take-INF-hold-INF-GER / **see-ATTR-COMP** FPT
'**Like gazing** at the pearls [I] have taken up in [my] hands...'

194. 14:3424.1-4 – Simotukeno
之母都家野 / 美可母乃夜麻能 / **許奈良能須** / 麻具波思兒呂波
simötukeNO / *mikamö-nö yama-nö* / ***kö-nara-nösu*** / *ma n-gupasi KO-rö pa*
TN / TN-GEN mountain-GEN / **DIM-oak-COMP** / true COP.INF-be.beautiful girl-DIM TPT
'[This] truly beautiful girl [who is] **like a little oak** on the mountain of Mikamo in Simotukeno...'

195. 14:3514.1-4 – UNP
多可伎祢尓 / 久毛能**都久能須** / 和礼左倍尓 / 伎美尓都吉奈那
taka-ki ne-ni / *kumo-nö **tuk-u-nösu*** / *ware sapey n-i* / *kimi-ni tuk-i-n-ana*
be.high-AVATTR peak-LOC / cloud-GEN **reach-ATTR-COMP** / 1.S RPT COP-INF / lord-LOC attach-INF-PERF-DES
'**Like** [how] clouds **reach** the high mountain peaks, even I have wanted to be close to [you, my] lord.'

196. 14:3541.1-3 – UNP
安受倍可良 / 古麻能**由胡能須** / 安也波刀文
anzu pey-kara / *koma-nö **yuk-o-nösu*** / *ayapa tomo*
crumbling.cliffs area-ABL / horse-GEN **go-ATTR-COMP** / dangerous CNJ
'Even though it is as dangerous **as riding** [my] horse from the edge of crumbling cliffs...'

197. 14:3561.3-5 – UNP
比賀刀礼婆 / 阿米乎**万刀能須** / 伎美乎等麻刀母
pi-nga tor-e-nba / *amey-wo* **mat-o-nösu** / *kimi-wo tö mat-o mö*
sun-POSS shine-EV-CONJ / rain-ACC **wait-ATTR-COMP** / lord-ACC FPT wait-ATTR EPT
'[I] wait for [you, my] lord, **as [one] waits** for the rain when the sun is shining.'

5.4.1.13.3 Examples of -*nö*

The comparative -*nö* is the most common of all the comparative forms, and it is attested in both EOJ and TSOJ. It is also well attested in WOJ. It appears after nominalized verbs and nouns, but unlike the comparatives -*nasu* and -*nösu*, it is unattested after the attributive form of verbs. This seems to be the primary distributional difference between the two forms in the AOJ dialects.

198. 20:4337.1-2 – Suruga
美豆等利乃 / **多知能**已蘇岐尔
mindu töri-nö / **tat-i-nö** *isong-i n-i*
water bird-GEN / **rise-NML-COMP** hurry-NML COP-INF
'Being in a rush [to leave], **like the ascent** of waterfowl...'

199. 14:3423.1-4 – Kamitukeno
可美都氣努 / 伊可抱乃祢呂尔 / 布路<u>与伎能</u> / 遊吉須宜可提奴
kamitukeyno / *ikapo-nö ne-rö-ni* / *pur-o* **yöki-nö** / *yuk-i-sungï-kande-n-u*
TN / TN-GEN peak-DIM-LOC / fall-ATTR **snow-COMP** / go-INF-pass.INF-POT-NEG-ATTR
'**Like** the falling **snow** on the peak of Ikapo in Kamitukeno, [I] cannot go past [it].'

200. 14:3376a.4-5 – Muzasi
宇家良我**波奈乃** / 伊呂尔豆奈由米
ukera-nga **pana-nö** / *irö-ni [i]nd-una yumey*
ukera-POSS **flower-COMP** / color/feelings-LOC go.out-NEG.IMP at.all
'**Like** the *ukera* **flowers**, do not let [your] face reveal even a hint of [your] true feelings [for me]!'

201. 14:3370.1-4 – Sagamu
安思我里乃 / 波故祢能祢呂乃 / 尓古**具佐能** / 波奈都豆麻奈礼也
asingari-nö / *pakone-nö ne-rö-nö* / *niko **n-gusa-nö*** / *pana tutu ma nar-e ya*
TN-GEN / TN-GEN peak-DIM-GEN / soft **COP.ATTR-grass-COMP** / flower earth wife be-EV QPT
'Are [you] a wife [who is] a flower of the earth, **like** the soft **grass** on the small peak of Pakone in Asigari? (Certainly not!)'

202. 20:4369 – Pitati
都久波祢乃 / **佐由流能波奈能** / 由等許尓母 / 可奈之家伊母曽 / 比留毛可奈之祁
tukupa ne-nö / ***sa-yuru-nö pana-nö*** / *yu tökö-ni mö* / *kanasi-ke imö sö* / *piru mo kanasi-ke*
TN peak-GEN / **LOC-lily-GEN flower-COMP** / night bed-LOC FPT / be.dear-AVATTR beloved.girl FPT / daytime FPT be.dear-AVATTR
'**Like the blossoms of a lily on the peaks of Mt. Tukupa**, [my] beloved girl, who is dear [to me] in bed at night, is also dear [to me] during the day.'

203. 20:4352 – Kamitupusa
美知乃倍乃 / 宇万良能宇礼尓 / 波保**麻米乃** / 可良麻流伎美乎 / 波可礼加由加牟
miti-nö pey-nö / *umara-nö ure-ni* / *pap-o **mamey-nö*** / *karam-ar-u kimi-wo* / *pakare ka yuk-am-u*
road-GEN side-GEN / briar-GEN tip-LOC / crawl-ATTR **bean-COMP** / wrap.around-PROG-ATTR lord-ACC / separate.from.INF QPT go-TENT-ATTR
'Should [I] go, separating from [you, my] lord, whom [I] wrap around **like the beans** that crawl on the tips of the briar on the side of the road?'

204. 14:3453.1-2 – UNP
可是能**等乃** / 登抱吉和伎母賀
*kanze-nö [o]**tö-nö*** / *töpo-ki wa-ng[a]-imö-nga*
wind-GEN **sound-COMP** / be.far-AVATTR 1.S-POSS-beloved.girl-POSS
'My beloved girl, who is far away **like the sound** of the wind. . .'

205. 14:3473.1-2 – UNP
左努夜麻尓 / 宇都也乎能**登乃**
sano yama-ni / *ut-u ya wonö [o]**tö-nö***
TN mountain-LOC / strike-ATTR EPT axe **sound-COMP**
'**Like the sound** of an axe striking on Sano mountain. . .'

206. 14:3493a.3-4 – UNP
牟可都乎能 / 四比乃**故夜提能**
*muka-tu wo-nö / sipi-nö **ko-yande-nö***
opposite.side-GEN.LOC mountain.ridge-GEN / chinquapin-GEN **DIM-branch-COMP**
'Like the **little branches** of the chinquapin trees on the mountain ridge across the way...'

Table 5.18: Attestations of the comparatives *-nasu* ~ *-nösu* ~ *-nö* across the provinces.

Form	TSOJ			EOJ								UNP
	Sin	Tö	Su	Kak	Mu	Sa	Mi	Sik	Pi	Sip	Kap	
-nasu	0	0	1	0	0	0	0	0	0	0	0	2
-nösu	0	0	0	1	1	0	0	1	0	0	0	5
-nö	0	0	2	1	2	5	0	0	1	1	3	37

5.4.1.13.4 Analytic comparative constructions

There are also purely analytic (periphrastic) means of expressing a comparative relation, in lieu of any morphology, though they are uncommon in the corpus.

207. 14:3509.1-2 – UNP
多久夫須麻 / 之良夜麻可是
taku-n-busuma / *sira yama kanze*
paper.mulberry-GEN-bed.covers / white mountain wind
'Wind from the white mountain, **[that is like] bed covers [made] of paper mulberry [cloth]**...'

208. 14:3392 – Pitati
筑波祢能 / 伊波毛等杼呂尔 / 於都留美豆 / 代尔毛多由良尔 / 和我於毛波奈久尔
tukupa ne-nö / ipa mo töndörö n-i / ot-uru mindu / YÖ-ni mo tayura n-i / wa-nga omop-an-aku n-i
TN peak-GEN / rock FPT thunderous COP-INF / fall-ATTR water / lifetime-LOC FPT wavering COP-INF / 1.S-POSS think-NEG.ATTR-NML COP-INF
'**[Like] the water that falls thunderously amid the rocks of the peaks of Mt. Tukupa**, I do not think that [I will] waver [in my love for you] in [my] lifetime.'

209. 20:4387.1-3 – Simotupusa
知波乃奴乃 / 古乃弖加之波能 / 保々麻例等
tipa-nö nu-nö / **ko-nö te** *kasipa-nö* / *popom-ar-e-ndö*
TN-GEN field-GEN / **child-GEN hand** oak-GEN / be.unopened-PROG-EV-CONC
'Although [the buds of] the oak trees in Tiba field, with leaves **[like] a child's hand**, have not yet blossomed. . .'

5.4.1.14 Directive *-ka* ~ *-ngari*

The directive case indicates a motion toward someone. There are two suffixes in the corpus: *-ka* and *-ngari*.

5.4.1.14.1 Example of *-ka*

The directive *-ka* is only attested once, in EOJ. I propose it is cognate with the Proto-Ryukyuan allative *-ka (Thorpe 1983: 214). This suffix is not attested in WOJ or TSOJ.

210. 20:4387.4-5 – Simotupusa
阿夜尓加奈之美 / 於枳弖他加枳奴
aya n-i kanasi-mi / *ok-i-te **ta-ka** k-i-n-u*
mysterious COP-INF be.dear-GER / leave.behind-INF-SUB **rice.field-DIR** come-INF-PERF-FIN
'[I] left [her] behind and came **to the rice field**, because [she] is mysteriously dear [to me].'

5.4.1.14.2 Examples of *-ngari*

The directive case marker *-ngari* is attested three times. Historically, it was formed with the directive *-ka* and the same *-ri* formant in the ablative pair *-yo* ~ *yori*. The initial voicing of *k > /ng/ seems to be secondary. It is not phonographically attested in WOJ (Vovin 2005: 188).

211. 14:3536.4-5 – UNP
伊可奈流勢奈可 / 和我理許武等伊布
ika nar-u se-na ka / ***wa**-**ngari** kö-m-u tö ip-u*
how be-ATTR beloved.man-DIM QPT / **1.S-DIR** come-TENT-FIN QUOT say-ATTR
'What kind of lover is [he], [who] says [he] shall come **to me**?'

212. 14:3549.3-5 – UNP

 伊豆由可母 / 加奈之伎世呂我 / **和賀利**可欲波牟

 *indu-yu kamö / kanasi-ki se-rö-nga / **wa-ngari** kayop-am-u*

 where-ABL EPT / be.dear-AVATTR beloved.man-DIM-POSS / **1.S-DIR** visit.frequently-TENT-ATTR

 '[I] wonder, from where shall [my] dearly beloved pay frequent visits **to me**?'

213. 14:3538b.3-5 – UNP

 己許呂能未 / **伊母我理**夜里弖 / 和波己許尓思天

 *kökörö nömï / **imö-ngari** yar-i-te / wa pa kökö n-i s-i-te*

 heart RPT / **beloved.girl-DIR** send-INF-SUB / 1.S TPT here COP-INF do-INF-SUB

 '[I] can only send [my] heart **to [my] beloved**, [as] I am here.'

Table 5.19: Attestations of the directive -*ka* ~ -*ngari* across the provinces.

Form	TSOJ			EOJ							UNP
	Sin	Tö	Su	Kak	Mu	Sa	Mi	Sik	Pi	Sip	Kap	
-*ka*	0	0	0	0	0	0	0	0	0	1	0	0
-*ngari*	0	0	0	0	0	0	0	0	0	0	0	3

5.4.2 Number suffixes

The AOJ dialects have a morphological category of number, but it is not consistent or pervasive. We do not find a plural marker used in AOJ in many contexts in which a language like English, with true morphological number, would require it. Additionally, the plural never attaches to body part terms (such as *te* 'hand' or *mey* 'eye'). The plural marker is -*ra*, there is no dual, and the singular is unmarked.

5.4.2.1 Plural -*ra*

The plural -*ra* is attested mainly in UNP. In EOJ, it is only found in the Kamitukeno topolect, whereas in TSOJ it is found in the Sinano and Suruga topolects. This, along with the fact it is quite uncommon and only attaches to a small set of roots, may indicate it is a TSOJ feature[142] that was borrowed by some EOJ topolects, such as

---

[142] It is also attested in WOJ (Vovin 2005: 93–96).

Kamitukeno. There are attestations of its usage attached to the roots *ko* 'child', *ne* 'summit', and *wo* 'cord'.

214. 20:4401.1-4 – Sinano
可良己呂武 / 須宗尒等里都伎 / 奈古古良乎 / 意伎弖曽伎怒也
kara körömu / *suso-ni tör-i-tuk-i* / *nak-o **ko-ra**-wo* / *ok-i-te sö k-i-n-o ya*
TN garment / hem-LOC take-INF-attach-INF / cry-ATTR **child-PLUR**-ACC / leave.behind-INF-SUB FPT come-INF-PERF-ATTR EPT
'Oh, [I] have come [here], leaving behind [my] sobbing **children** who clung to the hem of [my] Kara robes!'

215. 20:4345.3-5 – Suruga
宇知江須流 / 々々河乃祢良波 / 苦不志久米阿流可
uti-yes-uru / *surunga-nö **ne-ra** pa* / *kupusi-ku mey ar-u ka*
PREF-approach-ATTR / TN-GEN **peak-PLUR** TPT / be.longing-INF FPT exist-ATTR QPT
'How [I] long for the **peaks** of Suruga, where [the waves] crash!'

216. 14:3484.1-2 – UNP
安左乎良乎 / 遠家尒布須左尒
*asa **wo-ra**-wo* / *wo ke-ni pususa n-i*
hemp **cord-PLUR**-ACC / ramie container-LOC much COP-INF
'There are many hemp **threads** in the ramie container.'

Table 5.20: Attestations of the plural *-ra* across the provinces.

TSOJ			EOJ								UNP
Sin	Tö	Su	Kak	Mu	Sa	Mi	Sik	Pi	Sip	Kap	
1	0	1	3	0	0	0	0	0	0	0	6

5.4.3 Diminutive suffixes

There are five diminutive suffixes attested: *-ko*, *-na*, *-ra*, *-rö*, and *-nö*. These are found along with a few diminutive prefixes (described in §5.3.1).

5.4.3.1 Diminutive *-ko*

This diminutive is a grammaticalization of the noun *ko* 'child', as evidenced by the fact it is sometimes written logographically with the character 兒 in the MYS, which means 'child' in Chinese (an example is 14:3519.4 – UNP). It has a function of endearment, and it only attaches to two roots: *imo* 'beloved girl' and *se* 'beloved man'.

217. 20:4345.1-4 – Suruga
和伎米故等 / 不多利和我見之 / 宇知江須流 / 々々河乃祢良波
***wa-ng[a]-imey-ko**-tö* / *puta-ri wa-nga MI-si* / *uti-yes-uru* / *surunga-nö ne-ra pa*
1.S-POSS-**beloved.girl-DIM**-COM / two-CL 1.S-POSS see.INF-PST.ATTR PREF-approach-ATTR / TN-GEN peak-PLUR TPT
'The peaks of Suruga, where [the waves] crash, which I gazed upon with **my darling girl**.'

218. 20:4405.1-2 – Kamitukeno
和我伊母古我 / 志濃比尒西餘等
*wa-nga **imö-ko**-nga* / *sinup-i n-i se-yö tö*
1.S-POSS **beloved.girl-DIM**-POSS / yearn.for-NML COP-INF do-IMP QUOT
'My **dearly beloved** told [me] to yearn for [her]. . .'

219. 14:3379.1-2 – Muzasi
和我世故乎 / 安杼可母伊波武
*wa-nga **se-ko**-wo* / *andö kamö ip-am-u*
1.S-POSS **beloved.man-DIM**-ACC / what EPT say-TENT-ATTR
'[I] wonder, what could [I] say [about] my **beloved man**?'

220. 14:3363.1-2 – Sagamu
和我世古乎 / 夜麻登敝夜利弖
*wa-nga **se-ko**-wo* / *yamatö-pe yar-i-te*
1.S-POSS **beloved.man-DIM**-ACC / TN-ALL send-INF-SUB
'[I] sent my **darling man** to Yamatö.'

221. 20:4357.3-5 – Kamitupusa
和藝毛古我 / 蘇弖母志保々尒 / 奈伎志曽母波由
***wa-ng[a]-imo-ko**-nga* / *sonde mö sipopo n-i* / *nak-i-si sö [o]möp-ay-u*
1.S-POSS-**beloved.girl-DIM**-POSS / sleeve FPT soaked COP-INF / cry-INF-PST.ATTR FPT think-PASS-FIN
'[I] remember how my **darling girl** wept [for me] until her sleeves were sopping wet.'

222. 14:3445.1-4 – UNP
美奈刀能也 / 安之我奈可那流 / 多麻古須氣 / 可利己和我西古
*minato-nö ya / asi-nga naka-n[i] ar-u / tama-ko-sungey / kar-i kö wa-nga **se-ko***
harbor-GEN EPT / reed-POSS inside-LOC exist-ATTR / jewel-DIM-sedge / chop.down-INF come.IMP 1.S-POSS **beloved.man-DIM**
'Chop down the jewel[-like] little sedges that are among the reeds in the harbor and come [back here], my **darling man**.'

Example (222) is the only poem in the corpus to include both the diminutive prefix *ko-* (in line 3) and the diminutive suffix *-ko* (in line 4).

223. 14:3566.1-2 – UNP
和伎毛古尔 / 安我古非思奈婆
***wa-ng[a]-imo-ko**-ni / a-nga kopï sin-anba*
1.S-POSS-beloved.girl-DIM-DAT / 1.S-POSS long.for.NML die-COND
'If I die [from] longing for my **darling girl**...'

5.4.3.2 Diminutive *-na*

The diminutive *-na* attaches to the following roots: *se* 'beloved man', *tengo* 'maiden', *ko* 'girl', and *imo* 'beloved girl'. It is most commonly found attached to *se* 'beloved man' (14 out of 18 total attestations), so it appears to be a more typical diminutive for women addressing men. Like the diminutive *-ko*, it only has a meaning of endearment. The diminutive *-na* is notable because all examples of double diminutive marking in the corpus contain the diminutive *-na* as the first diminutive in the sequence.[143]

224. 14:3402.4-5 – Kamitukeno
勢奈能我素侶母 / 佐夜尓布良思都
***se-na-nö**-nga sonde mö / saya n-i pur-as-i-t-u*
beloved.man-DIM-DIM-POSS sleeve FPT / clear COP-INF wave-HON-INF-PERF-FIN
'[My] **dearly beloved** clearly waved [his] sleeve [at me].'

Example (224) shows a double diminutive suffixation on the root *se* 'beloved man'.

---

[143] Double diminutive marking is not attested in WOJ or TSOJ.

225. 20:4424.1-3 – Muzasi
伊呂夫可久 / **世奈**我許呂母波 / 曽米麻之乎
irö-n-buka-ku / ***se-na**-nga körömö pa* / *sömey-masi-wo*
color-GEN-be.deep-INF / **beloved.man-DIM**-POSS garment TPT / dye-SUBJ.ATTR-ACC
'[I] should like to dye my **darling man**'s garment in a deeply [saturated] color.'

226. 14:3384.1-4 – Simotupusa
可都思加能 / 麻末能**手兒奈**乎 / 麻許登賀聞 / 和礼爾余須等布
kandusika-nö / *mama-nö **teNGO-na**-wo* / *ma-kötö kamo* / *ware-ni yös-u tö [i] p-u*
TN-GEN / cliff-GEN **maiden-DIM**-ACC / INT-word EPT / 1.S-DAT make.approach-ATTR QUOT say-FIN
'[I] wonder, is it true that [some] say I am intimate with a **darling maiden** from the cliff in Kadusika?'

227. 20:4358.4-5 – Kamitupusa
和努等里都伎弖 / 伊比之**古奈**波毛
wano tör-i-tuk-i-te / *ip-i-si **ko-na** pa mo*
1.S take-INF-attach-INF-SUB / say-INF-PST.ATTR **girl-DIM** TPT EPT
'[What about] the **dear girl** who clung to me and said [all those things]?'

228. 14:3446.1-3 – UNP
伊毛奈呂我 / 都可布河泊豆乃 / 佐左良乎疑
***imo-na-rö**-nga* / *tukap-u kapa-n-du-nö* / *sasara wongï*
beloved.girl-DIM-DIM-POSS / use-ATTR river-GEN-harbor-GEN / little Amur.silver.grass
'The little Amur silver grass [growing] along the harbor of the river that [my] **darling, beloved girl** uses [for washing]...'

Example (228) is another example of two different diminutive suffixes attached to the same root, for an emphatic meaning.

229. 14:3463.3-5 – UNP
己許呂奈久 / 佐刀乃美奈可尓 / 安敞流**世奈**可毛
kökörö na-ku / *sato-nö mi-naka-ni* / *ap-er-u **se-na** kamo*
heart not.exist-INF / village-GEN HON-inside-LOC / meet-PROG-ATTR **beloved.man-DIM** EPT
'Oh [my] **darling beloved**, [with] whom [I] am meeting inconsiderately in the great center of the village!'

230. 14:3544.4-5 – UNP
勢奈那登布多理 / 左宿而久也思母
se-na-na-tö puta-ri / sa-NE-TE kuyasi-mö
beloved.man-DIM-DIM-COM two-CL / LOC-sleep.INF-SUB be.regretful.AVFIN-EXCL
'[I] slept there with my **dear, darling beloved**, [and now I] regret it!'

Example (230) is yet another example that shows two diminutives attached in succession, for an emphatic meaning.

231. 20:4428.1-2 – UNP
和我世奈乎 / 都久志波夜利弖
wa-nga **se-na**-wo / tukusi-pa yar-i-te
1.S-POSS **beloved.man-DIM**-ACC / TN-ALL make.go-INF-SUB
'[I] sent my **dearly beloved** to Tukusi…'

5.4.3.3 Diminutive -ra

The diminutive -ra is attested only in the Kamitukeno topolect of EOJ and in UNP. It only has a meaning of endearment. Since this form is also found in WOJ, the attestations in Kamitukeno are likely due to a borrowing from WOJ.

232. 14:3408.3-5 – Kamitukeno
和尓余曽利 / 波之奈流兒良師 / 安夜尓可奈思母
wa-ni yösör-i / pasi-n[i]-ar-u **KO-ra** si / aya n-i kanasi-mö
1.S-DAT be.attracted.to-INF / interval-LOC-be-ATTR **girl-DIM** EPT / mysterious COP-INF be.dear.AVFIN-EXCL
'[My] **darling girl** who is attracted to me, [but] will not commit [to me], is mysteriously dear [to me]!'

233. 14:3412.4-5 – Kamitukeno
可奈師家兒良尓 / 伊夜射可里久母
kanasi-ke **KO-ra**-ni / iya n-zakar-i-[i]k-umö
be.dear-AVATTR **girl-DIM**-DAT / more.and.more COP.INF-be.far.from-INF-go-EXCL
[I] am going further and further away from [my] dear, **darling girl**!'

234. 14:3537a.4-5 – UNP
安比見之**兒良**之 / 安夜尔可奈思母
*ap-i-MI-si **KO-ra** si / aya n-i kanasi-mö*
meet-INF-see.INF-PST.ATTR **girl-DIM** EPT / extreme COP-INF be.dear.AVFIN-EXCL
'The **sweet girl** who [I] met is extremely dear [to me].'

235. 20:4436.4-5 – UNP
伊都伎麻佐牟等 / 登比之**古良**波母
*indu k-i-mas-am-u tö / töp-i-si **ko-ra** pa mö*
when come-INF-HON-TENT-FIN QUOT / ask-INF-PST.ATTR **girl-DIM** TPT EPT
'Oh, [my] **darling girl**, who asked me, 'When will you come back?'.'

236. 14:3405a.4-5 – Kamitukeno
兒良波安波奈毛 / 比等理能未思弖
***KO-ra** pa ap-ana-m-o / pitö-ri nömï s-i-te*
girl-DIM TPT meet-DES-TENT-ATTR / one-CL RPT do-INF-SUB
'[I] want [my] **darling girl** to meet [me], [when she is] all alone.'

237. 14:3409.5 – Kamitukeno
伊射祢志米**刀羅**
*inza ne-simey **[i]to-ra***
well sleep-CAUS.INF **dear.one-DIM**
'Well, let's sleep [together], **deary**.'

238. 14:3518.5 – UNP
伊射祢之賣**刀良**
*inza ne-sime **[i]to-ra***
well sleep-CAUS.INF **dear.one-DIM**
'Well, let's sleep [together], **deary**.'

5.4.3.4 Diminutive -*rö*

The diminutive -*rö* is the most frequently attested diminutive in the AOJ corpus, though it is noticeably absent from TSOJ. There is one attestation in WOJ, but I consider that to be a separate development.[144] It can be reconstructed for Proto-EOJ

---

144 Vovin (2005: 210) notes this attestation occurs in NK 4. It is suffixed to the word *mey* 'eye, mesh'. This is the only attestation of the diminutive suffix -*ra* ~ -*rö* on this noun in OJ. It is probably the result of a synchronic progressive vowel assimilation, since *mey* is phonetically [məy], thus

as a reflex of PJe *-ra. The diminutive -rö occurs with both diminutive and endearment functions (as noted by Vovin 2005: 210–212).

5.4.3.4.1 Diminutive function

239. 14:3412.1-3 – Kamitukeno
   賀美都家野 / 久路保乃祢呂乃 / 久受葉我多
   kamitukeNO / *kuropo-nö* **ne-rö**-*nö* / *kunzu-PA-n-gata*
   TN / TN-GEN **peak-DIM**-GEN / kudzu-leaf-GEN-vine
   '[Like] the vines of kudzu leaves on the **small peak** of Kuropo in Kamitukeno...'

240. 14:3395.1-2 – Pitati
   乎豆久波乃 / 祢呂尓都久多思
   won-dukupa-nö / **ne-rö**-*ni tuku tas-i*
   DIM-TN-GEN / **peak-DIM**-LOC moon rise-INF
   'The moon rises on the **small peak** of Mt. Tukupa.'

241. 14:3383.1-2 – Kamitupusa
   宇麻具多能 / 祢呂尓可久里為
   umanguta-nö / **ne-rö**-*ni kakur-i-wi*
   TN-GEN / **peak-DIM**-LOC hide-INF-sit.NML
   '[I] remain hiding [away] **in the small peak** of Umaguta.'

242. 14:3495.1-2 – UNP
   伊波保呂乃 / 蘇比能和可麻都
   ipapo-rö-*nö* / *sopi-nö waka matu*
   boulder-DIM-GEN / beside-GEN young pine
   '[Like] the young pines growing beside **little rocks**...'

---

producing [məyrə] from [məyra]. This is similar to the sporadic assimilative reduction of the WOJ iterative suffix -*ap*- to -*öp*- when following certain verb roots that contain the vowel *ö*: an example is *pokör-öp*- 'boast-ITER' from MYS 5:892.17. As such, I consider it to be unrelated to the change of this suffix in Proto-EOJ, which occurred unconditionally at an earlier date.

5.4.3.4.2 Endearment function

243. 20:4406.1-2 – Kamitukeno
 和我**伊波呂**尓 / 由加毛比等母我
 *wa-nga **ipa-rö**-ni / yuk-am-o pitö mönga*
 1.S-POSS **house-DIM**-LOC / go-TENT-ATTR person DPT
 '[I] wish someone would go to my **dear home**.'

244. 14:3375.4-5 – Muzasi
 伊尓之与比欲利 / **世呂**尓安波奈布与
 *in-i-si yöpi-yori / **se-rö**-ni ap-an-ap-u yö*
 depart-INF-PST.ATTR evening-ABL / **beloved.man-DIM**-DAT meet-NEG-ITER-FIN EPT
 'Since the evening [he] departed, [I] have not met [my] **beloved**!'

245. 20:4419 – Muzasi
 伊波呂尓波 / 安之布多氣度母 / 須美与氣乎 / 都久之尓伊多里弖 / 古布志氣毛波母
 ***ipa-rö**-ni pa / asi-pu tak-ey-ndomö / sum-i yö-key-wo / tukusi-ni itar-i-te / kopusi-ngey [o]mop-am-ö*
 house-DIM-LOC TPT / reed-fire burn-EV-CONC / reside-NML be.good-AVATTR-ACC / TN-LOC arrive-INF-GER / be.longing.for-AVNML think-TENT-ATTR
 'Although [we] would burn reeds [to warm our] **modest home**, it was nice living there, so [I] am sure [I] will long for [it] after [I] arrive in Tukusi.'

246. 14:3368.4-5 – Sagamu
 余尓母多欲良尓 / **故呂**河伊波奈久尓
 *yö-ni mö tayora n-i / **ko-rö**-nga ip-an-aku n-i*
 lifetime-LOC FPT wavering COP-INF / **girl-DIM**-POSS say-NEG.ATTR-NML COP-INF
 'Although [my] **dear girl** will not say [her love for me] will waver in this lifetime...'

247. 20:4329.3-5 – Sagamu
 布奈可射里 / 安我世牟**比呂**乎 / 美毛比等母我毛
 *puna-kanzar-i / a-nga se-m-u **pi-rö**-wo / mi-m-o pitö mönngamo*
 boat-decorate-NML / 1.S-POSS do-TENT-ATTR **day-DIM**-ACC / see-TENT-ATTR person DPT
 '[I] wish someone would witness the **special day** when I do the boat-decorating.'

248. 14:3424.4-5 – Simotukeno
麻具波思**兒呂**波 / 多賀家可母多牟
ma n-gupasi **KO-rö** pa / ta-nga ke ka möt-am-u
true COP.INF-be.beautiful **girl-DIM** TPT / who-POSS container QPT hold-TENT-ATTR
'Whose [food] container shall the truly beautiful **girl** hold?'

249. 14:3446.1-3 – UNP
伊毛奈呂我 / 都可布河泊豆乃 / 佐左良乎疑
imo-na-rö-nga / tukap-u kapa-n-du-nö / sasara wongï
beloved.girl-DIM-DIM-POSS / use-ATTR river-GEN-harbor-GEN / little Amur.silver.grass
'The little Amur silver grass [growing] along the harbor of the river that [my] **darling, beloved girl** uses [for washing]...'

Example (249) shows the diminutive -rö follows the diminutive -na in the linear ordering of morphemes in a nominal word form.

250. 14:3564.1-2 – UNP
古須氣呂乃 / 宇良布久可是能
kosungey-rö-nö / ura puk-u kanze-nö
TN-DIM-GEN / bay blow-ATTR wind-COMP
'Like the winds that blow over the bay of **ol' Kosugey**...'

251. 20:4427.1-2 – UNP
伊波乃**伊毛呂** / 和乎之乃布良之
ipa-nö **imo-rö** / wa-wo sinöp-urasi
house-GEN **beloved.girl-DIM** / 1.S-ACC yearn.for-SUP
'It seems that [my] **darling girl** at home yearns for me.'

5.4.3.5 Diminutive -nö

I consider the diminutive -nö to be a phonetic variant of the diminutive -na, due to vowel centralization. This diminutive occurs only twice.

252. 14:3402.4-5 – Kamitukeno
勢奈能我素侶母 / 佐夜尔布良思都
se-na-nö-nga sonde mö / saya n-i pur-as-i-t-u
beloved.man-DIM-DIM-POSS sleeve FPT / clear COP-INF wave-HON-INF-PERF-FIN
'[My] **dearly beloved** clearly waved [his] sleeve [at me].'

Example (252) shows the diminutive -nö follows the diminutive -na in the linear ordering of morphemes in a nominal word form.

253. 14:3528.3-4 – UNP
 伊母能良尔 / 毛乃伊波受伎尔弖
 ***imö-nö**-ra-ni* / *monö ip-anz-u k-i-n-i-te*
 beloved.girl-DIM-PLUR-DAT / things say-NEG-INF come-INF-PERF-INF-SUB
 '[I] came without saying a thing to [my] **darling girls**.'

5.4.3.6 A comparison of the diminutive suffixes in AOJ

In Table 5.21 below, all attested diminutive suffixes are compared across the provinces.

Table 5.21: Attestations of all diminutive suffixes across the provinces.

Form	TSOJ			EOJ							UNP
	Sin	Tö	Su	Kak	Mu	Sa	Mi	Sik	Pi	Sip	Kap	
-ko	0	0	1	2	1	1	0	0	0	0	2	2
-na	0	0	0	2	3	0	0	0	0	2	1	10
-ra	0	0	0	3	0	0	0	0	0	0	0	3
-rö	0	0	0	7	3	5	0	1	4	0	2	33
-nö	0	0	0	1	0	0	0	0	0	0	0	1

These data demonstrate the most widely attested diminutive suffix in AOJ is -*rö*, with 55 attestations in EOJ and UNP (but none in TSOJ). Curiously, the only diminutive suffix attested in TSOJ is -*ko*. Apparently, diminutives were quite popular in the Kamitukeno topolect of EOJ, since all five diminutive suffixes are attested at least once.

5.5 Reduplication

Full noun reduplication occurs in the AOJ dialects, but it is infrequently attested. There are no attested examples of partial reduplication. The functions of this process are iteration and plurality. The onset of the reduplicated segment is prenasalized when used to indicate plurality, but not when used to indicate iteration. This prenasalization may have been the result of an analogical extension from the MODIFIER COP.ATTR-HEAD phrases that are common, but it is difficult to connect that with the meaning of plurality found in the reduplicated examples.

The reduplication of verbs is also attested. See §7.10 for examples.

5.5.1 Iteration function

The iteration function is attested just once.

254. 14:3481.2 – UNP
 佐恵佐恵之豆美
 sawe-sawe sindum-i
 rustle-REDUP become.quiet-NML
 'The **rustling** [of my departure] died down...'

UNP *sawe-sawe* 'rustling' appears to be a more archaic form of WOJ *sawi-sawi* 'id.' (Vovin 2012a: 196). There is also the word *sawawe* 'noisy' attested in 14:3552.2 – UNP. These words descend from a PJe onomatopoeia *sawai 'noise'. See the discussion in §4.5 for more details.

5.5.2 Plurality function

The plurality function is attested four times.

255. 20:4323.1-3 – Töpotuapumi
 等伎騰吉乃 / 波奈波左家登母
 töki-ndöki-nö / pana pa sak-e-ndömö
 time-REDUP-GEN / flower TPT bloom-EV-CONC
 'The **seasonal** [lit. 'of seasons' or 'of times'] flowers [all] bloom, but...'

256. 20:4381.1-3 – Simotukeno
 久尔具尓乃 / 佐岐毛利都度比 / 布奈能里弖
 kuni-nguni-nö / sakimori tundop-i / puna-nör-i-te
 province-REDUP-GEN / border.guard gather-INF / boat-ride-INF-SUB
 'Border guards from [many] **provinces** gather here, and sail [out] on a boat.'

257. 20:4391.1-3 – Simotupusa
 久尔具尓乃 / 夜之里乃加美尓 / 奴作麻都理
 kuni-nguni-nö / yasirö-nö kami-ni / nusa matur-i
 province-REDUP-GEN / shrine-GEN deity-DAT / paper.offering offer-INF
 '[I] make paper offerings to the deities in the shrines of [many] **provinces**.'

258. 20:4372.13-15 – Pitati
毛呂々々波 / 佐祁久等麻乎須 / 可閇利久麻弖尓
***morö-morö** pa / sake-ku tö mawos-u / kapeyr-i-k-u-mande-ni*
many-REDUP TPT / be.safe-AVINF QUOT say.HUM-FIN / return-INF-come-ATTR-TERM-LOC
'[I] will implore [the deities] to keep the **many, many** [people I left behind] safe until [I] return [home].'

Table 5.22: Attestations of reduplication in AOJ based on function.

Func	TSOJ			EOJ								UNP
	Sin	Tö	Su	Kak	Mu	Sa	Mi	Sik	Pi	Sip	Kap	
Iteration	0	0	0	0	0	0	0	0	0	0	0	1
Plurality	0	1	0	0	0	0	0	1	1	1	0	0

5.6 Pronouns

The pronoun system includes personal, demonstrative, interrogative, and collective pronouns.

5.6.1 Personal pronouns

The personal pronoun system of AOJ is somewhat unusual. On the one hand it is extremely minimal in terms of distinctions (such as those of person, inclusivity, or number), containing only the most basic one found in the languages of the world, which is that of first versus second person. On the other hand, there are multiple first and second person pronouns, some of which have no clear synchronic difference in meaning or function from one another. The full pronoun system is listed below in Table 5.23.

5.6.1.1 First-person pronouns

The first-person pronouns include *wa ~ ware*, *wano ~ wanu*, and *a ~ are*. The short forms *wa* and *a* can be used nearly in free variation with one another, and similarly the usage of the forms *ware* and *are* overlaps in most cases. In fact, two or more different first-person pronouns can be found in the same poem, sometimes even in adjacent lines. However, some important morphosyntactic and functional dis-

Table 5.23: Attested pronouns in the AOJ dialects.

	First-person		Second-person	
	TSOJ	EOJ	TSOJ	EOJ
Singular	*wa*	*wa*	*imasi*	*na*
	ware	*ware*		*nare*
	warö	*a*		
	are	*are*		
		wano		
		wanu		
Reflexive	–	–	–	*a*

tinctions between these various pronouns do exist, which will be discussed in the sections that follow.

5.6.1.1.1 *wa ~ ware ~ warö*

The first-person pronoun *wa* and its extended version *ware ~ warö* are always singular in AOJ, thus I gloss them as '1.S'. I will describe *wa* and *ware ~ warö* in separate sections below because they have some morphosyntactic differences.

5.6.1.1.1.1 *wa*

The form *wa* is attested with a suffixed possessive case *-nga*, dative case *-ni*, accusative case *-wo*, and directive case *-ngari*. It is also attested before the topic particle *pa* and directly before a verb.

259. 14:3399.5 – Sinano
   久都波氣<u>和我</u>世
   *kutu pak-ey **wa-nga** se*
   shoes put.on-IMP **1.S-POSS** beloved.man
   'Wear [your] shoes, **my** beloved.'

260. 20:4326.5 – Töpotuapumi
   <u>和我</u>伎多流麻弖
   ***wa-nga** k-i-tar-u-mande*
   1.S-POSS come-INF-PP-ATTR-TERM
   'Until **I** return [to them]...'

261. 20:4343.5 – Suruga
和加美可奈志母
wa-nga *mi kanasi-mö*
1.S-POSS wife be.sad.AVFIN-EXCL
'**My wife** [must] be so sad!'

262. 14:3420.4-5 – Kamitukeno
於也波佐久礼騰 / 和波左可流賀倍
oya pa sak-ure-ndö / ***wa pa*** *sakar-u ngapey*
parents TPT keep.apart-EV-CONC / **1.S TPT** be.far.from-ATTR IPT
'Although [our] parents keep [us] apart, will **I** be far from [you]? (No, I will not!)'

263. 20:4405.1-2 – Kamitukeno
和我伊母古我 / 志濃比尓西餘等
wa-nga *imö-ko-nga* / *sinup-i n-i se-yö tö*
1.S-POSS beloved.girl-DIM-POSS / yearn.for-NML COP-INF do-IMP QUOT
'**My** dearly beloved told [me] to yearn for [her]...'

264. 14:3378.5 – Muzasi
和尓奈多要曽祢
wa-ni *na-taye-sö-n-e*
1.S-DAT NEG.IMP-break.INF-do-DES-IMP
'Please do not break up **with me**.'

265. 20:4418.1-2 – Muzasi
和我可度乃 / 可多夜麻都婆伎
wa-nga *kando-nö* / *kata yama tubaki*
1.S-POSS gate-GEN / side mountain camellia
'The camellias near the mountain [off] the side of **my** gate...'

266. 14:3432.4 – Sagamu
和乎可豆佐祢母
wa-wo *kandus-an-e mö*
1.S-ACC abduct-DES-IMP EPT
'Please abduct **me**!'

267. 20:4382.3-5 – Simotukeno
阿多由麻比 / **和我**須流等伎尓 / 佐伎毛里尓佐酒
ata yum-ap-i / **wa-nga** *s-uru töki-ni* / *sakimori n-i sas-u*
sudden be.ill-ITER-NML / **1.S-POSS** do-ATTR time-LOC / border.guard COP-INF appoint-FIN
'When I am suffering from this sudden illness, [he] appoints [me] to be a border guard.'

268. 14:3392.4-5 – Pitati
代尓毛多由良尓 / **和我**於毛波奈久尓
YÖ-ni mo tayura n-i / **wa-nga** *omop-an-aku n-i*
lifetime-LOC FPT wavering COP-INF / **1.S-POSS** think-NEG.ATTR-NML COP-INF
'I do not think that [I will] waver [in my love for you] in [my] lifetime.'

269. 20:4368.5 – Pitati
和波可敝里許牟
wa pa *kaper-i-kö-m-u*
1.S TPT return-INF-come-TENT-FIN
'I shall return [to you].'

270. 14:3382.1-4 – Kamitupusa
宇麻具多能 / 祢呂乃佐左葉能 / 都由思母能 / 奴礼弖**和**伎奈婆
umanguta-nö / *ne-rö-nö sasa-PA-nö* / *tuyu simö-nö* / *nure-te* **wa** *k-i-n-anba*
TN-GEN / peak-DIM-GEN bamboo.grass-leaf-GEN / dew frost-GEN / get.wet.INF-SUB **1.S** come-INF-PERF-COND
'If I come [to you], wet [with] dew and frost from the bamboo grass leaves on the peaks of Umaguta...'

271. 20:4356.3-5 – Kamitupusa
和我可良尓 / 奈伎之許己呂乎 / 和須良延奴可毛
wa-nga *karani* / *nak-i-si kökörö-wo* / *wasur-aye-n-u kamo*
1.S-POSS because.of / cry-INF-PST.ATTR heart-ACC / forget-PASS-NEG-ATTR EPT
'[I] cannot forget how [my mother] wept from [her] heart because **of me**!'

272. 14:3539.3-5 – UNP
安夜抱可等 / 比等豆麻古呂乎 / 伊吉尓**和我**須流
ayapo-ka-ndö / *pitö-n-duma ko-rö-wo* / *iki-ni* **wa-nga** *s-uru*
be.dangerous-AVEV-CONC / person-GEN-spouse girl-DIM-ACC / breath-LOC **1.S-POSS** do-ATTR
'Although it is dangerous, I sigh for a dear girl [who is] another man's wife.'

273. 14:3549.3-5 – UNP
伊豆由可母 / 加奈之伎世呂我 / **和賀利**可欲波牟
indu-yu kamö / kanasi-ki se-rö-nga / **wa**-**ngari** *kayop-am-u*
where-ABL EPT / be.dear-AVATTR beloved.man-DIM-POSS / **1.S-DIR** visit.frequently-TENT-ATTR
'From where shall [my] dearly beloved pay frequent visits **to me**?'

274. 14:3563.4-5 – UNP
和乎可麻都那毛 / 伎曽毛己余必母
wa-**wo** *ka mat-unam-o / kisö mo köyöpi mö*
1.S-ACC QPT wait-TENT2-ATTR / last.night FPT this.evening FPT
'[You] almost certainly waited for **me** last night, and tonight [you will] as well?'

275. 20:4427.1-2 – UNP
伊波乃伊毛呂 / **和乎**之乃布良之
ipa-nö imo-rö / **wa**-**wo** *sinöp-urasi*
house-GEN beloved.girl-DIM / **1.S-ACC** yearn.for-SUP
'It seems that [my] darling girl at home yearns for **me**.'

5.6.1.1.1.2 *ware ~ warö*

The extended form *ware* is only attested in isolation, or before the topic particle *pa*. In two instances it functions as a first-person possessive pronoun. While there is an orthographic form *warö* attested once in the Suruga topolect of TSOJ, I do not view that as being phonemically (or phonetically) distinct from the form *ware*. Refer to §2.2.1.1 for a discussion.

5.6.1.1.1.2.1 Nominative function

In the examples below this pronoun functions as a first-person singular nominative form.

276. 20:4416.4-5 – Muzasi
伊波奈流**和礼波** / 比毛等加受祢牟
ipa-n[i] ar-u **ware pa** */ pimo tök-anz-u ne-m-u*
house-LOC exist-ATTR **1.S TPT** / cord undo-NEG-INF sleep-TENT-FIN
'**I**, who am at home, shall sleep without untying my cords.'

277. 20:4374.4-5 – Simotukeno
都久之乃之麻乎 / 佐之弖伊久**和例波**
tukusi-nö sima-wo / *sas-i-te ik-u* ***ware pa***
TN-GEN island-ACC / point.toward-INF-SUB go-ATTR **1.S TPT**
'I, who went pointing toward the island of Tukusi...'

278. 20:4370.4-5 – Pitati
須米良美久佐尓 / **和礼波**伎尓之乎
sumeyra mi-[i]kusa-ni / ***ware pa*** *k-i-n-i-si-wo*
emperor HON-army-LOC / **1.S TPT** come-INF-PERF-INF-PST.ATTR-ACC
'Since **I** came into the Emperor's great army...'

279. 14:3444.1-4 – UNP
伎波都久能 / 乎加能久君美良 / **和礼**都賣杼 / 故尓毛乃多奈布
kipatuku-nö / *woka-nö kuku-mira* / ***ware*** *tum-e-ndö* / *ko-ni mo nöt-an-ap-u*
TN-GEN / hill-GEN stem-leek / **1.S** pluck-EV-CONC / basket-LOC FPT fill.up-NEG-ITER-FIN
'**I** pluck the stem-leeks on Kipatuku hill, but the basket is not filling up.'

280. 14:3498.4-5 – UNP
伎美波和須良酒 / **和礼**和須流礼夜
kimi pa wasur-as-u / ***ware*** *wasur-ure ya*
lord TPT forget-HON-FIN / **1.S** forget-EV QPT
'[You, my] lord will forget [me]. Will **I** forget you? (No, I will not!)'

281. 14:3514.3-4 – UNP
和礼左倍尓 / 伎美尓都吉奈那
ware *sapey n-i* / *kimi-ni tuk-i-n-ana*
1.S RPT COP-INF / lord-LOC attach-INF-PERF-DES
'Even **I** have wanted to be close to [you, my] lord.'

5.6.1.1.1.2.2 Possessive function

In the examples that follow, the first-person pronoun *ware* acts as a possessive without any possessive morphology.

282. 20:4343.1-2 – Suruga
和呂多比波 / 多比等於米保等
warö *tanbi pa* / *tanbi tö omeyp-o-ndö*
1.S journey TPT / journey COP think-EV-CONC
'Although [I] know **my** journey will be an [arduous] one...'

Example (282) shows *ware* written as *warö*.

283. 20:4348.3-5 – Kamitupusa
 麻許等**和例** / 多非乃加里保尓 / 夜須久祢牟加母
 ma-kötö **ware** / *tanbï-nö kari-[i]po-ni* / *yasu-ku ne-m-u kamö*
 INT-word **1.S** / journey-GEN borrow.NML-hut-LOC / be.easy-AVINF sleep-TENT-ATTR EPT
 '[I] wonder, shall **I** truly sleep peacefully on [my] journey in a makeshift abode?'

Table 5.24: Attestations of the first-person pronouns *wa* ~ *ware* ~ *warö* across the provinces.

Form	TSOJ			EOJ								UNP
	Sin	Tö	Su	Kak	Mu	Sa	Mi	Sik	Pi	Sip	Kap	
wa	1	1	3	5	2	2	0	1	3	0	4	18
ware	0	0	1	0	1	0	0	2	1	0	1	3
warö	0	0	1	0	0	0	0	0	0	0	0	0

5.6.1.1.2 *wano* ~ *wanu*

The first-person pronoun *wano* ~ *wanu* is attested just three times, in EOJ and UNP. It is unattested in WOJ and TSOJ but is clearly cognate with the PR first-person pronoun *wanu (Thorpe 1983: 218).

284. 20:4358.4-5 – Kamitupusa
 和努等里都伎弖 / 伊比之古奈波毛
 wano *tör-i-tuk-i-te* / *ip-i-si ko-na pa mo*
 1.S take-INF-attach-INF-SUB / say-INF-PST.ATTR girl-DIM TPT EPT
 '[What about] the dear girl who clung **to me** and said [all those things]?'

Example (284) shows the pronoun *wano* used in a dative function, without a dative case suffix. In contrast, in example (285), we do find the dative suffix.

285. 14:3476a.1-2 – UNP
 宇倍兒奈波 / **和奴尓**故布奈毛
 unbey KO-na pa / **wanu-ni** *kop-unam-o*
 surely girl-DIM TPT / **1.S-DAT** long.for-TENT2-ATTR
 '[That] dear girl will surely long for **me**!'

286. 14:3476b.5 – UNP
和奴賀由乃敝波
wanu-nga yun-öp-e-nba
1.S-POSS sleep-ITER-EV-COND
'If **I** continue to sleep [with her]...'

Example (286) shows the pronoun *wanu* used with the possessive case *-nga*, to mark the subject of the sentence.

Table 5.25: Attestations of the first-person pronoun *wano ~ wanu* across the provinces.

TSOJ			EOJ								UNP
Sin	Tö	Su	Kak	Mu	Sa	Mi	Sik	Pi	Sip	Kap	
0	0	0	0	0	0	0	0	0	0	1	2

5.6.1.1.3 *a ~ are*

The first-person pronoun *a* and its extended variant *are* are always attested as singular, so I gloss them as '1.S'. These two forms have some morphosyntactic differences, so I describe them separately below.

5.6.1.1.3.1 *a*

The first-person pronoun *a* is usually attested suffixed by either the possessive *-nga*, the accusative *-wo*, or the dative *-ni*. In example (291) it is attested before the topic particle *pa*. In EOJ, this pronoun also has a special function as a second-person reflexive, described in §5.6.1.1.3.1.1 below.

287. 14:3404.5 – Kamitukeno
安抒加**安我**世牟
andö ka **a-nga** se-m-u
what QPT **1.S-POSS** do-TENT-ATTR
'What should **I** do?'

288. 20:4329.3-5 – Sagamu
布奈可射里 / **安我**世牟比呂乎 / 美毛比等母我毛
puna-kanzar-i / **a-nga** se-m-u pi-rö-wo / mi-m-o pitö möngamo
boat-decorate-NML / **1.S-POSS** do-TENT-ATTR day-DIM-ACC / see-TENT-ATTR person DPT
'[I] wish someone would witness the special day when **I** do the boat-decorating.'

289. 20:4366.3-5 – Pitati
阿我古比乎 / 志留志弖都祁弖 / 伊母尓志良世牟
***a*-nga** kopi-wo / sirus-i-te tuke-te / imö-ni sir-ase-m-u
1.S-POSS long.for.NML-ACC / record-INF-SUB attach.INF-SUB / beloved.girl-DAT know-CAUS-TENT-FIN
'Writing [a note describing] **my** love and [sending it] attached [to the goose] would let [my] beloved girl know [how I feel].'

290. 20:4391.4-5 – Simotupusa
阿加古比須奈牟 / 伊母賀加奈志作
***a*-nga** kopi s-unam-u / imö-nga kanasi-sa
1.S-POSS long.for.NML do-TENT2-ATTR / beloved.girl-POSS be.sad-ADJNML
'The sadness of **my** beloved who probably longs for [me]...'

291. 14:3519.1-2 – UNP
奈我波伴尓 / 己良例安波由久
na-nga papa-ni / *kör-are **a** pa yuk-u*
2.S-POSS mother-DAT / scold-PASS.INF **1.S** TPT go-FIN
'[I] was scolded by your mother and [now] **I** will leave.'

292. 14:3532.4-5 – UNP
安乎思努布良武 / 伊敝乃兒呂波母
***a*-wo** sinop-uram-u / ipe-nö KO-rö pa mö
1.S-ACC long.for-TENT2-ATTR / house-GEN girl-DIM TPT EPT
'Oh, [my] dear girl at home who must be longing for **me**.'

293. 14:3566.1-2 – UNP
和伎毛古尓 / 安我古非思奈婆
wa-ng[a]-imo-ko-ni / ***a*-nga** kopi sin-anba
1.S-POSS-beloved.girl-DIM-DAT / **1.S-POSS** long.for.NML die-COND
'If **I** die from longing for my darling girl...'

Example (293) shows the first-person pronouns *wa* and *a* attested in the same poem (*wa* in line 1, *a* in line 2), both with the same suffix (possessive *-nga*) attached.

294. 20:4430.5 – UNP
伊埿弖登阿我久流
*inde-te tö **a**-nga k-uru*
go.out.INF-SUB FPT **1.S-POSS** come-ATTR
'**I** went out and came [here].'

5.6.1.1.3.1.1 Usage as a second-person reflexive pronoun

There is one example of the pronoun *a* used as a second-person reflexive in EOJ (Takagi, Gomi, and Ōno 1962: 445).

295.   20:4420.4-5 – Muzasi
       安我弖等都氣呂 / 許礼乃波流母志
       ***a*-nga** te-tö tukey-rö / köre nö paru mös-i
       REFL-POSS hand-COM be.attached-IMP / this COP.ATTR needle hold-INF
       'Hold this needle and attach [the cords] with **your own** hands.'

This usage seems to be the beginning of what we find widespread in Middle Japanese. Although the first-person pronoun *a* is unattested in MJ, many of the MJ personal pronouns can also act as reflexive pronouns. For example, the MJ first-person pronoun *wa ~ ware* can act as a first or third-person reflexive, and the first-person pronoun *ono- ~ onore* can act as a second-person reflexive (Vovin 2003: 97–102).

5.6.1.1.3.2 *are*

The extended form *are* is usually attested in isolation or before the topic particle *pa*, just like the first-person pronoun *ware*. One notable difference between *ware* and *are* is that only *are* is attested with the accusative suffix *-wo* (shown in examples 296 and 304 below).

296.   14:3429.4-5 – Töpotuapumi
       安礼乎多能米弖 / 安佐麻之物能乎
       ***are*-wo** tanömey-te / as-amasi mönöwo
       1.S-ACC make.trust.INF-SUB / be.shallow-SUBJ CNJ
       '[You] made **me** trust [you], even though [your feelings for me] may be shallow.'

297.   20:4327.4-5 – Töpotuapumi
       多比由久阿礼波 / 美都都志努波牟
       tanbi yuk-u ***are pa*** / mi-tutu sinop-am-u
       journey go-ATTR **1.S TPT** / see.INF-COOR long.for-TENT-FIN
       'I [would take the picture with me] on my journey and long for [her] while looking [at it].'

298. 14:3361.5 – Sagamu
許呂**安礼**比毛等久
kö-rö **are** pimo tök-u
girl-DIM **1.S** cord undo-FIN
'[My] dear girl and I untie [our] cords. . .'

299. 20:4365.4-5 – Pitati
阿例波許藝奴等 / 伊母尓都岐許曽
are pa köng-i-n-u tö / imö-ni tung-i-kös-ö
1.S TPT row-INF-PERF-FIN QUOT / beloved.girl-LOC tell.INF-BEN-IMP
'Please tell [my] darling that I am rowing out!'

300. 20:4350.4 – Kamitupusa
阿例波伊波々牟
are pa ipap-am-u
1.S TPT pray-TENT-FIN
'I shall pray.'

301. 14:3440a.3-4 – UNP
奈礼毛**阿礼**毛 / 余知乎曽母弖流
nare mo **are** mo / yöti-wo sö möt-er-u
2.S FPT **1.S** FPT / same.age-ACC FPT hold-PROG-ATTR
'You and I both have [children] of the same age.'

Example (301) shows *are* used as a syntactic nominative. We also see this in (303) below.

302. 14:3496.5 – UNP
伊弓**安礼波**伊可奈
inde **are pa** ik-ana
well **1.S TPT** go-DES
'Well, I want to go [to her]!'

303. 14:3508.4-5 – UNP
安比見受安良婆 / **安礼**古非米夜母
ap-i-MI-nz-u ar-anba / **are** kopï-m-ey ya mö
meet-INF-see-NEG-INF exist-COND / 1.S love-TENT-EV QPT EPT
'If [I] had not met [you], would I be in love [with you]? (No, I would not!)'

304. 20:4426.5 – UNP
阿礼乎之毛波婆
***are*-wo** si [o]mop-anba
1.S-ACC EPT love-COND
'If [you] love **me**...'

Table 5.26: Attestations of the first-person pronoun *a ~ are* across the provinces.

Form	TSOJ			EOJ								UNP
	Sin	Tö	Su	Kak	Mu	Sa	Mi	Sik	Pi	Sip	Kap	
a	0	0	0	2	2	2	0	0	1	1	0	14
are	0	2	0	0	0	1	0	0	3	0	1	5

5.6.1.1.4 Summary of first-person pronouns

The following morphological distinctions can be seen among the various first-person pronouns.

Table 5.27: Attested morphological forms of the first-person pronouns in AOJ.

PRONOUN	Possessive -nga		Accusative -wo		Dative -ni		Directive -ngari	
	TSOJ	EOJ	TSOJ	EOJ	TSOJ	EOJ	TSOJ	EOJ
wa	wa-nga	wa-nga	–	wa-wo	–	wa-ni	–	wa-ngari
a	–	a-nga	–	a-wo	–	a-ni	–	–
ware	–	–	–	ware-wo	–	–	–	–
are	–	–	are-wo	are-wo	–	–	–	–
wano ~ wanu	–	wanu-nga	–	–	–	wanu-ni	–	–

We find the following pronouns in Table 5.28 attested as topicalized.

Table 5.28: First-person pronouns attested as topicalized with the particle *pa*.

PRONOUN	TSOJ	EOJ
wa	–	wa pa
a	a pa[145]	–

---

[145] The form *a pa* '1.S TPT' is only attested once in AOJ, in a UNP poem. The poem does not have any unique EOJ linguistic features, and instead looks like it was written in a TSOJ topolect, which is why I list it in this column.

Table 5.28 (continued)

PRONOUN	TSOJ	EOJ
ware	–	ware pa
are	are pa	are pa
wano ~ wanu	–	–

We find the following pronouns in Table 5.29 attested as a syntactic nominative.

Table 5.29: First-person pronouns attested as a syntactic nominative.

PRONOUN	TSOJ	EOJ
wa	–	–
a	–	–
ware	+	+
are	–	+
wano ~ wanu	–	+

5.6.1.2 Second-person pronouns

The second-person pronouns are *na* ~ *nare* and *imasi* ~ *masi*.

5.6.1.2.1 *na* ~ *nare*

The second-person pronoun *na* and its extended variant *nare* are always attested as singular, so I gloss them as '2.S'. These two forms have some morphosyntactic differences, so I describe them separately below.

5.6.1.2.1.1 *na*

The second-person pronoun *na* is attested suffixed with the possessive case *-nga*, the dative case *-ni*, the comitative case *-tö*, and the accusative case *-wo*. It is also attested followed by the topic particle *pa*. It is always attested with either a suffix attached or a following topic particle.

305. 14:3425.5 – Simotukeno
 奈我己許呂能礼
 na*-*nga kökörö nör-e
 2.S-POSS heart tell-IMP
 'Tell [me] **your** feelings.'

306. 14:3394.4-5 – Pitati
和須良延許婆古曽 / **那乎**可家奈波賣
wasura-kö-nba kosö / **na-wo** kake-n-ap-am-e
forget-come-COND FPT / **2.S-ACC** call.out-NEG-ITER-TENT-EV
'When [I] start to forget [our meeting there], [I] shall stop calling out for **you**!'

307. 14:3383.4-5 – Kamitupusa
久尓乃登保可婆 / **奈我**目保里勢牟
kuni-nö töpo-ka-nba / **na-nga** MEY por-i se-m-u
province-GEN be.far-AVEV-CONJ / **2.S-POSS** eye desire-NML do-TENT-FIN
'[I] dream of **your** eyes, since [your] province is far [away].'

308. 20:4347.3-5 – Kamitupusa
奈我波氣流 / 多知尓奈里弖母 / 伊波非弖之加母
na-nga pak-eyr-u / tati n-i nar-i-te mö / ipap-ï-te-si kamö
2.S-POSS wear-PROG-ATTR / long.sword COP-INF become-INF-SUB FPT / pray-INF-PERF-PST.ATTR EPT
'[I] want to become the long sword that **you** are wearing and pray for [you].'

309. 14:3478.5 – UNP
奈尓己曽与佐礼
na-ni kösö yösar-e
2.S-DAT FPT be.attracted.to-EV
'[I] am attracted to **you**.'

310. 14:3492.4-5 – UNP
奈里毛奈良受毛 / **奈等**布多里波毛
nar-i mo nar-anz-u mo / **na-tö** puta-ri pa mo
be-INF FPT be-NEG-INF FPT / **2.S-COM** two-CL TPT FPT
'Whatever may be, at least [I shall be] **with you**!'

311. 14:3494.4-5 – UNP
宿毛等和波毛布 / **汝波**安杼可毛布
NE-m-o tö wa pa [o]mop-u / **NA pa** andö ka [o]mop-u
sleep-TENT-ATTR COP 1.S TPT think-FIN / **2.S TPT** what QPT think-ATTR
'I think we should sleep [together]. What do **you** think?'

5.6.1.2.1.2 *nare*

The second-person pronoun *nare* is only attested in isolation. This appears to be the main difference between it and its unextended stem *na*.

312. 20:4418.3-5 – Muzasi
 麻己等**奈礼** / 和我弓布礼奈々 / 都知尔於知母可毛
 *ma-kötö **nare** / wa-nga te pure-na-na / tuti-ni oti-m-ö kamo*
 INT-word **2.S** / 1.S-POSS hand touch-NEG.ATTR-LOC / earth-LOC fall-TENT-ATTR EPT
 'Oh, I wonder if **you** would really fall to the ground without touching my hand.'

313. 14:3440a.3-4 – UNP
 奈礼毛阿礼毛 / 余知乎曽母弓流
 ***nare** mo are mo / yöti-wo sö möt-er-u*
 2.S FPT 1.S FPT / same.age-ACC FPT hold-PROG-ATTR
 '**You** and I both have [children] of the same age.'

Table 5.30: Attestations of the second-person pronoun *na ~ nare* across the provinces.

Form	TSOJ			TSOJ								UNP
	Sin	Tö	Su	Kak	Mu	Sa	Mi	Sik	Pi	Sip	Kap	
na	0	0	0	0	0	0	1	1	0	3		7
nare	0	0	0	0	1	0	0	0	0	0	0	1

5.6.1.2.2 *imasi ~ masi*

The second-person pronoun *imasi* is attested twice: once as *imasi*, and once as *masi* with an elided initial vowel (perhaps to avoid a hypermetrical line). It is unclear if this pronoun has any different meaning or pragmatic function in comparison with the second-person pronoun *na ~ nare*. In AOJ it is only attested in TSOJ and UNP, but it is well attested in WOJ.

314. 14:3359a.4-5 – Suruga
 伊麻思乎多能美 / 波播尔多我比奴
 ***imasi**-wo tanöm-i / papa-ni tangap-i-n-u*
 2.S-ACC trust-INF / mother-DAT defy-INF-PERF-FIN
 '[I] defied [my] mother and put [my] trust in **you**.'

315. 14:3440b.3-4 – UNP
麻之毛阿礼母/ 余知乎曽母弓流
masi* mo are mö / *yöti-wo sö möt-er-u
2.S FPT 1.S FPT / same.age-ACC FPT hold-PROG-ATTR
'**You** and I both have [children] of the same age.'

Table 5.31: Attestations of the second-person pronoun *imasi* ~ *masi* across the provinces.

TSOJ			EOJ								UNP
Sin	Tö	Su	Kak	Mu	Sa	Mi	Sik	Pi	Sip	Kap	
0	0	1	0	0	0	0	0	0	0	0	1

5.6.1.2.3 Summary of second-person pronouns

Table 5.32 below shows the morphological distinctions that can be seen among the various second-person pronouns.

Table 5.32: Attested morphological forms of the second-person pronouns.

PRONOUN	Possessive -*nga*		Accusative -*wo*		Dative -*ni*		Directive -*ngari*		Comitative -*tö*	
	TSOJ	EOJ	TSOJ	EOJ	TSOJ	EOJ	TSOJ	EOJ	TSOJ	EOJ
na	–	*na-nga*	–	*na-wo*	–	*na-ni*	–	–	*na-tö*[146]	
nare	–	–	–	–	–	–	–	–	–	–
imasi ~ *masi*	–	–	*imasi-wo*	–	–	–	–	–	–	–

In regard to topicalization, only the pronoun *na* is attested topicalized, as shown in Table 5.33 below.

Table 5.33: Second-person pronouns attested topicalized with the particle *pa*.

PRONOUN	TSOJ	EOJ
na	–	*na pa*
nare	–	–
imasi ~ *masi*	–	–

Table 5.34 below shows which pronouns are attested with the function of a syntactic nominative.

---

146 This only occurs once in 14:3492.5 – UNP, and it is unclear if the poem is written in TSOJ or EOJ.

Table 5.34: Second-person pronouns attested as a syntactic nominative.

PRONOUN	TSOJ	EOJ
na	–	–
nare	–	+
imasi ~ masi	+[147]	–

5.6.2 Demonstrative pronouns

The demonstrative pronoun system involves a three-way distinction between proximal, mesial, and distal. There is no distinction of plurality. This is illustrated in Table 5.35 below. Unfortunately, none of the demonstrative pronouns is attested in TSOJ.

Table 5.35: Attested demonstrative pronouns in AOJ.

	Pronominal		Modifying		Locational	
	TSOJ	EOJ	TSOJ	EOJ	TSOJ	EOJ
Proximal	–	*köre* 'this'	–	*könö* 'this'	–	*kökö* 'here'[148]
Mesial	–	*sö* 'that'[149]	–	*sönö* 'that'	–	–
Distal	–	*ka* 'that (over there)'	–	*kanö* 'that (over there)'[150]	–	–
				wote 'that (over there)'		

5.6.2.1 Proximal pronouns
The proximal pronouns include *könö ~ köre* 'this' and *kökö* 'here'.

5.6.2.1.1 *könö ~ köre* 'this'
Unlike in later forms of Japanese, there does not appear to be any speaker/addressee relation to the proximal pronoun *könö ~ köre* 'this', instead it simply refers to some-

---

[147] One UNP poem (see example 315) does show this pronoun used as a syntactic nominative, but the poem does not contain any EOJ linguistic features, thus it may have been written in a TSOJ topolect.
[148] Only attested once in an UNP poem, but the poem shows EOJ linguistic features.
[149] Only attested once in an UNP poem, but the poem shows EOJ linguistic features.
[150] Only attested once in an UNP poem, but the poem shows EOJ linguistic features.

thing nearby (Vovin 2005: 272). The proximal *kö-* 'this' is lexicalized in the word *köyöpi* 'tonight' (e.g., in 14:3469.2 – UNP), but otherwise does not occur, so I do not include it as a form in the synchronic grammar. The modifying form *könö* appears before all other nouns. An extended form *köre* 'this' is attested once, in isolation before the attributive copula *nö* (see example 317). The formant *-re* in this form is probably related to the formant *-re* we find in the personal pronouns *ware* '1.S', *are* '1.S', and *nare* '2.S', but synchronically there is no clear meaning for it.

316. 14:3361.1-3 – Sagamu
安思我良能 / 乎弓毛許乃母尓 / 佐須和奈乃
asingara-nö / *wote mo **könö mö**-ni* / *sas-u wana-nö*
TN-GEN / that side **this side**-LOC / thrust-ATTR trap-COMP
'Like the [noise from the] traps set **here** [lit. 'this side'] and there in Asigara...'

317. 20:4420.4-5 – Muzasi
安我弓等都氣呂 / 許礼乃波流母志
a-nga te-tö tukey-rö / ***köre** nö paru mös-i*
REFL-POSS hand-COM affix-IMP / **this** COP.ATTR needle hold-INF
'Hold **this** needle and attach [the cords] with your own hands.'

318. 20:4394.3-5 – Simotupusa
由美乃美他 / 佐尼加和多良牟 / 奈賀氣己乃用乎
yumi-nö mita / *sa-ne ka watar-am-u* / *nanga-key **könö** yo-wo*
bow-GEN together / LOC-sleep.NML QPT cross.over-TENT-ATTR / be.long-AVATTR **this** night-ACC
'Shall [I] get through **this** long night, sleeping together with [my] bow?'

319. 14:3460.1-2 – UNP
多礼曽許能 / 屋能戸於曽夫流
*tare sö **könö*** / *YA-nö TO osö-nbur-u*
who FPT **this** / house-GEN door push-shake-ATTR
'Who is knocking on the door of **this** house?'

320. 14:3506.5 – UNP
見延奴己能許呂
*MI-ye-n-u **könö** körö*
see-PASS-NEG-ATTR **this** time
'[It was during] **this** time that I could not see [my lord].'

Table 5.36: Attestations of the proximal pronoun *könö ~ köre* across the provinces.

Form	TSOJ			EOJ								UNP
	Sin	Tö	Su	Kak	Mu	Sa	Mi	Sik	Pi	Sip	Kap	
könö	0	0	0	0	0	1	0	0	0	1	0	6
köre	0	0	0	0	1	0	0	0	0	0	0	0

5.6.2.1.2 *kökö* 'here'

The proximal *kökö* 'here' is attested only once. It is not a reduplicated form of the pronoun *kö* 'this', rather it is historically from *kə kə[151] 'this place' (Vovin 2005: 279).

321. 14:3538b.3-5 – UNP
己許呂能未 / 伊母我理夜里弖 / 和波**己許**尓思天
*kökörö nömï / imö-ngari yar-i-te / wa pa **kökö** n-i s-i-te*
heart RPT / beloved.girl-DIR send-INF-SUB / 1.S TPT **here** COP-INF do-INF-SUB
'[I can] only send [my] heart to [my] darling, [as] I am **here**.'

5.6.2.2 Mesial pronoun *sö ~ sönö*

There does not appear to be any speaker/addressee relation to the mesial pronoun *sö* 'that', rather it indicates something that is somewhat remote (Vovin 2005: 285). It can also have an anaphoric usage (see example 324 below). The mesial *sö* 'that' is attested just once, before the accusative *-wo*, while the modifying form *sönö* is attested twice. Unlike the proximal *kö-* which has an extended stem *köre*, an extended stem *söre* is unattested in AOJ, though it is phonographically attested once in WOJ (Omodaka 1967: 407).

322. 14:3411.5 – Kamitukeno
曾能可抱与吉尓
***sönö** kapo yö-ki-ni*
that face be.good-AVATTR-LOC
'Since **that** [hidden] face [of his] is handsome. . .'

---

151 Or *kə ko, with progressive vowel assimilation.

323. 14:3386.4-5 – Simotupusa
曾能可奈之伎乎 / 刀尔多弖米也母
sönö kanasi-ki-wo / to-ni tate-m-ey ya mö
that be.dear-AVATTR-ACC / outside-LOC make.stand-TENT-EV QPT EPT
'Will [I] make **that** dear [girl] stand outside? (No, I will not)'

324. 14:3472.1-2 – UNP
比登豆麻等 / 安是可曾乎伊波牟
pitö-n-duma tö / anze ka **sö-wo** ip-am-u
person-GEN-spouse QUOT / why QPT **that**-ACC say-TENT-ATTR
'[That girl is] another man's wife – why should [I] say **that**?'

Table 5.37: Attestations of the mesial pronoun sö ~ sönö across the provinces.

TSOJ			EOJ								UNP
Sin	Tö	Su	Kak	Mu	Sa	Mi	Sik	Pi	Sip	Kap	
0	0	0	1	0	0	0	0	0	1	0	1

5.6.2.3 Distal pronouns
The distal pronouns include ka ~ kanö 'that (over there)' and wote 'that (over there)'.

5.6.2.3.1 Distal pronoun ka ~ kanö
The distal ka 'that (over there)' is attested once, and its modifying form kanö is also attested once. It refers to something or someone a considerable distance away.

325. 20:4384.1-2 – Simotupusa
阿加等伎乃 / 加波多例等枳尔
akatöki-nö / **ka** pa tare töki-ni
dawn-GEN / **that** TPT who time-LOC
'At dawn, when [one asks], 'Who [is] **that over there**?'.'

326. 14:3565.1-2 – UNP
可能古呂等 / 宿受夜奈里奈牟
kanö ko-rö-tö / NE-nz-u ya nar-i-n-am-u
that girl-DIM-COM / sleep-NEG-INF QPT be-INF-PERF-TENT-ATTR
'Shall [it] be that [I] will not sleep with **that** sweet girl?'

Table 5.38: Attestations of the distal pronoun *ka ~ kanö* across the provinces.

TSOJ			EOJ								UNP
Sin	Tö	Su	Kak	Mu	Sa	Mi	Sik	Pi	Sip	Kap	
0	0	0	0	0	0	0	0	0	1	0	1

5.6.2.3.2 Distal pronoun *wote*

The distal pronoun *wote* 'that (over there)' is attested just once. It modifies the following noun without any intervening morphology.

327. 14:3361.1-3 – Sagamu
 安思我良能 / **乎弓毛**許乃母尓 / 佐須和奈乃
 asingara-nö / ***wote mo** könö mö-ni* / *sas-u wana-nö*
 TN-GEN / **that side** this side-LOC / thrust-ATTR trap-COMP
 'Like the [noise from the] traps set here and **there** [lit. 'that side'] in Asigara...'

5.6.3 Interrogative pronouns

There are many interrogative pronouns, some of which are only attested in a few AOJ topolects. The full list is provided in Table 5.39 below. Unfortunately, only one is attested in TSOJ, though this is certainly a byproduct of the smaller size of its corpus.

Table 5.39: Attested interrogative pronouns of AOJ.

Pronoun	TSOJ	EOJ
who	–	*ta- ~ tare*
what	–	*andö, anze**
why	*nani*	*anze*
where	–	*indu*[152]
when	–	*itu*
which	–	*indure* *indusi*[153]
how	–	*ika*

*This form is only attested once with the indicated meaning

---

[152] Only attested once in an UNP poem, but the poem contains EOJ linguistic features.
[153] Only attested once in an UNP poem, but the poem contains EOJ linguistic features.

5.6.3.1 *ta-* ~ *tare* 'who'

The interrogative pronoun meaning 'who' has a bound stem *ta-* and an extended, free form *tare*. The bound stem *ta-* is only attested with a following possessive suffix *-nga*.

328. 14:3424.5 – Simotukeno
多賀家可母多牟
ta-nga *ke ka möt-am-u*
who-POSS container QPT hold-TENT-ATTR
'**Whose** [food] container shall [she] hold?'

329. 20:4425.1-3 – UNP
佐伎毛利尓 / 由久波多我世登 / 刀布比登乎
sakimori n-i / *yuk-u pa **ta-nga** se tö* / *top-u pitö-wo*
border.guard COP-INF / go-ATTR TPT **who-POSS** beloved.man QUOT / ask-ATTR person-ACC
'Those who ask, '**Whose** husband is that, going to be a border guard?'.'

330. 20:4384.1-2 – Simotupusa
阿加等伎乃 / 加波多例等枳尓
akatöki-nö / *ka pa **tare** töki-ni*
dawn-GEN / that TPT **who** time-LOC
'At dawn, when [one asks], '**Who** [is] that over there?'.'

331. 14:3460.1-2 – UNP
多礼曾許能 / 屋能戸於曾夫流
***tare** sö könö* / *YA-nö TO osö-nbur-u*
who FPT this / house-GEN door push-shake-ATTR
'**Who** is knocking on the door of this house?'

Table 5.40: Attestations of the interrogative pronoun *ta-* ~ *tare* across the provinces.

Form	TSOJ			EOJ								UNP
	Sin	Tö	Su	Kak	Mu	Sa	Mi	Sik	Pi	Sip	Kap	
ta-	0	0	0	0	0	0	0	1	0	0	0	1
tare	0	0	0	0	0	0	0	0	0	1	0	1

5.6.3.2 *nani* 'why, what'

The interrogative pronoun *nani* 'why, what' is attested just once in the corpus, in TSOJ.

332. 20:4323.3-5 – Töpotuapumi
 奈尓須礼曾 / 波々登布波奈乃 / 佐吉泥己受祁牟
 nani *s-ure sö* / *papa tö [i]p-u pana-nö* / *sak-i-nde-kö-nz-u-kem-u*
 why do-EV FPT / mother QUOT say-ATTR flower-GEN / bloom-INF-go.out.INF-come-NEG-INF-PST.TENT-ATTR
 '**Why** has the flower called 'mother' not come out in bloom?'

The usage of the phrase *nani s-ure sö* to mean 'why' may be a TSOJ innovation since it is not attested anywhere else in the MYS (Mizushima 2003: 105).

5.6.3.3 *anze* 'why, what'

The interrogative pronoun *anze* usually means 'why', but in one poem (example 338 below) it has a meaning of 'what'. It is an EOJ word. The WOJ cognate is *nanzö* (Vovin 2005: 333–334). All attested examples are given below.

333. 14:3434.5 – Kamitukeno
 安是加多延世武
 anze *ka taye-se-m-u*
 why QPT break.INF-CAUS-TENT-FIN
 '**Why** would [you] break [us] apart?'

334. 14:3369.3-5 – Sagamu
 須我麻久良 / 安是加麻可左武 / 許呂勢多麻久良
 sunga-makura / ***anze*** *ka mak-as-am-u* / *kö-rö se ta-makura*
 sedge-pillow / **why** QPT use.as.a.pillow-HON-TENT-ATTR / girl-DIM do.IMP hand-pillow
 '**Why** should [you] lay [your] head [on] a sedge pillow? Dear girl, use [my] arm as [your] pillow!'

335. 14:3469.3-5 – UNP
 和加西奈波 / 阿是曾母許与比 / 与斯呂伎麻左奴
 wa-nga se-na pa / ***anze*** *sö mö köyöpi* / *yös-i-rö-k-i-mas-an-u*
 1.S-POSS beloved.man-DIM TPT / **why** FPT EPT this.evening / approach-INF-UNC-come-INF-HON-NEG-ATTR
 'Oh, **why** does my beloved not come [to me] tonight?'

336. 14:3472.1-2 – UNP
比登豆麻等 / 安是可曾乎伊波牟
pitö-n-duma tö / ***anze** ka sö-wo ip-am-u*
person-GEN-spouse QUOT / **why** QPT that-ACC say-TENT-ATTR
'[That girl] is another man's wife – **why** should [I] call [her] that?'

337. 14:3513.4-5 – UNP
安是可多要牟等 / 伊比之兒呂波母
***anze** ka taye-m-u tö* / *ip-i-si KO-rö pa mö*
why QPT break-TENT-ATTR QUOT / say-INF-PST.ATTR girl-DIM TPT EPT
'Oh, this girl, who asked, '**Why** would [we] break up?'.'

338. 14:3517.2-3 – UNP
多要尓之伊毛乎 / 阿是西呂等
taye-n-i-si imo-wo / ***anze** se-rö tö*
break.INF-PERF-INF-PST.ATTR beloved.girl-ACC / **what** do-IMP QUOT
'[I am] thinking of **what** to do about [my] darling, who broke up with [me].'

339. 14:3576.5 – UNP
安是可加奈思家
***anze** ka kanasi-ke*
why QPT be.dear-AVATTR
'**Why** is [she] dear [to me]?'

Table 5.41: Attestations of the interrogative pronoun *anze* across the provinces.

TSOJ			EOJ								UNP
Sin	Tö	Su	Kak	Mu	Sa	Mi	Sik	Pi	Sip	Kap	
0	0	0	1	0	1	0	0	0	0	0	5

5.6.3.4 *andö* 'what'

This interrogative pronoun is unique to EOJ. Its initial vowel is attested once elided, which is shown in example (345) below. The WOJ cognate is *nandö* (Vovin 2005: 333).

340. 14:3404.5 – Kamitukeno
 安杼加安我世牟
 andö ka a-nga se-m-u
 what QPT 1.S-POSS do-TENT-ATTR
 '**What** should I do?'

341. 14:3379.1-2 – Muzasi
 和我世故乎 / 安杼可母伊波武
 wa-nga se-ko-wo / andö kamö ip-am-u
 1.S-POSS beloved.man-DIM-ACC / **what** EPT say-TENT-ATTR
 '[I] wonder, **what** could [I] say [about] my beloved man?'

342. 14:3397.5 – Pitati
 阿杼可多延世武
 andö ka taye-se-m-u
 what QPT break-CAUS-TENT-ATTR
 '**What** would make [us] break [up]?'

343. 14:3465.4 – UNP
 安杼世呂登可母
 andö se-rö tö kamö
 what do-IMP QUOT EPT
 '[I] wonder, **what** would [you] say [I] do?'

344. 14:3494.5 – UNP
 汝波安杼可毛布
 NA pa andö ka [o]mop-u
 2.S TPT **what** QPT think-ATTR
 '**What** do you think?'

345. 14:3556.5 – UNP
 那乎杼可母思武
 na-wo [a]ndö kamö si-m-u
 2.S-ACC **what** EPT do-TENT-ATTR
 '**What** should [I] do about you?'

Table 5.42: Attestations of the interrogative pronoun *andö* across the provinces.

TSOJ			EOJ								UNP
Sin	Tö	Su	Kak	Mu	Sa	Mi	Sik	Pi	Sip	Kap	
0	0	0	1	1	0	0	0	1	0	0	4

5.6.3.5 *ika* 'how, what kind'

This interrogative pronoun is only attested twice.

346. 14:3418.4-5 – Kamitukeno
 許登波佐太米都 / 伊麻波伊可尓世母
 *kötö pa sandamey-t-u / ima pa **ika** n-i se-m-ö*
 matter TPT determine.INF-PERF-FIN / now TPT how COP-INF do-TENT-ATTR
 '[They] have decided the matter [of who I will marry]. Now, **how** will [I] go through [with it]?'

347. 14:3536.4-5 – UNP
 伊可奈流勢奈可 / 和我理許武等伊布
 ***ika** nar-u se-na ka / wa-ngari kö-m-u tö ip-u*
 what.kind be-ATTR beloved.man-DIM QPT / 1.S-DIR come-TENT-FIN QUOT say-ATTR
 '**What kind** of lover is [he], [who] says [he] shall come to me?'

Table 5.43: Attestations of the interrogative pronoun *ika* across the provinces.

TSOJ			EOJ								UNP
Sin	Tö	Su	Kak	Mu	Sa	Mi	Sik	Pi	Sip	Kap	
0	0	0	1	0	0	0	0	0	0	0	1

5.6.3.6 *indu* 'where'

This interrogative pronoun is only attested once.

348. 14:3549.3-5 – UNP
 伊豆由可母 / 加奈之伎世呂我 / 和賀利可欲波牟
 ***indu**-yu kamö / kanasi-ki se-rö-nga / wa-ngari kayop-am-u*
 where-ABL EPT / be.dear-AVATTR beloved.man-DIM-POSS / 1.S-DIR visit.frequently-TENT-ATTR
 '[I] wonder, from **where** shall [my] dearly beloved pay frequent visits to me?'

5.6.3.7 *indusi* 'which'

The interrogative pronoun *indusi* 'which' is only attested once. Its WOJ cognate is *induti* 'which'. Since the sound change *t > s_i only occurred in the Muzasi, Simotukeno, Simotupusa, and Pitati topolects of EOJ, it is likely the below poem is written in one of those topolects.

349. 14:3474.3-5 – UNP
伊侶弓伊奈波 / **伊豆思**牟伎弓可 / 伊毛我奈氣可牟
inde-te in-anba / ***indusi*** *muk-i-te ka* / *imo-nga nangeyk-am-u*
go.out.INF-SUB depart-COND / **which** face-INF-SUB QPT / beloved.girl-POSS lament-TENT-ATTR
'When [I] go away, **which** [way] will [my] darling girl face to lament?'

5.6.3.8 *indure* 'which'

Like the pronoun *indusi*, the interrogative pronoun *indure* also means 'which' (Vovin 2005: 324). This word is attested once in EOJ.

350. 20:4392– Simotupusa
阿米都之乃 / **以都例**乃可美乎 / 以乃良波加 / 有都久之波々尓 / 麻多己等刀波牟
amey tusi-nö / ***indure*** *nö kami-wo* / *inör-anba ka* / *utukusi papa-ni* / *mata kötö top-am-u*
heaven earth-GEN / **which** COP.ATTR deity-ACC / pray-COND FPT / be.beloved.AVFIN mother-DAT / again word ask-TENT-ATTR
'If [I] pray, to **which** deities of heaven and earth [should I pray so I] could once again inquire after [my] beloved mother?'

5.6.3.9 *itu* 'when'

When the focus particle *mo* follows the interrogative pronoun *itu* 'when', its meaning is 'always'. A meaning of 'when' can also be expressed by certain verbal suffixes and conjunctions (discussed in Chapters 7 and 9). It is attested in EOJ and UNP.

351. 20:4386.3-5 – Simotupusa
以都母**以都**母 / 於毛加古比須々 / 奈理麻之都之母
itu *mö* ***itu*** *mö* / *omo-nga kopi s-u s-u* / *nar-i-mas-i-tusi mö*
when FPT when FPT / mother-POSS love.NML do-FIN do-FIN / make.a.living-INF-HON-INF-COOR FPT
'[My] mother **always** loves [me], even while working.'

Example (351) shows a syntactic inversion.

352. 20:4359.3-5 – Kamitupusa
 伊都之加毛 / 都加敝麻都里弖 / 久尓尓閇牟可毛
 itu si kamo / tukape-matur-i-te / kuni-ni pey muk-am-o
 when EPT EPT / serve.INF-HUM-INF-SUB / province-LOC prow face-TENT-ATTR
 '**When**, [I] wonder, [after] having served, will [the boat] face its prow towards [my home] province?'

353. 20:4436.4-5 – UNP
 伊都伎麻佐牟等 / 登比之古良波母
 itu k-i-mas-am-u tö / töp-i-si ko-ra pa mö
 when come-INF-HON-TENT-FIN QUOT / ask-INF-PST.ATTR girl-DIM TPT EPT
 'Oh, [my] darling girl, who asked [me], '**When** will you come back?'.'

Table 5.44: Attestations of the interrogative pronoun *itu* across the provinces.

TSOJ			EOJ								UNP
Sin	Tö	Su	Kak	Mu	Sa	Mi	Sik	Pi	Sip	Kap	
0	0	0	0	0	0	0	0	0	1	1	1

5.6.4 Collective pronouns

The collective pronouns are *mïna* 'all' and *mörö-mörö* 'many'.

5.6.4.1 *mïna* 'all'

The collective pronoun *mïna* 'all', is only attested once, in TSOJ.

354. 14:3398 – Sinano
 比等未奈乃 / 許等波多由登毛 / 波尔思奈能 / 伊思井乃手兒我 / 許登奈多延曽祢
 pitö mïna-nö / kötö pa tay-u tömo / panisina-nö / isiWI-nö teNGO-nga / kötö na-taye-sö-n-e
 person all-GEN / word TPT cease-FIN CNJ / TN-GEN / TN-GEN maiden-POSS / word NEG.IMP-cease.INF-do-DES-IMP
 'Even if **everyone** [else] goes silent, [there is] a maiden from Isiwi in Panisina [whose] words [I] wish would never cease!'

5.6.4.2 *morö-morö* 'many'

This pronoun is only attested in its reduplicated form. It is attested unreduplicated, as *mörö* 'many', in all WOJ texts except BS, where it is attested three times in its reduplicated form (see Vovin 2005: 342–343). It is only attested once in EOJ.

355. 20:4372.13-15 – Pitati
毛呂々々波 / 佐祁久等麻乎須 / 可閇利久麻弖尓
morö-morö pa / sake-ku tö mawos-u / kapeyr-i-k-u-mande-ni
many-REDUP TPT / be.safe-AVINF QUOT say.HUM-FIN / return-INF-come-ATTR-TERM-LOC
'I will implore [the deities] to keep the **many, many** [people I left behind] safe until [I] return [home].'

5.7 Numerals

Both cardinal and ordinal numbers are attested.

5.7.1 Cardinal numbers

There are five cardinal numbers attested: *pitö ~ pita* 'one', *puta* 'two', *itu* 'five', *nana* 'seven', and *ya* 'eight'. These are only attested in EOJ and UNP. Most of these are only attested with a classifier attached (*pitö ~ pita* 'one', *itu* 'five', *nana* 'seven', and *ya* 'eight'). Only *puta* 'two' is attested in isolation. An attestation of each numeral is provided below.

356. 14:3405a.4-5 – Kamitukeno
兒良波安波奈毛 / 比等理能未思弖
*KO-ra pa ap-ana-m-o / **pitö-ri** nömï s-i-te*
girl-DIM TPT meet-DES-TENT-ATTR / **one-CL** RPT do-INF-SUB
'[I] want [my] darling girl to meet [me], [when she is] all **alone**.'

357. 14:3435.5 – Kamitukeno
比多敝登於毛敝婆
***pita-pe** tö omop-e-nba*
one-CL QUOT think-EV-CONJ
'Since [I] think there is [just] **one layer**...'

358. 14:3526.3-5 – UNP
安我己許呂 / **布多**由久奈母等 / 奈与母波里曽祢
a-nga kökörö / ***puta** yuk-unam-ö tö* / *na-y-ömöp-ar-i-sö-n-e*
1.S-POSS heart / **two** go-TENT2-ATTR QUOT / NEG.IMP-EPEN-think-PROG-INF-do-DES-IMP
'Please do not think that my heart will go [after] **two** [women]!'

359. 20:4386.1-2 – Simotupusa
和加可都乃 / **以都毛等**夜奈枳
wa-nga kandu-nö / ***itu-motö** yanangi*
1.S-POSS gate-GEN / **five-CL** willow
'The **five** willows near my gate...'

360. 20:4431.3-5 – UNP
奈々弁加流 / 去呂毛尔麻世流 / 古侶賀波太波毛
***nana-pe** k-ar-u* / *körömo-ni mas-er-u* / *ko-rö-nga panda pa mo*
seven-CL wear-PROG-ATTR / robe-LOC be.superior-PROG-ATTR / girl-DIM-POSS skin TPT EPT
'Oh, [my] darling girl's skin [would] be better than the robes [I] am wearing in **seven layers**...'

361. 20:4379.5 – Simotukeno
夜多妣蘓弖布流
***ya-tanbi** sonde pur-u*
eight-CL sleeve wave-FIN
'[I shall] wave [my] sleeve **many times**.'[154]

5.7.1.1 Bound root *-so* 'ten'

The bound root *-so* is used to count tens, and the number that precedes it is multiplied by ten. While an unbound *so* 'ten' is unattested, an unbound number 'ten' in WOJ is attested as *töwo* (Vovin 2005: 364). The bound *-so* 'ten' is only attested in EOJ and UNP attached to the number *ya* 'eight', in a word form that idiomatically means 'many'.

---

[154] *Ya* 'eight' is used figuratively here and elsewhere in OJ to mean 'many' (Omodaka 1967: 754).

362. 20:4329.1-2 – Sagamu
夜蘇久尓波 / 奈尓波尓都度比
ya-so *kuni pa / nanipa-ni tundop-i*
eight-ten province TPT / TN-LOC gather-INF
'[Those from] **many provinces** gather in Nanipa...'

363. 20:4363.3 – Pitati
夜蘇加奴伎
ya-so *ka nuk-i*
eight-ten oar pierce-INF
'[We] pierced **many** oars [into the water]...'

364. 20:4349.4 – Kamitupusa
夜蘇志麻須義弖
ya-so *sima sungï-te*
eight-ten islands pass.INF-SUB
'Passing **many** islands...'

365. 14:3456.1-4 – UNP
宇都世美能 / 夜蘇許登能敷波 / 思氣久等母 / 安良蘇比可祢弖
utusemi-nö / ***ya-so*** *kötö-nö pe pa / singey-ku*[155] *tömö / arasop-i-kane-te*
the.world-GEN / **eight-ten** word-GEN leaf TPT / be.lush-AVINF CNJ / resist-INF-NEG.POT.INF-SUB
'Even though rumors **abound** in this world, [you] cannot resist [them].'

Table 5.45: Attestations of the bound root *-so* across the provinces.

TSOJ			EOJ								UNP
Sin	Tö	Su	Kak	Mu	Sa	Mi	Sik	Pi	Sip	Kap	
0	0	0	0	0	1	0	0	1	0	1	1

5.7.2 Ordinal numbers

The only ordinal number attested is *patu* 'first', which is attested just once.

---

[155] Literally, 'the leaves of eighty words are lush'.

366. 14:3468.1-2 – UNP
夜麻杼里乃 / 乎呂能**波都**乎尓 / 可賀美可家
yama-n-döri-nö / *wo-rö-nö **patu** wo-ni* / *kangami kake*
mountain-GEN-bird-GEN / tail-DIM-COMP **first** hemp-LOC / mirror hang.INF
'[I] hung the mirror on the **first** hemp [of the season], which is like the small tail of a mountain bird.'

5.7.3 Numeral classifiers

The numeral classifiers are *-tanbi, -ri, -motö, -tu,* and *-pe.*

5.7.3.1 Classifier *-tanbi*

The numeral classifier *-tanbi* indicates something done an X amount of times (where X is specified by the numeral to which the classifier attaches). The sole attestation in EOJ occurs after *ya* 'eight, many'.

367. 20:4379.5 – Simotukeno
夜多妣蘇弓布流
ya*-*tanbi *sonde pur-u*
eight-CL sleeve wave-FIN
'[I shall] wave [my] sleeve **many times**.'

5.7.3.2 Classifier *-ri*

The numeral classifier *-ri* is used to count a person or persons. It is only attested suffixed to the numbers *pitö* 'one' and *puta* 'two'. In the AOJ poetry, the form *puta-ri* 'two-CL' is used after the comitative suffix *-tö* to indicate the action of one person is done with someone else, and *pitö-ri* 'one-CL' is used to mean 'alone'.

368. 20:4345.1-4 – Suruga
和伎米故**等** / **不多利**和我見之 / 宇知江須流 / 々々河乃祢良波
*wa-ng[a]-imey-ko-**tö*** / ***puta-ri*** *wa-nga MI-si* / *uti-yes-uru* / *surunga-nö ne-ra pa*
1.S-POSS-beloved.girl-DIM-**COM** / **two-CL** 1.S-POSS see.INF-PST.ATTR / PREF-approach-ATTR / TN-GEN peak-PLUR TPT
'The peaks of Suruga, where [the waves] crash, which I gazed upon **with** my darling girl.'

369. 14:3405a.4-5 – Kamitukeno
 兒良波安波奈毛 / 比等理能未思弖
 KO-ra pa ap-ana-m-o / ***pitö-ri*** *nömï s-i-te*
 girl-DIM TPT meet-DES-TENT-ATTR / **one-CL** RPT do-INF-SUB
 '[I] want [my] darling girl to meet [me], [when she is] all **alone**.'

370. 14:3544.4-5 – UNP
 勢奈那**登布多理** / 左宿而久也思母
 *se-na-na-**tö puta-ri*** / *sa-NE-TE kuyasi-mö*
 beloved.male-DIM-DIM-**COM two-CL** / LOC-sleep.INF-SUB be.regretful.AVFIN-EXCL
 '[I] slept there **with** my dear, darling beloved, [and now I] regret it!'

371. 14:3550.4-5 – UNP
 伊多夫良思毛与 / 伎曽**比登里**宿而
 itanbur-asi-mo yö / *kisö **pitö-ri** NE-TE*
 tremble-SUP-EXCL EPT / last.night **one-CL** sleep.INF-SUB
 'Last night [I] slept **alone**, and oh, it seems [I] am trembling!'

Example (371) shows a syntactic inversion.

Table 5.46: Attestations of the classifier *-ri* across the provinces.

TSOJ			EOJ								UNP
Sin	Tö	Su	Kak	Mu	Sa	Mi	Sik	Pi	Sip	Kap	
0	0	1	1	0	0	0	0	0	0	0	3

5.7.3.3 Classifier *-motö*

The numeral classifier *-motö* is attested just once in EOJ, after the numeral *itu* 'five'. This example is used to count a type of tree. In contrast, the four WOJ examples provided in Vovin (2005: 385) are all used to count grassy plants.

372. 20:4386.1-2 – Simotupusa
 和加可都乃 / **以都毛等**夜奈枳
 wa-nga kandu-nö / ***itu-motö*** *yanangi*
 1.S-POSS gate-GEN / **five-CL** willow
 'The **five** willows near my gate...'

5.7.3.4 Classifier *-tu*

This numeral classifier *-tu* is used to count inanimate objects. It is only attested once.

373. 14:3526.1-2 – UNP
      奴麻**布多都** / 可欲波等里我栖
      *numa **puta-tu** / kayop-a töri-nga SU*
      marsh **two-CL** / go.back.and.forth-ATTR bird-POSS nest
      '[Like] the nests of a bird that shuttles between **two** marshes...'

5.7.3.5 Classifier *-pe*

This numeral classifier *-pe* is used to count layers.

374. 14:3435.5 – Kamitukeno
      比多敝登於毛敝婆
      ***pita-pe** tö omop-e-nba*
      one-CL QUOT think-EV-CONJ
      'Since [I] think there is [just] **one layer**...'

375. 20:4431.3-5 – UNP
      奈々弁加流 / 去呂毛尓麻世流 / 古侶賀波太波毛
      ***nana-pe** k-ar-u / körömo-ni mas-er-u / ko-rö-nga panda pa mo*
      seven-CL wear-PROG-ATTR / robe-LOC be.superior-PROG-ATTR / girl-DIM-POSS skin TPT EPT
      'Oh, [my] darling girl's skin [would] be better than the robes [I] am wearing in **seven layers**...'

Table 5.47: Attestations of the classifier *-pe* across the provinces.

TSOJ			EOJ								UNP
Sin	Tö	Su	Kak	Mu	Sa	Mi	Sik	Pi	Sip	Kap	
0	0	0	1	0	0	0	0	0	0	0	1

5.7.3.6 Classifier *-saka*

This classifier is used as a measurement of length: one *saka* equates to approximately 29.6cm. It is only attested once, in EOJ, suffixed to *ya-* 'eight, many'.

376. 14:3414.1-2 – Kamitukeno
伊香保呂能 / <u>夜左可</u>能為提尓
ikapo-rö-nö / ***ya-saka****-nö winde-ni*
TN-DIM-GEN / **eight-CL**-GEN dam-LOC
'Over the **tall** dam at Mt. Ikapo. . .'

6 Adjectives and adjectival verbs

In AOJ, as in WOJ, there are both adjectives and adjectival verbs. The former do not inflect, while the latter have a paradigm with several verbal suffixes. Most of these are exclusive to adjectival verbs, but a few are shared with regular verbs.

6.1 The basic syntax of adjectives and adjectival verbs

As is typical of SOV word order, the AOJ adjectives precede nominal heads. AOJ adjectival verbs can also precede nominal heads, but they must take an attributive suffix when functioning as a modifier. In addition, due to their verbal nature, adjectival verbs can also serve as the predicate of the sentence.

6.2 Adjectives

Adjectives in AOJ are true adjectives because they are uninflected. Historically, these seem to have been nouns (Vovin 2009a: 430). However, they cannot be followed by any of the nominal suffixes, so from a synchronic, morphological standpoint they are a distinct class from nouns.

6.2.1 Bare roots used as a modifier

Bare adjective roots can modify a noun on their own, and they are distinct from adjectival verbs in this regard because there is no attributive morphology attached. This appears to be a more archaic usage, indicating the morphology of adjectival verbs, and adjectival verbs as a distinct class, is a later development (as hypothesized by Vovin 2009a: 429). The adjectives attested as modifiers include *aka* 'red', *ara* 'rough', *ata* 'sudden', *awo* 'blue', *kanasi* 'dear, sad', *kupasi* 'beautiful', *ma* 'true', *nanga* 'long', *nipi* 'new', *opo* 'great', *osö* 'slow', *paya* 'fast', *posö* 'narrow', *puru* 'old', *sira ~ siro* 'white', *taka* 'high', *tökö* 'eternal', *utukusi* 'beloved', and *waka* 'young'. Among these, *ara* 'rough', *kanasi* 'dear, sad', *nanga* 'long', *paya* 'fast', *taka* 'high', and *utukusi* 'beloved' are also attested as adjectival verbs.

1. 14:3352.1-2 – Sinano
   信濃奈流 / 須我能**安良能**尔
   *sinanu-n[i] ar-u / sunga-nö **ara nö**-ni*
   TN-LOC exist-ATTR / TN-GEN **wild field**-LOC
   'In the **wild fields** of Suga in Sinano...'

2. 14:3429.1-3 – Töpotuapumi
   等保都安布美 / 伊奈佐**保曽江**乃 / 水乎都久思
   *töpotuapumi / inasa **posö YE**-nö / MIwo-tu kusi*
   TN / TN **narrow estuary**-GEN / channel-GEN.LOC stalk
   'The buoys in the channel of the **narrow estuary** of Inasa in Töpotuapumi...'

3. 20:4341.4-5 – Suruga
   道乃**長道**波 / 由伎加弖奴加毛
   *MITI nö **NANGA-NDI** pa / yuk-i-kate-n-u kamo*
   road COP.ATTR **long-road** TPT / go-INF-POT-NEG-ATTR EPT
   'The road [ahead] is **long**, and [I] fear I cannot traverse it!'

4. 14:3436.5 – Kamitukeno
   登許波尔毛我母
   ***tökö pa** n-i mongamö*
   eternal leaf COP-INF DPT
   '[I] wish [the trees] had **eternal leaves**...'

5. 20:4328.1-2 – Sagamu
   於保吉美能 / 美許等可之古美
   ***opo kimi**-nö / mi-kötö kasiko-mi*
   great lord-GEN / HON-word be.august-AVGER
   'Because [my] **sovereign**'s command is august...'

6. 20:4379.1-2 – Simotukeno
   之良奈美乃 / 与曽流波麻倍尔
   *sira **nami**-nö / yösör-u pama-pey-ni*
   white wave-GEN / draw.near-ATTR shore-side-LOC
   'On the side of the shore where the **white waves** draw near...'

7. 14:3424.4-5 – Simotukeno
麻**具波思兒**呂波 / 多賀家可母多年
ma **n-gupasi KO**-rö pa / ta-nga ke ka möt-am-u
true **COP.INF-beautiful girl**-DIM TPT / who-POSS container QPT hold-TENT-ATTR
'Whose [food] container shall the truly **beautiful girl** hold?'

8. 20:4392 – Simotupusa
阿米都之乃 / 以都例乃可美乎 / 以乃良波加 / **有都久之波々**尔 / 麻多己等刀波牟
amey tusi-nö / indure-nö kami-wo / inör-anba ka / **utukusi papa**-ni / mata kötö top-am-u
heaven earth-GEN / which-GEN deity-ACC / pray-COND FPT / **beloved mother**-DAT / again word ask-TENT-ATTR
'If [I] pray, to which deities of heaven and earth [should I pray so I] could once again inquire after [my] **beloved mother**?'

9. 14:3493a.1 – UNP
於曾波夜母
osö paya mö
slow fast FPT
'[Whether you are] **early or late**. . .'

10. 14:3495.1-2 – UNP
伊波保呂乃 / 蘓比能**和可麻都**
ipapo-rö-nö / sopi-nö **waka matu**
boulder-DIM-GEN / beside-GEN **young pine.tree**
'[Like] the **young pines** [growing] beside little rocks. . .'

11. 14:3514.5 – UNP
多可祢等毛比弖
taka ne tö [o]mop-i-te
high peak QUOT think-INF-SUB
'[I] think of [you] as a **high peak**.'

12. 14:3540.3-5 – UNP
安可故麻我 / 安我伎乎波夜美 / 許等登波受伎奴
aka koma-nga / a-n-gak-i-wo paya-mi / kötö tö [i]p-anz-u k-i-n-u
red horse-POSS / foot-GEN-scrape-NML-ABS be.fast-AVGER / word QUOT say-NEG-INF come-INF-PERF-FIN
'Because [my] **red horse**'s gallop is swift, [I] came [back] without saying a word.'

13. 14:3452.3-4 – UNP
    布流久佐尓 / 仁比久佐麻自利
    puru kusa*-ni** / ***nipi kusa *manzir-i*
    old grass-LOC / **new grass** mix-INF
    'Mix **new grass** with **old grass**…'

14. 14:3480.3-5 – UNP
    可奈之伊毛我 / 多麻久良波奈礼 / 欲太知伎努可母
    ***kanasi imo*-nga** / *ta-makura panare* / *yo-n-dat-i k-i-n-o kamö*
    dear beloved.girl-POSS / arm-pillow part.from.INF / night-LOC-rise-INF come-INF-PERF-ATTR EPT
    'Parting from [my] **dearly beloved's** arm [used as my] pillow and leaving in the night, [I] wonder, will [I] come [back]?'

Examples (7), (8), and (14) are debatable, since the final form of adjectival verbs can be used in an attributive function, and the final form of each of these is homophonous with their root. For example, the final form of *kanasi* 'be dear' is *kanasi* 'be.dear.AVFIN'. See §6.3.1 for further discussion. The fact that all three of these apparent adjectives are also attested as adjectival verbs further raises doubts as to whether these were used as true adjectives.

6.2.2 Usage followed by an attributive copula

An attributive copula *nö* (or its contracted form *n-*) may intervene between an adjective and the head it modifies. Syntactically, this forms a relative clause. For example, *niko n-gusa* 'soft COP.ATTR-grass' in example (16) below literally means 'grass that is soft'. The adjectives attested with an attributive copula before their head include *mandara* 'speckled', *niko* 'soft', *pirö* 'wide', *taka* 'high', *sikö* 'lowly', and *aka* 'red'.

15. 14:3354.1-3 – Töpotuapumi
    伎倍比等乃 / 萬太良夫須麻尓 / 和多佐波太
    kipey pitö-nö / ***mandara* n-*busuma*-ni** / *wata sapanda*
    TN person-GEN / **speckled COP.ATTR-bed.covers**-LOC / cotton amply
    '[Like] the cotton [that is] amply [placed] inside the **speckled bed covers** of the people from Kipey…'

16. 14:3370.1-3 – Sagamu
    安思我里乃 / 波故祢能祢呂乃 / <u>尓古具佐</u>能
    asingari-nö / *pakone-nö ne-rö-nö* / ***niko n-gusa**-nö*
    TN-GEN / TN-GEN peak-DIM-GEN / **soft COP.ATTR-grass**-COMP
    'Like the **soft grass** on the little peak of Mt. Pakone in Asigari...'

17. 20:4373.4 – Simotukeno
    之許乃美多弖等
    sikö nö mi-tate *tö*
    lowly COP.ATTR HON-shield COP
    'To be a **lowly soldier**...'

18. 20:4417.1-3 – Muzasi
    <u>阿加胡麻</u>乎 / 夜麻努尔波賀志 / 刀里加尔弖
    ***aka n-goma**-wo* / *yama no-ni pangas-i* / *tor-i-kani-te*
    red COP.ATTR-horse-ACC / mountain field-LOC let.go-INF / hold-INF-NEG.POT.INF-SUB
    '[I] set [my beloved's] **red horse** free [to roam] the mountains and fields, [but now I] cannot recapture [him]...'

19. 14:3497.1-2 – UNP
    可波加美能 / 祢自路<u>多可我夜</u>
    kapa kami-nö / *ne-n-ziro **taka n-gaya***
    river upper.part-GEN / root-GEN-white **high COP.ATTR-grass**
    'The **tall grass** [with] white roots in the upper area [of] the river...'

20. 14:3536.1-3 – UNP
    <u>安加胡麻</u>乎 / 宇知弖左乎尔吉 / 己許呂尔吉
    ***aka n-goma**-wo* / *ut-i-te sa-wo-n-bik-i* / *kökörö-n-bik-i*
    red COP.ATTR-horse-ACC / strike-INF-SUB LOC-string-GEN-pull-INF / heart-GEN-pull-INF
    'Just as [he] whips [his] **red horse** and tugs on the reins there, so [he] tugs on [my] heart.'

6.2.3 Multiple adjectives before a head

Multiple adjectives before a head are simply presented in order, with no morphology in between them.

21. 14:3497.1-2 – UNP
可波加美能 / 祢自路多可我夜
kapa kami-nö / **ne-n-ziro taka** n-gaya
river upper.part-GEN / **root-GEN-white high** COP.ATTR-grass
'The **tall** grass [with] **white roots** in the upper area [of] the river...'

6.2.4 *-ka* final adjectives

In WOJ, there are adjectives that end in the suffix *-ka* (Vovin 2009a: 440–443). These are not attested in TSOJ, and in EOJ we only find a single attestation of such an adjective, but it is one that is unattested in WOJ. This adjective is *sayaka* 'clear', which is only attested in WOJ as *saya* 'id.'. It should be noted the adjective *saya* 'clear' is also attested in EOJ (once in the Kamitukeno topolect and once in the Muzasi topolect). It is unclear what meaning this *-ka* adds.

22. 20:4424.5 – Muzasi
麻佐夜可尓美无
*ma-**sayaka** n-i mi-m-u*
INT-**clear** COP-INF see-TENT-FIN
'[I] would see [him] so **clearly**...'

6.2.5 *-nde* final adjectives

There is one adjective attested in AOJ that ends in the suffix *-nde*. This adjective is *masande* 'certain'. Its counterpart in WOJ is *masa* 'id.', which is unattested in AOJ. It is unclear what meaning this *-nde* adds.

23. 14:3521.3-5 – UNP
麻左侣尓毛 / 伎麻左奴伎美乎 / 許呂久等曽奈久
masande *n-i mo* / *k-i-mas-an-u kimi-wo* / *köröku tö sö nak-u*
certain COP-INF FPT / come-INF-HON-NEG-ATTR lord-ACC / caw-caw QUOT FPT cry-ATTR
'[The crow] will cry 'caw-caw' for [my] lord who **certainly** will not come.'

6.2.6 -nda final adjectives

There is one attestation of an AOJ adjective that ends in the suffix -nda. This adjective is *sapanda* 'many, much, amply'. Its counterpart in WOJ is *sapa* 'id.', which is unattested in AOJ. It is unclear what meaning this -nda adds.

24. 14:3354.1-3 – Töpotuapumi
  伎倍比等乃 / 萬太良夫須麻尓 / 和多**佐波太**
  kipey pitö-nö / *mandara n-busuma-ni* / *wata* **sapanda**
  TN person-GEN / speckled COP.ATTR-bed.covers-LOC / cotton **amply**
  '[Like] the cotton [that is] **amply** [placed] inside the speckled bed covers of the people from Kipey.'

6.2.7 Adjectival reduplication

There is only one instance of a reduplicated adjective. It is used before the copula infinitive *n-i* to create an adverbial phrase.

25. 14:3537a.3-5 – UNP
  波都々々尓 / 安比見之兒良之 / 安夜尓可奈思母
  patu-patu *n-i* / *ap-i-MI-si KO-ra si* / *aya n-i kanasi-mö*
  brief-REDUP COP-INF / meet-INF-see.INF-PST.ATTR girl-DIM EPT / extreme COP-INF be.dear.AVFIN-EXCL
  'The sweet girl that [I] met **briefly** is extremely dear [to me]!'

This is probably a reduplication of the *patu-* found in Late WOJ *patuka* 'slight, faint' (Omodaka 1967: 584).

6.3 Adjectival verbs

Adjectival verbs are adjectives that are verbal, and as such they take verbal morphology such as predication, evidentiality, tense, and aspect. In AOJ, adjectival verbs inflect for predication and evidentiality, but not tense or aspect. In order to add tense or aspect to an adjectival verb phrase, the auxiliary verb *ar-* 'exist' must follow the adjectival verb in the infinitive form. The addition of the auxiliary *ar-* 'exist' allows the affixation of whatever tense, aspect, or mood marker is needed for the adjectival verb. This can be seen in examples (33) and (34) in §6.3.3.1.1 below.

In addition, there are a number of gerund forms for adjectival verbs. All of the morphology will be discussed in the sections that follow.

6.3.1 Adjectival verb classes

There are two classes of adjectival verbs: those with roots that end with the syllable /si/, and those with roots that do not. Following Vovin (2009a: 444) I will refer to the former as Class 2 and the latter as Class 1. The only difference between the two is that Class 2 adjectival verbs have portmanteau final forms that are homophonous with their adjectival verb root. This is due to haplology of the sequence *si-si (Vovin 2009a: 444). Table 6.1 below shows the maximal inflectional paradigm[156] for the Class 1 adjectival verb *töpo-* 'be far' and the Class 2 adjectival verb *kuyasi-* 'be regretful'.

Table 6.1: Maximal inflectional paradigm for each class of adjectival verb in TSOJ and EOJ.

Form	*töpo-* 'be far' (CLASS 1)		*kuyasi-* 'be regretful' (CLASS 2)	
	TSOJ	EOJ	TSOJ	EOJ
Infinitive	töpo-ku	töpo-ku	kuyasi-ku	kuyasi-ku
Final	töpo-si	töpo-si	kuyasi	kuyasi
Attributive	töpo-ki	töpo-ke ~ töpo-ki	kuyasi-ki	kuyasi-ke ~ kuyasi-ki
Evidential	–[157]	töpo-ka-[158]	–[159]	kuyasi-ka-
Gerund	töpo-mi	töpo-mi	kuyasi-mi	kuyasi-mi

6.3.2 Prefixes

There is only one prefix attested, the intensifying *ma-*.

6.3.2.1 Intensifying prefix *ma-*

This prefix also attaches to nouns. It serves to intensify the meaning of the adjective or adjectival verb, and can in most cases be translated as 'so' or 'really'. See §5.3.4 for further discussion.

---

156 All of the suffixes listed are attested, but not all of them are attested attached to *töpo-* or *kuyasi-*.
157 Unattested, but based on TSOJ morphophonology we would expect the form *töpo-ke-*.
158 An evidential form *-ke* is attested once. See §6.3.3.5 for more discussion.
159 Unattested, but based on TSOJ morphophonology we would expect the form *kuyasi-ke-*.

26. 20:4424.5 – Muzasi
麻佐夜可尔美无
ma-sayaka n-i mi-m-u
INT-clear COP-INF see-TENT-FIN
'[I] would see [him] **so clearly**.'

27. 14:3366.1-2 – Sagamu
麻可奈思美 / 佐祢尓和波由久
ma-kanasi-mi / sa-ne-ni wa pa yuk-u
INT-be.dear-AVGER / LOC-sleep.NML-LOC 1.S TPT go-ATTR
'Since [she] is **truly dear** [to me], I will go and sleep [with her].'

28. 14:3488.3-4 – UNP
麻之波尔毛 / 能良努伊毛我名
ma-sinba n-i mo / nör-an-o imo-nga NA
INT-frequent COP-INF FPT / tell-NEG-ATTR beloved.girl-POSS name
'[My] beloved girl's name that [I] have not uttered **so frequently**...'

29. 14:3567.1-2 – UNP
於伎弖伊可婆 / 伊毛婆麻可奈之
ok-i-te ik-anba / imo pa ma-kanasi
leave.behind-INF-SUB go-COND / beloved.girl TPT INT-be.sad.AVFIN
'If [I] leave [her] behind and go [away], [my] beloved girl will be **so sad**.'

Table 6.2: Attestations of the intensifying prefix *ma-* across the provinces.

TSOJ			EOJ							UNP
Sin	Tö	Su	Kak	Mu	Sa	Mi	Sik	Pi	Sip	Kap	
0	0	0	0	2	1	0	0	0	0	0	3

6.3.3 Suffixes

The suffixes that attach to adjectival verb bases include the infinitive *-ku*, the nominalizer *-ku*, the final *-si*, the attributive *-ki* ~ *-ke*, the evidential *-ka* ~ *-ke*, the gerund *-mi*, the nominalizer *-sa*, the exclamative *-mo*, the conditional gerund *-anba*, the conjunctive gerund *-nba*, the concessive gerund *-ndö*, the nominalizer *-aku*, and the nominalizer *-nge*. Among these, the exclamative *-mo*, the conditional gerund *-anba*, the conjunctive gerund -*nba*, the concessive gerund -*ndö*, and the nominalizer -*aku* also attach to verbal word forms (see Chapter 7 for details).

6.3.3.1 Infinitive -*ku*

The infinitive -*ku* is the adjectival verb counterpart to the verbal infinitive -*i*. It can be used as a non-final predicate or as an adverbial modifier (Vovin 2009a: 457). In addition, it can be followed by the subordinative gerund auxiliary -*te*, just as we find with the infinitive -*i* in the verbal paradigm.

6.3.3.1.1 Usage as a non-final predicate

30. 20:4407.4-5 – Kamitukeno
伊毛賀**古比之久** / 和須良延奴加母
*imo-nga **kopisi-ku*** / *wasur-aye-n-u kamö*
beloved.girl-POSS **be.longing.for-AVINF** / forget-PASS-NEG-ATTR EPT
'[I] **began to miss** [my] beloved, and [I realized I] cannot forget [her]!'

31. 20:4424.1-3 – Muzasi
伊呂**夫可久** / 世奈我許呂母波 / 曽米麻之乎
*irö-n-**buka-ku*** / *se-na-nga körömö pa* / *sömey-masi-wo*
color-GEN-**be.deep-AVINF** / beloved.man-DIM-POSS garment TPT / dye-SUBJ-ACC
'Even though [I] should like to dye my darling man's garment in a **deeply** [saturated] color. . .'

32. 20:4373.1-2 – Simotukeno
祁布与利波 / 可敝理見**奈久**弖
kepu-yöri pa / *kaper-i-MI **na-ku**-te*
today-ABL TPT / return-INF-see.NML **not.exist-AVINF**-SUB
'From today, **without** looking back. . .'

33. 14:3476a.5 – UNP
故布思可流奈母
***kopusi-k[u]**-ar-unam-ö*
be.longing.for-AVINF-exist-TENT2-ATTR
'[She] **will long for** [me].'

34. 14:3482b.5 – UNP
    許等**多可**利都母
    *kötö [i]**ta-k[u]**-ar-i-t-umö*
    word **be.painful-AVINF**-exist-INF-PERF-EXCL
    'The rumors have been **painful**!'

6.3.3.1.2 Usage as an adverbial modifier

35. 20:4322.1-2 – Töpotuapumi
    和我都麻波 / **伊多久**古非良之
    *wa-nga tuma pa / **ita-ku** kopï-rasi*
    1.S-POSS spouse TPT / **be.extreme-AVINF** long.for-SUP
    'My wife must miss [me] **greatly**.'

36. 20:4346.1-3 – Suruga
    知々波々我 / 可之良加伎奈弖 / **佐久**阿例弖
    *titi papa-nga / kasira kaki-nande / **sa-ku** ar-e te*
    father mother-POSS / head TNG-caress.INF / **be.safe-AVINF** exist-IMP QUOT
    '[My] mother and father patted [me on] the head and told me to stay **safe**.'

37. 14:3415.4-5 – Kamitukeno
    賀久古非牟等夜 / 多祢物得米家武
    ***ka-ku** kopï-m-u tö ya / tane mötömey-kem-u*
    be.thus-AVINF long.for-TENT-FIN QUOT QPT / seed search.for.INF-PST.TENT-ATTR
    'Do [you] think [I] would long for [it] **so much** that [I] would have searched for [its] seeds?'

38. 20:4368.1-2 – Pitati
    久自我波々 / **佐氣久**阿利麻弖
    *kunzi-n-gapa pa / **sakey-ku** ari-mat-e*
    TN-GEN-river TPT / **be.safe-AVINF** DUR-wait-IMP
    'Keep waiting [for me] **safely**, [at] Kuzi river!'

39. 20:4389.3-4 – Simotupusa
    尓波志**久**母 / 於不世他麻保加
    ***nipasi-ku** mö / opuse-tamap-o ka*
    be.sudden-AVINF FPT / give.responsibility.INF-HON-ATTR QPT
    'Has [the emperor] **suddenly** given [me] an order?'

40. 20:4348.5 – Kamitupusa
夜須久祢牟加母
yasu-ku ne-m-u kamö
be.easy-AVINF sleep-TENT-ATTR EPT
'[I] wonder, shall [I] sleep **peacefully**?'

41. 14:3383.3-5 – Kamitupusa
可久太尔毛 / 久尔乃登保可婆 / 奈我目保里勢牟
ka-ku ndani mo / kuni-nö töpo-ka-nba / na-nga MEY por-i se-m-u
be.thus-AVINF RPT FPT / province-GEN be.far-AVEV-CONJ / 2.S-POSS eye desire-NML do-TENT-FIN
'[I] dream of your eyes, since [your] province is just **so** far [away].'

42. 14:3463.3-5 – UNP
己許呂奈久 / 佐刀乃美奈可尔 / 安敝流世奈可毛
kökörö na-ku / sato-nö mi-naka-ni / ap-er-u se-na kamo
heart not.exist-AVINF / village-GEN HON-inside-LOC / meet-PROG-ATTR beloved.man-DIM EPT
'Oh, [my] darling beloved, whom [I] am meeting **inconsiderately** in the great center of the village...'

43. 14.3487.3-5 – UNP
可久須酒曽 / 宿莫奈那里尔思 / 於久乎可奴加奴
ka-ku s-u s-u sö / NE-NA-na nar-i-n-i-si / oku-wo kan-u kan-u
be.thus-AVINF do-FIN do-FIN FPT / sleep-NEG.ATTR-LOC become-INF-PERF-INF-PST.ATTR / future-ACC worry.about-FIN worry.about-FIN
'Doing it **thusly** again and again, [I] worry about [our] future again and again, [because] it turned out that [we] did not sleep [together].'

44. 14:3522.5 – UNP
麻登保久於毛保由
ma-töpo-ku omop-oy-u
INT-be.far-AVINF think-PASS-FIN
'[I] suddenly think it **is so far** [away]...'

Table 6.3: Attestations of the infinitive -*ku* across the provinces.

TSOJ			EOJ								UNP
Sin	Tö	Su	Kak	Mu	Sa	Mi	Sik	Pi	Sip	Kap	
0	1	2	2	1	0	0	1	2	1	2	8

6.3.3.2 Nominalizer -*ku*

The nominalizer -*ku* is attested once in the corpus. This is probably just an extended function of the infinitive -*ku*, but since I list the nominalizer -*i* separate from the verbal infinitive -*i*, I do the same here in order to be consistent.

45. 14:3463.1-2 – UNP
     麻等保久能 / 野尔毛安波奈牟
     ma-töpo-ku nö / NO-ni mo ap-ana-m-u
     INT-be.far-AVNML COP.ATTR / field-LOC FPT meet-DES-TENT-FIN
     '[I] should like to meet [you] in the fields that are **quite a distance** [away].'

6.3.3.3 Final predication marker -*si*

The final suffix -*si* is not a final predication marker in the same strict sense that the verbal -*u* is a final predication marker because we find many examples of -*si* used in a purely attributive function. Due to this latter function, one might be tempted to think the adjectival verb final -*si* and the past-attributive auxiliary -*si* in the verbal morphology (described in §7.6.1.1.4) are related. This comparison is untenable due to the following facts: final -*si* is a suffix and past-attributive -*si* is an auxiliary; their semantics differ significantly; they cannot be followed by the same morphology; and while final -*si* can be used as an attributive, past-attributive -*si* is never used as a final. A better explanation was put forth by Vovin (2009a: 462), who claims final -*si* and attributive -*ki* were relatively new elements in the adjectival verb paradigm, leading to occasional confusion between the two. Due to the inability to reconstruct these forms in Proto-Ryukyuan, we can reconstruct them as morphological innovations in PJe. The final -*si* can be followed by the exclamatory suffix -*mo* (shown in examples 49 and 50 below).

6.3.3.3.1 Final function

The suffix -*si* is predominantly used as an adjectival verb final predication marker.

46. 20:4381.5 – Simotukeno
     伊刀母須敝**奈之**
     ito mö sunbe **na-si**
     really FPT way **not.exist-AVFIN**
     'Really, **it can't** be helped.'

47. 20:4351.4 – Kamitupusa
    奈保波太**佐牟之**
    *napo panda **samu-si***
    still skin **be.cold**-AVFIN
    'Still [my] skin **is cold**. . .'

48. 14:3478.1-2 – UNP
    等保斯等布 / 故奈乃思良祢尓
    ***töpo-si** tö [i]p-u / kona-nö sira ne-ni*
    be.far-AVFIN QUOT say-ATTR / TN-GEN white peak-LOC
    'On the white peaks of Kona which are said **to be far** [away]. . .'

49. 14:3530.4-5 – UNP
    兒呂我可奈門欲 / 由可久之**要思**母
    *KO-rö-nga kana-TO-yo / yuk-aku si **ye-si**-mö*
    girl-DIM-POSS metal-door-ABL / go.ATTR-NML FPT **be.good**-AVFIN-EXCL
    'Going through the metal gate of [my] darling girl's [home] **is** so **nice**!'

50. 14:3555.4 – UNP
    於等**太可思**母奈
    *otö-n-**daka-si**-mö na*
    sound-GEN-**be.high**-AVFIN-EXCL EPT
    'The sound is **loud**!'

6.3.3.3.2 Attributive function

The attributive function of *-si* is less commonly attested, and only occurs with two adjectival verbs: *na-* 'not.exist' and *ara-* 'be.rough'. A wider variety of adjectival verbs are attested with the final *-si* in an attributive function in WOJ (Vovin 2009a: 463–464).

51. 20:4401.5 – Sinano
    意母**奈志**尓志弖
    *omö **na-si** n-i s-i-te*
    mother **not.exist**-AVFIN COP-INF do-INF-SUB
    '[I] have left [them] **without** a mother. . .'

52. 20:4321.5 – Töpotuapumi
    伊牟**奈之**尔志弖
    *imu **na-si** n-i s-i-te*
    beloved.girl **not.exist-AVFIN** COP-INF do-INF-SUB
    '**Without** [my] beloved girl. . .'

53. 14:3405b.5 – Kamitukeno
    美流比登**奈思**尔
    *mi-ru pitö **na-si**-ni*
    see-ATTR person **not.exist-AVFIN**-LOC
    'When there **is no** one [there] who would see [him]. . .'

54. 20:4330.5 – Sagamu
    美流波々**奈之**尔
    *mi-ru papa **na-si**-ni*
    see-ATTR mother **not.exist-AVFIN**-LOC
    '[I ask] because [my] mother **is not here** to watch. . .'

55. 14:3442.4-5 – UNP
    夜麻尔可祢牟毛 / 夜杼里波**奈之**尔
    *yama-ni ka ne-m-u mo / yandör-i pa **na-si**-ni*
    mountain-LOC QPT sleep-TENT-ATTR FPT / lodge-NML TPT **not.exist-AVFIN**-LOC
    'Shall [I] sleep in the mountains being that **there is** no **lodging** [here]?'

The form *na-si-ni* 'not.exist-AVFIN-LOC' found in examples (53) – (55) is attested in both WOJ and EOJ, whereas the expected form *na-ki-ni* 'not.exist-AVATTR-LOC' is unattested.

56. 20:4372.5-6 – Pitati
    阿良志乎母 / 多志夜波婆可流
    ara-si wo mö / tas-i ya panbakar-u
    be.rough-AVFIN man FPT / stand-INF EPT hesitate-FIN
    'Even a **rough man** would stand and hesitate.'

57. 20:4430.1-2 – UNP
    阿良之乎乃 / 伊乎佐太波佐美
    ara-si wo-nö / i-wo-sa-n-da-pasam-i
    be.rough-AVFIN man-GEN / PREF-DIM-arrow-LOC-hand-pinch-INF
    '[Like a] **rough** man [with his] fingers pinching a small arrow. . .'

Table 6.4: Attestations of the final -*si* and its functions across the provinces.

Func	TSOJ			EOJ								UNP
	Sin	Tö	Su	Kak	Mu	Sa	Mi	Sik	Pi	Sip	Kap	
Final	1	0	0	0	0	0	0	1	0	0	2	6
Attributive	1	1	0	1	0	1	0	0	1	0	0	2

6.3.3.3.3 Final form of Class 2 adjectival verbs

As mentioned in §6.3.1, the final form of Class 2 adjectival verbs is homophonous with the adjectival verb root. Thus, it is morphologically null, and the root becomes portmanteau.

58. 20:4406.3-5 – Kamitukeno
久佐麻久良 / 多妣波**久流之**等 / 都氣夜良麻久母
*kusa makura / tanbi pa **kurusi** tö / tungey-yar-am-aku mö*
grass pillow / journey TPT **be.painful.AVFIN** QUOT / tell.INF-send-TENT.ATTR-NML FPT
'[I] **would send** [him] to tell [them] that [my] journey, [sleeping on] a grass pillow, is painful!'

59. 14:3556.1-2 – UNP
思保夫祢能 / 於可礼婆**可奈之**
*sipo-n-bune-nö / ok-ar-e-nba **kanasi***
tide-GEN-boat-COMP / leave.behind-PROG-EV-CONJ **be.sad.AVFIN**
'When [I] am leaving [you], [I] **am sad**, like [leaving] a boat in the tide.'

60. 14:3567.1-2 – UNP
於伎弖伊可婆 / 伊毛婆麻**可奈之**
*ok-i-te ik-anba / imo pa ma-**kanasi***
leave.behind-INF-SUB go-COND / beloved.girl TPT INT-**be.sad.AVFIN**
'If [I] leave [her] behind and go [away], [my] darling girl will **be** so **sad**.'

6.3.3.4 Attributive -*ki* ~ -*ke*

The adjectival verb attributive suffix has two main functions: adnominalization and final predication. Its usage as a final predication marker is triggered by certain attributive-triggering particles, described in §10.1.1. In addition, it can nominalize an adjectival verb, just as the verbal attributive suffix can nominalize a verb.

6.3 Adjectival verbs — 261

The adjectival verb attributive -*ki* and its variant -*ke* have been described quite extensively in the previous research on AOJ. The variant -*ke* is exclusive to EOJ,[160] and simply shows an unraised vowel, whereas the variant -*ki* is found in WOJ, TSOJ, and EOJ, and is the product of the vowel raising of *e > /i/. The adjectival attributive -*ki* ~ -*ke* can be followed by either the conditional gerund -*anba* or the nominalizer -*aku*.

6.3.3.4.1 -*ki* form

The form -*ki* is the only one attested in WOJ and TSOJ, but it is well attested in EOJ as well. I separate the attestations by function in the sections that follow below.

6.3.3.4.1.1 Adnominal function

Examples of the adnominal function follow below.

61. 14:3379.2;4-5 – Muzasi
安杼可母伊波武 /宇家良我波奈乃 / 登吉**奈伎**母能乎
*andö kamö ip-am-u / ukera-nga pana-nö / töki **na-ki** mönö-wo*
what EPT say-TENT-ATTR / okera-POSS blossoms-COMP /time **not.exist-AVATTR** thing-ACC
'[I] wonder, what could I say [about my beloved]? Considering [my love for him] **is timeless**, like the *ukera* blossoms...'

62. 20:4413.3-4 – Muzasi
麻**可奈之伎** / 西呂我馬伎己无
*ma-**kanasi-ki** / se-rö-nga mek-i-kö-m-u*
INT-**be.dear-AVATTR** / beloved.man-DIM-POSS walk-INF-come-TENT-ATTR
'[My] **dearly** beloved shall come walking [back].'

63. 14:3351.4-5 – Pitati
加奈思吉兒呂我 / 尓努保佐流可母
kanasi-ki *KO-rö-nga* / *nino pos-ar-u kamö*
be.dear-AVATTR girl-DIM-POSS / cloth dry-PROG-ATTR EPT
'[I] wonder [if my] **dear**, darling girl is drying a cloth.'

---

160 This is retained in Hachijō as -*ke* (Kaneda 2001: 85).

64. 20:4371.1-4 – Pitati
多知波奈乃 / 之多布久可是乃 / 可**具波志伎** /都久波能夜麻乎
tatinbana-nö / *sita puk-u kanze-nö* / *ka-n-**gupasi-ki*** / *tukupa-nö yama-wo*
mandarin.orange-GEN / below blow-ATTR wind-GEN / scent-GEN-**be.lovely-AVATTR** / TN-GEN mountain-ACC
'Tukupa mountain, **where** the scent of the wind that blows below the mandarin orange trees **is lovely**...'

65. 14:3452.1-2 – UNP
於毛思路伎 / 野乎婆奈夜吉曽
omosiro-ki / *NO-wonba na-yak-i-sö*
be.lovely-AVATTR / field-ACC.EMP NEG.IMP-burn-INF-do
'Do not burn the **lovely** field!'

66. 14:3453.1-2 – UNP
可是能等乃 / **登抱吉**和伎母賀
kanze-nö [o]tö-nö / ***töpo-ki*** *wa-ng[a]-imö-nga*
wind-GEN sound-COMP / **be.far-AVATTR** 1.S-POSS-beloved.girl-POSS
'My beloved girl, who **is far away** like the sound of the wind...'

6.3.3.4.1.2 Final predication due to an attributive-triggering particle

In the following examples, the attributive *-ki* is triggered due to a particle that induces this change.

67. 20:4321.1 – Töpotuapumi
可之古**伎**夜
kasiko-ki *ya*
be.august-AVATTR EPT
'**The august** [imperial command]!'

68. 20:4337.5 – Suruga
已麻叙**久夜志伎**
*ima nzö **kuyasi-ki***
now FPT **be.regretful-AVATTR**
'Now [I] **regret** it!'

69. 14:3504.3-4 – UNP
宇良夜須尓 / 左奴流夜曽**奈伎**
*ura yasu n-i / sa-n-uru YO sö **na-ki***
heart easy COP-INF / LOC-sleep-ATTR night FPT **not.exist-AVATTR**
'There **are no** nights when [I] sleep there with [my] heart at ease.'

6.3.3.4.1.3 Nominalization function

The nominalization function of the attributive -*ki* occurs just two times. In each instance a case marker is attached to this -*ki*.

70. 14:3386.4-5 – Simotupusa
曽能**可奈之伎**乎 / 刀尓多弖米也母
*sönö **kanasi-ki**-wo / to-ni tate-m-ey ya mö*
that **be.dear-AVATTR**-ACC / outside-LOC make.stand-TENT-EV QPT EPT
'Will [I] make that **dear** [girl] stand outside? (No, I will not!)'

71. 14:3411.5 – Kamitupusa
曽能可抱**与吉尓**
*sönö kapo **yö-ki**-ni*
that face **be.good-AVATTR**-LOC
'Since that [hidden] face [of his] **is handsome**. . .'

6.3.3.4.2 -*ke* form

The attributive -*ke* is exclusive to EOJ. In the sections that follow below, I separate the examples based on their primary function.

6.3.3.4.2.1 Adnominal function

The adnominal function of -*ke* is attested four times.

72. 14:3412.4-5 – Kamitukeno
可奈師家兒良尓 / 伊夜射可里久母
***kanasi-ke** KO-ra-ni / iya n-zakar-i-[i]k-umö*
be.dear-AVATTR girl-DIM-DAT / more.and.more COP.INF-be.far.from-INF-go-EXCL
'[I] am going further and further away from [my] **dear**, darling girl!'

73. 20:4382.1-2 – Simotukeno
布多富我美 / 阿志氣比等奈里
putapongami / **asi-key** pitö nar-i
PN / **be.bad-AVATTR** person be-FIN
'Putapogami is a **bad** person.'

74. 20:4394.3-5 – Simotupusa
由美乃美他 / 佐尼加和多良牟 / 奈賀氣己乃用乎
yumi-nö mita / sa-ne ka watar-am-u / **nanga-key** könö yo-wo
bow-GEN together / LOC-sleep.NML QPT cross.over-TENT-ATTR / **be.long-AVATTR** this night-ACC
'Shall [I] get through this **long** night, sleeping together with [my] bow?'

75. 14:3557.1-2 – UNP
奈夜麻思家 / 比登都麻可母与
nayam-asi-ke / pitö-tuma kamö yö
distress-ADJ-AVATTR / person-spouse FPT EPT
'[This] wife of another man **is** so **distressing** [to me]!'

6.3.3.4.2.2 Final predication due to an attributive-triggering particle

In the following examples, the attributive -*ke* is triggered due to a particle that induces this change.

76. 20:4369.4-5 – Pitati
由等許尓母 / 可奈之家伊母曽 / 比留毛可奈之祁
yu tökö-ni mö / **kanasi-ke** imöسö / piru mo **kanasi-ke**
night bed-LOC FPT / **be.dear-AVATTR** beloved.girl FPT / daytime FPT **be.dear-AVATTR**
'[My] beloved girl, who is dear [to me] in bed at night, is also **dear** [to me] during the day.'

77. 14:3483.4-5 – UNP
阿飛与流等可毛 / 欲流等家也須家
ap-ï-yor-u tö kamo / yoru töke-**yasu-ke**
meet-INF-approach-FIN QUOT EPT / night come.undone.INF-**be.easy-AVATTR**
'[I] wonder [if I] will meet with [my beloved]. [Our garment cords] **easily** come undone at night!'

6.3.3.4.2.3 Nominalization function

The nominalization function of the attributive -*ke* occurs just two times. In each instance the accusative case marker -*wo* is attached to -*ke*.

78. 20:4419.3-5 – Muzasi

須美**与氣**乎 / 都久之尓伊多里弖 / 古布志氣毛波母
*sum-i **yö-key**-wo* / *tukusi-ni itar-i-te* / *kopusi-ngey [o]mop-am-ö*
reside-NML **be.good-AVATTR**-ACC / TN-LOC arrive-INF-GER / be.longing.for-AVNML think-TENT-ATTR
'It **was nice** living there, so [I] am sure [I] will long for [it] after [I] arrive in Tukusi.'

79. 14:3500.3-4 – UNP

比等能兒能 / **宇良我奈之家**乎
pitö-nö KO-nö / ***ura-n-ganasi-ke**-wo*
person-GEN girl-GEN / **feelings-GEN-be.dear-AVATTR**-ACC
'[I] **have strong feelings** for [that] person's girl, but. . .'

6.3.3.4.3 Unclear examples

Before the conditional gerund -*anba* the vowel in the attributive will either fuse or elide. When it has elided, in the form -*k-anba* '-AVATTR-COND', we are unable to determine if the underlying form of the attributive is -*ki* or -*ke*. Thus, I mark such examples as being unclear.

80. 14:3410.4-5 – Kamitukeno

於久乎奈加祢曽 / 麻左可思**余加婆**
oku-wo na-kane-sö / *masaka si **yö-k-anba***
future-ACC NEG.IMP-worry.INF-do / present EPT **be.good-AVATTR-COND**
'Do not fret about the future, **if [things] are fine** now.'

In addition, the vowel of the attributive suffix elides before the nominalizer -*aku*, once again preventing us from determining the underlying vowel of the attributive in these forms.

81. 14:3489.3-4 – UNP

之牙**可久**尓 / 伊毛呂乎多弖天
***singe-k-aku**-ni* / *imo-rö-wo tate-te*
be.lush-AVATTR-NML-LOC / beloved.girl-DIM-ACC make.stand.INF-SUB
'[I] had [my] beloved girl stand in the **thicket**.'

Table 6.5: Attestations of the attributive -*ki* ~ -*ke* across the provinces.

Form	TSOJ			EOJ								UNP	Totals
	Sin	Tö	Su	Kak	Mu	Sa	Mi	Sik	Pi	Sip	Kap		
-*ki*	0	1	1	1	2	0	0	0	3	1	0	8	18
-*ke*	0	0	0	1	2	0	0	0	2	0	0	9	14
UNC	0	0	0	1	0	0	0	0	0	0	1	1	4

The data in Table 6.5 show the attributive -*ki* is slightly more common than the attributive -*ke*, and no province shows only the attributive -*ke*.

6.3.3.5 Evidential -*ka* ~ -*ke*

The EOJ adjectival verb evidential -*ka* corresponds to the WOJ adjectival verb evidential -*ke*. The latter is also attested once in EOJ, but I view this attestation, shown below in example (85), as the result of either scribal alteration or WOJ influence. Vovin (2009a: 476) makes a convincing argument that the WOJ form -*ke* developed from a fusional reduction of PJe *-*ki* ar-e* '-AVATTR exist-EV', with subsequent *r loss, though the PJe form of the adjectival verb attributive was *-*ke*, not *-*ki*. Accordingly, it is clear the EOJ form -*ka* is the result of V₁ elision of the medial PJe vowel sequence in *-*ke* ar-e* 'id.' with subsequent *r loss, rather than a fusional reduction of *ea > /e/. Neither suffix is attested in TSOJ. The evidential can be followed by the concessive gerund -*ndö[mo]* or the conjunctive gerund -*nba*.

82. 14:3383.4-5 – Kamitupusa
久尔乃**登保可婆** / 奈我目保里勢牟
*kuni-nö **töpo-ka-nba*** / *na-nga MEY por-i se-m-u*
province-GEN **be.far-AVEV-CONJ** / 2.S-POSS eye desire-NML do-TENT-FIN
'[I] dream of your eyes, **since** [your] province **is far** [away].'

83. 14:3473.3-5 – UNP
等抱可騰母 /祢毛等可兒呂賀 / 於由尔美要都留
töpo-ka-ndömö / *ne-m-o tö ka KO-rö-nga* / *oyu n-i mi-ye-t-uru*
be.far-AVEV-CONC / sleep-TENT-ATTR QUOT QPT girl-DIM-POSS / grow.older. NML COP-INF see-PASS.INF-PERF-ATTR
'**Although [she] is far** [away], [I] suddenly see [my] dear girl has grown older, asking [me], 'Shall [we] sleep [together]?'.'

84. 14:3539.3-5 – UNP
    安夜抱可等 / 比等豆麻古呂乎 / 伊吉尔和我須流
    ayapo-ka-ndö / *pitö-n-duma ko-rö-wo* / *iki-ni wa-nga s-uru*
    be.dangerous-AVEV-CONC / person-GEN-spouse girl-DIM-ACC / breath-LOC 1.S-POSS do-ATTR
    'Although it is dangerous, still I sigh for a dear girl [who is another] man's wife.'

85. 14:3376a.1-2;5 – Muzasi
    古非思家波 /素弖毛布良武乎 /伊呂尔豆奈由米
    kopïsi-ke-nba / *sonde mo pur-am-u-wo* / *irö-ni [i]nd-una yumey*
    be.longing.for-AVEV-CONJ / sleeve FPT wave-TENT-ATTR-ACC / color/feelings-LOC go.out-NEG.IMP at.all
    'When [you] are longing [for me], [I] shall wave [my] sleeves [for you], but do not let [your] face reveal even a hint of [your] true feelings [for me]!'

Table 6.6: Attestations of the evidential -*ka* ~ -*ke* across the provinces.

Form	TSOJ			EOJ								UNP
	Sin	Tö	Su	Kak	Mu	Sa	Mi	Sik	Pi	Sip	Kap	
-ka	0	0	0	0	0	0	0	0	0	0	1	2
-ke	0	0	0	0	1	0	0	0	0	0	0	0

6.3.3.6 Gerund -*mi*

The adjectival verb gerund -*mi* indicates a reason. It is the only gerund suffix that attaches directly to an adjectival verb root.

86. 20:4403.1-2 – Sinano
    意保枳美能 / 美己等**可之古美**
    opo kimi-nö / *mi-kötö* **kasiko-mi**
    great lord-GEN / HON-word **be.august-AVGER**
    'Because [my] sovereign's command **is august**...'

87. 14:3434.3 – Kamitukeno
    野乎**比呂美**
    NO-wo **pirö-mi**
    field-ABS **be.wide-AVGER**
    'Because the field **is wide**...'

88. 20:4422.3 – Muzasi
    宇都久之美
    utukusi-mi
    be.beloved-AVGER
    'Because [I] love [him]...'

89. 14:3366.1-2 – Sagamu
    麻可奈思美 / 佐祢尔和波由久
    ma-kanasi-mi / sa-ne-ni wa pa yuk-u
    INT-be.dear-AVGER / LOC-sleep.NML-LOC 1.S TPT go-ATTR
    'Since [she] is truly dear [to me], [I] will go and sleep [with her].'

90. 20:4328.1-2 – Sagamu
    於保吉美能 / 美許等**可之古美**
    *opo kimi-nö / mi-kötö **kasiko-mi***
    great lord-GEN / HON-word **be.august-AVGER**
    'Because [my] sovereign's command is **august**...'

91. 14:3426.1-3 – Mitinöku
    安比豆祢能 / 久尓乎**佐杼抱美** / 安波奈波婆
    apindu ne-nö / kuni-wo sa n-döpo-mi / ap-an-ap-anba
    TN peak-GEN / land-ABS thus COP.INF-be.far-AVGER / meet-NEG-ITER-COND
    'If [we] keep failing to meet **because** the land of the Apidu peaks **is so far** [away]...'

92. 20:4379.4-5 – Simotukeno
    伊刀毛須倍**奈美** / 夜多妣蘓弖布流
    *ito mo sunbey **na-mi** / ya-tanbi sonde pur-u*
    simply FPT way **not.exist-AVGER** / eight-CL sleeve wave-FIN
    '[I shall] wave [my] sleeve many times, **because** there **is** simply **nothing** [more I can] do!'

93. 20:4387.4-5 – Simotupusa
    阿夜尓**加奈之美** / 於枳弖他加枳奴
    *aya n-i **kanasi-mi** / ok-i-te ta-ka k-i-n-u*
    mysterious COP-INF **be.dear-AVGER** / leave.behind-INF-SUB rice.field-DIR come-INF-PERF-FIN
    '[I] left [her] behind and came to the rice field, **because [she] is** mysteriously **dear** [to me].'

94. 20:4358.1-2 – Kamitupusa
    於保伎美乃 / 美許等加志古美
    *opo kimi-nö / mikötö **kasiko-mi***
    great lord-GEN / command **be.august-AVGER**
    'Because [my] sovereign's command **is august**. . .'

95. 14:3468.4-5 – UNP
    刀奈布倍美許曽 / 奈尓与曽利鷄米
    ***tonap-unbey-mi** kösö / na-ni yösör-i-kem-ey*
    recite-DEB-AVGER FPT / 2.S-DAT have.feelings.for-INF-PST.TENT-EV
    'And just **because [I] had to recite** [the incantation], feelings for you welled up [inside me].'

In example (95) the adjectival verb gerund -*mi* attaches to the verbal debitive suffix -*unbey* which only allows adjectival verb morphology.

96. 14:3507.1-3 – UNP
    多尓世婆美 / 弥年尓波比多流 / 多麻可豆良
    *tani **senba-mi** / mi-ne-ni pap-i-tar-u / tama kandura*
    valley **be.narrow-AVGER** / HON-peak-LOC crawl-INF-PP-ATTR / jade vine
    '[It is like] the jade[-like] vines that crawl up the peak **because** the valley **is narrow**.'

97. 20:4428.3-4 – UNP
    宇都久之美 / 叡比波登加奈々
    ***utukusi-mi** / yenbi pa tök-ana-na*
    be.beloved-AVGER / sash TPT undo-NEG.ATTR-LOC
    '[And] **because [I] love** [him], [I shall sleep] without untying [my] sash.'

Table 6.7: Attestations of the gerund -*mi* across the provinces.

TSOJ			EOJ								UNP
Sin	Tö	Su	Kak	Mu	Sa	Mi	Sik	Pi	Sip	Kap	
1	0	0	1	2	2	1	1	0	2	1	7

6.3.3.7 Conditional gerund -*anba*

The conditional gerund -*anba* creates a conditional clause. It is one of the few suffixes that attaches to both verb and adjectival verb stems, though it is only attested once attached to an adjectival verb. While it can attach directly to a verb root, it attaches to the adjectival verb attributive suffix, rather than the root.

98. 14:3410.4-5 – Kamitukeno
     於久乎奈加祢曽 / 麻左可思**余加婆**
     *oku-wo na-kane-sö / masaka si **yö-k-anba***
     future-ACC NEG.IMP-worry.INF-do / present FPT **be.good-AVATTR-COND**
     'Do not fret about the future, **if [things] are fine** now.'

6.3.3.8 Conjunctive gerund -*nba*

The conjunctive gerund -*nba* indicates a reason, something akin to 'because' or 'since'. It can also be used in a temporal function, meaning 'when'. It is another suffix that attaches to both verb and adjectival verb stems. This gerund cannot attach directly to an adjectival verb root, instead it must attach to the adjectival verb evidential suffix -*ka* ~ -*ke*.

99. 14:3376a.1-2;5 – Muzasi
     古非思家波 / 素弖毛布良武乎 / 伊呂尓豆奈由米
     kopïsi-ke-nba / *sonde mo pur-am-u-wo* / *irö-ni [i]nd-una yumey*
     be.longing.for-AVEV-CONJ / sleeve FPT wave-TENT-ATTR-ACC / color/feelings-LOC go.out-NEG.IMP at.all
     '**When [you] are longing** [for me], [I] shall wave [my] sleeve [for you], but do not let [your] face reveal even a hint of [your] true feelings [for me]!'

100. 14:3383.4-5 – Kamitupusa
     久尓乃**登保可婆** / 奈我目保里勢牟
     *kuni-nö **töpo-ka-nba*** / *na-nga MEY por-i se-m-u*
     province-GEN **be.far-AVEV-CONJ** / 2.S-POSS eye desire-NML do-TENT-FIN
     '[I] dream of your eyes, **since** [your] province **is far** [away].'

Table 6.8: Attestations of the conjunctive gerund -*nba* across the provinces.

TSOJ			EOJ								UNP
Sin	Tö	Su	Kak	Mu	Sa	Mi	Sik	Pi	Sip	Kap	
0	0	0	0	1	0	0	0	0	0	1	0

6.3.3.9 Concessive gerund -ndö ~ -ndömo

This gerund creates a concessive clause (i.e., 'although. . .'). Like the conditional -anba and the conjunctive gerund -nba, the concessive gerund attaches to both verb and adjectival verb stems. When attaching to an adjectival verb stem, it follows the adjectival verb evidential suffix -ka- ~ -ke-.

101. 14:3473.3-5 – UNP
 等抱可騰母 / 祢毛等可兒呂賀 / 於由尓美要都留
 töpo-ka-ndömö / *ne-m-o tö ka KO-rö-nga* / *oyu n-i mi-ye-t-uru*
 be.far-AVEV-CONC / sleep-TENT-ATTR QUOT QPT girl-DIM-POSS / grow.older. NML COP-INF see-PASS.INF-PERF-ATTR
 '**Although [she] is far** [away], [I] suddenly see [my] dear girl has grown older, asking [me], 'Shall [we] sleep [together]?'.'

102. 14:3539.3-5 – UNP
 安夜抱可等 / 比等豆麻古呂乎 / 伊吉尓和我須流
 ayapo-ka-ndö / *pitö-n-duma ko-rö-wo* / *iki-ni wa-nga s-uru*
 be.dangerous-AVEV-CONC / person-GEN-spouse girl-DIM-ACC / breath-LOC 1.S-POSS do-ATTR
 '**Although it is dangerous**, still I sigh for a dear girl [who is another] man's wife.'

Table 6.9: Attestations of the concessive gerund -ndö ~ -ndömo across the provinces.

TSOJ			EOJ								UNP
Sin	Tö	Su	Kak	Mu	Sa	Mi	Sik	Pi	Sip	Kap	
0	0	0	0	0	0	0	0	0	0	0	2

6.3.3.10 Nominalizer -aku

The nominalizer *-aku* nominalizes the adjectival verb phrase, rather than just the adjectival verb. This is another suffix that attaches to both verbal and adjectival verbal stems. See §7.5.2.1.3.2 for a discussion of its usage with verbs. With adjectival verbs it must attach to the attributive suffix, and it can be followed by the case suffix *-ni*. It is only attested twice with an adjectival verb.

103. 14:3489.3-4 – UNP
之牙可久尓 / 伊毛呂乎多弖天
singe-k-aku*-ni / *imo-rö-wo tate-te
be.lush-AVATTR-NML-LOC / beloved.girl-DIM-ACC make.stand.INF-SUB
'[I] had [my] beloved girl stand in the **thicket**.'

This form (*singe-k-aku* 'be.lush-AVATTR-NML') is notable because it shows a vowel contraction common in AOJ verbal morphology (e.g., *-ke-aku* or *-ki-aku* > *-k-aku*), but uncommon in WOJ verbal morphology. More specifically, WOJ always fuses the adjectival verb attributive *-ki* and the nominalizer *-aku* into the portmanteau form *-keku* (Vovin 2009a: 763). Thus, we would find *singe-keku* 'be.lush-AVATTR.NML' in WOJ. Still, the usage of this suffix on adjectival verbs in AOJ is most likely due to borrowing from WOJ.

The other AOJ attestation, given in example (104) below, contains the WOJ form *-keku* '-AVATTR.NML', and therefore it is probably the result of borrowing from WOJ or a scribal alteration.

104. 14:3533.4-5 – UNP
安奈由牟古麻能 / 乎之家口母奈思
a nayum-u koma-nö / ***wosi-keku*** *mö na-si*
leg be.troubled.by-ATTR horse-GEN / **feel.sad**-AVATTR.NML FPT not.exist-AVFIN
'[I] do not **feel sad** for [my] horse who struggles with [its] legs.'

Table 6.10: Attestations of the nominalizer *-aku* across the provinces.

TSOJ			EOJ								UNP
Sin	Tö	Su	Kak	Mu	Sa	Mi	Sik	Pi	Sip	Kap	
0	0	0	0	0	0	0	0	0	0	0	2

6.3.3.11 Nominalizer *-sa*

The nominalizer *-sa* is attested three times. It nominalizes the adjectival verb, rather than the adjectival verb phrase. Unlike the nominalizer *-aku*, *-sa* suffixes directly to the adjectival verb root, and is exclusive to the adjectival verb morphology. The adjectival verb that takes *-sa* is always immediately preceded by a noun or adnominalized verb in the possessive case.

105. 20:4338.4-5 – Suruga
波々乎波奈例天 / 由久我加奈之佐
papa-wo panare-te / yuk-u-nga **kanasi-sa**
mother-ACC part.from.INF-SUB / go-ATTR-POSS be.sad-AVNML
'The **sadness** of parting from [my] mother and going [away]. . .'

106. 20:4391.4-5 – Simotupusa
阿加古比須奈牟 / 伊母賀加奈志作
a-nga kopi s-unam-u / imö-nga **kanasi-sa**
1.S-POSS long.for.NML do-TENT2-ATTR / beloved.girl-POSS be.sad-AVNML
'The **sadness** of my beloved girl who probably long for [me]. . .'

107. 20:4425.1-4 – UNP
佐伎毛利尓 / 由久波多我世登 / 刀布比登乎 / 美流我登毛之佐
sakimori n-i / yuk-u pa ta-nga se tö / top-u pitö-wo / mi-ru-nga **tömosi-sa**
border.guard COP-INF / go-ATTR TPT who-POSS beloved.man QUOT / ask-ATTR person-ACC / see-ATTR-POSS be.favored-AVNML
'The **enviousness** of looking at those who ask, 'Whose husband is that, going to be a border guard?'.'

Table 6.11: Attestations of the nominalizer *-sa* across the provinces.

TSOJ			EOJ							UNP
Sin	Tö	Su	Kak	Mu	Sa	Mi	Sik	Pi	Sip	Kap	
0	0	1	0	0	0	0	0	0	1	0	1

6.3.3.12 Nominalizer *-nge*

The nominalizer *-nge* nominalizes the adjectival verb and indicates a quality or feeling. This suffix is unattested in WOJ and TSOJ and appears to be the predecessor of the Middle Japanese nominalizer *-ge*,[161] which is described in Vovin (2003: 269–270). The voicing in the Middle Japanese form *-ge* may be secondary, but it is difficult to tell with just a single attestation of this suffix in EOJ, due to the fact that the phonogram 氣 could be used to write both /ke/ and /ⁿge/ in EOJ. I chose *-nge* due to the Middle Japanese cognate and because it is not homophonous with the adjectival attributive suffix *-ke*. There is only one clear attestation of this suffix.

---

[161] I am grateful to Alexander Vovin (personal communication) for this suggestion.

108. 20:4419.3-5 – Muzasi
須美与氣乎 / 都久之尓伊多里弖 / 古布志氣毛波母
*sum-i yö-key-wo / tukusi-ni itar-i-te / **kopusi-ngey** [o]mop-am-ö*
reside-NML be.good-AVATTR-ACC / TN-LOC arrive-INF-SUB / **be.longing.for-AVNML** think-TENT-ATTR
'It was nice living there, so [I] am sure [I] **will long for** [it] after [I] arrive in Tukusi.'

6.3.3.13 Exclamative *-mo*

I view the adjectival verb exclamative *-mo* as the result of a back-formation from the verbal exclamative suffix *-umo*, a suffix that was first described by Vovin (2009a: 695). It indicates an exclamation. This suffix attaches to the final suffix *-si* of Class 1 adjectival verbs and the portmanteau root-final form of Class 2 adjectival verbs.

109. 20:4343.5 – Suruga
和加美可奈志母
*wa-nga mi **kanasi-mö***
1.S-POSS wife **be.sad.AVFIN-EXCL**
'My wife [must] **be so sad**!'

110. 14:3408.5 – Kamitukeno
安夜尓可奈思母
*aya n-i **kanasi-mö***
mysterious COP-INF **be.dear.AVFIN-EXCL**
'[She] is mysteriously **dear** [to me]!'

111. 14:3350a.4-5 – Pitati
伎美我美家思志 / 安夜尓伎保思母
*kimi-nga mi-kesi si / aya n-i ki **posi-mö***
lord-POSS HON-garment EPT / extreme COP-INF wear.NML **be.desired-EXCL**
'[I] so desperately **want** to wear [my] lord's garment.'

112. 14:3481.5 – UNP
於毛比具流之母
*omop-i-n-**gurusi-mö***
think-NML-GEN-**be.painful.AVFIN-EXCL**
'Oh, **it is painful** to think [about that]!'

113. 14:3509.3-5– UNP
宿奈敝杼母 / 古呂賀於曽伎能 / 安路許曽**要志母**
NE-n-ap-e-ndömö / ko-rö-nga osöki-nö / ar-o kösö **ye-si-mö**
sleep-NEG-ITER-EV-CONC / girl-DIM-POSS upper.garment-GEN / exist-ATTR FPT **be.good-AVFIN-EXCL**
'Although [we] are not sleeping together, it is **so nice** to have [my] dear girl's upper garment!'

114. 14:3544.4-5 – UNP
勢奈那登布多理 / 左宿而**久也思母**
se-na-na-tö puta-ri / sa-NE-TE **kuyasi-mö**
beloved.male-DIM-DIM-COM two-CL / LOC-sleep.INF-SUB **be.regretful.AVFIN-EXCL**
'[I] slept there with [my] dear, darling beloved, and [now I] **regret** it!'

115. 14:3555.3-4 – UNP
可良加治乃 / 於等**太可思母**奈
kara kandi-nö / otö-n-**daka-si-mö** na
TN oar-COMP / sound-GEN-**be.high-AVFIN-EXCL** EPT
'The sound **is loud**, like [that of] Kara oars!'

116. 20:4429.5 – UNP
於伎弖**可奈之毛**
ok-i-te **kanasi-mo**
leave.behind-INF-SUB **be.sad.AVFIN-EXCL**
'Leaving [her] behind, **oh, [I] am sad**!'

Table 6.12: Attestations of the exclamative *-mo* across the provinces.

TSOJ			EOJ								UNP
Sin	Tö	Su	Kak	Mu	Sa	Mi	Sik	Pi	Sip	Kap	
0	0	1	1	0	0	0	0	0	0	0	10

6.3.4 Bound Auxiliaries

The only bound auxiliary in the adjectival verb morphology is the subordinative gerund *-te*, which also attaches to verbs.

6.3.4.1 Subordinative gerund -te

The auxiliary -te only occurs twice on an adjectival verb. It follows the infinitive form of the adjectival verb. Its function is simply that of subordination.

117. 20:4373 – Simotukeno
祁布与利波 / 可敝理見**奈久弖** / 意富伎美乃 / 之許乃美多弖等 / 伊埿多都和例波

*kepu-yöri pa / kaper-i-MI **na-ku-te** / opo kimi-nö / sikö nö mi-tate tö / inde-tat-u ware pa*

today-ABL TPT / return-INF-see.NML **not.exist-INF-SUB** / great lord-GEN / lowly COP.ATTR HON-shield COP / go.out.INF-rise-ATTR 1.S TPT

'I, who will set out from today, **without** looking back, to be a lowly soldier for [my] sovereign...'

118. 14:3524.1-3 – UNP
麻乎其母能 / 布能末**知可久弖** / 安波奈敝波

*ma-won-gömö-nö / pu-nö ma **tika-ku-te** / ap-an-ap-e-nba*

INT-DIM-wild.rice-GEN / joint-GEN space **be.near-INF-SUB** / meet-NEG-ITER-EV-CONJ

'Since, [like] the really small gaps in the [woven] wild rice [mat], [we] **are near** [one another], yet [we] do not meet...'

Table 6.13: Attestations of the subordinative gerund -te across the provinces.

TSOJ			EOJ								UNP
Sin	Tö	Su	Kak	Mu	Sa	Mi	Sik	Pi	Sip	Kap	
0	0	0	0	0	0	0	1	0	0	0	1

7 Verbs

Verbs are the most morphologically complex of all parts of speech in AOJ. Arguably the most notable characteristic of AOJ verbs is the rich system of mood markers. This chapter describes the verbal morphology from their forms to their functions.

7.1 The basic syntax of verbs

As all AOJ topolects are predominantly SOV, predicate verbs normally appear phrase-final and sentence-final. Verbs in the attributive or infinitive form may modify nouns, and in such cases the verb precedes the noun. Thus, relative clauses in the language are right-headed and left-branching, and there is no relative pronoun. Verbal auxiliaries follow the infinitive form of the verb stem. Syntactic inversions, in which a verbal phrase is moved before or after another phrase, are also attested, and are not especially rare.

7.2 Verbal grammatical categories

Before presenting detailed discussions of each verbal class and affix, I will first give an overview of the categories marked in the morphology of TSOJ and EOJ, and list the morphemes found in each. This can be viewed as a simplistic summary of the functions and their corresponding forms.

7.2.1 Polarity

The affirmative is marked by zero and the negative is marked by several different affixes. In the indicative mood we find the negative suffix -*an*- ~ -*n*- ~ -*anz*- ~ -*nz*- and the EOJ negative-attributive suffix -*ana*- ~ -*na*-. In the imperative mood we find the negative suffix -*una* and the negative prefix *na*-. The negative-tentative mood is indicated by the portmanteau suffix -*anzi*.

7.2.2 Aspect

There is one aspectual suffix in AOJ: the EOJ progressive -*ar*- and the TSOJ progressive -*er*- ~ -*ir*-. There are also a few bound aspectual auxiliaries: the perfectives -*n*- and -*te*- ~ -*t*-, and the perfective-progressive -*tar*-. The imperfective aspect is unmarked.

7.2.3 Tense

The only tense marked is the past, which is indicated by the following bound auxiliaries: the past -*kV*, the past-attributive -*si*, and the past-evidential -*sika*. In many instances, however, the past is unmarked.

7.2.4 Mood

Most of the mood markers are suffixes, but a few are bound auxiliaries. The mood suffixes include the imperative -*e* ~ -*ö* ~ -*i* ~ -*rö* ~ -*yö*, the tentative -*am*- ~ -*m*-, the tentative 2 -*uram*- (TSOJ) ~ -*unam*- (EOJ), the negative-tentative -*anzi*, the debitive -*unbe*-, the subjunctive -*amasi* ~ -*masi*, the suppositional -*urasi* ~ -*rasi* ~ -*asi*, and the desiderative -*ana* ~ -*an*- ~ -*n*-.

The bound auxiliaries include the benefactive -*kös*-, the potential -*kate*- (TSOJ) ~ -*kande*- (EOJ), and the negative-potential -*kane*-.

The indicative mood is unmarked.

7.2.5 Voice

There are three voices, two of which are morphologically marked. The passive voice is marked by the suffix -*are* ~ -*ar*- ~ -*aye* ~ -*ye*- ~ -*y*- and the causative voice is marked by the suffixes -*ase*- ~ -*se*- and -*asime*. The active voice is unmarked.

7.2.6 Retrospection

Retrospection is indicated by the bound auxiliaries -*kar*- (EOJ) and -*ker*- (TSOJ).

7.2.7 Iteration and Duration

The iterative is marked by the suffix *-ap-* ~ *-öp-*. Duration is indicated by the prefix *ari-* or the iterative *-ap-* ~ *-öp-* (only with certain verbs).

7.2.8 Predication

Both final and non-final predication are morphologically marked in AOJ. Final predication is completely suffixal, and is marked by either the final *-u*, the attributive *-uru* ~ *-ur-* ~ *-oro* ~ *-u* ~ *-o*, the attributive *-a*, the exclamative *-umo* ~ *-mo*, or the evidential *-ure* ~ *-re* ~ *-e* ~ *-o*.

Non-final predication is marked by both suffixes and bound auxiliaries. The suffixes include the infinitive *-i* ~ *-u*, the conditional gerund *-anba*, the conjunctive gerund *-nba*, the concessive gerund *-ndö*, and the negative-attributive *-ana-* ~ *-na-*. The bound auxiliaries include the subordinative gerund *-te* and the coordinative gerund *-tutu* ~ *-tusi* ~ *-tötö*.

7.2.9 Honorification

Honorification is marked by the suffix *-as-* ~ *-s-* ~ *-os-*, the auxiliaries *-tamap-* and *-mas-*, and the suppletive verb *imas-*.

7.2.10 Humbleness

Humbleness is marked by the auxiliary *-matur-* and the suppletive verbs *tamapar-* ~ *tanbar-*, *mawos-*, *mawi-*, and *kangapur-*.

7.3 Morphotactics

The verbal affix slots in EOJ are as follows (only one affix within a set of brackets can occur per word form):

[PREF]-ROOT-[PASS/CAUS]-[HON]-[PROG]-[NEG/DES]-[ITER]-[TENT/INF]-[EV/FIN/ATTR/NEG. ATTR/EXCL/IMP/SUBJ/SUP/NEG.TENT/NEG.IMP]-[CONJ/CONC/NML[162]]

---

[162] Only the nominalizer *-aku*.

A word form containing an affix in each of these slots is not attested (and some of the morphemes in the above structure cannot combine with preceding or following morphemes), but we can piece together the maximal word form by comparing the range of word forms attested in the corpus. There is one irregularity that is not explained by the affix order above: the iterative precedes the passive. Since this also occurs in WOJ, it may have been due to WOJ influence. The iterative is unattested in TSOJ, so it is unknown if it preceded (like WOJ) or followed (like EOJ) the negative and progressive suffixes, but otherwise TSOJ shows the same affix order. Although there are eight suffix slots, the longest verbal word forms we find in the corpus consist of a root with four suffixes. One combination is in the order ROOT-NEG-ITER-TENT-EV, shown below in example (1):

1. 14:3394.4-5 – Pitati
   和須良延許婆古曽 / 那乎**可家奈波賣**
   *wasura-kö-nba kosö / na-wo **kake-n-ap-am-e***
   forget-come-COND FPT / 2.S-ACC **call.out-NEG-ITER-TENT-EV**
   'When [I] start to forget [our meeting there], [I] **shall stop calling out** for you!'

Another attestation is in the order ROOT-CAUS-PROG-ITER-EXCL, shown below in example (2):

2. 14:3541.4-5 – UNP
   比登豆麻古呂乎 / 麻由可西良布母
   *pitö-n-duma ko-rö-wo / ma-**yuk-as-er-ap-umö***
   person-GEN-spouse girl-DIM-ACC / eye-**go-CAUS-PROG-ITER-EXCL**
   '**Time and again** [I] **let** [my] eyes **wander** toward [that] dear girl [who is] the wife of another man!'

I place the tentative and infinitive suffixes in the same slot because they cannot co-occur. The infinitive of a verb is used to allow the addition of one of many auxiliaries, creating long verbal complexes. An example of this is given below:

3. 20:4323.3-5 – Töpotuapumi
   奈尓須礼曽 / 波々登布波奈乃 / <u>佐吉泥己受祁牟</u>
   *nani s-ure sö / papa tö [i]p-u pana-nö / **sak-i-nde-kö-nz-u-kem-u***
   why do-EV FPT / mother QUOT say-ATTR flower-GEN / **bloom-INF-go.out.INF-come-NEG-INF-PST.TENT-ATTR**
   'Why **has** the flower called 'mother' **not come out in bloom**?'

7.4 Verbal classes

There are three main verbal classes: consonant-final stems, vowel-final stems, and irregular stems.

7.4.1 Consonant-final stem verbs

Consonant-final stems are by far the most numerous in TSOJ and EOJ. In addition, there is evidence that they were more numerous in EOJ than in WOJ or TSOJ. This is because some verbs that are vowel-final stems in WOJ, such as *arapare-* 'appear', are consonant-final stems in EOJ (cf. *arapar-* 'id.'). This probably indicates the consonant-final stems are more archaic, and WOJ innovatively changed some to vowel-final stems. Alternatively, it could show some EOJ topolects reanalyzed and analogically leveled some original vowel-final stem verbs to fit into the more regular consonant-final stem verbal conjugation. Perhaps both phenomena occurred.

In some TSOJ and EOJ topolects the attributive *-u* is syncretic with the final *-u* in consonant-final stems, which is the same situation we find in WOJ. The evidential and imperative syncretize to *-e* in EOJ after all consonant-final stems and after coronal-final stems in TSOJ. In TSOJ the evidential is *-o* (/o/) after labial-final stems; this creates syncretism between the evidential and attributive in those topolects that retained the unraised attributive *-o*. The evidential is orthographically attested only as *-e ~ -ey* after a velar-final stem in TSOJ, but I reconstruct it as *-ö* (/ə/) due to a sound change that occurred in Proto-TSOJ (see Chapter 2 for a detailed discussion). Table 7.1 below presents a labial-final stem, a coronal-final stem, and a velar-final stem in order to show the phonological differences in the imperative and evidential forms in TSOJ.

Table 7.1: The basic inflectional paradigm for the verbs *ap-* 'meet', *tat-* 'rise', and *kik-* 'hear'.

Form	TSOJ	EOJ ~ TSOJ	TSOJ
	ap- 'meet'	*tat-* 'rise'	*kik-* 'hear'
Infinitive	*ap-i*	*tat-i*	*kik-i*
Imperative	*ap-e*	*tat-e*	*kik-e*
Final	*ap-u*	*tat-u*	*kik-u*
Attributive	*ap-u ~ ap-o*	*tat-u ~ tat-o*	*kik-u ~ kik-o*
Negative	*ap-an-*	*tat-an-*	*kik-an*
Evidential	*ap-o*	*tat-e*	*kik-ö*
Tentative	*ap-am-*	*tat-am-*	*kik-am-*

While not every paradigmatic form of the three verbs in Table 7.1 is attested, every suffix is attested on at least one consonant-final stem verb in both EOJ and TSOJ. Thus, we can use these data to piece together the full paradigm of a single consonant-final stem verb.

7.4.2 Vowel-final stem verbs

Vowel-final stem verbs are the second most common verb type in AOJ. These verbs terminate their root in a vowel (which can be orthographically e ~ ey, ö, or i ~ï, depending on the verb and the dialect). There are three main features of vowel-final stem verbs that distinguish them from consonant-final stem verbs:
1) Vowel-final verbs have portmanteau infinitive forms that are homophonous with their root (e.g., the root *kane-* 'consider' and its infinitive form *kane* 'consider.INF').
2) The final vowel of a vowel-final verb is deleted when certain suffixes with "strong" initial vowels overtake them, such as the evidential *-ure* and the attributive *-uru*.
3) Due to historical *r loss in the consonant-final stem verb paradigm (Whitman 1985: 190–201), the attributive and evidential suffixes have different allomorphs in the vowel-final stem verb paradigm.

Table 7.2: The basic inflectional paradigm for the verb *wasure-* 'forget'.

Form	wasure- 'forget'	
	TSOJ	EOJ
Infinitive	wasure	wasure ~ wasura-[163]
Imperative	wasure	wasure
Final	wasur-u	wasur-u
Attributive	wasur-uru	wasur-uru
Negative	wasure-n-	wasure-n-
Evidential	wasur-ure	wasur-ure
Tentative	wasur-am-	wasur-am-

While not every word form in Table 7.2 above is attested, every suffix is attested on at least one vowel-final stem verb in the corpus. Thus, we can use these data to piece together the full paradigm of a single vowel-final stem verb.

---

[163] This form is only attested once and may be an archaism.

7.4.3 Irregular verbs

There are five classes of irregular verbs. These include strong vowel-final stems (such as *mi-* 'see'), *kö-* 'come', *se-* ~ *si-* ~ *-sö* 'do', *r*-root-final irregulars (e.g., *ar-* 'exist' and *wor-* 'exist, stay'), and a small number of defective verbs (e.g., copula *nö*).

7.4.3.1 Strong vowel-final verbs

There are only two strong vowel-final verbs attested in AOJ:[164] *mi-* 'see' and *ki-* 'wear'. They are termed "strong" because they do not delete their stem-final vowel in most instances where regular vowel-final stem verbs do. Due to this characteristic, these verbs display a striking three-way syncretism in their infinitive, final, and imperative forms. In addition, they have special allomorphs of the evidential and attributive suffixes not found on any other verb. The verb *ki-* 'wear' is attested in a causative form *ki-se-* (rather than *k-ase-*), just as it is in WOJ (Vovin 2009a: 864; also note the form *mi-se-* 'see-CAUS-' in Vovin (2009a: 865, 868)). A final important feature to mention is the attested EOJ progressive form of *ki-* 'wear' is *k-ar-* (compare WOJ *ker-*[165] 'wear.PROG-' with a fusion of the sequence *ia > /e/ (Vovin (2009a: 883–884)), with a deleted stem vowel, so in EOJ this verb was not "strong" in all paradigmatic forms. The progressive form of *mi-* 'see' is unattested.

Table 7.3: The basic inflectional paradigm for the strong vowel-final verb *mi-* 'see'.

Form	TSOJ ~ EOJ
	mi- 'see'
Infinitive	*mi*
Imperative	*[mi] ~ [mi-rö]*[166]
Final	*[mi]*
Attributive	*mi-ru*
Negative	*[mi-n-]*
Evidential	*mi-re*
Tentative	*mi-m-*

---

164 Others are attested in WOJ, such as *mï-* 'go around' and *isati-* 'sob'. See Vovin (2009a: 505–506) for an overview.
165 Though unattested, this is the form we would also expect in TSOJ.
166 The forms in brackets are unattested but are what we would expect based on a comparison of WOJ forms and other EOJ and TSOJ verb paradigms.

7.4.3.2 *kö-* 'come'

The verb *kö-* 'come' is irregular in a few ways. First, it has two alternating stems, *k-* and *kö-*, thus its paradigm is a mixture of consonant-final and vowel-final stem verb morphology. Second, there is a peculiar usage of what appears to be the final form *k-u* before the terminative case suffix *-mande*. This may be some form of *r-loss (different from the *r-loss described in Whitman (1985: 190–201)) exclusive to AOJ. This is because the form *k-uru* 'come-ATTR' is well attested in AOJ, but it is never attested before the terminative suffix *-mande*. Another explanation is that the terminative *-mande* was a postposition that originally followed the final suffix in PJe and *-u-mande* contains a fossilization of that, whereas WOJ innovated (through analogy with other case suffixes) to have it follow the attributive. This would explain why EOJ and TSOJ both show the same form, in contrast to WOJ. Although I favor this explanation, I still gloss the examples with *-u-mande-* as 'ATTR-TERM-' due to the lack of any other case suffixes that attach to the final suffix in the synchronic grammar. Note the following example from Kamitupusa province (the same form *k-u-mande* 'come-ATTR-TERM' can be found in 20:4339.4 – Suruga, 20:4340.5 – Suruga, 20:4404.2 – Kamitukeno, and 20:4372.15 – Pitati):

4. 20:4350.5 – Kamitupusa
   加倍理**久麻泥**尔
   *kapeyr-i-**k-u-mande**-ni*
   return-INF-**come-ATTR-TERM**-LOC
   '**Until** [I] **come** back [home]...'

Now compare this with the identical form 'come-ATTR-TERM' attested in WOJ, found in the following poem from MYS Book 15:

5. 15:3702.3-4 – WOJ
   和礼由伎弖 / 可敝里**久流末侶**
   *ware yuk-i-te / kaper-i-**k-uru-mande***
   1.S go-INF-SUB / return-INF-**come-ATTR-TERM**
   '**Until** I go and **come** back...'

A negative suffix is only attested attached to the root *kö-* 'come' two times: once in TSOJ as *kö-nz-* 'come-NEG-' (in 20:4323.5 – Töpotuapumi), and once in EOJ as *kö-na-* 'come-NEG.ATTR-' (shown in example 6 below).

6. 14.3461.3-5 – UNP
真日久礼弓 / 与比奈波**許奈尔** / 安家奴思太久流
MA-PI kure-te / *yöpi-na pa* ***kö-na-ni*** / *ake-n-o sinda k-uru*
INT-sun grow.dark.INF-SUB / evening-LOC TPT **come-NEG.ATTR-LOC** / dawn.
INF-PERF-ATTR CNJ come-ATTR
'[It is] **because [you] did not come** during the evening after the bright sun set, [you only] came when it dawned.'

Table 7.4 below shows the basic inflectional paradigm of this verb, which is identical in TSOJ and EOJ.

Table 7.4: The basic inflectional paradigm for the irregular stem verb *kö-* 'come'.

Form	TSOJ ~ EOJ
	kö- 'come'
Infinitive	*k-i*
Imperative	*kö*
Final	*k-u*
Attributive	*k-uru*
Negative	*kö-nz-*
Evidential	*k-ure*
Tentative	*kö-m-*

7.4.3.3 *se-* ~ *-sö* ~ 'do'

The verb meaning 'do' in AOJ is the most complex in terms of allomorphy, with four attested forms. While the allomorphs *s-*, *se-*, and *-sö*[167] are found across AOJ (and in WOJ), the form *si-* is only attested once in EOJ (shown in example 7 below) and is by all indications a variant specific to one topolect. Similarly, there is one attestation of EOJ *sö-* (in the Kamitupusa topolect of EOJ) that is not found in the negative-imperative construction (this is discussed in §2.3.7.1). I consider *se-* to be the underlying root in a synchronic sense, at least in most of the AOJ topolects, so I will refer to this morpheme by that root in the discussion that follows. I follow the proposal by Frellesvig and Whitman (2004: 294) that, historically, the root was *sö [sə].

The verb *se-* 'do' loses its vowel before the infinitive -*i*, the final -*u*, the attributive -*uru*, and evidential -*ure*. This is identical to vowel-final stem verbs, except for the

---

[167] Attested in the negative-imperative construction.

infinitive form, which patterns with consonant-final stem verbs. Before the negative *-an-* and mood markers such as the tentative *-am-*, it retains its vowel, again patterning with vowel-final stems. Since the form *-sö* is a bound auxiliary only used in the negative-imperative construction, it can be viewed as peripheral to the inflectional paradigm. The basic inflectional paradigm of this verb is identical in EOJ and TSOJ.

Table 7.5: The basic inflectional paradigm for the irregular stem verb *se-* 'do'.

Form	TSOJ ~ EOJ
	se- 'do'
Infinitive	*s-i*
Imperative	*se ~ -sö*
Final	*s-u*
Attributive	*s-uru*
Negative	*se-n-*
Evidential	*s-ure*
Tentative	*se-m-*

7. 14:3556.5 – UNP
   那乎杼可母**思武**
   *na-wo [a]ndö kamö **si-m-u***
   2.S-ACC what EPT **do-TENT-ATTR**
   'What should [I] **do** about you?'

The phonologically unique form of this verb in example (7) is due to vowel raising (*e > /i/) in this unknown topolect.

7.4.3.4 *r*-final irregular verbs

The *r*-final irregular verbs attested are *ar-* 'exist', *nar-* 'become', *por-* 'desire', and *nar-* 'be'. Their irregularity lies in the syncretism between their infinitive and final forms. They also exhibit syncretism between their imperative and evidential forms, like all other coronal-final stem verbs in AOJ. The basic inflectional paradigm of this verb class is identical in EOJ and TSOJ.

7.4 Verbal classes — 287

Table 7.6: The basic inflectional paradigm for the r-final stem irregular verb *ar-* 'exist'.

Form	TSOJ ~ EOJ
	ar- 'exist'
Infinitive	*ar-i*
Imperative	*ar-e*
Final	*ar-i*
Attributive	*ar-u ~ ar-o*
Negative	*ar-an-*
Evidential	*ar-e*
Tentative	*ar-am-*

7.4.3.5 Defective verbs

The defective verbs consist of three copulas. Compared to other verbs, defective verbs lack a complete inflectional paradigm.

7.4.3.5.1 Copula *nö*

The copula *nö* is attested in every AOJ topolect, and it always follows a nominal form (noun, adjective, or nominalized verb). It has just two forms in its defective paradigm: the infinitive *n-i* and the root *nö*, which is used in an attributive function.[168] In fact, it is the only verb in the language in which the root is used attributively. In addition, there is a contracted form *n-* 'COP.ATTR'. In WOJ, there is also a subordinative gerund infinitive form *n-i-te* attested (Vovin 2009a: 510), but this is not attested in AOJ.

7.4.3.5.1.1 Infinitive form *n-i*

The following examples show the infinitive form of the copula *nö*.

---

[168] Unlike Vovin (2005, 2009a, etc.), Russell (2006), and my previous research (Kupchik 2011, etc.), I do not analyze this copula's root as *n-*. This is because an attributive *-ö* is not attested with any other verb, and four other basic verbs in the language, *tö* 'COP', *rö* 'COP', *kö-* 'come', and *se-* (< **sö-*) 'do', also have roots that end in *ö*. Just like the copula *nö* and its infinitive form *n-i*, the infinitive forms of the latter two are *k-i* 'come-INF' and *s-i* 'do-INF', respectively. Furthermore, a verb root that consists of one consonant phoneme is not very likely in a language with (C)V phonotactics.

8. 20:4401.5 – Sinano
意母**奈志尔**志弖
omö **na-si n-i** s-i-te
mother **not.exist-AVFIN COP-INF** do-INF-SUB
'[I] have left [them] **without** a mother. . .'

In example (8) the adjectival verb final suffix -si is used in an attributive function (this is an irregular feature of the adjectival verb na-), which allows the copula nö to follow.

9. 14:3402.4-5 – Kamitukeno
勢奈能我素伱母 / **佐夜尔**布良思都
se-na-nö-nga sonde mö / **saya n-i** pur-as-i-t-u
beloved.man-DIM-DIM-POSS sleeve FPT / **clear COP-INF** wave-HON-INF-PERF-FIN
'[My] dearly beloved **clearly** waved [his] sleeve [at me].'

In example (9) the infinitive copula n-i is used after an adjective to adverbialize it. The same function is shown in example (10) below, where it adverbializes a nominalized verb.

10. 20:4405.1-2 – Kamitukeno
和我伊母古我 / **志濃比尔**西餘等
wa-nga imö-ko-nga / **sinup-i n-i** se-yö tö
1.S-POSS beloved.girl-DIM-POSS / **yearn.for-NML COP-INF** do-IMP QUOT
'My dearly beloved told [me] to **yearn for** [her]. . .'

11. 14:3374.3-5 – Muzasi
麻左弖尔毛/乃良奴伎美我名 / 宇良尔伱尔家里
masande n-i mo / nör-an-u kimi-nga NA / ura-ni [i]nde-n-i-ker-i
certain COP-INF FPT / tell-NEG-ATTR lord-POSS name / divination-LOC go.out.INF-PERF-INF-RETR-FIN
'[My] lord's name that [I] did not tell [them] **certainly** emerged from the divination.'

12. 14:3426.4-5 – Mitinöku
斯努比尔勢毛等 / 比毛牟須波佐祢
sinop-i n-i se-m-o tö / pimo musunb-as-an-e
yearn.for-NML COP-INF do-TENT-ATTR QUOT / cord tie-HON-DES-IMP
'[I] want [you] to tie [your] cords and **think [of me]** when [you] do!'

13. 14:3350a.4-5 – Pitati
伎美我美家思志 / **安夜尓**伎保思母
kimi-nga mi-kesi si / ***aya n-i** ki posi-mö*
lord-POSS HON-garment EPT / **extreme COP-INF** wear.NML be.desired-EXCL
'[I] **so desperately** want to wear [my] lord's garment.'

14. 14:3385.4-5 – Simotupusa
麻末乃於須比尓 / 奈美毛**登杼呂尓**
mama-nö osu-pi-ni / *nami mo **töndörö n-i***
cliff-GEN rocky.shore-side-LOC / wave FPT **thunderous COP-INF**
'Waves **were** also **roaring** on the side of the rocky shore [near] the cliffs...'

15. 20:4388.1-2 – Simotupusa
多飛等弊等 / 麻多妣**尓奈理奴**
tanbï tö [i]p-e-ndö / *ma-tanbi **n-i nar-i-n-u***
journey QUOT say-EV-CONC / INT-journey **COP-INF become-INF-PERF-FIN**
'Although [it] was said to be [just] 'a journey', [this] **has become** such a [trying] journey.'

16. 20:4349.1-3 – Kamitupusa
毛母久麻能 / 美知波紀尓志乎 / 麻多佐良**尓**
momö kuma-nö / *miti pa k-ï-n-i-si-wo* / *mata sara **n-i***
hundred bend.in.a.road-GEN / road TPT come-INF-PERF-INF-PST.ATTR-ACC / again more **COP-INF**
'Though [I] have come [this far] on roads with a hundred bends, still there **is** more [to travel].'

17. 20:4428.4-5 – UNP
叡比波登加奈々 / **阿夜尓**可毛祢牟
yenbi pa tök-ana-na / ***aya n-i** kamo ne-m-u*
sash TPT undo-NEG.ATTR-LOC / **unnatural COP-INF** EPT sleep-TENT-ATTR
'[I] shall sleep without untying [my] sash, **unnatural** [as it] may **be**!'

7.4.3.5.1.2 Attributive root form *nö*

The following examples show the attributive function of the root, which I gloss as 'COP.ATTR'.

18. 20:4420.5 – Muzasi
 許礼乃波流母志
 köre nö paru mös-i
 this COP.ATTR needle hold-INF
 'Hold **this needle**...'

19. 14:3363.4-5 – Sagamu
 安思我良夜麻乃 / 須疑乃木能末可
 *asingara yama-nö / **sungï nö KÖ**-nö ma ka*
 TN mountain-GEN / **cryptomeria COP.ATTR tree**-GEN space QPT
 '[Will his return be] through the **cryptomeria trees** of Mt. Asigara?'

20. 20:4373.3-4 – Simotukeno
 意富伎美乃 / 之許乃美多弖等
 *opo kimi-nö / **sikö nö mi-tate** tö*
 great lord-GEN / **despicable COP.ATTR HON-shield** COP
 'To be a **lowly soldier** for [my] sovereign...'

21. 14:3501.1-3 – UNP
 安波乎呂能 / 乎呂田尔於波流 / 多波美豆良
 apa wo-rö nö / wo-rö TA-ni op-ar-u / tapami-n-dura
 TN **hill-DIM COP.ATTR** / **hill-DIM** rice.field-LOC grow-PROG-ATTR / UNC-GEN-vine
 '[Like] the *tapami* vines that grow in the rice fields [on] **the small hills of Apa**...'

7.4.3.5.1.3 Contracted form *n-*

The following examples show the contracted form *n-* (a portmanteau morph), which may be 'COP.ATTR' or 'COP.INF'; only context can be our guide in these cases.

22. 14:3354.1-3 – Töpotuapumi
 伎倍比等乃 / 萬太良夫須麻尔 / 和多佐波太
 *kipey pitö-nö / **mandara n-busuma**-ni / wata sapanda*
 TN person-GEN / **speckled COP.ATTR-bed.covers**-LOC / cotton amply
 '[Like] the cotton [that is] amply [placed] inside the **speckled bed covers** of the people from Kipey...'

23. 14:3426.1-3 – Mitinöku
    安比豆祢能 / 久尔乎**佐杼抱美** / 安波奈波婆
    apindu ne-nö / *kuni-wo* **sa n-döpo-mi** / *ap-an-ap-anba*
    TN peak-GEN / land-ABS **thus COP.INF-be.far-AVGER** / meet-NEG-ITER-COND
    'If [we] keep failing to meet because the land of the Apidu peaks **is so far** [away]. . .'

24. 14:3561.1-2 – UNP
    可奈刀田乎 / **安良我伎**麻由美
    kana-to-N-DA-wo / ***ara n-gaki*** *ma-yu mi*
    metal-door-GEN-rice.field-ACC / **rough COP.ATTR-fence** space-ABL see.INF
    'Through a gap in the **rough fence**, [I] see the rice field [in front of] the metal gate.'

7.4.3.5.2 Copula *tö*

There are only two attestations of the copula *tö*: one in TSOJ and one in EOJ. It is not attested in an attributive function, which probably indicates WOJ *t-u* 'COP-ATTR' is a later innovation. One must be careful not to confuse this with the quotative particle *tö* (see §10.8).

25. 14:3400.3-5 – Sinano
    左射礼思母 / 伎弥之布美弖波 / 多麻**等**比呂波牟
    sanzare [i]si mö / *kimi si pum-i-te-nba* / *tama **tö** piröp-am-u*
    little stone FPT / lord EPT step-INF-PERF-COND / jade **COP** pick.up-TENT-FIN
    'When you have stepped on the small stones, [I] shall pick them up **as** jewels.'

26. 20:4373.4 – Simotukeno
    之許乃美多弖**等**
    *sikö nö mi-tate **tö***
    lowly COP.ATTR HON-shield **COP**
    '**To be** a lowly soldier. . .'

7.4.3.5.3 Copula *rö*

The copula *rö* is only attested once, in UNP. We might think this is due to WOJ influence (since it is attested in WOJ more than once), but it is attested in a poem, and a line, with some distinct EOJ features (such as the tentative 2 suffix -*unam*- and the attributive suffix -*o*), so possibly it is a retention from PJe.

27. 14:3552.1-4 – UNP
麻都我宇良尔 / 佐和恵宇良太知 / 麻比登其等 / 於毛抱須奈母呂
matu-nga ura-ni / *sawawe ura-n-dat-i* / *ma-pitö-n-götö* / *omop-os-unam-ö* **rö**
pine-POSS bay-LOC / noisy tip-LOC-rise-NML / INT-people-GEN-word / think-HON-TENT2-ATTR **COP**
'[You] **are** probably thinking of the rumors people [spread that are like] noisy [waves] rising to the tips [of the tree branches] in the bay of pines.'

7.5 Verbal affixes

Verbal affixes attach directly to the root, or to another affix. Both prefixes and suffixes are attested.

7.5.1 Prefixes

There are six verbal prefixes: the durative *ari-*, the tangible *kaki-*, the negative-imperative *na-*, the directive-locative *i-*, the intensifying prefix *ka-*, and the prefix *uti-*.

7.5.1.1 Durative *ari-*
The durative *ari-* is attested just once, in EOJ. I view it as a durative prefix because in its sole attestation it only has a meaning of a prolonged duration.

28. 20:4368.1-2 – Pitati
久自我波々 / 佐氣久阿利麻弖
kunzi-n-gapa pa / *sakey-ku* **ari-mat-e**
TN-GEN-river TPT / be.safe-AVINF **DUR-wait-IMP**
'**Keep waiting** for [me] safely, [at] Kunzi river!'

7.5.1.2 Tangible *kaki-*
I refer to *kaki-* as a tangible prefix because its meaning involves touching something with the hands. It is a grammaticalization of the infinitive or nominalized form of the verb *kak-* 'scratch'. It is only attested twice: once in TSOJ and once in EOJ.

29. 20:4346.1-3 – Suruga
知々波々我 / 可之良**加伎奈弖** / 佐久阿例弖
*titi papa-nga / kasira **kaki-nande** / sa-ku ar-e te*
father mother-POSS / head **TNG-caress.INF** / be.safe-AVINF exist-IMP QUOT
'[My] mother and father **patted** [me on] the head and told [me] to stay safe.'

30. 14:3404.1-3 – Kamitukeno
可美都氣努 / 安蘇能麻素武良 / **可伎武太伎**
*kamitukeyno / aso-nö ma-so mura / **kaki-mundak-i***
TN / TN-GEN INT-hemp group / **TNG-embrace-NML**
'[Like] **holding** a fine bundle of hemp from Aso [in] Kamitukeno **close to [my] bosom**. . .'

Table 7.7: Attestations of the tangible prefix *kaki-* across the provinces.

TSOJ			EOJ								UNP
Sin	Tö	Su	Kak	Mu	Sa	Mi	Sik	Pi	Sip	Kap	
0	0	1	1	0	0	0	0	0	0	0	0

7.5.1.3 Negative-imperative *na-*

The negative-imperative prefix *na-* attaches to a verb in the infinitive form, as the two examples below demonstrate. It usually occurs in the construction *na*-VERB-INF-*sö*, described in the next section.

31. 20:4385.1-2 – Simotupusa
由古作枳尓 / 奈美**奈等惠良比**
*yuk-o saki-ni / nami **na-töwerap-i***
go-ATTR ahead-LOC / wave **NEG.IMP-shake-INF**
'Waves, **do not shake** [me] as [I] go ahead!'

32. 14:3501.5 – UNP
安乎許等**奈多延**
*a-wo kötö **na-taye***
1.S-ACC word **NEG.IMP-break.INF**
'**Do not stop** speaking to me!'

7.5.1.3.1 Special construction *na*-VERB-INF-*sö*

Vovin (2009a: 572) and Russell (2006: 158, 290) refer to this construction as a circumfix in OJ. While I view *na*- as a prefix, I do not view the element -*sö* 'do' as a suffix because it attaches to the infinitive form of the verb, and not the verb stem.[169] Furthermore, if a segment (prefix or suffix) of a circumfix is attested on its own in a language, it normally has a meaning or function that is quite different from the circumfix (Spencer 2001: 129; Bauer 2004: 29), but *na*- is well attested as a negative-imperative without an accompanying -*sö*. For these reasons, I do not consider this construction to be a circumfix in OJ.

The semantics of the construction appear to be the same as that of the negative-imperative *na*-. The advantage of adding the auxiliary -*sö* 'do' is that it allows the addition of further affixation in the form of an optional desiderative and subsequent imperative suffix. In this sense, the auxiliary -*sö* 'do' is a dummy auxiliary like the auxiliary -*ar*- described in §7.6.2.3.1.

33. 14:3398.4-5 – Sinano
    伊思井乃手兒我 / 許登**奈多延曽袮**
    isiWI-nö te*NGO-nga* / *kötö* **na-taye-sö-n-e**
    TN-GEN maiden-POSS / word **NEG.IMP-cease.INF-do-DES-IMP**
    '[There is] a maiden [whose] words [I] **wish would never cease**!'

34. 14:3410.4-5 – Kamitukeno
    於久乎**奈加袮曽** / 麻左可思余加婆
    oku-wo **na-kane-sö** / *masaka si yö-k-anba*
    future-ACC **NEG.IMP-worry.INF-do** / present EPT be.good-AVATTR-COND
    '**Do not fret about** the future, if [things] are fine now.'

35. 14:3378.5 – Muzasi
    和尓**奈多要曽袮**
    wa-ni **na-taye-sö-n-e**
    1.S-DAT **NEG.IMP-break.INF-do-DES-IMP**
    '**Please do not break up** with me.'

---

[169] It should be noted that in WOJ, with the verb *se*- 'do', the negative-imperative construction *na*-VERB-*sö* irregularly attaches directly to the stem *se*- rather than to the infinitive form *s-i* (Vovin 2009a: 571). This is unattested in AOJ.

36. 14:3452.1-2 – UNP
於毛思路伎 / 野乎婆**奈夜吉曽**
*omosiro-ki / NO-wonba **na-yak-i-sö***
be.lovely-AVATTR / field-ACC.EMP **NEG.IMP-burn-INF-do**
'**Do not burn** the lovely field!'

37. 14:3526.3-5 – UNP
安我己許呂 / 布多由久奈母等 / **奈与母波里曽祢**
*a-nga kökörö / puta yuk-unam-ö tö / **na-y-ömöp-ar-i-sö-n-e***
1.S-POSS heart / two go-TENT2-ATTR QUOT / **NEG.IMP-EPEN-think-PROG-INF-do-DES-IMP**
'**Please do not think** that my heart will go after two (women)!'

Table 7.8: Attestations of the negative-imperative *na-* across the provinces.

Form	TSOJ			EOJ								UNP
	Sin	Tö	Su	Kak	Mu	Sa	Mi	Sik	Pi	Sip	Kap	
na-	0	0	0	0	0	0	0	0	0	1	0	1
na-VERB-INF-*sö*	1	0	0	2	1	0	0	0	0	0	0	2

7.5.1.4 Directive-locative focus *i-*

Vovin (2009a: 561) analyzes this prefix as a directive-locative focus marker that focalizes the direction or location of the verbal action. This is the analysis I follow here. An alternate hypothesis was presented by Yanagida and Whitman, in which *i-* is an active prefix that "only occurs with nominalized predicates…and infinitives with agentive *pro* subjects" (2009: 119).

Comparatively speaking, in WOJ this morpheme is attested preceding a verbal prefix, and never following it (Vovin 2009a: 561). It is not attested before or after any other prefix in AOJ. This prefix is attested in the Kamitukeno topolect of EOJ and in UNP.

38. 14:3409.1-2 – Kamitukeno
伊香保呂尓 / 安麻久母**伊都藝**
*ikapo-rö-ni / ama-kumö **i-tung-i***
TN-DIM-LOC / heavens-cloud **DLF-follow-INF**
'Clouds in the skies over Ikapo **pass by**…'

39. 14:3518.1-2 – UNP
    伊波能倍尓 / 伊可賀流久毛能
    ipa-nö [u]pey-ni / *i-kangar-u kumo-nö*
    rock-GEN above-LOC / **DLF-hang-ATTR** cloud-COMP
    'Like the clouds that **hang low,** above the rocks. . .'

40. 14:3540.1-2 – UNP
    左和多里能 / 手兒尓伊由伎安比
    sawatari-nö / te*NGO-ni **i-yuk-i-ap-i***
    TN-GEN / maiden-LOC **DLF-go-INF-meet-INF**
    '[I] **went over to meet** the maiden of Sawatari. . .'

Table 7.9: Attestations of directive-locative focus *i-* across the provinces.

TSOJ			EOJ								UNP
Sin	Tö	Su	Kak	Mu	Sa	Mi	Sik	Pi	Sip	Kap	
0	0	0	1	0	0	0	0	0	0	0	2

7.5.1.5 Intensifying *ka-*

The prefix *ka-* is well attested in WOJ adjectival verbs with the function of intensifying an action, but Vovin (2009a: 573–574) only lists one example where it attaches to a verb. There are two examples of this prefix in AOJ, one from the Sagamu topolect of EOJ and one from UNP, but both lines in which it appears are identical.

41. 14:3361.3-5 – Sagamu
    佐須和奈乃 / 可奈流麻之豆美 / 許呂安礼比毛等久
    sas-u wana-nö / ***ka-nar-u ma** sindum-i* / *kö-rö are pimo tök-u*
    set-ATTR trap-COMP / **INT-make.sound-ATTR interval** grow.quiet-INF/ girl-DIM 1.S string undo-FIN
    'The **sounds** fade away, like the **noise** from the traps set [here and there], and [my] dear girl and I untie [our] cords.'

42. 20:4430.4-5 – UNP
    可奈流麻之都美 / 伊湮弖登阿我久流
    ***ka-nar-u ma** sindum-i* / *inde-te tö a-nga k-uru*
    INT-make.sound-ATTR interval grow.quiet-INF / go.out.INF-SUB FPT 1.S-POSS come-ATTR
    '[After] **all** grew quiet, I went out and came [here].'

7.5 Verbal affixes

Table 7.10: Attestations of the intensifying prefix *ka-* across the provinces.

TSOJ			EOJ								UNP
Sin	Tö	Su	Kak	Mu	Sa	Mi	Sik	Pi	Sip	Kap	
0	0	0	0	0	1	0	0	0	0	0	1

7.5.1.6 Prefix *uti-*

This prefix is attested in the Suruga topolect of TSOJ and in UNP. It is also attested attaching to nouns (see §5.3.5 for examples). The meaning of this prefix is difficult to discern, so I gloss it as 'PREF'. It is possibly an intensifying prefix.

43. 20:4345.1-4 – Suruga
和伎米故等 / 不多利和我見之 / **宇知江須流** / 夕夕河乃祢良波
wa-ng[a]-imey-ko-tö / *puta-ri wa-nga MI-si* / **uti-yes-uru** / *surunga-nö ne-ra pa*
1.S-POSS-beloved.girl-DIM-COM / two-CL 1.S-POSS see.INF-PST.ATTR **PREF-approach-ATTR** / TN-GEN peak-PLUR TPT
'The peaks of Suruga, **where [the waves] crash**, which I gazed upon with my darling girl...'

44. 14:3562.1-3 – UNP
安里蘇夜尓 / 於布流多麻母乃 / **宇知奈婢伎**
ar[a]-iso ya-ni / *op-uru tama mö-nö* / **uti-nanbik-i**
rough-rock shore-LOC / grow-ATTR jewel seaweed-COMP / **PREF-stretch.out-INF**
'**Stretching out** like the seaweed that grows on the rocky shore...'

Table 7.11: Attestations of the prefix *uti-* across the provinces.

TSOJ			EOJ								UNP
Sin	Tö	Su	Kak	Mu	Sa	Mi	Sik	Pi	Sip	Kap	
0	0	1	0	0	0	0	0	0	0	0	1

7.5.2 Suffixes

Verbal suffixes are plentiful in AOJ. I separate them into the categories of sentence non-final, sentence-final, and word non-final.

7.5.2.1 Sentence non-final suffixes

The sentence non-final suffixes are those that can end a verbal word form, but not a sentence. They include the infinitive *-i ~ -u*, the gerunds *-[a]nba, -nba,* and *-ndö[mo]*, the nominalizers *-i* and *-aku*, and the adjectivizer *-asi*.

7.5.2.1.1 Infinitives
The infinitives are *-i ~ -u* and the orthographic infinitive *-e*.

7.5.2.1.1.1 Infinitive *-i ~ -u*
The infinitive *-i* has three functions. First, it can act as a gerund. Second, it can act as glue to link verbs and auxiliaries together in a string. Finally, it can act as a prenominal modifier. It has three allomorphs: the underlying form *-i* that occurs after consonant-final verb stems, the phonologically conditioned null form that occurs after vowel-final verb stems, and the morphologically conditioned allomorph *-u* described in §7.5.2.1.1.4. The null form is the product of the language's phonotactics: vowel sequences are not permitted within a word form. Thus, the infinitive is lost upon affixation to a vowel-final stem verb, which in turn creates a portmanteau verb form consisting of 'root.INF'.

The infinitive *-i* is one of the most common morphemes in the corpus, attested multiple times in every topolect. Due to this fact, I do not present a chart listing the number of attestations in each province.

7.5.2.1.1.1.1 Linking function
It is not possible to translate the infinitive into English in these examples. The infinitive acts as a linking element that allows the addition of various bound auxiliaries.

45. 14:3352.5 – Sinano
登伎須疑尔家里
*töki **sungï-n-i-ker-i***
time **pass.INF-PERF-INF-RETR-FIN**
'[I realize] time **has passed by**.'

46. 14:3354.4-5 – Töpotuapumi
伊利奈麻之母乃 / 伊毛我乎杼許尔
ir-i-n-amasi mönö / imo-nga won-dökö-ni
enter-INF-PERF-SUBJ CNJ / beloved.girl-POSS DIM-bed-LOC
'Although [I] **would like to [lay] in** the warm bed of [my] beloved...'

47. 14:3359a.4-5 – Suruga
伊麻思乎多能美 / 波播尓**多我比奴**
imasi-wo tanöm-i / *papa-ni **tangap-i-n-u***
2.S-ACC trust-INF / mother-DAT **defy-INF-PERF-FIN**
'[I] **defied** [my] mother and put [my] trust in you.'

48. 20:4341.4-5 – Suruga
道乃長道波 / **由伎加弖奴**加毛
MITI nö NANGA-NDI pa / ***yuk-i-kate-n-u** kamo*
road COP.ATTR long-road TPT / **go-INF-POT-NEG-ATTR** EPT
'The road [ahead] is long, and [I] fear **I cannot traverse** it.'

49. 14:3410.4-5 – Kamitukeno
於久乎奈**加祢**曽 / 麻左可思余加婆
*oku-wo na-**kane**-sö* / *masaka si yö-k-anba*
future-ACC NEG.IMP-**worry**.INF-do / present EPT be.good-AVATTR-COND
'Do not **fret about** the future, if [things] are fine now.'

50. 20:4415.4-5 – Muzasi
伊弊奈流伊母乎 / 麻多**美**弖毛母也
ipe-n[i] ar-u imö-wo / *mata **mi**-te-m-o mö ya*
house-LOC exist-ATTR beloved.girl-ACC / again **see.INF**-PERF-TENT-ATTR EPT EPT
'How [I] would like to **see** [my] darling, who is at home, again!'

51. 20:4330.3-4 – Sagamu
氣布能比夜 / **伊田**弖麻可良武
keypu-nö pi ya / ***inde**-te makar-am-u*
today-GEN day QPT / **go.out.INF**-SUB depart-TENT-ATTR
'Will [we] depart and **[sail] out** today?'

52. 14:3437.1-3 – Mitinöku
美知能久能 / 安太多良末由美 / **波自伎於伎**弖
mitinöku-nö / *andatara ma-yumi* / ***panzik-i-ok-i**-te*
TN-GEN / TN INT-bow / **take-off-INF-put-INF**-SUB
'[I] **take off** [the string on my] fine bow [from] Adatara in Mitinöku…'

53. 14:3425.4-5 – Simotukeno
蘇良由登**伎**努与 / 奈我己許呂能礼
*sora-yu tö **k-i**-n-o yö / na-nga kökörö nör-e*
sky-ABL FPT **come-INF**-PERF-ATTR EPT / 2.S-POSS heart tell-IMP
'[I] **came** from the sky! Tell [me] your feelings.'

54. 14:3385.1-3 – Simotupusa
可都思加能 / 麻萬能手兒奈我 / **安里**之波可
*kandusika-nö / mama-nö teNGO-na-nga / **ar-i**-si paka*
TN-GEN / cliff-GEN maiden-DIM-POSS / **exist-INF**-PST.ATTR place
'The place where the dear maiden from the cliffs of Kadusika **was**...'

55. 14:3460.3-5 – UNP
尓布奈未尓 / 和我世乎**夜里**弖 / 伊波布許能戸乎
*nipu-namï-ni / wa-nga se-wo **yar-i**-te / ipap-u könö TO-wo*
new-taste.NML-LOC / 1.S-POSS beloved.man-ACC **send-INF**-SUB / purify.oneself-ATTR this door-ACC
'[I] **sent** my beloved to the new harvest [festival], and [now I] purify myself [behind] this door.'

7.5.2.1.1.1.2 Gerund function

In the following examples the infinitive suffix functions as a gerund.

56. 20:4401.2-4 – Sinano
須宗尓**等里都伎** / 奈古古良乎 / 意伎弖曽伎怒也
*suso-ni **tör-i-tuk-i** / nak-o ko-ra-wo / ok-i-te sö k-i-n-o ya*
hem-LOC **take-INF-attach-INF** / cry-ATTR child-PLUR-ACC / leave.behind-INF-SUB FPT come-INF-PERF-ATTR EPT
'Oh, [I] have come [here], leaving behind [my] sobbing children who **clung** to the hem [of my Kara robes]!'

57. 20:4321.2-4 – Töpotuapumi
美許等**加我布理** / 阿須由利也 / 加曳我牟多祢牟
*mi-kötö **kangapur-i** / asu-yuri ya / kaye-nga muta ne-m-u*
HON-word **receive.HUM-INF** / tomorrow-ABL QPT / reed-POSS together sleep-TENT-ATTR
'**Having received** [my sovereign's] command, will [I] sleep among the reeds from tomorrow?'

58. 20:4414.3-5 – Muzasi
宇都久之氣 / 麻古我弓**波奈利** / 之末**豆多比**由久
utukusi-key / *ma-ko-nga te* **panar-i** / *sima-n-dutap-i yuk-u*
be.dear-AVATTR / INT-girl-POSS hand **be.separated-INF** / island-LOC-**pass.along-INF** go-FIN
'[I] will go and **pass by** island after island, **separated from** the hands of [my] dear and devoted girl.'

59. 20:4374.1-3 – Simotukeno
阿米都知乃 / 可美乎伊乃里弖 / 佐都夜**奴伎**
amey tuti-nö / *kami-wo inör-i-te* / *satu-ya* **nuk-i**
heaven earth-GEN / deity-ACC pray-INF-SUB / hunting-arrow **pull.out-INF**
'Praying to the deities of heaven and earth, and **pulling out** a hunting arrow...'

60. 14:3395.1-2 – Pitati
乎豆久波乃 / 祢呂尔都久**多思**
won-dukupa-nö / *ne-rö-ni tuku* **tas-i**
DIM-TN-GEN / peak-DIM-LOC moon **rise-INF**
'The moon **rises** on the small peak of Mt. Tukupa...'

61. 20:4363.1-3 – Pitati
奈尔波都尔 / 美布祢**於呂須恵** / 夜蘇加**奴伎**
nanipa tu-ni / *mi-pune* **orö-suwe** / *ya-so ka* **nuk-i**
TN harbor-LOC / HON-boat **lower-place.INF** / eight-ten oar **pierce-INF**
'[After] **lowering** the boat in Nanipa harbor **and fixing it in place**, [we] **pierced** many oars [into the water]...'

62. 14:3383.1-2 – Kamitupusa
宇麻具多能 / 祢呂尔**可久里為**
umanguta-nö / *ne-rö-ni* **kakur-i-wi**
TN-GEN / peak-DIM-LOC **hide-INF-sit.INF**
'[I] **am hiding** [away] in the small peak of Umaguta...'

63. 20:4350.1-4 – Kamitupusa
尔波奈加能 / 阿須波乃可美尔 / 古志波**佐之** / 阿例波伊波々牟
nipa naka-nö / *asupa-nö kami-ni* / *ko-sinba* **sas-i** / *are pa ipap-am-u*
garden middle-GEN / TN-GEN deity-DAT / DIM-bush **insert-INF** / 1.S TPT pray-TENT-FIN
'I shall **place** [some] sprigs [in the ground] **and** pray to the Asupa deity in the middle of the garden.'

64. 14:3445.1-4 – UNP
美奈刀能也 / 安之我奈可那流 / 多麻古須氣 / **可利**己和我西古
minato-nö ya / *asi-nga naka-n[i] ar-u* / *tama-ko-sungey* / **kar-i** *kö wa-nga se-ko*
harbor-GEN EPT / reed-POSS middle-LOC exist-ATTR / jewel-DIM-sedge / **chop.down**-INF come.IMP 1.S-POSS beloved.man-DIM
'**Chop down** the jewel[-like] small sedges that are among the reeds in the harbor and come [back here], [my] darling man.'

65. 20:4426.1-3 – UNP
阿米都之乃 / 可未尓奴佐**於伎** / 伊波比都々
amey tusi-nö / *kamï-ni nusa* **ok-i** / *ipap-i-tutu*
heaven earth-GEN / deity-LOC paper.offering **put**-INF / pray-INF-COOR
'**Leave** paper offerings to the deities of heaven and earth while praying...'

7.5.2.1.1.1.3 Adnominal function

In these examples the infinitive is used in an adnominal (or attributive) function, modifying the following noun.

66. 14:3411.1-3 – Kamitukeno
多胡能祢尓 / **与西都奈**波倍弖 / 与須礼騰毛
tango-nö ne-ni / **yöse tuna** *papey-te* / *yös-ure-ndömo*
TN-GEN peak-LOC / **approach.INF rope** stretch.out.INF-SUB / draw.near-EV-CONC
'Although [I] would pull him up the peak of Mt. Tago by stretching out a **rope**...'

67. 20:4407.1-3 – Kamitukeno
比奈久毛理 / 宇須比乃佐可乎 / **古延**志太尓
pi-na kumor-i / *usupi-nö saka-wo* / **koye sinda**-ni
sun-LOC become.cloudy-INF / TN-GEN slope-ACC / **cross.INF CNJ**-LOC
'**When [I] crossed** Usupi hill [with] clouds over the sun...'

Example (67) is of note because we normally find an attributive form of a verb before the conjunction *sinda* 'when'. See §9.6 for examples illustrating this.

68. 20:4393.3-5 – Simotupusa
知々波々乎 / **以波比弊**等於枳弖 / 麻為弖枳尓之乎
titi papa-wo / **ipap-i pe**-*tö ok-i-te* / *mawi-nde-k-i-n-i-si-wo*
father mother-ACC / **pray-INF pot**-COM leave.behind-INF-SUB / come.HUM.INF-go.out.INF-come-INF-PERF-INF-PST.ATTR-ACC
'[I] left [my] father and mother with a **praying pot** and came out [here].'

69. 20:4370.1-3 – Pitati
    阿良例布理 / 可志麻乃可美乎 / 伊能利都々
    arare pur-i / ***kasima**-nö kami-wo* / *inör-i-tutu*
    hail fall-INF / TN-GEN deity-ACC / pray-INF-COOR
    'While praying to the deity of **Kasima where the hail falls**...'

70. 14:3442.1-3 – UNP
    安豆麻治乃 / 手兒乃欲妣左賀 / 古要我祢弖
    anduma-ndi-nö / *teNGO-nö **yonb-i saka*** / *koye-ngane-te*
    TN-road-GEN / maiden-GEN **call-INF slope** / get.past.INF-NEG.POT.INF-SUB
    'Being unable to cross the maiden-**calling slope** on the road to Aduma...'

71. 14:3512.3-5 – UNP
    安乎祢呂尓 / 伊佐欲布久母能 / 余曽里都麻波母
    awo ne-rö-ni / *isayop-u kumö-nö* / ***yösör-i tuma** pa mö*
    green peak-DIM-LOC / hesitate-ATTR cloud-COMP / **rumored.to.be-INF spouse**
    TPT EPT
    '[She] is [only] **rumored to be [my] wife**, like the clouds that hesitate over the little green peak.'

7.5.2.1.1.1.4 Infinitive allomorph *-u*

The infinitive allomorph *-u* only follows the allomorph *-[a]nz-* of the negative suffix, an environment where the infinitive *-i* is blocked (this may be related to the fact that a form *-anzi* exists but is 'NEG.TENT'). We would expect the negative-infinitive form to be *-an-i*, however this is unattested in AOJ, even though it does occur in WOJ with a few verbs. Thus, this infinitive *-u* is a morphologically conditioned allomorph of the infinitive *-i*. As in WOJ, the nominalizer *-u* is also attested after the negative allomorph *-anz-* (in TSOJ, EOJ, and UNP). Similarly, we find the final form *-anz-u* '-NEG-FIN' (in TSOJ, EOJ, and UNP); an example is provided in (73) below for comparison. Due to this, Vovin (2009a: 716–717) analyzes *-u* as a suffix, rather than *-anzu* as a portmanteau morph. I adopt his analysis here.

72. 20:4323.3-5 – Töpotuapumi
    奈尓須礼曽 / 波々登布波奈乃 / 佐吉泥己受祁牟
    nani s-ure sö / *papa tö [i]p-u pana-nö* / *sak-i-nde-**kö-nz-u**-kem-u*
    why do-EV FPT / mother QUOT say-ATTR flower-GEN / bloom-INF-go.out.INF-
    come-NEG-INF-PST.TENT-ATTR
    'Why has the flower called 'mother' **not come** out in bloom?'

73. 20:4322.3-5 – Töpotuapumi
乃牟美豆尓 / 加其佐倍美曳弓 / 余尓和須良礼受
nöm-u mindu-ni / *kangö sapey mi-ye-te* / *yö-ni **wasur-are-nz-u***
drink-ATTR water-LOC / shadow RPT see-PASS.INF-SUB / lifetime-LOC **forget-PASS-NEG-FIN**
'So much as seeing her shadow in the water that [I] drink, [makes me realize I] **cannot forget** [her] in this lifetime.'

74. 20:4337.3-4 – Suruga
知々波々尓 / 毛能波須價尓弓
titi papa-ni / *monö **[i]p-anz-u** k-e-n-i-te*
father mother-DAT / things **say-NEG-INF** come-INF-PERF-INF-SUB
'[I] have come [out here] **without saying** a word to my father or mother!'

75. 20:4416.4-5 – Muzasi
伊波奈流和礼波 / 比毛等加受祢牟
ipa-n[i] ar-u ware pa / *pimo **tök-anz-u** ne-m-u*
house-LOC exist-ATTR 1.S TPT / string **undo-NEG-INF** sleep-TENT-FIN
'I, who am at home, shall sleep **without untying** my cords.'

76. 14:3370.5 – Sagamu
比母登可受祢牟
*pimö **tök-anz-u** ne-m-u*
string **undo-NEG-INF** sleep-TENT-ATTR
'[Why would I] sleep with [you] **without untying** [my] cords?'

77. 14:3425.1-4 – Simotukeno
志母都家努 / 安素乃河泊良欲 / 伊之布麻努受 / 蘓良由登伎努与
simötukeno / *aso-nö kapara-yo* / *isi **pum-anz-u*** / *sora-yu tö k-i-n-o yö*
TN / TN-GEN river.bank-ABL / stone **step-NEG-INF** / sky-ABL FPT come-INF-PERF-ATTR EPT
'[I] came from the sky **without stepping** [on] the stones from the riverbank of Aso in Simotukeno!'

78. 20:4371.4-5 – Pitati
都久波能夜麻乎 / 古比須安良米可毛
tukupa-nö yama-wo / ***kopi-nz-u** ar-am-ey kamo*
TN-GEN mountain-ACC / **long.for-NEG-INF** exist-TENT-EV EPT
'[I] wonder, shall [I] **not long for** Tukupa mountain?'

79. 14:3481.3-5 – UNP
伊敝能伊母尔 / 毛乃**伊波受**伎尓弖 / 於毛比具流之母
*ipe-nö imö-ni / monö **ip-anz-u** k-i-n-i-te / omop-i-n-gurusi-mö*
house-GEN beloved.girl-DAT / thing **say-NEG-INF** come-INF-PERF-INF-SUB / think-NML-GEN-be.painful.AVFIN-EXCL
'[I] came [here] **without saying** anything to [my] darling [I left] at home. . .oh, it is painful to think [about that]!'

80. 14:3508.4-5 – UNP
安比見受安良婆 / 安礼古非米夜母
***ap-i-MI-nz-u** ar-anba / are kopï-m-ey ya mö*
meet-INF-see-NEG-INF exist-COND / 1.S love-TENT-EV QPT EPT
'If [I] had **not met** [you], would I be in love [with you]? (No, I would not!)'

81. 20:4436.1-3 – UNP
夜未乃欲能 / 由久左伎**之良受** / 由久和礼乎
*yamï nö yo-nö / yuk-u saki **sir-anz-u** / yuk-u ware-wo*
darkness COP.ATTR night-GEN / go-ATTR ahead **know-NEG-INF** / go-ATTR 1.S-ACC
'I, [who] was going **without knowing** what lies ahead on this dark night. . .'

The infinitive allomorph -*u* may be followed by the subordinative gerund auxiliary -*te*, just like the infinitive allomorph -*i*. This is shown in the following two examples:

82. 20:4376.1-2 – Simotukeno
多妣由伎尓 / 由久等**之良受弖**
*tanbi yuk-i-ni / yuk-u tö **sir-anz-u-te***
journey go-NML-LOC / go-FIN QUOT **know-NEG-INF-SUB**
'**[I] did not know** that [I] would be going on a journey. . .'

83. 14:3447.4-5 – UNP
阿努波**由加受弖** / 阿良久佐太知奴
*ano pa **yuk-anz-u-te** / ara kusa-n-dat-i-n-u*
TN TPT **go-NEG-INF-SUB** / wild grass-GEN-rise-INF-PERF-FIN
'Wild grass has sprung up, [because] **no [one] goes** [to] Ano.'

7.5.2.1.1.2 Orthographic infinitive -*e*

The orthographic infinitive -*e* is only attested once, in the Suruga topolect of TSOJ. I refer to it as "orthographic" because it is most likely an illusion, being the result of a lack of contrast between *ki* and *ke* phonograms, after extensive raising of *ke > /ki/ occurred in this topolect. See §2.2.1.1 for a discussion.

84. 20:4337.3-4 – Suruga
知々波々尓 / 毛能波須價尓弖
*titi papa-ni / monö [i]p-anz-u **k-e-n-i-te***
father mother-DAT / thing say-NEG-INF **come-INF-PERF-INF-SUB**
'[I] **have come** [out here] without saying a word to [my] father or mother!'

7.5.2.1.2 Gerunds
The gerunds include the conditional gerund *-anba*, the conjunctive gerund *-nba*, and the concessive gerund *-ndö[mo]*.

7.5.2.1.2.1 Conditional gerund *-anba* ~ *-nba*
The conditional gerund *-anba* introduces a conditional clause, with the meaning of 'if X'. It has two allomorphs: *-anba* after consonant-final stems and *-nba* after vowel-final stems and most vowel-final suffixes and auxiliaries. There is also a special temporal construction involving the conditional *-anba*, described in §7.5.2.1.2.1.1.

85. 20:4324.1-4 – Töpotuapumi
等倍多保美 / 志留波乃伊宗等 / 尓閇乃宇良等 / 安比弖之**阿良婆**
*töpeytapomi / sirupa-nö iso-tö / nipey-nö ura-tö / ap-i-te si **ar-anba***
TN / TN-GEN rocky.shore-COM / TN-GEN bay-COM / meet-INF-SUB EPT **exist-COND**
'**If** only Töpeytapomi's rocky shore of Sirupa and Nipey bay **were** close to one another!'

86. 14:3414.5 – Kamitukeno
佐祢乎**佐祢弖婆**
*sa-ne-wo **sa-ne-te-nba***
LOC-sleep.NML-ACC **LOC-sleep.INF-PERF-COND**
'**If [only I] had slept there** [with you]...'

87. 14:3378.3-4 – Muzasi
伊波爲都良 / 比可**婆**奴流々々
*ipawi tura / **pik-anba** nur-u nur-u*
UNC vine / **pull-COND** come.loose-FIN come.loose-FIN
'The *ipawi* vines come loose smoothly **if [they are] pulled** [up].'

88. 20:4423.1-3 – Muzasi
   安之我良乃 / 美佐可尔多志弖 / 蕪塈**布良婆**
   *asingara-nö / mi-saka-ni tas-i-te / sonde **pur-anba***
   TN-GEN / HON-slope-LOC stand-INF-GER / sleeve **wave-COND**
   'If [I] **wave** [my] sleeve, standing on the slope of Asigara. . .'

89. 14:3426.1-3 – Mitinöku
   安比豆祢能 / 久尔乎佐杼抱美 / **安波奈波婆**
   *apindu ne-nö / kuni-wo sa n-döpo-mi / **ap-an-ap-anba***
   TN peak-GEN / land-ABS thus COP.INF-be.far-AVGER / **meet-NEG-ITER-COND**
   'If [we] **keep failing to meet** because the land of the Apidu peaks is so far [away]. . .'

90. 20:4379.1-3 – Simotukeno
   之良奈美乃 / 与曽流波麻倍尔 / **和可例奈婆**
   *sira nami-nö / yösör-u pama-pey-ni / **wakare-n-anba***
   white wave-GEN / draw.near-ATTR shore-side-LOC / **separate.INF-PERF-COND**
   'If [I] **part** [with you] at the side of the shore where the white waves draw near. . .'

91. 20:4392.1-3 – Simotupusa
   阿米都之乃 / 以都例乃可美乎 / **以乃良波**加
   *amey tusi-nö / indure-nö kami-wo / **inör-anba** ka*
   heaven earth-GEN / which-GEN deity-ACC / **pray-COND** QPT
   'If [I] **pray**, to which deities of heaven and earth [should I pray]?'

Example (91) shows the conditional *-anba* used in tandem with a preceding interrogative pronoun and a following question particle, to indicate uncertainty.

92. 14:3382.1-4 – Kamitupusa
   宇麻具多能 / 祢呂乃佐左葉能 / 都由思母能 / 奴礼弖和**伎奈婆**
   *umanguta-nö / ne-rö-nö sasa-PA-nö / tuyu simö-nö / nure-te wa **k-i-n-anba***
   TN-GEN / peak-DIM-GEN bamboo.grass-leaf-GEN / dew frost-GEN / get.wet.INF-SUB 1.S **come-INF-PERF-COND**
   'If I **come** [to you], wet [with] dew and frost from the bamboo grass leaves on the peaks of Umaguta. . .'

93. 14:3567.1-2 – UNP
於伎弖**伊可婆** / 伊毛婆麻可奈之
ok-i-te **ik-anba** / imo pa ma-kanasi
leave.behind-INF-SUB go-COND / beloved.girl TPT INT-be.sad.AVFIN
'**If [I] go** and leave [her] behind, [my] beloved girl will be so sad.'

94. 20:4426.3-5 – UNP
伊波比都々 / 伊麻世和我世奈 / 阿礼乎之**毛波婆**
ipap-i-tutu / imas-e wa-nga se-na / are-wo si [o]**mop-anba**
pray-INF-COOR / exist.HON-IMP 1.S-POSS beloved.man-DIM / 1.S-ACC EPT **love-COND**
'My dearly beloved, **if [you] love** me, then keep praying.'

7.5.2.1.2.1.1 Temporal construction with a following verb in the tentative mood
When the conditional -anba is followed by a predicate verb in the tentative mood, it can mean 'when', rather than 'if' (Vovin 2009a: 733). I could only find three clear examples of this in the AOJ corpus.

95. 14:3400.3-5 – Sinano
左射礼思母 / 伎弥之**布美弖波** / 多麻等**比呂波牟**
sanzare [i]si mö / kimi si **pum-i-te-nba** / tama tö **piröp-am-u**
little stone FPT / lord EPT **step-INF-PERF-COND** / jade COP **pick.up-TENT-FIN**
'**When** [you, my] lord **have stepped** on the small stones, [I] **shall pick [them] up** as jewels.'

96. 14:3394.4-5 – Pitati
和須良延許婆古曽 / 那乎**可家奈波賣**
wasura-kö-nba kosö / na-wo kake-n-ap-am-e
forget-come-COND FPT / 2.S-ACC call.out-NEG-ITER-TENT-EV
'**When [I] start to forget** [our meeting there], [I] **shall stop calling out** for you!'

97. 14:3477.2-4 – UNP
手兒乃欲婢佐可 / 古要弖**伊奈波** / 安礼波**古非牟**奈
teNGO-nö yonb-i saka / koye-te **in-anba** / are pa **kopï-m-u** na
maiden-GEN call-INF slope / cross.INF-SUB **depart-COND** / 1.S TPT **long.for-TENT-FIN** EPT
'**When** [you] **depart** and cross the maiden-calling slope, oh, I **shall long for** [you]!'

Table 7.12: Attestations of the conditional gerund *-anba* ~ *-nba* across the provinces.

TSOJ			EOJ								UNP
Sin	Tö	Su	Kak	Mu	Sa	Mi	Sik	Pi	Sip	Kap	
2	1	0	2	6	0	2	1	1	1	2	11

7.5.2.1.2.2 Conjunctive gerund *-nba*

The conjunctive gerund *-nba* has two functions: an expression of reason, and a temporal function. It is homophonous with the allomorph *-nba* of the conditional gerund. They are differentiated based on semantics as well as the stems to which they attach: the conjunctive gerund *-nba* only attaches to stems that end in the evidential suffix.

7.5.2.1.2.2.1 Expression of reason

The following examples show the conjunctive gerund used to express reason, something akin to 'because' or 'since'.

98. 20:4351.5 – Kamitupusa
    伊母尓志阿良祢婆
    *imö n-i si **ar-an-e-nba***
    beloved.girl COP-INF EPT **exist-NEG-EV-CONJ**
    '**Because it is not** [my] beloved [who will warm me up]!'

99. 14:3498.1-3 – UNP
    宇奈波良乃 / 根夜波良古須氣 / 安麻多安礼波
    *una-para-nö / NE yapara ko-sungey / amata **ar-e-nba***
    sea-field-GEN / root soft DIM-sedge / many **exist-EV-CONJ**
    '**Since** there **are** many [girls like] the small sedges [with] soft roots [growing near] the sea...'

7.5.2.1.2.2.2 Temporal function

The following examples show the conjunctive gerund used to indicate a meaning of 'when'.

100. 14:3352.3-4 – Sinano
保登等藝須 / 奈久許恵伎氣波
potötöngisu / *nak-u köwe* **kik-ey-nba**
cuckoo / cry-ATTR voice **hear-EV-CONJ**
'**When** [I] **hear** the crying voice [of] the cuckoo...'

101. 20:4375.1-2 – Simotukeno
麻都能氣乃 / 奈美多流美礼波
matu-nö key-nö / *nam-i-tar-u* **mi-re-nba**
pine-GEN tree-GEN / be.lined.up-INF-PP-ATTR **see-EV-CONJ**
'**When** [I] **look at** the pine trees lined up...'

102. 14:3397.1-4 – Pitati
比多知奈流 / 奈左可能宇美乃 / 多麻毛許曽 / 飛氣波多延須礼
pitati-n[i] ar-u / *nasaka-nö umi-nö* / *tama mo kösö* / **pïk-ey-nba** *taye-s-ure*
TN-LOC exist-ATTR / TN-GEN sea-GEN / jade seaweed FPT / **pull-EV-CONJ**
break-CAUS-EV
'**When** [I] **pull** [up] the jade seaweed from the sea of Nasaka in Pitati, it falls apart.'

103. 14:3450.1-4 – UNP
乎久左乎等 / 乎具佐受家乎等 / 斯抱布祢乃 / 那良敝弖美礼婆
wokusa wo-tö / *wongusa-n-suke-wo-tö* / *sipo pune-nö* / *naranbe-te* **mi-re-nba**
TN man-COM / TN-GEN-help-man-COM / tide boat-COMP / line.up.INF-SUB
see-EV-CONJ
'**When** [I] **see** the man [from] Wokusa and the assistant [from] Wogusa lined up like tide boats...'

104. 14:3476a.3-4 – UNP
多刀都久能 / 努賀奈敝由家婆
tat-o tuku-nö / **nongan-ape-yuk-e-nba**
rise-ATTR moon-GEN / **flow-ITER.INF-go-EV-CONJ**
'**Whenever** the rising moon **sets**...'

105. 20:4427.4-5 – UNP
由須比之比毛乃 / 登久良久毛倍婆
yusup-i-si pimo-nö / *tök-ur-aku [o]***mop-ey-nba**
tie-INF-PST.ATTR string-GEN / come.undone-ATTR-NML **think-EV-CONJ**
'**When** [I] **think** that the cord [she] tied has come undone...'

Table 7.13: Attestations of the conjunctive gerund -nba across the provinces.

TSOJ			EOJ								UNP
Sin	Tö	Su	Kak	Mu	Sa	Mi	Sik	Pi	Sip	Kap	
1	0	0	1	0	0	0	3	1	1	2	15

7.5.2.1.2.3 Concessive gerund -ndömo ~ -ndö

The concessive gerund has a meaning of 'however', 'although', or 'but'. It always attaches to the evidential suffix. Due to this we might be tempted to conclude there is no synchronic morpheme boundary between the two forms, but the fact that the evidential occurs on its own paired with the fact that other suffixes can attach to the evidential makes such a conclusion implausible.

There are two allomorphs: -ndö and -ndömo. The latter historically consists of a focus particle attached to the concessive, but as Vovin (2009a: 746) notes there is no difference in meaning or function on the synchronic level, so the allomorphs can be considered free variants.

The concessive gerund can also attach to the evidential forms of adjectival verbs. See §6.3.3.5 for those examples.

106. 20:4343.1-2 – Suruga
 和呂多比波 / 多比等於米保等
 *warö tanbi pa / tanbi tö **omeyp-o-ndö***
 1.S journey TPT / journey COP **think-EV-CONC**
 '**Although [I] know** my journey will be an [arduous] one...'

107. 14:3420.4 – Kamitukeno
 於也波佐久礼騰
 *oya pa **sak-ure-ndö***
 parents TPT **keep.apart-EV-CONC**
 '**Although** [our] parents **split [us] apart**...'

108. 20:4419.1-2 – Muzasi
 伊波呂尓波 / 安之布多氣度母
 *ipa-rö-ni pa / asi-pu **tak-ey-ndomö***
 house-DIM-LOC TPT / reed-fire **burn-EV-CONC**
 '**Although [we] would burn** reeds [to warm our] modest home...'

109. 20:4378.1-2 – Simotukeno
    都久比夜波 / 須具波由氣等毛
    tuku pi ya pa / ***sungu pa yuk-ey-ndömo***
    moon sun EPT TPT / **pass.NML TPT go-EV-CONC**
    'Oh, sun and moon! **Although [they] pass through** [their cycles]. . .'

110. 14:3350a.1-3 – Pitati
    筑波祢乃 / 尓比具波麻欲能 / 伎奴波安礼杼
    tukupa ne-nö / *nipi n-gupa mayo-nö* / *kinu pa **ar-e-ndö***
    TN peak-GEN / new COP.ATTR-wild.silkworm cocoon-GEN / robe TPT **exist-EV-CONC**
    '**Although [I have** robes [spun] from new wild silkworm cocoons from the peak of Mt. Tukupa. . .'

111. 20:4388.1-2 – Simotupusa
    多飛等弊等 / 麻多妣尓奈理奴
    *tanbï tö [i]**p-e-ndö*** / *ma-tanbi n-i nar-i-n-u*
    journey QUOT say-EV-**CONC** / INT-journey COP-INF become-INF-PERF-FIN
    '**Although** [it] was **said** to be [just] 'a journey', [this] has become such a [trying] journey.'

112. 20:4353.1-2 – Kamitupusa
    伊倍加是波 / 比尓々々布氣等
    ipey kanze pa / *pi-ni pi-ni **puk-ey-ndö***
    house wind TPT / day-LOC day-LOC **blow-EV-CONC**
    '**Although** the wind [from my] home **blows** [here] day by day. . .'

113. 14:3444.1-4 – UNP
    伎波都久能 / 乎加能久君美良 / 和礼都賣杼 / 故尓毛乃多奈布
    kipatuku-nö / *woka-nö kuku-mira* / *ware **tum-e-ndö*** / *ko-ni mo nöt-an-ap-u*
    TN-GEN / hill-GEN stem-leek / 1.S **pluck-EV-CONC** / basket-LOC FPT fill.up-NEG-ITER-FIN
    'I **pluck** the stem-leeks on Kipatuku hill, **but** the basket is not filling up.'

114. 14:3509.3-5 – UNP
宿奈敝杼母 / 古呂賀於曽伎能 / 安路許曽要志母
NE-n-ap-e-ndömö / *ko-rö-nga osöki-nö* / *ar-o kösö ye-si-mö*
sleep-NEG-ITER-EV-CONC / girl-DIM-POSS upper.garment-GEN / exist-ATTR FPT be.good-AVFIN-EXCL
'**Although [we] are not sleeping together**, it is so nice to have [my] dear girl's upper garment!'

115. 14:3550.2 – UNP
伊祢波**都可祢杼**
ine pa ***tuk-an-e-ndö***
rice.plant TPT **pound-NEG-EV-CONC**
'**Though [I] did not pound** the rice. . .'

Table 7.14: Attestations of the concessive gerund *-ndömö ~ -ndö* across the provinces.

TSOJ			EOJ							UNP
Sin	Tö	Su	Kak	Mu	Sa	Mi	Sik	Pi	Sip	Kap	
0	1	2	3	1	0	0	1	1	2	2	8

7.5.2.1.3 Nominalizers
The nominalizers are *-i ~ -u* and *-aku*.

7.5.2.1.3.1 Nominalizer *-i ~ -u*
The nominalizer *-i* is usually considered to be morphologically distinct from the infinitive *-i*, since the former is derivational, and the latter is inflectional. There are also some accentual differences between the two, but we can only see that in later forms of Japanese (cf. Martin 1987: 211, 1988: 884). There is no evidence such accentual differences were present in the AOJ dialects, since accent was not marked in the orthography. From a typological perspective it is not uncommon for an infinitive form of a verb to also act as a nominal form, but I will not stray from the usual analysis of considering the nominalizer *-i* a distinct morpheme from the infinitive *-i* in Old Japanese (Vovin 2009a: 753), as I see no benefit from doing so.

The nominalizer *-i* has the same allomorphy as the infinitive *-i*, including the morphologically conditioned allomorph *-u*.

116. 20:4337.1-2 – Suruga
    美豆等利乃 / **多知能已蘓岐**尔
    mindu töri-nö / **tat-i**-nö **isong-i** n-i
    water bird-GEN / **rise**-NML-COMP **rush**-NML COP-INF
    'Being in **a rush** [to leave], like the **ascent** of waterfowl. . .'

117. 14:3404.1-3 – Kamitukeno
    可美都氣努 / 安蘓能麻素武良 / **可伎武太伎**
    kamitukeyno / aso-nö ma-so mura / **kaki-mundak-i**
    TN / TN-GEN INT-hemp group / **TNG-embrace-NML**
    '[Like] **holding** a fine bundle of hemp from of Aso [in] Kamitukeno **close to** [my] **bosom**. . .'

118. 20:4405.1-2 – Kamitukeno
    和我伊母古我 / **志濃比**尔西餘等
    wa-nga imö-ko-nga / **sinup-i** n-i se-yö tö
    1.S-POSS beloved.girl-DIM-POSS / **yearn.for**-NML COP-INF do-IMP QUOT
    'My dearly beloved told [me] to **yearn for** [her]. . .'

119. 14:3374.1-2 – Muzasi
    武蔵野尔 / **宇良敝**可多也伎
    munzasi NO-ni / **urape** kata yak-i
    TN field-LOC / **divine.**NML shoulder burn-INF
    '**A diviner** burned a [deer] shoulder on Muzasi Plain. . .'

120. 20:4421.1-2 – Muzasi
    和我**由伎**乃 / 伊伎都久之可婆
    wa-nga **yuk-i**-nö / iki-n-dukus-i-k-anba
    1.S-POSS **go**-NML-GEN / breath-GEN-exhaust-INF-PST-COND
    'If [you] have exhausted [all your] breath due to my **departure**. . .'

121. 20:4329.3-5 – Sagamu
    布奈可射里 / 安我世牟比呂乎 / 美毛比等母我毛
    puna-kanzar-i / a-nga se-m-u pi-rö-wo / mi-m-o pitö möngamo
    boat-decorate-NML / 1.S-POSS do-TENT-ATTR day-DIM-ACC / see-TENT-ATTR person DPT
    '[I] wish someone would witness the special day when I do the **boat-decorating**.'

122. 14:3426.4-5 – Mitinöku
斯努比尔勢毛等 / 比毛牟須波佐祢
sinop-i n-i se-m-o tö / pimo musunb-as-an-e
yearn.for-NML COP-INF do-TENT-ATTR QUOT / cord tie-HON-DES-IMP
'[I] want [you] to tie [your] cords and **think [of me]** when [you] do!'

123. 20:4376.1-2 – Simotukeno
多妣由伎尓 / 由久等之良受弖
tanbi yuk-i-ni / yuk-u tö sir-anz-u-te
journey go-NML-LOC / go-FIN QUOT know-NEG-INF-SUB
'[I] did not know that [I] would be going on a **journey**...'

124. 20:4364.1-2 – Pitati
佐岐牟理尓 / 多々牟佐和伎尓
sakimuri-ni / tat-am-u sawak-i-ni
border.guard-LOC / depart-TENT-ATTR **make.noise**-NML-LOC
'In the **noisiness** of the departure of the border guards...'

125. 20:4391.4-5 – Simotupusa
阿加古比須奈牟 / 伊母賀加奈志作
a-nga kopi s-unam-u / imö-nga kanasi-sa
1.S-POSS **long.for**.NML do-TENT2-ATTR / beloved.girl-POSS be.sad-ADJNML
'The sadness of my beloved girl who probably **longs for** [me]...'

126. 14:3383.5 – Kamitupusa
奈我目保里勢牟
na-nga MEY por-i se-m-u
2.S-POSS eye **desire**-NML do-TENT-FIN
'[I] **dream of** your eyes.'

127. 20:4354.2-3 – Kamitupusa
多知乃佐和伎尓 / 阿比美弖之
tat-i-nö sawak-i-ni / ap-i-mi-te si
depart-NML-GEN **make.noise**-NML-LOC / meet-INF-see.INF-SUB EPT
'[We] met during the **noisiness** of [my] **departure**.'

128. 14:3442.4-5 – UNP
夜麻尓可祢牟毛 / <u>夜杼里</u>波奈之尓
yama-ni ka ne-m-u mo / **yandör-i** *pa na-si-ni*
mountain-LOC QPT sleep-TENT-ATTR FPT / **lodge-NML** TPT not.exist-AVFIN-LOC
'Shall [I] sleep in the mountains, since there is no **lodging** [here]?'

129. 14:3493a.3-5 – UNP
牟可都乎能 / 四比乃故夜提能 / <u>安比</u>波多我波自
muka-tu wo-nö / *sipi-nö ko-yande-nö* / **ap-i** *pa tangap-anzi*
opposite.side-GEN.LOC mountain.ridge-GEN / chinquapin-GEN DIM-branch-COMP / **meet-NML** TPT differ-NEG.TENT
'[Our] **meeting** shall be indistinguishable from how the small branches of the chinquapin trees on the mountain ridge across the way [touch each other].'

130. 14:3495.3 – UNP
可<u>藝里</u>登也
kangir-i *tö ya*
limit-NML QUOT QPT
'Is [this] the **end**?'

131. 14:3461.1-2 – UNP
安是登伊敝可 / 佐<u>宿</u>尓安波奈久尓
anze tö ip-e ka / *sa-**NE**-ni ap-an-aku n-i*
why QUOT say-EV QPT / LOC-**sleep.NML**-LOC meet-NEG.ATTR-NML COP-INF
'Why did [we] not meet to **sleep** together?'

Example (131) is a logographic attestation.

132. 20:4425.5 – UNP
毛乃<u>母比</u>毛世受
*monö [o]**möp-i** mo se-nz-u*
thing **think-NML** FPT do-NEG-FIN
'[I] do not **worry about** things.'

7.5.2.1.3.1.1 Allomorph -*u*

The nominalizer allomorph -*u* is attested three times in the entire corpus. Just as we find in WOJ, it only occurs after the negative suffix -*anz*-.

133. 20:4347.1-2 – Kamitupusa
伊閇尓之弖 / 古非都々**安良受**波
ipey n-i s-i-te / *kopï-tutu* **ar-anz-u** *pa*
house COP-INF do-INF-SUB / long.for.INF-COOR **exist-NEG-NML** TPT
'**Without** longing for you while I am at home. . .'

134. 14:3544.1-3 – UNP
阿須可河泊 / 之多尓其礼留乎 / **之良受**思天
asuka-n-gapa / *sita ningör-er-u-wo* / **sir-anz-u** *s-i-te*
TN-GEN-river / below be.muddy-PROG-ATTR-ACC / **know-NEG-NML** do-INF-SUB
'The bottom of Asuka river is muddy, but [I] **did not know** [that].'

135. 14:3565.1-2 – UNP
可能古呂等 / **宿受**夜奈里奈牟
kanö ko-rö-tö / **NE-nz-u** *ya nar-i-n-am-u*
that girl-DIM-COM / **sleep-NEG-NML** QPT be-INF-PERF-TENT-ATTR
'Shall it be **that [I] will not sleep** with that sweet girl?'

Table 7.15: Attestations of the nominalizer *-i ~ -u* across the provinces.

TSOJ			EOJ							UNP
Sin	Tö	Su	Kak	Mu	Sa	Mi	Sik	Pi	Sip	Kap	
2	0	2	4	2	1	1	1	1	1	4	24

7.5.2.1.3.2 Nominalizer *-aku*

Vovin (2005, 2009a) and Russell (2006) view *-aku* as a suffix in both WOJ and AOJ, though Vovin (2009a: 763) claims that it is not a true suffix. This is because it behaves more like a postposed noun, at least diachronically, in that it attaches to the attributive form of a verb. Another notable feature of *-aku* is that it nominalizes the entire verb phrase, rather than the verb root. This feature is more characteristic of an enclitic, but unlike an enclitic *-aku* is clearly integrated into the verbal paradigm, cannot be dislocated and moved to any other part of the sentence, and cannot have any particle intervene between it and the verb to which it attaches.

Synchronically, I agree that the suffix was *-aku*, but I propose it is a reflex of the concatenation of the PJ attributive *-a and a nominalizing postposition *ku. The attributive *-a* is attested elsewhere in EOJ (see §7.5.2.2.3 for a discussion), but not in

TSOJ or WOJ, where it is only fossilized in this suffix. This indicates the suffix can be projected back to PJe. Consider the following data from Vovin (2009a: 764), showing the attested (synchronic) WOJ forms, in comparison to my PJe (diachronic) analysis.

Table 7.16: Synchronic and diachronic analysis of the nominalizer -aku.

PRECEDING MORPHEME	VOVIN'S WOJ ANALYSIS	MY PJe ANALYSIS	ATTESTED IN AOJ?
NEGATIVE	-(a)n-aku	*-(a)n-a-ku	+
TENTATIVE	-(a)m-aku	*-(a)m-a-ku	+
ATTRIBUTIVE[170]	-(u)r-aku	*-(u)r-a-ku	+
PAST-FINAL	-keku (<*-ki-aku)	*-ki-aku (> -keku)[171]	-
PAST-ATTRIBUTIVE	-si-ku (<*-si-aku)	*-si-ku	-
RETROSPECTIVE	-ker-aku	*-ki-ar-a-ku (< -ker-aku)	-
ADJECTIVAL ATTRIBUTIVE	-keku (<*-ki-aku)	*-ki-aku[172]	+
CONSONANT-FINAL VERB STEM	-aku	*-a-ku	+

The advantage of my PJe analysis is that it offers a plausible explanation for why the WOJ past-attributive form is -si-ku instead of expected -s-aku or -seku. Since -si is already attributive and cannot be suffixed by the attributive -u ~ -uru, it is only natural that we would not find the attributive *-a in this form. However, if -aku were simply a monomorphemic nominalizing suffix in PJe, we would not expect its initial vowel to disappear only when it follows an attributive suffix. Francis-Ratte (2016: 149–150) earlier proposed a historical segmentation of -ku from -aku, but his analysis involves an adnominal -or- and a suffix -a which he claims was "a deverbal inflection[173] with a specific, non-active or resultative interpretation that becomes lexicalized and narrowed" (2016: 135), and he considers the -ku to be the adjectival verb infinitive suffix. His analysis does not explain the nominalized past-attributive form -si-ku.

The usage of this suffix on adjectival verbs must have been a later development, which is unsurprising since the attributive *-a can be projected back to PJ but the adjectival verb attributive *-ke only emerged in PJe. Thus, I consider its usage on adjectival verbs in the attributive to be based on a reanalysis of *-aku as a monomorphemic suffix. The EOJ form -k-aku '-AVATTR-NML' (attested once, in 14:3489.3 – UNP) shows the form -aku (not *-ku) is involved here. Since there

---

[170] The allomorph of the attributive that attaches to vowel-final verb stems. Historically this contains the PJe stative *-ur- (Russell (2006: 648–650) reconstructs PJ *-ʼura- for this stative).
[171] This form can only be projected back to WOJ, not PJe.
[172] This form can only be projected back to WOJ, not PJe.
[173] In simple terms, he is describing a nominalizer.

are only two attestations of the nominalizer -*aku* attached to adjectival verbs in AOJ, it is likely this usage was a recent loan from WOJ. The WOJ form is -*keku* (< *-ki-aku), the result of a fusion of the two adjacent medial vowels – a process that does not occur in the earlier paradigmatic forms of -*aku*, such as -*ur-aku* (instead of -*uroku* <*-uru-aku). This supports the idea this usage was an innovation in WOJ. The usage of this suffix on the past-final form of verbs similarly developed in WOJ after the morpheme boundary in *-a-ku was lost (because, by that time, the attributive *-a had been completely replaced in WOJ by -*u* ~ -*uru*). It applied to the past-final through a process of back-formation and analogy, and a fusion of -*ki-aku* > -*keku* occurred. This form is unattested in AOJ, which adds further support to the idea it was a later, innovative construction in WOJ.

As mentioned above, from the viewpoint of the synchronic grammar the nominalizer -*aku* attaches to the attributive form of verbs. The initial vowel of this suffix is strong, and as such it never deletes in a verbal word form in AOJ. In verbs that take the attributive allomorphs -*o* or -*u*, the attributive is rendered phonologically null upon the addition of -*aku*, and thus the preceding verbal suffix or root becomes portmanteau. Note the following examples:

136. 20:4406 – Kamitukeno
和我伊波呂尓 / 由加毛比等母我 / **久佐麻久良** / **多妣波久流之等** /
都氣夜良麻久母
wa-nga ipa-rö-ni / *yuk-am-o pitö mönga* / **kusa makura** / **tanbi pa kurusi tö** / **tungey-yar-am-aku mö**
1.S-POSS house-DIM-LOC / go-TENT-ATTR person DPT / grass pillow / journey TPT be.painful.AVFIN QUOT / tell.INF-send-**TENT.ATTR-NML FPT**
'[I] wish someone would go to my dear home! **[I] would have [him] tell [my] family] that [my] journey, [sleeping on] a grass pillow, is painful**!'

In example (136) the tentative suffix -*am*- becomes the portmanteau form 'TENT. ATTR' due to the following, phonologically null attributive suffix created upon suffixing the nominalizer -*aku*. We see a similar example below, with the negative suffix -*an*- becoming the portmanteau suffix 'NEG.ATTR' after the nominalizer -*aku* is added:

137. 20:4413.4-5 – Muzasi
西呂我馬伎己无 / 都久乃**之良奈久**
se-rö-nga mek-i-kö-m-u / *tuku-nö* **sir-an-aku**
beloved.man-DIM-POSS walk-INF-come-TENT-ATTR / month-GEN **know-NEG.ATTR-NML**
'**Not knowing** the month when [my] beloved shall come walking [back].'

In a different analysis, the attributive in these examples could also be considered a zero morph.

When *-aku* attaches to the attributive *-uru*, the attributive reduces to *-ur-*, as can be seen in the following example:

138. 20:4427.3-5 – UNP
麻由須比尓 / 由須比之比毛乃 / 登久良久毛倍婆
ma-yusup-i-ni / *yusup-i-si pimo-nö* / *tök-ur-aku* [o]*mop-ey-nba*
INT-tie-NML-LOC / tie-INF-PST.ATTR string-GEN / come.undone-ATTR-NML think-EV-CONJ
'When [I] think **that the cord [she] tied, in a tight knot, has come undone**...'

Further examples of the nominalizer *-aku* follow below:

139. 14:3368.4-5 – Sagamu
余尓母多欲良尓 / 故呂河**伊波奈久尓**
yö-ni mö tayora n-i / *ko-rö-nga **ip-an-aku** n-i*
lifetime-LOC FPT wavering COP-INF / girl-DIM-POSS say-NEG.ATTR-NML COP-INF
'Although [my] dear girl **will not say that** [her love for me] will waver in [this] lifetime...'

140. 20:4377.3-5 – Simotukeno
伊多太伎弖 / **美都良乃奈可尓** / 阿敞麻可麻久毛
itandak-i-te / ***mindura-nö naka-ni*** / *ape-mak-am-aku mo*
place.on.head-INF-SUB / **type.of.hairstyle-GEN inside-LOC** / join.INF-wrap-TENT.ATTR-NML FPT
'[I] would place [her] upon my head, **wrapping [her] up within [my] *mindura***...'

141. 14:3392.4-5 – Pitati
代尓毛多由良尓 / **和我於毛波奈久尓**
YÖ-ni mo tayura n-i / ***wa-nga omop-an-aku** n-i*
lifetime-LOC FPT wavering COP-INF / **1.S-POSS think-NEG.ATTR-NML** COP-INF
'**I do not think** that [my love for you] will waver in [this] lifetime.'

142. 20:4389.5 – Simotupusa
於毛波弊奈久尓
omop-ape-n-aku n-i
think-endure-NEG.ATTR-NML COP-INF
'[I] **cannot bear to think about it**.'

143. 20:4355.3-5 – Kamitupusa
奈尓波我多 / 久毛為尓美由流 / 志麻奈良奈久尓
nanipa-n-gata / *kumo wi-ni mi-y-uru* / *sima nar-an-aku n-i*
TN-GEN-tideland / cloud sit.NML-LOC see-PASS-ATTR / island be-NEG.ATTR-NML COP-INF
'Being that **it is not an island that** [one] **can see through the clouds sitting [over] the Nanipa tidelands**…'

144. 14:3500.3-5 – UNP
比等能兒能 / 宇良我奈之家乎 / 祢乎遠敝奈久尓
pitö-nö KO-nö / *ura-n-ganasi-ke-wo* / *ne-wo wope-n-aku n-i*
person-GEN girl-GEN / feelings-GEN-be.dear-AVATTR-ACC / **sleep.NML-ACC finish-NEG.ATTR-NML** COP-INF
'[I] have strong feelings for [that] person's girl, though [I] **have not slept with her completely**…'

145. 14:3530.4-5 – UNP
兒呂我可奈門欲 / 由可久之要思母
KO-rö-nga kana-TO-yo / *yuk-aku si ye-si-mö*
girl-DIM-POSS metal-door-ABL / **go.ATTR-NML** EPT be.good-AVFIN-EXCL
'**Going through the metal gate of** [my] **darling girl's [home] is so nice!**'

146. 14:3543.4-5 – UNP
古呂波伊敝杼母 / 伊末太年那久尓
ko-rö pa ip-e-ndömö / *imanda ne-n-aku n-i*
girl-DIM TPT say-EV-CONC / **not.yet sleep-NEG.ATTR-NML** COP-INF
'Although [that] dear girl speaks [as if we have], [the fact] is that [we] **still have not slept together**.'

Table 7.17: Attestations of the nominalizer *-aku* across the provinces.

TSOJ			EOJ								UNP
Sin	Tö	Su	Kak	Mu	Sa	Mi	Sik	Pi	Sip	Kap	
0	0	2	1	1	1	0	0	1	1	1	12

7.5.2.2 Sentence-final suffixes

The sentence-final suffixes end both a sentence and a verbal word form.

7.5.2.2.1 Final predication -*u* ~ -*i*

The final suffix -*u* is syncretic with the attributive suffix -*u* in consonant-final stem verbs. This suffix is semantically null because it only functions to mark the final predicate of the sentence. The final -*u* is one of the most common verb suffixes, attested in every AOJ topolect except Mitinöku. There is also an allomorph -*i* that occurs after -*r*-final stems.

147. 14:3398.1-2 – Sinano
 比等未奈乃 / **許等波多由**登毛
 pitö mïna-nö / ***kötö pa tay-u*** *tömo*
 people all-GEN / **word TPT cease-FIN** CNJ
 'Even if everyone [else] **goes silent**...'

148. 20:4325.3-5 – Töpotuapumi
 久佐麻久良 / 多妣波**由久**等母 / 佐々己弖由加牟
 kusa makura / *tanbi pa **yuk-u** tömö* / *sasangö-te yuk-am-u*
 grass pillow / journey TPT **go-FIN** CNJ / lift.up.above.head.INF-SUB go-TENT-ATTR
 '[I] would carry [them] above my head, even if [I] **went** on a journey, [sleeping on] a grass pillow.'

149. 14:3359a.4-5 – Suruga
 伊麻思乎多能美 / 波播尓**多我比奴**
 imasi-wo tanöm-i / *papa-ni **tangap-i-n-u***
 2.S-ACC trust-NML / mother-DAT **defy-INF-PERF-FIN**
 '[I] **defied** [my] mother and put [my] trust in you.'

150. 20:4342.5 – Suruga
 於米加波利**勢受**
 *omey kapar-i **se-nz-u***
 face change-NML **do-NEG-FIN**
 'With [your] face unchanging.'

151. 14:3402.4-5 – Kamitukeno
勢奈能我素侶母 / 佐夜尓**布良思都**
se-na-nö-nga sonde mö / saya n-i **pur-as-i-t-u**
beloved.man-DIM-DIM-POSS sleeve FPT / clear COP-INF **wave-HON-INF-PERF-FIN**
'[My] dearly beloved clearly **waved** [his] sleeve [at me].'

152. 20:4405.3-5 – Kamitukeno
都氣志非毛 / 伊刀尓**奈流**等母 / 和波等可自等余
tukey-si pïmo / ito n-i **nar-u** tömö / wa pa tök-anzi tö yö
affix.INF-PST.ATTR string / thread COP-INF **become-FIN** CNJ / 1.S TPT undo-NEG.TENT QUOT EPT
'Even if the cord that she tied [on me] **becomes** threadbare, still I think [I] probably will not untie it.'

153. 14:3378.3-4 – Muzasi
伊波爲都良 / 比可婆**奴流**々々
ipawi tura / pik-anba **nur-u nur-u**
UNC vine / pull-COND **come.loose-FIN come.loose-FIN**
'The *ipawi* vines **come loose smoothly** if [they are] pulled [up].'

154. 20:4424.4-5 – Muzasi
美佐可多婆良婆 / 麻佐夜可尓**美无**
mi-saka tanbar-anba / ma-sayaka n-i **mi-m-u**
HON-slope receive.HUM-COND / INT-clear COP-INF **see-TENT-FIN**
'If [he] received [permission to cross] the honored slope, [I] would **see** [him] so clearly.'

155. 14:3361.4-5 – Sagamu
可奈流麻之豆美 / 許呂安礼比毛**等久**
ka-nar-u ma sindum-i / kö-rö are pimo **tök-u**
PREF-make.sound-ATTR duration grow.quiet-INF / girl-DIM 1.S cord **untie-FIN**
'The sounds fade away, and [my] dear girl and I **untie** [our] cords.'

156. 20:4328.3-4 – Sagamu
伊蘓尓布理 / 宇能波良**和多流**
iso-ni pur-i / unö-para **watar-u**
rock-LOC touch-INF / sea-field **cross-FIN**
'[I] **cross** the open sea, touching the rocks [as I go].'

157. 20:4375.3-5 – Simotukeno
伊波比等乃 / 和例乎美於久流等 / 多々里之毛己呂
ipa-pitö-nö / ware-wo **mi-okur-u** tö / tat-ar-i-si mokörö
house-person-GEN / 1.S-ACC **see.INF-send.off-FIN** QUOT / stand-PROG-INF-PST.ATTR similarity
'[It is] similar to how how [my] family members were standing, intending to **see [me] off**.'

158. 20:4372.3-4 – Pitati
可閇理美須 / 阿例波久江由久
kapeyr-i-mi-nz-u / are pa **kuye-yuk-u**
return-INF-see-NEG-INF / 1.S TPT **cross.over.INF-go-FIN**
'I will **go and cross over** [it] without looking back.'

159. 14:3386.2-3 – Simotupusa
可豆思加和世乎 / 尓倍須登毛
kandusika wase-wo / **nipey s-u** tömo
TN early.rice-ACC / **food.offering do-FIN** CNJ
'Even though [she] **made an offering** of new rice from Kadusika. . .'

160. 20:4388.1-2 – Simotupusa
多飛等弊等 / 麻多妣尓奈理奴
tanbï tö [i]p-e-ndö / ma-tanbi n-i **nar-i-n-u**
journey COP say-EV-CONC / INT-journey COP-INF **become-INF-PERF-FIN**
'Although [it] was said to be [just] 'a journey', [this] **has become** such a [trying] journey.'

161. 14:3383.5 – Kamitupusa
奈我目保里勢牟
na-nga MEY **por-i se-m-u**
2.S-POSS eye **desire-NML do-TENT-FIN**
'[I] **dream of** your eyes.'

162. 20:4357.3-5 – Kamitupusa
和藝毛古我 / 蘓弖母志保々尓 / 奈伎志曽母波由
wa-ng[a]-imo-ko-nga / sonde mö sipopo n-i / nak-i-si sö [o]**möp-ay-u**
1.S-POSS-beloved.girl-DIM-POSS / sleeve FPT soaked COP-INF / cry-INF-PST.ATTR FPT **think-PASS-FIN**
'[I] **suddenly remember** how my darling cried [so much for me], even her sleeves were soaking wet!'

163. 14:3536.4-5 – UNP
伊可奈流勢奈可 / 和我理**許武**等伊布
*ika nar-u se-na ka / wa-ngari **kö-m-u** tö ip-u*
how be-ATTR beloved.man-DIM QPT / 1.S-DIR **come-TENT-FIN** QUOT say-ATTR
'What kind of lover is he, [who] says [he] **shall come** to me?'

164. 14:3549.1-2 – UNP
多由比加多 / 志保**美知和多流**
*tayupi kata / sipo **mit-i-watar-u***
TN tideland / tide **fill-INF-cross-FIN**
'The tide **spreads over** the Tayupi tideland.'

165. 14:3572.2-5 – UNP
阿自久麻夜末乃 / 由豆流波乃 / 布敷麻留等伎尓 / 可是**布可受**可母
*anzikuma yama-nö / yundurupa-nö / pupum-ar-u töki-ni / kanze **puk-anz-u** kamö*
TN mountain-GEN / false.daphne-GEN / be.unopened-PROG-ATTR time-LOC / wind **blow-NEG-FIN** EPT
'[I] wonder, **will** the wind **not blow** when the [buds] of the false daphne are [still] unopened, on Mt. Azikuma?'

166. 20:4425.5 – UNP
毛乃母比毛**世受**
*monö [o]möp-i mo **se-nz-u***
thing think-NML FPT **do-NEG-FIN**
'[I] **do not** worry about things.'

7.5.2.2.1.1 Final predication allomorph -*i*

The final predication allomorph -*i* occurs rather infrequently in the corpus. It only occurs after the retrospective auxiliary -*ker-* ~ -*kar-* and some *r*-irregular verbs (such as *nar-* 'become'). The use of the final suffix allomorph -*u* is blocked in these environments.

167. 14:3352.3-5 – Sinano
保登等藝須 / 奈久許恵伎氣波 / 登伎**須疑尓家里**
*potötöngisu / nak-u köwe kik-ey-nba / töki **sungï-n-i-ker-i***
cuckoo / cry-ATTR voice hear-EV-CONJ / time **pass.INF-PERF-INF-RETR-FIN**
'When [I] hear the crying voice [of] the cuckoo, [I realize] time **has passed by**.'

168. 14:3374.4-5 – Muzasi
乃良奴伎美我名 / 宇良尔**侣尔家里**
nör-an-u kimi-nga NA / ura-ni [i]nde-n-i-ker-i
tell-NEG-ATTR lord-POSS name / divination-LOC **go.out.INF-PERF-INF-RETR-FIN**
'[My] lord's name that [I] did not tell [them] **emerged** from the divination.'

169. 20:4382.1-2 – Simotukeno
布多富我美 / 阿志氣比等**奈里**
*putapongami / asi-key pitö **nar-i***
PN / be.bad-AVATTR person **be-FIN**
'Putapogami **is** a bad person.'

170. 20:4388.3-5 – Simotupusa
以弊乃母加 / 枳世之己呂母尔 / 阿可**都枳尔迦理**
*ipe-nö [i]mö-nga / ki-se-si körömö-ni / aka **tuk-i-n-i-kar-i***
house-GEN beloved.girl-POSS / wear-CAUS-PST.ATTR garment-LOC / dirt **attach-INF-PERF-INF-RETR-FIN**
'Dirt **is** stuck to the garment that [my] beloved at home had [me] wear.'

171. 14:3453.4-5 – UNP
多母登乃久太利 / **麻欲比伎尔家利**
*tamötö-nö kundar-i / **mayop-i-k-i-n-i-ker-i***
sleeve.edge-GEN descend-NML / **become.frayed-INF-come-INF-PERF-INF-RETR-FIN**
'The edge of the sleeve [of my robe] **has become frayed**.'

Table 7.18: Attestations of the final predication suffix *-u ~ -i* across the provinces.

TSOJ			EOJ								UNP
Sin	Tö	Su	Kak	Mu	Sa	Mi	Sik	Pi	Sip	Kap	
3	4	4	7	7	3	0	6	8	5	4	41

7.5.2.2.2 Attributive *-uru ~ -ur- ~ -ru- ~ -oro ~ -u ~ -o*
The attributive suffix is one of the most common verbal affixes. It is attested multiple times in every topolect. There is a large range of allomorphy for this morpheme, with five main allomorphs: *-uru, -ur-, -ru, -u,* and *-o*. These are all attested in EOJ, and all but *-ur-* are attested in TSOJ. The allomorph *-uru* attaches to vowel-final stem

verbs and it has two secondary allomorphs based on vowel elision: the form *-ru* attaches to strong vowel-final stems (like *mi-* 'see') and the form *-ur-* is only found before the nominalizer *-aku*. There is also a variant form *-oro* attested once in an EOJ topolect (for further discussion see §2.3.1.3). The allomorphs *-u* and *-o* attach to consonant-final stems. The allomorph *-o*[174] is common in EOJ and rare in TSOJ. Historically, the allomorph *-u* is a raised form of the allomorph *-o*. The forms *-oro* and *-o* are not attested in WOJ. An example of each allomorph is provided below:

Example of *-uru* ~ *-ur-*

172. 14:3359a.1-3 – Suruga
駿河能宇美 / 於思敝尓**於布流** / 波麻都豆良
surunga-nö umi / *osi-pe-ni* **op-uru** / *pama tundura*
TN-GEN sea / rock-shore-LOC **grow-ATTR** / shore vine
'[Like] the vines **that grow** on the rocky shore along the sea of Suruga. . .'

Example of *-oro*

173. 14:3419.3 – Kamitukeno
於毛比度路
omop-i-nd-oro
think-INF-emerge-ATTR
'**[I] recall**. . .'

Example of *-ru*

174. 20:4415.1-3 – Muzasi
志良多麻乎 / 弖尓刀里母之弖 / **美流**乃須母
sira tama-wo / *te-ni tor-i-mös-i-te* / **mi-ru**-nösu mö
white pearl-ACC / hand-LOC take-INF-hold-INF-SUB / **see-ATTR**-COMP FPT
'Like holding pearls in [my] hands and **gazing at** [them]. . .'

---

174 This is retained in Hachijō as *-o* (Kaneda 2001: 188).

Example of -*o*

175. 14:3426.4-5 – Mitinöku
 斯努比尔勢毛等 / 比毛牟須波佐祢
 sinop-i n-i se-m-o tö / *pimo musunb-as-an-e*
 yearn.for-NML COP-INF do-TENT-ATTR QUOT / cord tie-HON-DES-IMP
 '[I] want [you] to tie [your] cords and **think [of me] when [you] do**!'

Example of -*u*

176. 14:3352.1-2 – Sinano
 信濃奈流 / 須我能安良能尔
 sinanu-n[i] ar-u / *sunga-nö ara nö-ni*
 TN-LOC **exist-ATTR** / TN-GEN wild field-LOC
 'In the wild fields of Suga **in** Sinano...'

In the sections below I illustrate each function of this morpheme.

7.5.2.2.2.1 Adnominal function

One of the most common functions of the attributive is to allow a verb to modify a following noun phrase. This is commonly referred to as adnominalization. Morpho-syntactically, it creates a relative clause.

177. 20:4345.1-4 – Suruga
 和伎米故等 / 不多利和我見之 / 宇知江須流 / 々々河乃祢良波
 wa-ng-imey-ko-tö / *puta-ri wa-nga MI-si* / ***uti*-*yes*-*uru*** / *surunga-nö ne-ra pa*
 1.S-POSS-beloved.girl-DIM-COM / two-CL we-POSS see.INF-PST.ATTR / **PREF-approach-ATTR** / TN-GEN peak-PLUR TPT
 'The peaks of Suruga, **where [the waves] crash**, which I gazed upon with my darling girl...'

178. 14:3402.1-3 – Kamitukeno
 比能具礼尔 / 宇須比乃夜麻乎 / 古由流日波
 pi-nö kure-ni / *usupi-nö yama-wo* / ***koy*-*uru*** *PI pa*
 sun-GEN darken.NML-LOC / TN-GEN mountain-ACC / **cross-ATTR** day TPT
 '[On] the day [my beloved] **crossed over** Mt. Usupi during the sunset...'

179. 20:4406.1-2 – Kamitukeno
和我伊波呂尔 / **由加毛**比等母我
wa-nga ipa-rö-ni / **yuk-am-o** pitö mönga
1.S-POSS house-DIM-LOC / **go-TENT-ATTR** person DPT
'[I] wish someone **would go** to my dear home.'

180. 20:4380.3-5 – Simotukeno
可美佐夫流 / 伊古麻多可祢尔 / 久毛曽多奈妣久
kami sanb-uru / ikoma taka ne-ni / kumo sö tananbik-u
deity behave.like-ATTR / TN high peak-LOC / cloud FPT stream.out-ATTR
'[I see] clouds streaming out over the high peak [of] **the deific** Mt. Ikoma.'

181. 14:3392.1-3 – Pitati
筑波祢能 / 伊波毛等杼呂尔 / **於都留**美豆
tukupa ne-nö / ipa mo töndörö n-i / **ot-uru** mindu
TN peak-GEN / rock FPT thunderous COP-INF / **fall-ATTR** water
'The water **that falls** thunderously [on] the rocks of the peaks of [Mt.] Tukupa...'

182. 20:4366.1-2 – Pitati
比多知散思 / **由可牟**加里母我
pitati sas-i / **yuk-am-u** kari mönga
TN point.toward-INF / **go-TENT-ATTR** wild.goose DPT
'[I] wish [I had] a wild goose [I] **could send** to Pitati!'

183. 20:4385.1-2 – Simotupusa
由古作枳尔 / 奈美奈等恵良比
yuk-o saki-ni / nami na-töwerap-i
go-ATTR ahead-LOC / wave NEG.IMP-shake-INF
'Waves, do not shake [me] as [I] **go** ahead!'

184. 20:4355.3-5 – Kamitupusa
奈尔波我多 / 久毛為尔 **美由流** / 志麻奈良奈久尔
nanipa-n-gata / kumo wi-ni **mi-y-uru** / sima nar-an-aku n-i
TN-GEN-tideland / cloud sit.NML-LOC **see-PASS-ATTR** / island be-NEG.ATTR-NML COP-INF
'Being that it is not an island **that [one] can see** through the clouds sitting [over] the Nanipa tidelands...'

185. 14:3504.3-4 – UNP
宇良夜須尔 / 左奴流夜曽奈伎
ura yasu n-i / ***sa-n-uru*** *YO sö na-ki*
heart easy COP-INF / **LOC-sleep-ATTR** night FPT not.exist-AVATTR
'There are no nights **when [I] sleep there** with [my] heart at ease.'

186. 14:3405b.5 – Kamitukeno
美流比登奈思尔
mi-ru *pitö na-si-ni*
see-ATTR person not.exist-FIN-LOC
'When there's no one [there] **who would see** [him].'

7.5.2.2.2.2 Nominalization function

The attributive can also function as a nominalizer. In doing so, it allows the deverbal noun to take case suffixes.

187. 14:3395.3-5 – Pitati
安比太欲波 / 佐波太奈利怒乎 / 萬多祢天武可聞
apinda yo pa / *sapanda **nar-i-n-o**-wo* / *mata ne-te-m-u kamo*
interval night TPT / many **be-INF-PERF-ATTR**-ACC / again sleep.INF-PERF-TENT-ATTR EPT
'Since **there have been** many nights in between [our meetings], [I] wonder if [I] shall sleep [with her] again.'

188. 14:3376a.1-2;5 – Muzasi
古非思家波 / 素弖毛布良武乎 / 伊呂尔豆奈由米
kopïsi-ke-nba / *sonde mo **pur-am-u**-wo* / *irö-ni [i]nd-una yumey*
be.longing.for-AVEV-CONJ / sleeve FPT **wave-TENT-ATTR**-ACC / color/feelings-LOC go.out-NEG.IMP at.all
'When [you] are longing [for me], [I] **shall wave** [my] sleeves [for you], **but** do not let [your] face reveal even a hint of [your] true feelings [for me]!'

189. 14:3465.3-4 – UNP
奴流我倍尔 / 安杼世呂登可母
***n-uru**-nga [u]pey-ni* / *andö se-rö tö kamö*
sleep-ATTR-POSS above-LOC / what do-IMP QUOT EPT
'Besides **sleeping** [with you], [I] wonder, what would [you] say [I] do?'

190. 14:3509.4-5 – UNP
古呂賀於曾伎能 / 安路許曾要志母
ko-rö-nga osöki-nö / **ar-o** kösö ye-si-mö
girl-DIM-POSS upper.garment-GEN / **exist-ATTR** FPT be.good-AVFIN-EXCL
'It is so nice **to have** [my] dear girl's upper garment!'

191. 20:4425.1-3 – UNP
佐伎毛利尓 / 由久波多我世登 / 刀布比登乎
sakimori n-i / **yuk-u** pa ta-nga se tö / top-u pitö-wo
border.guard COP-INF / **go-ATTR** TPT who-POSS beloved.man QUOT / ask-ATTR person-ACC
'Those who ask, 'Whose husband is that, **going** to be a border guard?'.'

7.5.2.2.2.3 Usage as a final predicate due to an attributive-triggering particle

The attributive suffix is mandatory on a final predicate verb when certain particles appear before or after the verb. These are called *kakari* ('linking') particles in the Japanese tradition, but they are essentially a set of focus, emphatic, and interrogative particles. I refer to them as "attributive-triggering" particles. A full description of the attributive-triggering particles is presented in Chapter 10.

192. 20:4403.3-5 – Sinano
阿乎久牟乃 /等能妣久夜麻乎 / 古与弖伎怒加牟
awo kumu-nö / tönönbik-u yama-wo / koyö-te **k-i-n-o** kamu
blue cloud-GEN / stream.out-ATTR mountain-ACC / cross.INF-SUB **come-INF-PERF-ATTR** EPT
'Oh, [I] **came** [here], having crossed over the mountain where the blue clouds stream out...'

193. 20:4321.3-4 – Töpotuapumi
阿須由利也 / 加曳我牟多祢牟
asu-yuri ya / kaye-nga muta **ne-m-u**
tomorrow-ABL QPT / reed-POSS together **sleep-TENT-ATTR**
'**Will [I] sleep** among the reeds from tomorrow?'

194. 14:3379.1-2 – Muzasi
和我世故乎 / 安杼可母伊波武
wa-nga se-ko-wo / andö kamö **ip-am-u**
1.S-POSS beloved.man-DIM-ACC / what EPT **say-TENT-ATTR**
'[I] wonder, what **could [I] say** [about] my beloved man?'

195. 20:4330.3-4 – Sagamu
氣布能比夜 / 伊田弓**麻可良武**
keypu-nö pi ya / *inde-te* **makar-am-u**
today-GEN day QPT / go.out.INF-SUB **depart-TENT-ATTR**
'**Will [we] depart** and [sail] out today?'

196. 14:3424.4-5 – Simotukeno
麻具波思兒呂波 / 多賀家可**母多牟**
ma n-gupasi KO-rö pa / *ta-nga ke ka* **möt-am-u**
true COP.INF-beautiful girl-DIM TPT / who-POSS container QPT **hold-TENT-ATTR**
'Whose [food] container **shall** the truly beautiful girl **hold**?'

197. 20:4355.1-2 – Kamitupusa
余曽尓能美 / 々弓夜**和多良毛**
yösö-ni nömi / *mi-te ya* **watar-am-o**
elsewhere-LOC RPT / see.INF-SUB QPT **cross-TENT-ATTR**
'**Shall [I] cross over** [to the island, even though I] only gazed into the distance?'

198. 14:3500.1-2 – UNP
牟良佐伎波 / 根乎可母**乎布流**
murasaki pa / *NE-wo kamö* **wop-uru**
gromwell TPT / root-ACC EPT **finish-ATTR**
'[I] wonder, will [I] **reach the end** of the gromwell root?'

7.5.2.2.2.4 Usage as a final predicate without an attributive-triggering particle

Examples of the attributive used as a final predicate marker without an attributive-triggering particle anywhere in the poem, are attested, but are quite rare.

199. 14:3426.4-5 – Mitinöku
斯努比尓勢毛等 / 比毛牟須波佐祢
sinop-i n-i se-m-o tö / *pimo musunb-as-an-e*
yearn.for-NML COP-INF do-TENT-ATTR QUOT / cord tie-HON-DES-IMP
'[I] want [you] to tie [your] cords and **think [of me] when [you] do**!'

200. 20:4419.5 – Muzasi
古布志氣**毛波母**
kopusi-ngey [o]**mop-am-ö**
be.longing.for-AVNML **think-TENT-ATTR**
'[I] am sure [I] **will long for** [it] after [I] arrive in Tukusi.'

Examples like (199) and (200) probably show the early stage of the attributive suffix overtaking the final suffix as the final predicate marker, a change that was finalized centuries later in the history of the Japanese language.

Table 7.19: Attestations of the allomorphs of the attributive suffix across the provinces.

Form	TSOJ			EOJ							UNP
	Sin	Tö	Su	Kak	Mu	Sa	Mi	Sik	Pi	Sip	Kap	
-uru ~ -ur-	0	0	3	1	0	0	0	1	0	0	1	7
-oro	0	0	0	1	0	0	0	0	0	0	0	0
-ru	0	0	0	1	1	0	0	0	0	0	0	1
-o	2	0	1	6	6	2	1	2	2	3	4	26
-u	7	8	11	12	9	10	0	7	12	4	10	94

It is helpful to examine the phonological environments in which the attributives -o and -u occur in each province, since the attributive -o is unattested in WOJ.

The attributive -o occurs in Sinano once after /n/ and once after /k/.

Töpotuapumi is the only topolect to lack an attestation of the attributive -o.

In Suruga we find the attributive -o just once, after /n/.

In Kamitukeno, we find the attributive -o after /m/ and /r/, but the attributive -u is also found after /m/.

All six attestations of the attributive -o in Muzasi occur after a labial initial (/p/ or /m/). Unlike in the Kamitukeno topolect, there are no examples of the attributive -u in this environment. This may indicate the labial consonants disallowed the raising of the attributive -o to /u/ in this topolect.

The attestations of the attributive -o in Sagamu occur once after /k/ and once after /m/. There are multiple attestations of the attributive -u after /m/ in this topolect.

In Mitinöku the only verbal attributive attested is -o, and it occurs after /m/.

In Simotukeno the attributive -o is attested once after /m/ and once after /n/. The attributive -u is also attested after /m/ in this topolect.

In Pitati the attributive -o is attested once after /m/ and once after /n/. The attributive -u is also attested after /m/ in this topolect.

In Simotupusa the attributive -*o* is attested once after /k/, once after /s/, and once after /p/. Interestingly, there are three attestations of the attributive -*u* after /m/, and no attestations of the attributive -*o* after /m/, which is different from the other topolects.

In Kamitupusa the attributive -*o* is attested once after /p/ and three times after /m/. The attributive -*u* is also attested after /m/.

In sum, across the topolects the most common environment in which we find the attributive -*o* is after /m/. It appears the labiality of /m/ (and possibly also /p/) blocked, or at least slowed, the raising of *o > /u/ in many topolects. In the UNP poems we find the attributive /o/ attested after a range of consonants (/p/, /t/, /k/, /m/, /n/, /s/, /r/), but we also find the attributive /u/ in the same environments. There are no attestations of the attributive -*o* after a prenasalized voiced consonant. Interestingly, none of the UNP poems from MYS Book 20 contain an attributive /o/.

7.5.2.2.3 Attributive -*a*

The EOJ attributive -*a* has been pointed out in many previous works, including Fukuda (1965: 504), Hōjō (1966: 410), Mizushima (1986: 340), Ikier (2006: 101–106) and Vovin (2012a, 2013). In Kupchik (2011: 696–697) I argued against the existence of this suffix, but I have since changed my mind because, as I argue in §7.5.2.1.3.2 and §7.5.2.3.1.1, it helps to explain the historical origin of the nominalizer -*aku* (< PJe *-a-ku) and the negative-attributive -*ana* (< PJ *-an-a). There is only one synchronic example of this attributive, shown below.

201. 14:3526.1-2 – UNP
奴麻布多都 / **可欲波**等里我栖
numa puta-tu / ***kayop-a*** *töri-nga SU*
marsh two-CL / **go.back.and.forth-ATTR** bird-POSS nest
'[Like] the nests of a bird that **shuttles between** two marshes. . .'

This poem hails from an unknown Azuma province, but it was clearly an EOJ topolect because the poem contains both the EOJ progressive -*ar*- and the EOJ tentative 2 -*unam*-. This topolect is textually unique within OJ in exhibiting the attributive -*a* in its synchronic grammar. It is also possible this suffix was an infinitive, like AOJ -*i*, since AOJ infinitives also modify nouns in an adnominal function (see §7.5.2.1.1.1.3). If true, the most plausible etymological source would be the Old (or Proto-) Korean infinitive *-a.

7.5.2.2.4 Evidential *-ure ~ -re ~ -e ~ -o*

This morpheme indicates something evident to the speaker, and it seems to add emphasis. As Vovin (2009a: 637) notes, labelling this an "evidential" diverges from modern linguistic terminology, where "evidential" is used to refer to a marker of evidence-based experience. Despite this inconsistency, I continue to refer to this AOJ suffix as an evidential due to its history of use in the analysis of OJ grammar.

There are three allomorphs in EOJ, two of which[175] are also attested in TSOJ: *-ure*, *-re*, and *-e* (sometimes written as *-ey*). The first of these occurs after vowel-final stem verbs, while the allomorph *-re* is restricted to strong vowel-final stem verbs. The allomorph *-e* occurs after all consonant-final stem verbs in EOJ and after coronal-final stem verbs in TSOJ. There is an additional allomorph, *-o*, that only occurs in TSOJ after labial-final consonant stem verbs (see example 204 below), due to a sound change that occurred in Proto-TSOJ (see §2.2.4). Furthermore, due to this same sound change, the expected TSOJ allomorph after velar-final consonant stem verbs is /ə/ (*-ö*).[176]

Another possible allomorph, *-ore*, is only attested in the Kamitupusa topolect and in UNP (shown in examples 214 and 215 below), but both attestations are probably misspellings for *-ure*,[177] or possibly due to sporadic secondary vowel lowering (or assimilation) in certain EOJ topolects. Furthermore, it is unattested in WOJ, TSOJ, and Ryukyuan, therefore we do not have grounds to reconstruct *o in this morpheme in PJe or PJ.

202. 14:3352.3-4 – Sinano
 保登等藝須 / 奈久許恵**伎氣波**
 *potötöngisu / nak-u köwe **kik-ey-nba***
 cuckoo / cry-ATTR voice **hear-EV-CONJ**
 'When [I] hear the crying voice [of] the cuckoo...'

203. 20:4323.1-2 – Töpotuapumi
 等伎騰吉乃 / 波奈波**左家登母**
 *töki-ndöki-nö / pana pa **sak-e-ndömö***
 time-REDUP-GEN / flower TPT **bloom-EV-CONC**
 'The seasonal flowers [all] **bloom**, but...'

---

175 The strong vowel-final stem verb allomorph *-re* is not attested in TSOJ, but it is the expected form in the dialect.
176 The strong vowel-final stem verb allomorph *-re* is not attested in TSOJ, but it is the expected form in the dialect.
177 Phonograms for WOJ *key* and *kö* were both used to write the syllable /kə/ in TSOJ. Thus, the form *kik-ey-nba* in example (202) was phonemically /kikəᵐba/.

204. 20:4343.1-2 – Suruga
和呂多比波 / 多比等於米保等
*warö tanbi pa / tanbi tö **omeyp-o-ndö***
1.S journey TPT / journey COP **think-EV-CONC**
'**Although [I] know** my journey will be an [arduous] one...'

205. 14:3417.5 – Kamitukeno
伊麻許曽麻左礼
*ima kösö **mas-ar-e***
now FPT **be.superior-PROG-EV**
'Now [things] **are better**...'

206. 20:4419.1-2 – Muzasi
伊波呂尓波 / 安之布多氣度母
*ipa-rö-ni pa / asi-pu **tak-ey-ndomö***
house-DIM-LOC TPT / reed-fire **burn-EV-CONC**
'**Although [we] would burn** reeds [to warm our] modest home...'

207. 14:3370.4 – Sagamu
波奈都豆麻奈礼也
*pana tutu ma **nar-e** ya*
flower earth wife **be-EV** QPT
'**Are** [you] a wife [who is] a flower of the earth? (Certainly not!)'

Example (207) shows a special usage of the evidential suffix with the question particle *ya*. The two used in combination create an ironic question, where the answer is implied to be negative.

208. 14:3437.4-5 – Mitinöku
西良思馬伎那婆 / 都良波可馬可毛
*ser-asime-k-i-n-anba / tura **pak-am-e** kamo*
bend-CAUS.INF-come-INF-PERF-COND / bowstring **put.on-TENT-EV** EPT
'When [the bow] becomes warped, [I] wonder, **should [I] put on** a [new] string?'

Example (208) shows a special usage of the evidential suffix with the focus particle *kamo*. The two used in combination create a tentative question.

209. 20:4381.4-5 – Simotukeno
和可流乎**美礼婆** / 伊刀母須敞奈之
wakar-u-wo **mi-re-nba** / ito mö sunbe na-si
separate-ATTR-ACC **see-EV-CONJ** / really FPT way not.exist-AVFIN
'**When [I] see** [them] parting [from their families it is sad but] really, it can't be helped.'

210. 14:3394.4-5 – Pitati
和須良延許婆古曽 / 那乎**可家奈波賣**
wasura-kö-nba kosö / na-wo **kake-n-ap-am-e**
forget-come-COND FPT / 2.S-ACC **call.out-NEG-ITER-TENT-EV**
'When [I] start to forget [our meeting there], [I] **shall stop calling out** [for] you!'

211. 20:4371.4-5 – Pitati
都久波能夜麻乎 / 古比須**安良米**可毛
tukupa-nö yama-wo / kopi-nz-u **ar-am-ey** kamo
TN-GEN mountain-ACC / long.for-NEG-INF **exist-TENT-EV** EPT
'[I] wonder, **shall** [I] not long for Tukupa mountain?'

212. 14:3386.4-5 – Simotupusa
曽能可奈之伎乎 / 刀尓**多弖米**也母
sönö kanasi-ki-wo / to-ni **tate-m-ey** ya mö
that be.dear-AVATTR-ACC / outside-LOC **make.stand-TENT-EV** QPT EPT
'Will [I] **make** that dear [girl] **stand** outside? (No, I will not)'

213. 20:4393.1-2 – Simotupusa
於保伎美能 / 美許等尓**作例波**
opo kimi-nö / mi-kötö n-i **s[i]-ar-e-nba**
great lord-GEN / HON-word COP-INF **EPT-exist-EV-CONJ**
'**As it is** [my] great lord's command...'

214. 20:4351.1-3 – Kamitupusa
多妣己呂母 / 夜倍伎可佐祢弖 / **伊努礼等母**
tanbi körömö / ya-pey ki-kasane-te / **i-n-ore-ndömö**
journey garment / eight-CL wear.INF-pile.up.INF-SUB / **sleep-sleep-EV-CONC**
'**Although [I] sleep** wearing the many layers [of my] travel garment...'

215. 14:3466 – UNP
麻可奈思美 / **努礼婆**許登尓豆 / **佐祢奈敝波** / 己許呂乃緒呂尓 / 能里弖可奈思母
ma-kanasi-mi / **n-ore-nba** *kötö-ni [i]nd-u* / **sa-ne-n-ap-e-nba** / *kökörö-nö WO-rö-ni* / *nör-i-te kanasi-mö*
INT-be.dear-GER / **sleep-EV-CONJ** word-LOC go.out-FIN / **LOC-sleep-NEG-ITER-EV-CONJ** / heart-GEN string-DIM-LOC / ride-INF-SUB be.sad.AVFIN-EXCL
'When [I] **sleep** [with you], because [you] are so dear [to me], [people] start talking. When [I] **am not sleeping** [with you], [you] ride on the small strings in [my] heart and [I] am sad!'

216. 14:3476a.3-5 – UNP
多刀都久能 / **努賀奈敝由家婆** / 故布思可流奈母
tat-o tuku-nö / **nongan-ape-yuk-e-nba** / *kopusi-k[u]-ar-unam-ö*
rise-ATTR moon-GEN / **flow-ITER.INF-go-EV-CONJ** / be.longing.for-AVINF-exist-TENT2-ATTR
'**Whenever** the rising moon **sets**, [she] will long for [me].'

217. 14:3550.1-2 – UNP
於志弖伊奈等 / 伊祢波**都可祢杼**
os-i-te ina tö / *ine pa **tuk-an-e-ndö***
push-INF-SUB no QUOT / rice.plant TPT **pound-NEG-EV-CONC**
'[I] was pushed, and [I] said 'No,' **but [I] did not pound** the rice.'

218. 14:3572.1 – UNP
安杼**毛敝**可
*andö [o]**mop-e** ka*
what **think-EV** QPT
'What **do [you] think**?'

(218) is the only example in the corpus in which the evidential is directly followed by the question particle *ka*.

219. 20:4427.3-5 – UNP
麻由須比尓 / 由須比之比毛乃 / 登久良久**毛倍婆**
ma-yusup-i-ni / *yusup-i-si pimo-nö* / *tök-ur-aku [o]**mop-ey-nba***
INT-tie-NML-LOC / tie-INF-PST.ATTR cords-GEN / come.undone-ATTR-NML **think-EV-CONJ**
'When [I] **think** that the cord [she] tied, in a tight knot, has come undone...'

Table 7.20: Attestations of the evidential suffix across the provinces.

TSOJ			EOJ								UNP
Sin	Tö	Su	Kak	Mu	Sa	Mi	Sik	Pi	Sip	Kap	
1	2	3	5	1	1	1	4	5	5	4	33

7.5.2.2.5 Imperative *-e ~ -ö ~ -i ~ -rö ~ -yö*

In EOJ, the imperative *-e* is syncretic with the evidential *-e* due to the change of *ai > /e/. In TSOJ we find the same syncretism after coronal-final verb stems, however, the forms are distinct after labial and velar-final verb stems, with *-e* for the imperative and *-o ~ -ö* for the evidential. There is also a special allomorph *-ö* that only occurs following the benefactive auxiliary *-kös-*, which is shown in example (230) below. This allomorph is the product of a progressive vowel assimilation. In addition, there is a raised variant *-i* attested just once in EOJ, shown in example (231) below. Finally, two verbs can indicate an imperative meaning with either the suffix *-rö ~ -yö* or their bare root. This is discussed in §7.5.2.2.5.1 and §7.5.2.2.5.2 below.

220. 14:3399.5 – Sinano
 久都**波氣**和我世
 kutu **pak-ey** wa-nga se
 shoes **put.on-IMP** 1.S-POSS beloved.man
 '**Wear** [your] shoes, my beloved.'

While orthographically the vowel in example (220) indicates this should be the evidential *-ey*, contextually only the imperative *-e* makes sense, so we can attribute this discrepancy to a scribal error.

221. 20:4326.4-5 – Töpotuapumi
 母々与**伊弖麻勢** / 和我伎多流麻弖
 mömö yö **inde-mas-e** / wa-nga k-i-tar-u-mande
 hundred year **go.out.INF-HON-IMP** / 1.S-POSS come-INF-PP-ATTR-TERM
 '[I] **hope** [my parents] **live** for a hundred years, until I return [to them]!'

222. 20:4340.1-2 – Suruga
 等知波々江 / 已波比弖**麻多祢**
 töti papa ye / ipap-i-te **mat-an-e**
 father mother EPT / pray-INF-SUB **wait-DES-IMP**
 'Father, mother! **Please** pray and **wait for** [me]!'

223. 14:3416.5 – Kamitukeno
安乎**奈多要曽祢**
*a-wo **na-taye-sö-n-e***
1.S-ACC NEG.IMP-break.INF-do-DES-IMP
'**Please do not break** [up] with me.'

224. 14:3378.5 – Muzasi
和尓**奈多要曽祢**
*wa-ni **na-taye-sö-n-e***
1.S-DAT NEG.IMP-break.INF-do-DES-IMP
'**Please do not break** [up] with me.'

It is peculiar that examples (223) and (224) both have the same meaning, and the verb form is identical, yet in (223) the object is marked by the accusative -*wo*, while in (224) the object is marked by the dative -*ni*. Perhaps this was a grammatical difference between the two topolects.

225. 20:4421.3-5 – Muzasi
安之我良乃 / 美祢波保久毛乎 / 美等登**志努波祢**
*asingara-nö / mi-ne pap-o kumo-wo / mi-tötö **sinop-an-e***
TN-GEN / HON-peak crawl-ATTR cloud-ACC / see.INF-COOR **yearn.for-DES-IMP**
'**Please remember** [me] while [you] watch the clouds that go slowly over the great peak of [Mt.] Asigara.'

When the imperative follows the desiderative it conveys a request, as shown in examples (222) – (225) above and examples (226), (227), and (229) below.

226. 14:3432.4 – Sagamu
和乎**可豆佐祢**母
*wa-wo **kandus-an-e** mö*
1.S-ACC abduct-DES-IMP EPT
'Please **abduct** me!'

227. 14:3426.4-5 – Mitinöku
斯努比尓勢毛等 / 比毛**牟須波佐祢**
*sinop-i n-i se-m-o tö / pimo **musunb-as-an-e***
yearn.for-NML COP-INF do-TENT-ATTR QUOT / cord **tie-HON-DES-IMP**
'[I] **want [you] to tie [your] cords** and think [of me] when [you] do!'

228. 14:3425.5 – Simotukeno
奈我己許呂**能礼**
na-nga kökörö **nör-e**
2.S-POSS heart **tell-IMP**
'**Tell** [me] your feelings.'

229. 14:3388.4-5 – Pitati
伊伎豆久伎美乎 / 為祢弓**夜良佐祢**
ikinduk-u kimi-wo / wi-ne-te **yar-as-an-e**
sigh-ATTR lord-ACC / bring.INF-sleep.INF-SUB **send-HON-DES-IMP**
'**Please** bring [my] lord who sighs to sleep [with me], and then **send** [him back].'

230. 20:4363.4-5 – Pitati
伊麻波許伎奴等 / 伊母尓**都氣許曽**
ima pa köng-i-n-u tö / imö-ni **tungey-kös-ö**
now TPT row-INF-PERF-FIN QUOT / beloved.girl-DAT **tell.INF-BEN-IMP**
'**Please tell** [my] beloved girl that [I] have rowed out now!'

231. 14:3440a.5 – UNP
伊伃兒**多婆里尓**
inde KO **tanbar-i-n-i**
well girl **receive.HUM-INF-PERF-IMP**
'Well, **let [me] receive** [your] girl.'

232. 14:3444.5 – UNP
西奈等**都麻佐祢**
se-na-tö **tum-as-an-e**
beloved.man-DIM-COM **pluck-CAUS-DES-IMP**
'**Please let [me] pluck** [them] with [my] dearly beloved!'

233. 14:3526.5 – UNP
奈与母波里曽祢
na-y-ömöp-ar-i-sö-n-e
NEG.IMP-EPEN-think-PROG-INF-do-DES-IMP
'**Please do not think** [that]!'

234. 20:4426.3-5 – UNP
 伊波比都々 / 伊麻世和我世奈 / 阿礼乎之**毛波婆**
 ipap-i-tutu / *imas-e wa-nga se-na* / *are-wo si [o]**mop-anba***
 pray-INF-COOR / exist.HON-IMP 1.S-POSS beloved.man-DIM / 1.S-ACC EPT **love-COND**
 'My dearly beloved, **if [you] love** me, then keep praying.'

Table 7.21: Attestations of the imperative suffix *-e ~ -i ~ -ö* across the provinces.

Form	TSOJ			EOJ							UNP
	Sin	Tö	Su	Kak	Mu	Sa	Mi	Sik	Pi	Sip	Kap	
-e	2	1	4	1	2	1	1	1	3	0	0	4
-i	0	0	0	0	0	0	0	0	0	0	0	1
-ö	0	0	0	0	0	0	0	2	0	0	0	0

7.5.2.2.5.1 Imperative *-rö ~ -yö*

The imperative *-yö* is a common suffix in WOJ, but considering it is attested just once in the Kamitukeno topolect and the imperative exclusive to EOJ is *-rö* (which survives in Modern Japanese), this single attestation can likely be attributed to WOJ influence (either through borrowing, or through later scribal alterations of the text). The imperative *-rö* is an earlier form of *-yö*, which did not undergo the sporadic lenition of **r- > y-*. It is not very common, with only three attestations in the corpus.

235. 20:4420.4-5 – Muzasi
 安我弓等**都氣呂** / 許礼乃波流母志
 *a-nga te-tö **tukey-rö*** / *köre nö paru mös-i*
 REFL-POSS hand-COM **attach-IMP** / this COP.ATTR needle hold-INF
 'Hold this needle and **attach** [the cords] with your own hands.'

236. 14:3465.4 – UNP
 安杼**世呂**登可母
 *andö **se-rö** tö kamö*
 what **do-IMP** QUOT EPT
 '[I] wonder, what would [you] say [I] **do**?'

237. 14:3517.1-3 – UNP
思良久毛能 / 多要尔之伊毛乎 / 阿是西呂等
*sira kumo-nö / taye-n-i-si imo-wo / anze **se-rö** tö*
white cloud-COMP/ break.INF-PERF-INF-PST.ATTR beloved.girl-ACC / what **do-IMP** QUOT
'[I am] thinking of what to **do** about [my] darling, who broke up [with me] like how a white cloud [breaks up].'

238. 20:4405.1-2 – Kamitukeno
和我伊母古我 / 志濃比尔西餘等
*wa-nga imö-ko-nga / sinup-i n-i **se-yö** tö*
1.S-POSS beloved.girl-DIM-POSS / yearn.for-NML COP-INF **do-IMP** QUOT
'My dearly beloved told [me] **to** yearn for [her]. . .'

Table 7.22: Attestations of the imperative suffix *-rö ~ -yö* across the provinces.

Form	TSOJ			EOJ								UNP
	Sin	Tö	Su	Kak	Mu	Sa	Mi	Sik	Pi	Sip	Kap	
-rö	0	0	0	0	1	0	0	0	0	0	0	2
-yö	0	0	0	1	0	0	0	0	0	0	0	0

7.5.2.2.5.2 Zero imperative

A zero imperative, which involves the use of the verb root and no further morphology, is attested with the verbs *kö-* 'come' and *se-* 'do'. This appears to be functionally identical to the imperative *-rö ~ -yö*.

239. 14:3369.5 – Sagamu
許呂勢多麻久良
*kö-rö **se** ta-makura*
girl-DIM **do.IMP** hand-pillow
'Dear girl, **use** [my] arm **as** [your] pillow!'

240. 14:3445.3-4 – UNP
多麻古須氣 / 可利己和我西古
*tama-ko-sungey / kar-i **kö** wa-nga se-ko*
jewel-DIM-sedge / chop.down-INF **come.IMP** 1.S-POSS beloved.man-DIM
'Chop down the jewel[-like] small sedges and **come** [back here], my darling man.'

Table 7.23: Attestations of the zero imperative across the provinces.

TSOJ			EOJ								UNP
Sin	Tö	Su	Kak	Mu	Sa	Mi	Sik	Pi	Sip	Kap	
0	0	0	0	0	1	0	0	0	0	0	1

7.5.2.2.6 Negative-imperative -*una*

The negative-imperative -*una* is a portmanteau morpheme attested three times in the corpus. The initial vowel of this suffix is strong, and as such it is not attested deleted. When it follows a vowel-final stem, the stem vowel is deleted. It usually suffixes directly to the verb root, but it can also follow the causative -*asime*-. All examples in the corpus are given below.

241. 14:3399.3-4 – Sinano
 可里婆祢尓 / 安思布麻之牟奈
 karinba ne-ni / *asi* **pum-asim-una**
 sakura root-LOC / foot **step-CAUS-NEG.IMP**
 '**Do not let** [your] feet **step** on the *sakura* roots.'

242. 14:3376a.3-5 – Muzasi
 牟射志野乃 / 宇家良我波奈乃 / 伊呂尓豆奈由米
 munzasi NO-nö / *ukera-nga pana-nö* / *irö-ni [i]nd-una yumey*
 TN field-GEN / ukera-POSS flower-COMP / color/feelings-LOC **emerge-NEG.IMP** at.all
 'Like the *ukera* flowers on Muzasi plain, **do not let** [your face] **reveal** even a hint of [your] true feelings [for me]!'

243. 14:3456.5 – UNP
 安乎許登奈須那
 a-wo kötö **nas-una**
 1.S-ACC word **produce-NEG.IMP**
 '**Do not spread** rumors about me.'

Table 7.24: Attestations of the negative-imperative suffix -*una* across the provinces.

TSOJ			EOJ								UNP
Sin	Tö	Su	Kak	Mu	Sa	Mi	Sik	Pi	Sip	Kap	
1	0	0	0	1	0	0	0	0	0	0	1

7.5.2.2.7 Desiderative *-ana* ~ *-an-* ~ *-n-*

The desiderative suffix *-ana* indicates a desire for something. It has three allomorphs: *-ana*, *-an-*, and *-n-*. The allomorph *-ana* occurs word-finally and before the tentative suffix allomorph *-m-*, while the allomorph *-an-* occurs before the imperative *-e*. The allomorph *-n-* only occurs after the auxiliary verb *-sö* 'do'.

244. 14:3398.3-5 – Sinano
波尓思奈能 / 伊思井乃手兒我 / 許登**奈多延曽祢**
panisina-nö / *isiWI-nö* te*NGO-nga* / *kötö* **na-taye-sö-n-e**
TN-GEN / TN-GEN maiden-POSS / word NEG.IMP-cease.INF-do-DES-IMP
'[There is] a maiden from Isiwi in Panisina [whose] words [I] **wish would never cease**!'

245. 20:4340.1-2 – Suruga
等知波々江 / 已波比弖**麻多祢**
töti papa ye / *ipap-i-te* **mat-an-e**
father mother EPT / pray-INF-SUB **wait-DES-IMP**
'Father, mother! [I] **want [you] to pray and wait** [for me]!'

246. 14:3405a.4-5 – Kamitukeno
兒良波**安波奈毛** / 比等理能未思弖
KO-ra pa **ap-ana-m-o** / *pitö-ri nömï s-i-te*
girl-DIM TPT **meet-DES-TENT-ATTR** / one-CL RPT do-INF-SUB
'[I] **want** [my] darling girl **to meet** [me], [when she is] all alone.'

247. 14:3378.5 – Muzasi
和尓**奈多要曽祢**
wa-ni **na-taye-sö-n-e**
1.S-DAT NEG.IMP-break.INF-do-DES-IMP
'**Please do not break** [up] with me.'

248. 20:4421.3-5 – Muzasi
安之我良乃 / 美祢波保久毛乎 / 美等登**志努波祢**
asingara-nö / *mi-ne pap-o kumo-wo* / *mi-tötö* **sinop-an-e**
TN-GEN / HON-peak crawl-ATTR cloud-ACC / see.INF-COOR **yearn.for-DES-IMP**
'**Please remember** [me] while [you] watch the clouds that go slowly over the great peak of [Mt.] Asigara.'

249. 14:3432.4 – Sagamu
和乎可豆佐祢母
*wa-wo **kandus-an-e** mö*
1.S-ACC **abduct-DES-IMP** EPT
'Please **abduct** me!'

250. 14:3426.4-5 – Mitinöku
斯努比尔勢毛等 / 比毛牟須波佐祢
*sinop-i n-i se-m-o tö / pimo **musunb-as-an-e***
yearn.for-NML COP-INF do-TENT-ATTR QUOT / cord **tie-HON-DES-IMP**
'[I] **want [you] to tie [your] cords** and think [of me] when [you] do!'

251. 14:3388.4-5 – Pitati
伊伎豆久伎美乎 / 為祢弖夜良佐祢
*ikinduk-u kimi-wo / wi-ne-te **yar-as-an-e***
sigh-ATTR lord -ACC / bring.INF-sleep.INF-SUB **send-HON-DES-IMP**
'**Please** bring [my] lord who sighs to sleep with [me], and then **send** [him back].'

252. 20:4367.5 – Pitati
伊母波之奴波尼
*imö pa **sinup-an-e***
beloved.girl TPT **yearn.for-DES-IMP**
'[I] **want** [my] beloved **to yearn for** [me].'

253. 14:3496.5 – UNP
伊弓安礼波伊可奈
*inde are pa **ik-ana***
well 1.S TPT **go-DES**
'Well, I **want to go** [to her].'

254. 14:3514.3-4 – UNP
和礼左倍尓 / 伎美尓都吉奈那
*ware sapey n-i / kimi-ni **tuk-i-n-ana***
1.S RPT COP-INF / lord-LOC **attach-INF-PERF-DES**
'Even I **have wanted to be close to** [you, my] lord.'

Table 7.25: Attestations of the desiderative suffix *-ana ~ -an- ~ -n-* across the provinces.

TSOJ			EOJ								UNP
Sin	Tö	Su	Kak	Mu	Sa	Mi	Sik	Pi	Sip	Kap	
1	0	2	5	4	1	1	0	3	0	0	8

7.5.2.2.8 Negative-tentative *-anzi*

The negative-tentative *-anzi* indicates an action that probably will not occur. Historically, it developed from a fusion of the negative *-an-* and the suppositional *-asi* (Vovin 2009a: 686). There are only four attestations.

255. 20:4405.5 – Kamitukeno
  和波等可自等余
  *wa pa **tök-anzi** tö yö*
  1.S TPT untie-NEG.TENT QUOT EPT
  '[I] think I **probably will not untie** [it].'

256. 14:3451.5 – UNP
  和波素登毛波自
  *wa pa so tö [o]**mop-anzi***
  1.S TPT shoo QUOT think-NEG.TENT
  'I **would not think** to shoo [it away].'

257. 14:3493a.3-5 – UNP
  牟可都乎能 / 四比乃故夜提能 / 安比波多我波自
  *muka-tu wo-nö / sipi-nö ko-yande-nö / ap-i pa **tangap-anzi***
  opposite.side-GEN.LOC mountain.ridge-GEN / chinquapin-GEN DIM-branch-COMP / meet-NML TPT differ-NEG.TENT
  '[Our] meeting **shall be indistinguishable from** how the small branches of the chinquapin trees on the mountain ridge across the way [touch each other].'

Table 7.26: Attestations of the negative-tentative suffix *-anzi* across the provinces.

TSOJ			EOJ								UNP
Sin	Tö	Su	Kak	Mu	Sa	Mi	Sik	Pi	Sip	Kap	
0	0	0	1	0	0	0	0	0	0	0	3

7.5.2.2.9 Exclamative -*umo* ~ -*mo*

The exclamative -*umo* adds a heavy exclamatory emphasis to a verb phrase. This suffix has a complex and rather debatable origin that deserves some discussion. Vovin (2009a: 695–700) analyzes the exclamative as historically consisting of *-um-ə '-FIN-EXCL', and he considers it to be a suffix in both WOJ and AOJ. The only evidence that -*umo* is undeniably a suffix in WOJ is found in MYS 15:3684, shown below, from Vovin (2009b: 100). There is no such evidence in the AOJ corpus.

258. 15.3684.3-4
      奈曽許己波 / 伊能祢良要奴毛
      nanzö kökönba / *i-nö* **ne-raye-n-umo**
      why extremely / sleep-GEN **sleep-PASS-NEG-EXCL**
      '*Why* **can [I] not sleep** at all?'

Vovin's argument (2009a: 696–697) hinges on the fact that the final suffix is not -*u* after the negative -*n*, but rather it is -*i*. Thus, synchronically, he concludes the vowel -*u* in -*umo* in 15:3684.4 must be a part of an exclamative suffix -*umo*, rather than the sequence-*u-mo* '-FIN-EXCL'.

Vovin's second argument to support this idea is that the emphatic particle *mo* cannot directly follow the final form of a verb. This is not as strong evidence as his previous point because if one simply takes every instance of -*umo* in the corpus in which the -*u* is clearly a final and reanalyzes it as -*u mo* '-FIN EPT', then this particle does indeed follow the final form.

Ultimately, I do follow Vovin's analysis, due to the strong evidence from WOJ he presents, along with the fact that this suffix must have existed in PJe. However, I prefer the diachronic analysis of this suffix as *-u mə '-FIN EPT', which later became reanalyzed as a single exclamative final suffix. This is because an emphatic particle *mo* (< *mə) is attested in OJ, but an exclamative suffix -*ö* (< *-ə) is not. There is also no basis to reconstruct an exclamative suffix *-ə in PR or in PJ.

This is one of the few suffixes that attaches to both verbs and adjectival verbs. For the examples where it attaches to adjectival verbs, see §6.3.3.13. The main allomorph on verbs is -*umo*, however it loses its initial vowel when it attaches to a vowel-final stem, producing the allomorph -*mo*.

259. 14:3412.4-5 – Kamitukeno
      可奈師家兒良尓 / 伊夜射可里久母
      kanasi-ke KO-ra-ni / *iya* **n-zakar-i-[i]k-umö**
      be.dear-AVATTR girl-DIM-DAT / more.and.more **COP.INF-be.far.from-INF-go-EXCL**
      '[I] am going **further and further away from** [my] dear, darling girl!'

260. 14:3431.1-4 – Sagamu
阿之我里乃 / 安伎奈乃夜麻尓 / 比古布祢乃 / 斯利**比可志母**與
*asingari-nö / akina-nö yama-ni / pik-o pune-nö / siri **pik-asi-mö** yö*
TN-GEN / TN-GEN mountain-LOC / pull-ATTR boat-COMP / behind **pull-SUP-EXCL** EPT
'[I] **seem to be pulling** on the back of [my beloved], as if [he] were a boat being pulled up Mt. Akina!'

261. 20:4378.3-5 – Simotukeno
阿毛志志可 / 多麻乃須我多波 / 和須例**西奈布母**
*amo sisi-nga / tama-nö sungata pa / wasure **se-n-ap-umö***
mother father-POSS / jade-GEN appearance TPT / forget.NML **do-NEG-ITER-EXCL**
'[I] **will not** forget the jewel-like appearance of mother and father!'

262. 20:4384.4-5 – Simotupusa
己枳尓之布祢乃 / 他都枳**之良酒毛**
*köng-i-n-i-si pune-nö / tatuki **sir-anz-umo***
row-INF-PERF-INF-PST.ATTR boat-GEN / clue **know-NEG-EXCL**
'[I] **do not have** a clue about the boat that has rowed [out]!'

263. 14:3489.3-5 – UNP
之牙可久尓 / 伊毛呂乎多弖天 / 左祢度**波良布母**
*singe-k-aku-ni / imo-rö-wo tate-te / sa-ne n-do **parap-umö***
be.lush-AVATTR-NML-LOC / beloved.girl-DIM-ACC make.stand.INF-SUB / LOC-sleep.NML COP.ATTR-place **clear.away-EXCL**
'[I] had [my] beloved girl stand in the thicket, [as I] **clear away** a place for [us] to sleep!'

264. 14:3546.4-5 – UNP
西美度波久末受 / 多知度**奈良須母**
*se mindo pa kum-anz-u / tat-i-n-do **naras-umö***
rapids water TPT scoop-NEG-INF / stand-NML-GEN-place **flatten-EXCL**
'Without scooping up the river water, [I] **stamp flat** the place where [I] stand!'

265. 14:3565.4-5 – UNP
宇良野能夜麻尓 / 都久**可多与留母**
*uraNO yama-ni / tuku **katayör-umö***
TN mountain-LOC / moon **incline.toward-EXCL**
'The moon **is getting close to** Mt. Urano!'

Table 7.27: Attestations of the exclamative suffix *-umo ~ -mo* across the provinces.

TSOJ			EOJ								UNP
Sin	Tö	Su	Kak	Mu	Sa	Mi	Sik	Pi	Sip	Kap	
0	0	0	2	0	1	0	1	1	1	0	10

7.5.2.2.10 Subjunctive *-amasi ~ -masi*

The suffix *-amasi* marks the subjunctive mood. It also has an attributive quality, since it can take case markers and act as a prenominal modifier. It is only attested five times. It has the allomorphs *-amasi* and *-masi*. The former occurs after consonant-final stems, while the latter occurs after vowel-final stems.

266. 14:3354.4-5 – Töpotuapumi
伊利奈麻之母乃 / 伊毛我乎杼許尓
ir-i-n-amasi mönö / imo-nga won-dökö-ni
enter-INF-PERF-SUBJ CNJ / beloved.girl-POSS DIM-bed-LOC
'Although [I] **would like to [lay] in** the warm bed of [my] beloved. . .'

Example (266) shows a syntactic inversion.

267. 14:3429.4-5 – Töpotuapumi
安礼乎多能米弖 / 安佐麻之物能乎
are-wo tanömey-te / as-amasi mönöwo
1.S-ACC make.trust.INF-SUB / be.shallow-SUBJ CNJ
'[You] made me trust [you], even though [your feelings for me] **may be shallow**.'

268. 20:4424.1-3 – Muzasi
伊呂夫可久 / 世奈我許呂母波 / 曽米麻之乎
irö-n-buka-ku / se-na-nga körömö pa / sömey-masi-wo
color-GEN-be.deep-AVINF / beloved.man-DIM-POSS garment TPT / dye-SUBJ-ACC
'[I] **should like to dye** [my] darling man's garment in a deeply [saturated] color.'

269. 14:3486.5 – UNP
伊夜可多麻斯尓
iya kat-amasi-ni
extremely **win-SUBJ**-LOC
'There is no doubt [I] **will win**.'

Table 7.28: Attestations of the subjunctive suffix -*amasi* ~ -*masi* across the provinces.

TSOJ			EOJ								UNP
Sin	Tö	Su	Kak	Mu	Sa	Mi	Sik	Pi	Sip	Kap	
0	2	0	0	1	0	0	0	0	0	0	1

7.5.2.2.11 Suppositional -*urasi* ~ -*rasi* ~ -*asi*

The suppositional -*urasi* indicates conjecture (Vovin 2009a: 679). It has three allomorphs: -*urasi*, -*rasi*, and -*asi*. Unlike WOJ where -*asi* is only attested after *ar*- 'exist', *nar*- 'become', and *nar*- 'be' (Vovin 2009a: 682), in AOJ this allomorph is attested attached to *yör*- 'approach', *pik*- 'pull', and *itanbur*- 'tremble'. The allomorph -*urasi* follows consonant-final stem verbs. The allomorph -*rasi* is only attested once in TSOJ, where it follows a vowel-final stem verb. This is different from WOJ, where it is only possible to find -*rasi* after strong-vowel stem verbs (Vovin 2009a: 679).

270. 20:4322.1-2 – Töpotuapumi
 和我都麻波 / 伊多久<u>古非良之</u>
 wa-nga tuma pa / *ita-ku **kopï-rasi***
 1.S-POSS spouse TPT / be.extreme-AVINF **long.for-SUP**
 'My wife **must miss** [me] greatly.'

271. 14:3435.1-4 – Kamitukeno
 伊可保呂乃 / 蘇比乃波里波良 / 和我吉奴尓 / <u>都伎与良志母</u>与
 ikapo-rö-nö / *sopi-nö pari para* / *wa-nga kinu-ni* / ***tuk-i-yör-asi-mö*** *yö*
 TN-DIM-GEN / adjacent-GEN alder field / 1.S-POSS robe-LOC / **attach-INF-approach-SUP-EXCL** EPT
 'It **seems** the [flowers from the] field [of] alders beside Mt. Ikapo **cling to** my robes!'

272. 14:3431.2-4 – Sagamu
 安伎奈乃夜麻尓 / 比古布祢乃 / 斯利<u>比可志母</u>與
 akina-nö yama-ni / *pik-o pune-nö* / *siri **pik-asi-mö*** *yö*
 TN-GEN mountain-LOC / pull-ATTR boat-COMP / back **pull-SUP-EXCL** EPT
 '[I] **seem to be pulling** on the back of [my beloved], as if [he] were a boat being pulled up Mt. Akina!'

273. 14:3550. 4 – UNP
　　伊多夫良思毛与
　　itanbur-asi-mo yö
　　tremble-SUP-EXCL EPT
　　'Oh, **it seems [I] am trembling**!'

274. 14:3446.4-5 – UNP
　　安志等比登其等 / 加多理与良斯毛
　　asi tö pitö-n-götö / ***katar-i-yör-asi-mo***
　　be.bad.AVFIN QUOT people-GEN-word / **tell-INF-approach-SUP-EXCL**
　　'**It seems** that people **are saying** [the Amur silver grass] is bad!'

275. 20:4427.1-2 – UNP
　　伊波乃伊毛呂 / 和乎之乃布良之
　　ipa-nö imo-rö / *wa-wo **sinöp-urasi***
　　house-GEN beloved.girl-DIM / 1.S-ACC **yearn.for-SUP**
　　'It **seems** that [my] darling girl at home **yearns** for me.'

Table 7.29: Attestations of the suppositional *-urasi ~ -rasi ~ -asi* across the provinces.

TSOJ			EOJ								UNP
Sin	Tö	Su	Kak	Mu	Sa	Mi	Sik	Pi	Sip	Kap	
0	1	0	0	0	1	0	0	0	0	0	2

7.5.2.2.12 Verbal adjectivizer *-asi*

This suffix changes a verb into an adjectival verb and it is homophonous with the suppositional allomorph *-asi*. There is only one clear example of this suffix in the corpus. Some lexicalized adjectival verbs, like EOJ *kopusi* 'be longing for' < PJe *koposi (< *kopoi-asi 'long.for-ADJ'), contain this suffix historically.

276. 14:3557.1-2 – UNP
　　奈夜麻思家 / 比登都麻可母与
　　***nayam-asi*-ke** / *pitö-tuma kamö yö*
　　distress-ADJ-AVATTR / person-spouse EPT EPT
　　'[This] wife of another man **is so distressing** [to me]!'

7.5.2.3 Word non-final suffixes

The word non-final suffixes cannot terminate a word form. They include the negative *-an- ~ -anz- ~ -n- ~ -nz-*, the negative-attributive *-ana- ~ -na-*, the tentative *-am- ~ -m-*, the tentative 2 *-uram- ~ -unam-*, the iterative *-ap- ~ -öp-*, the passive *-are- ~ -ar- ~ -aye- ~ -ye- ~ -y-*, the honorific *-as- ~ -s- ~ -os-*, the causative *-asime-*, the causative *-ase-*, the debitive *-unbe-*, and the progressive *-ar- ~ -er- ~ -ir-*.

7.5.2.3.1 Negative suffix *-an- ~ -anz- ~ -n- ~ -nz-*

The negative suffix *-an-* has four allomorphs in EOJ and TSOJ: *-an-*, *-n-*, *-anz-*, and *-nz-*. In EOJ, there is also a special negative-attributive form *-ana-* that I describe separately in §7.5.2.3.1.1. Only *-anz-* and *-nz-* can occur before the final suffix *-u*. They are also the only allomorphs that occur before the infinitive allomorph *-u* and the nominalizer allomorph *-u*. The vowel-less variants *-n-* and *-nz-* attach to vowel-final stems.

Table 7.30: Sample AOJ paradigmatic forms of the negative suffix *-an- ~ -anz-* showing its allomorphy with the consonant-final stem verb *ip-* 'say' and the vowel-final stem verb *wasure-* 'forget'.

STEM \ SUFFIX	Attributive	Infinitive	Final	Evidential
ip-an- 'say-NEG-'	*ip-**an**-u*	*ip-**anz**-u*	*ip-**anz**-u*	*ip-**an**-e*
wasure-n- 'forget-NEG-'	*wasure-**n**-u*	*wasure-**nz**-u*	*wasure-**nz**-u*	*wasure-**n**-e*

There is also a form *-n-i* 'NEG-INF' (rather than *-nz-u* 'id.') that is attested just once, after the potential auxiliary *-kande-* (see example 287 below). Historically the form *-anz-* is a contraction of the construction VERB-*an-i se-* 'VERB-NEG-NML do-' (Vovin 2009c: 779). It is unclear why the infinitive is *-u* after *-anz-*, since the infinitive form of *se-* 'do' is *s-i* 'do-INF', and a form *-anzi* is not only phonologically possible in the language, it is also attested, as the negative-tentative suffix.

The negative suffix's allomorph *-an-* may be followed by these suffixes: the attributive *-u ~ -o*, the iterative *-ap-*, the infinitive *-i*, and the evidential *-e*. The fact that it precedes the iterative *-ap-* is very important to note[178] because the negative *-an-* is attested following, but never preceding, the iterative *-ap-* in WOJ. The

---

[178] This was first suggested by Ikier (2006: 100), though he did not accept this analysis, rather he settled on the form *-anap-* for the negative suffix, with no iterative involved.

negative suffix's allomorph -anz- can be followed by the final -u, the infinitive -u, and the nominalizer -u.

277. 20:4322.3-5 – Töpotuapumi
乃牟美豆尔 / 加其佐倍美曳弓 / 余尔和須良礼受
*nöm-u mindu-ni / kangö sapey mi-ye-te / yö-ni **wasur-are-nz-u***
drink-ATTR water-LOC / shadow RPT see-PASS.INF-SUB / lifetime-LOC **forget-PASS-NEG-FIN**
'So much as seeing her shadow in the water that [I] drink, [makes me realize I] **cannot forget** [her] in this lifetime.'

278. 20:4342.5 – Suruga
於米加波利勢受
*omey kapar-i **se-nz-u***
face change-NML **do-NEG-FIN**
'With [your] face **un**changing.'

279. 14:3404.4-5 – Kamitukeno
奴礼杼安加奴乎 / 安杼加安我世牟
*n-ure-ndö **ak-an-u**-wo / andö ka a-nga se-m-u*
sleep-EV-CONC **be.satisfied-NEG-ATTR**-ACC / what QPT 1.S-POSS do-TENT-ATTR
'[I] slept with [her], but [I] **am unsatisfied**. What should I do?'

280. 20:4407.4-5 – Kamitukeno
伊毛賀古比之久 / 和須良延奴加母
*imo-nga kopisi-ku / **wasur-aye-n-u** kamö*
beloved.girl-POSS be.longing.for-AVINF / **forget-PASS-NEG-ATTR** EPT
'[I] began to miss [my] beloved, and [I realized I] **cannot forget** [her]!'

281. 14:3375.4-5 – Muzasi
伊尓之与比欲利 / 世呂尔安波奈布与
*in-i-si yöpi-yori / se-rö-ni **ap-an-ap-u** yö*
depart-INF-PST.ATTR evening-ABL / beloved.man-DIM-DAT **meet-NEG-ITER-FIN** EPT
'Since the evening [he] departed, [I] **have not met** [my] beloved!'

282. 20:4413.4-5 – Muzasi
西呂我馬伎己无 / 都久乃之良奈久
se-rö-nga mek-i-kö-m-u / *tuku-nö **sir-an-aku***
beloved.man-DIM-POSS walk-INF-come-TENT-ATTR / moon-GEN **know-NEG.ATTR-NML**
'**Not knowing** the month when [my] beloved shall come walking back...'

283. 14:3368.4-5 – Sagamu
余尓母多欲良尓 / 故呂河伊波奈久尓
yö-ni mö tayora n-i / *ko-rö-nga **ip-an-aku** n-i*
lifetime-LOC FPT wavering COP-INF / girl-DIM-POSS **say-NEG.ATTR-NML** COP-INF
'Although [my] dear girl **will not say that** [her love for me] will waver in [this] lifetime...'

284. 14:3426.1-3 – Mitinöku
安比豆祢能 / 久尓乎佐杼抱美 / 安波奈波婆
apindu ne-nö / *kuni-wo sa n-döpo-mi* / ***ap-an-ap-anba***
TN peak-GEN / land-ABS thus COP.INF-be.far-AVGER / **meet-NEG-ITER-COND**
'If [we] **keep failing to meet** because the land of the Apidu peaks is so far [away]...'

285. 14:3425.1-4 – Simotukeno
志母都家努 / 安素乃河泊良欲 / 伊之布麻努受 / 蘓良由登伎努与
simötukeno / *aso-nö kapara-yo* / *isi **pum-anz-u*** / *sora-yu tö k-i-n-o yö*
TN / TN-GEN river.bank-ABL / stone **step-NEG-INF** / sky-ABL FPT come-INF-PERF-ATTR EPT
'[I] came from the sky **without stepping** [on] the stones from the riverbank of Aso in Simotukeno!'

286. 20:4378.3-5 – Simotukeno
阿毛志志可 / 多麻乃須我多波 / 和須例西奈布母
amo sisi-nga / *tama-nö sungata pa* / *wasure **se-n-ap-umö***
mother father-POSS / jade-GEN appearance TPT / forget.NML **do-NEG-ITER-EXCL**
'[I] **will not forget** the jewel-like appearance of my mother and father!'

287. 14:3388.1-3 – Pitati
筑波祢乃 / 祢呂尔可須美為 / **須宜可提尓**
*tukupa ne-nö / ne-rö-ni kasumi wi / **sungï-kande-n-i***
TN peak-GEN / peak-DIM-LOC mist sit.INF / **pass.INF-POT-NEG-INF**
'[I] **cannot pass through** the mist sitting on the smaller peak of Mt. Tukupa, so...'

288. 20:4371.4-5 – Pitati
都久波能夜麻乎 / **古比須**安良米可毛
*tukupa-nö yama-wo / **kopi-nz-u** ar-am-ey kamo*
TN-GEN mountain-ACC / **long.for-NEG-INF** exist-TENT-EV EPT
'I wonder, shall [I] **not long for** Tukupa mountain?'

289. 20:4351.4-5 – Kamitupusa
奈保波太佐牟之 / 伊母尔志**阿良祢婆**
*napo panda samu-si / imö n-i si **ar-an-e-nba***
still skin be.cold-FIN / beloved.girl COP-INF EPT **exist-NEG-EV-CONJ**
'Still [my] skin is cold, because it **is not** [my] beloved [who will warm me up]...'

290. 14:3532.1-3 – UNP
波流能野尓 / 久佐波牟古麻能 / 久知**夜麻受**
*paru-nö NO-ni / kusa pam-u koma-nö / kuti **yam-anz-u***
spring-GEN field-LOC / grass eat-ATTR horse-COMP / mouth **stop-NEG-INF**
'Like a horse eating grass on the spring fields [whose] mouth **does not stop**...'

291. 14:3546.4-5 – UNP
西美度波**久末受** / 多知度奈良須母
*se mindo pa **kum-anz-u** / tat-i-n-do naras-umö*
rapids water TPT **scoop-NEG-INF** / stand-NML-GEN-place flatten-EXCL
'**Without scooping up** the river water, [I] stamp flat the place where [I] stand!'

292. 14:3565.1-2 – UNP
可能古呂等 / **宿受**夜奈里奈牟
*kanö ko-rö-tö / **NE-nz-u** ya nar-i-n-am-u*
that girl-DIM-COM / **sleep-NEG-NML** QPT be-INF-PERF-TENT-ATTR
'Shall [it] be that [I] **will not sleep** with that sweet girl?'

293. 20:4436.1-2 – UNP
夜未乃欲能 / 由久左伎之良受
yamï nö yo-nö / yuk-u saki **sir-anz-u**
darkness COP.ATTR night-GEN / go-ATTR ahead **know-NEG-INF**
'**Without knowing** what lies ahead on [this] dark night...'

Table 7.31: Attestations of the negative suffix *-an-* ~ *-anz-* ~ *-n-* ~ *-nz-* across the provinces.

TSOJ			EOJ							UNP
Sin	Tö	Su	Kak	Mu	Sa	Mi	Sik	Pi	Sip	Kap	
1	2	4	7	4	3	1	4	7	2	5	51

7.5.2.3.1.1 Negative-Attributive *-ana-* ~ *-na-*

This suffix is only attested in EOJ and UNP, in the allomorphs *-ana-* (after consonant-final stems) and *-na-* (after vowel-final stems). Historically, it is a combination of the negative *-an- and the attributive *-a.[179] Synchronically, a morpheme boundary cannot be drawn (much like the case of the AOJ nominalizer *-aku*, which contains the same attributive morpheme), since the attributive *-a is only attested attached to a morpheme other than the negative suffix in one UNP poem (see §7.5.2.2.3).

This suffix is always attested with a following locative *-na* or *-ni*, thus it only survived in certain special grammatical constructions (described in §5.4.1.5.4 and §5.4.1.6.1). Hōjō (1966: 492–497, 502–503) proposed a connection between this suffix and the Ryukyuan negative suffix *-ada*. I think this is a plausible comparison if we reconstruct PJ *-an-a '-NEG-ATTR' with a sporadic change in PR to *-aⁿda. This form was analogically levelled out in WOJ, replaced by *-anz-u n-i* -NEG-INF COP-INF 'without (doing)' and *-an-u-ni* -NEG-ATTR-LOC 'because not (doing)'.

294. 14:3408.2 – Kamitukeno
祢尓波都可奈那
ne-ni pa tuk-ana-na
peak-LOC TPT reach-NEG.ATTR-LOC
'**Without reaching** the peak...'

---

[179] Ikier (2006: 102–103) was the first to propose this form contains an attributive *-a*, though his morphological analysis is synchronic rather than diachronic.

295. 14:3436.4-5 – Kamitukeno
 宇良賀礼勢奈那 / 登許波尓毛我母
 ura-n-gare se-na-na / tökö pa n-i mongamö
 top.branch-GEN-wither.NML do-NEG.ATTR-LOC / eternal leaf COP-INF DPT
 'I wish [the trees] had eternal leaves, **without withered top branches**.'

296. 20:4422.3-5 – Muzasi
 宇都久之美 / 於妣波等可奈々 / 阿也尓加母祢毛
 utukusi-mi / **onbi pa tök-ana-na** / aya n-i kamö ne-m-o
 be.beloved-AVGER / **sash TPT untie-NEG.ATTR-LOC** / strange COP-INF EPT sleep-TENT-ATTR
 '[I] shall sleep strangely, **without untying [my] sash**, because [I] love [him].'

297. 14:3487.4-5 – UNP
 宿莫奈那里尓思 / 於久乎可奴加奴
 NE-NA-na nar-i-n-i-si / oku-wo kan-u kan-u
 sleep-NEG.ATTR-LOC become-INF-PERF-INF-PST.ATTR / future-ACC worry.about-FIN worry.about-FIN
 '[I] worry about [our] future again and again, [because] it turned out that [we] **did not sleep** [together].'

298. 14:3557.4-5 – UNP
 和須礼波勢奈那 / 伊夜母比麻須尓
 wasure pa se-na-na / iya [o]möp-i mas-u-ni
 forget.NML TPT do-NEG.ATTR-LOC / more.and.more think-NML increase-ATTR-LOC
 '[I] think of [her] more and more, **without forgetting** [anything about her].'

299. 14:3461.3-5 – UNP
 真日久礼弖 / 与比奈波**許奈尓** / 安家奴思太久流
 MA-PI kure-te / yöpi-na pa **kö-na-ni** / ake-n-o sinda k-uru
 INT-sun grow.dark.INF-SUB / evening-LOC TPT **come-NEG.ATTR-LOC** / dawn.INF-PERF-ATTR CNJ come-ATTR
 '[It is] **because [you] did not come** during the evening after the bright sun set, [you only] came when it dawned.'

Table 7.32: Attestations of the negative-attributive suffix -ana- ~ -na- across the provinces.

TSOJ			EOJ								UNP
Sin	Tö	Su	Kak	Mu	Sa	Mi	Sik	Pi	Sip	Kap	
0	0	0	2	2	0	0	0	0	0	0	5

7.5.2.3.2 Tentative -*am*- ~ -*m*-

The tentative mood suffix -*am*- ~ -*m*- is one of the most common mood markers in the AOJ dialects. It usually indicates an action that 'shall', 'should', 'would', 'will', or 'probably (will)' be done (or was done), but in some contexts it is not translatable in English. The allomorphy is quite basic, with the shortened form -*m*- occurring after vowel-final stem verbs, irregular verbs, and vowel-final suffixes. In TSOJ, when it follows the past tense -*kV* the two fuse into the portmanteau form -*kem*-, shown in example (301) below; although it is unattested, in EOJ we would expect to find -*k-am*-.

300. 14:3400.3-5 – Sinano
 左射礼思母 / 伎弥之布美弓波 / 多麻等**比呂波牟**
 *sanzare [i]si mö / kimi si pum-i-te-nba / tama tö **piröp-am-u***
 little stone FPT / lord EPT step-INF-PERF-COND / jewel COP **pick.up-TENT-FIN**
 'When [you, my] lord have stepped on the small stones, [I] **shall pick [them] up** as jewels.'

301. 20:4323.3-5 – Töpotuapumi
 奈尓須礼曽 / 波々登布波奈乃 / **佐吉泥己受祁牟**
 *nani s-ure sö / papa tö [i]p-u pana-nö / **sak-i-nde-kö-nz-u-kem-u***
 why do-EV FPT / mother QUOT say-ATTR flower-GEN / **bloom-INF-go.out. INF-come-NEG-INF-PST.TENT-ATTR**
 'Why **has** the flower called 'mother' **not come out in bloom**?'

302. 20:4344.1 – Suruga
 和須良牟弓
 ***wasur-am-u** te*
 try.to.forget-TENT-FIN QUOT
 '[I] thought [I] **would try to forget** [them].'

303. 14:3405b.4-5 – Kamitukeno
世奈**波安波奈母** / 美流比登奈思尓
se-na pa **ap-ana-m-ö** / mi-ru pitö na-si-ni
beloved.man-DIM TPT **meet-DES-TENT-ATTR** / see-ATTR person not.exist-AVFIN-LOC
'[I] **want** [my] beloved man **to meet** [me], when there is no one [there] who would see [him].'

304. 20:4406.4-5 – Kamitukeno
多妣波久流之等 / **都氣夜良麻久**母
tanbi pa kurusi tö / **tungey-yar-am-aku** mö
journey TPT be.painful.AVFIN QUOT / **tell.INF-send-TENT.ATTR-NML** FPT
'[I] **would send** [him] to tell [them] that [my] journey is painful!'

305. 14:3379.1-2 – Muzasi
和我世故乎 / 安杼可母**伊波武**
wa-nga se-ko-wo / andö kamö **ip-am-u**
1.S-POSS man-DIM-ACC / what EPT **say-TENT-ATTR**
'[I] wonder, what **could** [I] **say** [about] my beloved man?'

306. 20:4416.4-5 – Muzasi
伊波奈流和礼波 / 比毛等加受**祢牟**
ipa-n[i] ar-u ware pa / pimo tök-anz-u **ne-m-u**
house-LOC exist-ATTR 1.S TPT / cord undo-NEG-INF **sleep-TENT-FIN**
'I, who am at home, **shall sleep** without untying [my] cord.'

307. 14:3369.3-4 – Sagamu
須我麻久良 / 安是加**麻可左武**
sunga-makura / anze ka **mak-as-am-u**
sedge-pillow / why QPT **use.as.a.pillow-HON-TENT-ATTR**
'Why **should** [you] **lay** [your] **head** [on] a sedge pillow?'

308. 20:4329.3-5 – Sagamu
布奈可射里 / 安我**世牟**比呂乎 / **美毛**比等母我毛
puna-kanzar-i / a-nga **se-m-u** pi-rö-wo / **mi-m-o** pitö möngamo
boat-decorate-NML / 1.S-POSS **do-TENT-ATTR** day-DIM-ACC / **see-TENT-ATTR** person DPT
'[I] wish someone **would witness** the special day when I **do** the boat-decorating.'

309. 14:3426.4-5 – Mitinöku
斯努比尓勢毛等 / 比毛牟須波佐祢
sinop-i n-i se-m-o tö / pimo musunb-as-an-e
yearn.for-NML COP-INF **do**-TENT-ATTR QUOT / cord **tie**-HON-DES-IMP
'[I] want [you] to tie [your] cords and **think** [of me] **when** [you] **do**!'

310. 14:3424.4-5 – Simotukeno
麻具波思兒呂波 / 多賀家可**母多牟**
*ma n-gupasi KO-rö pa / ta-nga ke ka **möt-am-u***
true COP.INF-beautiful girl-DIM TPT / who-POSS container QPT **hold**-TENT-ATTR
'Whose [food] container **shall** the truly beautiful girl **hold**?'

311. 20:4383.4-5 – Simotukeno
多志埿毛等伎尓 / 阿母我米母我母
tas-i-nde-m-o töki-ni / amö-nga mey möngamö
rise-INF-**go.out**-TENT-ATTR time-LOC / mother-POSS eye DPT
'When [we] **rise and set out**, [I] long for [my] mother's eyes.'

312. 14:3394.4-5 – Pitati
和須良延許婆古曽 / 那乎**可家奈波賣**
*wasura-kö-nba kosö / na-wo **kake-n-ap-am-e***
forget-come-COND FPT / 2.S-ACC **call.out**-NEG-ITER-TENT-EV
'When [I] start to forget [our meeting there], [I] **shall stop calling out** for you!'

313. 20:4372.12 – Pitati
阿例波**伊波々牟**
*are pa **ipap-am-u***
1.S TPT **pray**-TENT-ATTR
'I **will pray**...'

314. 14:3386.4-5 – Simotupusa
曽能可奈之伎乎 / 刀尓**多弖米**也母
*sönö kanasi-ki-wo / to-ni **tate-m-ey** ya mö*
that be.dear-AVATTR-ACC / outside-LOC **make.stand**-TENT-EV QPT EPT
'**Will** [I] **make** that dear [girl] **stand** outside? (No, I will not)'

315. 20:4392.4-5 – Simotupusa
有都久之波々尓 / 麻多己等**刀波牟**
*utukusi papa-ni / mata kötö **top-am-u***
beloved mother-DAT / again word **ask-TENT-ATTR**
'[So I] **could** once again **inquire** after [my] beloved mother...'

316. 14:3383.4-5 – Kamitupusa
久尓乃登保可婆 / 奈我目**保里勢牟**
*kuni-nö töpo-ka-nba / na-nga MEY **por-i se-m-u***
province-GEN be.far-AVEV-CONJ / 2.S-POSS eye **desire-NML do-TENT-FIN**
'[I] **dream of** your eyes, since [your] province is far [away].'

317. 20:4349.4-5 – Kamitupusa
夜蘓志麻須義弖 / 和加例加**由可牟**
*ya-so sima sungï-te / wakare ka **yuk-am-u***
eight-ten island pass.INF-SUB / be.separated.INF QPT **go-TENT-ATTR**
'Going past many islands, **shall [I] go** [ahead], further away [from home]?'

318. 14:3463.1-2 – UNP
麻等保久能 / 野尓毛**安波奈牟**
*ma-töpo-ku nö / NO-ni mo **ap-ana-m-u***
INT-be.far-NML COP.ATTR / field-LOC FPT **meet-DES-TENT-FIN**
'[I] **would like to meet** [you] in the fields that are quite a distance [away].'

319. 14:3472.4-5 – UNP
刀奈里乃伎奴乎 / 可里弖**伎奈波毛**
*tonari-nö kinu-wo / kar-i-te **ki-n-ap-am-o***
neighbor-GEN robe-ACC / borrow-INF-SUB **wear.INF-PERF-ITER-TENT-ATTR**
'Borrowing [my] neighbor's robes, [I] **shall wear [them] again and again**.'

320. 14:3474.3-5 – UNP
伊伱弖伊奈波 / 伊豆思牟伎弖可 / 伊毛我**奈氣可牟**
*inde-te in-anba / indusi muk-i-te ka / imo-nga **nangeyk-am-u***
go.out.INF-SUB leave-COND / which face-INF-SUB QPT / beloved.girl-POSS **lament-TENT-ATTR**
'When [I] go away, which [way] **will** [my] darling girl face to **lament**?'

321. 20:4436.4 – UNP
伊都**伎麻佐牟**等
itu **k-i-mas-am-u** tö
when **come-INF-HON-TENT-FIN** QUOT
'When **will [you] come** [back]?'

Table 7.33: Attestations of the tentative suffix -am- ~ -m- across the provinces.

TSOJ			EOJ							UNP
Sin	Tö	Su	Kak	Mu	Sa	Mi	Sik	Pi	Sip	Kap	
1	6	1	10	11	5	2	3	10	3	7	38

7.5.2.3.3 Tentative 2 -uram- ~ -unam-

I refer to the suffix -uram- ~ -unam- as "tentative 2" due to the fact there is a tentative suffix -am- attested. The meaning of this suffix is difficult to distinguish from the tentative -am-, but Vovin (2009a: 814) presents ample evidence that it is a "non-past" tentative in WOJ, since, unlike the tentative -am-, it cannot combine with the past tense -kV. Thus, the tentative 2 suffix may only be used to indicate present or future actions. In AOJ we find the same picture, so I adopt Vovin's analysis here. I hesitate to mark this as a "non-past" tentative morpheme in the glossing, however, because the language otherwise does not overtly mark the non-past in the morphology.[180]

This suffix is -uram- in TSOJ and -unam- in EOJ. Both forms are attested in UNP: poems with -unam- are written in an EOJ topolect, but poems with -uram- are either written in a TSOJ topolect or an EOJ topolect exhibiting WOJ influence. The medial -n- in the EOJ form is the result of a regressive nasal assimilation that occurred in Proto-EOJ. I have segregated the two forms in the examples provided below.

7.5.2.3.3.1 Examples of TSOJ and UNP -uram-

322. 20:4343.3-5 – Suruga
己比尓志弖 / 古米知**夜須良牟** / 和加美可奈志母
ipi n-i s-i-te / ko meyt-i **yas-uram-u** / wa-nga mi kanasi-mö
house COP-INF do-INF-SUB / girl hold-INF **become.emaciated-TENT2-ATTR** / 1.S-POSS wife be.sad.AVFIN-EXCL
'My wife, who is at home, holding the children **and probably becoming emaciated**, [must] be so sad!'

---

180 Historically, however, this contains a non-past stative suffix *-ur- (Russell 2006: 650).

323. 14:3505.2-5 – UNP
美夜能瀬河泊能 / 可保婆奈能 / 孤悲天香**眠良武** / 伎曽母許余比毛
*miyanöSE kapa-nö / kapo-n-bana-nö / kopï-te ka **N-Uram-u** / kisö mö köyöpi mo*
TN river-GEN / face-GEN-blossom-COMP / long.for.INF-SUB QPT **sleep-TENT2-ATTR** / last.night FPT this.evening FPT
'**Did [she fall] asleep** longing for [me] last night, like the morning glories along Miyanöse river, and [will she do so again] tonight?'

324. 14:3532.4-5 – UNP
安乎**思努布良武** / 伊敝乃兒呂波母
*a-wo **sinop-uram-u** / ipe-nö KO-rö pa mö*
1.S-ACC **long.for-TENT2-ATTR** / house-GEN girl-DIM TPT EPT
'[My] darling girl back home, who **must be longing** for me...'

7.5.2.3.3.2 Examples of EOJ *-unam-*

325. 14:3366.4-5 – Sagamu
美奈能瀬河泊尓 / 思保**美都奈武**賀
*minanöSE kapa-ni / sipo **mit-unam-u** ka*
TN river-LOC / tide **fill-TENT2-ATTR** QPT
'**Will** the tide **wash** into Minanöse river?'

326. 20:4390.4-5 – Simotupusa
以毛加去ゝ里波 / **阿用久奈米**加母
*imo-nga kökörö pa / **ayok-unam-ey** kamö*
beloved.girl-POSS heart TPT / **waver-TENT2-EV** EPT
'[I] wonder, **will** [my] beloved girl's feelings **waver**?'

327. 20:4391.4-5 – Simotupusa
阿加**古比須奈牟** / 伊母賀加奈志作
*a-nga **kop-i s-unam-u** / imö-nga kanasi-sa*
1.S-POSS **long.for-NML do-TENT2-ATTR** / beloved.girl-POSS be.sad-AVNML
'The sadness of my beloved girl who **probably longs for** [me]...'

328. 14:3476a.5 – UNP
故布思可流奈母
kopusi-k[u]-ar-unam-ö
be.longing.for-AVINF-exist-TENT2-ATTR
'[She] **will long for** [me].'

329. 14:3496.1-3 – UNP
多智婆奈乃 / 古婆乃波奈里我 / **於毛布奈牟**
*tatinbana-nö / konba-nö panari-nga / **omop-unam-u***
TN-GEN / TN-GEN long.parted.hair-POSS / **love-TENT2-ATTR**
'[The girl] from Koba in Tatibana with long, parted hair **probably loves** [me].'

330. 14:3526.3-5 – UNP
安我己許呂 / 布多**由久奈母**等 / 奈与母波里曾祢
*a-nga kökörö / puta **yuk-unam-ö** tö / na-y-ömöp-ar-i-sö-n-e*
1.S-POSS heart / two **go-TENT2-ATTR** QUOT / NEG.IMP-EPEN-think-PROG-INF-do-DES-IMP
'Please do not think that my heart **will go** [after] two [women]!'

331. 14:3552.1-4 – UNP
麻都我宇良尓 / 佐和恵宇良太知 / 麻比登其等 / **於毛抱須奈母呂**
*matu-nga ura-ni / sawawe ura-n-dat-i / ma-pitö-n-götö / **omop-os-unam-ö** rö*
pine-POSS bay-LOC / noisy tip-LOC-rise-NML / INT-people-GEN-word / **think-HON-TENT2-ATTR** COP
'[You] are **probably thinking** of the rumors people [spread that are like] noisy [waves] rising to the tips [of the tree branches] in the bay of pines.'

332. 14:3563.4-5 – UNP
和乎可**麻都那毛** / 伎曽毛己余必母
*wa-wo ka **mat-unam-o** / kisö mo köyöpi mö*
1.S-ACC QPT **wait-TENT2-ATTR** / last.night FPT this evening FPT
'**Will [you] wait** for me tonight, [as you did] last night?'

Table 7.34: Attestations of the tentative 2 suffix *-uram-* ~ *-unam-* across the provinces.

Form	TSOJ			EOJ								UNP
	Sin	Tö	Su	Kak	Mu	Sa	Mi	Sik	Pi	Sip	Kap	
-uram-	0	0	1	0	0	0	0	0	0	0	0	3
-unam-	0	0	0	0	0	1	0	0	0	2	0	6

7.5.2.3.4 Iterative *-ap-* ~ *-öp-*

The iterative *-ap-* indicates an action is done multiple times. With verbs that have semantics involving a continuous state, such as *mat-* 'wait' and *wasure-* 'forget', the iterative is used in a durative function. Due to this later function, Russell (2006: 167–168) views this suffix as a pure durative, though Vovin (2009a: 820) and Bentley (2001: 200–203) prefer to classify it as an iterative. I follow Vovin and Bentley in regard to the classification of this suffix's underlying (or primary) function, noting the durative function pointed out by Russell is intrinsically linked with the semantics of some verbs.

The iterative has two allomorphs: -*ap*- and -*öp*-. The former is used everywhere except when directly following a verb root that contains the vowel *ö* (see example 341 below). If a suffix comes between the iterative and a root, the iterative remains -*ap*- even if the root has the vowel *ö*. Example (338) below illustrates this.

In regard to morphotactics, the iterative follows the negative and progressive suffixes in EOJ.[181] This is very important to note because only the opposite morpheme orders (-ITER-NEG-, -ITER-PROG-) are found in WOJ (Vovin 2009a: 820-827). I view these opposite morpheme orders as the result of the independent grammaticalizations of the iterative suffix in WOJ and EOJ, from a PJe auxiliary. The iterative is not attested in TSOJ.

333. 14:3419.5 – Kamitukeno
和須礼西奈布母
wasure se-n-ap-umö
forget.NML do-NEG-ITER-FIN-EXCL
'[I] **will not forget** [you]!'

334. 14:3375.4-5 – Muzasi
伊尓之与比欲利 / 世呂尓**安波奈布**与
in-i-si yöpi-yori / *se-rö-ni **ap-an-ap-u*** *yö*
depart-INF-PST.ATTR evening-ABL / beloved.man-DIM-DAT **meet-NEG-ITER-FIN** EPT
'Since the evening [he] departed, [I] **have not met** [my] beloved!'

335. 14:3426.1-3 – Mitinöku
安比豆祢能 / 久尓乎佐杼抱美 / **安波奈波婆**
apindu ne-nö / *kuni-wo sa n-döpo-mi* / ***ap-an-ap-anba***
TN peak-GEN / land-ABS thus COP.INF-be.far-AVGER / **meet-NEG-ITER-COND**
'If [we] **keep failing to meet** because the land of the Apidu peaks is so far [away]. . .'

---

[181] This was first suggested by Ikier (2006: 100), though he did not accept this analysis, rather he settled on the form -*anap*- for the negative suffix, with no iterative involved.

336. 20:4378.3-5 – Simotukeno
阿毛志志可 / 多麻乃須我多波 / 和須例西奈布母
*amo sisi-nga / tama-nö sungata pa / wasure **se-n-ap-umö***
mother father-POSS / jade-GEN appearance TPT / forget.NML **do-NEG-ITER-EXCL**
'[I] will **not forget** the jewel-like appearance of [my] mother and father.'

337. 14:3394.4-5 – Pitati
和須良延許婆古曾 / 那乎可家奈波賣
*wasura-kö-nba kosö / na-wo **kake-n-ap-am-e***
forget-come-COND FPT / 2.S-ACC **call.out-NEG-ITER-TENT-EV**
'When [I] start to forget [our meeting there], [I] **shall stop calling out** for you!'

338. 14:3444.1-4 – UNP
伎波都久能 / 乎加能久君美良 / 和礼都賣杼 / 故尓毛乃多奈布
*kipatuku-nö / woka-nö kuku-mira / ware tum-e-ndö / ko-ni mo **nöt-an-ap-u***
TN-GEN / hill-GEN stem-leek / 1.S pluck-EV-CONC / basket-LOC FPT **fill.up-NEG-ITER-FIN**
'I pluck the stem-leeks on Kipatuku hill, but the basket **is not filling up**.'

339. 14:3448.1-2 – UNP
波奈治良布 / 己能牟可都乎乃
*pana-**n-dir-ap-u** / könö muka-tu wo nö*
flower-**GEN-scatter-ITER-ATTR** / this opposite.side-GEN.LOC mountain.ridge COP.ATTR
'It is the mountain ridge across the way, where the flower petals **are scattering**.'

340. 14:3525.4-5 – UNP
許等乎呂波敝而 / 伊麻太宿奈布母
*kötö-wo-rö pape-TE / imanda **NE-n-ap-umö***
word-string-DIM stretch.INF-SUB / not.yet **sleep-NEG-ITER-EXCL**
'[I] spoke effusively [to my beloved girl], [but we] **are** still **not sleeping** [together]!'

341. 14:3529.5 – UNP
波伴尓許呂波要
*papa-ni **kör-öp-aye***
mother-DAT **scold-ITER-PASS.INF**
'[I] **was repeatedly scolded** by [her] mother...'

Table 7.35: Attestations of the iterative -*ap*- ~ -*öp*- across the provinces.

TSOJ			EOJ								UNP
Sin	Tö	Su	Kak	Mu	Sa	Mi	Sik	Pi	Sip	Kap	
0	0	0	1	1	0	1	2	1	0	0	11

7.5.2.3.4.1 Iterative-infinitive -*ape* ~ -*öpe*

There is a special iterative-infinitive morph -*ape* attested in UNP poems that contain unique EOJ linguistic features, but not in poems that contain unique linguistic features found in TSOJ. So, I consider it to be an EOJ form. I view this as a single portmanteau morph -*ape* rather than two segmentable morphs (i.e., -*ap-e*) due to the fact an infinitive -*e* is unattested anywhere else in AOJ (except one purely orthographic example from Suruga, described in §7.5.2.1.1.2) or any other Japonic language variety. Also, the WOJ reflex -*apey* indicates the PJe form was *-apai, not *-ape. Vovin (2009a: 820) similarly views the WOJ reflex as a portmanteau morph.

There is also one example that may contain the iterative allomorph -*ap*- followed by the nominalizer -*i*, which is shown below:

342. 20:4382.3 – Simotukeno
 阿多由麻比
 ata yum-ap-i
 sudden be.ill-ITER-NML
 'A sudden illness.'

An alternate analysis is that this is the product of vowel raising (*-ape > -api), in which case a unique allomorph of the iterative-infinitive is involved.

The behavior of the iterative -*ap*- and the iterative-infinitive -*ape* likely shows that the iterative had two stems: a consonant-final stem -*ap*- and a vowel-final stem -*ape*. The stems may have been topolect-specific, or they may have been variants competing for dominance across the topolects. Unlike in WOJ, where the iterative form that precedes the perfective -*n*- is -*ap-i*- '-ITER-INF-' (Vovin 2009a: 937), the attested form in AOJ is -*ape*- '-ITER.INF-' (see example 345 below).

The form -*ape*, like the infinitive -*i* and the attributive suffixes, can also modify a following nominal. In addition, it can act as a nominalized form, like vowel-final verb stems with a phonologically null nominalizer -*i*. Lastly, there is a form -*öpe* attested twice (see examples 344 and 349), which shows vowel centralization in the first syllable. In these cases, the sound change is not assimilatory because -*öpe* does not follow a root with the vowel *ö*.

7.5.2.3.4.1.1 Linking function
The linking function is attested three times.

343. 14:3476a.3-5 – UNP
 多刀都久能 / **努賀奈敝**由家婆 / 故布思可流奈母
 tat-o tuku-nö / ***nongan*-*ape**-yuk-e-nba* / *kopusi-k[u]-ar-unam-ö*
 rise-ATTR moon-GEN / **flow-ITER.INF**-go-EV-CONJ / be.longing.for-AVINF-exist-TENT2-ATTR
 'Whenever the rising moon **sets**, [she] will long for [me]!'

344. 14:3476b.4-5 – UNP
 奴我奈敝由家杼 / 和奴賀**由乃敝**波
 nungan-ape-yuk-e-ndö / *wanu-nga **yun-öpe**-nba*
 flow-ITER.INF-go-EV-CONC / 1.S-POSS **sleep-ITER**-COND
 'Although [the moon] **sets day after day**, if I **continue to sleep** [with her]...'

345. 20:4432.1-2 – UNP
 佐弁奈弁奴 / 美許登尓阿礼婆
 sape-n-ape-n-u / *mi-kötö n-i ar-e-nba*
 obstruct-NEG-ITER.INF-PERF-FIN / HON-word COP-INF exist-EV-CONJ
 'Since [these] are commands [from the emperor], [I] **will not interfere with** [them].'

There is a syntactic inversion in example (345).

7.5.2.3.4.1.2 Adnominal function
The adnominal (or attributive) function is attested four times. This suffix may modify a noun or a conjunction.

346. 14:3483.1-2 – UNP
 比流等家波 / **等家奈敝**比毛乃
 piru tök-e-nba / ***töke-n-ape** pimo-nö*
 daytime undo-EV-CONJ / **come.undone-NEG-ITER.INF** string-GEN
 '[His] cords **that do not come undone** if [I try] to untie [them in] the daytime...'

347. 14:3529.3-5 – UNP
乎佐乎左毛 / 祢奈敝古由恵尓 / 波伴尓許呂波要
wosawosa mo / ***ne-n-ape*** *ko yuwe n-i* / *papa-ni kör-öp-aye*
enough FPT / **sleep-NEG-ITER.INF** girl reason COP-INF / mother-DAT scold-ITER-PASS.INF
'Due to **not sleeping with** a [certain] girl [often] enough, [I] was repeatedly scolded by [her] mother...'

348. 14:3555.5 – UNP
宿莫敝兒由恵尓
NE-N-Ape KO yuwe n-i
sleep-NEG-ITER.INF girl reason COP-INF
'Due to a girl [I] **am not sleeping with**...'

349. 14:3478.3-5 – UNP
阿抱思太毛 / 安波能敝思太毛 / 奈尓己曽与佐礼
ap-o sinda mo / ***ap-an-öpe*** *sinda mo* / *na-ni kösö yösar-e*
meet-ATTR CNJ FPT / **meet-NEG-ITER.INF** CNJ FPT / 2.S-DAT FPT be.attracted.to-EV
'When [we] meet, and even when [we] **are not meeting**, [I] am attracted to you.'

7.5.2.3.4.1.3 Nominalization function

This function is attested just once, though example (342) may include another attestation.

350. 14:3482b.4-5 – UNP
祢奈敝乃可良尓 / 許等多可利都母
ne-n-ape-*nö karani* / *kötö [i]ta-k[u]-ar-i-t-umö*
sleep-NEG-ITER.NML-GEN because.of / word be.painful-AVINF-exist-INF-PERF-EXCL
'Because of [our] **not sleeping** [together], the rumors have been painful!'

Table 7.36: Attestations of the iterative-infinitive suffix -*ape* ~ -*öpe* across the provinces.

	TSOJ			EOJ							UNP
Sin	Tö	Su	Kak	Mu	Sa	Mi	Sik	Pi	Sip	Kap	
0	0	0	0	0	0	0	0	0	0	0	9

7.5.2.3.5 Passive *-are-* ~ *-ar-* ~ *-aye-* ~ *-ye-* ~ *-y-*

The passive has two main allomorphs: *-are-* and *-aye-*. In other grammars of OJ (e.g., Vovin 2009a), these are treated as separate suffixes, but I view them as synchronic phonetic variants because there is no functional difference between them. The allomorph *-aye-* developed later through the sporadic lenition of *-r- > -y- (Vovin 2009a: 839); see §7.5.2.2.5.1 for another example of this in WOJ.

The allomorph *-are-* is also attested in the phonologically reduced form *-ar-* that only occurs when suffixed by the attributive *-uru*. The allomorph *-aye-* has two phonologically reduced forms: *-ye-* and *-y-*. Like many other AOJ suffixes that begin and end with a vowel, it can lose either vowel depending on the type of verb stem it follows and the suffix it precedes. Strong vowel-final verb stems, like *mi-* 'see', always contract the first vowel of the allomorph *-aye-*, while the attributive suffix *-uru* and the final suffix *-u* contract its final vowel. The passive can be followed by the infinitive *-i*, but in this case the infinitive becomes phonologically null and the passive becomes the portmanteau morph *-are* ~ *-aye* 'PASS.INF'. This is shown in examples (355) and (356) below.

The passive has three functions: passive, potential, and spontaneous action. I show examples of each in separate sections below.

7.5.2.3.5.1 Potential function

The potential function is only attested when the negative *-n-* ~ *-nz-* follows the passive.

351. 20:4322.4-5 – Töpotuapumi
 加其佐倍美曳弓 / 余尓和須良礼受
 *kangö sapey mi-ye-te / yö-ni **wasur-are-nz-u***
 shadow RPT see-PASS.INF-SUB / lifetime-LOC **forget-PASS-NEG-FIN**
 'So much as seeing [her] shadow, [makes me realize I] **cannot forget** [her] in this lifetime.'

352. 20:4407.4-5 – Kamitukeno
 伊毛賀古比之久 / 和須良延奴加母
 *imo-nga kopisi-ku / **wasur-aye-n-u** kamö*
 beloved.girl-POSS be.longing.for-AVINF / **forget-PASS-NEG-ATTR** EPT
 '[I] began to miss [my] beloved, and [I realized I] **cannot forget** [her]!'

353. 14:3506.4-5 – UNP
穂尓弓之伎美我 / **見延奴**已能許呂
PO-ni [i]nde-si kimi-nga / ***MI-ye-n-u*** *könö körö*
head.of.grain-LOC go.out.INF-PST.ATTR lord-POSS / **see-PASS-NEG-ATTR** this time
'[It was during] this time that [I] **was unable to see** my lord who opened up [to me].'

354. 14:3530.3-5 – UNP
見要受等母 / 兒呂我可奈門欲 / 由可久之要思母
MI-ye-nz-u *tömö* / *KO-rö-nga kana-TO-yo* / *yuk-aku si ye-si-mö*
see-PASS-NEG-FIN CNJ / girl-DIM-POSS metal-door-ABL / go.ATTR-NML EPT be.good-AVFIN-EXCL
'Even though [I] **cannot see** [her], going through the metal gate of [my] darling girl's [home] is so nice!'

7.5.2.3.5.2 Passive function

The passive function is attested twice. The oblique agent is marked by the dative *-ni*.

355. 14:3519.1-2 – UNP
奈我波伴尓 / **己良例**安波由久
na-nga papa-ni / ***kör-are*** *a pa yuk-u*
2.S-POSS mother-DAT / **scold-PASS.INF** 1.S TPT go-FIN
'[I] **was scolded** by your mother and [now] I will leave.'

356. 14:3529.5 – UNP
波伴尓**許呂波要**
*papa-ni **kör-öp-aye***
mother-DAT **scold-ITER-PASS.INF**
'[I] **was repeatedly scolded** by [her] mother…'

7.5.2.3.5.3 Spontaneous action function

The function of the passive indicating a spontaneous action is the most frequently attested in AOJ.

357. 14:3372.4-5 – Sagamu
兒良波可奈之久 / **於毛波流留**可毛
KO-ra pa kanasi-ku / ***omop-ar-uru*** *kamo*
girl-DIM TPT be.dear-AVINF / **think-PASS-ATTR** EPT
'[I] **suddenly think** of how dear [my] beloved girl is [to me]!'

358. 20:4322.3-5 – Töpotuapumi
乃牟美豆尔 / 加其佐倍**美曳弖** / 余尔和須良礼受
*nöm-u mindu-ni / kangö sapey **mi-ye-te** / yö-ni wasur-are-nz-u*
drink-ATTR water-LOC / shadow RPT **see-PASS.INF-SUB** / lifetime-LOC forget-PASS-NEG-FIN
'So much as **seeing** [her] shadow in the water that [I] drink, [**makes me realize** I] cannot forget her in this lifetime.'

359. 20:4357.3-5 – Kamitupusa
和藝毛古我 / 蕤弖母志保々尓 / 奈伎志曽**母波由**
*wa-ng[a]-imo-ko-nga / sonde mö sipopo n-i / nak-i-si sö [o]**möp-ay-u***
1.S-POSS-beloved.girl-DIM-POSS / sleeve FPT soaked COP-INF / cry-INF-PST.ATTR FPT **think-PASS-FIN**
'[I] **suddenly remember** how my darling cried [so much for me], even her sleeves were soaking wet!'

360. 14:3522.5 – UNP
麻登保久**於毛保由**
*ma-töpo-ku **omop-oy-u***
INT-be.far-AVINF **think-PASS-FIN**
'[I] **suddenly think** it is very far [away].'

In example (360) we find an allomorph *-oy(e)-* in this unknown topolect, due to assimilation to the vowel of the verb root. This is the only allomorph of the passive attested after the verb *omop-* 'think' in WOJ (Vovin 2009a: 829). Compare the EOJ forms in (357) and (359) that do not show an assimilated vowel allomorph after this verb. Clearly, WOJ is more innovative here.

361. 14:3471.3-5 – UNP
伊米能未尓 / 母登奈**見要都追** / 安乎祢思奈久流
*imey nömï n-i / mötöna **MI-ye-tutu** / a-wo ne si nak-uru*
dream RPT COP-INF / incessantly **see-PASS.INF-COOR** / 1.S-ACC voice EPT make.cry-ATTR
'[They] are just dreams, [but you] **appear** [in them] incessantly, and it makes me cry!'

362. 14:3473.4-5 – UNP
祢毛等可兒呂賀 / 於由尓美要都留
*ne-m-o tö ka KO-rö-nga / oyu n-i **mi-ye-t-uru***
sleep-TENT-ATTR QUOT QPT girl-DIM-POSS / grow.older.NML COP-INF **see-PASS.INF-PERF-ATTR**
'[I] **suddenly see** [my] dear girl has grown older, asking [me], 'Shall [we] sleep [together]?'.'

Table 7.37: Attestations of the passive suffix *-are-* ~ *-ar-* ~ *-aye-* ~ *-ye-* ~ *-y-* across the provinces.

Form	TSOJ			EOJ								UNP
	Sin	To	Su	Kak	Mu	Sa	Mi	Sik	Pi	Sip	Kap	
-are- ~ *-ar-*	0	1	0	0	0	1	0	0	0	0	0	1
-aye- ~ *-ye-* ~ *-y-*	0	0	0	1	0	0	0	0	0	0	3	7

The data in Table 7.37 show the allomorphs with *-y-* are more common than the phonologically conservative allomorphs that retain PJ *-r-*. There are two plausible hypotheses for this: either the allomorph *-aye-* developed in PJe through the sporadic intervocalic lenition of PJ *-(r)arai- > *-(r)ayai-*, or this lenition occurred in WOJ as *-are-* > *-aye-* (Vovin 2009a: 839) and was subsequently borrowed into EOJ. It is difficult to decide between these two, but the presence of *-(r)are-* and absence of *-(r)aye-* in TSOJ, MJ, Hachijō, PR, and possibly also NOJ (see Vovin 2021a: 167 and the discussion in Kupchik 2022) supports the hypothesis it is a WOJ loanword in EOJ.

7.5.2.3.6 Honorific *-as-* ~ *-s-* ~ *-os-*

The honorific is attached to verbs that are connected to agents that the speaker honors or reveres, such as a parent or a spouse. This suffix has three allomorphs: *-as-*, *-s-*, and *-os-*. The form *-as-* occurs after consonant-final stems, while the form *-s-* occurs after vowel-final stems. The form *-os-* only occurs after the verb *omop-* 'think' (see example 369 below), due to a progressive vowel assimilation that occurred in PJe.

363. 14:3402.4-5 – Kamitukeno
勢奈能我素伱母 / 佐夜尓布良思都
*se-na-nö-nga sonde mö / saya n-i **pur-as-i-t-u***
beloved.man-DIM-DIM-POSS sleeve FPT / clear COP-INF **wave-HON-INF-PERF-FIN**
'My dearly beloved clearly **waved** [his] sleeve [at me].'

364. 14:3426.4-5 – Mitinöku
斯努比尔勢毛等 / 比毛**牟須波佐祢**
sinop-i n-i se-m-o tö / pimo **musunb-as-an-e**
yearn.for-NML COP-INF do-TENT-ATTR QUOT / cord tie-HON-DES-IMP
'[I] **want [you] to tie [your] cords** and think [of me] when [you] do!'

365. 14:3369.3-5 – Sagamu
須我麻久良 / 安是加**麻可左武** / 許呂勢多麻久良
sunga-makura / anze ka **mak-as-am-u** / kö-rö se ta-makura
sedge-pillow / why QPT **pillow-HON-TENT-ATTR** / girl-DIM do.IMP hand-pillow
'Why **should [you] lay [your] head** [on] a sedge-pillow? Dear girl, use [my] arm as [your] pillow!'

366. 14:3388.4-5 – Pitati
伊伎豆久伎美乎 / 為祢弖**夜良佐祢**
ikinduk-u kimi-wo / wi-ne-te **yar-as-an-e**
sigh-ATTR lord-ACC / bring.INF-sleep.INF-SUB send-HON-DES-IMP
'**Please** bring [my] lord who sighs to sleep [with me], then **send** [him back].'

367. 14:3484.4 – UNP
阿須伎西**佐**米也
asu **ki-se-s-am-ey** ya
tomorrow **wear-CAUS-HON-TENT-EV** QPT
'Will [you] make [me] **wear** [it] tomorrow? (No, you won't)'

368. 14:3498.4-5 – UNP
伎美波**和須良酒** / 和礼和須流礼夜
kimi pa **wasur-as-u** / ware wasur-ure ya
lord TPT **forget-HON-FIN** / 1.S forget-EV QPT
'[You, my] lord, will **forget** [me]. Will I forget [you]? (No, I will not!)'

369. 14:3552.1-4 – UNP
麻都我宇良尔 / 佐和恵宇良太知 / 麻比登其等 / 於毛抱須奈母呂
matu-nga ura-ni / sawawe ura-n-dat-i / ma-pitö-n-götö / **omop-os-unam-ö** rö
pine-POSS bay-LOC / noisy tip-LOC-rise-NML / INT-people-GEN-word / **think-HON-TENT2-ATTR** COP
'[You] are **probably thinking** of the rumors people [spread that are like] noisy [waves] rising to the tips [of the tree branches] in the bay of pines.'

Table 7.38: Attestations of the honorific suffix -as- ~ -s- ~ -os- across the provinces.

TSOJ			EOJ								UNP
Sin	Tö	Su	Kak	Mu	Sa	Mi	Sik	Pi	Sip	Kap	
0	0	0	1	0	1	1	0	1	0	0	4

7.5.2.3.7 Causative -asime- ~ -asim- ~ -sime-

The causative -asime- is attested four times. It has three allomorphs: -asime-, -asim-, and -sime-. The underlying form -asime- occurs after consonant-final stems. The form -asim- only occurs once in the Sinano topolect of TSOJ, before the negative-imperative -una, while the form -sime- occurs after vowel-final stems.

The causative -asime- can be followed by the negative-imperative -una and the infinitive -i (which becomes phonologically null due to the morphophonological rules of the language).

370. 14:3399.3-4 – Sinano
 可里婆祢尓 / 安思**布麻之牟奈**
 karinba ne-ni / *asi **pum-asim-una***
 sakura root-LOC / foot **step-CAUS-NEG.IMP**
 'Do not **let** [your] feet **step** on the *sakura* roots.'

371. 14:3437.4-5 – Mitinŏku
 西良思馬伎那婆 / 都良波可馬可毛
 ser-asime-k-i-n-anba / *tura pak-am-e kamo*
 bend-CAUS.INF-come-INF-PERF-COND / string put.on-TENT-EV EPT
 '**When [the bow] becomes warped**, [I] wonder, should [I] put on a [new] string?'

372. 14:3409.5 – Kamitukeno
 伊射**祢志米**刀羅
 *inza **ne-simey** [i]to-ra*
 well **sleep-CAUS.INF** dear.one-DIM
 'Well, **let's** sleep [together], deary.'

373. 14:3518.5 – UNP
 伊射**祢之賣**刀良
 *inza **ne-sime** [i]to-ra*
 well **sleep-CAUS.INF** dear.one-DIM
 'Well, **let's** sleep [together], deary.'

Table 7.39: Attestations of the causative suffix *-asime-* ~ *-asim-* ~ *-sime-* across the provinces.

TSOJ			EOJ								UNP
Sin	Tö	Su	Kak	Mu	Sa	Mi	Sik	Pi	Sip	Kap	
1	0	0	1	0	0	1	0	0	0	0	1

7.5.2.3.8 Causative *-ase-* ~ *-as-* ~ *-se-*

The causative *-ase-* is more common than the causative *-asime-*, but there are still relatively few examples of it in the corpus. This suffix has three allomorphs: *-ase-* and *-as-* after consonant-final stems, and *-se-* after vowel-final stems. The allomorph *-as-* only occurs before the desiderative *-ana*.[182] The causative *-ase-* can also be followed by the tentative *-m-*, the honorific *-s-*, and the past-attributive *-si*.

374. 14:3434.5 – Kamitukeno
 安是加**多延世武**
 anze ka **taye-se-m-u**
 why QPT **break-CAUS-TENT-FIN**
 'Why would [you] **break** [us] apart?'

375. 14:3397.5 – Pitati
 阿杼可**多延世武**
 andö ka **taye-se-m-u**
 what QPT **break-CAUS-TENT-ATTR**
 'What **would make** [us] **break** [up]?'

376. 20:4366.3-5 – Pitati
 阿我古比乎 / 志留志弖都祁弖 / 伊母尔**志良世牟**
 a-nga kopi-wo / sirus-i-te tuke-te / imö-ni **sir-ase-m-u**
 1.S-POSS love.NML-ACC / record-INF-SUB attach.INF-SUB / beloved.girl-DAT **know-CAUS-TENT-FIN**
 'Writing [a note with] my love and [sending it] attached [to the goose] would **let** [my] beloved girl **know** [how I feel].'

---

[182] The form *-as-an(a)-* '-CAUS-DES-' is unattested in WOJ (Vovin 2009a: 863–864).

377. 20:4388.3-5 – Simotupusa
以弊乃母加 / **枳世之**己呂母尓 / 阿可都枳尓迦理
ipe-nö [i]mö-nga / **ki-se-si** *körömö-ni* / *aka tuk-i-n-i-kar-i*
house-GEN beloved.girl-POSS / **wear-CAUS-PST.ATTR** garment-LOC / dirt attach-INF-PERF-INF-RETR-FIN
'Dirt is stuck to the garment that [my] beloved at home **had [me] wear**.'

378. 14:3444.5 – UNP
西奈等**都麻佐祢**
se-na-tö **tum-as-an-e**
beloved.man-DIM-COM **pluck-CAUS-DES-IMP**
'Please **let [me] pluck** [them] with [my] dearly beloved!'

379. 14:3453.3-5 – UNP
吉西斯伎奴 / 多母登乃久太利 / 麻欲比伎尓家利
ki-se-si *kinu* / *tamötö-nö kundar-i* / *mayop-i-k-i-n-i-ker-i*
wear-CAUS-PST.ATTR robe / sleeve.edge-GEN descend-NML / fray-INF-come-INF-PERF-INF-RETR-FIN
'The edge of the sleeve of the robe [that my beloved] **had [me] wear** has become frayed.'

380. 14:3484.4 – UNP
阿須**伎西佐米**也
asu **ki-se-s-am-ey** *ya*
tomorrow **wear-CAUS-HON-TENT-EV** QPT
'Will [you] **make [me] wear** [it] tomorrow? (No, you will not)'

Table 7.40: Attestations of the causative suffix *-ase-* ~ *-as-* ~ *-se-* across the provinces.

	TSOJ			EOJ							UNP
Sin	Tö	Su	Kak	Mu	Sa	Mi	Sik	Pi	Sip	Kap	
0	0	0	0	0	0	0	0	2	1	0	4

7.5.2.3.9 Debitive *-unbe-*

The debitive suffix *-unbe-* indicates obligation or necessity. It is only attested twice: once in the Pitati topolect of EOJ and once in UNP. This may be due to the fact it was still in the process of being grammaticalized, as shown by its use as a free adverb in example (381) below:

381. 14:3476a.1-2 – UNP
   宇倍兒奈波 / 和奴尓故布奈毛
   unbey KO-na pa / wanu-ni kop-unam-o
   surely girl-DIM TPT / 1.S-DAT long.for-TENT2-ATTR
   '[That] dear girl will **surely** long for me.'

The debitive -*unbe*- differs morphologically from most other verbal suffixes, in that it has the paradigm of an adjectival verb. It is attested suffixed by the adjectival verb attributive -*ki* and the adjectival verb gerund -*mi*.

382. 20:4364.3-5 – Pitati
   伊敝能伊牟何 / 奈流敝伎己等乎 / 伊波須伎奴可母
   ipe-nö imu-nga / **nar-unbe-ki** kötö-wo / ip-anz-u k-i-n-u kamö
   house-GEN beloved.girl-POSS / **make.a.living-DEB-AVATTR** word-ACC / say-NEG-INF come-INF-PERF-ATTR EPT
   '[I] may have come [here] without telling my darling at home that she **must make a living**.'

383. 14:3468.4-5 – UNP
   刀奈布倍美許曽 / 奈尓与曽利鷄米
   tonap-unbey-mi kösö / na-ni yösör-i-kem-ey
   recite-DEB-AVGER FPT / 2.S-DAT have.feelings.for-INF-PST.TENT-EV
   'And just **because [I] had to recite** [the incantation], feelings for you welled up [inside me].'

Table 7.41: Attestations of the debitive suffix -*unbe*- across the provinces.

TSOJ			EOJ							UNP
Sin	Tö	Su	Kak	Mu	Sa	Mi	Sik	Pi	Sip	Kap	
0	0	0	0	0	0	0	0	1	0	0	1

7.5.2.3.10 Progressive -*ar*- ~ -*er*- ~ -*ir*-

The progressive aspect indicates an action is in the process of occurring. It also has a secondary function of acting as a perfective marker. There are three progressive markers in the AOJ corpus: -*ar*-, -*er*-, and -*ir*-. The progressive -*ar*- is only found in EOJ,[183] while the progressive -*er*- is the WOJ form. The progressive -*ir*- is only

---

183 This is retained in Hachijō, as -*ar*- (Kaneda 2001: 206).

attested in the Suruga topolect of TSOJ. These forms are the result of different morphophonological processes after the split from PJe. In EOJ *-ar-* was formed through a V_1 elision of the PJe sequence **-i ar-* '-INF exist-,' while WOJ *-er-* is the result of a fusion of **-i ar-* > *-er-*. The formation of Suruga's progressive *-ir-* is due to fusion of **-i ar-* > **-er*, followed by vowel raising to *-ir-*, as is common in the topolect. Attestations of *-er-* in EOJ poetry are either due to scribal alterations or borrowing from WOJ. In the case of UNP poems, it is possible some of these reflect genuine forms in the Sinano and Töpotuapumi topolects of TSOJ, which most likely had *-er-*, rather than *-ir-*.

The progressives *-ar-*, *-er-*, and *-ir-* are attested followed by the evidential *-e*, the infinitive *-i*, the attributive *-u ~ -o*, and the conditional gerund *-anba*.

7.5.2.3.10.1 EOJ progressive *-ar-*
Examples of the progressive *-ar-* follow below.

384. 20:4375.3-5 – Simotukeno
伊波比等乃 / 和例乎美於久流等 / 多々里之毛己呂
ipa-pitö-nö / ware-wo mi-okur-u tö / **tat-ar-i-si** mokörö
house-person-GEN / 1.S-ACC see.INF-send.off-FIN QUOT / **stand-PROG-INF-PST.ATTR** similarity
'[It is] similar to how how [my] family members **were standing**, intending to see me off.'

385. 14:3351.1-2 – Pitati
筑波祢尓 / 由伎可母**布良留**
tukupa ne-ni / yuki kamö **pur-ar-u**
TN peak-LOC / snow EPT **fall-PROG-ATTR**
'[I] wonder [if] snow **is falling** on Mt. Tukupa.'

386. 20:4387.1-3 – Simotupusa
知波乃奴乃 / 古乃弖加之波能 / **保々麻例等**
tipa-nö nu-nö / ko-nö te kasipa-nö / **popom-ar-e-ndö**
TN-GEN field-GEN / child-GEN hand oak-GEN / **be.unopened-PROG-EV-CONC**
'Although [the buds of] the oak trees in Tiba field, with leaves [like] a child's hand, **have not yet blossomed. . .**'

387. 20:4352.4-5 – Kamitupusa
可良麻流伎美乎 / 波可礼加由加牟
***karam-ar-u** kimi-wo* / *pakare ka yuk-am-u*
wrap.around-PROG-ATTR lord-ACC / be.separated.NML QPT go-TENT-ATTR
'Should [I] go away from [my] lord, whom [I] **am wrapped around**?'

388. 14:3469.1-2 – UNP
由布氣尔毛 / 許余比登**乃良路**
yupu key-ni mo / *köyöpi tö **nör-ar-o***
evening fortunetelling-LOC FPT / this.evening QUOT **tell-PROG-ATTR**
'At the evening fortunetelling [they] **told** [me] tonight [would be the night].'

Example (388) shows the perfective aspect function of this suffix.

389. 14:3546.1-3 – UNP
安乎楊木能 / **波良路**可波刀尓 / 奈乎麻都等
awo yaNGÏ-nö / ***par-ar-o** kapa to-ni* / *na-wo mat-u tö*
green willow-GEN / **stretch-PROG-ATTR** river door-LOC / 2.S-ACC wait-FIN QUOT
'At the estuary where the green willows **are stretching** [over], [I] say [to myself] '[I will] wait for you'.'

390. 14:3556.1-2 – UNP
思保夫祢能 / **於可礼婆**可奈之
sipo-n-bune-nö / ***ok-ar-e-nba** kanasi*
tide-GEN-boat-COMP / **leave-PROG-EV-COND** be.sad.AVFIN
'When [I] **am leaving** you like a tide boat, [I] am sad.'

391. 14:3572.3-5 – UNP
由豆流波乃 / **布敷麻留**等伎尔 / 可是布可受可母
yundurupa-nö / ***pupum-ar-u** töki-ni* / *kanze puk-anz-u kamö*
false.daphne-GEN / **be.unopened-PROG-ATTR** time-LOC / wind blow-NEG-FIN EPT
'[I] wonder, will the wind not blow when the [buds] of the false daphne **are [still] unopened**?'

392. 20:4431.3-5--- UNP
奈々弁加流 / 去呂毛尓麻世流 / 古侶賀波太波毛
*nana-pe **k-ar-u** / körömo-ni mas-er-u / ko-rö-nga panda pa mo*
seven-CL **wear-PROG-ATTR** / robe-LOC be.superior-PROG-ATTR / girl-DIM-POSS skin TPT EPT
'Oh, my darling girl's skin [would] be better than the robes [I] **am wearing** in seven layers...'

This poem contains both an *-ar-* and an *-er-* progressive.

7.5.2.3.10.2 WOJ/TSOJ progressive *-er-*
Examples of the progressive *-er-* follow below.

393. 14:3413.4-5 – Kamitukeno
奈美尓安布能須 / 安敝流伎美可母
*nami-ni ap-u-nösu / **ap-er-u** kimi kamö*
wave-DAT meet-ATTR-COMP / **meet-PROG-ATTR** lord EPT
'Oh, **meeting** [you, my] lord, [is] like encountering a wave!'

394. 20:4347.3-4 – Kamitupusa
奈我波氣流 / 多知尓奈里弖母
*na-nga **pak-eyr-u** / tati n-i nar-i-te mö*
2.S-POSS **wear-PROG-ATTR** / long.sword COP-INF become-INF-SUB FPT
'Becoming the long sword that you are **wearing**...'

395. 14:3463.4-5 – UNP
佐刀乃美奈可尓 / 安敝流世奈可毛
*sato-nö mi-naka-ni / **ap-er-u** se-na kamo*
village-GEN HON-inside-LOC / **meet-PROG-ATTR** beloved.man-DIM EPT
'Oh [my] darling beloved, whom [I] **am meeting** in the great center of the village.'

396. 14:3503.1-3 – UNP
安齊可我多 / 志保悲乃由多尓 / 於毛敝良婆
*anzeka-n-gata / sipo pï-nö yuta n-i / **omop-er-anba***
TN-GEN-tideland / tide ebb.NML-COMP leisure COP-INF / **think-PROG-COND**
'When [I] **am thinking** leisurely, like the ebb of the tide in the Azeka tideland...'

397. 14:3544.1-3 – UNP
阿須可河泊 / 之多**尔其礼留**乎 / 之良受思天
asuka-n-gapa / sita **ningör-er-u**-wo / sir-anz-u s-i-te
TN-GEN-river / below **be.muddy-PROG-ATTR**-ACC / know-NEG-INF do-INF-SUB
'The bottom of Asuka river **is muddy**, but [I] did not know [that].'

398. 20:4431.3-5 – UNP
奈々弁加流 / 去呂毛尓**麻世流** / 古侶賀波太波毛
nana-pe k-ar-u / körömo-ni **mas-er-u** / ko-rö-nga panda pa mo
seven-CL wear-PROG-ATTR / robe-LOC **be.superior-PROG-ATTR** / girl-DIM-POSS skin TPT EPT
'Oh, [my] darling girl's skin [would] **be better than** the robes [I] am wearing in seven layers...'

7.5.2.3.10.3 Suruga TSOJ progressive -ir-

The progressive -ir- is only attested once, in the Suruga topolect of TSOJ.

399. 20:4342.1-3 – Suruga
麻氣婆之良 / 寶米弖**豆久利留** / 等乃能其等
ma-key n-basira / pomey-te **tukur-ir-u** / tönö-nö ngötö
INT-tree COP.ATTR-pillar / bless.INF-SUB **make-PROG-ATTR** / mansion-GEN like
'Like the mansion with pillars of hearty timber that were blessed **during construction**...'

Table 7.42: Attestations of the progressive suffixes -ar-, -er-, and -ir- across the provinces.

Form	TSOJ			EOJ								UNP	TOTAL
	Sin	Tö	Su	Kak	Mu	Sa	Mi	Sik	Pi	Sip	Kap		
-ar-	0	0	0	0	0	0	0	1	1	1	2	9	14
-er-	0	0	0	1	0	0	0	0	0	0	1	6	8
-ir-	0	0	1	0	0	0	0	0	0	0	0	0	1

From the data in Table 7.42 we see that attestations of -ar- are nearly double that of -er-. While it may be tempting to attribute all of the -er- attestations to later scribal alterations, it is possible that the forms were in free variation (due to borrowing), or the -er- form was considered more prestigious or prescriptively ideal in EOJ due to its WOJ provenance.

7.6 Auxiliaries

There are many verbal auxiliaries. They can be segregated into two groups: bound and lexical.

7.6.1 Bound auxiliaries

The bound auxiliaries consist of two groups: word-final and word non-final.

7.6.1.1 Word-final bound auxiliaries
The word-final bound auxiliaries are those that can end a word form but cannot occur on their own in a sentence. They include the subordinative gerund -*te*, the coordinative gerund -*tutu* ~ -*tusi* ~ -*tötö*, the past tense -*kV*, the past-attributive -*si*, and the past-evidential -*sika*. Most of these do not allow the affixation of any further verbal morphology. The exceptions are the past-tense -*kV* the past-attributive -*si*.

7.6.1.1.1 Subordinative gerund -*te*
The gerund -*te* subordinates a verbal phrase. It follows the infinitive form of a verb. It does not allow any further suffixes, such as case markers, to follow it. Due to this, it can be considered a purely verbal gerund.

400. 20:4403.3-5 – Sinano
 阿乎久牟乃 / 等能妣久夜麻乎 / <u>古与弖</u>伎怒加牟
 awo kumu-nö / tönönbik-u yama-wo / **koyö-te** *k-i-n-o kamu*
 blue cloud-GEN / stream.out-ATTR mountain-ACC / **cross.INF-SUB** come-INF-PERF-ATTR EPT
 'Oh, [I] came [here], **having crossed over** the mountain where the blue clouds stream out...'

401. 14:3429.4-5 – Töpotuapumi
 安礼乎多能米弖 / 安佐麻之物能乎
 are-wo **tanömey-te** */ as-amasi mönöwo*
 1.S-ACC **make.trust.INF-SUB** / be.shallow-SUBJ CNJ
 '[You] **made** me **trust** [you], even though [your feelings for me] may be shallow.'

402. 20:4321.3-5 – Töpotuapumi
阿須由利也 / 加曳我牟多祢牟 / 伊牟**奈之尓志弖**
asu-yuri ya / kaye-nga muta ne-m-u / imu **na-si n-i s-i-te**
tomorrow-ABL QPT / reed-POSS together sleep-TENT-ATTR / beloved.girl not. exist-FIN COP-INF **do-INF-SUB**
'Will [I] sleep among the reeds from tomorrow, **without** [my] beloved girl?'

403. 20:4339.5 – Suruga
已**波比弖**麻多祢
ipap-i-te mat-an-e
pray-INF-SUB wait-DES-IMP
'Please **pray and** wait for [me]…'

404. 14:3411.1-3 – Kamitukeno
多胡能祢尓 / 与西都奈**波倍弖** / 与須礼騰毛
tango-nö ne-ni / yöse tuna ***papey-te*** / yös-ure-ndömo
TN-GEN peak-LOC / approach.INF rope **stretch.out.INF-SUB** / draw.near-EV-CONC
'Although [I] **would** pull him up the peak of Mt. Tago **by stretching out** a rope…'

405. 20:4404.1-2 – Kamitukeno
奈尓波治乎 / **由伎弖**久麻弖等
nanipa-ndi-wo / ***yuk-i-te*** k-u-mande tö
TN-road-ACC / **go-INF-SUB** come-ATTR-TERM QUOT
'Until [I] returned [from my] **journey** on Nanipa road…'

406. 20:4417.3-5 – Muzasi
刀里加尓弖 / 多麻能余許夜麻 / 加志由加也良牟
tor-i-kani-te / tama-nö yökö yama / kasi-yu ka yar-am-u
hold-INF-NEG.POT.INF-SUB / TN-GEN horizontal mountain / go.on.foot-ABL QPT send-TENT-ATTR
'[Now I] **cannot recapture** [his horse]…shall [I] send [my beloved to traverse] Tama's flat mountain on foot?'

407. 14:3363.1-2 – Sagamu
和我世古乎 / 夜麻登敝**夜利弖**
wa-nga se-ko-wo / yamatö-pe ***yar-i-te***
1.S-POSS beloved.man-DIM-ACC / TN-ALL **send-INF-SUB**
'[I] **sent** my darling beloved to Yamatö.'

408. 20:4330.1-2 – Sagamu
奈尔波都尔 / 余曾比**余曽比弖**
nanipa tu-ni / yösöp-i-**yösöp-i-te**
TN harbor-LOC / prepare-INF-**prepare-INF-SUB**
'**Preparing** [the boats] in Nanipa harbor. . .'

Example (408) demonstrates that when a verb form has been reduplicated for an iterative meaning, the subordinative gerund only attaches to the infinitive suffix at the end.

409. 14:3437.1-3 – Mitinöku
美知能久能 / 安太多良末由美 / **波自伎於伎弖**
mitinöku-nö / andatara ma-yumi / **panzik-i-ok-i-te**
TN-GEN / TN INT-bow / **take.off-INF-put-INF-SUB**
'[I] **take off** [the string from my] fine bow [from] Adatara in Mitinöku. . .'

410. 20:4376.3-5 – Simotukeno
阿母志志尔 / 己等**麻乎佐受弖** / 伊麻叙久夜之氣
amö sisi-ni / kötö **mawos-anz-u-te** / ima nzö kuyasi-key
mother father-DAT / word **say.HUM-NEG-INF-SUB** / now FPT be.regretful-AVATTR
'[I] **did not inform** [my] mother and father, and oh, now [I] regret it!'

411. 14:3388.4-5 – Pitati
伊伎豆久伎美乎 / **爲祢弖**夜良佐祢
ikinduk-u kimi-wo / **wi-ne-te** yar-as-an-e
sigh-ATTR lord-ACC / **bring.INF-sleep.INF-SUB** send-HON-DES-IMP
'Please **bring** [my] lord who sighs **to sleep** with [me], then send [him back].'

412. 20:4366.3-5 – Pitati
阿我古比乎 / **志留志弖都祁弖** / 伊母尓志良世牟
a-nga kopi-wo / **sirus-i-te tuke-te** / imö-ni sir-ase-m-u
1.S-POSS love.NML-ACC / **record-INF-SUB attach.INF-SUB** / beloved.girl-DAT know-CAUS-TENT-FIN
'**Writing** [a note with] my love and [sending it] **attached to** [the goose] would let [my] beloved girl know [how I feel].'

413. 20:4393.3-4 – Simotupusa
知々波々乎 / 以波比弊等<u>於枳弖</u>
titi papa-wo / *ipap-i pe-tö* **ok-i-te**
father mother-ACC / pray-INF pot-COM **leave.behind-INF-SUB**
'[I] **left** [my] father and mother with a praying pot. . .'

414. 14:3382.3-4 – Kamitupusa
都由思母能 / <u>奴礼弖</u>和伎奈婆
tuyu simö-nö / **nure-te** *wa k-i-n-anba*
dew frost-GEN / **get.wet.INF-SUB** 1.S come-INF-PERF-COND
'If I come [to you], **wet** [with] dew and frost. . .'

415. 20:4356.1-2 – Kamitupusa
和我波々能 / 蘓天<u>母知奈弖氏</u>
wa-nga papa-nö / *sonde* **möt-i-nande-te**
1.S-POSS mother-GEN / sleeve **hold-INF-caress.INF-SUB**
'[I] **held and caressed** my mother's sleeve.'

416. 14:3489.3-5 – UNP
之牙可久尓 / 伊毛呂乎<u>多弖天</u> / 左祢度波良布母
singe-k-aku-ni / *imo-rö-wo* **tate-te** / *sa-ne n-do parap-umö*
be.lush-AVATTR-NML-LOC / beloved.girl-DIM-ACC **make.stand.INF-SUB** / LOC-sleep.NML COP.ATTR-place clear.away-EXCL
'[I] **had** [my] beloved girl **stand** in the thicket, [as I] clear away a place for [us] to sleep!'

417. 14:3551.3-5 – UNP
比良湍尓母 / 比毛登久毛能可 / 加奈思家乎<u>於吉弖</u>
pira se-ni mö / *pimo tök-u monö ka* / *kanasi-ke-wo* **ok-i-te**
normal beloved.man-LOC FPT / cord untie-ATTR thing QPT / be.dear-AVATTR-ACC **leave.behind-INF-SUB**
'Will [I] untie cords with an ordinary lover? [I] **left** behind [a man] who is dear [to me].'

418. 14:3567.1-2 – UNP
<u>於伎弖</u>伊可婆 / 伊毛婆麻可奈之
ok-i-te *ik-anba* / *imo pa ma-kanasi*
leave.behind-INF-SUB go-COND / beloved.girl TPT INT-be.sad.AVFIN
'If [I] go **and leave [her] behind**, [my] beloved girl will be so sad.'

419. 20:4428.1-2 – UNP
和我世奈乎 / 都久志波<u>夜利弖</u>
wa-nga se-na-wo / tukusi-pa **yar-i-te**
1.S-POSS beloved.man-DIM-ACC / TN-ALL **send-INF-SUB**
'[I] sent my dearly beloved **to Tukusi**.'

Table 7.43: Attestations of the subordinative gerund -te across the provinces.

TSOJ			EOJ							UNP
Sin	Tö	Su	Kak	Mu	Sa	Mi	Sik	Pi	Sip	Kap
2	4	8	2	5	2	1	8	5	3	14	43

7.6.1.1.2 Coordinative gerund -tutu ~ -tusi ~ -tötö

The coordinative gerund -*tutu* indicates the meaning of 'while (doing something)'. There are two additional EOJ topolect variants attested: -*tusi* and -*tötö*. In WOJ and TSOJ we only find -*tutu*.

420. 20:4327 – Töpotuapumi
和我都麻母 / 畫尓可伎等良无 / 伊豆麻母加 / 多比由久阿礼波 / <u>美都都</u>志努波牟
wa-nga tuma mö / WE-ni kak-i-tör-am-u / ituma mönga / tanbi yuk-u are pa / **mi-tutu** sinop-am-u
1.S-POSS spouse FPT / picture-LOC draw-INF-take-TENT-ATTR / spare.time DPT / journey go-ATTR 1.S TPT / **see.INF-COOR** long.for-TENT-FIN
'[I] wish [I had] some free time to draw a picture of my wife. I [would take it with me] on my journey and long for [her] **while looking** [at it].'

421. 14:3416.3-4 – Kamitukeno
伊波為都良 / 比可波<u>奴礼都追</u>
ipawi tura / pik-anba **nure-tutu**
UNC vine / pull-COND **untangle.INF-COOR**
'If [one] pulls up the *ipawi* vines **while untangled**. . .'

422. 20:4367.3-5 – Pitati
都久波尼乎 / <u>布利佐氣美都々</u> / 伊母波之奴波尼
tukupa ne-wo / **purisakey-mi-tutu** / imö pa sinup-an-e
TN peak-ACC / **look.up.INF-see.INF-COOR** / beloved.girl TPT yearn.for-DES-IMP
'[I] want [my] beloved to yearn for [me], **while looking up** at the peaks of Tukupa.'

423. 20:4370.1-3 – Pitati
阿良例布理 / 可志麻乃可美乎 / **伊能利都々**
arare pur-i / *kasima-nö kami-wo* / **inör-i-tutu**
hail fall-INF / TN-GEN deity-ACC / **pray-INF-COOR**
'**While praying** to the deity of Kasima where the hail falls...'

424. 20:4347.1-2 – Kamitupusa
伊閇尓之弖 / **古非都々**安良受波
ipey n-i s-i-te / **kopï-tutu** *ar-anz-u pa*
house COP-INF do-INF-SUB / **long.for.INF-COOR** exist-NEG-NML TPT
'[I] am at home, and **while [I] am longing for** [you], [I] am not with [you].'

425. 14:3471.1-2 – UNP
思麻良久波 / **祢都追**母安良牟乎
simaraku pa / **ne-tutu** *mö ar-am-u-wo*
for.a.while TPT / **sleep.INF-COOR** FPT exist-TENT-ATTR-ACC
'Although [I] **will sleep** for a while...'

426. 14:3515.4-5 – UNP
祢尓多都久毛乎 / **見都追**思努波西
ne-ni tat-u kumo-wo / **MI-tutu** *sinop-as-e*
peak-LOC rise-ATTR cloud-ACC / **see.INF-COOR** long.for-HON-IMP
'Long for [me] **while watching** the clouds that rise over the peaks!'

427. 14:3520.3-5 – UNP
於抱野呂尓 / 多奈婢久君母乎 / **見都追**思努波牟
opo NO-rö-ni / *tananbik-u kumö-wo* / **MI-tutu** *sinop-am-u*
great plain-DIM-LOC / stream.out-ATTR cloud-ACC / **see.INF-COOR** long.for-TENT-FIN
'[I] shall long for [you] **while watching** the clouds that stream out over the great plains.'

428. 20:4426.1-3 – UNP
阿米都之乃 / 可未尓奴佐於伎 / **伊波比都々**
amey tusi-nö / *kamï-ni nusa ok-i* / **ipap-i-tutu**
heaven earth-GEN / deity-LOC paper.offering leave-INF / **pray-INF-COOR**
'Leave paper offerings to the deities of heaven and earth **and keep praying**...'

7.6.1.1.2.1 Variant -tusi

The variant -tusi is only attested in the Simotupusa topolect of EOJ.

429. 20:4386.3-5 – Simotupusa
以都母以都母 / 於毛加古比須々 / **奈理麻之都之**母
itu mö itu mö / *omo-nga kopi s-u s-u* / ***nar-i-mas-i-tusi*** *mö*
when FPT when FPT / mother-POSS love.NML do-FIN do-FIN / **make.a.living-INF-HON-INF-COOR** FPT
'[My] mother always loves [me], **even while working**.'

7.6.1.1.2.2 Variant -tötö

The variant -tötö is attested once in the Muzasi topolect of EOJ.

430. 20:4421.3-5 – Muzasi
安之我良乃 / 美祢波保久毛乎 / **美等登**志努波祢
asingara-nö / *mi-ne pap-o kumo-wo* / ***mi-tötö*** *sinop-an-e*
TN-GEN / HON-peak crawl-ATTR cloud-ACC / **see.INF-COOR** yearn.for-DES-IMP
'Please remember [me] **while [you] watch** the clouds that move slowly over the great peak of Mt. Asigara.'

Table 7.44: Attestations of the coordinative gerund -tutu and its variant forms across the provinces.

Form	TSOJ			EOJ								UNP
	Sin	Tö	Su	Kak	Mu	Sa	Mi	Sik	Pi	Sip	Kap	
-tutu	0	1	0	1	0	0	0	0	2	0	1	6
-tusi	0	0	0	0	0	0	0	0	0	1	0	0
-tötö	0	0	0	0	1	0	0	0	0	0	0	0

7.6.1.1.3 Past tense -kV

The past tense -kV is not used in many cases where a past tense would be required, so the category of tense in the language was either not fully developed or was eroding away. The cognate form in WOJ is -ki, but there is not a single example in AOJ that shows us the underlying vowel in this morpheme. Since EOJ shows *ke* in other cases that are *ki* in WOJ, both -ke and -ki are possible in those topolects, and *-ke is possible for PJe. For TSOJ, I consider -ki to be more likely due to the dialect's extensive raising of *e > /i/.

Although it is never actually attested word-final in AOJ, I include it among the other word-final bound auxiliaries because it is a suppletive allomorph of the past-attributive -si (which is attested word-final) and it is attested word-final in

WOJ (Vovin 2009a: 919). In this case the lack of such an attestation in AOJ is most likely due to the size of the AOJ corpus. As regards allomorphy, in TSOJ, as in WOJ, it fuses its underlying vowel with the vowel of a following suffix to create portmanteau forms such as -kem- 'PST.TENT', as shown in example (431). In EOJ, its underlying vowel elides before a following suffix (see example 433), which is unattested in WOJ. The presence of the form -kem- in the Kamitukeno topolect of EOJ (example 432) is probably due to borrowing from a neighboring TSOJ topolect or WOJ.[184]

431. 20:4323.3-5 – Töpotuapumi
奈尔須礼曽 / 波々登布波奈乃 / 佐吉泥己受祁牟
nani s-ure sö / papa tö [i]p-u pana-nö / **sak-i-nde-kö-nz-u-kem-u**
why do-EV FPT / mother QUOT say-ATTR flower-GEN / **bloom-INF-go.out.INF-come-NEG-INF-PST.TENT-ATTR**
'Why **has** the flower called 'mother' **not come out in bloom**?'

432. 14:3415.4-5 – Kamitukeno
賀久古非牟等夜 / 多祢物得米家武
ka-ku kopï-m-u tö ya / tane **mötömey-kem-u**
be.thus-AVINF long.for-TENT-FIN QUOT QPT / seed **search.for.INF-PST.TENT-ATTR**
'Do [you] think [I] would long for [it] so much that [I] **would have searched for [its] seeds**?'

433. 20:4421.1-2 – Muzasi
和我由伎乃 / 伊伎都久之可婆
*wa-nga yuk-i-nö / iki-n-***dukus-i-k-anba**
1.S-POSS go-NML-GEN / breath-GEN-**exhaust-INF-PST-COND**
'If [you] **have exhausted** [all your] breath due to my departure...'

434. 14:3468.4-5 – UNP
刀奈布倍美許曽 / 奈尔与曽利鷄米
tonap-unbey-mi kösö / na-ni **yösör-i-kem-ey**
recite-DEB-AVGER FPT / 2.S-DAT **have.feelings.for-INF-PST.TENT-EV**
'And just because [I] had to recite [the incantation], **feelings for you welled up** [inside me].'

---

184 If the PJe form were *-ke and EOJ retained it as -ke, then this could be analyzed as -ke-m- (i.e., V₂ elision) rather than a fusional reduction of *ia > /e/ which otherwise does not occur in EOJ. If so, then it would not be borrowed from TSOJ or WOJ.

Table 7.45: Attestations of the past tense -kV across the provinces.

TSOJ			EOJ								UNP
Sin	Tö	Su	Kak	Mu	Sa	Mi	Sik	Pi	Sip	Kap	
0	2	0	1	1	0	0	0	0	0	0	1

7.6.1.1.4 Past-attributive -si

The past-attributive -si is suppletive with the past tense -kV because among the two only -si may function as a past-attributive (Vovin 2009a: 919). There is one other important distinction between the two in AOJ: while -kV allows the addition of verbal morphology (such as the tentative -am-), -si only allows case suffixes,[185] since attributives can function as nominal forms.

435. 20:4346.4-5 – Suruga
伊比之氣等婆是 / 和須礼加祢豆流
ip-i-si *keytönba nze* / *wasure-kane-t-uru*
say-INF-PST.ATTR word FPT / forget.INF-NEG.POT.INF-PERF-ATTR
'[I] have not been able to forget the words [they] **said**.'

436. 14:3417.4-5 – Kamitukeno
与曽尓見之欲波 / 伊麻許曽麻左礼
*yösö-ni **MI-si**-yo pa* / *ima kösö mas-ar-e*
elsewhere-LOC **see.INF-PST.ATTR**-ABL TPT / now FPT be.superior-PROG-EV
'Now [things] are better than [when I] **was looking** elsewhere.'

437. 20:4404.3-5 – Kamitukeno
和藝毛古賀 / 都氣之非毛我乎 / 多延尓氣流可毛
wa-ng-imo-ko-nga / ***tukey-si*** *pïmo-nga wo* / *taye-n-i-keyr-u kamo*
1.S-POSS-beloved.girl-DIM-POSS / **affix.INF-PST.ATTR** cords-POSS string / break.INF-PERF-INF-RETR-ATTR EPT
'Oh, the cord that my beloved girl **tied** [over my robes] has come undone!'

---

[185] In WOJ, however, the conditional gerund -anba may attach to the past-attributive -si, which creates the form -senba. The nominalizer -aku also suffixes to -si, producing the form -si-ku.

438. 14:3375.4-5 – Muzasi
伊尔之与比欲利 / 世呂尔安波奈布与
in-i-si *yöpi-yori* / *se-rö-ni ap-an-ap-u yö*
depart-INF-PST.ATTR evening-ABL / beloved.man-DIM-DAT meet-NEG-ITER-FIN EPT
'Since the evening [he] **departed**, [I] have not met [my] beloved!'

439. 20:4375.3-5 – Simotukeno
伊波比等乃 / 和例乎美於久流等 / **多々里之**毛己呂
ipa-pitö-nö / *ware-wo mi-okur-u tö* / ***tat-ar-i-si*** *mokörö*
house-person-GEN / 1.S-ACC see.INF-send.off-FIN QUOT / **stand-PROG-INF-PST.ATTR** similarity
'[It is] similar to how my family members **were standing**, intending to see me off.'

440. 20:4370.4-5 – Pitati
須米良美久佐尔 / 和礼波**伎尔之**乎
sumeyra mi-[i]kusa-ni / *ware pa* ***k-i-n-i-si***-*wo*
emperor HON-army-LOC / 1.S TPT **come-INF-PERF-INF-PST.ATTR**-ACC
'Since I **came** into the Emperor's great army...'

441. 20:4388.3-5 – Simotupusa
以弊乃母加 / **枳世之**己呂母尔 / 阿可都枳尔迦理
ipe-nö [i]mö-nga / ***ki-se-si*** *körömö-ni* / *aka tuk-i-n-i-kar-i*
house-GEN beloved.girl-POSS / **wear-CAUS-PST.ATTR** garment-LOC / dirt attach-INF-PERF-INF-RETR-FIN
'Dirt is stuck to the garment that [my] beloved at home **had [me] wear**.'

442. 20:4358.3-5 – Kamitupusa
伊弖久礼婆 / 和努等里都伎弖 / **伊比之**古奈波毛
inde-k-ure-nba / *wano tör-i-tuk-i-te* / ***ip-i-si*** *ko-na pa mo*
go.out.INF-come-EV-CONJ / 1.S take-INF-attach-INF-SUB / **say-INF-PST.ATTR** girl-DIM TPT EPT
'Since [I] left [home] and came [here], oh, [what about] the dear girl who clung to me and **said** [all those things]?'

443. 14:3487.4-5 – UNP
宿莫奈**那里尔思** / 於久乎可奴加奴
*NE-NA-na **nar-i-n-i-si*** / *oku-wo kan-u kan-u*
sleep-NEG.ATTR-LOC **be-INF-PERF-INF-PST.ATTR** / future-ACC worry.about-FIN worry.about-FIN
'[I] worry about [our] future again and again, [because] **it turned out that** [we] did not sleep [together].'

444. 14:3506.4-5 – UNP
穗尔弖之伎美我 / 見延奴己能許呂
***PO-ni [i]nde-si** kimi-nga* / *MI-ye-n-u könö körö*
head.of.grain-LOC go.out.INF-PST.ATTR lord-POSS / see-PASS-NEG-ATTR this time
'[It was during] this time that [I] was unable to see my lord who **opened up** [to me].'

445. 20:4436.3-5 – UNP
由久和礼乎 / 伊都伎麻佐牟等 / **登比之**古良波母
yuk-u ware-wo / *itu k-i-mas-am-u tö* / ***töp-i-si** ko-ra pa mö*
go-ATTR 1.S-ACC / when come-INF-HON-TENT-FIN QUOT / **ask-INF-PST.ATTR** girl-DIM TPT EPT
'Oh, [my] darling girl, who **asked** me [as I] left, 'When will [you] come [back]?'.'

Table 7.46: Attestations of the past-attributive *-si* across the provinces.

TSOJ			EOJ								UNP
Sin	Tö	Su	Kak	Mu	Sa	Mi	Sik	Pi	Sip	Kap	
0	0	2	4	1	0	0	1	1	4	4	14

7.6.1.1.5 Past-evidential *-sika*

The past-evidential form *-sika* is another suppletive allomorph of the past tense *-kV*. At first glance it seems to contain the past-attributive *-si*. Thus, one might conclude there should be a morpheme boundary between *-si* and *-ka*, especially considering *-ka* (PJe *-kia) is an adjectival verb evidential suffix in EOJ. However, upon careful consideration of both internal evidence and comparative evidence from WOJ, it soon becomes apparent that this idea does not stand up to scrutiny. First, this suffix also exists in WOJ, as *-sika*, and furthermore it is far more common in WOJ than in AOJ. However, there is no adjectival verb evidential suffix *-ka* attested in WOJ (rather, in that dialect the adjectival verb evidential is *-ke* or *-kere*). Second, the past tense auxiliary -*si* cannot be followed by any morphological marker exclusive to the adjectival verb paradigm. With these two points in mind, it is best not to draw a boundary inside this morpheme.[186] Instead, it is preferable to conclude that it is synchronically a portmanteau morph (Vovin 2009a: 919–922). There are only three attestations of this morpheme in the corpus, all in UNP poems.

446. 14:3522.1-2 – UNP
 伎曽許曽波 / 兒呂等**左宿之香**
 *kisö kösö pa / KO-rö-tö **sa-NE-sika***
 last.night FPT TPT / girl-DIM-COM **LOC-sleep.INF-PST.EV**
 'Last night [I] **slept together** with [my] darling girl.'

447. 14:3531.1-2 – UNP
 伊母乎許曽 / 安比美尓**許思可**
 *imö-wo kösö / ap-i-mi-ni **kö-sika***
 beloved.girl-ACC FPT / meet-INF-see.NML-LOC **come-PST.EV**
 '[I] **came** to see [my] beloved girl.'

448. 14:3497.5 – UNP
 己登尓弖尓思可
 kötö-ni [i]nde-n-i-sika
 word-LOC go.out.INF-PREF-INF-PST.EV
 '[People] **have been talking** [about us].'

Table 7.47: Attestations of the past-evidential -*sika* across the provinces.

TSOJ			EOJ							UNP
Sin	Tö	Su	Kak	Mu	Sa	Mi	Sik	Pi	Sip	Kap	
0	0	0	0	0	0	0	0	0	0	0	3

7.6.1.2 Word non-final auxiliaries

The word non-final auxiliaries include the perfectives -*n*- and -*te*- ~ -*t*-, the perfective-progressive -*tar*-, the retrospective -*ker*- ~ -*kar*-, the potential -*kate*- ~ -*kande*-, the negative-potential -*kane*-, and the benefactive -*kös*-.

---

186 Some morphologists may still prefer to analyze -*sika* 'PST.EV' as two segments due to a clearly segmentable past tense morpheme -*si*. Thus -*si-ka* '-PST-EV', with the -*ka* being a morphologically conditioned allomorph of the verbal evidential unrelated to the adjectival verb evidential -*ka*.

7.6.1.2.1 Perfectives -*n*- and -*te*- ~ -*t*-

The perfective auxiliaries -*n*- and -*te*- ~ -*t*- indicate the perfective aspect. More specifically, an action that is complete, or will be complete in the future. The perfective -*te*- ~ -*t*- is in lexical complementary distribution with the allomorph -*n*-. In other words, -*te*- ~ -*t*- only occurs with a certain set of verbs, and -*n*- only occurs with another set of verbs. There is good evidence to believe that the distinction between these two perfective markers was originally a matter of animacy in PJe, where -*n*- occurred with inanimate subjects, and -*te*- ~ -*t*- with animate subjects (see Vovin 2003: 305 for a thorough overview of the subject), however in AOJ we do not find such a distinction still firmly in place – both are attested with animate and inanimate subjects. This is an important difference in comparison to WOJ, where -*te*- ~ -*t*- is never found with an inanimate subject, as noted by Vovin (2009a: 960). In addition, while both perfectives can attach to transitive and intransitive verbs, the perfective -*n*- mainly occurs with intransitive verbs.

A final point worth mentioning is these two perfective markers have different combinatorial characteristics in WOJ, notably only the perfective -*te*- can combine with imperatives and causatives (Vovin 2009a: 950). However, in AOJ, the perfective -*te*- is not attested in combination with an imperative or causative.

7.6.1.2.1.1 Perfective -*n*-

The perfective -*n*- is attested occurring after the infinitive form of the following verbs: *sungï*- 'pass by', *kö*- 'come', *ir*- 'enter', *tangap*- 'differ', *taye*- 'break', *wakare*- 'separate', *nar*- 'be', *nar*- 'become', *ok*- 'leave behind', *köng*- 'row', *tuk*- 'attach', *tanbar*- 'receive.HUM', *tat*- 'rise', *ake*- 'brighten', *ap*- 'meet', *kos*- 'cross', *sape*- 'obstruct', and *inde*- 'go out'.

In both TSOJ and EOJ the attributive allomorph that follows the perfective -*n*- is always -*u* ~ -*o*, rather than -*uru*. This is a major difference compared to WOJ, where the attributive is always -*uru* after the perfective -*n*- (Vovin 2009a: 936). This supports the idea that the WOJ form -*n-uru* '-PERF-ATTR' is innovative (Vovin 2021a: 178). Other than the attributive, the perfective -*n*- is attested followed by the subjunctive -*amasi*, the conditional gerund -*anba*, the final -*u*, and the infinitive -*i*.

449. 14:3352.5 – Sinano
登伎須疑尓家里
töki **sungï-n-i-ker-i**
time **pass.INF-PERF-INF-RETR-FIN**
'[I realize] time **has passed by**.'

450. 20:4403.3-5 – Sinano
阿乎久牟乃 /等能妣久夜麻乎 / 古与弓伎怒加牟
*awo kumu-nö / tönönbik-u yama-wo / koyö-te **k-i-n-o** kamu*
blue cloud-GEN / stream.out-ATTR mountain-ACC / cross.INF-SUB **come-INF-PERF-ATTR** EPT
'Oh, [I] **came** [here], having crossed over the mountain where the blue clouds stream out. . .'

451. 14:3354.4-5 – Töpotuapumi
伊利奈麻之母乃 / 伊毛我乎杼許尓
ir-i-n-amasi *mönö / imo-nga won-dökö-ni*
enter-INF-PERF-SUBJ CNJ / beloved.girl-POSS DIM-bed-LOC
'Although [I] **would like to [lay] in** the warm bed of [my] beloved. . .'

Example (451) shows a syntactic inversion.

452. 14:3359a.4-5 – Suruga
伊麻思乎多能美 / 波播尓多我比奴
*imasi-wo tanöm-i / papa-ni **tangap-i-n-u***
2.S-ACC trust-INF / mother-DAT **defy-INF-PERF-FIN**
'[I] **defied** [my] mother and put [my] trust in you.'

453. 20:4337.3-4 – Suruga
知々波々尓 / 毛能波須價尓弓
*titi papa-ni / monö [i]p-anz-u **k-e-n-i-te***
father mother-DAT / things say-NEG-INF **come-INF-PERF-INF-SUB**
'[I] **have come** [out here] without saying a word to [my] father or mother.'

454. 14:3434.4-5 – Kamitukeno
波比尓思物能乎 / 安是加多延世武
pap-i-n-i-si *mönöwo / anze ka taye-se-m-u*
crawl-INF-PERF-INF-PST.ATTR CNJ / why QPT break-CAUS-TENT-ATTR
'Considering [the vines] **have crawled** [across the field], why would [you] break [us] apart?'

455. 20:4404.3-5 – Kamitukeno
和藝毛古賀 / 都氣之非毛我乎 / **多延尓氣流**可毛
*wa-ng-imo-ko-nga / tukey-si pïmo-nga wo / **taye-n-i-keyr-u** kamo*
1.S-POSS-beloved.girl-DIM-POSS / affix.INF-PST.ATTR string-POSS cord / **break.INF-PERF-INF-RETR-ATTR** EPT
'Oh, the cord that my darling girl tied [over my robes] **has come undone**!'

456. 14:3374.4-5 – Muzasi
乃良奴伎美我名 / 宇良尓**伱尓家里**
*nör-an-u kimi-nga NA / ura-ni [i]**nde-n-i-ker-i***
tell-NEG-ATTR lord-POSS name / divination-LOC **emerge.INF-PERF-INF-RETR-FIN**
'[My] lord's name that [I] did not tell [them] **emerged** from the divination.'

457. 14:3437.4-5 – Mitinöku
西良思馬伎那婆 / 都良波可馬可毛
***ser-asime-k-i-n-anba** / tura pak-am-e kamo*
bend-CAUS.INF-come-INF-PERF-COND / string put.on-TENT-EV EPT
'**When [the bow] becomes warped**, [I] wonder, should [I] put on a [new] string?'

458. 14:3425.1-4 – Simotukeno
志母都家努 / 安素乃河泊良欲 / 伊之布麻努受 / 蘓良由登**伎努**与
*simötukeno / aso-nö kapara-yo / isi pum-anz-u / sora-yu tö **k-i-n-o** yö*
TN / TN-GEN river.bank-ABL / stone step-NEG-INF / sky-ABL FPT **come-INF-PERF-ATTR** EPT
'[I] **came** from the sky without stepping [on] the stones from the riverbank of Aso in Simotukeno!'

459. 20:4379.1-3 – Simotukeno
之良奈美乃 / 与曽流波麻倍尓 / **和可例奈婆**
*sira nami-nö / yösör-u pama-pey-ni / **wakare-n-anba***
white wave-GEN / draw.near-ATTR shore-side-LOC / **separate.INF-PERF-COND**
'**If [I] part** [with you] at the side of the shore where the white waves draw near...'

460. 14:3395.3-4 – Pitati
安比太欲波 / 佐波太**奈利怒**乎
*apinda yo pa / sapanda **nar-i-n-o-wo***
interval night TPT / many **be-INF-PERF-ATTR-ACC**
'Since **there have been** many nights in between [our meetings]...'

461. 20:4365.4-5 – Pitati
阿例波**許藝奴**等 / 伊母尓都岐許曽
*are pa **köng-i-n-u** tö / imö-ni tung-i-kös-ö*
1.S TPT **row-INF-PERF-FIN** QUOT / beloved.girl-LOC tell.INF-BEN-IMP
'Please tell [my] darling that I **am rowing out**!'

462. 20:4384.4-5 – Simotupusa
己枳尓之布祢乃 / 他都枳之良酒毛
***köng-i-n-i-si** pune-nö / tatuki sir-anz-umo*
row-INF-PERF-INF-PST.ATTR boat-GEN / clue know-NEG-EXCL
'[I] do not have a clue about the boat that **has rowed** [out]!'

463. 20:4388 – Simotupusa
多飛等弊等 / 麻多妣尓**奈理奴** / 以弊乃母加 / 枳世之己呂母尓 / 阿可**都枳尓迦理**
*tanbï tö [i]p-e-ndö / ma-tanbi n-i **nar-i-n-u** / ipe-nö [i]mö-nga / ki-se-si körömö-ni / aka **tuk-i-n-i-kar-i***
journey QUOT say-EV-CONC / INT-journey COP-INF **become-INF-PERF-FIN** / house-GEN beloved.girl-POSS / wear-CAUS-PST.ATTR garment-LOC / dirt **attach-INF-PERF-INF-RETR-FIN**
'Although [it] was said to be [just] 'a journey', this **has become** such a [trying] journey. Dirt **is stuck** to the garment that [my] beloved at home had [me] wear.'

464. 20:4393.3-5 – Simotupusa
知々波々乎 / 以波比弊等於枳弖 / **麻為弓枳尓之乎**
*titi papa-wo / ipap-i pe-tö ok-i-te / **mawi-nde-k-i-n-i-si-wo***
father mother-ACC / pray-INF pot-COM leave.behind-INF-SUB / **come.HUM.INF-go.out.INF-come-INF-PERF-INF-PST.ATTR-ACC**
'[I] left [my] father and mother with a praying pot and **came out** [here]…'

465. 14:3382.3-4 – Kamitupusa
都由思母能 / 奴礼弖和**伎奈婆**
*tuyu simö-nö / nure-te wa **k-i-n-anba***
dew frost-GEN / get.wet.INF-SUB 1.S come-INF-PERF-COND
'If I **come** [to you], wet [with] dew and frost…'

466. 20:4349.1-3 – Kamitupusa
毛母久麻能 / 美知波**紀尔志乎** / 麻多佐良尔
momö kuma-nö / miti pa **k-i-n-i-si**-wo / mata sara n-i
hundred bend.in.a.road-GEN / road TPT **come-INF-PERF-INF-PST.ATTR**-ACC / still more COP-INF
'Though [I] **have come** [this far on] roads with a hundred bends, still there is more [to go].'

467. 14:3447.4-5 – UNP
阿努波由加受弓 / 阿良久佐**太知奴**
ano pa yuk-anz-u-te / ara kusa-**n-dat-i-n-u**
TN TPT go-NEG-INF-SUB / wild grass-**GEN-rise-INF-PERF-FIN**
'Wild grass **has sprung** up, [because] no [one] goes [to] Ano.'

468. 14:3461.5 – UNP
安家努思太久流
ake-n-o sinda k-uru
brighten.INF-PERF-ATTR CNJ come-ATTR
'[You only] came when **it dawned**.'

469. 20:4432.1-2 – UNP
佐弁奈弁奴 / 美許登尔阿礼婆
sape-n-ape-n-u / mi-kötö n-i ar-e-nba
obstruct-NEG-ITER.INF-PERF-FIN / HON-word COP-INF exist-EV-CONJ
'Since [these] are commands [from the emperor], [I] **will not interfere with** [them].'

7.6.1.2.1.2 Perfective -te- ~ -t-

The perfective -te- ~ -t- is attested after the infinitive form of the following verbs: pum- 'step', sandamey- 'decide', mi- 'see', ne- 'sleep', katamey- 'strengthen', and ar- 'exist'. It may also follow the negative-potential -kane-, as shown in example (471) below. Like many other vowel-final verbal morphemes, the perfective -te- loses its vowel when it precedes strong vowel-initial suffixes, creating the shortened allomorph -t-.

Unlike the perfective -n-, the attributive allomorph that attaches to the perfective -te- ~ -t- is -uru. An orthographic form -tö- is also attested once in the Simotupusa topolect of EOJ, which is shown in example (475) below. Other than the attributive, the perfective -te- ~ -t- is attested followed by the conditional gerund -nba, the final -u, the evidential -ure, the exclamative -umo, the tentative -m-, and the past-attributive -si.

470. 14:3400.1-4 – Sinano

信濃奈留 / 知具麻能河泊能 / 左射礼思母 / 伎弥之**布美弓波**

sinanu-n[i] ar-u / *tinguma-nö kapa-nö* / *sanzare [i]si mö* / *kimi si* **pum-i-te-nba**

TN-LOC exist-ATTR / TN-GEN river-GEN / little stone FPT / lord EPT **step-INF-PERF-COND**

'When [you, my] lord **have stepped** on the small stones in Tiguma river in Sinano. . .'

471. 20:4346.4-5 – Suruga

伊比之氣等婆是 / **和須礼加祢豆流**

ip-i-si keytönba nze / **wasure-kane-t-uru**

say-INF-PST.ATTR word FPT / **forget.INF-NEG.POT.INF-PERF-ATTR**

'[I] **have not been able to forget** the words [they] said.'

472. 14:3418.3-4 – Kamitukeno

武良奈倍尓 / 許登波**佐太米都**

mura-napey-ni / *kötö pa* **sandamey-t-u**

divination-seedling-LOC / matter TPT **decide.INF-PERF-FIN**

'[They] **have decided** the matter [of who I will marry based] on the divination seedlings.'

473. 20:4415.4-5 – Muzasi

伊弊奈流伊母乎 / 麻多**美弓毛**母也

ipe-n[i] ar-u imö-wo / *mata* **mi-te-m-o** *mö ya*

house-LOC exist-ATTR beloved.girl-ACC / again **see.INF-PERF-TENT-ATTR** EPT EPT

'How [I] **would like to see** [my] darling, who is at home, again!'

474. 14:3395.5 – Pitati

萬多**祢天武**可聞

mata **ne-te-m-u** *kamo*

again **sleep.INF-PERF-TENT-ATTR** EPT

'[I] wonder if [I] **shall sleep** [with her] again.'

475. 20:4390.3-5 – Simotupusa

加多米等之 / 以毛加去々里波 / 阿用久奈米加母

katamey-tö-si / *imo-nga kökörö pa* / *ayok-unam-ey kamö*

strengthen.INF-PERF.INF-PST.ATTR / beloved.girl-POSS heart TPT / waver-TENT2-EV EPT

'[I] wonder, will the **strengthened** feelings of [my] beloved girl waver?'

In example (475) the perfective form is difficult to explain from a phonological perspective, but I offer a discussion of some possibilities in §2.3.6.1.1. In addition, it must contain a phonologically null infinitive since the past-attributive -*si* that follows it only attaches to infinitive forms.

476. 14:3473.4-5 – UNP
祢毛等可兒呂賀 / 於由尓美要都留
*ne-m-o tö ka KO-rö-nga / oyu n-i **mi-ye-t-uru***
sleep-TENT-ATTR QUOT QPT girl-DIM-POSS / grow.older.NML COP-INF **see-PASS.INF-PERF-ATTR**
'[I] **suddenly see** [my] dear girl has grown older, asking [me], 'Shall [we] sleep [together]?'.'

477. 14:3482b.4-5 – UNP
祢奈敝乃可良尓 / 許等多可利都母
ne-n-ape-nö karani / kötö [i]ta-k[u]-ar-i-t-umö
sleep-NEG-ITER.NML-GEN because.of / word **be.painful-AVINF-exist-INF-PERF-EXCL**
'Because of [our] not sleeping [together], the rumors **have been painful**!'

Example (477) shows the perfective -*te*- used with an inanimate subject.

478. 14:3556.3-4 – UNP
左宿都礼婆 / 比登其等思氣志
*sa-**NE-t-ure-nba** / pitö-n-götö singey-si*
LOC-sleep-PERF-EV-CONJ / people-GEN-word be.lush-AVFIN
'**Because [I] had slept** there with [you], people really talked about it.'

Table 7.48: Attestations of the perfective morphemes across the provinces.

Form	TSOJ			EOJ								UNP
	Sin	Tö	Su	Kak	Mu	Sa	Mi	Sik	Pi	Sip	Kap	
-n-	5	1	3	2	1	0	1	2	5	6	2	22
-te- ~ -t-	1	0	1	4	1	0	0	0	2	1	0	5

7.6.1.2.2 Perfective/Progressive -*tar*-

The perfective/progressive -*tar*- is only attested three times. Rather than having a meaning of both perfective and progressive simultaneously, it indicates either perfective or progressive, depending on the context (Vovin 2009a: 964). Historically, this form is the result of a concatenation of the subordinative gerund *-te and the auxiliary *-ar- 'exist' (Vovin 2009a: 963). Examples (479) and (481) show the perfective function, while example (480) shows the progressive function.

479. 20:4326.5 – Töpotuapumi
和我**伎多流**麻弖
wa-nga **k-i-tar-u**-mande
1.S-POSS **come-INF-PP-ATTR**-TERM
'Until I **return** [to them]...'

480. 20:4375.1-2 – Simotukeno
麻都能氣乃 / **奈美多流**美礼波
matu-nö key-nö / **nam-i-tar-u** mi-re-nba
pine-GEN tree-GEN / **be.lined.up-INF-PP-ATTR** see-EV-CONJ
'When [I] look at the pine trees **lined up**...'

481. 14:3507.1-3 – UNP
多尓世婆美 / 弥年尓**波比多流** / 多麻可豆良
tani senba-mi / mi-ne-ni **pap-i-tar-u** / tama kandura
valley be.narrow-AVGER / HON-peak-LOC **crawl-INF-PP-ATTR** / jade vine
'[It is like] the jade[-like] vines **that crawl** up the peak because the valley is narrow...'

Table 7.49: Attestations of the perfective/progressive -tar- across the provinces.

TSOJ			EOJ							UNP
Sin	Tö	Su	Kak	Mu	Sa	Mi	Sik	Pi	Sip	Kap	
0	1	0	0	0	0	0	1	0	0	0	1

7.6.1.2.3 Retrospective -ker- ~ -kar-

In WOJ, the retrospective -ker- indicates neither tense nor aspect, rather it refers to an event experienced either directly or indirectly, and it may refer to the past, present, or future; it is also used to indicate a sudden realization of a fact (Vovin 2009a: 978). In AOJ, it is attested referencing the past or present, with the same semantics. The EOJ form -kar- is attested just once. The form -ker- is attested in both TSOJ and EOJ. This is the expected reflex of PJe *-ki-ar- in TSOJ, but not in EOJ. The attestations of -ker- in EOJ are therefore either due to dialect borrowing (from TSOJ or WOJ) or later scribal alterations in the text.

482. 14:3352.5 – Sinano
登伎須疑尓家里
töki **sungï-n-i-ker-i**
time **pass.INF-PERF-INF-RETR-FIN**
'[I realize] time **has passed by**.'

483. 20:4404.3-5 – Kamitukeno
和藝毛古賀 / 都氣之非毛我乎 / 多延尓氣流 可毛
wa-ng-imo-ko-nga / tukey-si pïmo-nga wo / **taye-n-i-keyr-u** kamo
1.S-POSS-beloved.girl-DIM-POSS / affix.INF-PST.ATTR cord-POSS string / **break.INF-PERF-INF-RETR-ATTR** EPT
'Oh, the cord that my darling girl tied [over my robes] **has come undone**!'

484. 14:3374.4-5 – Muzasi
乃良奴伎美我名 / 宇良尓伊尓家里
nör-an-u kimi-nga NA / ura-ni [i]**nde-n-i-ker-i**
tell-NEG-ATTR lord-POSS name / divination-LOC go.out.INF-PERF-INF-RETR-FIN
'[My] lord's name that [I] did not tell [them] **emerged** from the divination.'

485. 14:3453 – UNP
可是能等乃 / 登抱吉和伎母賀 / 吉西斯伎奴 / 多母登乃久太利 / 麻欲比伎尓家利
kanze-nö [o]tö-nö / töpo-ki wa-ng[a]-imö-nga / ki-se-si kinu / tamötö-nö kundar-i / **mayop-i-k-i-n-i-ker-i**
wind-GEN sound-COMP / be.far-AVATTR 1.S-POSS-beloved.girl-POSS / wear-CAUS-PST.ATTR robe / sleeve.edge-GEN descend-NML / **fray-INF-come-INF-PERF-INF-RETR-FIN**
'The edge of the sleeve of the robe that my beloved girl, who is far away like the sound of the wind, had [me] wear **has become frayed**.'

7.6.1.2.3.1 EOJ form -*kar*-

The EOJ form -*kar*- is attested once, in the Simotupusa topolect.

486. 20:4388.3-5 – Simotupusa
以弊乃母加 / 枳世之己呂母尓 / 阿可都枳尓迦理
ipe-nö [i]mö-nga / ki-se-si körömö-ni / aka **tuk-i-n-i-kar-i**
house-GEN beloved.girl-POSS / wear-CAUS-PST.ATTR garment-LOC / dirt **attach-INF-PERF-INF-RETR-FIN**
'Dirt **is stuck** to the garment that [my] beloved at home had [me] wear.'

Table 7.50: Attestations of the retrospective -*ker*- ~ -*kar*- across the provinces.

Form	TSOJ			EOJ							UNP
	Sin	Tö	Su	Kak	Mu	Sa	Mi	Sik	Pi	Sip	Kap	
-*ker*-	1	0	0	1	0	0	1	0	0	0	0	1
-*kar*-	0	0	0	0	0	0	0	0	0	1	0	0

7.6.1.2.4 Potential -*kate*- ~ -*kande*-

The potential auxiliary indicates an action that one can do. The TSOJ form is -*kate*-, like in WOJ,[187] but the EOJ form is -*kande*- which is the product of secondary prenasalization on the medial consonant. There are only three examples of this morpheme in the corpus, and all of them precede the negative -*n*-.

487. 20:4341.4-5 – Suruga
道乃長道波 / 由伎加弖奴加毛
MITI nö NANGA-NDI pa / **yuk-i-kate-n-u** *kamo*
road COP.ATTR long-road TPT / **go-INF-POT-NEG-ATTR** EPT
'The road [ahead] is long, and [I] fear **I cannot traverse** it!'

488. 14:3423.1-4 – Kamitukeno
可美都氣努 / 伊可抱乃祢呂尔 / 布路与伎能 / 遊吉須宜可提奴
kamitukeyno / *ikapo-nö ne-rö-ni* / *pur-o yöki-nö* / **yuk-i-sungï-kande-n-u**
TN / TN-GEN peak-DIM-LOC / fall-ATTR snow-COMP / **go-INF-pass.INF-POT-NEG-ATTR**
'Like the falling snow on the little peak of Ikapo in Kamitukeno, [I] **cannot go past** [it].'

489. 14:3388.3 – Pitati
須宜可提尔
sungï-kande-n-i
pass.INF-POT-NEG-INF
'[I] **cannot pass** through [it]. . .'

---

187 WOJ also has the phonetic variant -*ngate*- (Vovin 2009a: 988).

Table 7.51: Attestations of the potential auxiliary -kate- ~ -kande- across the provinces.

TSOJ			EOJ								UNP
Sin	Tö	Su	Kak	Mu	Sa	Mi	Sik	Pi	Sip	Kap	
0	0	1	1	0	0	0	0	1	0	0	0

7.6.1.2.5 Negative-potential-infinitive -kane- ~ -ngane-

The negative-potential-infinitive auxiliary -kane- indicates an action that one cannot do. In all attestations it functions as an infinitive form, without an overt infinitive morpheme present, because the infinitive always becomes phonologically null when it attaches to a vowel-final verbal morpheme.

The existence of a portmanteau negative-potential-infinitive auxiliary is a bit peculiar considering there are also three attestations of the potential -kate- followed by the negative -n-. In fact, we find that combination as well as the negative-potential-infinitive -kane- attested in the same topolect (see example 487 from Suruga in §7.6.1.2.4, compared with example 490 from Suruga below). This morpheme is unusual in another way: as Vovin (2009a: 951) pointed out it often precedes the perfective auxiliary -te-, which is not expected. One possibility for the origin of the auxiliary -kane- is that it is the result of the nasal from the negative suffix in the sequence *-kate-n- '-POT-NEG-' spreading regressively and fusing inside the preceding potential auxiliary, thus PJe *-kate-n- > *-kane-.

In addition to the form -kane-, the Muzasi topolect shows a variant -kani- that has undergone vowel raising (*e > /i/), and three UNP poems show a variant with a prenasalized voiced onset (-ngane-).

490. 20:4346.4-5 – Suruga
 伊比之氣等婆是 / 和須礼加祢豆流
 ip-i-si keytönba nze / ***wasure-kane-t-uru***
 say-INF-PST.ATTR word FPT / **forget.INF-NEG.POT.INF-PERF-ATTR**
 '[I] **have not been able to forget** the words [they] said.'

491. 20:4417.1-3 – Muzasi
 阿加胡麻乎 / 夜麻努尓波賀志 / 刀里加尓弖
 aka n-goma-wo / *yama no-ni pangas-i* / ***tor-i-kani-te***
 red COP.ATTR-horse-ACC / mountain field-LOC let.go-INF / **hold-INF-NEG. POT.INF-SUB**
 '[I] set [my beloved's] red horse free [to roam] the mountains and fields, [but now I] **cannot recapture** [him]. . .'

492. 14:3442.1-3 – UNP
安豆麻治乃 / 手兒乃欲姃左賀 / 古要我祢弖
anduma-ndi-nö / te*NGO-nö yonb-i saka* / ***koye-ngane-te***
TN-road-GEN / maiden-GEN call-INF slope / **cross.INF-NEG.POT.INF-SUB**
'**Being unable to cross** the maiden-calling slope on the road to Aduma. . .'

493. 14:3456.1-4 – UNP
宇都世美能 / 夜蘓許登能敷波 / 思氣久等母 / 安良蘓比可祢弖
utusemi-nö[188] / *ya-so kötö-nö pe pa* / *singey-ku tömö* / ***arasop-i-kane-te***
this.world-GEN / eight-ten word-GEN leaf TPT / be.lush-AVINF CNJ / **resist-INF-NEG.POT.INF-SUB**
'Even though rumors abound in this world, [you] **cannot resist** [them].'

494. 14:3485.2-3 – UNP
身尓素布伊母乎 / 等里見我祢
MÏ-ni sop-u imö-wo / ***tör-i-MI-ngane***
body-LOC accompany-ATTR beloved.girl-ACC / **take-INF-see.INF-NEG.POT.INF**
'[I] **cannot take care** of [my] beloved girl, who [always] accompanies me.'

495. 14:3528.5 – UNP
於毛比可祢都毛
omop-i-kane-t-umo
think-INF-NEG.POT.INF-PERF-EXCL
'[I] **cannot think** [of them]!'

Table 7.52: Attestations of the negative-potential-infinitive -*kane*- ~ -*ngane*- across the provinces.

TSOJ			EOJ								UNP
Sin	Tö	Su	Kak	Mu	Sa	Mi	Sik	Pi	Sip	Kap	
0	0	1	0	1	0	0	0	0	0	0	6

7.6.1.2.6 Benefactive -*kös*-

The benefactive auxiliary -*kös*- indicates an action is done for someone's benefit. It only occurs twice in the corpus, in the Pitati topolect of EOJ. In both examples it

---

[188] *Utu semi* literally means 'empty cicada (shell)', and its use here to mean 'this world' is metaphorical.

precedes the imperative -*ö*, which is a special allomorph of -*e* caused by progressive vowel assimilation. Another allomorph, -*köse*-, is attested in WOJ.

496. 20:4363.4-5 – Pitati
 伊麻波許伎奴等 / 伊母尔**都氣許曽**
 ima pa köng-i-n-u tö / *imö-ni **tungey-kös-ö***
 now TPT row-INF-PERF-FIN QUOT / beloved.girl-DAT **tell.INF-BEN-IMP**
 '**Please tell** [my] beloved girl that [I] have rowed out now!'

497. 20:4365.4-5 – Pitati
 阿例波許藝奴等 / 伊母尔**都岐許曽**
 are pa köng-i-n-u tö / *imö-ni **tungi-kös-ö***
 1.S TPT row-INF-PERF-FIN QUOT / beloved.girl-LOC **tell.INF-BEN-IMP**
 '**Please tell** [my] beloved girl that I have rowed out!'

Table 7.53: Attestations of the benefactive auxiliary -*kös*- across the provinces.

TSOJ			EOJ								UNP
Sin	Tö	Su	Kak	Mu	Sa	Mi	Sik	Pi	Sip	Kap	
0	0	0	0	0	0	0	0	2	0	0	0

7.6.1.2.7 Conjectural -*mer*-

The conjectural -*mer*- can be translated as 'it seems that'. This morpheme is only attested once in AOJ, in the example shown below. It is unattested in WOJ. This is clearly the predecessor to the Middle Japanese conjectural suffix -*umer*-, which is described in Vovin (2003: 295–298).

498. 14:3450.5 – UNP
 乎具佐**可利馬利**
 *wongusa **kat-i-mer-i***
 TN **win-INF-CNJC-FIN**
 '**It seems that** [the assistant from] Wongusa **will win**.'

7.6.2 Lexical auxiliaries

There is a wide range of lexical auxiliaries, including honorific, humble, resultative, and directive auxiliaries. Some of these are bound, but many can also appear as independent verbs. However, when used as an auxiliary they do not have the same lexical meaning as when they appear independently, so they require a dedicated discussion.

7.6.2.1 Honorific auxiliaries
There are two honorific auxiliaries: -*tamap*- and -*mas*-.

7.6.2.1.1 Honorific auxiliary -*tamap*-
The honorific auxiliary -*tamap*- is attested just once in the corpus, in the Simotupusa topolect of EOJ. As it is only attested in reference to the emperor, it likely indicated a very strong honorification. In WOJ as well, it is most often used in reference to emperors and deities (Vovin 2009a: 1004).

499. 20:4389.4-5 – Simotupusa
於不世他麻保加 / 於毛波弊奈久尓
opuse-tamap-o ka / omop-ape-n-aku n-i
give.responsibility.HON.INF-HON-ATTR QPT / think-endure-NEG.ATTR-NML COP-INF
'Has [the emperor] **given [me] an order**? [I] cannot bear to think about it.'

7.6.2.1.2 Honorific auxiliary -*mas*-
The honorific auxiliary -*mas*- probably had a lower level of honorification compared to the honorific auxiliary -*tamap*-, as it is attested more frequently, is used in reference to common people (such as a child to a mother, shown in example 501 below), is unattested in reference to the emperor,[189] and developed from the honorific verb *imas*- 'exist.HON', which is also attested independently (see §7.7.1 for examples). It is attested in both TSOJ and EOJ.

500. 20:4326.1-4 – Töpotuapumi
父母我 / 等能々志利弊乃 / 母々余具佐 / 母々与**伊弓麻勢**
TITI PAPA-nga / tönö-nö siri pe-nö / mömö-yö-n-gusa / mömö-yö **inde-mas-e**
father mother-POSS / mansion-GEN back side-GEN / hundred-petal-GEN-grass / hundred year **go.out.INF-HON-IMP**
'Like the flowers with a hundred petals in the back of [our] mansion, [I] **hope** [my] parents **live** for a hundred years!'

---

[189] In WOJ, in contrast, there do exist attestations of this auxiliary used in reference to the emperor, though overall its usage suggests a lower level of honorification than -*tamap*-, in that we see it most often used as a more general honorific (Vovin 2009a: 1012).

501. 20:4386.3-5 – Simotupusa
以都母以都母 / 於毛加古比須々 / 奈理麻之都之母
itu mö itu mö / omo-nga kopi s-u s-u / **nar-i-mas-i-tusi** mö
when FPT when FPT / mother-POSS love.NML do-FIN do-FIN / **make.a.living-INF-HON-INF-COOR** FPT
'[My] mother always loves [me], **even while working**.'

502. 14:3469.4-5 – UNP
阿是曾母許与比 / 与斯呂**伎麻左奴**
anze sö mö köyöpi / yös-i-rö-**k-i-mas-an-u**
why FPT EPT this.evening / approach-INF-UNC-come-INF-HON-NEG-ATTR
'Oh, why **does [my beloved] not come** [to me] tonight?'

503. 14:3495.4-5 – UNP
伎美我**伎麻左努** / 宇良毛等奈久文
kimi-nga **k-i-mas-an-o** / ura motö na-ku mo
lord-POSS **come-INF-HON-NEG-ATTR** / feelings base not.exist-AVINF FPT
'[My] lord **did not come**, and [so I] feel empty.'

504. 14:3521.4-5 – UNP
伎麻左奴伎美乎 / 許呂久等曾奈久
k-i-mas-an-u kimi-wo / köröku tö sö nak-u
come-INF-HON-NEG-ATTR lord-ACC / caw-caw QUOT FPT cry-ATTR
'[The crow] will cry 'caw-caw' for [my] lord who **will not come**.'

Table 7.54: Attestations of the honorific auxiliary -*[i]mas*- across the provinces.

TSOJ			EOJ								UNP
Sin	Tö	Su	Kak	Mu	Sa	Mi	Sik	Pi	Sip	Kap	
0	1	0	0	0	0	0	0	0	1	0	3

7.6.2.2 Humble auxiliaries
Humble auxiliaries lower the speaker in relation to some other person or entity. There is only one humble auxiliary attested, the auxiliary -*matur*-.

7.6.2.2.1 Humble auxiliary -*matur*-
The humble auxiliary *matur*- is attested just once, in the Kamitupusa topolect of EOJ.

505. 20:4359.4-5 – Kamitupusa
都加敝麻都里弖 / 久尔尓閇牟可毛
tukape-matur-i-te / *kuni-ni pey muk-am-o*
serve.INF-HUM-INF-SUB / province-LOC prow face-TENT-ATTR
'[After] **doing [my] service**, will [the boat] face its prow towards [my] province?'

7.6.2.3 Other auxiliaries

The other auxiliaries attested in AOJ are the dummy auxiliary *-ar-*, the resultative auxiliary *-ok-*, the auxiliary of difficulty *-ngata-*, and the directive auxiliaries *-kö-*, *-yuk-* ~ *-ik-*, *-nde-*, *-yör-*, and *-tuk-*.

7.6.2.3.1 Dummy auxiliary *-ar-*

The auxiliary *-ar-*, grammaticalized from the verb *ar-* 'exist', is semantically null, and as such it is little more than a dummy auxiliary (Vovin 2009a: 1057-1058). It simply functions as a linking element that allows further suffixes to be concatenated to a verbal form. It is particularly useful with adjectival verbs, which cannot take mood markers on their own. The vowel of this auxiliary is strong and thus never deletes, but it may cause the deletion of a preceding /u/, as seen in examples (508) and (509) below. It is well attested in WOJ, but unattested in TSOJ.

506. 20:4371.4-5 – Pitati
都久波能夜麻乎 / 古比須安良米可毛
tukupa-nö yama-wo / **kopi-nz-u-ar-am-ey** *kamo*
TN-GEN mountain-ACC / **long.for-NEG-INF-exist-TENT-EV** EPT
'[I] wonder, shall [I] **not long for** Tukupa mountain?'

507. 14:3508.4-5 – UNP
安比見受安良婆 / 安礼古非米夜母
ap-i-MI-nz-u-ar-anba / *are kopï-m-ey ya mö*
meet-INF-see-NEG-INF-exist-COND / 1.S love-TENT-EV QPT EPT
'**If [I] had not met** [you], would I be in love [with you]? (No, I would not!)'

508. 14:3476a.3-5 – UNP
多刀都久能 / 努賀奈敝由家婆 / 故布思可流奈母
tat-o tuku-nö / *nongan-ape-yuk-e-nba* / **kopusi-k[u]-ar-unam-ö**
rise-ATTR moon-GEN / flow-ITER.INF-go-EV-CONJ / **be.longing.for-AVINF-exist-TENT2-ATTR**
'Whenever the rising moon sets, [she] **will long for** [me].'

509. 14:3482b.4-5 – UNP
祢奈敝乃可良尓 / 許等**多可利都母**
ne-n-ape-nö karani / *kötö **[i]ta-k[u]-ar-i-t-umö***
sleep-NEG-ITER.NML-GEN because.of / word **be.painful-AVINF-exist-INF-PERF-EXCL**
'Because of [our] not sleeping [together], the rumors **have been painful**!'

510. 20:4432.1-2 – UNP
佐弁奈弁奴 / 美許登**尓阿礼婆**
sape-n-ape-n-u / *mi-kötö **n-i ar-e-nba***
obstruct-NEG-ITER.INF-PERF-FIN / HON-word **COP-INF exist-EV-CONJ**
'**Since [these] are** commands [from the emperor], [I] will not interfere with [them].'

Table 7.55: Attestations of the dummy auxiliary *-ar-* across the provinces.

	TSOJ					EOJ					UNP
Sin	Tö	Su	Kak	Mu	Sa	Mi	Sik	Pi	Sip	Kap	
0	0	0	0	0	0	0	0	1	0	0	4

7.6.2.3.2 Resultative auxiliary *-ok-*

The resultative auxiliary *-ok-*, a grammaticalization of the verb *ok-* 'put', is used to indicate an action's effects will continue afterwards (Vovin 2009a: 1096). This auxiliary is attested just once, in the easternmost EOJ topolect, Mitinöku.

511. 14:3437.3-4 – Mitinöku
波自伎於伎弖 / 西良思馬伎那婆
*panzik-i-**ok**-i-te* / *ser-asime-k-i-n-anba*
take.off-INF-put-INF-SUB / bend-CAUS.INF-come-INF-PERF-COND
'When [I] **take off** the [string] and [the bow] becomes warped...'

7.6.2.3.3 Auxiliary *-ngata* 'difficult to do' and two similar forms

The auxiliary *-ngata* is added to indicate the verb's action is difficult to do. Unlike most other auxiliaries, it attaches to the verb root, rather than to the infinitive. This differs from WOJ, where it attaches to the nominalized form of the verb root (Vovin 2009a: 1099). It is attested just once, in EOJ.

512. 14:3431.5 – Sagamu
    許己波**胡賀多**尔
    *kökönba **ko-ngata** n-i*
    extremely **come-difficult.to.do** COP-INF
    'It is extremely **difficult to come** [here].'

Unlike in WOJ, there are also two additional constructions attested in AOJ which may or may not involve auxiliaries similar to -*ngata*. It is hard to claim definitively that they are auxiliaries due to a lack of attestations. Alternatively, they may have been collocations involving a particular verb. The first is the adjectival verb *kurusi-* 'be.painful' which is added to the genitive form of a nominalized verb to indicate that verb's action is painful to do. It is shown in example (513) below.

513. 14:3481.5 – UNP
    於毛比**具流之母**
    *omop-i-**n-gurusi-mö***
    think-NML-GEN-**be.painful.AVFIN-EXCL**
    '**Oh**, it **is painful** to think [about that]!'

The second is the adjectival verb *yasu-* 'be.easy', which attaches to the infinitive form of a verb to indicate that verb's action is easy to do. It is also only attested once, shown in example (514) below.

514. 14:3483.3-5 – UNP
    和賀西奈尓 / 阿飛与流等可毛 / 欲流**等家也須家**
    *wa-nga se-na-ni / ap-i-yör-u tö kamo / yoru **töke-yasu-ke***
    1.S-POSS beloved.man-DIM-DAT / meet-INF-approach-FIN QUOT EPT / night
    come.undone.INF-be.easy-AVATTR
    '[I] wonder, will [I] meet with my dearly beloved? [Our garment cords] **easily come undone** at night.'

The construction *VERB-yasu-* is used in Modern Japanese with the same meaning.

7.6.2.3.4 Directive auxiliaries

Directive auxiliaries are used to indicate a verb's action is directed upwards, downwards, forwards, backwards, inwards, or outwards, either in space or in time.

7.6.2.3.4.1 Directive auxiliary -kö-

The directive auxiliary -kö-, which is a grammaticalization of the verb kö- 'come', is used to indicate an action occurs toward the speaker's location. However, in example (517) below it indicates an action toward the listener's location, a usage that is unattested in WOJ. This auxiliary may also indicate an action that developed toward the present moment (Vovin 2009a: 1068), as found in example (521) below, or the start of an action (shown in example 518). It is attested in TSOJ and EOJ.

515. 20:4323.3-5 – Töpotuapumi
奈尓須礼曽 / 波々登布波奈乃 / 佐吉泥己受祁牟
nani s-ure sö / papa tö [i]p-u pana-nö / **sak-i-nde-kö-nz-u-kem-u**
why do-EV FPT / mother QUOT say-ATTR flower-GEN / **bloom-INF-go.out.INF-come-NEG-INF-PST.TENT-ATTR**
'Why **has** the flower called 'mother' **not come out in bloom**?'

516. 14:3437.3-4 – Mitinöku
波自伎於伎弖 / 西良思馬伎那婆
panzik-i-ok-i-te / **ser-asime-k-i-n-anba**
take.off-INF-put-INF-SUB / **bend-CAUS.INF-come-INF-PERF-COND**
'When [I] take off the [string] and [the bow] **becomes warped**...'

517. 20:4368.4-5 – Pitati
麻可知之自奴伎 / 和波可敝里許牟
ma-kandi sinzi nuk-i / wa pa **kaper-i-kö-m-u**
INT-oar constantly pierce-INF / 1.S TPT **return-INF-come-TENT-FIN**
'Constantly thrusting the oar [on the tide boat], I **shall return** [to you].'

518. 14:3394.4-5 – Pitati
和須良延許婆古曽 / 那乎可家奈波賣
wasura-kö-nba kosö / na-wo kake-n-ap-am-e
forget-come-COND FPT / 2.S-ACC call.out-NEG-ITER-TENT-EV
'When [I] **start to** forget [our meeting there], [I] shall stop calling out for you!'

519. 20:4393.3-5 – Simotupusa
知々波々乎 / 以波比弊等於枳弖 / 麻為弖枳尓之乎
titi papa-wo / ipap-i pe-tö ok-i-te / **mawi-nde-k-i-n-i-si-wo**
father mother-ACC / pray-INF pot-COM leave.behind-INF-SUB / **come.HUM.INF-go.out.INF-come-INF-PERF-INF-PST.ATTR-ACC**
'[I] left [my] father and mother with a praying pot and **came out** [here].'

520. 20:4358.3-5 – Kamitupusa
伊弖久礼婆 / 和努等里都伎弖 / 伊比之古奈波毛
inde-k-ure-nba / wano tör-i-tuk-i-te / ip-i-si ko-na pa mo
go.out.INF-**come**-EV-CONJ / 1.S take-INF-attach-INF-SUB / say-INF-PST.ATTR girl-DIM TPT EPT
'Since [I] **left** [home] **and came** [here], oh, [what about] the dear girl who clung to me and said [all those things]?'

521. 14:3453.4-5 – UNP
多母登乃久太利 / 麻欲比伎尔家利
tamötö-nö kundar-i / **mayop-i-k-i-n-i-ker-i**
sleeve.edge-GEN descend-NML / **fray-INF-come-INF-PERF-INF-RETR-FIN**
'The edge of the sleeve [of my robe] **has become frayed**.'

522. 14:3469.3-5 – UNP
和加西奈波 / 阿是曽母許与比 / 与斯呂伎麻左奴
wa-nga se-na pa / anze sö mö köyöpi / **yös-i-rö-k-i-mas-an-u**
1.S-POSS beloved.man-DIM TPT / why FPT EPT this.evening / **approach-INF-UNC-come-INF-HON-NEG-ATTR**
'Oh, why **does** my beloved **not come** [to me] tonight?'

Table 7.56: Attestations of the directive auxiliary -kö- across the provinces.

TSOJ			EOJ								UNP
Sin	Tö	Su	Kak	Mu	Sa	Mi	Sik	Pi	Sip	Kap	
0	1	0	0	0	0	1	0	2	1	1	2

7.6.2.3.4.2 Directive auxiliary -yuk- ~ -ik-

The directive auxiliary -yuk- ~ -ik-, a grammaticalization of the verb yuk- ~ ik- 'go', indicates an action is directed away from the speaker. It may also indicate an action will occur into the future (Vovin 2009a: 1073).

523. 14:3412.4-5 – Kamitukeno
可奈師家兒良尔 / 伊夜射可里久母
kanasi-ke KO-ra-ni / iya n-zakar-i-**[i]k-umö**
be.dear-AVATTR girl-DIM-DAT / more.and.more COP.INF-be.far.from-INF-**go-EXCL**
'[I] **am going further and further away** from [my] dear, darling girl!'

524. 20:4372.3-4 – Pitati
可問理美須 / 阿例波**久江由久**
kapeyr-i-mi-nz-u / *are pa* **kuye-yuk-u**
return-INF-see-NEG-INF / 1.S TPT **cross over.INF-go-FIN**
'I will **go and cross over** without looking back.'

525. 14:3476a.3-5 – UNP
多刀都久能 / **努賀奈敝由家婆** / 故布思可流奈母
tat-o tuku-nö / **nongan-ape-yuk-e-nba** / *kopusi-k[u]-ar-unam-ö*
rise-ATTR moon-GEN / **flow-ITER.INF-go-EV-CONJ** / be.longing.for-AVINF-exist-TENT2-ATTR
'**Whenever** the rising moon **sets**, [she] will long for [me].'

526. 14:3476b.3-5 – UNP
多刀都久能 / **奴我奈敝由家杼** / 和奴賀由乃敝波
tat-o tuku-nö / **nungan-ape-yuk-e-ndö** / *wanu-nga yun-öpe-nba*
rise-ATTR moon-GEN / **flow-ITER.INF-go-EV-CONC** / 1.S-POSS sleep-ITER-COND
'**Although** the rising moon **sets day after day**, if I continue to sleep [with her]...'

Table 7.57: Attestations of the directive auxiliary *-ik-* ~ *-yuk-* across the provinces.

TSOJ			EOJ								UNP
Sin	Tö	Su	Kak	Mu	Sa	Mi	Sik	Pi	Sip	Kap	
0	0	0	1	0	0	0	0	1	0	0	2

7.6.2.3.4.3 Directive auxiliary *-nde-*

The directive auxiliary *-nde-*, grammaticalized from the verb *inde-* 'go out', indicates an action occurs outward. It is attested in TSOJ and EOJ.

527. 14:3401.1-3 – Sinano
中麻奈尔 / 宇伎乎流布祢能 / **許藝弓奈婆**
tinguma na-ni / *uk-i-wor-u pune-nö* / **köng-i-nde-n-anba**
TN river-LOC / float-INF-exist-ATTR boat-GEN / **row-INF-go.out.INF-PERF-COND**
'If the boat floating in Tiguma river **rows out**...'

528. 20:4323.3-5 – Töpotuapumi
奈尔須礼曽 / 波々登布波奈乃 / 佐吉泥己受祁牟
*nani s-ure sö / papa tö [i]p-u pana-nö / **sak-i-nde-kö-nz-u-kem-u***
why do-EV FPT / mother QUOT say-ATTR flower-GEN / **bloom-INF-go.out. INF-come-NEG-INF-PST.TENT-ATTR**
'Why **has** the flower called 'mother' **not come out in bloom**?'

529. 14:3419.3 – Kamitukeno
於毛比度路
omop-i-nd-oro
think-INF-emerge-ATTR
'[I] **recall**...'

530. 20:4380.1-2 – Simotukeno
奈尔婆刀乎 / 己岐涅弖美例婆
*naninba to-wo / **köng-i-nde-te** mi-re-nba*
TN door-ACC / **row-INF-go.out.INF-SUB** look-EV-CONJ
'When [I] **row out** of Nanipa harbor and look [back]...'

Table 7.58: Attestations of the directive auxiliary *-nde-* across the provinces.

TSOJ			EOJ								UNP
Sin	Tö	Su	Kak	Mu	Sa	Mi	Sik	Pi	Sip	Kap	
1	1	0	1	0	0	0	1	0	0	0	0

7.6.2.3.4.4 Directive auxiliary *-yör-*

The directive auxiliary *-yör-*, grammaticalized from the verb *yör-* 'approach', indicates an action occurs near someone or something.

531. 14:3435.3-4 – Kamitukeno
和我吉奴尔 / 都伎与良志母与
*wa-nga kinu-ni / **tuk-i-yör-asi-mö** yö*
1.S-POSS robe-LOC / **attach-INF-approach-SUP-EXCL** EPT
'It seems [the flowers] **cling to** my robes!'

532. 14:3446.4-5 – UNP
安志等比登其等 / 加多理与良斯毛
asi tö pitö-n-götö / **katar-i-yör-asi-mo**
be.bad.AVFIN QUOT people-GEN-word / **tell-INF-approach-SUP-EXCL**
'**It seems** that people **are saying** [the Amur silver grass] is bad!'

533. 14:3483.3-5 – UNP
和賀西奈尓 / 阿飛与流等可毛 / 欲流等家也須家
wa-nga se-na-ni / **ap-ï-yör-u** *tö kamo* / *yoru töke-yasu-ke*
1.S-POSS beloved.man-DIM-DAT / **meet-INF-approach-FIN** QUOT EPT / night come.undone.INF-be.easy-AVATTR
'[I] wonder, will [I] **meet** with my dearly beloved? [Our garment cords] easily come undone at night.'

Table 7.59: Attestations of the directive auxiliary *-yör-* across the provinces.

TSOJ			EOJ							UNP
Sin	Tö	Su	Kak	Mu	Sa	Mi	Sik	Pi	Sip	Kap	
0	0	0	1	0	0	0	0	0	0	0	2

7.6.2.3.4.5 Directive auxiliary *tuk-*

The directive auxiliary *tuk-*, grammaticalized from the verb *tuk-* 'attach', indicates an action makes contact with someone or something. It is attested in TSOJ and EOJ.

534. 20:4401.1-4 – Sinano
可良己呂武 / 須宗尓等里都伎 / 奈古古良乎 / 意伎弖曽伎怒也
kara körömu / *suso-ni* **tör-i-tuk-i** / *nak-o ko-ra-wo* / *ok-i-te sö k-i-n-o ya*
TN garment / hem-LOC **take-INF-attach-INF** / cry-ATTR child-PLUR-ACC / leave.behind-INF-SUB FPT come-INF-PERF-ATTR EPT
'Oh, [I] have come [here], leaving behind [my] sobbing children who **clung to** the hem of [my] Kara robes!'

535. 20:4358.3-5 – Kamitupusa
伊弖久礼婆 / 和努等里都伎弖 / 伊比之古奈波毛
inde-k-ure-nba / *wano* **tör-i-tuk-i-te** / *ip-i-si ko-na pa mo*
go.out.INF-come-EV-CONJ / 1.S **take-INF-attach-INF-SUB** / say-INF-PST.ATTR girl-DIM TPT EPT
'Since [I] left [home] and came [here], oh, [what about] the dear girl who **clung to** me and said [all those things]?'

Table 7.60: Attestations of the directive auxiliary -*tuk*- across the provinces.

TSOJ			EOJ							UNP
Sin	Tö	Su	Kak	Mu	Sa	Mi	Sik	Pi	Sip	Kap
1	0	0	0	0	0	0	0	0	1	0

7.7 Suppletive honorific and humble verbs

There are five suppletive verbs that indicate honorification or humbleness.

7.7.1 Honorific *imas*-

The honorific verb *imas*- also occurs as an honorific auxiliary, but when it is in its free form it is an honorific verb that means 'exist' or 'be'. In WOJ it can also mean 'go' or 'come' (Vovin 2009a: 1015). It is only attested in the imperative form. Both attested examples are provided below.

536. 20:4342.1-4 – Suruga
 麻氣婆之良 / 寶米弖豆久利留 / 等乃能其等 / 已麻勢波々刀自
 *ma-key n-basira / pomey-te tukur-ir-u / tönö-nö ngötö / **imas**-e papa tonzi*
 INT-tree COP.ATTR-pillar / bless.INF-SUB make-PROG-ATTR / mansion-GEN like / **exist.HON-IMP** mother mistress.of.house
 'Dear mother! **Be** like the mansion with pillars of hearty timber that were blessed during construction.'

537. 20:4426.1-4 – UNP
 阿米都之乃 / 可未尓奴佐於伎 / 伊波比都々 / 伊麻世和我世奈
 *amey tusi-nö / kamï-ni nusa ok-i / ipap-i-tutu / **imas**-e wa-nga se-na*
 heaven earth-GEN / deity-LOC paper.offering leave-INF / pray-INF-COOR / **exist.HON-IMP** 1.S-POSS beloved.man-DIM
 'Leave paper offerings to the deities of heaven and earth and **keep** praying, my beloved.'

7.7.2 Humble *tamapar-* ~ *tanbar-*

The humble verb *tamapar-* means 'receive'. There is also a contracted form *tanbar-*. All three attested examples are given below.

538.   20:4372.1-4 – Pitati
阿之加良能 / 美佐加**多麻波理** / 可閇理美須 / 阿例波久江由久
asingara-nö / *mi-saka **tamapar-i*** / *kapeyr-i-mi-nz-u* / *are pa kuye-yuk-u*
TN-GEN / HON-slope **receive.HUM-INF** / return-INF-see-NEG-INF / 1.S TPT cross.over.INF-go-FIN
'**Receiving** [permission to cross] the great slope of Asigara, I will go and cross over without looking back.'

539.   20:4424.4-5 – Muzasi
美佐可**多婆良婆** / 麻佐夜可尓美无
*mi-saka **tanbar-anba*** / *ma-sayaka n-i mi-m-u*
HON-slope **receive.HUM-COND** / INT-clear COP-INF see-TENT-FIN
'**If [he] received** [permission to cross] the great slope, [I] would see [him] so clearly.'

540.   14:3440a.4-5 – UNP
余知乎曽母弖流 / 伊伄兒**多婆里尓**
yöti-wo sö möt-er-u / *inde KO **tanbar-i-n-i***
same.age-ACC FPT hold-PROG-ATTR / well girl **receive.HUM-INF-PERF-IMP**
'[We] have [children] of the same age. Well, let [me] **receive** [your] child.'

7.7.3 Humble *mawos-*

This verb is a humble form of the verb *ip-* 'say'. Both attested examples are given below.

541.   20:4376.3-5 – Simotukeno
阿母志志尓 / **己等麻乎佐受弖** / 伊麻叙久夜之氣
amö sisi-ni / ***kötö mawos-anz-u-te*** / *ima nzö kuyasi-key*
mother father-DAT / **word say.HUM-NEG-INF-SUB** / now FPT be.regretful-AVATTR
'[I] **did not inform** [my] mother and father, and oh, now [I] regret it!'

542. 20:4372.13-15 – Pitati
    毛呂々々波 / 佐祁久等**麻乎須** / 可閇利久麻弖尓
    *morö-morö pa / sake-ku tö **mawos-u** / kapeyr-i-k-u-mande-ni*
    many-REDUP TPT / be.safe-AVINF QUOT **say.HUM-FIN** / return-INF-come-ATTR-TERM-LOC
    '[I] **will implore** [the deities] to keep the many, many [people I left behind] safe until [I] return [home].'

7.7.4 Humble *mawi-*

This verb is a humble form of the verb *kö-* 'come'. It is attested just once, in EOJ.

543. 20:4393.3-5 – Simotupusa
    知々波々乎 / 以波比弊等於枳弖 / **麻為**弖枳尓之乎
    *titi papa-wo / ipap-i pe-tö ok-i-te / **mawi**-nde-k-i-n-i-si-wo*
    father mother-ACC / pray-INF pot-COM leave.behind-INF-SUB / **come.HUM.INF**-go.out.INF-come-INF-PERF-INF-PST.ATTR-ACC
    '[I] left [my] father and mother with a praying pot and **came** out [here].'

7.7.5 Humble *kangapur-*

This humble verb means 'receive'. It is attested only once, in TSOJ.

544. 20:4321.2-4 – Töpotuapumi
    美許等**加我布利** / 阿須由利也 / 加曳我牟多祢牟
    *mi-kötö **kangapur-i** / asu-yuri ya / kaye-nga muta ne-m-u*
    HON-word **receive.HUM-INF** / tomorrow-ABL QPT / reed-POSS together sleep-TENT-ATTR
    '**Having received** [my sovereign's] command, will [I] sleep among the reeds from tomorrow?'

7.8 Serial verb constructions

Normal serial verb constructions in AOJ are formed as shown in examples (545) – (547) below. In these constructions the first verb is in the infinitive form, allowing it to connect to a following verb to indicate two actions occur in sequence.

545. 20:4323.3-5 – Töpotuapumi
奈尔須礼曽 / 波々登布波奈乃 / **佐吉泥己受祁牟**
*nani s-ure sö / papa tö [i]p-u pana-nö / **sak-i-nde-kö-nz-u-kem-u***
why do-EV FPT / mother QUOT say-ATTR flower-GEN / **bloom-INF-go.out. INF-come-NEG-INF-PST.TENT-ATTR**
'Why **has** the flower called 'mother' **not come out in bloom**?'

546. 20:4356.1-2 – Kamitupusa
和我波々能 / 藨天**母知奈弖氏**
*wa-nga papa-nö / sonde **möt-i-nande-te***
1.S-POSS mother-GEN / sleeve **hold-INF-caress.INF-SUB**
'[I] **held and caressed** my mother's sleeve.'

547. 14:3388.4-5 – Pitati
伊伎豆久伎美乎 / **為祢弖**夜良佐祢
*ikinduk-u kimi-wo / **wi-ne-te** yar-as-an-e*
sigh-ATTR lord-ACC / **bring.INF-sleep.INF-SUB** send-HON-DES-IMP
'Please **bring** [my] lord who sighs **to sleep** [with me], and then send [him back].'

Examples (548) – (550) below are unusual because they contain serial verb constructions in which the first verb is not in the infinitive form. All attestations are from EOJ or UNP. The constructions in examples (548) and (549) are likely archaic, remnants of a time before the infinitive suffix's linking function fully integrated into the verbal paradigms. Example (550), however, is better explained as a later V_1 elision of the vocalic sequence *-i-a (for more discussion, see §2.3.6.1), which caused the infinitive suffix -i to disappear.

548. 20:4363.1-2 – Pitati
奈尔波都尔 / 美布祢**於呂須恵**
*nanipa tu-ni / mi-pune **orö-suwe***
TN harbor-LOC / HON-boat **lower-place.INF**
'[After] **lowering** the boat in Nanipa harbor and **fixing it in place**…'

549. 14:3460.1-2 – UNP
多礼曽許能 / 屋能戸於曽夫流
tare sö könö / *YA-nö TO **osö-nbur-u***[190]
who FPT this / house-GEN door **push-shake-ATTR**
'Who is knocking [lit. '**pushing and shaking**'] on the door of this house?'

550. 20:4389.5 – Simotupusa
於毛波弊奈久尓
omop-ape-n-aku *n-i*
think-endure-NEG.ATTR-NML COP-INF
'[I] **cannot bear to think about it**.'

There is also one example (551) of a directive auxiliary verb attached to the preceding verb root, instead of the expected infinitive form of the verb. Once again, this is likely an archaism fossilized in poetry.

551. 14:3394.4-5 – Pitati
和須良延許婆古曽 / 那乎可家奈波賣
wasura-kö-nba *kosö* / *na-wo kake-n-ap-am-e*
forget-come-COND FPT / 2.S-ACC call.out-NEG-ITER-TENT-EV
'**When [I] start to forget** [our meeting there], [I] shall stop calling out for you!'

7.9 Light verb constructions

Light verb constructions in AOJ are formed with the light verb *se-* 'do' and a preceding nominal, which is often a nominalized verb. This nominal is not marked by the accusative *-wo*. The topic particle *pa* may intervene between the light verb and the nominal, as shown in example (554). Similarly, the focus particle *kösö* may intervene, as shown in example (557). When *se-* 'do' is in the imperative mood as *se* 'do. IMP', it may be fronted before the nominal, as shown in example (558).

---

190 This is also attested once in WOJ (in KK 2). It is unclear why *pur-* 'shake' is voiced to *nbur-* here.

552. 20:4344.4-5 – Suruga
和我知々波々波 / 和須例勢努加毛
wa-nga titi papa / **wasure se-n-o** kamo
1.S-POSS father mother / **forget.NML do-NEG-ATTR** EPT
'[I] **could never forget** my father and mother!'

553. 14:3436.4-5 – Kamitukeno
宇良賀礼勢奈那 / 登許波尓毛我母
ura-n-gare se-na-na / tökö pa n-i mongamö
top.branch-GEN-wither.NML do-NEG.ATTR-LOC / eternal leaf COP-INF DPT
'I wish [the trees] had eternal leaves, **without withered top branches**.'

554. 14:3557.4-5 – UNP
和須礼波勢奈那 / 伊夜母比麻須尓
wasure pa se-na-na / iya [o]möp-i mas-u-ni
forget.NML TPT do-NEG.ATTR-LOC / more.and.more think-NML increase-ATTR-LOC
'[I] think of [her] more and more, **without forgetting** [anything about her].'

555. 14:3386.2-3 – Simotupusa
可豆思加和世乎 / 尓倍須登毛
kandusika wase-wo / **nipey s-u** tömo
TN early.rice-ACC / **food.offering do-FIN** CNJ
'Even though [she] **made an offering** of new rice from Kadusika...'

556. 20:4416.2-3 – Muzasi
多比由苦世奈我 / 麻流祢世波
tanbi yuk-u se-na-nga / **maru-ne se-nba**[191]
journey go-ATTR beloved.man-DIM-POSS / **round-sleep.NML do-COND**
'If [my] beloved man, who will go on a journey, **sleeps with [his] clothes on**...'

---

[191] EOJ *maru-ne se-* 'round-sleep.NML do-' means 'to sleep with one's clothes on' (Omodaka 1967: 692–693; Mizushima 2003: 717).

557. 14:3419.3-5 – Kamitukeno
於毛比度路 / 久麻許曽之都等 / 和須礼西奈布母
omop-i-nd-oro / **kuma kösö s-i-t-u** *tö* / **wasure se-n-ap-umö**
think-INF-emerge-ATTR / **offering.to.the.deities FPT do-INF-PERF-FIN** QUOT / **forget.NML do-NEG-ITER-EXCL**
'[I] recall **making the offering to the deities** – [I] **will not forget** [you]!'

Example (557) contains two light verb constructions.

558. 14:3369.5 – Sagamu
許呂**勢多麻久良**
kö-rö se ta-makura
girl-DIM **do.IMP hand-pillow**
'Dear girl, **use [my] arm as [your] pillow**!'

7.10 Verbal reduplication

Verbal reduplication is attested in EOJ and UNP, but not in TSOJ. It indicates an iterative action. Since there are few examples of this in the corpus and the grammaticalization of the iterative suffix *-ap-* appears to be a late development (see §2.3.9), this was probably the original means of indicating an iterative action in PJe and PJ.

Only full reduplication is attested. In most examples the final form of the verb is reduplicated, but in example (559) the infinitive form is reduplicated. Suffixes are reduplicated with the root, but auxiliaries are not: they only attach to the end of the entire reduplicated form, as shown in example (559).

559. 20:4330.1-2 – Sagamu
奈尓波都尓 / 余曽比余曽比弖
nanipa tu-ni / **yösöp-i-yösöp-i-te**
TN harbor-LOC / **prepare-INF-prepare-INF-SUB**
'**Preparing** [the boats] in Nanipa harbor...'

560. 14:3378.3-4 – Muzasi
伊波為都良 / 比可婆**奴流々々**
ipawi tura / pik-anba **nur-u nur-u**
UNC vine / pull-COND **come.loose-FIN come.loose-FIN**
'The *ipawi* vines **come loose smoothly** if [they are] pulled [up].'

561. 20:4386.3-5 – Simotupusa
以都母以都母 / 於毛加**古比須々** / 奈理麻之都之母
itu mö itu mö / *omo-nga* **kopi s-u s-u** / *nar-i-mas-i-tusi mö*
when FPT when FPT / mother-POSS **love.NML do-FIN do-FIN** / make.a.living-INF-HON-INF-COOR FPT
'[My] mother always **loves** [me], even while working.'

562. 14:3487.3-5 – UNP
可久**須酒**曽 / 宿莫奈那里尔思 / 於久乎**可奴加奴**
ka-ku **s-u s-u** *sö* / *NE-NA-na nar-i-n-i-si* / *oku-wo* **kan-u kan-u**
be.thus-AVINF **do-FIN do-FIN** FPT / sleep-NEG.ATTR-LOC be-INF-PERF-INF-PST.ATTR / future-ACC **worry.about-FIN worry.about-FIN**
'[I] **do** it in the same manner **again and again**. [Likewise, I] **worry about** [our] future **over and over again**, [because] it turned out that [we] did not sleep [together].'

563. 14:3501.4-5 – UNP
比可婆**奴流奴留** / 安乎許等奈多延
pik-anba **nur-u nur-u** / *a-wo kötö na-taye*
pull-COND **come.loose-FIN come.loose-FIN** / 1.S-ACC word NEG.IMP-break.INF
'If [I] pull [them] up [they] **come loose smoothly**, [so] do not stop speaking to me!'

8 Adverbs

There are both adverbial constructions and pure adverbs. The adverbial constructions are formed either through an adjective followed by the infinitive copula *n-i*, or through an adjectival verb in the infinitive form ('ROOT-*ku*'). These are discussed in other chapters (see sections §7.4.3.5.1.1 and §6.3.3.1.2), so I will not describe them again here. Instead, I will focus only on pure adverbs in this chapter.

Pure adverbs in AOJ include *ito* ~ *itö* 'simply, very, really', *kökönba* 'extremely', *sapanda* 'many, much, amply', *mata* 'again', *iya* 'plentifully, certainly', *napo* 'still', *imanda* 'yet, still', *motöna* 'incessantly, at random', *tanda* 'directly', *nökinde* 'extremely', *sinzi* 'constantly', *simaraku* 'for a while', *köngötö* 'greatly', *unbey* 'surely', *yumey* '[not] at all', and *wosawosa* '[not] enough, [not] properly'. Adverbs normally precede the verb or adjectival verb they modify. The only exception is *yumey* '[not] at all', which follows the verb. In this chapter I provide every attested example of each adverb in AOJ.

8.1 *ito* 'simply, very, really'

This adverb is attested in EOJ and UNP. In the Simotukeno topolect it is written *ito* and is consistently followed by the focus particle *mo*, while in the UNP example it is used in isolation and written as *itö*, which is probably just a misspelling.

1. 20:4379.4-5 – Simotukeno
   伊刀毛須倍奈美 / 夜多妣蘇弖布流
   ito *mo sunbey na-mi* / *ya-tanbi sonde pur-u*
   simply FPT way not.exist-AVGER / eight-CL sleeve wave-FIN
   '[I] shall wave [my] sleeve many times, because there is **simply** nothing [more I can] do!'

2. 20:4381.4-5 – Simotukeno
   和可流乎美礼婆 / 伊刀母須敝奈之
   wakar-u-wo mi-re-nba / ***ito*** *mö sunbe na-si*
   separate-ATTR-ACC see-EV-CONJ / **really** FPT way not.exist-AVFIN
   'When [I] see [them] parting [from their families it is sad but] **really**, it can't be helped.'

3. 14:3548.3-5 – UNP
   伊等能伎提 / 可奈思家世呂尓 / 比等佐敝余須母
   itö nökinde / kanasi-ke se-rö-ni / pitö sape yös-umö
   very extremely / be.dear-AVATTR beloved.man-DIM-DAT / person RPT approach-EXCL
   'Even [other] people approach [my] beloved man who is so **very** dear [to me]!'

8.2 *kökönba* 'extremely'

This adverb is attested in EOJ and UNP. It is a cognate of WOJ *kökönba* 'id.' (attested just once, and also attested once as *kökönbaku*) and it seems that it shares a root *kökö-* with the WOJ adverbs *kökönda* 'id.' and *kökondaku* 'id.' (Vovin 2009a: 1107).

4. 14:3431.5 – Sagamu
   許己波胡賀多尓
   kökönba ko-n-gata n-i
   extremely come.NML-GEN-difficult COP-INF
   'It is **extremely** difficult to come [here].'

5. 14:3517.5 – UNP
   許己婆可那之家
   kökönba kanasi-ke
   extremely be.dear-AVATTR
   '[She] is **extremely** dear [to me]. . .'

8.3 *sapanda* 'many, much, amply'

This adverb is attested in TSOJ and EOJ. While it is not attested in WOJ, the WOJ adverb *sapa* 'id.' clearly shares the same root.

6. 14:3354.1-3 – Töpotuapumi
   伎倍比等乃 / 萬太良夫須麻尓 / 和多佐波太
   kipey pitö-nö / mandara n-busuma-ni / wata sapanda
   TN person-GEN / speckled COP.ATTR-bed.covers -LOC / cotton **amply**
   '[Like] the cotton [that is] **amply** [placed] inside the speckled bed covers of the people from Kipey.'

7. 14:3395.3-5 – Pitati
   安比太欲波 / <u>佐波太</u>奈利怒乎 / 萬多祢天武可聞
   apinda yo pa / ***sapanda*** *nar-i-n-o-wo* / *mata ne-te-m-u kamo*
   interval night TPT / **many** be-INF-PERF-ATTR-ACC / again sleep.INF-PERF-TENT-ATTR EPT
   'Since there have been **many** nights in between [our meetings], [I] wonder if [I] shall sleep [with her] again.'

8.4 *mata* 'again'

The adverb *mata* 'again' is attested four times, all in EOJ topolects.

8. 20:4415.4-5 – Muzasi
   伊弊奈流伊母乎 / <u>麻多</u>美弓毛母也
   ipe-n[i] ar-u imö-wo / ***mata*** *mi-te-m-o mö ya*
   house-LOC exist-ATTR beloved.girl-ACC / **again** see.INF-PERF-TENT-ATTR EPT EPT
   'How [I] would [like] to see [my] darling **again**, who is at home!'

9. 14:3395.5 – Pitati
   <u>萬多</u>祢天武可聞
   mata *ne-te-m-u kamo*
   again sleep.INF-PERF-TENT-ATTR EPT
   '[I] wonder if [I] shall sleep [with her] **again**.'

10. 20:4392.4-5 – Simotupusa
    有都久之波々尓 / <u>麻多</u>己等刀波牟
    utukusi papa-ni / ***mata*** *kötö top-am-u*
    beloved mother-DAT / **again** word ask-TENT-ATTR
    '[So I] could **once again** inquire after [my] beloved mother…'

11. 20:4349.1-3 – Kamitupusa
    毛母久麻能 / 美知波紀尓志乎 / <u>麻多</u>佐良尓
    momö kuma-nö / *miti pa k-ï-n-i-si-wo* / ***mata*** *sara n-i*
    hundred bend.in.a.road-GEN / road TPT come-INF-PERF-INF-PST.ATTR-ACC / **again** more COP-INF
    'Though [I] have come [this far on] roads with a hundred bends, **still** there is more [to go].'

8.5 *iya* 'plentifully, certainly'

The adverb *iya* 'plentifully, certainly', is attested twice, in UNP.

12. 14:3486.5 – UNP
    伊夜可多麻斯尔
    ***iya** kat-amasi-ni*
    certainly win-SUBJ-LOC
    'There is **no doubt** [I] will win.'

13. 14:3557.5 – UNP
    伊夜母比麻須尔
    ***iya** [o]möp-i-mas-u-ni*
    plentifully think-INF-increase-ATTR-LOC
    '[I] think [of her] **more and more**.'

8.6 *napo* 'still'

The adverb *napo* 'still', is attested just once, in EOJ.

14. 20:4351.4 – Kamitupusa
    奈保波太佐牟之
    ***napo** panda samu-si*
    still skin be.cold-AVFIN
    '[My bare] skin is **still** cold.'

8.7 *imanda* 'yet, still'

This adverb is only attested modifying a negative verb, in UNP. In WOJ, it is attested a few times modifying a verb in the affirmative (Vovin 2009a: 1125).

15. 14:3525.5 – UNP
    伊麻太宿奈布母
    ***imanda** NE-n-ap-umö*
    still sleep-NEG-ITER-EXCL
    '[We] are **still** not sleeping [together]!'

16. 14:3543.4-5 – UNP
古呂波伊敝杼母 / **伊末太**年那久尔
ko-rö pa ip-e-ndömö / **imanda** ne-n-aku n-i
girl-DIM TPT say-EV-CONC / **still** sleep-NEG.ATTR-NML COP-INF
'Although [that] dear girl says [we have], [the fact] is that [we] **still** have not slept together.'

8.8 *motöna* 'incessantly, at random'

The adverb *motöna* 'incessantly, at random' is attested just once, in UNP.

17. 14:3471.3-5 – UNP
伊米能未尔 / **母登奈**見要都追 / 安乎祢思奈久流
imey nömï n-i / **mötöna** MI-ye-tutu / a-wo ne si nak-uru
dream RPT COP-INF / **incessantly** see-PASS.INF-COOR / 1.S-ACC voice EPT make.cry-ATTR
'[They] are just dreams, [but] you appear [in them] **incessantly**, and it makes me cry!'

8.9 *tanda* 'directly'

The adverb *tanda* 'directly', is only attested once, in EOJ.

18. 14:3413.1-3 – Kamitukeno
刀祢河泊乃 / 可波世毛思良受 / **多太**和多里
tone-n-gapa-nö / kapa-se mo sir-anz-u / **tanda** watar-i
TN-GEN-river-GEN / river-rapids FPT know-NEG-INF / **directly** cross-INF
'**Directly** crossing Tone river without knowing of the river rapids. . .'

8.10 *nökinde* 'extremely'

The adverb *nökinde* 'extremely', always follows the adverb *ito* in WOJ, and in its sole attestation in UNP we find the same usage. The combination of these two adverbs is due to the influence of a Chinese proverb presented in the preface to MYS poem 5:897, in which superfluous suffering is involved. In WOJ poems it is used in phrases such as 'to cut the end of a short thing even shorter' or 'to sprinkle salt on a wound'. See Vovin (2011a: 137, 150) for a discussion.

19. 14:3548.3-5 – UNP
伊等**能伎提** / 可奈思家世呂尓 / 比等佐敝余須母
*itö **nökinde*** / *kanasi-ke se-rö-ni* / *pitö sape yös-umö*
very **extremely** / be.dear-AVATTR beloved.man-DIM-DAT / person RPT approach-EXCL
'Even [other] people approach [my] beloved man who is very, **extremely** dear [to me]!'

8.11 *sinzi* 'constantly'

The adverb *sinzi* 'constantly', is only attested once, in EOJ.

20. 20:4368.4-5 – Pitati
麻可知**之自奴伎** / 和波可敝里許牟
*ma-kandi **sinzi** nuk-i* / *wa pa kaper-i-kö-m-u*
INT-oar **constantly** pierce-INF / 1.S TPT return-INF-come-TENT-FIN
'**Constantly** thrusting the oar [on the tide boat], I shall return [to you].'

8.12 *simaraku* 'for a while'

The adverb *simaraku* 'for a while' is attested just once. It is phonographically unattested in WOJ, though WOJ *simasi(-ku)* 'for a while' clearly shares the same root *sim(a)-*.

21. 14:3471.1-2 – UNP
思麻良久波 / 祢都追母安良牟乎
***simaraku** pa* / *ne-tutu mö ar-am-u-wo*
for.a.while TPT / sleep.INF-COOR FPT exist-TENT-ATTR-ACC
'Although [I] will be sleeping **for a while**...'

8.13 *köngötö* 'greatly'

The adverb *köngötö* 'greatly' is attested just once, in UNP. It is unattested in WOJ. It may be related to WOJ *kökönda* 'extremely' through progressive vowel assimilation and different voicing on the medial consonants, if we reconstruct PJe *kəkəta 'greatly'.

22. 14:3502.4-5 – UNP
    等思佐倍**己其登** / 和波佐可流我倍
    *tösi sapey **köngötö*** / *wa pa sakar-u ngapey*
    year RPT **greatly** / 1.S TPT be.far.from-ATTR IPT
    'Will I be away from [her] even [after] **many** years? (No, I will not)'

8.14 *unbey* 'surely'

The adverb *unbey* 'surely' is attested just once. It also grammaticalized into the debitive suffix -*unbe* described in §7.5.2.3.9.

23. 14:3476a.1-2 – UNP
    宇倍兒奈波 / 和奴尓故布奈毛
    ***unbey** KO-na pa* / *wanu-ni kop-unam-o*
    surely girl-DIM TPT / 1.S-DAT long.for-TENT2-ATTR
    '[That] dear girl will **surely** long for me!'

8.15 *yumey* '[not] at all'

The adverb *yumey* is attested just once, in EOJ. It indicates a strong refutation, something akin to '[not] at all'. In this attestation it follows the negative-imperative suffix -*una*. This construction appears to be used for a stronger negative meaning. In WOJ it functions the same way, but in one example (19:4227.8), it comes before the verb, rather than after it (Vovin 2009a: 1122).

24. 14:3376a.4-5 – Muzasi
    宇家良我波奈乃 / 伊呂尓豆奈**由米**
    ukera-nga pana-nö / *irö-ni [i]nd-una **yumey***
    ukera-POSS flower-COMP / color/feelings-LOC go.out-NEG.IMP **at.all**
    'Like the *ukera* flowers, do not let [your face] reveal **even a hint of** your true feelings [for me]!'

8.16 *wosawosa* '[not] enough, [not] properly'

This adverb is only attested once, in UNP. It is not attested in WOJ, but it is attested in MJ. Diachronically it appears to be the result of a reduplication, though it is not clear what *wosa* meant by itself. Like *yumey*, this adverb co-occurs with a verb in the negative form.

25. 14:3529.3-5 – UNP
    <u>乎佐乎左</u>毛 / 祢奈敝古由惠尓 / 波伴尓許呂波要
    ***wosawosa** mo / ne-n-ape ko yuwe n-i / papa-ni kör-öp-aye*
    enough FPT / sleep-NEG-ITER.INF girl reason COP-INF / mother-DAT scold-ITER-PASS.INF
    'Due to not sleeping with a [certain] girl [often] **enough**, [I] was repeatedly scolded by [her] mother...'

9 Conjunctions

There are six conjunctions in AOJ, which connect verbal phrases in complex sentences. This is their major difference from particles (Vovin 2009a: 1133).

9.1 *tömo* 'even if, even though'

This conjunction always follows the final form of verbs and the infinitive form of adjectival verbs.

1. 14:3398.1-2 – Sinano
   比等未奈乃 / 許等波多由登毛
   *pitö mïna-nö / kötö pa tay-u **tömo***
   people all-GEN / word TPT cease-FIN **CNJ**
   '**Even if** everyone [else] goes silent. . .'

2. 20:4325.3-5 – Töpotuapumi
   久佐麻久良 / 多妣波由久等母 / 佐々己弖由加牟
   *kusa makura / tanbi pa yuk-u **tömö** / sasangö-te yuk-am-u*
   grass pillow / journey TPT go-FIN **CNJ** / lift.up.above.head.INF-SUB go-TENT-ATTR
   '[I] would carry [them] above my head, **even if** [I] went on a journey, [sleeping on] a grass pillow.'

3. 20:4405.3-5 – Kamitukeno
   都氣志非毛 / 伊刀尓奈流等母 / 和波等可自等余
   *tukey-si pïmo / ito n-i nar-u **tömö** / wa pa tök-anzi tö yö*
   attach.INF-PST.ATTR string / thread COP-INF become-FIN **CNJ** / 1.S TPT undo-NEG.TENT QUOT EPT
   '**Even if** the cord [she] tied [on me] becomes threadbare, [still] I think I probably will not untie it.'

4. 14:3386.2-3 – Simotupusa
   可豆思加和世乎 / 尓倍須登毛
   *kandusika wase-wo / nipey s-u **tömo***
   TN early.rice-ACC / food.offering do-FIN **CNJ**
   '**Even though** [she] made an offering of new rice from Kadusika. . .'

5. 14:3477.4-5 – UNP
安礼波古非牟奈 / 能知波安比奴**登母**
are pa kopï-m-u na / *nöti pa ap-i-n-u **tömö***
1.S TPT long.for-TENT-FIN EPT / later TPT meet-INF-PERF-FIN **CNJ**
'Oh, I shall long for [you]! **Even though** [we will] meet later...'

6. 14:3484.1-3 – UNP
安左乎良乎 / 遠家尓布須左尓 / 宇麻受**登毛**
asa wo-ra-wo / *wo ke-ni pususa n-i* / *um-anz-u **tömö***
hemp cord-PLUR-ACC / ramie container-LOC many COP-INF / spin.thread-NEG-FIN **CNJ**
'There are many small hemp threads in the ramie container, **even though** they are not [all] spun [together].'

7. 14:3456.1-4 – UNP
宇都世美能 / 夜蘓許登能敞波 / 思氣久**等母** / 安良蘓比可祢弖
utusemi-nö / *ya-so kötö-nö pe pa* / *singey-ku **tömö*** / *arasop-i-kane-te*
the.world-GEN / eight-ten word-GEN leaf TPT / be.lush-AVINF **CNJ** / resist-INF-NEG.POT.INF-SUB
'**Even though** rumors abound in this world, [you] cannot resist [them].'

8. 14:3530.3-5 – UNP
見要受**等母** / 兒呂我可奈門欲 / 由可久之要思母
*MI-ye-nz-u **tömö*** / *KO-rö-nga kana-TO-yo* / *yuk-aku si ye-si-mö*
see-PASS-NEG-FIN **CNJ** / girl-DIM-POSS metal-door-ABL / go.ATTR-NML EPT be.good-AVFIN-EXCL
'**Even though** [I] cannot see [her], going through the metal gate of [my] darling girl's [home] is so nice!'

Table 9.1: Attestations of the conjunction *tömo* across the provinces.

TSOJ			EOJ								UNP
Sin	Tö	Su	Kak	Mu	Sa	Mi	Sik	Pi	Sip	Kap	
1	1	0	1	0	0	0	0	0	1	0	5

9.2 *monö ~ monöwo* 'although, but, considering'

The conjunction *monö ~ monöwo*[192] is attested after the attributive and subjunctive forms of verbs. It is attested in both TSOJ and EOJ.

9. 14:3354.4-5 – Töpotuapumi
   伊利奈麻之**母乃** / 伊毛我乎杼許尔
   *ir-i-n-amasi **mönö*** / *imo-nga won-dökö-ni*
   enter-INF-PERF-SUBJ **CNJ** / beloved.girl-POSS DIM-bed-LOC
   '**Although** [I] would like to [lay] in the warm bed of [my] beloved. . .'

10. 14:3434.4-5 – Kamitukeno
    波比尔思**物能乎** / 安是加多延世武
    *pap-i-n-i-si **mönöwo*** / *anze ka taye-se-m-u*
    crawl-INF-PERF-INF-PST.ATTR **CNJ** / why QPT break-CAUS-TENT-FIN
    '**Considering** [the vines] have crawled [across the field], why would [you] break [us] apart?'

Table 9.2: Attestations of the conjunction *monö ~ monöwo* across the provinces.

TSOJ			EOJ								UNP
Sin	Tö	Su	Kak	Mu	Sa	Mi	Sik	Pi	Sip	Kap	
0	1	0	1	1	0	0	0	0	0	0	0

9.3 *monökara* 'although'

This conjunction follows the attributive form of verbs. It is only attested once, in UNP.

11. 14:3512.1-2 – UNP
    比登祢呂尔 / 伊波流**毛能可良**
    pitö ne-rö n-i / *ip-ar-u **monökara***
    one peak-DIM COP-INF / say-PROG-ATTR **CNJ**
    '**Although** [people] say [we] are one peak. . .'

---

[192] The form *monöwo* contains a fossilized accusative suffix *-wo* (Vovin 2009a: 1138).

9.4 *ngani* 'so that'

This conjunction is only attested once, in UNP. The WOJ form is *ngane*, thus the UNP form shows a raised vowel in the final syllable. As in WOJ, this conjunction follows the attributive form of verbs (Vovin 2009a: 1147–1148).

12. 14:3452.3-5 – UNP
     布流久佐尓 / 仁比久佐麻自利 / 於非波於布流**我尓**
     *puru kusa-ni / nipi kusa manzir-i / opï pa op-uru **ngani***
     old grass-LOC / new grass mix-INF / grow.NML TPT grow-ATTR **CNJ**
     'Mix new grass with old grass, **so that** [they] will grow.'

9.5 *ngani* 'like'

This conjunction is only attested once, in UNP. As in WOJ, it follows the final form of verbs (Vovin 2009a: 1149–1150).

13. 14:3543.1-3 – UNP
     武路我夜能 / 都留能都追美能 / 那利奴**賀尓**
     *murongaya-nö / turu-nö tutumi-nö / nar-i-n-u **ngani***
     TN-GEN / TN-GEN embankment-GEN / become-INF-PERF-FIN **CNJ**
     '**Like** [how] the embankment of Turu in Murogaya had been established...'

9.6 *sinda* 'when'

The conjunction *sinda* 'when' introduces a temporal clause and it always follows either a verb or an adjectival verb. In most cases the verb or adjectival verb is in the attributive form, but in two cases (examples 14 and 16 below) it is in the infinitive form, which can function as an adnominal modifier (see §7.5.2.1.1.1.3 for examples). This conjunction may be followed by the locative suffix -*ni*, as shown in example (14) below.

This conjunction is attested in EOJ and UNP, but not in TSOJ or WOJ. For a discussion of its etymology, see §4.3.1.5.1. All examples in the corpus are presented below.

14. 20:4407.1-3 – Kamitukeno
    比奈久毛理 / 宇須比乃佐可乎 / 古延志太尓
    pi-na kumor-i / *usupi-nö saka-wo* / *koye **sinda**-ni*
    sun-LOC become.cloudy-INF / TN-GEN slope-ACC / cross.INF **CNJ**-LOC
    '**When** [I] crossed Usupi hill [with] clouds over the sun...'

15. 20:4367.1-2 – Pitati
    阿我母弖能 / 和須例母之太波
    a-nga [o]möte-nö / *wasure-m-ö **sinda** pa*
    1.S-POSS face-GEN / forget-TENT-ATTR **CNJ** TPT
    '**When** [she] forgets my countenance...'

16. 14:3478.3-5 – UNP
    阿抱思太毛 / 安波能敝思太毛 / 奈尓己曽与佐礼
    *ap-o **sinda** mo* / *ap-an-öpe **sinda** mo* / *na-ni kösö yösar-e*
    meet-ATTR **CNJ** FPT / meet-NEG-ITER.INF **CNJ** FPT / 2.S-DAT FPT be.attracted.to-EV
    '**When** [we] meet, and even **when** [we] are not meeting, [I] am attracted to you.'

17. 14:3515.1-2 – UNP
    阿我於毛能 / 和須礼牟之太波
    a-nga omo-nö / *wasure-m-u **sinda** pa*
    1.S-POSS face-GEN / forget-TENT-ATTR **CNJ** TPT
    '**When** [you] forget my countenance...'

18. 14:3520.1-2 – UNP
    於毛可多能 / 和須礼牟之太波
    omo kata-nö / *wasure-m-u **sinda** pa*
    face shape-GEN / forget-TENT-ATTR **CNJ** TPT
    '**When** [I] forget the features of [your] countenance...'

19. 14:3533.1-2 – UNP
    比登乃兒能 / 可奈思家之太波
    pitö-nö KO-nö / *kanasi-ke **sinda** pa*
    person-GEN girl-GEN / be.dear-AVATTR **CNJ** TPT
    '**When** [I think of] how dear [that] person's girl is...'

20. 14:3363 – Sagamu
    和我世古乎 / 夜麻登敝夜利弖 / 麻都之太須 / 安思我良夜麻乃 / 須疑乃木能末可
    *wa-nga se-ko-wo / yamatö-pe yar-i-te / mat-u **sinda** s-u / asingara yama-nö / sungï nö KÖ-nö ma ka*
    1.S-POSS beloved.man-DIM-ACC / TN-ALL send-INF-SUB / wait-ATTR **CNJ** do-FIN / TN mountain-GEN / cryptomeria COP.ATTR tree-GEN space QPT
    '[I] sent my darling beloved to Yamatö, and **when** [I] wait [for my beloved to come back], I do [it]…[will his return be] through the cryptomeria trees of Mt. Asigara?'

21. 14:3461.5 – UNP
    安家努思太久流
    *ake-n-o **sinda** k-uru*
    brighten.INF-PERF-ATTR **CNJ** come-ATTR
    '[You only] came **when** it dawned.'

Table 9.3: Attestations of the conjunction *sinda* across the provinces.

TSOJ			EOJ								UNP
Sin	Tö	Su	Kak	Mu	Sa	Mi	Sik	Pi	Sip	Kap	
0	0	0	1	0	1	0	0	1	0	0	6

10 Particles

Particles are a fundamental aspect of the grammar of the AOJ dialects. The particles can be separated into seven classes: focus particles, emphatic particles, question particles, restrictive particles, desiderative particles, ironic particles, and quotative particles.

10.1 The basic syntax of particles

Particles always follow the phrase to which they attach. When two particles attach to the same phrase, their order is fixed (such orders are described in the relevant sections below). Some particles are restricted in their movement, for example some only occur after the predicate verb. Other particles are much freer and may follow nearly anything.

10.1.1 Attributive-triggering particles (*kakari musubi*)

The Japanese term *kakari musubi* refers to the phenomenon of a particle triggering a preceding or following verb to take an attributive, rather than a final, suffix ending. Much has been written about this phenomenon in Old Japanese (see Ōno 1993; Serafim and Shinzato 2000, 2005; Vovin 2009a: 1156–1292). In keeping with their behavior, I refer to these particles as "attributive-triggering". The particles that cause this phenomenon are the focus particle *sö ~ nzö ~ nze ~ tö*, the question particles *ka* and *ya*, and the emphatic particle *kamo*.

10.1.2 Evidential-triggering particles

The focus particle *kösö* triggers the evidential form of a following verb. The emphatic particle *kamo* may also trigger the evidential.

10.2 Focus particles

The focus particles include *pa, mo, sö ~ nzö ~ nze ~ tö,* and *kösö*.

10.2.1 Topic particle *pa*

The topic particle *pa* is amply attested in the corpus. Its function is to topicalize a preceding noun (phrase) and shift the focus to the remainder of the sentence (Martin 1988: 52; Vovin 2009a: 1156). It is important to understand this particle, like the Modern Japanese topic particle *wa*, does not mark the subject of a sentence. In the translations that follow below, I have bolded the part of the sentence where the focus has shifted.

1. 14:3398.1-2 – Sinano
   比等未奈乃 / 許等波多由登毛
   *pitö mïna-nö / kötö **pa** tay-u tömo*
   people all-GEN / word **TPT** cease-FIN CNJ
   '**Even if** everyone [else] **goes** quiet...'

2. 20:4402.4-5 – Sinano
   伊波布伊能知波 / 意毛知々可多米
   *ipap-u inöti **pa** / omo titi-nga tamey*
   pray-ATTR life **TPT** / mother father-POSS benefit
   '[I] prayed for the lives of [my] **mother and father**.'

3. 20:4322.1-2 – Töpotuapumi
   和我都麻波 / 伊多久古非良之
   *wa-nga tuma **pa** / ita-ku kopï-rasi*
   1.S-POSS spouse **TPT** / be.extreme-AVINF long.for-SUP
   'My wife **must miss [me] greatly**.'

4. 20:4343.1-2 – Suruga
   和呂多比波 / 多比等於米保等
   *warö tanbi **pa** / tanbi tö omeyp-o-ndö*
   1.S journey **TPT** / journey QUOT think-EV-CONC
   '**Although [I] know** my journey **will be an [arduous] one**...'

5. 14:3418.3-4 – Kamitukeno
   武良奈倍尓 / 許登波佐太米都
   *mura-napey-ni / kötö **pa** sandamey-t-u*
   divination-seedling-LOC / matter **TPT** determine.INF-PERF-FIN
   '[They] **have decided** the matter [of who I will marry based] on the divination seedlings.'

6. 20:4406.3-5 – Kamitukeno
    久佐麻久良 / 多妣**波**久流之等 / 都氣夜良麻久母
    *kusa makura / tanbi **pa** kurusi tö / tungey-yar-am-aku mö*
    grass pillow / journey **TPT** be.awful.AVFIN QUOT / tell.INF-send-TENT.ATTR-NML FPT
    '[I] would send [him] to tell [them] that [my] journey, [sleeping on] a grass pillow, **is painful**!'

7. 20:4422.4 – Muzasi
    於妣**婆**等可奈々
    *onbi **pa** tök-ana-na*
    sash **TPT** undo-NEG.ATTR-LOC
    '[I shall sleep], **without untying** [my] sash. . .'

8. 14:3366.1-2 – Sagamu
    麻可奈思美 / 佐祢尓和**波**由久
    *ma-kanasi-mi / sa-ne-ni wa **pa** yuk-u*
    INT-be.dear-AVGER / LOC-sleep.NML-LOC 1.S **TPT** go-ATTR
    'Since [she] is truly dear [to me], [I] **will go** and sleep [with her].'

9. 20:4329.1-2 – Sagamu
    夜蘇久尓**波** / 奈尓波尓都度比
    *ya-so kuni **pa** / nanipa-ni tundop-i*
    eight-ten province **TPT** / TN-LOC gather-INF
    '[Those from] many provinces **gather in Nanipa**. . .'

10. 14:3424.4-5 – Simotukeno
    麻具波思兒呂**波** / 多賀家可母多牟
    *ma n-gupasi KO-rö **pa** / ta-nga ke ka möt-am-u*
    true COP.INF-be.beautiful girl-DIM **TPT** / who-POSS container QPT hold-TENT-ATTR
    '**Whose [food] container shall** the truly beautiful girl **hold**?'

11. 20:4378.3-5 – Simotukeno
    阿毛志志可 / 多麻乃須我多**波** / 和須例西奈布母
    *amo sisi-ka / tama-nö sungata **pa** / wasure se-n-ap-umö*
    mother father-POSS / jewel-GEN appearance **TPT** / forget.NML do-NEG-ITER-EXCL
    '[I] **will not forget** the jewel-like appearance of [my] mother and father!'

12. 14:3395.3-5 – Pitati
    安比太欲**波** / 佐波太奈利怒乎 / 萬多祢天武可聞
    *apinda yo **pa** / sapanda nar-i-n-o-wo / mata ne-te-m-u kamo*
    interval night **TPT** / many be-INF-PERF-ATTR-ACC / again sleep.INF-PERF-TENT-ATTR EPT
    '**Since there have been many** nights in between [our meetings], [I] wonder if [I] shall sleep [with her] again...'

13. 20:4370.4-5 – Pitati
    須米良美久佐尓 / 和礼**波**伎尓之乎
    *sumeyra mi-[i]kusa-ni / ware **pa** k-i-n-i-si-wo*
    emperor HON-army-LOC / **1.S TPT** come-INF-PERF-INF-PST.ATTR-ACC
    '**Since I came** into the Emperor's great army...'

14. 20:4385.3-5 – Simotupusa
    志流敞尓**波** / 古乎等都麻乎等 / 於枳弖等母枳奴
    *siru pe-ni **pa** / ko-wo-tö tuma-wo-tö / ok-i-te tö mö k-i-n-u*
    behind area-LOC **TPT** / child-ACC-COM spouse-ACC-COM / leave.behind-INF-SUB FPT EPT come-INF-PERF-FIN
    '[I] **left [my] wife and child** behind to come [out here].'

15. 20:4349.1-2 – Kamitupusa
    毛母久麻能 / 美知**波**紀尓志乎 /
    *momö kuma-nö / miti **pa** k-ï-n-i-si-wo*
    hundred bend.in.a.road-GEN / road **TPT** come-INF-PERF-INF-PST.ATTR-ACC
    '**Though [I] have come** [this far on] roads with a hundred bends...'

16. 14:3476a.1-2 – UNP
    宇倍兒奈**波** / 和奴尓故布奈毛
    *unbey KO-na **pa** / wanu-ni kop-unam-o*
    surely girl-DIM **TPT** / 1.S-DAT long.for-TENT2-ATTR
    '[That] dear girl will surely **long for me**!'

17. 14:3494.1-4 – UNP
    兒毛知夜麻 / 和可加敞流弖能 / 毛美都麻弖 / 宿毛等**波**毛布
    *KOmoti yama / waka kaperute-nö / momit-u-mande / NE-m-o tö wa **pa** [o]mop-u*
    TN mountain / young maple-GEN / leaves.turn.color-ATTR-TERM / sleep-TENT-ATTR QUOT **1.S TPT** think-FIN
    'I **think** [we] should sleep [together] until the leaves of the young maples on Mt. Komoti turn red.'

18. 20:4425.1-2 – UNP
    佐伎毛利尓 / 由久**波**多我世登
    *sakimori n-i / yuk-u **pa** ta-nga se tö*
    border.guard COP-INF / go-ATTR **TPT** who-POSS beloved.man QUOT
    '**Whose husband** [is that], going to be a border guard?'

As in WOJ (Vovin 2020: 1075–1076), two topic particles can be used in the same sentence. When this occurs in EOJ both particles mark topics and the meaning is not contrastive, as demonstrated by examples (19) and (20) below.

19. 20:4378.1-2 – Simotukeno
    都久比夜**波** / 須具**波**由氣等毛
    *tuku pi ya **pa** / sungu **pa** yuk-ey-ndömo*
    month day EPT **TPT** / pass.NML **TPT** go-EV-CONC
    '**Although** the months and days **pass** [by]...'

20. 14:3382.5 – Kamitupusa
    汝**者**故布**婆**曽母
    *NA **PA** kopu **pa** sö-m-ö*
    2.S **TPT** long.for.NML **TPT** do-TENT-ATTR
    'You **shall love** [me].'

Table 10.1: Attestations of the topic particle *pa* across the provinces.

TSOJ			EOJ								UNP
Sin	Tö	Su	Kak	Mu	Sa	Mi	Sik	Pi	Sip	Kap	
4	4	6	12	5	2	0	7	14	3	7	42

10.2.2 Focus particle *mo*

The focus particle *mo* places a focus on that which comes before it, and thus indicates the opposite focus of the topic particle *pa* (Martin 1988: 52; Vovin 2009a: 1172).

21. 14:3400.3-5 – Sinano
    左射礼思**母** / 伎弥之布美弓波 / 多麻等比呂波牟
    *sanzare [i]si **mö** / kimi si pum-i-te-nba / tama tö piröp-am-u*
    little stone FPT / lord EPT step-INF-PERF-COND / jewel COP pick.up-TENT-FIN
    'When [you, my] lord have stepped on the **small stones**, [I] shall pick [them] up as jewels.'

22. 20:4325.1-2 – Töpotuapumi
    知々波々母 / 波奈尔母我毛夜
    titi papa mö / pana n-i möngamo ya
    father mother FPT / blossom COP-INF DPT EPT
    'Oh, [I] wish [my] **father and mother** were flowers!'

23. 14:3358c.3-5 – Suruga
    古布良久波 / 布自乃多可祢尔 / 布流由伎奈須毛
    kop-ur-aku pa / punzi-nö taka ne-ni / **pur-u yuki-nasu mo**
    long.for-ATTR-NML TPT / TN-GEN high peak-LOC / **fall-ATTR snow-COMP FPT**
    '[My] longing [for you] is **like the snow that falls** on Mt. Puzi's highest peak.'

24. 14:3402.4-5 – Kamitukeno
    勢奈能我素侶母 / 佐夜尔布良思都
    se-na-nö-nga sonde mö / saya n-i pur-as-i-t-u
    beloved.man-DIM-DIM-POSS sleeve FPT / clear COP-INF wave-HON-INF-PERF-FIN
    '[My] **dearly beloved** clearly waved [his] **sleeve** [at me].'

25. 20:4406.3-5 – Kamitukeno
    久佐麻久良 / 多妣波久流之等 / 都氣夜良麻久母
    kusa makura / tanbi pa kurusi tö / **tungey-yar-am-aku mö**
    grass pillow / journey TPT be.awful.AVFIN QUOT / **tell.INF-send-TENT.ATTR-NML FPT**
    '[I] **would send [him] to tell** [them] that [my] journey, [sleeping on] a grass pillow, is painful!'

26. 14:3374.3-5 – Muzasi
    麻左弖尔毛 / 乃良奴伎美我名 / 宇良尔侶尔家里
    masande n-i mo / nör-an-u kimi-nga NA / ura-ni [i]nde-n-i-ker-i
    certain COP-INF FPT / tell-NEG-ATTR lord-POSS name / divination-LOC go.out.INF-PERF-INF-RETR-FIN
    '[My] lord's name that [I] did not tell [them] **certainly** emerged from the divination.'

27. 20:4415.1-3 – Muzasi
    志良多麻乎 / 弖尔刀里母之弖 / 美流乃須母
    sira tama-wo / te-ni tor-i-mös-i-te / **mi-ru-nösu mö**
    white pearl-ACC / hand-LOC take-INF-hold-INF-GER / **see-ATTR-COMP FPT**
    '**Like** taking and holding pearls in [my] hands and **gazing at them**.'

28. 14:3368.4-5 – Sagamu
余尓母多欲良尓 / 故呂河伊波奈久尓
yö-ni mö tayora n-i / *ko-rö-nga ip-an-aku n-i*
lifetime-LOC FPT wavering COP-INF / girl-DIM-POSS say-NEG.ATTR-NML COP-INF
'Although [my] dear girl will not say that [her love for me] will waver **in [this] lifetime**...'

29. 20:4377.1-2 – Simotukeno
阿母刀自母 / 多麻尓毛賀毛夜
amö tonzi mö / *tama n-i mongamo ya*
mother housewife FPT / jade COP-INF DPT FPT
'Oh, how [I] wish [my] **dear mother** were a jewel!'

30. 14:3392.4-5 – Pitati
代尓毛多由良尓 / 和我於毛波奈久尓
YÖ-ni mo tayura n-i / *wa-nga omop-an-aku n-i*
lifetime-LOC FPT wavering COP-INF / 1.S-POSS think-NEG.ATTR-NML COP-INF
'I do not think that [I will] waver [in my love for you] **in [my] lifetime**.'

31. 20:4369.4-5 – Pitati
由等許尓母 / 可奈之家伊母曽 / 比留毛可奈之祁
yu tökö-ni mö / *kanasi-ke imö sö* / *piru mo kanasi-ke*
night bed-LOC FPT / be.dear-AVATTR beloved.girl FPT / daytime FPT be.dear-AVATTR
'[My] beloved girl, who is dear [to me] **in bed at night**, is also dear [to me] during the day.'

32. 14:3385.4-5 – Simotupusa
麻末乃於須比尓 / 奈美毛登杼呂尓
mama-nö osu-pi-ni / **nami mo** *töndörö n-i*
cliff-GEN rocky.shore-side-LOC / wave FPT thunderous COP-INF
'**Waves** were **also** roaring on the side of the rocky shore [near] the cliffs.'

33. 20:4386.3-5 – Simotupusa
以都母以都母 / 於毛加古比須々 / 奈理麻之都之母
itu mö itu mö / *omo-nga kopi s-u s-u* / *nar-i-mas-i-tusi mö*
when FPT when FPT / mother-POSS love.NML do-FIN do-FIN / make.a.living-INF-HON-INF-COOR FPT
'[My] mother **always** loves [me], **even while working**.'

34. 14:3383.3-5 – Kamitupusa
可久太尔毛 / 久尔乃登保可婆 / 奈我目保里勢牟
ka-ku ndani mo / kuni-nö töpo-ka-nba / na-nga MEY por-i se-m-u
be.thus-AVINF RPT FPT / province-GEN be.far-AVEV-CONJ / 2.S-POSS eye desire-NML do-TENT-FIN
'[I] dream of your eyes, since [your] province is **just so** far [away].'

35. 20:4347.3-5 – Kamitupusa
奈我波氣流 / 多知尔奈里弖母 / 伊波非弓之加母
na-nga pak-eyr-u / **tati n-i nar-i-te mö** / ipap-ï-te-si kamö
2.S-POSS wear-PROG-ATTR / **long.sword COP-INF become-INF-SUB FPT** / pray-INF-PERF-PST.ATTR EPT
'[I] want to **become the long sword that** you are wearing and pray for [you].'

36. 14:3440a.3-4 – UNP
奈礼毛阿礼毛 / 余知乎曽母弖流
nare mo are mo / yöti-wo sö möt-er-u
2.S FPT 1.S FPT / same.age-ACC FPT hold-PROG-ATTR
'**You and I** both have [children] of the same age.'

37. 14:3478.3-5 – UNP
阿抱思太毛 / 安波能敝思太毛 / 奈尔己曽与佐礼
ap-o sinda mo / **ap-an-öpe sinda mo** / na-ni kösö yösar-e
meet-ATTR CNJ FPT / **meet-NEG-ITER.INF CNJ FPT** / 2.S-DAT FPT be.attracted.to-EV
'[I] am attracted to you **when [we] meet, and even when [we] do not meet**.'

38. 14:3561.3-5 – UNP
比賀刀礼婆 / 阿米乎万刀能須 / 伎美乎等麻刀母
pi-nga tor-e-nba / amey-wo mat-o-nösu / **kimi-wo tö mat-o mö**
sun-POSS shine-EV-CONJ / rain-ACC wait-ATTR-COMP / **lord-ACC FPT wait-ATTR FPT**
'[I] **wait for [you, my] lord**, as [one] waits for the rain when the sun is shining.'

39. 20:4425.5 – UNP
毛乃母比毛世受
monö [o]möp-i mo se-nz-u
thing think-NML FPT do-NEG-FIN
'[I] do not **worry about things**.'

Table 10.2: Attestations of the focus particle *mo* across the provinces.

TSOJ			EOJ								UNP
Sin	Tö	Su	Kak	Mu	Sa	Mi	Sik	Pi	Sip	Kap	
1	2	2	6	3	2	0	2	4	5	4	25

10.2.3 Focus particle *sö ~ nzö ~ nze ~ tö*

The exact type of focus that this particle indicates is unclear. It appears to place a focus on that which comes before it, like the focus particle *mo*. In AOJ this particle is never preceded by any other particle, and there is only one instance where it is followed by the emphatic particle *mo* (shown in example 52 below). In comparison, Vovin (2009a: 1187) notes that in WOJ the focus particle *sö* combines with both the topic particle *pa* and the focus particle *mo*, and thus he concludes the focus particle *sö* must have indicated some other type of focus different from those two particles. Synchronically, there are four phonetic variants in AOJ (three of which are attested in EOJ, while two are attested in TSOJ), though historically there were two etymologically distinct particles in PJe (*sə ~ *nzə and *tə) and PJ (*sə and *tə). See §2.3.4.3 for a discussion of the historical development of the different forms.

The focus particle *sö* always triggers the attributive suffix on the verb or adjectival verb that follows.

40. 20:4401.1-4 – Sinano
可良己呂武 / 須宗尔等里都伎 / **奈古古良乎** / 意伎弖曽伎怒也
kara körömu / *suso-ni tör-i-tuk-i* / **nak-o ko-ra-wo** / *ok-i-te sö k-i-n-o ya*
TN garment / hem-LOC take-INF-attach-INF / **cry-ATTR child-PLUR-ACC** / **leave.behind-INF-SUB FPT** come-INF-PERF-ATTR EPT
'Oh, [I] have come [here], **leaving behind [my] sobbing children** who clung to the hem of [my] Kara robes!'

41. 20:4323.3-5 – Töpotuapumi
奈尔須礼曽 / 波々登布波奈乃 / 佐吉泥己受祁牟
nani s-ure sö / *papa tö [i]p-u pana-nö* / *sak-i-nde-kö-nz-u-kem-u*
why do-EV FPT / mother QUOT say-ATTR blossom-GEN / bloom-INF-go.out.INF-come-NEG-INF-PST.TENT-ATTR
'**Why** has the flower called 'mother' not come out in bloom?'

42. 20:4380.3-5 – Simotukeno
可美佐夫流 / 伊古麻多可祢尓 / **久毛曽**多奈妣久
kami sanb-uru / *ikoma taka ne-ni* / ***kumo sö*** *tananbik-u*
deity behave.like-ATTR / TN high peak-LOC / **cloud FPT** stream.out-ATTR
'[I see] **clouds** streaming out over the high peak [of] the deific Mt. Ikoma.'

43. 20:4369.4-5 – Pitati
由等許尓母 / **可奈之家伊母曽** / 比留毛可奈之祁
yu tökö-ni mö / ***kanasi-ke imö sö*** / *piru mo kanasi-ke*
night bed-LOC FPT / **be.dear-AVATTR beloved.girl FPT** / daytime FPT be.dear-AVATTR
'[My] **beloved girl**, who is dear [to me] in bed at night, is also dear [to me] during the day.'

44. 20:4357.3-5 – Kamitupusa
和藝毛古我 / 蘓弖母志保々尓 / **奈伎志曽**母波由
wa-ng[a]-imo-ko-nga / *sonde mö sipopo n-i* / ***nak-i-si sö*** *[o]möp-ay-u*
1.S-POSS-beloved.girl-DIM-POSS / sleeve FPT soaked COP-INF / **cry-INF-PST.ATTR FPT** think-PASS-FIN
'[I] suddenly remember how my darling **cried** [so much for me], even her sleeves were soaking wet!'

45. 14:3460.1-2 – UNP
多礼曽許能 / 屋能戸於曽夫流
tare sö *könö* / *YA-nö TO osö-nbur-u*
who FPT this / house-GEN door push-shake-ATTR
'**Who** is knocking on the door of this house?'

46. 14:3504.3-4 – UNP
宇良夜須尓 / 左奴流**夜曽**奈伎
ura yasu n-i / *sa-n-uru **YO sö*** *na-ki*
heart easy COP-INF / LOC-sleep-ATTR **night FPT** not.exist-AVATTR
'There are no **nights** when [I] sleep with [my] heart at ease.'

47. 14:3511.4-5 – UNP
物能乎曽於毛布 / 等思乃許能己呂
mönö-wo sö *omop-u* / *tösi-nö könö körö*
thing-ACC FPT think-ATTR / year-GEN this time
'[I] ponder [many] **things** this time of year.'

10.2.3.1 Variant *nzö*

The variant form *nzö* probably originated due to a sporadic intervocalic voicing of *sö* > *nzö* (Omodaka 1967: 399). It is only attested once, in the Simotukeno topolect of EOJ.

48. 20:4376.3-5 – Simotukeno
阿母志志尓 / 已等麻乎佐受弖 / 伊麻叙久夜之氣
amö sisi-ni / *kötö mawos-anz-u-te* / **ima nzö** *kuyasi-key*
mother father-DAT / word say.HUM-NEG-INF-SUB / **now FPT** be.regretful-AVATTR
'[I] did not inform [my] mother and father, and **oh, now** [I] regret it!'

10.2.3.2 Variant *nze*

The variant form *nze* is attested only in the Suruga topolect of TSOJ. It is unattested in WOJ.

49. 20:4337.4-5 – Suruga
知々波々尓 / 毛能波須價尓弖 / 已麻叙久夜志伎
titi papa-ni / *monö [i]p-anz-u k-e-n-i-te* / **ima nzö** *kuyasi-ki*
father mother-DAT / thing say-NEG-INF come-INF-PERF-INF-SUB / **now FPT** be.regretful-AVATTR
'[I] have come [out here] without saying a word to [my] father or mother, and **oh, now** [I] regret it!'

While written *nzö* in example (49), I view this Suruga form as being phonemically /ⁿze/. See §2.2.1.1 for the phonological data supporting this analysis.

50. 20:4346.4-5 - Suruga
伊比之氣等婆是 / 和須礼加祢豆流
ip-i-si keytönba nze / *wasure-kane-t-uru*
say-INF-PST.ATTR word **FPT** / forget.INF-NEG.POT.INF-PERF-ATTR
'[I] have not been able to forget the **words [they] said**.'

10.2.3.3 Variant *tö*

The variant *tö* is attested four times in the corpus, in EOJ and UNP. It is unattested in WOJ. A diachronic and comparative discussion of this particle is presented in §2.3.4.3.

51. 14:3425.1-4 – Simotukeno
    志母都家努 / 安素乃河泊良欲 / 伊之布麻努受 / **蘓良由登**伎努与
    simötukeno / *aso-nö kapara-yo* / *isi pum-anz-u* / ***sora-yu tö*** *k-i-n-o yö*
    TN / TN-GEN river.bank-ABL / stone step-NEG-INF / **sky-ABL FPT** come-INF-PERF-ATTR EPT
    '[I] came **from the sky** without stepping [on] the stones from the riverbank of Aso in Simotukeno!'

52. 20:4385.3-5 – Simotupusa
    志流敝尔波 / 古乎等都麻乎等 / **於枳弖等**母枳奴
    siru pe-ni pa / *ko-wo-tö tuma-wo-tö* / ***ok-i-te tö*** *mö k-i-n-u*
    behind area-LOC TPT / child-ACC-COM spouse-ACC-COM / **leave.behind-INF-SUB FPT** EPT come-INF-PERF-ATTR
    '[I] **left** [my] wife and child behind to come [out here].'

53. 20:4430.5 – UNP
    伊埿弖登阿我久流
    inde-te tö *a-nga k-uru*
    go.out.INF-SUB FPT 1.S-POSS come-ATTR
    'I **went out** and came [here].'

54. 14:3561.3-5 – UNP
    比賀刀礼婆 / 阿米乎万刀能須 / **伎美乎等**麻刀母
    pi-nga tor-e-nba / *amey-wo mat-o-nösu* / ***kimi-wo tö*** *mat-o mö*
    sun-POSS shine-EV-CONJ / rain-ACC wait-ATTR-COMP / **lord-ACC FPT** wait-ATTR FPT
    '[I] wait for [you, my] **lord**, as one waits for the rain when the sun is shining.'

Table 10.3: Attestations of the focus particle *sö* ~ *nzö* ~ *nze* ~ *tö* across the provinces.

Form	TSOJ			EOJ								UNP
	Sin	Tö	Su	Kak	Mu	Sa	Mi	Sik	Pi	Sip	Kap	
sö	1	1	0	0	0	0	0	1	1	0	1	11
nzö	0	0	0	0	0	0	0	1	0	0	0	0
nze	0	0	2	0	0	0	0	0	0	0	0	0
tö	0	0	0	0	0	0	0	1	0	1	0	2

10.2.4 Focus particle *kösö*

The focus particle *kösö*, like the focus particles *mo* and *sö*, emphasizes that which precedes it. It indicates the strongest emphasis of any focus particle attested in AOJ (Vovin 2009a: 1202). This particle usually triggers the evidential on the following predicate verb, but there are two examples in EOJ in which it precedes an adjectival verb or verb predicate (examples 56 and 59 below) and the following verb or adjectival verb is in the final form. This is different from WOJ where we only find the attributive occurring on adjectival verbs when preceded by this particle (Vovin 2009a: 1202).

55. 14:3417.4-5 – Kamitukeno
与曽尓見之欲波 / **伊麻許曽**麻左礼
yösö-ni MI-si-yo pa / ***ima kösö** mas-ar-e*
elsewhere-LOC see.INF-PST.ATTR-ABL TPT / **now FPT** be.superior-PROG-EV
'**Now** [things] are better than when [I] was looking elsewhere.'

56. 14:3419.3-5 – Kamitukeno
於毛比度路 / **久麻許曽**之都等 / 和須礼西奈布母
omop-i-nd-oro / ***kuma kösö** s-i-t-u tö* / *wasure se-n-ap-umö*
think-INF-emerge-ATTR / **offering.to.the.deities FPT** do-INF-PERF-FIN QUOT / forget.NML do-NEG-ITER-EXCL
'[I] recall making **the offering to the deities** – [I] will not forget [you]!'

57. 14:3394.4-5 – Pitati
和須良延許婆古曽 / 那乎可家奈波賣
wasura-kö-nba kosö / *na-wo kake-n-ap-am-e*
forget-come-COND FPT / 2.S-ACC call.out-NEG-ITER-TENT-EV
'**When [I] start to forget** [our meeting there], [I] shall stop calling out for you!'

58. 14:3493a.1-2 – UNP
於曽波夜母 / **奈乎許曽**麻多賣
osö paya mö / ***na-wo kösö** mat-am-e*
slow fast FPT / **2.S-ACC FPT** wait-TENT-EV
'Whether [you come] early or late, [I] shall wait **for you**.'

59. 14:3509.3-5 – UNP
宿奈敝杼母 / 古呂賀於曽伎能 / **安路許曽**要志母
NE-n-ap-e-ndömö / *ko-rö-nga osöki-nö* / **ar-o kösö** *ye-si-mö*
sleep-NEG-ITER-EV-CONC / girl-DIM-POSS upper.garment-GEN / **exist-ATTR FPT** be.good-AVFIN-EXCL
'Although [we] are not sleeping together, it is so nice **to have** [my] dear girl's upper garment!'

60. 14:3531.1-2 – UNP
伊母乎許曽 / 安比美尓許思可
imö-wo kösö / *ap-i-mi-ni kö-sika*
beloved.girl-ACC FPT / meet-INF-see.NML-LOC come-PST.EV
'[I] came to see [my] **beloved girl**.'

Table 10.4: Attestations of the focus particle *kösö* across the provinces.

TSOJ			EOJ								UNP
Sin	Tö	Su	Kak	Mu	Sa	Mi	Sik	Pi	Sip	Kap	
0	0	0	2	0	0	0	0	2	0	0	7

10.3 Emphatic particles

The emphatic particles include *kamo, si, mo, ya, yö, ye, na,* and *we*.

10.3.1 Emphatic particle *kamo*

The emphatic particle *kamo* has two functions: exclamation and uncertainty (Vovin 2009a: 1235). Due to the fact it historically contains the question particle *ka*, the particle *kamo* usually triggers an attributive suffix on the predicate verb regardless of whether it appears before or after *kamo*. In WOJ, this is a strict rule without exceptions (as noted by Vovin). However, there are several examples in EOJ of it triggering the evidential suffix on a preceding verb (including examples 71 and 75 below), as well as one example in which it follows the final form of a verb (76). None of these is attested in TSOJ. In addition, there is a variant form *kamu* with a raised final vowel attested once in the Sinano topolect of TSOJ (see example 61).

10.3.1.1 Exclamation function

61. 20:4403.3-5 – Sinano
    阿乎久牟乃 / 等能妣久夜麻乎 / 古与伎怒**加牟**
    awo kumu-nö / tönönbik-u yama-wo / koyö-te k-i-n-o **kamu**
    blue cloud-GEN / stream.out-ATTR mountain-ACC / cross.INF-SUB come-INF-PERF-ATTR **EPT**
    '**Oh**, [I] came [here], having crossed over the mountain where the blue clouds stream out...'

62. 20:4341.4-5 – Suruga
    道乃長道波 / 由伎加弓奴**加毛**
    MITI nö NANGA-NDI pa / yuk-i-kate-n-u **kamo**
    road COP.ATTR long-road TPT / go-INF-POT-NEG-ATTR **EPT**
    'The road [ahead] is long, and [I] **fear** I cannot traverse it!'

63. 14:3413.4-5 – Kamitukeno
    奈美尓安布能須 / 安敝流伎美**可母**
    nami-ni ap-u-nösu / ap-er-u kimi **kamö**
    wave-DAT meet-ATTR-COMP / meet-PROG-ATTR lord **EPT**
    '**Oh**, meeting [you, my] lord, [is] like encountering a wave!'

64. 20:4404.3-5 – Kamitukeno
    和藝毛古賀 / 都氣之非毛我乎 / 多延尓氣流**可毛**
    wa-ng-imo-ko-nga / tukey-si pïmo-nga wo / taye-n-i-keyr-u **kamo**
    1.S-POSS-beloved.girl-DIM-POSS / attach.INF-PST.ATTR cord-POSS string / break.INF-PERF-INF-RETR-ATTR **EPT**
    '**Oh**, the cord that my beloved girl tied [over my robes] has come undone!'

65. 20:4354.4-5 – Kamitupusa
    伊母加己己呂波 / 和須礼世奴**可母**
    imö-nga kökörö pa / wasure se-n-u **kamö**
    beloved.girl-POSS heart TPT / forget.NML do-NEG-ATTR **EPT**
    '[I] will not forget about [my] beloved's feelings!'

66. 14:3463.3-5 – UNP
己許呂奈久 / 佐刀乃美奈可尓 / 安敝流世奈**可毛**
kökörö na-ku / *sato-nö mi-naka-ni* / *ap-er-u se-na **kamo***
heart not.exist-INF / village-GEN HON-inside-LOC / meet-PROG-ATTR beloved.man-DIM **EPT**
'**Oh** [my] darling beloved, whom [I] am meeting inconsiderately in the great center of the village!'

67. 14:3527.4-5 – UNP
伊伎豆久伊毛乎 / 於伎弖伎努**可母**
ikinduk-u imo-wo / *ok-i-te k-i-n-o **kamö***
sigh-ATTR beloved.girl-ACC / leave.behind-INF-SUB come-INF-PERF-ATTR **EPT**
'[I] left behind [my] beloved girl who sighs [for me] and came [here]!'

68. 20:4428.4-5 – UNP
叡比波登加奈々 / 阿夜尓**可毛**祢牟
yenbi pa tök-ana-na / *aya n-i **kamo** ne-m-u*
sash TPT untie-NEG.ATTR-LOC / unnatural COP-INF **EPT** sleep-TENT-ATTR
'[I] shall sleep without untying [my] sash, unnatural [as it] **may** be!'

10.3.1.2 Uncertainty function

69. 14:3379.1-2 – Muzasi
和我世故乎 / 安杼**可母**伊波武
wa-nga se-ko-wo / *andö **kamö** ip-am-u*
1.S-POSS beloved.man-DIM-ACC / what **EPT** say-TENT-ATTR
'[I] **wonder**, what could [I] say [about] my beloved man?'

70. 20:4423.4-5 – Muzasi
伊波奈流伊毛波 / 佐夜尓美毛**可母**
ipa-n[i] ar-u imo pa / *saya n-i mi-m-o **kamö***
house-LOC exist-ATTR beloved.girl TPT / clear COP-INF see-TENT-ATTR **EPT**
'[I] **wonder** if [my] darling at home will see [me] clearly.'

71. 14:3437.5 – Mitinöku
都良波可馬**可毛**
*tura pak-am-e **kamo***
string put.on-TENT-EV **EPT**
'[I] **wonder**, should [I] put on a [new] string?'

72. 14:3351 – Pitati
筑波祢尔 / 由伎**可母**布良留 / 伊奈乎**可母** / 加奈思吉兒呂我 / 尓努保佐流**可母**
*tukupa ne-ni / yuki **kamö** pur-ar-u / ina wo **kamö** / kanasi-ki KO-rö-nga / nino pos-ar-u **kamö***
TN peak-LOC / snow **EPT** fall-PROG-ATTR / no yes **EPT** / be.dear-AVATTR girl-DIM-POSS / cloth dry-PROG-ATTR **EPT**
'[I] **wonder**, is snow falling on Mt. Tukupa? Yes or no? [And I] **wonder if** [my] dear, darling girl is drying [some] cloth...'

Example (72) is notable for the fact that it contains three *kamo* particles, more than any other poem in the AOJ corpus.

73. 20:4364.3-5 – Pitati
伊敝能伊牟何 / 奈流敝伎己等乎 / 伊波須伎奴**可母**
*ipe-nö imu-nga / nar-unbe-ki kötö-wo / ip-anz-u k-i-n-u **kamö***
house-GEN beloved.girl-POSS / make.a.living-DEB-AVATTR word-ACC / say-NEG-INF come-INF-PERF-AVATTR **EPT**
'[I] **wonder**, did [I] come [here] without telling [my] darling at home what [she] must do to make a living?'

74. 14:3384.3-4 – Simotupusa
麻許登**賀聞** / 和礼尓余須等布
*ma-kötö **kamo** / ware-ni yös-u tö [i]p-u*
INT-word **EPT** / 1.S-DAT bring.close-ATTR QUOT say-FIN
'[I] **wonder**, [is it] true, [that some] say I am intimate [with her]?'

75. 20:4390.4-5 – Simotupusa
以毛加去々里波 / 阿用久奈米**加母**
*imo-nga kökörö pa / ayok-unam-ey **kamö***
beloved.girl-POSS heart TPT / waver-TENT2-EV **EPT**
'[I] **wonder**, will [my] beloved girl's feelings waver?'

76. 14:3572.5 – UNP
可是布可受**可母**
*kanze puk-anz-u **kamö***
wind blow-NEG-FIN **EPT**
'[I] **wonder**, will the wind not blow?'

10.3.1.3 Special construction *-te-si kamo*

There is a special construction *-te-si kamo* '-PERF-PST.ATTR EPT' that indicates something the speaker wants to do. It is only attested once in the corpus, but it is widely attested in WOJ (Vovin 2009a: 1243–1245).

77. 20:4347.3-5 – Kamitupusa
    奈我波氣流 / 多知尓奈里弖母 / **伊波非弖之加母**
    *na-nga pak-eyr-u / tati n-i nar-i-te mö / **ipap-ï-te-si kamö***
    2.S-POSS wear-PROG-ATTR / long.sword COP-INF become-INF-SUB FPT / **pray-INF-PERF-PST.ATTR EPT**
    '[I] **want** to become the long sword that you are wearing and **pray for** [you].'

Table 10.5: Attestations of the emphatic particle *kamo ~ kamu* across the provinces.

Form	TSOJ			EOJ								UNP
	Sin	To	Su	Kak	Mu	Sa	Mi	Sik	Pi	Sip	Kap	
kamo	0	0	2	3	4	0	1	0	6	2	5	14
kamu	1	0	0	0	0	0	0	0	0	0	0	0

10.3.2 Emphatic particle *si*

Vovin (2009a: 1248) considers the emphatic particle *si* to be some kind of discourse particle, and I am unable to expand on that definition. It is difficult to pinpoint an exact meaning other than a general indication of emphasis on the preceding word or phrase. It precedes the emphatic particle *kamo* when both occur in the same line.

78. 14:3400.3-5 – Sinano
    左射礼思母 / 伎弥<u>之</u>布美弖波 / 多麻等比呂波牟
    *sanzare [i]si mö / kimi **si** pum-i-te-nba / tama tö piröp-am-u*
    little stone FPT / lord **EPT** step-INF-PERF-COND / jewel COP pick.up-TENT-FIN
    'When [you, my] lord have stepped on the small stones, [I] shall pick them up as jewels.'

10.3 Emphatic particles

79. 20:4324 – Töpotuapumi
等倍多保美 / 志留波乃伊宗等 / 尓閇乃宇良等 / 安比弓之阿良婆 / 己等母加
由波牟
töpeytapomi / sirupa-nö iso-tö / nipey-nö ura-tö / ap-i-te **si** ar-anba / kötö mö
kayup-am-u
TN / TN-GEN rocky.shore-COM / TN-GEN bay-COM / meet-INF-SUB **EPT** exist-
COND / word FPT go.back.and.forth-TENT-FIN
'If **only** Töpeytapomi's rocky shore of Sirupa and Nipey bay were close to one
another! [Then we] could exchange words. . .'

80. 14:3410.4-5 – Kamitukeno
於久乎奈加祢曽 / 麻左可思余加婆
oku-wo na-kane-sö / masaka **si** yö-k-anba
future-ACC NEG.IMP-worry.INF-do / present **EPT** be.good-AVATTR-COND
'Do not fret about the future, if [things] are fine now.'

81. 14:3350a.4-5 – Pitati
伎美我美家思志 / 安夜尓伎保思母
kimi-nga mi-kesi **si** / aya n-i ki posi-mö
lord-POSS HON-garment **EPT** / extreme COP-INF wear.NML be.desired-EXCL
'[I] so desperately want to wear [my] lord's garment!'

82. 14:3537b.3-5 – UNP
波都波都尓 / 仁必波太布礼思 / 古呂之可奈思母
patu-patu n-i / nipi panda pure-si / ko-rö **si** kanasi-mö
slight-REDUP COP-INF / new skin touch.INF-PST.ATTR / girl-DIM **EPT** be.dear.
AVFIN-EXCL
'The sweet girl whose virgin skin [I] touched [only] briefly is dear [to me]!'

83. 14:3504.5 – UNP
兒呂乎之毛倍婆
KO-rö-wo **si** [o]mop-ey-nba
girl-DIM-ACC **EPT** think-EV-CONJ
'Because [I] am thinking of a sweet girl. . .'

84. 14:3530.4-5 – UNP
兒呂我可奈門欲 / 由可久之要思母
KO-rö-nga kana-TO-yo / yuk-aku **si** ye-si-mö
girl-DIM-POSS metal-door-ABL / go.ATTR-NML **EPT** be.good-AVFIN-EXCL
'Going through the metal gate of [my] darling girl's home is so nice!'

85. 20:4426.5 – UNP
阿礼乎之毛波婆
are-wo **si** *[o]mop-anba*
1.S-ACC **EPT** love-COND
'If [you] love me. . .'

Table 10.6: Attestations of the emphatic particle *si* across the provinces.

TSOJ			EOJ								UNP
Sin	To	Su	Kak	Mu	Sa	Mi	Sik	Pi	Sip	Kap	
1	1	0	2	0	0	0	0	1	0	3	9

10.3.3 Emphatic particle *mo*

As Vovin (2009a: 1256) demonstrates, we must be careful to differentiate the emphatic particle *mo* from the homophonous focus particle *mo*. While the particles have different semantics, combinatorial information is especially helpful in discerning the two. Other than the fact that among the two particles only the emphatic particle *mo* can occur sentence-final, the emphatic particle *mo* is almost always attested after another particle. Table 10.7 below shows the differences when the focus particle *mo* and the emphatic particle *mo* combine with other particles.

Table 10.7: Combinatorial differences between the focus particle *mo* and the emphatic particle *mo* in EOJ[193].

	ya 'EPT'	*ya* 'QPT'	*pa* 'TPT'	*nzö* 'FPT'
mo 'FPT'	–	–	–	–[194]
mo 'EPT'	*mo ya*	*ya mo*	*pa mo*	*nzö mo ~ tö mo*

---

193 Unfortunately, none of these combinations is attested in TSOJ.
194 The combination of these particles is not attested in EOJ or TSOJ, but it is attested in WOJ as *mo nzö* (Vovin 2009a: 1173).

10.3 Emphatic particles

Examples:

86. 20:4415.4-5 – Muzasi
    伊弊奈流伊母乎 / 麻多美弖毛**母**也
    ipe-n[i] ar-u imö-wo / mata mi-te-m-o **mö** ya
    house-LOC exist-ATTR beloved.girl-ACC / again see.INF-PERF-TENT-ATTR **EPT** EPT
    'Oh, **how** [I] would like to see [my] beloved girl again, who is at home!'

87. 14:3386.4-5 – Simotupusa
    曾能可奈之伎乎 / 刀尓多弖米也**母**
    sönö kanasi-ki-wo / to-ni tate-m-ey ya **mö**
    that be.dear-AVATTR-ACC / outside-LOC make.stand-TENT-EV QPT **EPT**
    'Will [I] make that dear [girl] stand outside? (No, I will not!)'

88. 20:4385.3-5 – Simotupusa
    志流敝尓波 / 古乎等都麻乎等 / 於枳弖等**母**枳奴
    siru pe-ni pa / ko-wo-tö tuma-wo-tö / ok-i-te tö **mö** k-i-n-u
    behind area-LOC TPT / child-ACC-COM spouse-ACC-COM / leave.behind-INF-SUB FPT **EPT** come-INF-PERF-ATTR
    '[I] left [my] wife and child behind to come [out here]!'

89. 20:4358.4-5 – Kamitupusa
    和努等里都伎弖 / 伊比之古奈波**毛**
    wano tör-i-tuk-i-te / ip-i-si ko-na pa **mo**
    1.S take-INF-attach-INF-SUB / say-INF-PST.ATTR girl-DIM TPT **EPT**
    'Oh, [what about] the dear girl who clung to me and said [all those things]?'

90. 14:3469.3-5 – UNP
    和加西奈波 / 阿是曽**母**許与比 / 与斯呂伎麻左奴
    wa-nga se-na pa / anze sö **mö** köyöpi / yös-i-rö-k-i-mas-an-u
    1.S-POSS beloved.man-DIM TPT / why FPT **EPT** this.evening / approach-INF-UNC-come-INF-HON-NEG-ATTR
    'Oh, why does my beloved not come [to me] tonight?'

91. 14:3532.4-5 – UNP
    安乎思努布良武 / 伊敝乃兒呂波**母**
    a-wo sinop-uram-u / ipe-nö KO-rö pa **mö**
    1.S-ACC long.for-TENT2-ATTR / house-GEN girl-DIM TPT **EPT**
    'Oh, the sweet girl from [my] home who must be longing for me!'

92. 20:4436.4-5 – UNP
伊都伎麻佐牟等 / 登比之古良波母
*itu k-i-mas-am-u tö / töp-i-si ko-ra pa **mö***
when come-INF-HON-TENT-FIN QUOT / ask-INF-PST.ATTR girl-DIM TPT **EPT**
'**Oh**, [my] darling girl, who asked [me], 'When will [you] come [back]?'.'

Table 10.8: Attestations of the emphatic particle *mo* across the provinces.

TSOJ			EOJ							UNP
Sin	To	Su	Kak	Mu	Sa	Mi	Sik	Pi	Sip	Kap
0	0	0	0	1	0	0	0	0	2	1	7

10.3.4 Emphatic particle *ya*

The emphatic particle *ya* should not be confused with the homophonous question particle *ya* (described in §10.4.1). One clear distinguishing feature is the emphatic particle *ya* does not trigger the attributive form of predicate verbs, but it can follow attributive verb clauses. Desiderative particles and the emphatic particle *mo* precede it, but it can be found directly after the final form of verbs. One difference between WOJ and EOJ is that in WOJ the emphatic particle *ya* always follows the topic particle *pa* (Vovin 2009a: 1262), but in EOJ the opposite order is found, as shown in example (100). These particles are not attested next to each other in TSOJ.

93. 20:4401.1-4 – Sinano
可良己呂武 / 須宗尓等里都伎 / 奈古古良乎 / 意伎弖曽伎怒也
*kara körömu / suso-ni tör-i-tuk-i / nak-o ko-ra-wo / ok-i-te sö k-i-n-o **ya***
TN garment / hem-LOC take-INF-attach-INF / cry-ATTR child-PLUR-ACC leave.behind-INF-SUB FPT come-INF-PERF-ATTR **EPT**
'**Oh**, I have come [here], leaving behind [my] sobbing children who clung to the hem of [my] Kara robes.'

94. 20:4325.1-2 – Töpotuapumi
知々波々母 / 波奈尓母我毛夜
*titi papa mö / pana n-i möngamo **ya***
father mother FPT / flower COP-INF DPT **EPT**
'**Oh**, [I] wish [my] father and mother were flowers!'

95. 20:4372.5-6 – Pitati
阿良志乎母 / 多志**夜**波婆可流
ara-si wo mö / *tas-i* **ya** *panbakar-u*
be.rough-AVFIN man FPT / stand-INF **EPT** hesitate-FIN
'Even a rough man would stand and hesitate.'

96. 20:4377.1-2 – Simotukeno
阿母刀自母 / 多麻尔毛賀毛**夜**
amö tonzi mö / *tama n-i mongamo* **ya**
mother housewife FPT / jewel COP-INF DPT **EPT**
'**Oh, how** [I] wish [my] dear mother were a jewel!'

97. 14:3458.1 – UNP
奈勢能古**夜**
na se nö ko **ya**
2.S beloved.man COP.ATTR child **EPT**
'**Oh**, you, [my] young beloved!'

Examples (98) and (99) below demonstrate that the emphatic particle *ya* can come between a verb in the attributive form and the noun that attributivized verb is modifying.

98. 14:3530.1-2 – UNP
左乎思鹿能 / 布須**也**久草無良
sa-wo-siKA-nö / *pus-u* **ya** *kusa mura*
LOC-male-deer-GEN / lie.down-ATTR **EPT** grass group
'The patch of grass where a stag lies down...'

99. 14:3473.1-2 – UNP
左努夜麻尔 / 宇都**也**乎能登乃
sano yama-ni / *ut-u* **ya** *wonö [o]tö-nö*
TN mountain-LOC / strike-ATTR **EPT** axe sound-COMP
'Like the sound of an axe striking on Sano mountain...'

100. 20:4378.1-2 – Simotukeno
都久比**夜**波 / 須具波由氣等毛
tuku pi **ya** *pa* / *sungu pa yuk-ey-ndömo*
month day **EPT** TPT / pass.NML TPT go-EV-CONC
'Although the months and days pass [by]...'

Table 10.9: Attestations of the emphatic particle *ya* across the provinces.

TSOJ			EOJ								UNP
Sin	To	Su	Kak	Mu	Sa	Mi	Sik	Pi	Sip	Kap	
1	1	0	0	0	0	0	2	0	0	0	5

10.3.5 Emphatic particle *yö*

The emphatic particle *yö* expresses exclamation (Vovin 2009a: 1267). This particle follows the emphatic particle *kamö* and the quotative particle *tö* and is almost always attested sentence-final.

101. 14:3435.1-4 – Kamitukeno
 伊可保呂乃 / 蘓比乃波里波良 / 和我吉奴尓 / 都伎与良志母**与**
 ikapo-rö-nö / sopi-nö pari para / wa-nga kinu-ni / tuk-i-yör-asi-mö **yö**
 TN-DIM-GEN / adjacent-GEN alder field / 1.S-POSS robe-LOC / attach-INF-approach-SUP-EXCL **EPT**
 'It seems the [flowers from the] field [of] alders beside Mt. Ikapo cling to my robes!'

102. 20:4405.5 – Kamitukeno
 和波等可自等**余**
 wa pa tök-anzi tö **yö**
 1.S TPT undo-NEG.TENT QUOT **EPT**
 '[I] think I probably will not untie it!'

103. 14:3375.4-5 – Muzasi
 伊尓之与比欲利 / 世呂尓安波奈布**与**
 in-i-si yöpi-yori / se-rö-ni ap-an-ap-u **yö**
 depart-INF-PST.ATTR evening-ABL / beloved.man-DIM-DAT meet-NEG-ITER-FIN **EPT**
 'Since the evening [he] departed, [I] have not met [my] beloved!'

10.3 Emphatic particles — 465

104. 14:3431.1-4 – Sagamu
阿之我里乃 / 安伎奈乃夜麻尓 / 比古布祢乃 / 斯利比可志母**與**
asingari-nö / *akina-nö yama-ni* / *pik-o pune-nö* / *siri pik-asi-mö* **yö**
TN-GEN / TN-GEN mountain-LOC / pull-ATTR boat-COMP / back pull-SUP-EXCL **EPT**
'[I] seem to be pulling on the back of [my beloved], as if [he] were a boat being pulled up Mt. Akina in Asigari!'

105. 14:3425.3-4 – Simotukeno
伊之布麻受 / 蘓良由登伎努**與**
isi pum-anz-u / *sora-yu tö k-i-n-o* **yö**
stone step-NEG-FIN / sky-ABL FPT come-INF-PERF-ATTR **EPT**
'[I] came from the sky without stepping [on] the stones!'

106. 14:3458.4 – UNP
安乎祢思奈久**與**
a-wo ne si nak-u **yö**
1.S-ACC voice EPT make.cry-FIN **EPT**
'[It] makes me cry out loud!'

107. 14:3550.4 – UNP
伊多夫良思毛**與**
itanbur-asi-mo **yö**
tremble-SUP-EXCL **EPT**
'**Oh,** it seems [I] am trembling!'

108. 14:3557.1-2 – UNP
奈夜麻思家 / 比登都麻可母**與**
nayam-asi-ke / *pitö tuma kamö* **yö**
distress-ADJ-AVATTR / person spouse EPT **EPT**
'[This] wife of another man is so distressing [to me]!'

Table 10.10: Attestations of the emphatic particle *yö* across the provinces.

Sin	To	Su	Kak	Mu	Sa	Mi	Sik	Pi	Sip	Kap	UNP
0	0	0	1	1	1	0	1	0	0	0	3

10.3.6 Emphatic particle *ye*

The emphatic particle *ye* is only attested once, in the Suruga topolect of TSOJ. It is unattested in WOJ. It may have developed from the emphatic particle *yö*, through the fronting of *ə > /e/ after a palatal onset (see §2.2.1.1).

109. 20:4340.1-2 – Suruga
 等知波々<u>江</u> / 已波比弖麻多祢
 töti papa **ye** / *ipap-i-te mat-an-e*
 father mother **EPT** / pray-INF-SUB wait-DES-IMP
 '**Father, mother**! [I] want you to pray and wait [for me].'

10.3.7 Emphatic particle *na*

The emphatic particle *na* expresses exclamation (Vovin 2009a: 1270). As in WOJ, it can follow the final form of verbs, but unlike in WOJ, it can also follow the exclamatory suffix *-umo* (Vovin 2009a: 1272). It can also precede the emphatic particle *kamo*, which is unattested in WOJ. All attestations are provided in the examples below.

110. 14:3477.4-5 – UNP
 安礼波古非牟<u>奈</u> / 能知波安比奴登母
 are pa kopï-m-u **na** / *nöti pa ap-i-n-u tömö*
 1.S TPT long.for-TENT-FIN **EPT** / later TPT meet-INF-PERF-FIN CNJ
 '**Oh**, I shall long for [you]! Even though [we will] meet later. . .'

111. 14:3555.3-5 – UNP
 可良加治乃 / 於等太可思母<u>奈</u>
 kara kandi-nö / *otö-n-daka-si-mö* **na**
 TN oar-COMP / sound-GEN-be.high-AVFIN-EXCL **EPT**
 '**Oh**, the sound is loud, like [that of] Kara oars!'

112. 14:3499.5 – UNP
 祢呂等敝<u>奈</u>香母
 ne-rö tö [i]p-e **na** *kamö*
 sleep-IMP QUOT say-EV **EPT** EPT
 '**Oh**, [I] wonder [if you] will tell [me] to sleep [with you]!'

Example (112) is the only example in the corpus where the particle *na* follows the evidential form of a verb or precedes the emphatic particle *kamo*. The emphatic particle *kamo* can follow the evidential form of the verb and it is attested following the emphatic particle *si* in both WOJ (Vovin 2009a: 1242) and EOJ (20:4347.5 – Kamitupusa), so its following a different emphatic particle does not seem unusual. In WOJ, Vovin (2009a:1270) states the emphatic particle *na* never occurs before another particle, and always occurs sentence-final. However, particles in WOJ and AOJ do not behave exactly the same, so we cannot take the WOJ evidence as proof.

Table 10.11: Attestations of the emphatic particle *na* across the provinces.

TSOJ			EOJ								UNP
Sin	Tö	Su	Kak	Mu	Sa	Mi	Sik	Pi	Sip	Kap	
0	0	0	0	0	0	0	0	0	0	0	3

10.3.8 Emphatic particle *we*

This particle is only clearly attested once, in the Kamitukeno topolect of EOJ. It seems to act as confirmation of a declarative sentence (Omodaka 1967: 826).

113. 14:3406.4-5 – Kamitukeno
 安礼波麻多牟**恵** / 許登之弥受登母
 *are pa mat-am-u **we** / kötösi mi-nz-u tömö*
 1.S TPT wait-TENT-FIN **EPT** / this.year see-NEG-FIN CNJ
 'Even if [I] do not see [you] this year, I will wait for [you]!'

Another possible attestation is discussed in §2.3.5.1.

10.4 Question particles

There are two question particles: the yes/no question particle *ya* and the question particle *ka*.

10.4.1 Yes/no question particle *ya*

This question particle can be found in the sentence-final position (following either the evidential form of a verb or another particle), but it can also be moved to non-final sections of the sentence. The latter usage is more common than the former. When it is in the sentence-final position it follows the quotative particle *tö* or the evidential form of the verb. The examples with the evidential are used to make ironic questions and are described in §10.4.1.1. When this particle is fronted to a pre-verbal position, the verb form must take the attributive suffix (see examples 114, 116, 117, and 119 below). Unlike in WOJ, where *ya* is amply attested directly after the final form of a verb or the final exclamative *-umo* (Vovin 2009a: 1211), such usages are unattested in AOJ. There are two examples of *ya* after the quotative particle *tö* (examples 115 and 118).

114. 20:4321.3-4 – Töpotuapumi
 阿須由利也 / 加曳我牟多祢牟
 asu-yuri ya / kaye-nga muta ne-m-u
 tomorrow-ABL **QPT** / reed-POSS together sleep-TENT-ATTR
 'Will [I] sleep among the reeds from tomorrow?'

115. 14:3415.2-4 – Kamitukeno
 伊可保乃奴麻尓 / 宇恵古奈宜 / 賀久古非牟等夜
 ikapo-nö numa-ni / uwe ko-nangi / ka-ku kopï-m-u tö ya
 TN-GEN swamp-LOC / plant.INF DIM-pickerelweed / be.thus-INF long.for-TENT-FIN QUOT **QPT**
 'Do [you] think [I] would long for the little pickerelweeds planted in the swamp of Ikapo so much?'

116. 20:4330.3-4 – Sagamu
 氣布能比夜 / 伊田弖麻可良武
 keypu-nö pi ya / inde-te makar-am-u
 today-GEN day **QPT** / go.out.INF-SUB depart-TENT-ATTR
 'Will [we] depart and [sail] out today?'

117. 20:4355.1-2 – Kamitupusa
 余曽尓能美 / 々弖夜和多良毛
 yösö-ni nömi / mi-te ya watar-am-o
 other.place-LOC RPT / see.INF-SUB **QPT** cross-TENT-ATTR
 'Shall [I] cross over [to the island, even though I] only gazed into the distance?'

118. 14:3495.1-3 – UNP
 伊波保呂乃 / 蘓比能和可麻都 / 可藝里登也
 ipapo-rö-nö / sopi-nö waka matu / kangir-i tö **ya**
 boulder-DIM-GEN / side-GEN young pine / limit-NML QUOT **QPT**
 '[Like] the young pines growing beside small rocks, [I] am thinking, is [this] the end?'

119. 14:3565.1-2 – UNP
 可能古呂等 / 宿受夜奈里奈牟
 kanö ko-rö-tö / NE-nz-u **ya** *nar-i-n-am-u*
 that girl-DIM-COM / sleep-NEG-NML **QPT** be-INF-PERF-TENT-ATTR
 'Shall it be that [I] will not sleep with that sweet girl?'

10.4.1.1 Usage in ironic questions

When following the evidential form of a verb, the question particle *ya* is used to create an ironic question. Essentially, it implies the opposite answer to the question posed. The emphatic particle *mo* can follow *ya* to emphasize the irony in these constructions.

120. 14:3370.1-4 – Sagamu
 安思我里乃 / 波故祢能祢呂乃 / 尓古具佐能 / 波奈都豆麻奈礼也
 asingari-nö / pakone-nö ne-rö-nö / niko n-gusa-nö / pana tutu ma nar-e **ya**
 TN-GEN / TN-GEN peak-DIM-GEN / soft COP.ATTR-grass-COMP / flower earth wife be-EV **QPT**
 'Are [you] a wife [who is] a flower of the earth, like the soft grass on the small peak of Pakone in Asigari? (**Certainly not!**)'

121. 14:3386.4-5 – Simotupusa
 曽能可奈之伎乎 / 刀尓多弖米也母
 sönö kanasi-ki-wo / to-ni tate-m-ey **ya** *mö*
 that be.dear-AVATTR-ACC / outside-LOC make.stand-TENT-EV **QPT** EPT
 'Will [I] make that dear [girl] stand outside? (**No, I will not!**)'

122. 14:3484.4 – UNP
 阿須伎西佐米也
 asu ki-se-s-am-ey **ya**
 tomorrow wear-CAUS-HON-TENT-EV **QPT**
 'Will [you] make [me] wear [it] tomorrow? (**No, you will not!**)'

123. 14:3503.4-5 – UNP
    宇家良我波奈乃 / 伊呂尓弓米也毛
    *ukera-nga pana-nö / irö-ni [i]nde-m-ey **ya** mo*
    ukera-POSS flower-COMP / color-LOC emerge-TENT-EV **QPT** EPT
    'Would [I] reveal my feelings [for you], as the flowers of the *ukera* reveal their colors? (**No, I would not!**)'

124. 14:3508.4-5 – UNP
    安比見受安良婆 / 安礼古非米夜母
    *ap-i-MI-nz-u ar-anba / are kopï-m-ey **ya** mö*
    meet-INF-see-NEG-INF exist-COND / 1.S love-TENT-EV **QPT** FPT
    'If [I] had not met [you], would I be in love [with you]? (**No, I would not!**)'

Table 10.12: Attestations of the yes/no question particle *ya* across the provinces.

TSOJ			EOJ							UNP
Sin	Tö	Su	Kak	Mu	Sa	Mi	Sik	Pi	Sip	Kap	
0	1	1	1	0	2	0	0	0	1	1	7

10.4.2 Question particle *ka*

The question particle *ka* is mainly used to form *wh-* questions, but it is also attested in yes/no questions, overlapping with the usage of the question particle *ya*. Due to this, I classify the particle *ka* as a general question marker. In WOJ this particle can be used to form alternative questions (i.e., 'X or Y?') (Vovin 2009a: 1227), but this usage is unattested in AOJ. This particle also participates in a special emphatic construction, described in §10.4.2.1. The question particle *ka* always forces the main verb to take an attributive suffix, regardless of whether it follows or precedes the verb.

125. 14:3404.5 – Kamitukeno
    安杼加安我世牟
    *andö **ka** a-nga se-m-u*
    what **QPT** 1.S-POSS do-TENT-ATTR
    'What should I do?'

126. 20:4417.4-5 – Muzasi
多麻能余許夜麻 / 加志由加也良牟
*tama-nö yökö yama / kasi-yu **ka** yar-am-u*
TN-GEN horizontal mountain / go.on.foot-ABL **QPT** send-TENT-ATTR
'Shall [I] send [my beloved to traverse] Tama's flat mountain on foot?'

127. 14:3363.3-5 – Sagamu
麻都之太須 / 安思我良夜麻乃 / 須疑乃木能末可
*mat-u sinda s-u / asingara yama-nö / sungï nö KÖ-nö ma **ka***
wait-ATTR CNJ do-FIN / TN mountain-GEN / cryptomeria COP.ATTR tree-GEN space **QPT**
'When [I] wait [for my beloved to come back], [I] do [it]. . .will [his return be] through the cryptomeria trees of Mt. Asigara?'

128. 14:3424.5 – Simotukeno
多賀家可母多牟
*ta-nga ke **ka** möt-am-u*
who-POSS container **QPT** hold-TENT-ATTR
'Whose [food] container shall [she] hold?'

129. 14:3397.5 – Pitati
阿杼可多延世武
*andö **ka** taye-se-m-u*
what **QPT** break-CAUS-TENT-ATTR
'What would make [us] break [up]?'

130. 20:4389.4 – Simotupusa
於不世他麻保加
*opuse-tamap-o **ka***
assign.INF-HON-ATTR **QPT**
'Has [the emperor] given [me] an order?'

131. 20:4349.4-5 – Kamitupusa
夜蘇志麻須義弖 / 和加例加由可牟
*ya-so sima sungï-te / wakare **ka** yuk-am-u*
eight-ten islands pass.INF-SUB / be.separated.INF **QPT** go-TENT-ATTR
'Going past many islands, shall [I] go [ahead], further away [from home]?'

132. 14:3442.4-5 – UNP
夜麻尓可祢牟毛 / 夜杼里波奈之尓
*yama-ni **ka** ne-m-u mo / yandör-i pa na-si-ni*
mountain-LOC **QPT** sleep-TENT-ATTR FPT / lodge-NML TPT not.exist-AVFIN-LOC
'Shall [I] sleep in the mountains since there is no lodging [here]?'

133. 14:3494.5 – UNP
汝波安杼可毛布
*NA pa andö **ka** [o]mop-u*
2.S TPT what **QPT** think-ATTR
'What do you think?'

134. 14:3563.4 – UNP
和乎可麻都那毛 / 伎曽毛己余必母
*wa-wo **ka** mat-unam-o / kisö mo köyöpi mö*
1.S-ACC **QPT** wait-TENT2-ATTR / last.night FPT this.evening FPT
'[You] almost certainly waited for me last night, and tonight [you will] as well?'

10.4.2.1 Usage in a special emphatic construction

There is a special emphatic construction that is formed by an adjectival verb in the infinitive (*-ku*) followed by *mo ar-u ka* 'FPT exist-ATTR QPT'. This construction is not attested in EOJ, but it is attested once in TSOJ. A few examples can be found in WOJ as well, such as MYS 17:3922.5 (Vovin 2016: 50)[195].

135. 20:4345.3-5 – Suruga
宇知江須流 / 々々河乃祢良波 / 苦不志久米阿流可
*uti-yes-uru / surunga-nö ne-ra pa / **kupusi-ku mey ar-u ka***
PREF-approach-ATTR / TN-GEN peak-PLUR TPT / **be.longing-INF FPT exist-ATTR QPT**
'**How [I] long for** the peaks of Suruga, where [the waves] crash!'

Although written *mey*, I analyze the Suruga focus particle in example (135) as /mo/. See §2.2.1.1 for discussion.

---

[195] Vovin analyzes it here as an emphatic function of the particle *ka*, but it seems he did not notice the recurrent construction I describe here is necessary to create the emphatic meaning because there are no examples in OJ of an emphatic *ka* outside of this construction. Vovin's emphatic *ka* is not mentioned in his WOJ grammar (Vovin 2009a, 2020).

Table 10.13: Attestations of the question particle *ka* across the provinces.

TSOJ			EOJ								UNP
Sin	Tö	Su	Kak	Mu	Sa	Mi	Sik	Pi	Sip	Kap	
0	0	1	2	1	1	0	1	1	3	2	18

10.5 Restrictive particles

The restrictive particles are *nömi*, *ndani*, and *sapey*.

10.5.1 Restrictive particle *nömi*

The restrictive particle *nömi* has a meaning akin to 'only' or 'just' (Vovin 2009a: 1274). This particle is a true particle in AOJ, unlike in WOJ. In WOJ it precedes the accusative suffix *-wo* and the locative suffix *-ni* (Vovin 2009a: 1274), and particles cannot precede suffixes in a word form. In AOJ, on the other hand, *nömi* follows the case marker *-ni* (see example 137 below), as expected of a true particle. The restrictive particle *nömi* precedes the focus particle *sö* when the two occur in the same line. This particle is attested in EOJ and UNP. All attested examples follow below.

136. 14:3405a.4-5 – Kamitukeno
    兒良波安波奈毛 / 比等理能未思弖
    *KO-ra pa ap-ana-m-o / pitö-ri **nömi** s-i-te*
    girl-DIM TPT meet-DES-TENT-ATTR / one-CL **RPT** do-INF-SUB
    '[I] want [my] darling girl to meet [me], [when she is] **all** alone.'

137. 20:4355.1-2 – Kamitupusa
    余曽尓能美 / 々弖夜和多良毛
    *yösö-ni **nömi** / mi-te ya watar-am-o*
    elsewhere-LOC **RPT** / see.INF-SUB QPT cross.over-TENT-ATTR
    'Shall [I] cross over [to the island, even though I] **only** gazed into the distance?'

138. 14:3471.3-5 – UNP
    伊米**能未**尓 / 母登奈見要都追 / 安乎祢思奈久流
    *imey **nömï** n-i* / *mötöna MI-ye-tutu* / *a-wo ne si nak-uru*
    dream **RPT** COP-INF / incessantly see-PASS.INF-COOR / 1.S-ACC sound EPT make.cry-ATTR
    '[They] are **just** dreams, [but] you appear [in them] incessantly, and it makes me cry!'

139. 14:3538b.3-4 – UNP
    己許呂**能未** / 伊母我理夜里弖
    *kökörö **nömï*** / *imö-ngari yar-i-te*
    heart **RPT** / beloved.girl-DIR send-INF-SUB
    '[I] can **only** send [my] heart to [my] beloved.'

140. 14:3560.4-5 – UNP
    伊波奈久**能未**曽 / 安我古布良久波
    *ip-an-aku **nömï** sö* / *a-nga kop-ur-aku pa*
    say-NEG.ATTR-NML **RPT** FPT / 1.S-POSS long.for-ATTR-NML TPT
    'I am longing for [you], **only** [I] do not say it.'

Table 10.14: Attestations of the restrictive particle *nömi* across the provinces.

TSOJ			EOJ								UNP
Sin	Tö	Su	Kak	Mu	Sa	Mi	Sik	Pi	Sip	Kap	
0	0	0	1	0	0	0	0	0	0	1	3

10.5.2 Restrictive particle *ndani*

The restrictive particle *ndani* indicates a minimum representation, something akin to 'at least', 'even', 'just', or 'as little as' (Vovin 2009a: 1275). It can be followed by the focus particle *mo*. This particle is only attested once, in EOJ.

141. 14:3383.3-5 – Kamitupusa
    可久**太尓**毛 / 久尓乃登保可婆 / 奈我目保里勢牟
    *ka-ku **ndani** mo* / *kuni-nö töpo-ka-nba* / *na-nga MEY por-i se-m-u*
    be.thus-AVINF **RPT** FPT / province-GEN be.far-AVEV-CONJ / 2.S-POSS eye desire-NML do-TENT-FIN
    '[I] dream of your eyes, since [your] province is **just** so far [away].'

10.5.3 Restrictive particle *sapey*

The restrictive particle *sapey* indicates a maximum representation and is thus the opposite of the restrictive particle *ndani*. It can be translated as 'even (as much as)', 'even...in addition to' (Vovin 2009a: 1285) or 'so much as'. It is attested in TSOJ and UNP. All attested examples are given below.

142. 20:4322.3-5 – Töpotuapumi
乃牟美豆尓 / 加其<u>佐倍</u>美曳弖 / 余尓和須良礼受
*nöm-u mindu-ni / kangö **sapey** mi-ye-te / yö-ni wasur-are-nz-u*
drink-ATTR water-LOC / shadow RPT see-PASS.INF-SUB / lifetime-LOC forget-PASS-NEG-FIN
'**So much as** seeing [her] shadow in the water that [I] drink, [makes me realize I] cannot forget her in this lifetime.'

143. 14:3474.1-2 – UNP
宇恵太氣能 / 毛登<u>左倍</u>登与美
*uwe-n-dakey-nö / motö **sapey** töyöm-i*
plant.NML-GEN-bamboo-GEN / root RPT resound-INF
'**Even** the roots of the planted bamboo resound [when I go away].'

144. 14:3502.4-5 – UNP
等思<u>佐倍</u>己其登 / 和波佐可流我倍
*tösi **sapey** köngötö / wa pa sakar-u ngapey*
year RPT many / 1.S TPT be.away.from-ATTR IPT
'Will I be away from [her] **even** [after] many years? (No, I will not.)'

145. 14:3514.3-4 – UNP
和礼<u>左倍</u>尓 / 伎美尓都吉奈那
*ware **sapey** n-i / kimi-ni tuk-i-n-ana*
1.S RPT COP-INF / lord-LOC attach-INF-PERF-DES
'**Even** I have wanted to be close to [you, my] lord.'

146. 14:3548.4-5 – UNP
可奈思家世呂尓 / 比等<u>佐敝</u>余須母
*kanasi-ke se-rö-ni / pitö **sape** yös-umö*
be.dear-AVATTR beloved.man-DIM-DAT / person RPT approach-EXCL
'**Even** [other] people approach [my] dear, darling beloved!'

Table 10.15: Attestations of the restrictive particle *sapey* across the provinces.

TSOJ			EOJ							UNP
Sin	Tö	Su	Kak	Mu	Sa	Mi	Sik	Pi	Sip	Kap
0	1	0	0	0	0	0	0	0	0	0	4

10.6 Desiderative particle *monga[mo]*

The desiderative particle *mongamo* and its shortened variant *monga*[196] simply indicate a want or wish. It appears to only indicate the speaker's desire. It precedes the emphatic particle *ya* when the two occur in the same line.

147. 20:4325.1-2 – Töpotuapumi
      知々波々母 / 波奈尓**母我毛**夜
      *titi papa mö / pana n-i **möngamo** ya*
      father mother FPT / blossom COP-INF **DPT** EPT
      'Oh, [I] **wish** [my] father and mother were flowers!'

148. 14:3436.5 – Kamitukeno
      登許波尓**毛我母**
      *tökö-pa n-i **mongamö***
      constant-leaf COP-INF **DPT**
      '[I] **wish** [the trees] had eternal leaves. . .'

149. 20:4406.1-2 – Kamitukeno
      和我伊波呂尓 / 由加毛比等**母我**
      *wa-nga ipa-rö-ni / yuk-am-o pitö **mönga***
      1.S-POSS house-DIM-LOC / go-TENT-ATTR person **DPT**
      '[I] **wish** someone would go to my dear home.'

---

[196] The term "shortened variant" is used strictly in a synchronic sense. Historically, *mongamo* is the variant, and it is an extended one, consisting of the desiderative particle *monga* and the emphatic particle *mo* (Vovin 2009a: 1230).

150. 20:4329.3-5 – Sagamu
布奈可射里 / 安我世牟比呂乎 / 美毛比等**母我毛**
puna-kanzar-i / a-nga se-m-u pi-rö-wo / mi-m-o pitö **möngamo**
boat-decorate-NML / 1.S-POSS do-TENT-ATTR day-DIM-ACC / see-TENT-ATTR person DPT
'[I] **wish** someone would witness the special day when I do the boat-decorating.'

151. 20:4383.5 – Simotukeno
阿母我米**母我母**
amö-nga mey **möngamö**
mother-POSS eye DPT
'[I] **long for** [my] mother's eyes.'

152. 20:4366.1-2 – Pitati
比多知散思 / 由可牟加里**母我**
pitati sas-i / yuk-am-u kari **mönga**
TN point.toward-INF / go-TENT-ATTR wild.goose DPT
'[I] **wish** [I had] a wild goose [I] could send to Pitati!'

153. 14:3448.3-5 – UNP
乎那能乎能 / 比自尔都久麻提 / 伎美我与**母賀母**
wona-nö wo-nö / pinzi-ni tuk-u-mande / kimi-nga yö **möngamö**
TN-GEN mountain.ridge-GEN / sandbar-LOC reach-ATTR-TERM / lord-POSS life DPT
'[I] **want** [my] lord's life [to last] until the Wona mountain ridge reaches a sandbar.'

154. 14:3567.4-5 – UNP
安都佐能由美乃 / 由都可尔**母我毛**
andusa-nö yumi-nö / yun-duka n-i **möngamo**
catalpa-GEN bow-GEN / bow-grip COP-INF DPT
'[I] **wish** [she] were the grip of [my] catalpa bow.'

Table 10.16: Attestations of the desiderative particle *monga[mo]* across the provinces.

TSOJ			EOJ								UNP
Sin	Tö	Su	Kak	Mu	Sa	Mi	Sik	Pi	Sip	Kap	
0	1	0	2	0	1	0	2	1	0	0	2

10.7 Ironic particle *ngape*

The ironic particle *ngape* seems to indicate irony the same way that the combination of a verb in the evidential and the question particle *ya* does in WOJ and AOJ. It is attested in EOJ and UNP, but it is unattested in WOJ and TSOJ, so it may have been a Proto-EOJ innovation. All attested examples follow below.

155. 14:3420.4-5 – Kamitukeno
      於也波佐久礼騰 / 和波左可流**賀倍**
      *oya pa sak-ure-ndö / wa pa sakar-u **ngapey***
      parents TPT keep.apart-EV-CONC / 1.S TPT be.far.from-ATTR **IPT**
      'Although [our] parents keep [us] apart, will I stay away [from you]? (**No, I will not.**)'

156. 14:3502.4-5 – UNP
      等思佐倍己其登 / 和波佐可流**我倍**
      *tösi sapey köngötö / wa pa sakar-u **ngapey***
      year RPT greatly / 1.S TPT be.far.from-ATTR **IPT**
      'Will I be away from [her] even [after] many years? (**No, I will not.**)'

157. 20:4429.1-3 – UNP
      宇麻夜奈流 / 奈波多都古麻乃 / 於久流**我弁**
      *uma-ya-n[i] ar-u / napa tat-u koma-nö / okur-u **ngape***
      horse-house-LOC exist-ATTR / rope cut-ATTR horse-GEN / remain-ATTR **IPT**
      'Would a horse that has broken the ropes in [its] stable remain [there]? (**No, it would not.**)'

Table 10.17: Attestations of the ironic particle *ngape* across the provinces.

TSOJ			EOJ								UNP
Sin	To	Su	Kak	Mu	Sa	Mi	Sik	Pi	Sip	Kap	
0	0	0	1	0	0	0	0	0	0	0	2

10.8 Quotative particle *tö ~ te*

When this particle directly precedes a verb, the verb is always one with a meaning related to speech or thought, such as *ip-* 'say', *top-* 'ask', *omop-* 'think', or *nör-* 'tell'.

Additionally, the quotative particle *tö* can be used on its own without a following verb, as a means of quoting speech or thoughts.

This particle is attested orthographically twice as *te* in the Suruga topolect of TSOJ (an example is provided in 159 below). This is due to a change of *ə > /e/ that occurred after coronal onsets in the Suruga topolect. See §2.2.1.1 for a discussion.

158. 20:4323.3-5 – Töpotuapumi
 奈尔須礼曽 / 波々登布波奈乃 / 佐吉泥己受祁牟
 *nani s-ure sö / papa **tö** [i]p-u pana-nö / sak-i-nde-kö-nz-u-kem-u*
 why do-EV FPT / mother **QUOT** say-ATTR flower-GEN / bloom-INF-go.out.INF-come-NEG-INF-PST.TENT-ATTR
 'Why has the flower **called** 'mother' not come out in bloom?'

159. 20:4344.1 – Suruga
 和須良牟弖
 *wasur-am-u **te***
 try.to.forget-TENT-FIN **QUOT**
 '[I] **thought** [I] would try to forget [them].'

160. 20:4343.1-2 – Suruga
 和呂多比波 / 多比等於米保等
 *warö tanbi pa / tanbi **tö** omeyp-o-ndö*
 1.S journey TPT / journey **QUOT** think-EV-CONC
 '**Although [I] know** my journey will be an [arduous] one...'

161. 14:3435.5 – Kamitukeno
 比多敝登於毛敝婆
 *pita-pe **tö** omop-e-nba*
 one-CL **QUOT** think-EV-CONJ
 'Since [I] **think** there is [just] one layer...'

162. 20:4406.3-5 – Kamitukeno
 久佐麻久良 / 多妣波久流之等 / 都氣夜良麻久母
 *kusa makura / tanbi pa kurusi **tö** / tungey-yar-am-aku mö*
 grass pillow / journey TPT be.painful.AVFIN **QUOT** / tell.INF-send-TENT.ATTR-NML FPT
 '[I] would send [him] **to tell** [them] that [my] journey, [sleeping on] a grass pillow, is painful.'

163. 20:4404.1-2 – Kamitukeno
奈尔波治乎 / 由伎弓久麻弓等
nanipa-ndi-wo / yuk-i-te k-u-mande tö
TN-road-ACC / go-INF-SUB come-ATTR-TERM **QUOT**
'[My beloved girl] **said**, 'Until [you] return [from your] journey on Nanipa road'...'

164. 20:4375.4-5 – Simotukeno
和例乎美於久流等 / 多々里之毛己呂
ware-wo mi-okur-u tö / tat-ar-i-si mokörö
1.S-ACC see.INF-send.off-FIN **QUOT** / stand-PROG-INF-PST.ATTR similarity
'[It is] similar to how [my] family members were standing, **intending** to see me off.'

165. 20:4363.4-5 – Pitati
伊麻波許伎奴等 / 伊母尔都氣許曽
ima pa köng-i-n-u tö / imö-ni tungey-kös-ö
now TPT row-INF-PERF-FIN **QUOT** / beloved.girl-DAT tell.INF-BEN-IMP
'Please tell [my] beloved girl **that** [I] have rowed out now!'

166. 14:3384.1-4 – Simotupusa
可都思加能 / 麻末能手兒奈乎 / 麻許登賀聞 / 和礼尔余須等布
kandusika-nö / mama-nö teNGO-na-wo / ma-kötö kamo / ware-ni yös-u tö [i]p-u
TN-GEN / cliff-GEN maiden-DIM-ACC / INT-word EPT / 1.S-DAT bring.close-ATTR **QUOT** say-FIN
'[I] wonder, is it true that [some] **say** I am intimate with a darling maiden from the cliff in Kadusika?'

167. 20:4388.1-2 – Simotupusa
多飛等弊等 / 麻多妣尔奈理奴
tanbï tö [i]p-e-ndö / ma-tanbi n-i nar-i-n-u
journey **QUOT** say-EV-CONC / INT-journey COP-INF become-INF-PERF-FIN
'Although [it] was **said** to be [just] 'a journey', [this] has become such a [trying] journey.'

10.8 Quotative particle *tö ~ te*

168. 14:3446.3-5 – UNP
 佐左良乎疑 / 安志**等**比登其等 / 加多理与良斯毛
 *sasara wongï / asi **tö** pitö-n-götö / katar-i-yör-asi-mo*
 little Amur.silver.grass / be.bad.AVFIN QUOT people-GEN-word / tell-INF-approach-SUP-EXCL
 'It seems that people **say** the little Amur silver grass is bad!'

169. 14:3465.4-5 – UNP
 安杼世呂**登**可母 / 安夜尓可奈之伎
 *andö se-rö **tö** kamö / aya n-i kanasi-ki*
 what do-IMP QUOT EPT / extreme COP-INF be.dear-AVATTR
 '[I] wonder, what would [you] **say** [I] do? [You] are extremely dear [to me].'

170. 14:3469.1-2 – UNP
 由布氣尓毛 / 許余比**登**乃良路
 *yupu key-ni mo / köyöpi **tö** nör-ar-o*
 evening fortunetelling-LOC FPT / this.evening QUOT tell-PROG-ATTR
 'At the evening fortunetelling [they] **told** [me] tonight [would be the night].'

171. 20:4425.1-4 – UNP
 佐伎毛利尓 / 由久波多我世**登** / 刀布比登乎 / 美流我登毛之佐 / 毛乃母比毛世受
 *sakimori n-i / yuk-u pa ta-nga se **tö** / top-u pitö-wo / mi-ru-nga tömosi-sa*
 border.guard COP-INF / go-ATTR TPT who-POSS beloved.man QUOT / ask-ATTR person-ACC / see-ATTR-POSS be.favored-AVNML
 '[Oh,] the enviousness of looking at those who **ask**, 'Whose husband is that, going to be a border guard?'.'

172. 14:3447.1-2 – UNP
 久佐可氣乃 / 安努奈由可武**等**
 *kusa kangey-nö / ano-na yuk-am-u **tö***
 grass shadow-GEN / TN-LOC go-TENT-FIN QUOT
 '[I] **thought** [I] would go to Ano, [a place] of grass and shade.'

173. 14:3473.4-5 – UNP
祢毛<u>等</u>可兒呂賀 / 於由尓美要都留
*ne-m-o **tö** ka KO-rö-nga / oyu n-i mi-ye-t-uru*
sleep-TENT-ATTR **QUOT** QPT girl-DIM-POSS / grow.older.NML COP-INF see-PASS.INF-PERF-ATTR
'[I] suddenly see [my] dear girl has grown older, **asking** [me], 'Shall [we] sleep [together]?'.'

Table 10.18: Attestations of the quotative particle *tö* across the provinces.

TSOJ			EOJ								UNP
Sin	To	Su	Kak	Mu	Sa	Mi	Sik	Pi	Sip	Kap	
0	1	2	3	0	0	0	1	1	2	0	7

Appendix A – A classification of poems in MYS Book 14 based on linguistic features

This appendix contains all of the poems from MYS Book 14 in numerical order. I list which dialect region the poem belongs to, separating those written in an Azuma (AOJ) or Nara-Asuka (WOJ) dialect. The potential AOJ linguistic features – which are those features (lexical, grammatical, morphological, or phonological) not phonographically attested in WOJ, including "misspellings" that are unattested in WOJ – are also listed to substantiate the classification of a poem. All poems classified as WOJ were excluded from the study presented in this book.

Poem	Province	Dialect Region	K[197]	V[198]	Potential AOJ linguistic features
3348	Kamitupusa	WOJ			
3349	Simotupusa	AOJ			*mama* 'cliff'[199]
3350a	Pitati	AOJ		W	*mayo* 'cocoon'[200]
3350b	Pitati	WOJ			
3350c	Pitati	WOJ			
3351	Pitati	AOJ			*-ar-* 'PROG' (twice),[201] *nino* 'cloth',[202] *-rö* 'DIM'[203]
3352	Sinano	AOJ		W	*nö* 'field'[204]
3353	Töpotuapumi	WOJ			
3354	Töpotuapumi	AOJ			*sapanda* 'many, much, amply'[205]

---

[197] Classification in Kupchik (2011: 16–20), if it differs from this study. E= EOJ (=AOJ in this study), W=WOJ, Ab=Absent.
[198] Classification in Vovin (2012a), if it differs from this study. E= EOJ (=AOJ in this study), W=WOJ.
[199] Unattested in WOJ.
[200] There are no clear phonographic attestations in WOJ. There is a *kungana* attestation in MYS 12.2495.3, written as 眉 *mayo* ~ *mayu* 'eyebrow' (see Omodaka 1967: 691).
[201] Cf. WOJ *-er-* 'id.'.
[202] No phonographic attestations in WOJ, but cf. MJ *nuno* 'id.'.
[203] Cf. WOJ *-ra* 'id.'.
[204] Vovin (2012a: 33) considers this a misspelling due to a later copyist, but I was unable to find any similar misspellings of WOJ *no* 'field' in a WOJ text, so it meets my criteria for a "misspelling" not attested in WOJ, and thus is a potential Azuma dialect feature.
[205] Cf. WOJ *sapa* 'id.'.

(continued)

Poem	Province	Dialect Region	K	V	Potential AOJ linguistic features
3355	Suruga	WOJ			
3356	Suruga	WOJ			[o]yönb- 'reach'[206]
3357	Suruga	WOJ			
3358a	Suruga	WOJ			
3358b	Suruga	WOJ			
3358c	Suruga	AOJ	W		-e '-EV'[207]
3359a	Suruga	AOJ			osi 'rock, rocky shore'[208]
3359b	Suruga	AOJ	W		osi 'rock, rocky shore'[209]
3360a	Idu	WOJ			
3360b	Idu	WOJ			
3361	Sagamu	AOJ			kö-rö 'girl-DIM'[210]
3362a	Sagamu	WOJ		E	
3362b	Sagamu	WOJ		E	
3363	Sagamu	AOJ			sinda 'CNJ'[211]
3364a	Sagamu	WOJ			
3364b	Sagamu	WOJ			
3365	Sagamu	WOJ			
3366	Sagamu	AOJ			-unam- 'TENT2',[212] wa pa '1.S TPT'[213]

---

206 This word is not attested with its initial vowel elided in WOJ, and synchronic V_2 elision, which caused this form, was widespread in Azuma (refer to Chapter 3). However, V_2 elision was not exclusive to Azuma and it also occurred in WOJ in conditions that are not fully understood. For that reason, I still tentatively classify the poem as WOJ.
207 Cf. WOJ -ey 'id.'. I was unable to find a single misspelling of the evidential in WOJ texts (including MYS Book 15), but it is "misspelled" many times in Book 14.
208 Cf. WOJ iso 'id.', EOJ osu 'id.'.
209 Cf. WOJ iso 'id.', EOJ osu 'id.'.
210 Regressive vowel assimilation exclusive to the Sagamu topolect of EOJ. The cognate WOJ form is ko-ra, and other AOJ topolects show ko-rö.
211 Unattested in WOJ.
212 Cf. WOJ, TSOJ -uram- 'id.'.
213 This sequence wa pa is unattested in WOJ (a single attestation in MYS 20:4408.76 is clearly in imitation of a *Sakimori* poem), and thus I consider it to be a potential Azuma grammatical feature (see also Vovin 2012a: 68).

(continued)

Poem	Province	Dialect Region	K	V	Potential AOJ linguistic features
3367	Sagamu	WOJ			
3368	Sagamu	AOJ			*tayora n-i* 'wavering COP-INF'[214]
3369	Sagamu	AOJ			*mama* 'cliff',[215] *kö-rö* 'girl-DIM'[216]
3370	Sagamu	AOJ			*-rö* 'DIM',[217] *tutu* 'earth',[218] *ma* 'wife'[219]
3371	Sagamu	WOJ			
3372	Sagamu	AOJ	W	W	*omop-ar-uru* 'think-PASS-ATTR'[220]
3373	Muzasi	WOJ			
3374	Muzasi	AOJ			*masande n-i* 'clearly'[221]
3375	Muzasi	AOJ			*-rö* 'DIM',[222] *-an-ap-* 'NEG-ITER'[223]
3376a	Muzasi	AOJ			*ukera* 'Atractylodes japonica'[224]
3376b	Muzasi	AOJ	Ab		*ukera* 'Atractylodes japonica'[225]
3377	Muzasi	WOJ		E[226]	

---

[214] Vovin (2012a: 59), based on Takagi, Gomi, and Ōno (1959: 413–414) and Nakanishi (1981: 247), suggests this is *tayor-an-i* 'cease-NEG-INF', but the sound correspondences with AOJ/WOJ *taye-* 'cease, break' are irregular. It is not attested in WOJ.
[215] Unattested in WOJ.
[216] Regressive vowel assimilation exclusive to the Sagamu topolect of EOJ. The cognate WOJ form is *ko-ra*, and other AOJ topolects show *ko-rö*.
[217] Cf. WOJ *-ra* 'id.'.
[218] Cf. WOJ *tuti* 'id.'.
[219] Cf. WOJ *me* 'id.', Suruga TSOJ *mi* 'id.'.
[220] There are no attestations of *omop-* 'think' combining with the passive form *-are* in WOJ, but there are over one hundred attestations of *omop-oye* 'think-PASS' in WOJ. Furthermore, there are 46 attestations of WOJ *omop-oy-uru* 'think-PASS-ATTR' in the MYS. Therefore, this Sagamu form can be considered an EOJ feature (a retention).
[221] Only attested in WOJ as *masa n-i* 'clearly'.
[222] Cf. WOJ *-ra* 'id.'.
[223] In WOJ the order of these morphemes is reversed.
[224] A perennial grass in the chrysanthemum family. This word is not phonographically attested in WOJ, and the MJ word is *wokera* (cf. Modern Japanese *okera*).
[225] A perennial grass in the chrysanthemum family. This word is not phonographically attested in WOJ, and the MJ word is *wokera* (cf. Modern Japanese *okera*).
[226] Vovin (2012a: 68) considers this poem to be written in EOJ based on *WA PA* '1.S TPT'. He is correct that that is an EOJ grammatical feature, however, this attestation is logographic, and we cannot be sure it was not *A PA* '1.S TPT', which is phonographically attested once in WOJ and once in AOJ (in 14:3519.2 – UNP).

(continued)

Poem	Province	Dialect Region	K	V	Potential AOJ linguistic features
3378	Muzasi	AOJ			wa-ni '1.S-DAT',[227] ipawi-tura 'rock-vine'[228]
3379	Muzasi	AOJ			andö 'what'[229]
3380	Muzasi		WOJ		
3381	Muzasi		WOJ		
3382	Kamitupusa	AOJ			kopu pa sö-m-ö 'long.for.NML TPT do-TENT-ATTR'[230]
3383	Kamitupusa	AOJ			-rö 'DIM',[231] -ka- '-AVEV'[232]
3384	Simotupusa	AOJ			mama 'cliff',[233] tengo 'maiden, third daughter',[234] -na 'DIM'[235]
3385	Simotupusa	AOJ			mama 'cliff',[236] teNGO 'maiden, third daughter',[237] -na '-DIM',[238] paka 'place',[239] osi-pi 'rocky shore-side'[240]
3386	Simotupusa	AOJ		W	wase 'early rice'[241]
3387	Simotupusa	AOJ			a 'foot',[242] mama 'cliff'[243]

---

[227] This sequence of morphemes is unattested in WOJ, thus it may be an AOJ grammatical feature.
[228] Unattested in WOJ.
[229] Cf. WOJ nandö 'why', nani 'what'.
[230] Two AOJ features are present here: the nominalized form kopu 'long.for.NML' (< PJe *kopoi), and the verb sö- 'do'.
[231] Cf. WOJ -ra 'id.'.
[232] Cf. WOJ -ke- 'id.'.
[233] Unattested in WOJ.
[234] tengo 'maiden, third daughter' is an EOJ word (see Kupchik 2016 for more discussion).
[235] Cf. WOJ -ra 'id.'.
[236] Unattested in WOJ.
[237] tengo 'maiden, third daughter' is an EOJ word (see Kupchik 2016 for more discussion), though it is attested only partially phonographically here.
[238] Cf. WOJ -ra 'id.'.
[239] Only attested in WOJ as -n-baka '-GEN-place'.
[240] The cognate WOJ form is iso-pe (each morpheme is attested phonographically in WOJ, but the compound is only attested once logographically in MYS 11:2444.2), while the TSOJ form is osu-pe.
[241] This word is not phonographically attested in WOJ.
[242] Attested in WOJ as asi and a-; the latter is a bound form only found in compounds, but in EOJ it was the free form.
[243] Unattested in WOJ.

(continued)

Poem	Province	Dialect Region	K	V	Potential AOJ linguistic features
3388	Pitati	AOJ			-rö 'DIM'[244]
3389	Pitati	AOJ	Ab		potö 'time'[245]
3390	Pitati	WOJ	Ab		
3391	Pitati	WOJ	Ab		
3392	Pitati	AOJ			tayura n-i 'wavering COP-INF'[246]
3393	Pitati	WOJ	Ab		
3394	Pitati	AOJ			-rö 'DIM',[247] wasura-kö- 'forget-come',[248] -n-ap- 'NEG-ITER'[249]
3395	Pitati	AOJ			-rö 'DIM',[250] tuku 'moon',[251] tas-i 'rise-INF',[252] -o '-ATTR',[253] sapanda 'many, much, amply'[254]
3396	Pitati	WOJ	Ab		
3397	Pitati	AOJ			andö 'what'[255]
3398	Sinano	AOJ			teNGO 'maiden, third daughter'[256]
3399	Sinano	AOJ			karinba 'sakura bark',[257] pak-ey 'put.on-IMP'[258]

---

244 Cf. WOJ -ra 'id.'.
245 The WOJ cognate is potö 'time'. The AOJ form may show progressive vowel assimilation, or it may just be a misspelling.
246 Vovin (2012a: 59), based on Takagi, Gomi, and Ōno (1959: 413–414) and Nakanishi (1981: 247), suggests this is tayur-an-i 'cease-NEG-INF', but the sound correspondences with AOJ/WOJ taye- 'cease, break' are irregular. It is not attested in WOJ.
247 Cf. WOJ -ra 'id.'.
248 The phonological form wasura- 'forget' is exclusive to EOJ.
249 In WOJ the order of these morphemes is reversed.
250 Cf. WOJ -ra 'id.'.
251 Cf. WOJ tukï 'moon' (WOJ tuku- is only attested in compounds).
252 Cf. WOJ tat-i 'id.'.
253 Cf. WOJ -u 'id.'.
254 Cf. WOJ sapa 'many'.
255 Cf. WOJ nandö 'why', nani 'what'.
256 tengo 'maiden, third daughter' is an EOJ word (see Kupchik 2016 for more discussion), though it is attested only partially phonographically here.
257 This is a borrowing of Ainu karinpa 'sakura' (see §4.3.1.3). The form in WOJ is kaninba, which shows regressive nasal assimilation.
258 Cf. WOJ pak-e 'id.'.

(continued)

Poem	Province	Dialect Region	K	V	Potential AOJ linguistic features
3400	Sinano	AOJ			*piröp-* 'pick up',[259] *sanzaresi* 'pebble'[260]
3401	Sinano	AOJ	W		*na* 'river'[261]
3402	Kamitukeno	AOJ			*-na-nö* '-DIM-DIM'[262]
3403	Kamitukeno		WOJ		
3404	Kamitukeno	AOJ			*andö* 'what',[263] *mundak-* 'embrace'[264]
3405a	Kamitukeno	AOJ			*-o* '-ATTR'[265]
3405b	Kamitukeno	AOJ			*-na* 'DIM',[266] *-o* 'ATTR'[267]
3406	Kamitukeno	AOJ		W	*kuku-* 'stem'[268]
3407	Kamitukeno	AOJ		W	*makirapasi* 'be blinding',[269] *ma-[i]to* 'true-dear'[270]
3408	Kamitukeno	AOJ			*wa-ni* '1.S-DAT',[271] *-ana-na* 'NEG.ATTR-LOC'[272]
3409	Kamitukeno	AOJ			*-rö* '-DIM',[273] *otap-* 'sing',[274] *tö* 'FPT',[275] *[i]to-ra* 'dear-DIM',[276] *ka-numa* 'deer-marsh'[277]

---

259 The WOJ form *pirip-* is the product of progressive vowel assimilation.
260 Cf. WOJ *sanzare isi* 'pebble'.
261 Borrowing of Ainu *nay* 'river' (see §4.3.1.3). Unattested in WOJ.
262 Both diminutives are exclusive to EOJ and the usage of two diminutives in succession is an EOJ grammatical feature.
263 Cf. WOJ *nandö* 'why', *nani* 'what'.
264 Cf. WOJ *undak-* 'id.', MJ *idak-* 'id.'.
265 Cf. WOJ *-u* 'id.'.
266 Cf. WOJ *-ra* 'id.'.
267 Cf. WOJ *-u* 'id.'.
268 No phonographic attestations in WOJ. Cf. WOJ *kukï* 'id.'.
269 Unattested in WOJ.
270 The noun *ito* 'dear (one)' is unattested in WOJ.
271 This sequence of morphemes is unattested in WOJ, so it may be an EOJ grammatical feature.
272 Cf. WOJ *-nz-u n-i* '-NEG-INF COP-INF'.
273 Cf. WOJ *-ra* 'id.'.
274 Cf. WOJ *utap-* 'id.'.
275 Cf. WOJ *sö ~ nzö* 'id.'.
276 The noun *ito* 'dear (one)' is unattested in WOJ.
277 Another possibility is 'upper marsh' (Mizushima 1986: 155), as a contraction of *kami-numa.

(continued)

Poem	Province	Dialect Region	K	V	Potential AOJ linguistic features
3410	Kamitukeno	AOJ			-rö '-DIM',[278] -ka- '-AVEV-'[279]
3411	Kamitukeno	AOJ			ani 'what'[280]
3412	Kamitukeno	AOJ			-rö '-DIM',[281] -ke '-AVATTR'[282]
3413	Kamitukeno	AOJ			-nösu '-COMP'[283]
3414	Kamitukeno	AOJ			-rö '-DIM',[284] nonzi 'rainbow',[285] arapar- 'appear',[286] -o '-ATTR'[287]
3415	Kamitukeno	AOJ			uwe 'plant.INF'[288]
3416	Kamitukeno	AOJ		W	ipawi-tura 'rock-vine'[289]
3417	Kamitukeno	AOJ		W	opowi n-gusa 'bulrush COP.ATTR-grass'[290]
3418	Kamitukeno	AOJ			mura 'divination',[291] -ö 'ATTR'[292]
3419	Kamitukeno	AOJ			-n-ap- '-NEG-ATTR',[293] nangaNAKAsingey 'UNC',[294] omop-i-nd-oro 'think-INF-go.out-ATTR'[295]

278 Cf. WOJ -ra 'id.'.
279 Cf. WOJ -ke- 'id.'.
280 Cf. WOJ nani 'id.', TSOJ nani 'id.', Hachijō ani 'id.'.
281 Cf. WOJ -ra 'id.'.
282 Cf. WOJ -ki 'id.'.
283 Cf. WOJ -nasu 'id.'.
284 Cf. WOJ -ra 'id.'.
285 Cf. MJ nizi 'id.'. It is not phonographically attested in WOJ.
286 Cf. WOJ arapare- 'id.'.
287 Cf. WOJ -u 'id.'.
288 This is one of several examples attested in EOJ in which the infinitive form of a verb is used in an adnominal function to modify a following noun and create a relative clause. This usage of the infinitive is not attested in WOJ.
289 Unattested in WOJ.
290 Cf. MJ ofowi 'id.'. Unattested in WOJ.
291 Cf. WOJ ura 'divination'.
292 Cf. WOJ -u 'id.'.
293 The order of these morphemes is reversed in WOJ.
294 I tentatively analyze this as na-nga NAK-Asi-ngey 2.S-POSS cry-ADJ-NML 'You feel like crying'. The adjectival verb nominalizer -ngey is unattested in WOJ.
295 In WOJ we would expect omöp-i-nd-uru 'id.'.

(continued)

Poem	Province	Dialect Region	K	V	Potential AOJ linguistic features
3420	Kamitukeno	AOJ			*puna-pasi* 'boat-bridge',[296] *wa pa* '1.S TPT',[297] *ngapey* 'IPT'[298]
3421	Kamitukeno	WOJ			
3422	Kamitukeno	WOJ			
3423	Kamitukeno	AOJ			*-rö* '-DIM',[299] *-o* 'ATTR',[300] *yöki* 'snow'[301]
3424	Simotukeno	AOJ			*-rö* '-DIM',[302] *kö-* 'DIM',[303] *-nösu* '-COMP', *ke* 'container'[304]
3425	Simotukeno	AOJ			*tö* 'FPT'
3426	Mitinöku	AOJ			*-an-ap-* '-NEG-ITER',[305] *-o* 'ATTR'[306]
3427	Mitinöku	WOJ			
3428	Mitinöku	WOJ			
3429	Töpotuapumi	AOJ		W	*as-* 'make shallow'[307]
3430	Suruga	WOJ			
3431	Sagamu	AOJ			*-o* 'ATTR',[308] *kökönba* 'extremely'[309]

---

296 Each morpheme is attested in WOJ, but the compound is not.
297 In WOJ *wa* '1.S' is unattested preceding the topic particle *pa*, therefore it is an EOJ grammatical feature (Vovin 2012a: 68).
298 Unattested in WOJ.
299 Cf. WOJ *-ra* 'id.'.
300 Cf. WOJ *-u* 'id.'.
301 Cf. WOJ *yuki* 'id.'.
302 Cf. WOJ *-ra* 'id.'.
303 Probably a misspelling of *ko-* 'DIM'. It may also be the word *kö-* 'tree', but the morpheme order in the hypothetical compound *kö-nara* 'tree-oak' is the opposite of what we would expect.
304 Cf. WOJ *key* 'id.'.
305 In WOJ the order of these morphemes is reversed.
306 Cf. WOJ *-u* 'id.'.
307 A vowel-final stem verb *ase-* 'make shallow' is attested in WOJ, but only logographically. There are no clear attestations of *as-* 'make shallow' in WOJ.
308 Cf. WOJ *-u* 'id.'.
309 There is only one attestation of this in WOJ, in MYS 15.3684.3 (Vovin 2009a: 1107). MYS Book 15 shows one other EOJ word not attested elsewhere in WOJ (*andö* 'what' in 15.3639.3).

(continued)

Poem	Province	Dialect Region	K	V	Potential AOJ linguistic features
3432	Sagamu	AOJ			*kandu* 'paper.mulberry',[310] *kandusanemö* 'UNC',[311] *kandusakanzu* 'UNC'[312]
3433	Sagamu	WOJ			
3434	Kamitukeno	AOJ			*anze* 'why'[313]
3435	Kamitukeno	AOJ			*-rö* '-DIM',[314] *pita* 'one'[315]
3436	Kamitukeno	AOJ			*siratöpopu* 'UNC',[316] *-na-na* 'NEG.ATTR-LOC'[317]
3437	Mitinöku	AOJ			*ser-* 'bend'[318]
3438a	Unspecified Province	WOJ	Ab		
3438b	Unspecified Province	WOJ	Ab		
3438c	Unspecified Province	WOJ	Ab		
3439	Unspecified Province	WOJ	Ab		
3440a	Unspecified Province	AOJ		W	*-n-i* '-PERF-IMP'[319]
3440b	Unspecified Province	AOJ		W	*-n-i* '-PERF-IMP'[320]
3441a	Unspecified Province	WOJ			

---

310 Cf. WOJ *kandi* 'id.'.
311 Possibly contains a verb root *kandus-* 'abduct'. Unattested in WOJ.
312 Possibly contains a verb root *kandus-* 'abduct'. Unattested in WOJ.
313 Cf. WOJ *nanzö* 'id.'.
314 Cf. WOJ *-ra* 'id.'.
315 Cf. WOJ *pitö* 'id.'.
316 An MK attested only in this poem, of unclear meaning.
317 Cf. WOJ *-nz-u n-i* '-NEG-INF COP-INF'.
318 An earlier form of MJ *sor-* 'id.'. Unattested in WOJ.
319 Cf. WOJ *-te-yö* '-PERF-IMP'. I tentatively follow Mizushima (1986: 207) here. An alternative explanation (Omodaka 1965: 134–135) maintains this is the locative suffix *-ni* on the nominalized verb *tanbar-i* 'receive-NML', in which case it would not be an AOJ feature. The weakness of that hypothesis is that it necessitates a predicate, such as *yuk-* 'to go', was omitted from the line. Due to the unclear nature of this form, I include it as a potential AOJ feature.
320 See the footnote above.

(continued)

Poem	Province	Dialect Region	K	V	Potential AOJ linguistic features
3441b	Unspecified Province	WOJ	Ab		
3442	Unspecified Province	AOJ		W	te*NGO-nö yonb-i saka* 'maiden-GEN call-INF hill',[321] *-ngane-* 'NEG.POT.INF'[322]
3443	Unspecified Province	WOJ			
3444	Unspecified Province	AOJ			*kuku* 'stem',[323] *nöt-* 'fill',[324] *-an-ap-* '-NEG-ITER',[325] *-e* '-EV'[326]
3445	Unspecified Province	AOJ			*pendas-i* 'be.separated-NML'[327]
3446	Unspecified Province	AOJ			*-na-rö* '-DIM-DIM',[328] *sasara* 'little'[329]
3447	Unspecified Province	AOJ			*-na* '-LOC'[330]
3448	Unspecified Province	AOJ			*pinzi* 'sandbank'[331]
3449	Unspecified Province	WOJ	E		

---

321 This phrase, which we can translate as 'hill where maidens call out', is not attested in WOJ. *Tengo* 'maiden, third daughter' is an EOJ word (see Kupchik 2016 for more discussion), though it is attested only partially phonographically here. Furthermore, the use of the infinitive form of a verb in an attributive function is an EOJ grammatical feature.
322 Cf. WOJ *-kane-* 'id.'; the form *-ngane-* is unattested in WOJ.
323 Cf. WOJ *kukï* 'id.'.
324 Possibly related to WOJ *mit-* 'id.', but the sound correspondences are irregular.
325 In WOJ the order of these morphemes is reversed.
326 Cf. WOJ *-ey* 'id.'.
327 Cf. WOJ *pendat-i* 'id.'.
328 Both diminutive suffixes are exclusive to EOJ, and the usage of two diminutives in succession is an EOJ grammatical feature.
329 Probably cognate with the WOJ and Sinano TSOJ word *sanzare* 'id.'.
330 Unattested in WOJ. Cf. WOJ/AOJ *-ni* 'id.'.
331 Unattested in WOJ. It is a borrowing of Ainu *pis* 'shore' or *pis-i* 'its shore' (Vovin 2012a: 140).

Appendix A – A classification of poems in MYS Book 14 — 493

(continued)

Poem	Province	Dialect Region	K	V	Potential AOJ linguistic features
3450	Unspecified Province	AOJ			suke 'assistant',[332] naranbe- 'line up',[333] -mer- 'CNJC'[334]
3451	Unspecified Province	AOJ	W		wa pa '1.S TPT'[335]
3452	Unspecified Province	AOJ			ngani 'CNJ'[336]
3453	Unspecified Province	AOJ		W	mayop- 'become frayed'[337]
3454	Unspecified Province	WOJ	E		
3455	Unspecified Province	WOJ			
3456	Unspecified Province	AOJ			pe 'leaf'[338]
3457	Unspecified Province	WOJ			
3458	Unspecified Province	AOJ			ikunduk- 'catch one's breath'[339]
3459	Unspecified Province	WOJ	E		
3460	Unspecified Province	AOJ			nipu 'new',[340] nami- 'taste'[341]

---

[332] Cf. WOJ sukey 'id.'.
[333] Cf. WOJ naranbey- 'id.'.
[334] A conjectural verbal auxiliary unattested in WOJ. In AOJ, it is only attested this one time. It is later attested in MJ as the conjectural suffix -umer-.
[335] In WOJ wa '1.S' is unattested preceding the topic particle pa, therefore it is an EOJ grammatical feature (Vovin 2012a: 68).
[336] Cf. WOJ ngane 'id.'.
[337] No phonographic attestations in WOJ.
[338] Cf. WOJ pa 'id.'.
[339] Cf. WOJ ikinduk- 'id.'. The AOJ form is probably the result of sporadic regressive vowel assimilation.
[340] Cf. WOJ nipi 'id.'. The EOJ form is probably the result of sporadic backing and rounding of *i > /u/ after /p/, since Ryukyuan evidence supports PJ *i in the final syllable.
[341] Cf. WOJ namey- 'id.', nipi napey 'new harvest [festival]'.

(continued)

Poem	Province	Dialect Region	K	V	Potential AOJ linguistic features
3461	Unspecified Province	AOJ			*anze* 'why',[342] *-e* '-EV',[343] *-na* '-LOC',[344] *kö-na-ni* 'come-NEG.ATTR-LOC',[345] *sinda* 'CNJ'[346]
3462	Unspecified Province		WOJ		
3463	Unspecified Province	AOJ			*-na* '-DIM'[347]
3464	Unspecified Province	AOJ		W[348]	*wa pa* '1.S TPT'[349]
3465	Unspecified Province	AOJ			*andö* 'what',[350] *-rö* '-IMP'[351]
3466	Unspecified Province	AOJ			*-n-ap-* '-NEG-ITER',[352] *-rö* '-DIM',[353] *-e* '-EV'[354]
3467	Unspecified Province		WOJ		
3468	Unspecified Province	AOJ			*-rö* '-DIM',[355] *kake-* 'hang.INF-'[356]

---

[342] Cf. WOJ *nanzö* 'id.'.
[343] Cf. WOJ *-ey* 'id.'.
[344] Unattested in WOJ.
[345] Cf. WOJ *kö-n-u-ni* 'come-NEG-ATTR-LOC'.
[346] Unattested in WOJ.
[347] Cf. WOJ *-ra* 'id.'.
[348] Although erroneously listed as WOJ in the classification list, this poem was treated as EOJ in Kupchik (2011), and an example was cited (on page 501).
[349] In WOJ *wa* '1.S' is unattested preceding the topic particle *pa*, therefore it is an EOJ grammatical feature (Vovin 2012a: 68).
[350] Cf. WOJ *nandö* 'why', *nani* 'what'.
[351] Cf. WOJ *-yö* 'id.'.
[352] The order of these morphemes is reversed in WOJ.
[353] Cf. WOJ *-ra* 'id.'.
[354] Cf. WOJ *-ey* 'id.'.
[355] Cf. WOJ *-ra* 'id.'.
[356] Cf. WOJ *kakey-* 'id.'.

(continued)

Poem	Province	Dialect Region	K	V	Potential AOJ linguistic features
3469	Unspecified Province	AOJ			-o '-ATTR',[357] yösörö 'UNC',[358] -na '-DIM',[359] anze 'why'[360]
3470	Unspecified Province	WOJ			
3471	Unspecified Province	AOJ		W	simara-ku 'be for a while-AVINF'[361]
3472	Unspecified Province	AOJ			anze 'why',[362] -o '-ATTR',[363] -n-ap- '-NEG-ITER'[364]
3473	Unspecified Province	AOJ			-ka- 'AVEV',[365] -o '-ATTR',[366] -rö '-DIM',[367] oyu 'grow.older.NML'[368]
3474	Unspecified Province	AOJ			indusi 'where'[369]
3475	Unspecified Province	WOJ			

---

[357] Cf. WOJ -u 'id.'.
[358] Possibly a sporadic metathesis of the last two vowels in yösör-i 'approach-INF' (Vovin 2012a: 156), though I tentatively analyze it as yös-i-rö 'approach-INF-UNC'.
[359] Unattested in WOJ.
[360] Cf. WOJ nanzö 'id.'.
[361] Not attested as an inflected adjective in WOJ. There is a single phonographic attestation of simara-ku in the Nihon Ryōiki (Early Middle Japanese). Cf. WOJ simasi 'id.'.
[362] Cf. WOJ nanzö 'id.'.
[363] Cf. WOJ -u 'id.'.
[364] The order of these morphemes is reversed in WOJ.
[365] Cf. WOJ -ke- 'id.'.
[366] Cf. WOJ -u 'id.'.
[367] Cf. WOJ -ra 'id.'.
[368] Cf. WOJ oyi 'id.'.
[369] Cf. WOJ induti 'id.'.

(continued)

Poem	Province	Dialect Region	K	V	Potential AOJ linguistic features
3476a	Unspecified Province	AOJ			-na '-DIM',[370] -o '-ATTR' (twice),[371] tuku 'moon',[372] nongan- 'flow',[373] kopusi- 'be longing for',[374] -unam- '-TENT2' (twice),[375] -ö '-ATTR',[376] wanu '1.S' (twice),[377] -e '-EV' (twice)[378]
3476b	Unspecified Province	AOJ			wanu '1.S',[379] -an-öp- '-NEG-ITER',[380] yun- 'sleep'[381]
3477	Unspecified Province	AOJ		W	teNGO-nö yonb-i saka 'maiden-GEN call-INF hill'[382]
3478	Unspecified Province	AOJ			yösar- 'be attracted to',[383] sinda 'CNJ',[384] -an-öpe 'NEG-ITER.INF',[385] -o '-ATTR'[386]
3479	Unspecified Province	WOJ			

---

370 Unattested in WOJ.
371 Cf. WOJ -u 'id.'.
372 Cf. WOJ tukï 'id.'.
373 Cf. WOJ nangare- 'id.'.
374 Cf. WOJ kopïsi-, koposi- 'id.'.
375 Cf. WOJ -uram- 'id.'.
376 Cf. WOJ -u 'id.'.
377 EOJ oblique first-person pronoun unattested in WOJ and TSOJ.
378 Cf. WOJ -ey 'id.'.
379 Unattested in WOJ.
380 The order of these morphemes is reversed in WOJ.
381 Unattested in WOJ, but compare MJ o-yor- 'sleep' (Vovin 2012a: 165).
382 This phrase, which we can translate as 'hill where maidens call out', is not attested in WOJ, and contains two EOJ features: teNGO 'maiden; third daughter' is an EOJ word (see Kupchik 2016 for more discussion), though it is attested only partially phonographically here; the use of the infinitive form of a verb in an adnominal function is an EOJ grammatical feature.
383 Cf. WOJ yösör- 'id.'.
384 Unattested in WOJ. A borrowing of Ainu hi-ta 'time-LOC' (Vovin 2009c).
385 The order of these morphemes is reversed in WOJ, and the usage of the infinitive in an adnominal function is an EOJ grammatical feature.
386 Cf. WOJ -u 'id.'.

(continued)

Poem	Province	Dialect Region	K	V	Potential AOJ linguistic features
3480	Unspecified Province	AOJ			-n-o '-PERF-ATTR'[387]
3481	Unspecified Province	AOJ			sawe-sawe 'rustle-REDUP'[388]
3482a	Unspecified Province	AOJ	W	W	uti-kapey 'PREF-cross over.INF'[389]
3482b	Unspecified Province	AOJ			-an-ap- '-NEG-ITER',[390] -an-öpe '-NEG-ITER.INF',[391] kötö [i]ta- 'word be.painful',[392] -e '-EV'[393]
3483	Unspecified Province	AOJ			-e '-EV',[394] -ke 'AVATTR',[395] töke- 'get.untied',[396] -n-ape- '-NEG-ITER',[397] -na '-DIM'[398]
3484	Unspecified Province	AOJ			ke 'container',[399] pususa 'many'[400]
3485	Unspecified Province	AOJ	W		teNGO 'maiden',[401] -ngane- '-NEG.POT.INF-'[402]
3486	Unspecified Province	AOJ		W	yun-duka 'bow-handle'[403]

---

387 Cf. WOJ -n-uru 'id.'.
388 Cf. WOJ sawi-sawi 'id.'.
389 Unattested in WOJ, where we only find uti-kap- 'id.' (Mizushima 1986: 272).
390 The order of these morphemes is reversed in WOJ.
391 The order of these morphemes is reversed in WOJ, and the usage of the infinitive in an adnominal function is an EOJ grammatical feature.
392 The V_2 elision in this phrase is an EOJ feature. In WOJ we find köt[ö] ita- 'id.', with V_1 elision.
393 Cf. WOJ -ey 'id.'.
394 Cf. WOJ -ey 'id.'.
395 Cf. WOJ -ki 'id.'.
396 Cf. WOJ tökey- 'id.'.
397 The order of these morphemes is reversed in WOJ.
398 Cf. WOJ -ra 'id.'.
399 Cf. WOJ key 'id.'.
400 Unattested in WOJ.
401 An EOJ word unattested in WOJ except in a few poems that directly reference Azuma.
402 Cf. WOJ -kane- 'id.'.
403 A contraction of yumi 'bow' and tuka 'handle'. This contraction is not phonographically attested in WOJ.

(continued)

Poem	Province	Dialect Region	K	V	Potential AOJ linguistic features
3487	Unspecified Province	AOJ			*s-u s-u* 'do-FIN do-FIN',[404] *-NA-na* '-NEG.ATTR-LOC'[405]
3488	Unspecified Province	AOJ	W		*op-u* 'grow-ATTR',[406] *-o* '-ATTR'[407]
3489	Unspecified Province	AOJ			*-k-aku-* 'AVATTR-NML',[408] *singe-* 'be. overgrown'[409]
3490	Unspecified Province	WOJ			
3491	Unspecified Province	WOJ			
3492	Unspecified Province	AOJ		W	*na-tö* '2.S-COM'[410]
3493a	Unspecified Province	AOJ			*-e* '-EV',[411] *yande* 'branch'[412]
3493b	Unspecified Province	WOJ			
3494	Unspecified Province	AOJ			*andö* 'what',[413] *-o* '-ATTR',[414] *wa pa* '1.S TPT',[415] *kaperute* 'maple tree'[416]

---

404 A reduplication of the verbal form *s-u* 'do-FIN', which is unattested in WOJ. It indicates a repeated action or an action occurring over an extended duration.
405 Cf. WOJ *-nz-u n-i* '-NEG.INF COP-INF'.
406 Cf. WOJ *op-uru* 'id.'. In WOJ, this verb is a vowel-final stem, *opï-* 'grow', whereas in AOJ it is a consonant-final stem.
407 Cf. WOJ *-u* 'id.'.
408 Cf. WOJ *-keku* 'id.'.
409 Cf. WOJ *singey-* 'id.'.
410 The comitative suffix is not phonographically attested after *na* '2.S' in WOJ, and thus may be an AOJ grammatical feature.
411 Cf. WOJ *-ey* 'id.'.
412 Cf. WOJ *yenda* 'id.'. The AOJ form shows sporadic vowel metathesis.
413 Cf. WOJ *nandö* 'why', *nani* 'what'.
414 Cf. WOJ *-u* 'id.'.
415 In WOJ *wa* '1.S' is unattested preceding the topic particle *pa*, therefore it is an EOJ grammatical feature (Vovin 2012a: 68).
416 Unattested in WOJ.

(continued)

Poem	Province	Dialect Region	K	V	Potential AOJ linguistic features
3495	Unspecified Province	AOJ			-rö '-DIM'[417]
3496	Unspecified Province	AOJ			-unam- '-TENT2-'[418]
3497	Unspecified Province	AOJ	W	W	ne-n-ziro taka n-gaya 'root-GEN-white high COP.ATTR-thatching.reed'[419]
3498	Unspecified Province	AOJ		W	yapara 'soft'[420]
3499	Unspecified Province	AOJ			-rö '-IMP',[421] nangöya 'soft'[422]
3500	Unspecified Province	AOJ			wope- 'finish',[423] -ke '-AVATTR'[424]
3501	Unspecified Province	AOJ			-rö '-DIM' (twice),[425] -ar- '-PROG-',[426] op- 'grow'[427]
3502	Unspecified Province	AOJ			ma 'wife',[428] köngötö 'many',[429] meynd- 'love',[430] wa pa '1.S TPT',[431] ngapey 'IPT'[432]

---

417 Cf. WOJ -ra 'id.'.
418 Cf. WOJ and TSOJ -uram- 'id.'.
419 This phrase is unattested in other OJ texts, and it is unusual because it contains two occurrences of morpheme-based *rendaku* in one line of verse (I could not find any examples of that in WOJ).
420 There are no phonographic attestations in WOJ.
421 Cf. WOJ -yö 'id.'.
422 Cf. WOJ nangoya 'id.'.
423 Cf. WOJ wopey- 'id.'.
424 Cf. WOJ -ki 'id.'.
425 Cf. WOJ -ra 'id.'.
426 Cf. WOJ -er- 'id.'.
427 Cf. WOJ opï- 'id.'.
428 The EOJ cognate of WOJ *me* 'wife', TSOJ *mi* 'id.' < PJe *mia 'id.', with expected V_1 elision of *ia in EOJ (cf. the same correspondence in EOJ *ipa* 'house', WOJ *ipe* 'id.', TSOJ *ipi* 'id.' < PJe *ipia 'id.').
429 Unattested in WOJ.
430 Cf. WOJ meynde- 'id.'.
431 In WOJ *wa* '1.S' is unattested preceding the topic particle *pa*, therefore it is an EOJ grammatical feature (Vovin 2012a: 68).
432 Unattested in WOJ.

(continued)

Poem	Province	Dialect Region	K	V	Potential AOJ linguistic features
3503	Unspecified Province	AOJ			*ukera* 'Atractylodes japonica'[433]
3504	Unspecified Province	AOJ			*-rö* '-DIM'[434]
3505	Unspecified Province	AOJ		W	*kisö* 'last night',[435] *sat-* 'shine'[436]
3506	Unspecified Province	AOJ			*köndök-* 'UNC'[437]
3507	Unspecified Province	AOJ		W	*senba-* 'be narrow'[438]
3508	Unspecified Province	AOJ		W	*NEtuko-* 'UNC'[439]
3509	Unspecified Province	AOJ			*osöki* 'garment',[440] *-rö* '-DIM',[441] *-o* '-ATTR',[442] *-n-ap-* '-NEG-ITER',[443] *-e* '-EV'[444]
3510	Unspecified Province	WOJ			
3511	Unspecified Province	AOJ			*-rö* '-DIM',[445] *isayop-* 'hesitate'[446]

---

433 A perennial grass in the chrysanthemum family. This word is not phonographically attested in WOJ, and the MJ word is *wokera* (cf. MdJ *okera*).
434 Cf. WOJ *-ra* 'id.'.
435 Cf. WOJ *kinzö* 'id.'.
436 There is a single attestation in WOJ written in *kungana* (MYS 13:3295.1).
437 Unattested in WOJ.
438 Phonographically unattested in WOJ.
439 Unattested in WOJ. It refers to some type of grass.
440 Unattested in WOJ. Its etymology is unclear, but the element *ki* is perhaps the nominalized form of the verb *ki-* 'wear'.
441 Cf. WOJ *-ra* 'id.'.
442 Cf. WOJ *-u* 'id.'.
443 The order of these morphemes is reversed in WOJ.
444 Cf. WOJ *-ey* 'id.'.
445 Cf. WOJ *-ra* 'id.'.
446 Only one partially phonographic attestation in WOJ (MYS 3.428.4).

(continued)

Poem	Province	Dialect Region	K	V	Potential AOJ linguistic features
3512	Unspecified Province	AOJ			-rö '-DIM' (twice),[447] isayop- 'hesitate',[448] -ar- '-PROG-'[449]
3513	Unspecified Province	AOJ			-rö '-DIM',[450] anze 'why',[451] nino 'cloth'[452]
3514	Unspecified Province	AOJ			-nösu '-COMP'[453]
3515	Unspecified Province	AOJ			sinda 'CNJ'[454]
3516	Unspecified Province	AOJ			kamu 'deity',[455] -an-ap- '-NEG-ITER-',[456] -o '-ATTR'[457]
3517	Unspecified Province	AOJ			anze 'why',[458] -rö '-IMP',[459] kökönba 'extremely',[460] -ke '-AVATTR'[461]
3518	Unspecified Province	AOJ			otap- 'sing',[462] -sime- '-CAUS-',[463] [i]to-ra 'dear-DIM',[464] ka-numa 'deer-marsh'[465]

---

447 Cf. WOJ -ra 'id.'.
448 Only one partially phonographic attestation in WOJ (MYS 3.428.4).
449 Cf. WOJ -er 'id.'.
450 Cf. WOJ -ra 'id.'.
451 Cf. WOJ nanzö 'id.'.
452 No phonographic attestations in WOJ, but cf. MJ nuno 'id.'.
453 Cf. WOJ -nasu 'id.'.
454 Unattested in WOJ.
455 Cf. WOJ kamï 'id.'. WOJ kamu- is attested, but only as a compounding form.
456 The order of these morphemes is reversed in WOJ.
457 Cf. WOJ -u 'id.'.
458 Cf. WOJ nanzö 'id.'.
459 Cf. WOJ -yö 'id.'.
460 There is only one attestation of this in WOJ, in MYS 15.3684.3 (Vovin 2009a: 1107). MYS Book 15 shows one other EOJ word not attested elsewhere in WOJ (andö 'what' in 15.3639.3).
461 Cf. WOJ -ki 'id.'.
462 Cf. WOJ utap- 'id.'.
463 Cf. WOJ -simey- 'id.'.
464 Unattested in WOJ.
465 Another possibility is 'upper marsh', with ka- being a reduced form of kami 'upper'.

(continued)

Poem	Province	Dialect Region	K	V	Potential AOJ linguistic features
3519	Unspecified Province	AOJ		W	kör-are 'scold-PASS.INF'[466]
3520	Unspecified Province	AOJ			-rö '-DIM',[467] sinda 'CNJ'[468]
3521	Unspecified Province	AOJ			wosö 'lie',[469] köröku 'caw-caw',[470] masande 'really'[471]
3522	Unspecified Province	AOJ			kisö 'last night',[472] -rö '-DIM'[473]
3523	Unspecified Province		WOJ		
3524	Unspecified Province	AOJ			-an-ap- '-NEG-ITER-',[474] -e '-EV'[475]
3525	Unspecified Province	AOJ			-o '-ATTR',[476] -nösu '-COMP',[477] -rö '-DIM',[478] -n-ap- '-NEG-ITER-'[479]
3526	Unspecified Province	AOJ			-a '-ATTR',[480] -unam- '-TENT2-',[481] -y- '-EPEN-',[482] -ar- '-PROG-',[483] -ö '-ATTR'[484]

---

466 In WOJ we do not find the passive allomorph -are on the verb stem kör- 'scold'.
467 Cf. WOJ -ra 'id.'.
468 Unattested in WOJ.
469 Cf. Late WOJ woso 'id.'.
470 Imitation of the sound of a crow, unattested in WOJ.
471 Cf. WOJ masa 'id.'.
472 Cf. WOJ kinzö 'id.'.
473 Cf. WOJ -ra 'id.'.
474 The order of these morphemes is reversed in WOJ.
475 Cf. WOJ -ey 'id.'.
476 Cf. WOJ -u 'id.'.
477 Cf. WOJ -nasu 'id.'.
478 Cf. WOJ -ra 'id.'.
479 The order of these morphemes is reversed in WOJ.
480 Unattested in WOJ.
481 Cf. WOJ -uram- 'id.'.
482 An epenthetic consonant used to break up the vowel cluster in the form na-omöp- 'NEG.IMP-think-'. This is a phonological phenomenon that is not uncommon among the world's languages but is otherwise unattested in AOJ. Therefore, it is likely a feature of this specific Azuma topolect.
483 Cf. WOJ -er- 'id.'.
484 Cf. WOJ -u 'id.'.

(continued)

Poem	Province	Dialect Region	K	V	Potential AOJ linguistic features
3527	Unspecified Province	AOJ			-o '-ATTR',[485] -n-o '-PERF-ATTR'[486]
3528	Unspecified Province	AOJ			-nö '-DIM'[487]
3529	Unspecified Province	AOJ			wosangi 'hare',[488] -ar- '-PROG',[489] -n-ape '-NEG-ITER.INF',[490] wosawosa '[not] enough'[491]
3530	Unspecified Province	AOJ			-rö '-DIM'[492]
3531	Unspecified Province	AOJ			kö-sika 'come-PST.EV',[493] -rö '-DIM'[494]
3532	Unspecified Province	AOJ			-rö '-DIM'[495]
3533	Unspecified Province	AOJ			-ke '-AVATTR',[496] sinda 'CNJ',[497] a 'foot',[498] nayum- 'worry'[499]
3534	Unspecified Province		WOJ		
3535	Unspecified Province		WOJ		

[485] Cf. WOJ -u 'id.'.
[486] Cf. WOJ -n-uru 'id.'.
[487] Cf. WOJ -ra 'id.'.
[488] Cf. WOJ usangi 'id.'.
[489] Cf. WOJ -er- 'id.'.
[490] The order of these morphemes is reversed in WOJ. Also, this infinitive form functions as an attributive, which is an EOJ grammatical feature.
[491] Unattested in WOJ, but cf. MJ wosawosa 'id.'.
[492] Cf. WOJ -ra 'id.'.
[493] Irregular past tense evidential form. There is no purely phonographic attestation in WOJ, but a partially phonographic attestation can be found in MYS 9:1751 (Vovin 2009a: 920).
[494] Cf. WOJ -ra 'id.'.
[495] Cf. WOJ -ra 'id.'.
[496] Cf. WOJ -ki 'id.'.
[497] Unattested in WOJ.
[498] Cf. WOJ asi, a- (in compounds only) 'id.'.
[499] Cf. WOJ nayam- 'id.'.

(continued)

Poem	Province	Dialect Region	K	V	Potential AOJ linguistic features
3536	Unspecified Province	AOJ			-na '-DIM'[500]
3537a	Unspecified Province	AOJ			kupe 'fence',[501] mungi 'barley'[502]
3537b	Unspecified Province	AOJ			uma-se 'horse-fence',[503] -rö '-DIM'[504]
3538a	Unspecified Province	AOJ	W		wa pa '1.S TPT'[505]
3538b	Unspecified Province	AOJ			pasasangey 'make (something or someone) run into (something)',[506] wa pa '1.S TPT'[507]
3539	Unspecified Province	AOJ			anzu 'crumbling cliff',[508] upe 'top',[509] ayapo- 'be.dangerous-',[510] -rö '-DIM',[511] -ka- '-AVEV-'[512]
3540	Unspecified Province	AOJ			teNGO 'maiden'[513]

---

500 Cf. WOJ -ra 'id.'.
501 Unattested in WOJ.
502 No phonographic attestation in WOJ.
503 No phonographic attestation in WOJ. The -se morpheme is not attested outside of this compound.
504 Cf. WOJ -ra 'id.'.
505 The topic particle pa is not attested after the pronoun wa in WOJ.
506 This word form is unattested in WOJ. It probably consists of pas(e)-ase-angey 'run-CAUS-raise.up.INF' (Vovin 2012a: 227).
507 The topic particle pa is not attested after the pronoun wa in WOJ.
508 Unattested in WOJ.
509 Cf. WOJ upey 'id.'.
510 Unattested in WOJ, but cf. MJ ayafu- 'id.'.
511 Cf. WOJ -ra 'id.'.
512 Cf. WOJ -ke- 'id.'.
513 Unattested in WOJ except in a handful of poems that directly reference Azuma.

(continued)

Poem	Province	Dialect Region	K	V	Potential AOJ linguistic features
3541	Unspecified Province	AOJ			*anzu* 'crumbling cliff',[514] *pey* 'side',[515] *-o* '-ATTR',[516] *-nösu* '-COMP',[517] *ayapa* 'dangerous',[518] *tomo* 'CNJ',[519] *-er-ap-* '-PROG-ITER-'[520]
3542	Unspecified Province	WOJ	E		
3543	Unspecified Province	AOJ			*-e* '-EV',[521] *-rö* '-DIM'[522]
3544	Unspecified Province	AOJ			*-na-na* '-DIM-DIM'[523]
3545	Unspecified Province	WOJ	E		
3546	Unspecified Province	AOJ			*-ar-* '-PROG-',[524] *-o* '-ATTR-',[525] *se* 'clear',[526] *mindo* 'water'[527]
3547	Unspecified Province	WOJ			
3548	Unspecified Province	AOJ			*kötu* 'wooden debris',[528] *-rö* '-DIM' (twice),[529] *-ke* '-AVATTR'[530]

---

514 Unattested in WOJ.
515 Cf. WOJ *pe* 'id.'.
516 Cf. WOJ *-u* 'id.'.
517 Cf. WOJ *-nasu* 'id.'.
518 This is probably the result of a progressive vowel assimilation in EOJ *ayapo-* 'id.' (Vovin 2012a: 230). This word is unattested in WOJ, but cf. MJ *ayafu-* 'id.'.
519 Cf. WOJ *tömö* 'id.'.
520 In WOJ the order of these morphemes is reversed.
521 Cf. WOJ *-ey* 'id.'.
522 Cf. WOJ *-ra* 'id.'.
523 Cf. WOJ *-ra* 'id.'. The usage of two diminutive suffixes in sequence is an EOJ grammatical feature.
524 Cf. WOJ *-er-* 'id.'.
525 Cf. WOJ *-u* 'id.'.
526 Cf. WOJ *si* 'id.'.
527 Cf. WOJ *mindu* 'id.'.
528 Cf. WOJ *kötumi* 'id.'.
529 Cf. WOJ *-ra* 'id.'.
530 Cf. WOJ *-ki* 'id.'.

(continued)

Poem	Province	Dialect Region	K	V	Potential AOJ linguistic features
3549	Unspecified Province	AOJ			*indu* 'where',[531] *-rö* '-DIM'[532]
3550	Unspecified Province	AOJ		W	*kisö* 'last night'[533]
3551	Unspecified Province	AOJ			*-ke* '-AVATTR'[534]
3552	Unspecified Province	AOJ			*-o* '-ATTR',[535] *-ö* '-ATTR',[536] *-nösu* '-COMP',[537] *-unam-* '-TENT2-',[538] *sawawe* 'UNC',[539] *rö* 'UNC',[540] *ura* 'upper branches of a tree'[541]
3553	Unspecified Province	AOJ			*kötetanzukumoka* 'UNC'[542]
3554	Unspecified Province		WOJ		
3555	Unspecified Province	AOJ			*-N-Ape* '-NEG-ITER.INF'[543]

---

531 Cf. WOJ *induku* 'id.'.
532 Cf. WOJ *-ra* 'id.'.
533 Cf. WOJ *kinzö* 'id.'.
534 Cf. WOJ *-ki* 'id.'.
535 Cf. WOJ *-u* 'id.'.
536 Cf. WOJ *-u* 'id.'.
537 Cf. WOJ *-nasu* 'id.'.
538 Cf. WOJ *-uram-* 'id.'.
539 Unattested in WOJ. Etymologically related to AOJ *sawe-sawe* 'rustle-REDUP', indicating a noisy event.
540 This is either the copula *rö* or an AOJ emphatic particle *rö* (Cf. WOJ *yö* 'id.') (Vovin 2012a: 240). I prefer the analysis it is a copula.
541 Cf. WOJ *ure* 'id.'.
542 This line (the fourth in the poem) remains completely unintelligible, though there is no shortage of linguistically implausible hypotheses (see Mizushima 1986: 381–382).
543 The order of these morphemes is reversed in WOJ, and the usage of the infinitive in an adnominal function is an EOJ grammatical feature.

(continued)

Poem	Province	Dialect Region	K	V	Potential AOJ linguistic features
3556	Unspecified Province	AOJ			[a]ndö 'what',[544] si- 'do',[545] -ar- '-PROG-'[546]
3557	Unspecified Province	AOJ			-ke '-AVATTR',[547] -na-na '-NEG.ATTR-LOC'[548]
3558	Unspecified Province	WOJ			
3559	Unspecified Province	WOJ			
3560	Unspecified Province	AOJ			söpo 'red soil or pigment'[549]
3561	Unspecified Province	AOJ			tor- 'shine',[550] -nösu '-COMP',[551] -o '-ATTR-' (twice),[552] tö 'FPT',[553] mö 'EPT'[554]
3562	Unspecified Province	AOJ		W	ya ni 'UNC'[555]

---

544 Cf. WOJ *nandö* 'why', *nani* 'what'. Also, the synchronic V_2 elision of the initial vowel in this form is an EOJ grammatical feature.
545 Cf. WOJ *se-* 'id.'. This secondary raising of *se 'do' > /si/ appears to be isolated to the topolect attested in this poem.
546 Cf. WOJ *-er-* 'id.'.
547 Cf. WOJ *-ki* 'id.'.
548 Cf. WOJ *-nz-u n-i* '-NEG-INF COP-INF'.
549 Cf. WOJ *sopi* 'light red color'. The AOJ form is probably the result of progressive vowel assimilation. This word is likely related to pseudo-Koguryŏ *sapu* ~ *sapï* and Paekche *sopi*, all meaning 'red' (Vovin 2012a: 246).
550 Cf. WOJ *ter-* 'id.'. The vowel change in the AOJ form appears to be isolated to the topolect attested in this poem.
551 Cf. WOJ *-nasu* 'id.'.
552 Cf. WOJ *-u* 'id.'.
553 Cf. WOJ *sö* ~ *nzö* 'id.'.
554 This emphatic particle is well attested in WOJ, but its usage after the attributive form a verb is an EOJ grammatical feature.
555 Unattested in WOJ. It is probably *ya-ni* 'shore-LOC', with a borrowing of Ainu *ya* 'shore' (Vovin 2012a: 248).

(continued)

Poem	Province	Dialect Region	K	V	Potential AOJ linguistic features
3563	Unspecified Province	AOJ			-unam- '-TENT2-',[556] -o '-ATTR',[557] mindaye- 'be confused',[558] kisö 'last night'[559]
3564	Unspecified Province	AOJ			-rö '-DIM',[560] andö 'what',[561] ura 'upper branches of a tree',[562] s-u s-u 'do-FIN do-FIN',[563] -ke '-AVATTR',[564] sungos- 'to pass'[565]
3565	Unspecified Province	AOJ			-rö '-DIM',[566] tuku 'moon'[567]
3566	Unspecified Province	AOJ	Ab[568]		söwape 'UNC'[569]
3567	Unspecified Province	AOJ		W	yun-duka 'bow-handle'[570]
3568	Unspecified Province	WOJ			

---

[556] Cf. WOJ -uram- 'id.'.
[557] Cf. WOJ -u 'id.'.
[558] Cf. WOJ mindare- 'id.'.
[559] Cf. WOJ kinzö 'id.'.
[560] Cf. WOJ -ra 'id.'.
[561] Cf. WOJ nandö 'why', nani 'what'.
[562] Cf. WOJ ure 'id.'.
[563] This reduplication of s-u 'do-FIN' is unattested in WOJ, but it is attested twice in AOJ. It indicates an action is done repeatedly.
[564] Cf. WOJ -ki 'id.'.
[565] Cf. WOJ sungus- 'id.', MJ sugos- 'id.'.
[566] Cf. WOJ -ra 'id.'.
[567] Cf. WOJ tukï 'id.'.
[568] Although mistakenly omitted in the classification list, examples from this poem were used in Kupchik (2011).
[569] Unattested in WOJ. So far, no plausible internal etymology or meaning has been proposed, though in terms of morphology it appears to contain a verb stem söwe- with the iterative suffix -ape attached.
[570] Both morphemes are attested in WOJ, but the compound with a reduced form (yun-) of yumi 'bow' is only phonographically attested in AOJ.

(continued)

Poem	Province	Dialect Region	K	V	Potential AOJ linguistic features
3569	Unspecified Province	WOJ	E		
3570	Unspecified Province	WOJ			
3571	Unspecified Province	WOJ			
3572	Unspecified Province	AOJ			*andö* 'what',[571] *-e* '-EV',[572] *-ar-* '-PROG-'[573]
3573	Unspecified Province	WOJ	E		
3574	Unspecified Province	WOJ			
3575	Unspecified Province	WOJ			
3576	Unspecified Province	AOJ			*anze* 'why',[574] *-ke* '-AVATTR'[575]
3577	Unspecified Province	WOJ	Ab		

---

571 Cf. WOJ *nandö* 'why', *nani* 'what'.
572 Cf. WOJ *-ey* 'id.'.
573 Cf. WOJ *-er* 'id.'.
574 Cf. WOJ *nanzö* 'id.'.
575 Cf. WOJ *-ki* 'id.'.

References

Anderson, Stephen. 1975. The description of nasal consonants and the internal structure of segments. In Charles A. Ferguson, Larry M. Hyman & John J. Ohala (eds.), *Nasálfest: Papers from a Symposium on Nasals and Nasalization*, 1–26. Stanford: Stanford University, Department of Linguistics.

Aoki, Michiko Y. 1997. *Records of Wind and Earth: A Translation of Fudoki with Introduction and Commentaries*. Ann Arbor: The Association for Asian Studies.

Arisaka, Hideyo. 1955. *Jōdai on'in kō* [A study of ancient Japanese phonology]. Tokyo: Sanseidō.

Asanuma, Ryōji. 1999. *Hachijō-jima no hōgen jiten* [A dictionary of the dialect of Hachijō Island]. Tokyo: Asahi Shimbun Shuppan Sābisu.

Bauer, Laurie. 2004. *A Glossary of Morphology*. Washington D.C.: Georgetown University Press.

Baxter, William & Laurent Sagart. 2014. *Old Chinese: A New Reconstruction*. New York: Oxford University Press.

Bentley, John R. 2001. *A Descriptive Grammar of Early Old Japanese Prose*. Leiden: Brill.

Bentley, John R. 2002. The spelling of /mo/ in Old Japanese. *Journal of East Asian Linguistics* 11(4). 349–374.

Bentley, John R. 2006. *The Authenticity of Sendai Kuji Hongi: A New Examination of Texts, with a Translation and Commentary*. Leiden: Brill.

Bentley, John R. 2016. *ABC Dictionary of Ancient Japanese Phonograms*. Honolulu: University of Hawai'i Press.

Blust, Robert. 2007. The prenasalized trills of Manus. In Jeff Siegel, John Lynch & Diana Eades (eds.), *Language Description, History and Development: Linguistic Indulgence in Memory of Terry Crowley*, 297–311. Amsterdam/Philadelphia: John Benjamins.

Doi, Tadao (ed.). 1985. *Jidai betsu kokugo daijiten – Muromachi jidai-hen ichi* [A large dictionary of the Japanese language by periods – Muromachi period, volume 1]. Tokyo: Sanseidō.

Francis-Ratte, Alexander. 2016. *Proto-Korean-Japanese: A new reconstruction of the common origin of the Japanese and Korean languages*. PhD dissertation, Ohio State University.

Frellesvig, Bjarke. 2021. On otsu-rui Ci_2 and Ce_2 and root-final consonants in Pre-Old Japanese. In John Kupchik, José Andrés Alonso de la Fuente & Marc Hideo Miyake (eds.), *Studies in Asian Historical Linguistics, Philology and Beyond*, 35–48. Leiden: Brill.

Frellesvig, Bjarke & John Whitman. 2004. The vowels of Proto-Japanese. *Japanese Language and Literature* 38. 281–299.

Frellesvig, Bjarke & John Whitman. 2008. Evidence for seven vowels in proto-Japanese. In *Proto-Japanese: Issues and Prospects*, 15–41. Amsterdam: John Benjamins.

Fukuda, Yoshisuke. 1965. *Nara jidai azuma hōgen no kenkyū* [A study of the Nara period Azuma dialects]. Tokyo: Kazama Shoin.

Hamada, Atsushi. 1952. *Hatsuon to dakuon to no sōkansei no mondai* [The problem of the correlation between pronunciation and voicing]. *Kokugo Kokubun* 21(4). 18–32.

Hashimoto, Shinkichi. 1932. *Kokugo ni okeru biboin* [Nasalized vowels in Japanese]. *Hōgen* 2(1).

Hattori, Shirō. 1978–1979. *Nihon sogo ni tsuite* [On the proto-language of Japan]. *Gekkan Gengo* 7(1)–8(12).

Hattori, Shirō (ed.). 1964. *Ainugo hōgen jiten* [An Ainu dialect dictionary with Ainu, Japanese and English indexes]. Tokyo: Iwanami Shoten.

Hattori, Shirō. 1968. *Hachijō hōgen ni tsuite* [On the Hachijō dialect]. *Kotoba no uchū* 11. 92–95.

Hendricks, Peter. 1994. Adverbial modification in Old Japanese. In Noriko Akatsuka (ed.), *Japanese/Korean Linguistics* 4, 239–255. Stanford University: Center for the Study of Language and Information.

Hino, Sukenari. 2003. *Nihon sogo no boin taikei—jōdai azuma-hōgen shiryō ni yoru saikō* [A reconstruction of the Proto-Japanese vowel system based on the data from Eastern Old Japanese]. In Toshiki Osada & Alexander Vovin (eds.), *Nihongo keitōron no genzai/Perspectives on the Japanese language origins*, 187–205. Kyoto: Nichibunken.

Hirayama, Teruo, Ichirō Ōshima & Masachie Nakamoto. 1966. *Ryūkyū hōgen no sōgōteki kenkyū* [Comprehensive research on the Ryukyuan dialects]. Tokyo: Meiji Shoin.

Hōjō, Tadao. 1966. *Jōdai tōgoku hōgen no kenkyū* [A study of the dialects of the eastern provinces of the ancient period]. Tokyo: Maruzen.

Ikema, Nae. 2003. *Yonaguni-go jiten* [Dictionary of the Yonaguni language]. Yonaguni: Privately published manuscript.

Ikier, Steven. 2006. *On the attributive and final predicate forms in Eastern Old Japanese*. MA thesis, University of Hawai'i at Mānoa.

Itabashi, Yoshizō. 1991. The origin of the Old Japanese lative case suffix *-gari*. *Ural-Altaische Jahrbücher Neue Folge* Band 10. 143–158.

Itō, Haku. 1995–2000. *Man'yōshū shakuchū* [The annotated *Man'yōshū*]. Tokyo: Shūeisha.

Kakubayashi, Fumio. 1998. HAYATO: An Austronesian speaking tribe in southern Japan. *The Bulletin of the Institute of Japanese Culture, Kyoto Sangyo University* 3. 426–442.

Kaneda, Akihiro. 2001. *Hachi hōgen dōshi no kiso kenkyū* [Research on the basic elements of the verbs of the Hachijō dialect]. Tokyo: Kasama Shoin.

Kayano, Shigeru. 2002 (1996). *Kayano Shigeru no Ainu-go jiten – zōhoban* [Shigeru Kayano's Ainu dictionary – Enlarged edition]. Tokyo: Sanseidō.

Kenstowicz, Michael. 2003. Review Article: The role of perception in loanword phonology. A review of *Les emprunts linguistiques d'origine européenne en Fon*, by Flavien Gbéto (2000), Köln: Rüdiger Köppe Verlag. *Studies in African Linguistics* 32(1). 95–112.

Kiku, Chiyo & Toshizō Takahashi. 2005. *Yoron hōgen jiten* [Yoron dialect dictionary]. Tokyo: Musashino Shoin.

Kinoshita, Masayoshi. 1988. *Man'yōshū zenchū, kan dai* 20 [A complete commentary of the *Man'yōshū*, Book 20]. Tokyo: Yūhikaku.

Kinoshita, Masatoshi (ed.). 2001. *Man'yōshū CD-ROM-han* [*Man'yōshū*: The CD-ROM edition]. Tokyo: Hanawa Shobō.

Kojima, Noriyuki, Masatoshi Kinoshita & Akihiro Satake (eds.). 1971–1975: *Man'yōshū* 1–4. *Nihon koten bungaku zenshū* [A complete collection of Classical Japanese literature], vol. 2–5. Tokyo: Shōgakukan.

Kubota, Utsuho (ed.). 1967 (1943–1952). *Man'yōshū hyōshaku* VII [A commentary on the *Man'yōshū*, vol. VII]. Tokyo: Tōkyōdō.

Kumar, Ann & Phil Rose. 2000. Lexical evidence for early contact between Indonesian languages and Japanese. *Oceanic Linguistics* 39(2). 219–255.

Kupchik, John. 2007. A comprehensive study of *mwo, mö, mye, mey, po, pye,* and *pey* syllables in the Eastern Old Japanese dialects. *University of Hawai'i Working Papers in Linguistics* 38(7). 1–33.

Kupchik, John. 2011. *A grammar of the Eastern Old Japanese dialects*. PhD dissertation, University of Hawai'i at Mānoa.

Kupchik, John. 2012. Morpheme-based *rendaku* as a rhythmic stabilizer in Eastern Old Japanese poetry. *Acta Linguistica Asiatica* 2(1). 9–22.

Kupchik, John. 2013a. The rhythmic effects of *rendaku* and hiatal elision in Western Old Japanese poetry. Paper presented at the NINJAL International Conference on Phonetics and Phonology (ICPP 2013), Tachikawa City, Tokyo, Japan, 25 January, 2013.

Kupchik, John. 2013b. Hypermetricality and synchronic vowel elision in hiatus contexts in Eastern Old Japanese poetry. *Cahiers de Linguistique Asie Orientale* 42(1). 2–32.

Kupchik, John. 2016. On the etymology of the Eastern Japanese word *tego*. *The Journal of the American Oriental Society* 136(4). 733–743.

Kupchik, John. 2021a. Ainu loanwords in Hachijō. In John Kupchik, José Andrés Alonso de la Fuente & Marc Hideo Miyake (eds.), *Studies in Asian Historical Linguistics, Philology and Beyond*, 91–102. Leiden: Brill.

Kupchik, John. 2021b. Austronesian lights the way: The origins of the words for 'sun' and other celestial vocabulary in Old Ryukyuan. *International Journal of Eurasian Linguistics* 3(2). 245–265.

Kupchik, John. 2022. Review of *Man'yōshū, Book 16. A New English Translation Containing the Original Text, Kana Transliteration, Romanization, Glossing and Commentary*, by Alexander Vovin (2021), Leiden: Brill. *The Journal of the American Oriental Society* 142(4). 1014–1016.

Lawrence, Wayne. 2013. *Mama wo tazunete sanzenri – Hachijō hōgen no keitōteki ichi ni tsuite* [3000 leagues in search of mama: On the genealogical position of the Hachijō dialect]. In Nobuko Kibe (ed.), *Kiki hōgen no chōsa – Hozon no tame no sōgōteki kenkyū: Hachijō hōgen chōsa hōkokusho* [General research for the study and conservation of endangered dialects in Japan: Survey report on the Hachijō dialect], 71–75. Tokyo: NINJAL.

Maeara, Tōru. 2011. *Taketomi hōgen jiten* [Taketomi dialect dictionary]. Ishigaki: Nanzansha.

Mair, Victor H. 1991. What is a Chinese "dialect/topolect"? Reflections on some key Sino-English linguistic terms. *Sino-Platonic Papers* 29. 1–31.

Majtczak, Tomasz. 2008. *Japońskie klasy czasownikowe v perspektiwie diachronicznej* [Japanese verbal classes in a diachronic perspective]. Kraków: Wydawnictwo Uniwersytetu Jagiellońskiego.

Martin, Samuel E. 1966. Lexical evidence relating Korean to Japanese. *Language* 42(2). 185–251.

Martin, Samuel E. 1987. *The Japanese Language Through Time*. New Haven: Yale University Press.

Martin, Samuel E. 1988 (1972). *A Reference Grammar of Japanese*. Honolulu: University of Hawai'i Press.

Miyake, Marc Hideo. 2003. *Old Japanese: A Phonetic Reconstruction*. London: Routledge.

Mizushima, Yoshiharu. 1972. *Kōchū Man'yōshū azuma uta sakimori uta* [Azuma poems and border guard poems in the *Man'yōshū*]. Tokyo: Kasama Shoin.

Mizushima, Yoshiharu. 1984a. *Man'yōshū Azuma uta no kokugogaku-teki kenkyū* [A linguistic study of the Azuma poems in the *Man'yōshū*]. Tokyo: Kasama Shoin.

Mizushima, Yoshiharu. 1984b. *Man'yōshū Azuma uta honbun kenkyū narabi ni sōsakuin* [Indexes to and research on the original text of the Azuma poems in the *Man'yōshū*]. Tokyo: Kasama Shoin.

Mizushima, Yoshiharu. 1984c. *Man'yōshū Azuma uta no kenkyū* [Research on the Azuma poems in the *Man'yōshū*]. Tokyo: Kasama Shoin.

Mizushima, Yoshiharu. 1986. *Man'yōshū zenchū, kan dai 14* [A complete commentary of the *Man'yōshū*, Book 14]. Tokyo: Yūhikaku.

Mizushima, Yoshiharu. 1996. *Kōchū Man'yōshū azuma uta sakimori uta: shin zōho kaiteiban* [Azuma poems and border guard poems in the *Man'yōshū*: New reprint with additions and emendations]. Tokyo: Kasama Shoin.

Mizushima, Yoshiharu. 2003. *Man'yōshū sakimori uta zenchūshaku* [A complete commentary on the *Man'yōshū* border guard poems]. Tokyo: Kasama Shoin.

Mizushima, Yoshiharu. 2005. *Man'yōshū sakimori uta no kokugogaku-teki kenkyū* [A linguistic study of the border guard poems in the *Man'yōshū*]. Tokyo: Kasama Shoin.

Mizushima, Yoshiharu. 2009. *Man'yōshū sakimori uta no kenkyū* [Research on the border guard poems in the *Man'yōshū*]. Tokyo: Kasama Shoin.
Murayama, Shichirō. 1962. *Nihongo oyobi Kōkurigo no sūshi: Nihongo no keitō mondai ni tsuite* [The numerals of Japanese and Goguryeo: A problem of affinity]. *Kokugogaku* 48. 1–11.
Murayama, Shichirō. 1970. *Shinateru – terushino no kō* [Thoughts on *shinateru* and *terushino*]. *Kokugaku* 82. 15–28.
Murayama, Shichirō. 1975. *Hayato no gengo* [The language of Hayato]. In Taryō Ōbayashi (ed.), *Hayato: nihon kodai bunka no tankyū* [Hayato: The search for the ancient culture of Japan], 249–263. Tokyo: Shakai Shisōsha.
Murayama, Shichirō. 1976. The Malayo-Polynesian component in the Japanese language. *The Journal of Japanese Studies* 2(2). 413–436.
Naitō, Shigeru. 1979. *Hachijō-jima no hōgen* [The dialect of Hachijō Island]. Tokyo: Privately published manuscript.
Nakagawa, Hiroshi. 1995. *Ainu-go Chitose hōgen jiten* [A dictionary of the Chitose dialect of Ainu]. Tokyo: Sōfūkan.
Nakagawa, Hiroshi & Mutsuko Nakamoto. 1997. *CD Ekusupuresu Ainugo* [CD Express Ainu language]. Tokyo: Hakusuisha.
Nakanishi, Susumu. 1978–1983. *Man'yōshū zen chūshaku genbun tsuki* [*Man'yōshū* with a complete commentary and the original text]. Tokyo: Kadokawa.
Nakanishi, Susumu. 1985. *Man'yōshū jiten* [The *Man'yōshū* encyclopedia]. Tokyo: Kōdansha.
Nishimura, Shinji. 1922. *Yamato jidai* [The Yamato era]. (*Kokumin no nihonshi* 1). Tokyo: Waseda University Press.
NKD (*Nihon kokugo daijiten* [A comprehensive dictionary of the Japanese language]). 2006. Digital Edition. Tokyo: Shogakukan.
Omodaka, Hisataka. 1965. *Man'yōshū chūshaku* [Commentary on the *Man'yōshū*], vol. 14. Tokyo: Chuō Kōronsha.
Omodaka, Hisataka (ed.). 1967. *Jidai betsu kokugo daijiten – jōdai-hen* [A large dictionary of the Japanese language by periods – Old Japanese volume]. Tokyo: Sanseidō.
Omodaka, Hisataka. 1968. *Man'yōshū chūshaku* [Commentary on the *Man'yōshū*], vol. 20. Tokyo: Chuō Kōronsha.
Ōno, Susumu, Akihiro Satake & Kingorō Maeda (eds). 1990 (1974). *Iwanami kogo jiten – Hotei-ban* [Iwanami dictionary of Classical Japanese – Revised edition]. Tokyo: Iwanami Shoten.
Ōno, Susumu. 1993. *Kakari musubi no kenkyū* [Research on *kakari musubi*]. Tokyo: Iwanami.
Osada, Suma & Nahoko Suyama. 1977. *Amami hōgen bunrui jiten – jōkan* [A categorical dictionary of the Amami dialect – First volume]. Tokyo: Kasama Shoin.
Osada, Suma, Nahoko Suyama & Misako Fujii. 1980. *Amami hōgen bunrui jiten – gekan* [A categorical dictionary of the Amami dialect – Second volume]. Tokyo: Kasama Shoin.
Osterkamp, Sven. 2011. Digraphic transcriptions of monosyllabics in Old Japanese and their implications. *Proceedings of Linguistics in the 7th symposium of the Nordic Association of Japanese and Korean Studies*, ca. 22 S.
Pellard, Thomas. 2008. Proto-Japonic *e and *o in Eastern Old Japanese. *Cahiers de Linguistique Asie Orientale* 37(2). 133–158.
Pellard, Thomas. 2013. Ryukyuan perspectives on the Proto-Japonic vowel system. In Bjarke Frellesvig & Peter Sells (eds.), *Japanese/Korean Linguistics* 20, 81–96. Stanford: CSLI Publications.

Pellard, Thomas. 2015. The linguistic archeology of the Ryukyu Islands. In Patrick Heinrich, Shisho Miyara & Michinori Shimoji (eds.), *Handbook of the Ryukyuan Languages*, 13–37. Berlin: De Gruyter Mouton.
Pellard, Thomas. 2016. *Nichi-ryū sogo no bunki nendai* [The date of separation of the Proto-Japonic language]. In Yukinori Takubo, John Whitman & Tatsuya Hirako (eds.), *Ryūkyū shogo to Kodai Nihongo: Nichiryū sogo no saiken ni mukete* [Ryukyuan and premodern Japanese: Toward the reconstruction of Proto-Japanese-Ryukyuan], 99–124. Tokyo: Kuroshio.
Piggott, Joan R. 1990. *Mokkan*. Wooden documents from the Nara period. *Monumenta Nipponica* 45(4). 449–470.
Ramsey, S. Robert & J. Marshall Unger. 1972. Evidence of a consonant shift in 7th century Japanese. *UC Berkeley Papers in Japanese Linguistics* 1(2). 278–295.
Russell, Kerri. 2006. *A reconstruction and morphophonemic analysis of Proto-Japonic verbal morphology*. PhD dissertation, University of Hawai'i at Mānoa.
Sansom, George B. 1958. *A History of Japan to 1334*. Stanford: Stanford University Press.
Satake, Akihiro, Hideo Yamada, Rikio Kudō, Masao Ōtani & Yoshiyuki Yamazaki (eds.). 1999–2003. *Man'yōshū. Shin nihon koten bungaku taikei* [New series on Classical Japanese literature], vol 1–4. Tokyo: Iwanami Shoten.
Satō, Ryōichi (ed.). 2003. *Nihon hōgen jiten – Hyōjungo-biki* [Japanese dialect dictionary – with a Standard Japanese index]. Tokyo: Shōgakukan.
Schuessler, Axel. 2007. *ABC Etymological Dictionary of Old Chinese*. Honolulu: University of Hawai'i Press.
Schuessler, Axel. 2009. *Minimal Old Chinese and Late Han Chinese*. Honolulu: University of Hawai'i Press.
Serafim, Leon A. 1999. Why Proto-Japonic had at least six, not four vowels. Paper presented at the University of Hawai'i at Mānoa Linguistics Department Tuesday Seminar.
Serafim, Leon A. 2008. The uses of Ryukyuan in understanding Japanese language history. In Bjarke Frellesvig & John Whitman (eds.), *Proto-Japanese: Issues and Prospects*, 79–99. Amsterdam: John Benjamins.
Serafim, Leon A. & Rumiko Shinzato. 2000. Reconstructing the proto-Japonic *kakari musubi* *ka . . .-(a)m-wo*. *Gengo Kenkyū* 118. 81–118.
Serafim, Leon A. & Rumiko Shinzato. 2005. On the Old Japanese *kakari* (focus) particle *k̲o̲s̲o̲*: Its origin and structure. *Gengo Kenkyū* 127. 1–49.
Serafim, Leon A. & Rumiko Shinzato. 2013. *Synchrony and Diachrony of Okinawan Kakari Musubi in Comparative Perspective with Premodern Japanese*. Leiden: Brill.
Shinmura, Izuru 1927. *Tōhō gengo shi sōkō* [Collection of research on the history of East Asian languages]. Tokyo: Iwanami.
Silverman, Daniel. 1995. Optional, conditional, and obligatory prenasalization in Bafanji. *Journal of West African Languages* 25(2). 57–62.
Smith, Jennifer L. 2006. Loan phonology is not all perception: evidence from Japanese loan doublets. In Timothy J. Vance (ed.), *Japanese/Korean Linguistics* 14, 63–74. Stanford: CSLI.
Spencer, Andrew. 2001. Morphophonological operations. In Andrew Spencer & Arnold Zwicky (eds.), *The Handbook of Morphology*, 123–143. Hoboken, N.J.: John Wiley & Sons.
Takagi, Ichinosuke, Tomohide Gomi & Susumu Ōno (eds.). 1957–1962. *Man'yōshū*, vol. 1–4, *Nihon koten bungaku taikei* [Series on Japanese Classical Literature], vol. 4–7. Tokyo: Iwanami Shoten.
Tamura, Suzuko. 1996. *Ainu-go Saru hōgen jiten* [A dictionary of the Saru dialect of Ainu]. Tokyo: Sōfūkan.
Tateno, Kazumi. 2012. *'Kojiki' to mokkan ni mieru kokumei hyōki no taihi* [A comparison of the transcription of province names found in *Kojiki* and *mokkan*]. *Kodaigaku* (*Nara Joshi Daigaku Kodaigaku Gakujutsu Kenkyū Sentā*) 4. 17–25.

Thorpe, Maner L. 1983. *Ryukyuan language history*. PhD dissertation, University of Southern California.
Tokuyama, Shun'ei & Kenan Celik. 2020. *Minami Ryūkyū Miyako-go Tarama hōgen jiten* [A dictionary of the Tarama dialect of the Southern Ryukyuan language Miyako]. Tokyo: NINJAL.
Tomihama, Sadayoshi. 2013. *Miyako Irabu hōgen jiten* [Dictionary of the Irabu dialect of Miyako]. Naha: Okinawa Times Company.
Torii, Ryūzō. 1918. *Yūshi izen no nihon* [Prehistoric Japan]. Tokyo: Isobe Kōyōdō.
Tsuchiya, Fumiaki (ed.). 1975–1977. *Man'yōshū shichū* [A private commentary on the *Man'yōshū*], vol. 1–10. Tokyo: Chikuma Shobō.
Uffmann, Christian. 2015. Loanword adaptation. In Patrick Honeybone & Joseph Salmons (eds.), *The Oxford Handbook of Historical Phonology*, 644–665. Oxford: University of Oxford Press.
Unger, J. Marshall. 1975. *Studies in early Japanese morphophonemics*. PhD dissertation, Yale University.
Unger, J. Marshall. 1993 [1977]. *Studies in Early Japanese Morphophonemics*. Second edition. Bloomington: Indiana University Linguistics Club.
van Hinloopen Labberton, D. 1924. Preliminary results of researches into the original relationship between the Nipponese and the Malay-Polynesian languages. *The Journal of the Polynesian Society* 33(4). 244–280.
Vovin, Alexander. 2003. *A Reference Grammar of Classical Japanese Prose*. New York: Routledge Curzon.
Vovin, Alexander. 2005. *A Descriptive and Comparative Grammar of Western Old Japanese – Part 1: Phonology, Script, Lexicon and Nominals*. Folkestone: Global Oriental.
Vovin, Alexander. 2009a. *A Descriptive and Comparative Grammar of Western Old Japanese – Part 2: Adjectives, Verbs, Adverbs, Conjunctions, Particles, Postpositions*. Folkestone: Global Oriental.
Vovin, Alexander. 2009b. *Man'yōshū, Book 15. A New English Translation Containing the Original Text, Kana Transliteration, Romanization, Glossing and Commentary*. Folkestone: Global Oriental.
Vovin, Alexander. 2009c. *Man'yōshū to Fudoki ni mirareru fushigina kotoba to jōdai Nihon rettō ni okeru Ainugo no bunpu* [Strange words in the *Man'yōshū* and *Fudoki* and the distribution of the Ainu language in the Japanese islands in prehistory]. Kyoto: Kokusai Nihon Bunka Kenkyū Sentā.
Vovin, Alexander. 2010. *Koreo-Japonica: A Re-evaluation of a Common Genetic Origin*. Honolulu: University of Hawai'i Press.
Vovin, Alexander. 2011a. *Man'yōshū, Book 5. A New English Translation Containing the Original Text, Kana Transliteration, Romanization, Glossing and Commentary*. Folkestone: Global Oriental.
Vovin, Alexander. 2011b. On one more source of Old Japanese i_2. *Journal of East Asian Linguistics* 20(3). 219–228.
Vovin, Alexander. 2012a. *Man'yōshū, Book 14. A New English Translation Containing the Original Text, Kana Transliteration, Romanization, Glossing and Commentary*. Folkestone: Global Oriental.
Vovin, Alexander. 2012b. *Ryūkyū sogo no gochū ni okeru yūsei shi'in no saiken ni tsuite* [On the reconstruction of voiced medial consonants in Proto-Ryukyuan]. Paper presented at NINJAL, Tokyo, 7 August, 2012.
Vovin, Alexander. 2013. *Man'yōshū, Book 20. A New English Translation Containing the Original Text, Kana Transliteration, Romanization, Glossing and Commentary*. Folkestone: Global Oriental.
Vovin, Alexander. 2016. *Man'yōshū, Book 17: A New English Translation Containing the Original Text, Kana Transliteration, Romanization, Glossing and Commentary*. Leiden: Brill.
Vovin, Alexander. 2018. On the etymology of the name of Mt. Fuji. In Alexander Vovin & William McClure (eds.), *Studies in Japanese and Korean Historical and Theoretical Linguistics and Beyond: A Festschrift to Honor Prof. John B. Whitman on the Occasion of His 60th Birthday*, 80–89. Leiden: Brill.
Vovin, Alexander. 2020. *A Descriptive and Comparative Grammar of Western Old Japanese, vol. 1 and 2*. Second revised edition. (Handbuch der Orientalistik). Leiden: Brill.

Vovin, Alexander. 2021a. *Man'yōshū, Book 16. A New English Translation Containing the Original Text, Kana Transliteration, Romanization, Glossing and Commentary*. Leiden: Brill.
Vovin, Alexander. 2021b. Austronesians in the northern waters? *International Journal of Eurasian Linguistics* 3(2). 272–300.
Wenck, Günther. 1959. *Japanische Phonetik, Band IV. Erscheinungen und Probleme des Japanischen Lautwandels*. Wiesbaden: Otto Harrassowitz.
Whitman, John. 1985. *The phonological basis for the comparison of Japanese and Korean*. PhD dissertation, Harvard University.
Whitman, John. 2012a. Northeast Asian linguistic ecology and the advent of rice agriculture in Korea and Japan. *Rice* 4(3–4). 149–158.
Whitman, John. 2012b. The relationship of Japanese and Korean. In Nicolas Tranter (ed.), *The Languages of Japan and Korea*, 24–38. London: Routledge.
Yamada, Heiuemon. 2010. *Kiete iku shima kotoba: Hachijō-go no keishō to sonzoku o negatte* [Vanishing island words: Wishing for the succession and continuance of the Hachijō language]. Tokyo: Ikuhōsha.
Yamada, Yoshio. 1954 (1912). *Nara chō bunpō shi* [History of Nara-period grammar]. Tokyo: Hōbunkan.
Yanagida, Yūko & John Whitman. 2009. Alignment and word order in Old Japanese. *Journal of East Asian Linguistics* 18. 101–144.

Index (supplement to the Extended Table of Contents)

accent 3, 313
agglutinative 3, 156
Ainu 4, 116, 119, 123–140, 147, 156, 487n257, 488n261, 492n331, 496n384, 507n555
Altaic 141n126
Amami 138
Amis 4, 142
analogical levelling 34, 75, 80
analogy 54, 284, 319
Apa province 2, 17, 94n80
Arisaka, Hideyo 6
Asuka period 126n105
Asuka topolect 3, 43–44, 483
Austronesian 4, 24n24, 119, 127n108, 141–142
Azuma 1, 2, 4, 10n14, 11, 17, 20, 23, 42, 94, 117, 123, 127, 134, 140–141, 334, 483, 484n206, 484n213, 497n401, 502n482, 504n513
Azuma-uta 4

back-formation 274, 319
Batanic 141–142
Baxter, William 12n15
Bentley, John R. 12, 124n103, 366
borrowing 18, 50n43, 54–55, 70n64, 82, 85, 101, 120–121, 123, 128–130, 132–133, 138, 140–142, 147, 156, 157n137, 186, 202, 272, 342, 380, 383, 391, 403, 487n257, 488n261, 492n331, 496n384, 507n555

chōka 3
circumfix 294
Classical Japanese → see Middle Japanese
coda 11, 132
cognate 15, 26n27, 35n33, 37, 41, 50–51, 57, 60, 62n59, 71–73, 81, 84, 92, 94, 97, 117, 119, 121n100, 122, 136, 137n120, 138, 142n128–129, 180, 196, 215, 231, 233, 235, 273, 390, 428, 484n210, 485n216, 486n240, 487n245, 492n329
comparative method 28

dialect 1–6, 16–17, 21, 23, 28–29, 32, 41–42, 44, 47–48, 52n48, 54, 58, 77, 94–96, 98, 109, 111–112, 116, 119, 125, 127, 131–132, 137, 140–143, 158, 183, 186, 193, 197, 207, 282, 313, 335n175–176, 359, 390, 394, 403, 441, 483
dialect chain 1
dialect mixing 42
diphthong 6, 25–27, 36–37, 40, 46–47, 49, 55–56, 59, 67–69, 73, 78, 85, 90, 93, 131, 141
diphthongization 111
drift 89

Early Middle Chinese (EMC) 11–12, 140
Edo period 126n105
enclitic 317

Fijian 24n24
Finnish 64, 116
fortition 72, 89
Francis-Ratte, Alexander 121, 318
free variation 6–8, 29, 31–33, 38, 45, 49, 51, 62–64, 67, 74, 80, 86, 183, 209, 383
Frellesvig, Bjarke 7, 25n25, 45n39, 88, 285
Fukuda, Yoshisuke 5, 48, 334
fusion 39, 47, 62, 92n75, 99, 121n97, 157, 168, 174, 266, 283, 319, 347, 380, 391n184

geminate consonant 3

Hachijō 2, 21, 23, 32, 39, 45n39, 52, 71, 93n76, 93n78, 93n79, 94, 131, 137, 261n160, 327n174, 379n183, 489n280
Hamada, Atsushi 112
hapax legomenon 43, 128–136, 138–139
Hashimoto, Shinkichi 112
Hateruma 64
Hawaiian 59
Hayato → see Payatö
Heian period 14, 15n18, 16, 29, 41, 47, 57, 77, 84n68, 107n87–88, 122n102, 126

Hendricks, Peter 191
Hino, Sukenari 23, 35n33, 48, 96
Hitachi Fudoki → see *Pitati Fudoki*
Hōjō, Tadao 5, 334, 357
homorganic 101n83
hypermetrical 81, 110–112, 115, 182, 222
hypermetricality 3, 58n57
hypometrical 114

Idu province 1, 19, 96
Iejima Okinawan 71
Ikier, Steven 5, 96, 334, 353n178, 357n179, 366n181
Irabu dialect 39

kakari musubi 441
Kamakura period 16, 84n68
Kamitukeno topolect 42, 56–57, 60, 65, 76, 98–99, 101, 121, 126, 179, 197, 202, 207, 250, 295, 333, 342, 391, 467
Kamitupusa topolect 66, 69, 80, 139, 285, 335, 410
kana 29, 107n87–88
Kapï province 2, 17
Kapï topolect 94
Keichū 129
Kindaichi, Kyōsuke 5
Kofun period 24
Koguryŏ 507n549
Kubota, Utsuho 134
Kumasö 4
kungana 12, 33n31, 126, 129, 131, 483n200, 500n436
Kupchik, John 25n25–26, 28, 35–36, 42, 48, 71, 85, 94, 98, 101, 105–106, 112, 114n90, 122–123, 127n108, 128, 137, 287n168, 334, 374, 483n197, 486n234, 486n237, 487n256, 492n321, 494n348, 496n382, 508n568
Kyōto dialect 41, 47, 77, 137
Kyūshū 4, 138
Kyūshū Old Japanese (KOJ) 3–4, 95, 128, 138

Late Han Chinese (LH) 11, 12n15, 140
lenition 5, 55, 103, 121, 342, 371, 374
lexeme 17n19, 26, 37, 47, 76, 90
loan blend 137
loanword 4, 21, 55, 90, 119–123, 127n108, 128, 130, 132–133, 136, 140–141, 374

logogram 5–7, 13, 16
logographic 8n12, 16, 81, 107n87–88, 114, 152, 198, 316, 485n226, 486n240, 490n307
look-alike 141–142

Majtczak, Tomasz 25n25
Malayo-Polynesian 141n126, 142n129
Manus Island 24n24
Man'yōgana 5, 105
Man'yōshū (MYS) 4, 9n13, 10n14, 15–17, 20, 107n87–88
marginal phoneme 24, 40
Martin, Samuel E. 6, 23, 45n39, 120n95, 147n133, 313
meter 3, 27, 58n57, 112
merger 6, 15, 26, 26–30, 32, 36, 38–40, 46–47, 55, 60, 62, 67–68, 73, 76, 79, 85, 90, 93
Middle Japanese (MJ) 2, 14–16, 29, 50, 53n52, 54, 62n59, 77, 78n67, 91–92, 100, 116, 119, 126n106, 218, 273, 374, 408, 433, 483n202, 485n224–225, 488n264, 489n285, 489n290, 491n318, 493n334, 495n361, 496n381, 500n433, 501n452, 503n491, 504n510, 505n518, 508n565
Middle Korean 120–121, 133
Mikawa dialect 142n128
Miller, Roy Andrew 5
Mitinöku topolect 94
Miyake, Marc Hideo 6–7, 23, 25n25, 26, 28, 109
Miyako 39, 121n100, 122
Mizushima, Yoshiharu 5, 20, 57n56, 69n62, 72, 122, 126, 131, 133–134, 136–137, 491n319, 506n542
Modern Japanese 6, 20, 32, 88, 112, 132, 137, 342, 413, 442, 485n224–225
mokkan 126–127
monophthong 6, 25, 27, 36,
monophthongization 37–39, 47, 142
mora 3n8
morpheme 17, 20–21, 35n33, 47, 49, 50n46, 52, 55, 78, 82–83, 93–94, 96, 98n82, 112, 114–115, 130n113, 132, 140–141, 157, 183, 206–207, 277, 280, 285, 295, 298, 311, 313, 318–319, 326, 328, 335, 344, 357, 363, 366, 390, 394–395, 400, 405–406, 408, 485n223, 486n227, 486n240, 487n249, 488n271, 489n293, 490n296, 490n303, 490n305,

492n325, 494n352, 495n364, 496n380, 496n385, 497n390–391, 497n397, 499n419, 500n443, 501n456, 502n474, 502n479, 503n490, 504n503, 505n520, 506n543, 508n570
Murayama, Shichirō 4, 45n39, 127n108, 141n126
Muromachi period 16–17, 142n128
Muzasi topolect 35, 60, 62, 67, 99, 102, 117, 235, 250, 390, 406

Nagasaki dialect 137
Nara dialect 1, 137, 483
Nara period 1–3, 5, 42n38, 57, 59, 89, 126
Nara topolect 3
Northern Ryukyuan → see Ryūkyū Islands
Nōtō Old Japanese (NOJ) 3–4, 95, 374

Oceanic languages 24n24
Okinawan 71, 138n122
Okuyama dialect 137
Old Chinese 12n15
Old Javanese 141
Old Korean 116, 120–121, 134, 334
Old Okinawan → see Old Ryukyuan
Old Ryukyuan 100, 141n126
Omodaka, Hisataka 5, 8, 20, 72, 133, 141, 483n200, 491n319
ongana 7, 129, 131
Ōno, Susumu 5, 441
onset 8, 14, 33, 89, 101n83, 112, 115, 127–129, 147–148, 157, 174, 207, 406, 466
orthography 3, 5, 28, 31–32, 37, 39, 147n132, 313
Osterkamp, Sven 3n8

Paekche 507n549
parallel innovation 77, 89
Payatö 4
Pellard, Thomas 2, 25n25, 26n28
Philippine languages → see Batanic
phoneme 23–28, 36, 40, 46–47, 55, 59–60, 67, 73, 78, 85, 90, 92–93, 141–142, 287n168
phonogram 5–12, 16–17, 28–36, 38, 40, 43, 45, 48, 49–51, 56, 60, 62–64, 67–68, 71, 73–74, 76, 79–80, 83–87, 90–91, 98, 125–126, 129, 131, 273, 306
phonographic 10n14, 16–17, 62n59, 77, 78n67, 84n68, 119, 120n96, 126, 140, 145, 196,

227, 432, 483, 485n224–226, 486n237, 486n240–241, 487n256, 488n268, 489n285, 492n321, 493n337, 495n361, 496n382, 497n403, 498n410, 499n420, 500n433, 500n446, 501n448, 501n452, 503n493, 504n502–503, 508n570
phonotactics 3, 101n83, 278n168, 298
Pitati Fudoki 4–5, 129
Pitati topolect 41, 73, 76, 98n82, 102, 117, 235, 378, 407
portmanteau morph 3, 252, 260, 272, 274, 277, 282, 290, 298, 303, 319, 344, 359, 368, 371, 391, 395, 406
Proto-EOJ 21, 23, 35n33, 42, 45n39, 47–49, 52, 54–56, 59–60, 62–68, 73, 77–79, 82–83, 85–86, 88n73, 90–91, 93–96, 98n82, 99, 101, 104, 132, 135, 191, 203, 204n144, 363, 478
Proto-Korean 121, 147n133, 334
Proto-Malayo-Polynesian 141n126
Proto-Polynesian 59
Proto-Ryukyuan (PR) 2–3, 23–24, 26, 39, 50, 52, 61, 72, 95, 136, 137n120, 138n122, 142, 179–180, 183, 196, 215, 257, 348, 357, 374
Proto-TSOJ 7, 21, 23, 30, 32, 34, 36, 40, 46–48, 78, 127, 281, 335

reflex 23, 24n23, 26, 28, 31, 33n30, 35, 39, 41, 45, 47, 49, 50n43, 50n45, 52–53, 55, 57, 59, 60n58, 62, 68–70, 73, 75, 77–80, 82, 84, 87–88, 92n75, 94, 97–99, 101, 131, 137–139, 142, 157n137, 185, 204, 317, 368, 403
romanization 6
root 28, 33–34, 35n34, 45n39, 46, 49, 51–53, 56, 62, 68, 80, 87, 91, 94, 97, 99, 102–103, 115–117, 133, 140, 145, 149–150, 156, 186, 197–201, 204n144, 238, 245, 248, 252, 260, 267, 270, 272, 274, 280, 282, 284, 285, 287, 289, 292, 294n169, 317, 319, 339, 343–344, 366, 368, 373, 412, 423, 425, 428, 432, 491n311–312
Russell, Kerri 294, 317–318, 365–366
Ryūkyū Islands 4, 138
Ryukyuan → see Ryukyuan languages
Ryukyuan languages 21, 23, 26n28, 39, 50, 52–53, 64, 71, 94–95, 99, 122, 132, 138, 180, 335, 357, 493n340

Sagamu topolect 16, 57, 60, 64, 98, 117, 124, 130–131, 296, 484n210, 485n216
Sagart, Laurent 12n15
Sakanöupey nö Tamuramarö 4
Sakimori-uta 4
Schuessler, Axel 11–12
semantic change 126n107, 130
Serafim, Leon A. 23, 25n25, 72, 441
Sesoko Okinawan 138n122
shift 27–28
Shinzato, Rumiko 72, 441
Simotukeno topolect 67, 92, 94, 99, 101–102, 139, 185, 235, 427, 451
Simotupusa topolect 10n14, 41, 66, 102, 135, 235, 390, 400, 404, 409
Sinano topolect 1n4, 7, 16, 30, 33, 37–38, 49, 70, 197, 376, 380, 454
sonorant 24
Southern Ryukyuan 64, 89
stem 34, 38, 52, 223, 227, 230, 269–271, 281–286, 298, 306, 309, 318n170, 322, 326–327, 335, 339, 344, 348, 350–351, 357, 359, 368, 371, 374, 376–377, 490n307, 498n406, 502n466, 508n569
subdialect 48, 60, 65
subgroup → see subgrouping
subgrouping 1n4, 21, 23, 60, 93–96
suppletion → see suppletive
suppletive 279, 390, 392, 394, 419
Suruga topolect 7, 9n13, 16, 20, 30, 35, 38–39, 42, 48, 72, 89, 131, 179n139, 197, 213, 297, 305, 380, 383, 451, 466, 479
syllable 3, 6–8, 9n13, 10n14, 12, 14–16, 20, 26–39, 41, 45–47, 50–54, 56, 58–60, 62, 64, 71, 74, 76, 79, 81–86, 100–101, 105, 110–115, 117, 120n96, 126, 129–131, 136–137, 139, 252, 335n177, 368, 438, 493n340
syllable-timed 3, 28
syncretic 157, 281, 322, 339
syncretism 281, 283, 286, 339
syntactic inversion 236, 241, 278, 350, 369, 397

Takachi dialect 137
Taketomi 138
tanka 3
Tarama Miyako 121n100, 122

Thorpe, Maner L. 24n21, 52, 72, 180, 183
timing → see syllable-timed
Tokunoshima 138n122
Tongan 59, 64
topolect 1–3, 7, 9n13, 10n14, 16–17, 20–21, 23, 28–30, 32–45, 47–51, 53–57, 59–90, 92, 94–99, 101–102, 105, 107, 109, 111, 117, 121, 124, 126, 130–131, 135, 137–139, 156, 163–164, 168, 173, 179, 183, 185, 191, 197, 202, 207, 213, 220n145, 225n147, 229, 235, 250, 277, 281, 285–287, 295–298, 305–306, 322, 326–327, 333–335, 340, 342, 363, 368, 373, 376, 378, 380, 383, 388, 390–391, 400, 404, 406–407, 409–410, 412, 427, 429, 451, 454, 466–467, 479, 484n210, 485n216, 502n482, 507n545, 507n550
Töpotuapumi topolect 9n13, 30, 33–34, 42–43, 48–49, 70, 380
transliteration 1n5, 5–12, 20, 107n87–88

Unger, J. Marshall 23, 112

verse 27, 112, 115, 499n419
Vovin, Alexander 4–5, 10n14, 20, 24n21, 25n25, 35, 41, 43, 49n41, 51–52, 53, 57n54, 85n70, 87, 88n73, 98, 103, 117n93, 120–142, 145, 147, 149, 156, 181–182, 186, 191n141, 203n144, 237, 241, 245, 252, 257, 266, 274, 283, 287n168, 294–296, 303, 311, 317–318, 334–335, 348, 363, 366, 368, 374, 396, 406, 408, 431, 441, 449, 454, 458, 460, 467, 472n195, 483n204, 485n214, 485n226, 487n246
vowel fusion → see fusion
vowel sequence 25, 27, 46, 105, 110–111, 141, 266, 298

Wakayama dialect 137
Whitman, John 7, 23, 25n25, 88, 120–121, 123, 284, 285, 295

Yanagida, Yūko 295
Yayoi period 24
Yonaguni 39
Yoron 122, 138

zero morph 320

www.ingramcontent.com/pod-product-compliance
Lightning Source LLC
Chambersburg PA
CBHW051532230426
43669CB00015B/2572